OUR GUARANTEE: If you are not satisfied with **EMPLOYMENT LAW REPORT** for any reason, we will refund the unused portion of your subscription payment.

Use the attached order cards to order your own or extra subscriptions to the **EMPLOYMENT LAW REPORT** . . . the monthly ~~newsletter~~ reporting the very latest employment cases and ~~late-breaking legislation.~~

The attached order cards may be rem~~oved~~ ~~the book~~ for your order.

W9-AXQ-633

Yes, please send me _____ subscriptions to the **EMPLOYMENT LAW REPORT** . . . the monthly newsletter service reporting the very latest employment cases and late-breaking legislation.

☐ Send two years at $210.00 (your best price)

☐ Send one year at $120.00

Name _____

Title_____

Organization _____

Address _____

City _____ State _____ Zip _____

Purchase Order Number, if needed _____

Send order and check payable to : DATA RESEARCH, INC.,
P.O. BOX 490, ROSEMOUNT, MN 55068 or call
toll free 800-365-4900 or 612-452-8267;
FAX 612-452-8694

Yes, please send me _____ subscriptions to the **EMPLOYMENT LAW REPORT** . . . the monthly newsletter service reporting the very latest employment cases and late-breaking legislation.

☐ Send two years at $210.00 (your best price)

☐ Send one year at $120.00

Name _____

Title_____

Organization _____

Address _____

City _____ State _____ Zip _____

Purchase Order Number, if needed _____

Send order and check payable to : DATA RESEARCH, INC.,
P.O. BOX 490, ROSEMOUNT, MN 55068 or call
toll free 800-365-4900 or 612-452-8267;
FAX 612-452-8694

DESKBOOK ENCYCLOPEDIA
OF
EMPLOYMENT LAW

FOURTH EDITION

"This publication is designed to provide accurate and authoritative information in regard to the subject matter covered. It is sold with the understanding that the publisher is not engaged in rendering legal, accounting or other professional service. If legal advice or other expert assistance is required, the service of a competent professional person should be sought." -*from a Declaration of Principles jointly adopted by a Committee of the American Bar Association and a Committee of Publishers and associations.*

Published by Data Research, Inc.
P.O. Box 490
Rosemount, Minnesota 55068

OTHER TITLES PUBLISHED
BY DATA RESEARCH, INC.:

Deskbook Encyclopedia of American School Law
Deskbook Encyclopedia of American Insurance Law
Students with Disabilities and Special Education
U.S. Supreme Court Education Cases
U.S. Supreme Court Employment Cases
Deskbook Encyclopedia of Public Employment Law
Private School Law in America
Statutes, Regulations and Case Law
    Protecting Individuals with Disabilities

Copyright © 1996 by Data Research, Inc.

All rights reserved
Printed in the United States of America

ISBN 0-939675-55-2

The Library of Congress has catalogued this book as follows:

Employment - 4th ed.
          p.   cm.
    Includes bibliographical references and index.
    ISBN 0-939675-55-2
    1. Labor laws and legislation--United States--Digests.
  I. Data Research, Inc.
KF3314.D47   1996
344.73'01—dc20
[347.3041]   94-441
                                        CIP

Library of Congress Catalog Card Number: 94-441

PREFACE

The *Deskbook Encyclopedia of Employment Law* is an up-to-date compilation of state and federal court decisions which affect employment in the private sector. These decisions have been selected and edited by the editorial staff of Data Research, Inc., publishers of the *Employment Law Report*. From hiring and employment practices to termination of employment and workers' compensation, this volume examines a broad spectrum of legal issues in American employment law.

Employment law is a blend of well-settled principles which are unlikely to change, and new issues finding their way into the courts. There are a great many federal and state statutes which regulate various aspects of employment, but there is also a large body of judge-made law which has established standards for employers and employees in the workplace.This volume will give the reader a comprehensive guide to employment law.

EDITORIAL STAFF
DATA RESEARCH, INC.

INTRODUCTORY NOTE ON
THE JUDICIAL SYSTEM

In order to allow the reader to determine the relative importance of a judicial decision, the cases included in the *Deskbook Encyclopedia of Employment Law* identify the particular court from which a decision has been issued. For example, a case decided by a state supreme court generally will be of greater significance than a state circuit court case. Hence a basic knowledge of the structure of our judicial system is important to an understanding of employment law.

Almost all the reports in this volume are taken from appellate court decisions. Although most employment law decisions occur at trial court and administrative levels, appellate court decisions have the effect of binding lower courts and administrators so that appellate court decisions have the effect of law within their court systems.

State and federal court systems generally function independently of each other. Each court system applies its own law according to statutes and the determinations of its highest court. However, judges at all levels often consider opinions from other court systems to settle issues which are new or arise under unique fact situations. Similarly, lawyers look at the opinions of many courts to locate authority which supports their clients' cases.

Once a lawsuit is filed in a particular court system, that system retains the matter until its conclusion. Unsuccessful parties at the administrative or trial court level generally have the right to appeal unfavorable determinations of law to appellate courts within the system. When federal law issues or Constitutional grounds are present, lawsuits may be appropriately filed in the federal court system. In those cases, the lawsuit is filed initially in the federal district court for that area.

On rare occasions, the U.S. Supreme Court considers appeals from the highest courts of the states if a distinct federal question exists and at least four justices agree on the question's importance. The federal courts occasionally send cases to state courts for application of state law. These situations are infrequent and in general, the state and federal court systems should be considered separate from each other.

The most common system, used by nearly all states and also the federal judiciary, is as follows: a legal action is commenced in district court (sometimes called trial court, county court, common pleas court or superior court) where a decision is initially reached. The case may then be appealed to the court of appeals (or appellate court), and in turn this decision may be appealed to the supreme court.

Several states, however, do not have an intermediate court of appeals; lower court decisions are appealed directly to the state's supreme court. Additionally, some states have labeled their courts in a nonstandard fashion.

In Maryland, the highest state court is called the Court of Appeals. In the state of New York, the trial court is called the Supreme Court. Decisions of this court may be appealed to the Supreme Court, Appellate Division. The highest court in New York is the Court of Appeals. Pennsylvania has perhaps the most complex court system. The lowest state court is the Court of Common Pleas. Depending on the circumstances of the case, appeals may be taken to either the Commonwealth Court or the Superior Court. In certain instances the Commonwealth Court functions as a trial court as well as an appellate court. The Superior Court, however, is strictly an intermediate appellate court. The highest court in Pennsylvania is the Supreme Court.

While supreme court decisions are generally regarded as the last word in legal matters, it is important to remember that trial and appeals court decisions also create important legal precedents. For the hierarchy of typical state and federal court systems, please see the diagram below.

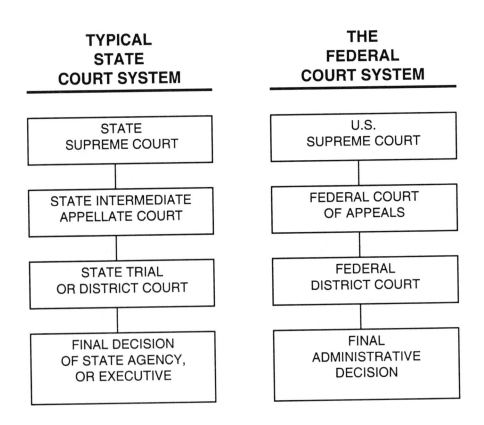

TYPICAL STATE COURT SYSTEM	THE FEDERAL COURT SYSTEM
STATE SUPREME COURT	U.S. SUPREME COURT
STATE INTERMEDIATE APPELLATE COURT	FEDERAL COURT OF APPEALS
STATE TRIAL OR DISTRICT COURT	FEDERAL DISTRICT COURT
FINAL DECISION OF STATE AGENCY, OR EXECUTIVE	FINAL ADMINISTRATIVE DECISION

Federal courts of appeal hear appeals from the district courts which are located in their circuits. Below is a list of states matched to the federal circuits in which they are located.

First Circuit	—	Puerto Rico, Maine, New Hampshire, Massachusetts, Rhode Island
Second Circuit	—	New York, Vermont, Connecticut
Third Circuit	—	Pennsylvania, New Jersey, Delaware, Virgin Islands
Fourth Circuit	—	West Virginia, Maryland, Virginia, North Carolina, South Carolina
Fifth Circuit	—	Texas, Louisiana, Mississippi
Sixth Circuit	—	Ohio, Kentucky, Tennessee, Michigan
Seventh Circuit	—	Wisconsin, Indiana, Illinois
Eighth Circuit	—	North Dakota, South Dakota, Nebraska, Arkansas, Missouri, Iowa, Minnesota
Ninth Circuit	—	Alaska, Washington, Oregon, California, Hawaii, Arizona, Nevada, Idaho, Montana, Northern Mariana Islands, Guam
Tenth Circuit	—	Wyoming, Utah, Colorado, Kansas, Oklahoma, New Mexico
Eleventh Circuit	—	Alabama, Georgia, Florida
District of Columbia Circuit	—	Hears cases from the U.S. District Court for the District of Columbia.
Federal Circuit	—	Sitting in Washington, D.C., the U.S. Court of Appeals, Federal Circuit, hears patent and trade appeals and certain appeals on claims brought against the federal government and its agencies.

TABLE OF CONTENTS

TABLE OF CASES

TABLE OF CASES

TABLE OF CASES

TABLE OF CASES

TABLE OF CASES

TABLE OF CASES

TABLE OF CASES BY STATE

TABLE OF CASES BY STATE

FLORIDA

GEORGIA

HAWAII

TABLE OF CASES BY STATE

TABLE OF CASES BY STATE

TABLE OF CASES BY STATE

TABLE OF CASES BY STATE

TABLE OF CASES BY STATE

CHAPTER ONE

DISCRIMINATION

I. RACE AND NATIONAL ORIGIN DISCRIMINATION

Title VII of the Civil Rights Act of 1964 and 42 U.S.C. § 1981 are important federal laws against employment discrimination on the basis of race, sex and national origin. Further, the passage of the Civil Rights Act of 1991 (amending the Civil Rights Act of 1964) reversed the impact of certain recent U.S. Supreme Court cases which reduced the scope and effectiveness of civil rights protections. State legislation also protects workers from employment discrimination.

A. Federal Statutes and Supreme Court Interpretations

Title VII applies to any entity engaged in an industry affecting commerce which has 15 or more employees. Its coverage is limited to employment discrimination based upon race, color, sex, religion or national origin. The U.S. Equal Employment Opportunity Commission (EEOC) is empowered to enforce Title VII through investigation and administrative complaint procedures or federal court lawsuits. Indeed, a private individual alleging discrimination must pursue administrative remedies within the EEOC before the individual will be allowed to file suit against an employer under Title VII. Plaintiffs who prevail in an employment discrimination lawsuit will be entitled, where appropriate, to backpay, front pay, accumulated seniority and other benefits, and attorney's fees. Further, Title VII allows the recovery of monetary damages for intentional discrimination. There is an exception for race discrimination lawsuits, however, because of the availability of monetary damages under 42 U.S.C. § 1981. Title VII is found at 42 U.S.C. § 2000e, *et seq.*

§ 2000e-2. Unlawful employment practices

(a) Employer practices

It shall be an unlawful employment practice for an employer—
(1) to fail or refuse to hire or to discharge any individual, or otherwise to discriminate against any individual with respect to his compensation, terms, conditions, or privileges of employment, because of such individual's race, color, religion, sex, or national origin; or
(2) to limit, segregate, or classify his employees or applicants for employment in any way which would deprive or tend to deprive any individual of employment opportunities or otherwise adversely affect his status as an employee, because of such individual's race, color, religion, sex, or national origin.

* * *

(e) Businesses or enterprises with personnel qualified on basis of religion, sex, or national origin; educational institutions with personnel of particular religion

Notwithstanding any other provision of this subchapter, (1) it shall not be an unlawful employment practice for any employer to hire and employ employees, for an employment agency to classify, or refer for employment any individual, for a labor organization to classify its membership or to classify or refer for employment any individual, or for an employer, labor organization or joint labor-management committee controlling apprenticeship or other training or retraining programs to admit or employ any individual in any such program, on the basis of his religion, sex, or national origin in those certain instances where religion, sex, or national origin is a bona fide occupational qualification reasonably necessary to the normal operation of that particular business or enterprise, and (2) it shall not be an unlawful employment practice for a school, college, university, or other educational institution or institution of learning to hire and employ employees of a particular religion if such school, college, university, or other educational institution or institution of learning is, in whole or in substantial part, owned, supported, controlled, or managed by a particular religion or by a particular religious corporation, association, or society, or if the curriculum of such school, college, university, or other educational institution or institution of learning is directed toward the propagation of a particular religion.

* * *

42 U.S.C. § 1981
Equal rights under the law

(a) All persons within the jurisdiction of the United States shall have the same right in every State and Territory to make and enforce contracts, to sue, be parties, give evidence, and to the full and equal benefit of all laws and proceedings for the security of persons and property as is enjoyed by white citizens, and shall be subject to like punishment, pains, penalties, taxes, licenses, and exactions of every kind, and to no other.

(b) For purposes of this section, the term 'make and enforce contracts' includes the making, performance, modification, and termination of contracts, and the enjoyment of all benefits, privileges, terms, and conditions of the contractual relationship.

(c) The rights protected by this section are protected against impairment by nongovernmental discrimination and impairment under color of State law.

Section 1 of the Civil Rights Act of 1871, which is codified at 42 U.S.C. § 1983, provides the basis for a federal court lawsuit to any individual whose constitutional rights, or federal statutory rights, have been violated by the government or its officials. Compensatory damages, punitive damages, injunctions and attorney's fees may be awarded under § 1983. Two elements are required for a successful § 1983 lawsuit: 1) action by the state or by a person or institution acting "under color of" state law, which 2) deprives an individual of federally guaranteed rights.

42 U.S.C. § 1983
Civil action for deprivation of rights

Every person who, under color of any statute, ordinance, regulation, custom, or usage, of any State or Territory or the District of Columbia, subjects, or causes to be subjected, any citizen of the United States or other person within the jurisdiction thereof to the deprivation of any rights, privileges, or immunities secured by the Constitution and laws, shall be liable to the party injured in an action at law, suit in equity, or other proper proceeding for redress. For the purposes of this section, any Act of Congress applicable exclusively to the District of Columbia shall be considered to be a statute of the District of Columbia.

One of the most important Supreme Court cases in the area of civil rights is *Griggs v. Duke Power Co.*, where the Court held that Title VII forbids not only practices adopted with a discriminatory motive, but also those which have a discriminatory effect. In *Griggs,* a group of black employees at a North Carolina power plant sued under Title VII of the Civil Rights Act of 1964, challenging their employer's requirement that employees possess a high school diploma or pass an intelligence test as a condition of employment in or transfer to jobs at the plant. Section 703 of the Act authorized the use of an ability test, so long as it was not intended or used to discriminate. The district court held that the employer's prior policy of racial discrimination had ended, and the Court of Appeals upheld that determination. The employees appealed to the U.S. Supreme Court.

The Supreme Court held that Title VII requires the elimination of artificial, arbitrary, and unnecessary barriers to employment that discriminate on the basis of race. If a practice excludes minorities and that practice cannot be shown to be related to job performance, it is prohibited, even if the employer lacked discriminatory intent. Title VII does not preclude the use of testing or measuring procedures so long as they are demonstrably a reasonable measure of job performance. In this case, the procedures were not related to job performance. Therefore, they violated Title VII. *Griggs v. Duke Power Co.,* 401 U.S. 424, 91 S.Ct. 849, 28 L.Ed.2d 158 (1971).

The Supreme Court case which first discussed the shifting burden of proof standard for Title VII discrimination lawsuits is *McDonnell Douglas Corp. v. Green.* In this case, a black civil rights activist engaged in disruptive and illegal activity against his former employer as part of his protest that his discharge and the employer's general hiring practices were racially motivated. Soon after, the employer advertised for qualified personnel, but rejected the activist's re-employment application on the grounds of his illegal conduct. The activist filed a complaint with the EEOC claiming a Title VII violation. The EEOC found that there was reasonable cause to believe that the decision violated § 704(a) of Title VII, which forbids discrimination against applicants or employees for protesting against discriminatory employment conditions. The activist then filed suit against the employer, and a Missouri federal district court ruled that the activist's illegal activity was not protected by § 704(a). The court dismissed the § 703 claim because the EEOC had made no finding with respect to that section. The court of appeals affirmed the ruling with respect to § 704(a), but reversed the dismissal of the § 703(a)(1) claim. The employer sought review from the U.S. Supreme Court.

The Supreme Court held that a reasonable cause finding by the EEOC is not necessary in order for a party to raise § 703(a)(1) at trial. It further held that in a private, nonclass-action complaint under Title VII the complaining party has the burden of establishing a *prima facie* case for employment discrimination. This can be satisfied by showing that the complaining party belongs to a racial minority, has applied and was qualified for a job the employer was trying to fill, was rejected, and the employer continued to seek applicants with the complainant's qualifications. Even though the employee had done this, the employer had responded to the activist's *prima facie* case by showing that it had a reason for rejecting the applicant. The Court remanded the case, with instructions to provide the activist an opportunity to establish his ultimate burden to show that the employer's reason for refusal was simply a pretext for a racially discriminatory decision. *McDonnell Douglas Corp. v. Green*, 411 U.S. 792, 93 S.Ct. 1817, 36 L.Ed.2d 668 (1973).

The Federal Lands Highway Division, part of the U.S. Department of Transportation, awarded a highway construction contract to a Colorado contractor. The contractor received additional compensation for hiring a subcontractor controlled by "socially and economically disadvantaged individuals." The highway division construed the relevant federal statute as containing a presumption that African-American, Hispanic, Asian-Pacific, Subcontinent Asian, Native American, and female individuals were socially and economically disadvantaged. The contractor rejected the low bidder on the subcontract, because it was not controlled by disadvantaged persons. The subcontractor filed suit in a federal district court, claiming that the race-based presumption violated its right to equal protection. The district court granted the U.S. government's motion for summary judgment, and the U.S. Court of Appeals, Tenth Circuit, affirmed. The subcontractor appealed to the U.S. Supreme Court.

The Supreme Court reversed the Tenth Circuit decision, ruling that the standard of review for federal, state and local governments should be strict scrutiny. The Court held that the Fifth and Fourteenth Amendments require that all racial classifications be narrowly tailored to further a compelling government interest. The Court rejected the government's plea for a less rigorous standard, ruling that only strict scrutiny would submit racial classifications to a sufficiently detailed examination. It noted that heightened scrutiny would "smoke out illegitimate uses of race by assuring that the legislative body is pursuing a goal important enough to warrant use of a highly suspect tool." The Court reversed and remanded the case to determine whether the use of the subcontractor compensation clauses could be properly described as compelling. *Adarand Constructors, Inc. v. Pena*, 115 S.Ct. 2097, 132 L.Ed.2d 158 (1995).

A Missouri halfway house employed an African-American correctional officer. After being demoted and ultimately discharged, the officer filed suit alleging that these actions had been taken because of his race in violation of Title VII of the Civil Rights Act of 1964. At trial, a federal district court found that the officer had established, by a preponderance of the evidence, a *prima facie* case of racial discrimination and that the employer's stated reasons for its actions were pretextual. However, the district court held that the officer had failed to carry his ultimate burden of proving that the adverse actions were racially motivated and found for the halfway house. The officer then appealed to the U.S. Court of Appeals, Eighth Circuit. The Eighth Circuit reversed the decision of the trial court and held that the officer was entitled to judgment as a matter of law once he proved that all of the employer's reasons were pretextual. The halfway house appealed to the U.S. Supreme Court.

The Supreme Court reinstated the district court's decision, stating that the judge's rejection of an employer's asserted reasons for its actions does not entitle a plaintiff to judgment as a matter of law. Under *McDonnell Douglas Corp. v. Green*, above, once the officer established a *prima facie* case of discrimination, a presumption arose that the employer unlawfully discriminated against him, requiring judgment in his favor unless the employer came forward with an explanation. This presumption placed upon the employer the burden of proving that the adverse actions were taken for legitimate, nondiscriminatory reasons. However, the ultimate burden of persuasion remained at all times with the employee. The trier of fact was required to decide whether the employee had proven that the employer had intentionally discriminated against him. Accordingly, the Supreme Court upheld the district court's decision. *St. Mary's Honor Center v. Hicks*, 113 S.Ct. 2742, 125 L.Ed.2d 407 (1993).

A group of black employees sued their North Carolina employer and the employees' union for Title VII violations. The major issues were the plant's seniority system, its program of employment testing, and backpay. The federal district court found that the employees had been locked in the lower paying job classifications and ordered a new system of plant-wide seniority. The court refused to order backpay. It also refused to limit the plant's testing program, stating that the tests were job related. The employees appealed the backpay and employment issues and the court of appeals ruled in their favor. The plant appealed to the U.S. Supreme Court. The Supreme Court held that if there is unlawful discrimination, backpay should only be denied for reasons that would not frustrate the purposes of Title VII. The absence of bad faith on the employer's part is not a sufficient reason for denying backpay. In this case, however, there was some question about the timing of the demand for backpay and so the issue would remain open on remand. With regard to testing, the Court stated that testing must be correlated with important elements of work behavior which comprise the job or are relevant to the job. The test in this case failed to meet these standards. *Albermarle Paper Co. v. Moody*, 422 U.S. 405, 95 S.Ct. 2362, 45 L.Ed.2d 280 (1975).

The United States government sued a nationwide common carrier of motor freight, and a union representing a large group of the company's employees, claiming that the company engaged in a pattern of discriminating against blacks and Hispanics. A federal district court in Texas held that the union and company had violated Title VII and enjoined both from committing further violations thereof. Review was sought from the U.S. Supreme Court. The Supreme Court held that the government had successfully shown that discrimination had occurred. The Court also held that retroactive seniority may be awarded, even if the seniority system agreement makes no provision for such relief. However, it stated that the union's conduct in agreeing to the seniority system did not violate Title VII. Employees who suffered only pre-Title VII discrimination were not entitled to relief, and no person could be given retroactive seniority to a date earlier than the Act's effective date. Therefore, the injunction was vacated. A bona fide seniority system does not become unlawful simply because it perpetuates pre-Title VII discrimination. The seniority system was made in good faith and applied to all members. *International Brotherhood of Teamsters v. U.S.*, 433 U.S. 324, 97 S.Ct. 1843, 52 L.Ed.2d 396 (1977).

A sheet metal workers union and its apprenticeship committee engaged in a continuing practice of discrimination toward black and Hispanic individuals for a number of years. After numerous court orders were unsuccessful in reversing the practice of the union, the EEOC initiated an action against the union under Title VII. The district court ordered the union to end its discriminatory practices, and established a 29 percent nonwhite membership goal (based on the percentage of nonwhites in the relevant labor pool in New York City). After several more court actions, the union was found guilty of civil contempt for disobeying earlier court orders. The court then imposed a fine on the union to be placed in a special fund for increasing nonwhite membership in the union. The court of appeals affirmed, and the union appealed to the U.S. Supreme Court. On appeal, the Supreme Court noted that Title VII allowed the kind of affirmative, race-conscious relief which the district court had ordered in this case. A court need not order relief only for actual victims of past discrimination, but can also order relief of a broader scope to satisfy the purposes of Title VII. The Supreme Court also found that the imposition of fines and the creation of the special fund had been designed to coerce compliance and were appropriate remedies for civil contempt. It affirmed the lower courts' decisions. *Local 28 of Sheet Metal Workers v. EEOC,* 478 U.S. 421, 106 S.Ct. 3019, 92 L.Ed.2d 344 (1986).

In 1973, individual employees of a steel company brought suit against their employer and their collective bargaining agents, asserting racial discrimination claims under Title VII and 42 U.S.C. § 1981. A federal district court held that the six-year statute of limitations governing contract claims was the appropriate limitation period to be applied in § 1981 claims. It further held that both the employer and the agents had discriminated against the employees in certain respects. On appeal to the U.S. Court of Appeals, Third Circuit, it was held that Pennsylvania's two-year statute of limitations governing personal injury actions was the applicable limitations period. The finding of liability against the employer and the agents was affirmed. The U.S. Supreme Court granted certiorari and affirmed the Third Circuit's ruling. It noted that § 1981 actions related to more than just personal rights to contract; § 1981 also speaks to rights to sue and testify, and acts to secure equal rights under all laws for the security of persons and property. The Court then noted that the courts below had properly found both the agents and the employer to have violated Title VII and § 1981. There had been more than mere passive acquiescence by the unions in the employer's acts of discrimination. The unions had deliberately chosen not to process grievances by African-Americans. *Goodman v. Lukens Steel Co.*, 482 U.S. 656, 107 S.Ct. 2617, 96 L.Ed.2d 572 (1987).

A Texas woman of African-American heritage was rejected in favor of white applicants for four promotions to supervisory positions in the bank where she worked. Rather than use specified standards in the selection process, the bank relied on the judgment of various white supervisors. The employee sued the bank in a federal district court, alleging violations of Title VII. The district court dismissed her claim, holding that she had not met her burden of proving that the bank had acted with the intent to discriminate against her personally. The U.S. Court of Appeals, Fifth Circuit, affirmed. The employee sought review from the U.S. Supreme Court. On appeal, she argued that the district court should have applied a "disparate impact" analysis to her claims. In other words, she would only have to show that the bank had adopted a facially neutral policy *without a discriminatory motive* which had the effect of discriminating against her. The Supreme Court held that, when analyzing subjective or discretionary employment practices, a court may, in appropriate cases, analyze the practice under the disparate impact approach. This would solve the problem of prohibited conduct caused by subconscious stereotypes and prejudices. The Court remanded the case for evaluation under the disparate impact approach. *Watson v. Fort Worth Bank and Trust*, 487 U.S. 977, 108 S.Ct. 2777, 101 L.Ed.2d 827 (1988).

A black woman was employed by a North Carolina credit union as a teller and file coordinator for ten years. After being laid off, she filed suit against her employer in federal district court, alleging violations of 42 U.S.C. § 1981. The U.S. Supreme Court held that § 1981 did not apply to conduct which occurs after the formation of a contract and which does not impair the right of the complaining party to enforce established contract obligations. The racial harassment complained of here would be actionable under Title VII of the Civil Rights Act, but the employee could not seek relief under § 1981. *Patterson v. McLean Credit Union,* 491 U.S. 164, 109 S.Ct. 2363, 105 L.Ed.2d 132 (1989). The passage of the Civil Rights Act of 1991 changed the result of this case by expressly allowing the application of § 1981 to post-formation conduct.

The case returned to the lower courts, and after additional appeals and motions, the district court granted the employer's summary judgment motion. The case came before the U.S. Court of Appeals, Fourth Circuit, which held that the Supreme Court's standard required a showing by the African-American employee that her promotion must amount to the formation of a new and distinct relationship between herself and the employer in order to avail herself of § 1981. The district court had properly ruled that the two jobs were not greatly different and had only a slight difference in pay. Accordingly, the promotion was insufficient to change the relationship between the employer and employee to transform their contractual relationship and trigger § 1981. The court of appeals affirmed summary judgment for the employer. *Patterson v. McLean Credit Union*, 39 F.3d 515 (4th Cir.1994).

Two companies operated salmon canneries in Alaska. The unskilled cannery jobs were filled predominately by nonwhites, and the skilled noncannery jobs were filled predominantly with white workers. A lawsuit followed in which a group of cannery workers alleged that the companies used hiring and promotion practices which caused workplace segregation, creating a disparate impact that violated Title VII. The question of how to analyze the claims eventually came before the U.S. Supreme Court. The Supreme Court held that to make out a *prima facie* disparate impact case, the proper comparison is between the jobs at issue and the racial composition of the qualified labor market. Here, the case would have to be remanded for such a comparison. The court then decided that if a *prima facie* case of disparate impact was shown, the employer would have to produce evidence of a business justification that was more than merely insubstantial for the employer's practice to be upheld as permissible. *Wards Cove Packing Co. v. Atonio*, 490 U.S. 642, 109 S.Ct. 2115, 104 L.Ed.2d 733 (1989). The Civil Rights Act of 1991 strengthened the standard from "business justification" to "business necessity," the standard enunciated in *Griggs v. Duke Power Co.*, and placed the burden of proof on the employer to show the necessity for the practice.

On remand, the district court concluded that none of the specific employment practices that the workers identified had created an adverse impact. The court found that the outward appearance of nepotism among upper level employees had no substantive basis. The workers again appealed to the U.S. Court of Appeals, Ninth Circuit. Ten months after the district court dismissed the case, but before the appeal was argued, Congress enacted the Civil Rights Act of 1991. The act contains a section which states:

Certain disparate impact cases — Notwithstanding any other provision of this act, nothing in this act shall apply to any disparate impact case for which a complaint was filed before March 1, 1975, and for which an initial decision was rendered after October 30, 1983.

This case is the only one to meet the criteria prescribed by this section for exemption from the statute. The workers contended that this section was unconstitutional. The court of appeals disagreed. It held that the rational basis test would be used to determine if the section was unconstitutional because the section's target was a particular case and not a racial class or other cadre subject to special constitutional protection. Further, the court determined that there was a rational basis to exempt this case. The court then remanded the case for a determination of whether separate hiring channels existed (which could be discriminatory). *Atonio v. Wards Cove Packing Co.*, 10 F.3d 1485 (9th Cir.1993).

A naturalized U.S. citizen, born in Lebanon and working in Saudi Arabia, was discharged by his employer, a Delaware Corporation. He filed a charge of discrimination with the EEOC, and filed suit in a Texas federal district court, seeking relief under Title VII of the 1964 Civil Rights Act. The court dismissed his suit, holding that it could not hear the case because Title VII's protections do not extend to U.S. citizens employed abroad by American employers. The U.S. Court of Appeals, Fifth Circuit, affirmed, and the case came before the U.S. Supreme Court. The employee asserted that the language of Title VII evinced a congressional intent to legislate extraterritorially. The Court, however, disagreed. It found that the language of Title VII was ambiguous, and that this did not overcome the presumption against extraterritorial application of the statute. *EEOC v. Arabian American Oil Co.,* 499 U.S. 808, 111 S.Ct. 1227, 113 L.Ed.2d 274 (1991). The Civil Rights Act of 1991 now mandates Title VII and Americans with Disabilities Act coverage for American citizens working abroad for American companies.

The U.S. Supreme Court held that § 101 of the Civil Rights Act of 1991, which defines § 1981's "make and enforce contracts" phrase to embrace all phases and incidents of the contractual relationship, did not apply to an Ohio case that arose before it was enacted. In this case, two garage mechanics were discharged and brought suit alleging that the firings had been because of their race in violation of 42 U.S.C. § 1981. Their claims were dismissed because of the decision in *Patterson v. McLean Credit Union,* which held that § 1981 did not apply to conduct which occurred after the formation of a contract and which did not interfere with the right to enforce established contract obligations. While their appeal was pending, the Civil Rights Act of 1991 became law. Section 101 of the act provided that § 1981's prohibition against racial discrimination in the making and enforcement of contracts applied to all phases and incidents of the contractual relationship, including discriminatory contract terminations. The U.S. Court of Appeals ruled that § 1981 as interpreted in *Patterson* governed the case. The Supreme Court affirmed this decision and denied retroactive application of the act. *Rivers v. Roadway Express, Inc.,* 114 S.Ct. 1510, 128 L.Ed.2d 274 (1994).

A union and a company entered into a collective bargaining agreement which included an affirmative action plan designed to raise the percentage of black craftworkers in the company's plants to the percentage of blacks in the local labor force. After some junior black employees were selected for in-plant craft training programs over some senior white employees, a lawsuit was brought in a Louisiana federal district court, alleging that the affirmative action program was in violation of Title VII. The court held that the plan violated Title VII, and the U.S. Court of Appeals affirmed. The U.S. Supreme Court then granted certiorari.

The Court first stated that Title VII's prohibition against racial discrimination did not condemn all private, voluntary, race-conscious affirmative action plans. To do so would defeat the very purpose of Title VII. The Court then noted that the affirmative action plan in this case was permissible. It opened employment opportunities for blacks in areas which were traditionally closed to them; it did not unnecessarily trammel the interests of white employees; nor did it create an absolute bar. Finally, the Court stated that the plan was a temporary measure, designed only to eliminate a manifest racial imbalance. The Court reversed the court of appeals' decision and upheld the plan. *United Steelworkers, Etc. v. Weber*, 443 U.S. 193, 99 S.Ct. 2721, 61 L.Ed.2d 480 (1979).

Two white employees of a transportation company were discharged for misappropriating cargo from one of the company's shipments. However, a black employee, charged with the same offense, was not fired. After grievance proceedings were unsuccessful, the two employees sued the company and their union for discriminating against them by retaining the black employee while letting them go. A Texas federal district court dismissed the complaint, finding that 42 U.S.C. § 1981 (which prohibits discrimination in the making and enforcement of contracts) did not apply to discrimination against whites, and also finding that no valid claim had been stated under Title VII. The U.S. Court of Appeals affirmed, and the case came before the U.S. Supreme Court.

The Supreme Court held that both Title VII and § 1981 apply to whites as much as to nonwhites in the private employment context. While theft of cargo may warrant discharging an employee, such a policy must be applied evenly to both whites and nonwhites or Title VII is violated. Here, if all other things were equal, then the union and the company would have unlawfully discriminated against the employees—the union by shirking its duty to properly represent the employees, and the company by discharging only the white employees. Since the case should not have been dismissed, the Court reversed and remanded it. *McDonald v. Santa Fe Trail Transp. Co.*, 427 U.S. 273, 96 S.Ct. 2574, 49 L.Ed.2d 493 (1976).

B. Race Discrimination

A Nigerian immigrant with extensive college coursework in accounting worked in the laundry of an Arizona hotel. He took the job after being told that he could seek a transfer to the hotel accounting department after six months, but the hotel repeatedly rejected his applications for transfer or promotion over the next two years. It twice employed less-qualified white applicants for accounting and auditing positions, and twice employed persons who had not even applied for jobs for which the Nigerian applied. An administrative employee told him to "go back to Africa where you came from," and another advised him to find work at a "black business." The employee filed a race and national origin discrimination complaint against the hotel in the U.S. District Court for the District of Arizona, which found that the hotel had discriminated against him. The U.S. Court of Appeals, Ninth Circuit, reversed and remanded the case for more specific findings. The district court issued findings, and the hotel appealed.

The court of appeals found no error in district court findings that in four contested promotional opportunities the hotel had violated the employee's rights under Title VII. In one case, the hotel had also violated 42 U.S.C. § 1981 under the standard applicable prior to the enactment of the Civil Rights Act of 1991. The hotel's argument that the employee had failed to mitigate his damages was without merit, and awards of backpay, front pay, and compensatory damages were justified. The court remanded the case for further findings on the compensatory damage award and the award of attorney's fees. *Odima v. Westin Tucson Hotel*, 53 F.3d 1484 (9th Cir.1995).

A union representing steamship clerks in the Boston area adopted a membership policy that required prospective union members to be sponsored by existing union members. During a six-year period, 30 new white members were admitted into the union, usually sponsored by relatives, but no African-Americans or Hispanics gained entry. The U.S. Equal Employment Opportunity Commission (EEOC) filed a lawsuit against the union in the U.S. District Court for the District of Massachusetts, claiming that the union had discriminated against African-American and Hispanic laborers in violation of Title VII of the Civil Rights Act of 1964. The court encouraged the parties to attempt a settlement but awarded summary judgment to the EEOC without providing further notice after they failed to settle within 30 days. Both parties appealed unfavorable aspects of the judgment to the U.S. Court of Appeals, First Circuit.

The court of appeals found no error in the district court's finding that the union's policy had an unlawful disparate impact on African-Americans and Hispanics, who composed a significant part of the local labor market and yet obtained no union memberships during the relevant period. The court rejected the union's arguments that the case should be dismissed because no minority applicants had actually sought union membership and that the district court had confused nepotism with racial discrimination. Despite the small number of memberships at stake and the lack of evidence concerning particular applicants, the district court's judgment had been based on sufficient legal grounds, and its order to discontinue the membership policy was affirmed. However, it vacated the remainder of the district court judgment and gave the parties an opportunity to argue for appropriate relief. *EEOC v. Steamship Clerks Union, Local 1066*, 48 F.3d 594 (1st Cir.1995).

U.S. Department of Transportation Regulations disqualify persons using controlled substances such as marijuana from operating commercial motor vehicles. The regulations also require mandatory drug testing for all employees holding commercial motor vehicle drivers' licenses. An African-American heavy equipment operator tested positive for illegal drug use in mandatory drug testing administered under the regulations. He was immediately suspended from driving as required. When the laboratory results of his retest were returned negative, his employment was reinstated. However, a retest six months later detected marijuana use and he was again immediately suspended. Within days, the employer fired the driver and refused to consider evidence that his retest was negative. He sought to file a grievance against the employer through his collective bargaining association, which refused to take action. He filed a lawsuit against the employer for racial discrimination and against the union for breach of the duty of fair representation in the U.S. District Court for the Middle District of Alabama. The employer and union filed summary judgment motions.

The court noted that the testing had been performed by an independent laboratory, undercutting the employee's argument that the employer had used fraudulent testing procedures on the basis of his race. The employer had asserted legitimate, nondiscriminatory reasons for discharging the employee, complying with federal regulations which made drug abusers unqualified to hold commercial licenses. The duty of fair representation claim against the union was dismissed because it was barred by the statute of limitations, and the court granted summary judgment to the employer and union. *Grooms v. Wiregrass Electric Cooperative, Inc.*, 877 F.Supp. 602 (M.D.Ala.1995).

An African-American aerospace worker was reassigned to a position with which he was dissatisfied. He filed a race discrimination complaint under the company's internal employment procedure. Although the company found no unlawful discrimination, the employee took a medical leave of absence and was subsequently denied promotional opportunities. Although the employee was scheduled for a promotion that year, an assistant manager learned that his performance was not good and asked the employee's immediate supervisor to make a further investigation. The supervisor confirmed that the employee's performance was unsatisfactory and did not recommend a promotion. The supervisor then claimed that a management employee harassed him for refusing to document inadequate performance by the African-American employee. The supervisor accepted an employment offer from another employer, and together with the African-American employee, sued the company in a California trial court for racial discrimination and retaliation. A jury awarded substantial amounts to the employees for lost wages and work-related benefits, plus $40 million each in punitive damages. The Los Angeles County Superior Court, Appellate Department, found that the employees' attorneys had engaged in inappropriate conduct, including inflammatory remarks to the jury, which required a new trial. There were a number of substantial problems in the employees' evidence and the punitive damage award was excessive. The court granted the employer's motion for a new trial. *Lane v. Hughes Aircraft Co., Inc.*, 40 Cal.Rptr.2d 97 (Cal.Super.— Los Angeles County 1994).

A former pizza delivery man filed an employment discrimination claim against his ex-employer. He alleged that the employer discriminated against him on the basis of race when it fired him for failure to appear clean-shaven in compliance with the company's no-beard policy. The no-beard policy was established nationwide by the pizza's franchiser. He alleged that he suffered from pseudofolliculitis barbae (PFB), a skin condition affecting approximately 50 percent of African males, half of whom cannot shave at all. The delivery man claimed that the no-beard policy deprived him and other African-American males suffering from PFB of equal employment opportunities in violation of Title VII. The trial court analyzed the record in light of *Wards Cove Packing Co. v. Atonio*, above, and found for the employer on the question of business justification. Accordingly, the court denied the relief, and the EEOC appealed to the U.S. Court of Appeals, Eighth Circuit.

The EEOC contended that because it sought relief from the employer's ongoing no-beard policy, the Civil Rights Act of 1991 governed in this case and the district court erred by applying the *Wards Cove* standard to determine the business necessity issue. Since the 1991 act expressly reinstated the law of business necessity as it existed before *Wards Cove* was decided, the 1991 act returned the burden of persuasion regarding business necessity to the defendant employer. The court of appeals agreed. The court further stated that the EEOC had demonstrated that the employer had failed to show the business necessity for its inflexible no-beard policy. The employer's evidence was speculative and conclusory. The court further stated that the company was free to establish any grooming and dress standard that it wished. However, the court held that a reasonable accommodation must be made for members of the protected class who suffer from PFB. Accordingly, the court reversed and remanded the district court's decision. *Bradley v. Pizzaco of Nebraska, Inc.*, 7 F.3d 795 (8th Cir.1993).

An African-American man began as an assistant accountant at an aircraft company and continued in that position for over six years. He had applied for several promotions but received none. In 1986, he was informed that he was to be laid off due to a shortage of work. After he complained about the layoff and obtained legal counsel, he was told that his layoff had been delayed. His department supervisor was ordered to create a position for him. The department supervisor then began to keep a separate file concerning the accountant's productivity. In 1989, the accountant was informed that he was a candidate for a company-wide reduction in force. He then filed this suit alleging racial discrimination in a California state court. The jury entered judgment in favor of the accountant and awarded punitive damages in the amount of $3.5 million. However, the accountant accepted a reduction of punitive damages to $1 million. The employer then appealed to the California Court of Appeal, Second District.

The aircraft company contended that the evidence did not support the finding of intentional racial discrimination because the employee failed to produce direct evidence. The company alleged that evidence of unfair treatment alone was insufficient and that intentional discrimination must be shown either by racially derogatory remarks or statistical evidence. However, the court determined that an employee may present any admissible evidence to prove either that it was more likely that the reason for the adverse employment action was due to racial discrimination or that the employer's stated reason was unworthy of credence. In the present case, the jury could fairly conclude that the employee had been subjected to a pattern of unfair treatment. *Harris v. Hughes Aircraft Co.*, 23 Cal.Rptr.2d 343 (Cal.App.1993).

An insurance company in Wisconsin employed an African-American sales manager who alleged that he experienced physical problems from job-related stress and abusive conduct by his white supervisor. In addition to race-neutral name calling, the sales manager alleged that the supervisor used the word "nigger" twice in his presence and stated, "you black guys are too fucking dumb to be insurance agents." The supervisor increased the size of an open account serviced by the sales manager, and the manager resigned. After bringing unsuccessful discrimination complaints before state and federal equal rights agencies, the sales manager sued the insurance company for unlawful racial harassment under Title

VII. The court held that the insurance company had violated Title VII by maintaining a racially hostile work environment, and had constructively discharged the sales manager by creating work-related stress. It awarded the sales manager over $101,000 and ordered the insurance company to pay him a pension plan annuity. It denied the sales manager's claim for front pay and both parties appealed to the U.S. Court of Appeals, Seventh Circuit.

The court held that the use of an unambiguously racial epithet by a supervisor in the presence of subordinates created an abusive working environment that violated Title VII. The fact that African-American employees may have also used the term "nigger" in the workplace did not mitigate the supervisor's use of the word. Title VII "does not permit supervisors to use this type of blanket criticism of the intelligence of a racially-defined class of employees as a motivational technique." The court rejected the insurance company's argument that the resignation was attributable to stress from the increased workload. It affirmed the finding of constructive discharge, the award of backpay and the annuity. It also affirmed the denial of the front pay award based on the sales manager's refusal to accept reemployment by the insurance company. *Rodgers v. Western — Southern Life Ins. Co.*, 12 F.3d 668 (7th Cir.1993).

An Alabama health maintenance organization hired an African-American secretary at the rate of $14,996 annually. She replaced a white female who had been hired nine months earlier at the rate of $16,000 per year. Over the next two years, she unsuccessfully applied for several positions of increasing responsibility. She then resigned. A white female was hired as the secretary's replacement; she had neither a college degree nor any prior work experience. The health maintenance organization had only employed two African-Americans: the secretary and another employee. The other employee filed a charge with the EEOC and received a right to sue letter. The secretary then filed a timely motion to intervene in a federal district court. After a two-day bench trial, the court permitted the secretary to intervene. However, the court found that her wage discrimination claim was time-barred, reasoning that the wage discrimination was the product of a single act which occurred on the day she began her employment. The secretary then appealed to the U.S. Court of Appeals, Eleventh Circuit.

On appeal, the secretary argued that the race-based wage discrimination was a continuing act and was not barred by the 180-day Title VII statute of limitations. The court concluded that race-based discriminatory wage payments constituted a continuing violation of Title VII. Since the claim was one for discriminatory wage, the violation existed every single day the employee worked, not merely the date the secretary was hired. Accordingly, the appellate court reversed the decision of the trial court and remanded the case for a determination of damages. *Calloway v. Partners National Health Plan*, 986 F.2d 446 (11th Cir.1993).

After a Maryland corporation hired a minority worker, a rejected white applicant sued it for reverse discrimination in a federal district court. The corporation had instituted an affirmative action program after an EEOC audit revealed violations of various federal fair employment statutes and regulations.

The affirmative action plan required that the employee be competent and qualified, but that there would be a preference for minority workers. The white employee alleged that the corporation refused to hire him solely on the basis of his race in violation of 42 U.S.C. § 1981. The corporation alluded to its affirmative action plan as a legitimate nondiscriminatory reason for the hiring decision. Thus, the burden of persuasion rested on the white employee to prove that the affirmative action plan was not bona fide. The court noted that the corporation had satisfied its burden and that the affirmative action plan was bona fide. The affirmative action plan was a response to a conspicuous racial imbalance and reasonably tailored to cure this imbalance. Thus, the corporation's motion for summary judgment was granted. *Stock v. Universal Foods Corporation*, 817 F.Supp. 1300 (D.Md.1993).

An African-American repair shop employee began working for a trailer manufacturer in Louisiana in 1966. He was denied a pay raise that was awarded to white employees in 1988 and when the company's ownership changed hands, he was not considered for continuing employment. A supervisor hired a 19-year-old white applicant instead. The employee then filed a complaint with the EEOC for age and race discrimination and was issued a right-to-sue letter. He sued the new company and the former company. The new company declared bankruptcy and was dismissed from the lawsuit. A federal court then found the selling company liable for discriminatory acts which deprived the employee of a pay raise and the opportunity to seek employment. The company appealed to the U.S. Court of Appeals, Fifth Circuit. The selling company contended that it could not be held liable for discrimination because the supervisor was not acting as its agent. The court noted that the employer was only liable for the acts of its servants committed while in the scope of employment. The court noted that the supervisor checked applications and interviewed potential employees for the purchasing company, not the selling company. Therefore, the court concluded that the supervisor was acting solely for the benefit of the new company and the discriminatory acts could not be attributed to the selling company. The court reversed the judgment against the selling company despite the racially discriminatory acts committed by the employee. *Moham v. Steego Corp.*, 3 F.3d 873 (5th Cir.1993).

A Washington African-American employee worked at a packaging company. The labor agreement in effect from 1985-1988 contained an explicit antidiscrimination clause. Despite this clause, repeated racial jokes, cartoons, comments and other forms of hostility directed at almost every racial and ethnic group, particularly blacks, were common at the plant. The union was aware of the racial atmosphere at the plant. The employee complained to a fellow employee who was a union official and asked three times to file a grievance concerning the plant's racial atmosphere. Nevertheless, the union rejected the idea that any union member should be disciplined by the packaging company for racial harassment. The employee brought an action in a U.S. district court against the packaging company and the union alleging violations of federal and state law. The court found that the union officials participated in the harassment and had constructive knowledge of the racial harassment at the plant. The court held that the union had violated the duty of fair representation and state tort law. It ordered the union to pay general, special and punitive damages to the employee. The union appealed both judgments to the U.S. Court of Appeals, Ninth Circuit. The court determined that the union officials were acting within the scope of their employment. Therefore, the court upheld the district court's decision. *Woods v. Graphic Communications,* 925 F.2d 1195 (9th Cir.1991).

A black Indiana man was laid off his job for economic reasons. Although he was considered a good or average employee, he was never recalled. The man notified the corporation's secretaries of his continued interest in employment, filed a complaint with the Gary Human Relations Committee, and expressed a willingness to return to work at a fact finding conference. In addition, another employee of the corporation suggested to a supervisor that he be rehired. The racial makeup of the employees consisted of only two black employees out of 28 labor gang employees working two job assignments. Moreover, the current work crew consisted of one black employee, one Hispanic employee and two white employees who were replaced with another white employee. A U.S. magistrate judge held that although the corporation could not be held liable for discrimination in the discharge, it had violated Title VII by failing to recall the black employee. The corporation appealed to the U.S. Court of Appeals, Seventh Circuit. On appeal, the court agreed that the corporation's failure to recall the black employee amounted to race discrimination. The court affirmed the ruling for the employee. *Smith v. BMI, Inc.,* 957 F.2d 462 (7th Cir.1992).

A black Illinois woman worked for the Chicago Tribune for 25 years. She started as a part-time ad-taker and earned a series of promotions within the advertising department. Eventually, she was transferred to the position of EEO employment manager. However, her immediate superior became dissatisfied with her work after receiving complaints from managers of other departments. He decided to transfer her back to the advertising department. She accepted the transfer and was also given a $2,000 raise. Her performance in her new position was unsatisfactory to her new supervisor, and he issued her a memo seeking responses to various criticisms. Instead, she resigned. She then brought suit against the newspaper for violations of Title VII.

Before the U.S. District Court for the Northern District of Illinois, she asserted that she had been demoted discriminatorily and that she had been constructively discharged. The court determined that she had not been demoted because she had received a raise of $2,000. Further, the memo from her superior was not onerous enough to amount to a constructive discharge. It merely sought a reply to various criticisms of her performance. Accordingly, the court ruled for the newspaper and found no discrimination. *Harriston v. Chicago Tribune Co.,* 771 F.Supp. 933 (N.D.Ill.1991).

A manufacturing company with a plant located in Chicago relied almost exclusively on word-of-mouth advertising in order to fill its entry-level jobs. The jobs were low paying, and did not require English language fluency. When the EEOC discovered that only six percent of the company's employees were black, it brought suit against the company in a federal district court, asserting that the company had engaged in discriminatory hiring and recruiting practices with respect to blacks. The company stated that there simply weren't many blacks interested in the jobs it offered. The EEOC, however, presented statistical evidence which showed that the percentage of entry-level workers in Chicago who were black was 36 percent, and argued that the statistical probability of the company's hiring so few blacks, in the absence of racial bias, was virtually zero. The district court agreed, and held for the EEOC. The company appealed to the U.S. Court of Appeals, Seventh Circuit.

On appeal, the court rejected the EEOC's assertion that intentional discrimination against blacks must have occurred because of two variables which had not been included in the district court's findings. First, because the jobs were so low-paying, commuting time had not been properly taken into account. Second, the fact that English fluency was not required was a factor which would raise the level of interest among people who did not speak English well. The EEOC had not shown that there were many blacks who were interested in the jobs but who were not hired. The court reversed the district court's decision and held for the company. *EEOC v. Chicago Miniature Lamp Works,* 947 F.2d 292 (7th Cir. 1991).

A black woman was hired by a department store chain to work as a receiving department clerk in its Mobile, Alabama, store. At the time she was hired, a white female was the receiving manager. Subsequently, two other white women served as receiving managers for the store. When the job next became available, employees who were interested in promotion were informally identified by store managers. One of the qualified interested candidates was the black woman who had been working at the store for 18 months. Another potential candidate was a white male who had been working at the store for approximately nine months. Since the store had no formal application procedure for promotions, the store's management committee conducted a meeting to determine which candidate would be best for the job. They selected the white male. The black woman then brought suit in a federal district court, claiming that the store had discriminated against her in violation of Title VII. The court ruled for the store, and the woman appealed to the U.S. Court of Appeals, Eleventh Circuit.

The court of appeals noted that the white male had been a chief petty officer in the Coast Guard for 15 years and had eleven years of supervisory experience. He had also supervised a maintenance crew that worked at a chain of grocery stores. The members of the management committee who had participated in the promotion decision had all testified that the white male was their unanimous choice to be the next receiving manager. Further, the store had a good record of promoting blacks to management positions. Accordingly, the court found that the store's reasons for not promoting the black employee were not a pretext for discrimination, and it affirmed the ruling of the district court. *Moulds v. Wal-Mart Stores Inc.*, 935 F.2d 252 (11th Cir.1991).

An Indiana African-American, employed for several years, received numerous disciplinary notices and incident reports from his employer. Citations included "poor work record, volatility, inability to get along with co-workers, and lack of appropriate leadership abilities." Upon application for a supervisor position, the employee was not recommended by the selection committee. The basis of the decision rested on the employee's past record of violations. The employee claimed the basis was race. A magistrate heard the allegation and found in favor of the employer. The employee appealed, and his employer cross-appealed, arguing that the employee's claims were frivolous. On appeal, the U.S. Court of Appeals, Seventh Circuit, affirmed the magistrate's decision in favor of the employer. Additionally, the court awarded the employer attorney's fees and costs as sanctions against the frivolous appeal by the employee's attorney. *Tyson v. Laughlin Steel Corporation,* 958 F.2d 556 (7th Cir.1992).

C. National Origin Discrimination

Title VII prohibits discrimination on the basis of national origin by employers, but discrimination against noncitizens on the basis of alienage has been upheld by the U.S. Supreme Court.

A Massachusetts man born in Israel applied for a position with his wife's company in directory advertising sales. During his interview, a company official indicated that his sales experience in Israel was too far removed in time from the application date to satisfy the experience requirement. He then filed a new application and was told that he would be interviewed within the coming year. He was called in for a test and an interview. He stated that during the interview, the interviewer asked if he was from Israel and he observed a look of disgust on her face. He filed yet another application and was told that the company had adopted a policy of not hiring employees' spouses. During this time, the company hired several individuals who did not meet the stated screening criteria of having a college degree and sales experience. He then brought a discrimination suit for race and national origin discrimination. The federal district court entered judgment for the applicant and the company appealed to the U.S. Court of Appeals, First Circuit. The court noted that the applicant had made out a *prima facie* case of discrimination. The company claimed that the events did not establish race discrimination. However, the court disagreed, noting that the jury could have determined that the company discriminated against the applicant on the basis of his race. The company further contended that it had hired several Jews for advertising positions. However, the court noted that the relevant issue in a discrimination claim was whether the defendant discriminated against the plaintiff on an improper basis. The fact that the company hired other members of the protected class was evidence that the jury could consider, but was not dispositive. The evidence was not so heavily weighted in the company's favor to justify setting aside the jury verdict. The court upheld the decision of the trial court and found for the applicant. *Sinai v. New England Telephone and Telegraph Co.*, 3 F.3d 471 (1st Cir.1993).

A Japanese corporation operated subsidiaries in the United States which sold heavy construction equipment. An American-born regional manager for one of the subsidiaries sold equipment and was required to entertain customers. The subsidiary was to reimburse him for entertainment and meal expenses based upon his expense reports. The manager's expense reports came under scrutiny and his supervisor ordered an audit. The manager admitted in a meeting with the human resources manager that he had altered some of his receipts, but claimed that he could account for the irregularities as legitimate business expenses. The subsidiary terminated the manager's employment for falsifying his expense reports. The manager was replaced by a Japanese employee who had formerly worked for the subsidiary's parent company. The discharged manager sued the subsidiary in the U.S. District Court for the Northern District of Illinois, claiming national origin discrimination. The court considered the subsidiary's motion for summary judgment. It determined that national origin discrimination complaints by U.S.-born individuals were recognized under Title VII of the Civil Rights Act. However, the employee had failed to allege facts that indicated he was fired for any reason other than preparing false expense account records. Although the manager alleged that the subsidiary was engaged in a plot to replace him with a Japanese-born employee, there was no evidence in the record to indicate any impermissible motive by the employer. The court granted the subsidiary's motion for summary judgment. *Bagnell v. Komatsu Dresser Co.*, 838 F.Supp. 1279 (N.D.Ill.1993).

A Hispanic operator of an asphalt paving machine was called a "wetback" and a "Mexican" by his supervisor. When the supervisor asked the Mexican-American to leave the machine and help with some shoveling, the employee walked off the work site and went to the main office to speak with the employee complaints manager. However, the employee did not mention the racial comments. After several days, the manager offered to let the employee return to work at a lower rate of pay. The employee filed a complaint with the EEOC claiming racial discrimination, which was later denied. Nevertheless, the employee filed suit in a Texas federal district court for constructive discharge pursuant to Title VII. The district court granted summary judgment to the employer, and the employee appealed to the U.S. Court of Appeals, Fifth Circuit.

The employer argued that the employee's allegations did not rise to the level of severe and pervasive harassment necessary to support a claim for constructive discharge. Further, the employer alleged that even if the ethnic slurs were severe and pervasive enough to support a constructive discharge, the employee's claim would still fail because he did not give the employer a chance to remedy the alleged harassment. In order to establish that he was constructively discharged, the employee had to prove that his working conditions were so unpleasant that a reasonable person would have felt compelled to resign. After reviewing the record, the court did not find evidence to suggest that a reasonable person in the employee's position would have felt compelled to resign. For this reason, the appellate court upheld the grant of summary judgment in favor of the employer. *Ugalde v. W. A. McKenzie Asphalt Co.*, 990 F.2d 239 (5th Cir.1993).

A Hispanic woman worked as a supervisor at a developmental disability center. She and the employee who worked with her were responsible for performing bed checks every 30 minutes. However, during her shift, a patient for whom her subordinate was responsible opened his window and fell to the ground. He was not discovered until after the supervisor's shift had ended. He subsequently died as a result of hypothermia. The superintendent of the facility conducted a complete investigation of the occurrence and decided to fire both the employee who had not made the bed check and the supervisor. The superintendent did not fire the supervisor of the following shift who had failed to discover the missing patient at the start of her shift. The Hispanic supervisor then filed an action in a Colorado federal district court, claiming that her discharge had been discriminatory under 42 U.S.C. § 1981 and under Title VII. The district court granted summary judgment to the employer on the § 1981 claim and dismissed the Title VII claim. The supervisor appealed.

On appeal to the U.S. Court of Appeals, Tenth Circuit, the court noted that § 1981 "prohibits racial discrimination in the making and enforcing of contracts." Conduct which occurred after the contract was made did not fall within the protections of § 1981. For the type of racial discrimination alleged in this case, Title VII provided an adequate remedy. However, the court then agreed with the district court's holding that the supervisor had not established a *prima facie* case of discrimination because she was unqualified for the position from which she was terminated. The other supervisor (who had not been fired) was found to have fulfilled her supervisory responsibilities. The court thus affirmed the district court's holding in favor of the employer. *Trujillo v. Grand Junction Regional Center*, 928 F.2d 973 (10th Cir.1991).

A citizen of Mexico, who resided lawfully in the United States, sought employment as a seamstress with a manufacturing company. Her application was rejected due to a long-standing policy against the employment of aliens. After exhausting her administrative remedies with the EEOC, the applicant sued the company in a Texas federal district court, asserting that the company had discriminated against her on the basis of national origin in violation of Title VII. The court granted summary judgment to the applicant, but the U.S. Court of Appeals, Fifth Circuit, reversed. It determined that the phrase "national origin" did not include citizenship. The case then came before the U.S. Supreme Court.

The Supreme Court held that the company's refusal to hire the woman because of her citizenship was not discrimination on the basis of national origin in violation of Title VII. Even though Title VII protects aliens against discrimination because of race, color, religion, sex, or national origin, it does not prohibit discrimination against aliens on the basis of alienage. Here, the company had not refused to hire the applicant because of her Mexican ancestry, but because she was not a United States citizen. This was not forbidden by Title VII. The Court affirmed the court of appeals' decision against the applicant. *Espinoza v. Farah Manufacturing Co.,* 414 U.S. 86, 94 S.Ct. 334, 38 L.Ed.2d 287 (1973).

II. GENDER DISCRIMINATION

Gender discrimination, like race discrimination, violates Title VII of the Civil Rights Act. The shifting burden of proof analysis applied by the courts in Title VII race discrimination cases also applies to sex discrimination cases. Where an employee proves under Title VII that his or her employer has engaged in unlawful intentional discrimination on the basis of sex, the employee will be entitled to recover monetary damages in addition to equitable relief. Another important statute with respect to gender discrimination is the Equal Pay Act.

A. Title VII

A Florida woman sued a company under Title VII claiming that she had been denied employment because of her sex. The company refused to accept job applications from women with pre-school age children. The district court granted summary judgment to the company, noting that 70-75 percent of the applicants were women and 75-80 percent of those hired for the position were women. It reasoned that no question of bias was thus presented. The court of appeals affirmed. The U.S. Supreme Court granted review. The Court stated that § 703(a) of the Civil Rights Act of 1964 requires that persons of like qualifications be given employment opportunities irrespective of their sex. There cannot be one hiring policy for women and one for men. The requirement could only be justified if it was a bona fide occupational qualification that was reasonably necessary to the normal operation of the business. The court remanded for full development of the issue. *Phillips v. Martin Marietta Corp.,* 400 U.S. 542, 91 S.Ct. 496, 27 L.Ed.2d 613 (1971).

An applicant for employment at an Alabama prison was rejected because she failed to meet its 120-pound weight requirement. The statute which established that requirement also established a minimum height of five feet two inches. She sued the employer in a federal district court, challenging the requirements as establishing gender criteria for assigning correctional counselors to "contact" positions. The court found for the applicant, noting that 40 percent of the female population, but only one percent of the male population, would be excluded by the requirements. The court rejected the employer's bona fide occupational qualification defense, ruling that being a male was not a legitimate qualification. The U.S. Supreme Court held that the district court was correct with regard to the finding of discrimination. The applicant had established a *prima facie* case which the employer failed to rebut. The employer had produced no evidence correlating the job requirements with the requisite amount of strength thought essential to good job performance. However, the Court held that the BFOQ defense should apply to this case. Alabama maintains a prison system where violence is rampant and small persons were unsuitable for employment. *Dothard v. Rawlinson*, 433 U.S. 321, 97 S.Ct. 2720, 53 L.Ed.2d 786 (1977).

Under a collective bargaining agreement (CBA), seniority at a corporation was determined by years of plantwide service. However, in 1979, under a new CBA, the manner of computing seniority was changed so that employees promoted to higher positions would have their seniority tested as of the date of promotion. Three women were selected for demotion during an economic downturn who would not have been demoted under the old system. They sued the corporation after receiving right-to-sue letters from the EEOC, but an Illinois federal district court granted summary judgment to the employer. They appealed unsuccessfully to the U.S. Court of Appeals, and further appealed to the U.S. Supreme Court, which held that a seniority system having a disparate impact on men and women is not unlawful unless discriminatory intent is proven. The system did not discriminate on its face or as it was applied. If it had been adopted with a discriminatory intent, the statute of limitations had run in the years since the CBA had been entered into. The Court affirmed the decision in favor of the employer. *Lorance v. AT & T Technologies, Inc.,* 490 U.S. 900, 109 S.Ct. 2261, 104 L.Ed.2d 961 (1989). The 1991 Civil Rights Act overrules the result of this case by stating that the statute of limitations under Title VII will begin to run not just when the employer's rule is adopted, but also whenever an individual is subjected to it, and whenever a person is aggrieved by the rule's application.

A senior manager at a nationwide professional accounting firm was refused admission as a partner. She brought suit against the firm in a federal district court under Title VII, charging that the firm had discriminated against her on the basis of sex in its partnership decisions. The district court found that the firm had discriminated against the manager, but held that it could avoid equitable relief if it could prove by clear and convincing evidence that it would have made the same decision in the absence of a discriminatory motive. The U.S. Court of Appeals, District of Columbia Circuit, affirmed, and noted that the firm could avoid liability if it showed by clear and convincing evidence that it would have made the same decision without the discrimination. The case came before the U.S. Supreme Court. The Supreme Court held that under Title VII, the employer could avoid liability if it showed by a mere preponderance of the evidence that it would have made the same decision even if it had not taken the manager's gender into account. This preserved the employer's right to freedom of choice. The court then reversed and remanded the case for a determination of whether the same decision would have been made absent the discrimination. *Price Waterhouse v. Hopkins,* 490 U.S. 228, 109 S.Ct. 1775, 104 L.Ed.2d 268 (1989). Under the Civil Rights Act of 1991, if it is shown that discrimination is a contributing factor in the employment decision, then (assuming that the employer can show that it would have made the same decision absent the discrimination) courts will be prohibited from ordering certain injunctive relief—like reinstatement. However, money damages may still be available.

A flight attendant for an airline company was forced to resign in 1968 when she married. When the airline's policy of "single only" flight attendants was found to be violative of Title VII, it abated the policy. The flight attendant was rehired by the airline in 1972 as a new employee, without seniority from her days with the airline prior to 1968. She sued the company in an Illinois federal district court, alleging that, by refusing to credit her with pre-1972 seniority, the airline was guilty of a present, continuing violation of Title VII. The court dismissed the case, but the U.S. Court of Appeals reversed. The U.S. Supreme Court agreed to review the case and noted that the violation alleged by the flight attendant was not a continuing violation. This was because she had not asserted that the seniority system discriminated against female employees or that it treated former employees who were discharged for discriminatory reasons differently from other former employees. Since the flight attendant had not shown intentional discrimination on the part of the airline. It is permissible to treat employees differently if done according to a bona fide seniority system, and if the differences are not the result of intentional discrimination. The Court reversed the court of appeals' decision. *United Air Lines, Inc. v. Evans,* 431 U.S. 553, 97 S.Ct. 1885, 52 L.Ed.2d 571 (1977).

A group of job applicants claimed that an airline refused to hire them because they did not meet its minimum height requirement of five feet two inches. They stated that the height requirement had a disparate impact on women based on statistical evidence that women were 66 times more likely to be excluded from being hired as a result of the requirement than men. They filed a lawsuit against the airline in a Minnesota trial court claiming that the hiring practice violated the state civil rights act. The court conducted a trial at which expert evidence was introduced supporting the applicants' argument. The court also considered evidence that the height requirement was related to important business purposes including customer service, passenger safety and reduced flight attendant injury based on less reaching. The court determined that the airline's stated reasons justified the policy, even though it had an adverse impact on women. The applicants appealed the finding that the height requirement was justified and the airline appealed the finding that the requirement had an adverse impact on women. The Court of Appeals of Minnesota determined that a challenged employment practice may be upheld if it serves a legitimate employment goal of an employer in a significant way. Accordingly, the trial court's finding that the height requirement was justified was not erroneous. Even though the requirement created an adverse impact on women, the airline had shown that it furthered a legitimate business interest. The court of appeals also upheld the trial court's determination not to certify the action as a class action. *Novack v. Northwest Airlines, Inc.*, 525 N.W.2d 592 (Minn.App.1995).

A Tennessee bookstore employee claimed that his immediate supervisor was a homosexual who harassed him on the basis of his sex. He filed a complaint with the EEOC, which filed a sexual harassment claim on his behalf against the employer in the U.S. District Court for the Middle District of Tennessee. The commission argued that Title VII of the Civil Rights Act of 1964 prohibits sexual harassment by supervisors against same-sex subordinates. The court noted that a number of federal courts had considered the issue with inconsistent results. Although the U.S. Supreme Court had never considered a same-sex harassment claim, language from its recent decisions indicated that Title VII contained a congressional intent to strike at the entire spectrum of workplace harassment. The court agreed with the employee's argument that Title VII prohibited sex discrimination by homosexual supervisors because a subordinate who was harassed on the basis of sex would not otherwise be treated differently than opposite-sex coworkers. *EEOC v. Walden Book Co., Inc.*, 885 F.Supp. 1100 (M.D.Tenn.1995).

The U.S. District Court for the District of Nevada dismissed a claim involving hostile work environment sex harassment. In that case, a group of employees claimed that their supervisors harassed them by writing about, drawing and explicitly discussing homosexual sex acts on the job which created a hostile work environment that materially hampered their ability to work. The court held that in order to prevail in their hostile work environment sexual harassment case, the employees would have to demonstrate that the work environment was hostile to men and not hostile on the basis of sexual orientation or preference. The court held that same-sex harassment was not legally recognized under Title VII in the absence of evidence that the employees were humiliated or ridiculed. Any hostile work environment case would be difficult to prove where same-sex harassment was alleged because an employee's reaction to homosexual conduct was a matter of sexual orientation, not sex discrimination. *Fox v. Sierra Development Co.*, 876 F.Supp. 1169 (D.Nev.1995).

A sales representative worked for a family-owned screen printing and designing business. The sales representative was regarded as an independent contractor and she also worked for other employers. The representative was paid commissions and received a 1099 tax form rather than a W-2. She paid her own expenses, received no leave time and was ineligible for unemployment or workers' compensation benefits. Although the representative reported to supervisors daily and received comments from them, she set her own schedule and solicited her own customers. She claimed that the company president made offensive and abusive statements of a sexual nature and called her "fat." She left the company, then sued it and its president in the U.S. District Court for the Eastern District of Virginia, which considered dismissal motions by the president and company.

The court agreed with the company president that Title VII does not impose personal liability on supervisors. Because the president was not an employer, he was entitled to dismissal of the complaint against him. Title VII protections extend only to employees, and not to independent contractors. The test of determining whether an individual is an employee or an independent contractor requires consideration of economic realities including the kind of occupation, duration of work, level of skill, method of payment, whether the work is an integral part of the employer's business and the employer's control over the individual. In this case a number of factors indicated that the sales representative was an independent contractor, particularly her description of her occupation as "self sales" on her tax forms. The court dismissed the Title VII complaint and other claims advanced under Virginia law, ruling also that being called fat did not constitute a breach of the peace under a state law prohibiting insults intended to cause violence. *Lane v. David P. Jacobson & Co., Ltd.*, 880 F.Supp. 1091 (E.D.Va.1995).

A New York accounting employee submitted medical claims on behalf of her husband under her employer's group health package, which covered spouses to the extent that their own coverage was insufficient. The employee represented that her husband had only hospitalization insurance and submitted over $700 in claims for reimbursement of medical expenses. The company later fired her, alleging that she had falsified the claims, that her husband had applicable coverage, and that the employee had failed to submit proof of her husband's other available insurance. Following her discharge, the state department of labor approved the employee's claim for unemployment benefits, finding no misconduct. The employee filed a discrimination complaint against the employer with the U.S. EEOC, which was rejected. She filed suit in the U.S. District Court for the Eastern District of New York, claiming that the employer had violated Title VII of the Civil Rights Act of 1964 and 42 U.S.C. § 1981. The court granted summary judgment to the employer, and the employee appealed to the U.S. Court of Appeals, Second Circuit. The court observed that the district court had based its dismissal on the employee's reliance upon two conflicting theories of liability. On the one hand, she argued that she had committed no wrong, and on the other, she argued that she had been treated differently than white and male employees for wrongful behavior. The court observed that the Federal Rules of Civil Procedure permit alternative pleadings, and that the district court had improperly dismissed the claim that the employee was not guilty of misconduct. Although the district court had correctly ruled that there was no evidence of disparate treatment among black, white or male employees, the court reversed and remanded the case for reconsideration of the misconduct charges. *Henry v. Daytop Village Inc.*, 42 F.3d 89 (2d Cir.1994).

A Texas employee alleged that a plant foreman who was not his supervisor grabbed his crotch area and made sexual motions from behind him. The employee reported this to his union steward and then filed a complaint with the EEOC. The plant manager reprimanded the foreman and warned him that further harassment would result in termination of his employment. The employee nonetheless filed a lawsuit against his employer's parent company, plant foreman and plant manager. The U.S. District Court for the Northern District of Texas granted summary judgment for the company, manager and foreman, and the employee appealed to the U.S. Court of Appeals, Fifth Circuit. The court of appeals stated that Title VII prohibits sex discrimination by an "employer." The term "employer" is defined as a person engaged in an industry affecting commerce with 15 or more employees, including a corporation. The district court had properly dismissed the parent corporation from the lawsuit, rejecting the employee's argument that his employer and its parent were a single, integrated enterprise. For the purposes of Title VII, only the subsidiary was the employee's "employer." Title VII was also inapplicable to the supervisor and foreman, who were mere coworkers. Accordingly, summary judgment had been appropriate. The district court also correctly determined that harassment by a male supervisor against a male subordinate did not state a claim under Title VII, despite sexual overtones. *Garcia v. Elf Atochem North America*, 28 F.3d 446 (5th Cir.1994).

A Delaware temporary employment agency maintained a list of more than 1,000 temporary workers but employed only six to eight permanent employees. Three permanent employees claimed sexual harassment by the agency and filed a lawsuit against it under Title VII of the Civil Rights Act of 1964 in the U.S. District Court for the District of Delaware. The court considered the agency's motion to dismiss the case based on lack of subject matter jurisdiction. Title VII prohibits employers and employment agencies from discriminating against employees for certain enumerated reasons, including sexual harassment. However, coverage under Title VII applies only to employers of 15 or more employees. The court rejected the argument that the agency should be considered an employer based on the large number of temporary workers it placed. Applying common law agency principles, the court found that the agency did not exercise significant control over temporary workers and did not direct, supervise or evaluate their performance. Since the temporary workers could not be considered employees of the agency, it did not meet the requirements for Title VII coverage, and the trial court granted the agency's motion to dismiss the lawsuit. *Kellam v. Snelling Personnel Serv.*, 866 F.Supp. 812 (D.Del.1994).

An Arkansas woman filed suit in a federal district court against a publishing company claiming gender discrimination. The district court ruled in favor of the employer. It concluded that the employer had presented a legitimate, nondiscriminatory reason for employment termination and the woman had not met her burden of showing that the reason was pretextual. The woman appealed to the U.S. Court of Appeals, Eighth Circuit. The court noted that a plaintiff in a sex discrimination suit may proceed under two theories, the *Price Waterhouse* theory and the *McDonnell Douglas* theory. Under the *Price Waterhouse* theory, often called the mixed-motive analysis, once an employee has established that gender was a motivating factor in the employment decision, the burden of persuasion shifts to the employer to show that "it would have made the same decision even if it had not taken the illegitimate criterion into account." However, if the plaintiff is unable to produce evidence that the employer used an illegitimate criterion, the employee may proceed under the three-step framework described in *McDonnell Douglas*. The woman contended that the district court had failed to address the applicability of *Price Waterhouse*. The employer argued that since the trial court had found that the employer had offered a legitimate reason for the employment decision, the court's omission was harmless error. However, the appellate court noted that a finding that the employer's reason was not pretextual did not satisfy the *Price Waterhouse* standard. Accordingly, the appellate court remanded the case to the trial court with instructions to evaluate it under the mixed-motive analysis of *Price Waterhouse*. *Stacks v. Southwestern Bell Yellow Pages, Inc.*, 996 F.2d 200 (8th Cir.1993).

A Michigan food service company had a grooming policy applicable to both males and females that provided that all hair be restrained by a baseball cap or a hair net, and that all hair be tucked under a hat so that it was not on the forehead or visible from the front of the hat. The hair length of male employees was required to be at or above the collar. A male employee was fired after he refused to cut his hair in compliance with the policy. He sued the company, alleging violation of state and federal civil rights acts by applying the grooming policy in a disparate manner in requiring only men to cut their hair at or above the collar. On the company's motion for summary judgment, the court found in the company's favor, finding no disparate treatment in the grooming policy, even though the company had modified its policy to provide for sex specific grooming policies. The employee appealed.

The Court of Appeals of Michigan held that sex-differentiated hair length grooming requirements do not constitute sex discrimination under Title VII of the Civil Rights Act. Here there was no allegation that each sex's individual grooming requirements were not enforced evenhandedly. The man did not contend that the overall grooming policy burdened one sex over the other, so as to give favorable treatment to one sex over the other. Because there was no evidence to the contrary, the court found that the company's grooming policy was not in violation of either the state or federal civil rights acts. It affirmed the decision of the trial court. *Bedker v. Domino's Pizza, Inc.*, 491 N.W.2d 275 (Mich.App.1992).

An employee executed an application for securities industry registration which included an arbitration agreement when she became a securities dealer. Subsequently, she filed a sex discrimination claim against her employer under the District of Columbia Human Rights Act. The employer moved to compel arbitration, but the trial court denied the motion on the grounds that the 1991 Civil Rights Act did not supplant the employee's rights under Title VII. The employer appealed to the District of Columbia Court of Appeals. The court of appeals held that compulsory arbitration agreements are binding for employment discrimination claims such as the one presented here. The court looked to *Gilmer v. Interstate/Johnson Lane Corp.*, 500 U.S. 20, 111 S.Ct. 1647, 114 L.Ed.2d 26 (1991), which held that employers may compel arbitration of an age discrimination claim, and followed the reasoning in that case, noting that the 1991 Civil Rights Act did not overrule the *Gilmer* holding. If anything, the act encouraged the use of alternative dispute resolution procedures in employment discrimination claims. The court reversed the trial court's decision, and held that the employee could be required to arbitrate her claim. *Benefits Communication Corp. v. Klieforth*, 642 A.2d 1299 (D.C.App.1994).

B. The Equal Pay Act

Enacted by Congress in 1963, the Equal Pay Act requires that employers pay males and females the same wages for equal work. As such, the Act applies only to sex discrimination in pay, and thus race-based equal pay claims must be litigated under the more general provisions of Title VII. Because the Equal Pay Act is part of the Fair Labor Standards Act, employees are protected by the Act as long as the employer is engaged in an industry affecting interstate commerce (in contrast to Title VII's 15-employee minimum for triggering coverage). The courts have consistently interpreted the "interstate commerce" requirement in a liberal fashion in favor of finding Equal Pay Act coverage. See, e.g., *Usery v. Columbia University,* 568 F.2d 953 (2d Cir.1977). The employee's burden of proof under the Act has been interpreted by the courts to require only that the jobs under comparison be "substantially" equal. Strict equality of the jobs under comparison is not required.

The Equal Pay Act, 29 U.S.C. § 206(d), provides in relevant part as follows:

(d) Prohibition of sex discrimination

(1) No employer having employees subject to any provisions of this section shall discriminate, within any establishment in which such employees are employed, between employees on the basis of sex by paying wages to employees in such establishment at a rate less than the rate at which he pays wages to employees of the opposite sex in such establishment for equal work on jobs the performance of which requires equal skill, effort, and responsibility, and which are performed under similar working conditions, except where such payment is made pursuant to (i) a seniority system; (ii) a merit system; (iii) a system which measures earnings by quantity or quality of production; or (iv) a differential based on any other factor other than sex: *Provided,* That an employer who is paying a wage rate differential in violation of this subsection shall not, in order to comply with the provisions of this subsection, reduce the wage rate of any employee.

* * *

A computer company hired a Florida woman as a technical writer. The writer learned that she and a female coworker were earning less than the male technical writers at the facility. She complained to her supervisor about the pay disparity and was subsequently placed on probation because of declining work performance and absenteeism. She filed a complaint with the EEOC and was later given an unsatisfactory performance rating. Eventually, she resigned, claiming that her supervisors had engaged in a pattern of harassment that constituted constructive discharge in retaliation for complaining about the unequal pay. She sued the employer in a federal district court for discrimination under the Equal Pay Act and also asserted that her employer had discriminated against her under Title VII and had retaliated against her under that statute as well. She won on all her claims and the employer appealed to the U.S. Court of Appeals, Eleventh Circuit.

The court of appeals affirmed the holding under the Equal Pay Act but reversed on the Title VII discrimination claim. Under the Equal Pay Act, once the pay disparity between substantially similar jobs is demonstrated, the burden shifts to the employer to prove that a factor other than sex is responsible for the differential. The employee need not prove discriminatory intent. However, under Title VII, the employee must prove that the employer had a discriminatory intent. Here, the lower court had never made a finding of intentional discrimination. Accordingly, the case had to be remanded so that issue could be resolved. Next, the court noted that the employee's claims of constructive discharge and retaliation were supported by the evidence. Here, the employee was engaged in statutorily protected expression when she contacted the EEOC, and had suffered an adverse employment action. There was also evidence of a causal relation between the two events. The court affirmed in part, reversed in part, and remanded the case. *Meeks v. Computer Associates International*, 15 F.3d 1013 (11th Cir.1994).

A supermarket chain in Florida hired a woman in 1976, promoting her to various positions in the company until she attained the position of grocery buyer. As the company's only female buyer, she was paid approximately $200 less per week than male buyers. Her year-end bonuses were also substantially smaller than those of her male counterparts. Eventually, the company terminated her position and offered her a head cashier job for $8.00 per hour (about $100 less per week). She filed suit against the company under Title VII and the Equal Pay Act. A federal district court ruled for the employee under Title VII, but granted summary judgment for the company under the Equal Pay Act, and both parties appealed to the U.S. Court of Appeals, Eleventh Circuit.

On appeal, the court noted that the burdens of proof under the two laws are different. Under the Equal Pay Act—which was directed only at wage discrimination between the sexes, forbidding the specific practice of paying unequal wages for equal work—the employee had to meet the fairly strict standard of proving that she performed "substantially similar work for less pay." However, under the more relaxed standard of similarity under Title VII, the employee only had to prove that the company intended to discriminate against her on the basis of her sex. The court then agreed with the district court that the employee had carried her burden of proof under Title VII, establishing that the company had discriminated against her because of her gender. Next, the court held that summary judgment against the employee on the Equal Pay Act claim had been improper because there was a genuine issue of material fact as to the similarity of the jobs held by the employee and the male buyer whose duties were most similar. The court reversed the grant of summary judgment on this issue, and remanded the case for a trial. It affirmed the holding under Title VII and the award of $52,000 in backpay. *Miranda v. B & B Cash Grocery Store, Inc.,* 975 F.2d 1518 (11th Cir.1992).

C. Pregnancy Discrimination

The Pregnancy Discrimination Act (42 U.S.C. § 2000e(k)) amended Title VII of the Civil Rights Act in 1978 to include pregnancy in its general prohibition of discrimination on the basis of sex. The act prohibits less favorable treatment of pregnancy-related conditions than that afforded to other medical conditions and disabilities. Covered employers must provide the same benefits to pregnant employees as those afforded to other workers with temporary and long-term disabilities. The U.S. Court of Appeals, Eleventh Circuit, reversed and remanded a decision of the U.S. District Court for the Northern District of Alabama, which had ruled against a pregnant employee because of her inability to show that the employer had dealt with her pregnancy-related absences differently than other employee illnesses. The court rejected this analysis, finding that the pregnant employee was not required to present specific evidence that she was dissimilarly treated. The court reasoned that the employer's policies were presumed to be followed, and required no further proof that the employer did not discharge other nonpregnant employees for taking their allotted sick leave. *Byrd v. Lakeshore Hospital*, 30 F.3d 1380 (11th Cir.1994).

A contrary result was reached by the U.S. Court of Appeals, Seventh Circuit, which affirmed the dismissal of a case filed by an Illinois employee who was fired the day before she took maternity leave. The employee had been frequently absent or late for work prior to her leave. The court affirmed the judgment of the U.S. District Court for the Northern District of Illinois, which granted the employer's summary judgment motion because of the employee's inability to produce evidence of dissimilar treatment of nonpregnant employees. The court stated that this failure of evidence left the court with no inference that the employee was a victim of pregnancy discrimination. The Pregnancy Discrimination Act did not require employers to offer maternity leave or preferential treatment to pregnant employees. *Troupe v. May Dept. Stores Co.*, 20 F.3d 734 (7th Cir.1994).

AT & T offered its eligible employees a retirement plan designed to encourage early retirement by crediting retirees with five extra years of service or age. A 43-year-old employee with 26 years of service believed that she would qualify for the early retirement package because the additional five years would give her over 30 years of service. However, after retiring, the company determined that because the employee had taken nine months of maternity leave during 1966-67, she had worked less than 30 years and had to wait until the age of 65 to receive her retirement benefits. She filed a lawsuit against the company in the U.S. District Court for the Southern District of Ohio, alleging violations of the Pregnancy Discrimination Act (part of Title VII of the Civil Rights Act of 1964), the Equal Pay Act provisions of the Fair Labor Standards Act, and ERISA. The court considered the parties' summary judgment motions.

The court found that the company's treatment of pregnant employees taking temporary leave differed from its treatment of other employees taking leave for temporary disability. The system violated Title VII because it credited other employees for temporary disability leave but gave no credit for temporary pregnancy leave. Because federal regulations incorporated retirement benefits into the term "wages," the denial of credit for pregnancy leave created a valid claim under the Equal Pay Act, and the employee was entitled to receive pension benefits on the same terms that would have been available without the discrimination. The employee had also made out a claim for violation of ERISA, because discrimination constituted a breach of fiduciary duties under that act. The court granted summary judgment to the employee. *Carter v. American Telephone and Telegraph Co.*, 870 F.Supp. 1438 (S.D.Ohio 1994).

A Texas automobile dealership hired a customer service representative for a 90-day probationary period. At the time of hire, the representative was about one month pregnant, a fact that she revealed after six weeks on the job. She was then reassigned. However, after the representative suffered a fall resulting in a sprained ankle, she was told to stay home. The company then generated back-dated paperwork documenting her termination. She filed a claim with the EEOC for discrimination because of her sex and pregnancy under Title VII of the Civil Rights Act of 1964, 42 U.S.C. § 2000e *et seq.* and hired a private attorney who filed additional state law claims. The U.S. District Court for the Southern District of Texas submitted a form to the jury for advisory findings, which the jury answered in favor of the dealership. The court rejected the jury findings and held that the dealership had violated Title VII. The court awarded backpay, denied a request for attorney's fees, dismissed the state law claims and denied certain post-trial motions. The dealership appealed to the U.S. Court of Appeals, Fifth Circuit.

The court found that it had been proper for the district court to consider the jury's verdict as only advisory. This was because there was no right to a jury trial in Title VII cases until the effective date of the Civil Rights Act of 1991. The act was passed after the representative's termination action and had no retroactive application. There was sufficient evidence for the district court to determine that the dealership had wrongfully discharged the former representative because of her pregnancy. It had been appropriate for the district court to deny the former employee's request for attorney's fees of over $132,000. *EEOC v. Clear Lake Dodge*, 25 F.3d 265 (5th Cir.1994).

A North Carolina woman worked as a field clerk for a company which built residential housing. When the company was sold, her position was eliminated, and she was offered an opportunity to train as a project superintendent. Although she had little construction industry experience, she was hired for the position. The company terminated her employment shortly after she notified it that she was pregnant. The employer stated that it was discharging her for lack of construction skills, complaints from customers, and because she lacked the behavior traits to be an effective superintendent. She then sued the company, alleging violations of Title VII based on her gender and status as a pregnant woman. A North Carolina federal district court, after hearing all the evidence, determined that the employee had not been terminated based on her gender or her status as a pregnant female. The court found the employee lacked the behavior traits necessary to be an effective superintendent, and that this was a legitimate, nondiscriminatory reason for her discharge. The court held that no discrimination had occurred. *Radovanic v. Centex Real Estate Corp.*, 767 F.Supp. 1322 (W.D.N.C.1991).

A California woman, hired by a company in 1967, took a pregnancy-related leave in 1972. This was prior to the enactment of the Pregnancy Discrimination Act. At that time, the company required employees disabled by pregnancy to take personal leaves. After the act was passed, the company changed its policy and allowed employees to take disability leaves for pregnancies. In 1987, the company instituted an early retirement plan for which the woman applied. The company informed her that she was not eligible, however, because she had spent time on personal leave. If she had been granted temporary disability leave, she would have been eligible for the early retirement benefits. She brought a lawsuit against the company asserting that its plan discriminated against her on the basis of gender and pregnancy in violation of the act. A federal district court interpreted the woman's complaint to allege only that discrimination had occurred prior to 1979, when the law did not require employers to treat pregnant women as temporarily disabled. The court dismissed her claim.

On appeal to the U.S. Court of Appeals, Ninth Circuit, the woman asserted that the company was discriminating against her in 1987 by denying her retirement benefits because of her 1972 pregnancy. The appellate court agreed. It noted that even though the company's action against the woman in 1972 was not actionable, the company was liable for discrimination against the woman in 1987 on the basis of her pregnancy. The court determined that the woman had stated a valid claim, and remanded the case to the district court for trial. *Pallas v. Pacific Bell*, 940 F.2d 1324 (9th Cir.1991).

A company manufactured batteries, the primary ingredient of which was lead. As a result, in 1982, the company began a policy of excluding pregnant women and women capable of bearing children from jobs involving lead exposure. In 1984, a group of affected employees initiated a class action suit against the company, challenging its fetal protection policy as sex discrimination that violated Title VII. A Wisconsin federal district court granted summary judgment to the company, finding that it had established a business necessity defense. The U.S. Court of Appeals, Seventh Circuit, affirmed, and the employees petitioned the U.S. Supreme Court for review.

The Court noted that there was a clear bias in the company's policy, allowing fertile men but not women the choice of risking their reproductive health. Thus, there was clear sex discrimination involved. Even though there was no malevolent motive involved, the policy could not be termed "neutral." Accordingly, the only way for the company to justify the discrimination was by establishing that gender was a bona fide occupational qualification (BFOQ). The Court then stated that the company could not show a valid BFOQ. Decisions about the welfare of future children must be left to parents rather than employers. Since the company complied with the lead standard developed by the Occupational Safety and Health Administration and issued warnings to its female employees about the dangers of lead exposure, it was not negligent and it would be difficult for a future court to find liability against the company. The Court therefore reversed the lower court decisions and struck down the company's fetal protection policy. *International Union, UAW v. Johnson Controls, Inc.*, 499 U.S. 187, 111 S.Ct. 1196, 113 L.Ed.2d 158 (1991).

D. Sexual Harassment

The U.S. Supreme Court has held that sexual harassment is a form of gender discrimination which violates Title VII. Harassment that creates a hostile work environment because of the employee's sex will be considered unlawful sexual harassment.

A female employee at a Texas plant operated a machine that produced plastic bags. A fellow employee repeatedly harassed her with inappropriate remarks and physical contact. Her complaints to her immediate supervisor resulted in no relief, but when she reported the incidents to the personnel manager, he conducted an investigation, reprimanded the other employee, and transferred him to another department. Four days later the employee quit her job. She filed a charge with the EEOC which determined that she had likely been the victim of sexual harassment creating a hostile work environment in violation of Title VII, but concluded that her employer had adequately remedied the violation. It issued a notice of right to sue. She then sued her employer alleging constructive discharge. A federal district court found that she had been sexually harassed, but held that her employment was not terminated in violation of Title VII. Also, because Title VII did not then authorize any other form of relief, the court dismissed her complaint. While her appeal was pending, the Civil Rights Act of 1991 became law. Section 102 of that act included provisions that created a right to recover compensatory and punitive damages for intentional discrimination violative of Title VII. The U.S. Court of Appeals affirmed the district court decision and rejected the employee's argument that her case should be remanded for a jury trial on damages under § 102.

On further appeal to the U.S. Supreme Court, it was held that § 102 did not apply to a Title VII case that was pending on appeal when the 1991 act was enacted. The Court reasoned that because the president had vetoed a 1990 version of the act partly because of perceived unfairness in the bill's elaborate retroactivity provision, it was likely that the omission of comparable language in the 1991 act was a compromise that resulted in passage of the act. Here, the Court found that the new statute would impair the rights that employers possessed and increase their liability for past conduct or impose new duties with respect to transactions already completed if it was given retroactive effect. The Court affirmed the decision against the employee. *Landgraf v. U.S.I. Film Products*, 114 S.Ct. 1483, 128 L.Ed.2d 229 (1994).

A woman worked for a District of Columbia bank in various capacities over a four-year period. Her supervisor allegedly harassed her during this period, demanding sexual favors, and she accused him of forcibly raping her on several occasions. When the employee took an indefinite sick leave, the bank discharged her. She then brought suit against the bank, claiming that she had been subjected to sexual harassment in violation of Title VII. A federal district court ruled for the bank, finding that the bank did not have notice of any harassment, and that its policies forbade such behavior. The U.S. Court of Appeals reversed, and appeal was taken to the U.S. Supreme Court. The Supreme Court first noted that sexual harassment is clearly a form of sex discrimination prohibited by Title VII. It then stated that while absence of notice of harassment will not necessarily shield an employer from liability, employers are not always liable automatically for sexual harassment by their supervisory employees. The court determined that Congress intended agency principles to apply to some extent. The Court affirmed the court of appeals' holding, and remanded the case. *Meritor Savings Bank, FSB v. Vinson*, 477 U.S. 57, 106 S.Ct. 2399, 91 L.Ed.2d 49 (1986).

A Tennessee woman worked as a manager of a rental equipment company. The president of the company often insulted her because of her gender and frequently made her the target of unwanted sexual innuendoes. The employee quit and sued the company, claiming that the president's conduct had created an abusive work environment because of her gender. A federal district court found that the president's conduct did not create an abusive environment because while some of the conduct would offend a reasonable woman, it was not so severe as to seriously affect the manager's psychological well-being. The U.S. Court of Appeals, Sixth Circuit, affirmed this decision and the manager appealed to the U.S. Supreme Court. The Court reaffirmed the standard set forth in *Meritor Savings Bank v. Vinson*, above. "Title VII is violated when the workplace is permeated with discriminatory behavior that is sufficiently severe or pervasive to create a hostile environment." The Court noted that the standard required showing only an objectively hostile environment — one that a reasonable person would find hostile — as well as the victim's subjective perception that the environment was abusive. Further, the court held that whether the environment was hostile could only be determined by looking at all the circumstances. The court reversed and remanded the case with instructions for the trial court to consider the psychological harm to the victim as but one factor to be considered in looking at all the circumstances. *Harris v. Forklift Systems, Inc.,* 114 S.Ct. 367, 126 L.Ed.2d 295 (1993).

An Illinois secretary complained that her supervisor sexually harassed her by making suggestive comments to her over a seven-month period. She filed a lawsuit against the employer in the U.S. District Court for the Northern District of Illinois under Title VII of the Civil Rights Act of 1964, attempting to hold it liable for the supervisor's actions. The court awarded the secretary $25,000 in damages, and the employer appealed to the U.S. Court of Appeals, Seventh Circuit. The court of appeals noted that the employer had taken reasonable steps to protect the secretary from harassment by her supervisor after she had made his comments known. Once the behavior was reported, the director of the department withheld a salary increase from the supervisor and instructed him to immediately quit making harassing comments. Because the supervisor's comments were more reasonably characterized as vulgarity than harassment, and because the supervisor stopped making them as soon as they were reported to management, no reasonable jury could have found that the remarks created a hostile working environment. The court reversed and remanded the district court's judgment, ruling that an employer's legal duty to prevent sexual harassment is fulfilled if the employer takes reasonable steps to discover and rectify the harassment. *Baskerville v. Culligan Intern. Co.*, 50 F.3d 428 (7th Cir.1995).

A California research specialist claimed that her supervisor sexually harassed and assaulted her on the job. She also stated that her repeated complaints to the company's president and chief executive officer were ignored and that the company fired her in retaliation for taking a one-month leave of absence to avoid further harassment. She filed a lawsuit against the company and the supervisor in a California trial court under the state Fair Employment and Housing Act (FEHA). The trial court held that the supervisor could not be held personally liable for sexual harassment in violation of the FEHA. The employee appealed to the California Court of Appeal, Third District, which considered the language of the state civil rights act. It determined that the FEHA prohibited sexual harassment by an employer, labor organization, employment agency, training program or any other person. This broad language indicated legislative intent to bring supervisors within FEHA coverage. The court rejected the supervisor's arguments that the act did not apply to individuals and that the court should apply federal law under the analogous portions of Title VII of the Civil Rights Act of 1964. The court granted the employee's requested order and vacated the trial court order. *Page v. Superior Court*, 37 Cal.Rptr.2d 529 (Cal.App.3d Dist.1995).

A New Jersey cable company closed its door-to-door sales department and released all employees of that department after settling a federal court discrimination complaint by one of the department's employees. The employee's mother, sister, and two close friends had also been employed in the department. Eighteen months later, the company resumed door-to-door sales, but refused to rehire three of the former department employees. The former employees filed a lawsuit against the company in a New Jersey trial court, asserting violation of the state law against discrimination. The court dismissed the complaint, but the New Jersey Superior Court, Appellate Division, reversed and remanded the case. The employer appealed to the Supreme Court of New Jersey, which found that the state law against discrimination protected friends and family members of complaining parties against retaliatory discharge in discrimination complaints. An amendment to the law expanded the class of protected employees to those persons who have aided or encouraged other persons to assert their rights. In this case, the door-to-door sales department was small and cohesive and the complaining parties constituted almost the entire department. Some of the employees had participated in the earlier discrimination claim by giving testimony adverse to the employer, and the law was intended to protect such individuals from reprisal. The court affirmed the decision for the former employees. *Craig v. Suburban Cablevision, Inc.*, 140 N.J. 623, 660 A.2d 505 (1995).

The office manager of a small Wisconsin supply company alleged that the company's owner and president created a sexually harassing work environment by using sexually explicit language and attempting to brush up against female employees. After she confronted the owner/president about his conduct, he fired her. She filed a lawsuit for retaliatory discharge in the U.S. District Court for the Eastern District of Wisconsin, claiming violations of the Age Discrimination in Employment Act (ADEA) and Title VII of the Civil Rights Act of 1964. A trial was held and the jury returned a backpay award of $80,000. However, the court refused to award front pay and reduced the amount of claimed attorney's fees from over $122,000 to $66,000. The court denied the company and owner's motion for judgment as a matter of law, and the parties appealed unfavorable aspects of the district court decision to the U.S. Court of Appeals, Seventh Circuit.

The court affirmed the district court's finding that the owner had created a hostile work environment. It also upheld the damage award, finding some merit to the owner's argument that the discharged employee had failed to energetically pursue a new job after being fired. It was permissible for the jury to award an amount less than the $147,000 in salary and bonuses allegedly paid to the manager's replacement during the 27 months after the firing. The court reversed and remanded the question of the district court's decision to reduce the attorney's fee award, finding no basis for the reduction in claimed fees. *Hutchison v. Amateur Electronic Supply, Inc.*, 42 F.3d 1037 (7th Cir.1994).

Four female restaurant employees claimed that their supervisors repeatedly harassed them by asking them for sexual favors and commenting on sexual topics. All of them quit their jobs, and filed a lawsuit against the employer and several management employees in the U.S. District Court for the Middle District of Alabama, which considered the employer's summary judgment motions. The court considered voluminous evidence of unwanted touching, sexual comments, and propositions including an offer by one manager to pay one of the employees $200 for sex, all of which combined to create a sufficiently strong enough case for hostile working environment sexual harassment to survive a pretrial motion for dismissal. The court also refused to dismiss a claim by one former employee that she had been denied promotional opportunities on the basis of her sex in violation of Title VII. However, the court granted the employer's summary judgment motion against two employees who had not alleged sufficient facts to establish their claim that they had been denied promotions or raises due to their sex. The court determined that there was evidence that the conduct of supervisory employees could be imputed to the company, which was deemed to be on notice of the sexually harassing environment which the supervisors had created. This was the case even though none of the employees had reported the harassing behavior to higher ranking management employees. *Splunge v. Shoney's, Inc.* 874 F.Supp. 1258 (M.D.Ala.1994).

The Illinois Constitution protects individuals from discrimination on the basis of race, color, creed, national ancestry and sex in hiring and promotional practices. However, the constitution grants the state legislature the power to establish reasonable exemptions to these guaranteed rights. The Illinois Human Rights Act protects individuals from discrimination, including employment discharge, but its scope is limited to employers of 15 or more employees during 20 or more calendar weeks of the year preceding an alleged violation. A tavern employee who alleged sex discrimination in her employment termination filed a lawsuit against her employer in an Illinois trial court, seeking compensatory damages. Because the tavern employed less than 15 employees, she sought to file a direct action under the state constitution, bypassing the human rights act. The trial court dismissed the lawsuit, and the Appellate Court of Illinois affirmed. The employee appealed to the Supreme Court of Illinois. The supreme court rejected the employee's argument that a direct cause of action for employment discrimination existed under the state constitution. The legislature intended to protect small employers from discrimination complaints. The act defined "employer" as only those entities employing 15 or more people. Creating a private right of action under the constitution disregarded the legislative intent of excluding small employers from the statutory definition. The court affirmed the trial court's dismissal of the lawsuit. *Baker v. Miller*, 159 Ill.2d 249, 636 N.E.2d 551 (1994).

A Michigan security officer alleged that her supervisor made sexual comments to her and then raped her, causing her to resign. She filed a lawsuit against the security company, claiming that she had been sexually harassed and that the supervisor's actions were attributable to the company. The trial court granted the employer's summary judgment motion on the grounds that the supervisor did not have direct authority to hire and fire employees. The former employee appealed to the Court of Appeals of Michigan. The court of appeals disagreed with the trial court's finding that the supervisor's lack of control over hiring, firing and discipline precluded company liability. It was sufficient that the supervisor wielded significant control over conditions of employment. However, the former employee's complaint did not allege sufficient facts under Michigan's Elliott-Larsen Civil Rights Act to support a claim against the company for sexual harassment. This was because the statute required a showing that submission to sexual advances was a factor in employment decisions. Because no decision affecting the security officer's employment had been made as a result of the improper conduct, the conduct did not fall within the prohibition of the civil rights act. The court affirmed the trial court's decision in favor of the employer. *Champion v. Nationwide Security, Inc.*, 517 N.W.2d 777 (Mich.App.1994).

A Washington woman worked for a janitorial service company as part of a three-member crew. The company was under contract to provide janitorial services to a federal courthouse. During a work shift, a court security officer informed the woman that the elevators were malfunctioning and needed to be fixed. Because her supervisor was not around, she went to a locked basement room to check the switches which controlled the elevators. When she unlocked the door and turned on the lights, she discovered her supervisor masturbating at a table. She left work and claimed that she could not work for her supervisor any longer. Her supervisor resigned, but she was unable to return to work for two weeks. She eventually refused to return to work when her coworker was appointed to act in the supervisor's place and she was informed that she would be reprimanded for reporting the matter to a federal employee. She sued the company for sexual harassment and retaliation, and a Washington trial court directed a verdict for her employer. She appealed to the Court of Appeals of Washington.

The court of appeals affirmed the lower court's ruling in favor of the company. Here, the employee had failed to present competent evidence that her gender was the motivating factor for her supervisor's conduct. Under Washington's Law Against Discrimination, the gender of the plaintiff-employee must be the motivating factor for the unlawful harassment. There was no indication that her supervisor singled her out to witness his conduct; in fact, her appearance on the scene came as a complete surprise. He did not intend for her to see him at all. Further, the employee had also failed to show that the company had retaliated against her. Because the supervisor's conduct in the basement room was not a practice forbidden by Washington's Law Against Discrimination, the employee's opposition to his conduct was not protected opposition activity. *Coville v. Cobarc Services, Inc.*, 869 P.2d 1103 (Wash.App.Div.3 1994).

A California creative editor filed a complaint alleging that he was subjected to sexual harassment and discrimination by his supervisor, the president of a motion picture company. The editor alleged that the president offered him money in exchange for sexual acts. The trial court dismissed the action and the editor appealed to the California Court of Appeal. California Government Code § 12940 prohibits discrimination on the basis of gender, including asking for sexual favors in return for favorable treatment in the workplace. The employer alleged that same gender sexual harassment could not be the basis of a cause of action under § 12940. The appellate court found no basis in the statutory language for the contention that the legislature intended to limit the protection from sexual harassment to male-female harassment. Accordingly, it vacated the dismissal and held that same gender sexual harassment may be a basis for a cause of action for sexual harassment. *Mogilefsky v. Superior Court*, 26 Cal.Rptr.2d 116 (Cal.App.1993).

A Texas corporation hired a contractor to provide janitorial services. For six years, the contractor sent a woman to perform cleaning duties at the corporation. During the course of the six years, a corporation employee made numerous sexual advances toward her. The woman testified that she considered the remarks to be unwelcome and degrading. The woman reported the employee's conduct to the corporation's human relations department. After the woman made her complaint, she stated that the employee continued to follow her around and take notes. The woman filed suit against the corporation alleging that it had a duty to maintain a work environment for all persons that was free of sexual harassment. The trial court granted the corporation's motion for a directed verdict, stating that the corporation did not owe a duty to the woman. The woman then appealed to the Court of Appeals of Texas.

The woman claimed that because the corporation was the owner and occupier of the premises, it owed a duty to employees of contractors working at the facility to provide a safe place to work. However, the court noted that the dangerous condition of sexual harassment was an unforeseeable intentional tort and thus was the sole intervening cause of any injuries suffered by her. The appellate court upheld the general rule that a premises owner is not legally responsible to protect a contractor's employee against the unforeseeable intentional tortious acts of third parties. Accordingly, the appellate court upheld the decision of the trial court and granted a directed verdict in favor of the corporation. *Graham v. Atlantic Richfield Company*, 848 S.W.2d 747 (Tex.App.1993).

A New York woman began working for an electronic score-keeping manu-facturer. She alleged that the owner repeatedly asked her to have his baby, gave her full-body hugs and joked about sex. All of the alleged acts occurred in the presence of other employees. The woman eventually resigned from her job and filed suit in a federal district court alleging sexual harassment. The question was whether the employer's conduct unreasonably interfered with the woman's work performance or created an intimidating, hostile, or offensive working environ-ment. The woman had the burden of proving that: 1) the alleged sexual harassment actually occurred; 2) that it was sufficiently severe so as to create an abusive working environment; and 3) that the advances were unwelcome. The court noted that even if it assumed the woman's testimony to be true, the work environment appeared to involve some casual discussion among the employees about having a baby, some sexual references and full body hugs on many occasions. Although these activities were inappropriate, they did not rise to the level of being sufficiently severe so as to alter the conditions of employment or create an abusive working environment. Therefore, the court found for the employer and dismissed the suit. *Currie v. Kowalewski*, 810 F.Supp. 31 (N.D.N.Y.1993).

An Illinois woman was employed as an inside sales representative. She alleged that her sales manager made unsolicited and nonconsensual sexual advances toward her and that she made numerous reports of his conduct to his superiors. According to the sales representative, the company took no action against the manager. The company then fired the sales representative. She filed suit in a state trial court alleging that the company had fired her in retaliation for her failure to comply with the manager's sexual advances and for her attempts to inform the company about his actions. The trial court dismissed the action against the company and the sales representative appealed to the Appellate Court of Illinois. The sales representative argued that the trial court should have recog-nized an employer's duty to make a reasonable sexual harassment investigation into the employment history of a prospective manager. The court agreed and noted that there was a foreseeable hazard of harassment occurring upon hiring a new manager of a staff comprised primarily of persons not of the manager's gender. Accordingly, the court determined that the employer had a duty to inquire into the manager's past sexual harassment history. The sales representative also argued that the trial court erred in dismissing her negligent retention claim. She claimed that Illinois law established an employer's duty to protect employees from other employees with sexual harassment propensities. The court determined that the sales representative sufficiently pleaded a cause of action for negligent retention. Thus, the court reversed the trial court's dismissal and remanded the case. *Geise v. Phoenix Co. of Chicago, Inc.*, 615 N.E.2d 1179 (Ill.App.1993).

A female New Jersey employee worked as a systems analyst for a toy company. Her supervisor exhibited allegedly offensive sexual conduct to the employee and to other female workers. She reported the conduct to her supervisor's immediate boss and to other corporate personnel. Eventually, the employee resigned and filed a sexual harassment claim under the New Jersey Law Against Discrimination (LAD) against her former employer and supervisor. The trial court concluded that the supervisor's conduct did not constitute sexual harassment under the LAD and that the employer could not be held liable. The employee appealed. On appeal, the Appellate Division for the Superior Court of New Jersey reversed the lower court's decision and remanded the case. The court held that the employee need not show that the supervisor "acted intentionally to harass." Rather, the employee could show that the supervisor's conduct was "unwelcome, intentional, and sexually oriented to the extent that it would not have occurred but for the fact that plaintiff was a woman." Additionally, the court held that the employer would be held liable for the supervisor's acts of sexual harassment. *T.L. v. Toys 'R' Us, Inc.*, 605 A.2d 1125 (N.J.Super.A.D.1992).

Six waitresses worked at a Washington truck stop under the supervision of a male manager. The waitresses complained to the owners' agents that the manager stared at them as though he were mentally undressing them, constantly touched them despite being told to keep his hands to himself, and made suggestive remarks. The manager apologized for his actions, but they continued unabated without further action from the truck stop owners. Subsequently, the waitresses walked off their jobs and picketed the restaurant. The manager resigned shortly thereafter. While on the picket line, two owners taunted the waitresses, and one allegedly stated that he would make sure that none of them worked in the area again. Two of the waitresses were thereafter offered their jobs back; all of them found employment elsewhere. They brought claims against the truck stop owners for sexual harassment and unlawful retaliation. A jury found in favor of the waitresses. The truck stop owners appealed.

The Court of Appeals of Washington noted that to establish a work-related sexual harassment claim, an employee must prove: (1) the harassment was unwelcome, (2) the harassment was because of sex, (3) the harassment affected terms or conditions of employment, and (4) the harassment could be imputed to the employer. The court found that the waitresses had satisfied all of these elements. It also found that the unlawful retaliation claim was not preempted by federal law. The waitresses' choice of effectively opposing the sexual harassment by refusing to work was statutorily protected, the owners' replacement of the waitresses constituted adverse employment action, and the retaliation was a substantial factor in the denial of reemployment to four of the waitresses. Accordingly, the court of appeals affirmed the judgment of the trial court. *Delahunty v. Cahoon,* 832 P.2d 1378 (Wash.App.Div.3 1992).

A New York not-for-profit corporation founded a shelter for the homeless. The shelter provided food, shelter, counseling and peace-keeping functions to area homeless people. The chairwoman of the board of directors and a shelter employee became romantically involved. The chairwoman had no power to fire or hire employees for the shelter. In 1990, the employee advised the chairwoman that he wished to end the relationship. At this time, the chairwoman asked the employee to resign his position at the shelter. He was informed by the board and the director that his job was not in jeopardy. The chairwoman repeatedly attempted to renew the relationship and frequently contacted the employee at work. The employee then submitted his resignation and filed this action in a federal district court alleging sexual harassment.

The court noted that although there was a history of sexual tension between the chairwoman and the employee, the tension was the result of a failed relationship, not sexual harassment in the workplace. The court found that there was no evidence that the alleged sexual harassment was so severe as to cause a constructive discharge or to create a hostile work environment in violation of Title VII. To establish a hostile environment, the sexual harassment must be sufficiently severe or pervasive to alter the condition of employment and create an abusive work environment. The court stated that even if it could be shown that it had become difficult or embarrassing for the chairwoman and the employee to work together after the end of a turbulent love affair, this simply was not enough to make a case under Title VII. *Carter v. Caring for the Homeless of Peekskill Inc.,* 821 F.Supp. 225 (S.D.N.Y.1993).

A South Dakota woman worked for a grocery store as an hourly employee and engaged in a personal relationship with her shift supervisor, a relationship that lasted approximately three months. Upon learning that she had commenced a new relationship with another coworker, the supervisor, as well as his friends and relatives, harassed and criticized the employee. The employee ultimately lodged a sexual harassment complaint with the South Dakota Division of Human Rights. In response, management tried to alleviate problems by moving the employee to a different shift. The employee, however, returned to her original third shift, and continued to have problems with the supervisor's friends and relatives. (The supervisor himself had been fired for having sexual relations with a different hourly employee.) Following two incidents, the employee requested and received a two week leave of absence. She was threatened and harassed at her home, and did not return to work following her leave of absence. As a result, she was fired. The circuit court dismissed her complaint in the lawsuit which followed, and the employee appealed to the South Dakota Supreme Court.

On appeal, the court held for the employer, noting that once management became aware of the sexual harassment, a number of remedial steps were implemented. These steps included the termination of the supervisor, granting the employee a leave of absence, and informing the employee's new shift supervisor of the situation. For these reasons, the lower court decision was affirmed. *Huck v. McCain Foods,* 479 N.W.2d 167 (S.D.1991).

III. AGE DISCRIMINATION

The use of an individual's age as a criterion for employment generally is forbidden by federal law. Only where age is a bona fide occupational qualification may it be used as a factor in employment decisions.

Age Discrimination in Employment Act

Like the Equal Pay Act, the Age Discrimination in Employment Act of 1967 (ADEA) (29 U.S.C. § 621 *et seq.*) is part of the Fair Labor Standards Act. It applies to institutions which have 20 or more employees and which affect interstate commerce. The ADEA extends its protection to any individual 40 years old or older.

Relevant provisions of the ADEA are as follows:

§ 623. Prohibition of age discrimination

(a) Employer practices

It shall be unlawful for an employer—

(1) to fail or refuse to hire or to discharge any individual or otherwise discriminate against any individual with respect to his compensation, terms, conditions, or privileges of employment, because of such individual's age;

(2) to limit, segregate, or classify his employees in any way which would deprive or tend to deprive any individual of employment opportunities or otherwise adversely affect his status as an employee, because of such individual's age; or

(3) to reduce the wage rate of any employee in order to comply with this chapter.

* * *

(f) Lawful practices; age an occupational qualification; other reasonable factors; laws of foreign workplace; seniority system; employee benefit plans; discharge or discipline for good cause.

It shall not be unlawful for an employer, employment agency, or labor organization—

(1) to take any action otherwise prohibited under subsections (a), (b), (c), or (e) of this section where age is a bona fide occupational qualification

reasonably necessary to the normal operation of the particular business, or where the differentiation is based on reasonable factors other than age, or where such practices involve an employee in a workplace in a foreign country, and compliance with such subsections would cause such employer, or a corporation controlled by such employer, to violate the laws of the country in which such workplace is located;

(2) to take any action otherwise prohibited under subsection (a), (b), (c), or (e) of this section—

(A) to observe the terms of a bona fide seniority system that is not intended to evade the purposes of this chapter, except that no such seniority system shall require or permit the involuntary retirement of any individual specified by section 631(a) of this title because of the age of such individual; or

(B) to observe the terms of a bona fide employee benefit plan—

(i) where, for each benefit or benefit package, the actual amount of payment made or cost incurred on behalf of an older worker is no less than that made or incurred on behalf of a younger worker, as permissible under section 1625.10, title 29, Code of Federal Regulations (as in effect on June 22, 1989); or

(ii) that is a voluntary early retirement incentive plan consistent with the relevant purpose or purposes of this chapter.

Notwithstanding clause (i) or (ii) of subparagraph (B), no such employee benefit plan or voluntary early retirement incentive plan shall excuse the failure to hire any individual, and no such employee benefit plan shall require or permit the involuntary retirement of any individual specified by section 631(a) of this title, because of the age of such individual. An employer, employment agency, or labor organization acting under subparagraph (A), or under clause (i) or (ii) of subparagraph (B), shall have the burden of proving that such actions are lawful in any civil enforcement proceeding brought under this chapter; or

(3) to discharge or otherwise discipline an individual for good cause.

* * *

§ 631. Age limits

(a) Individuals at least 40 years of age

The prohibitions in this chapter shall be limited to individuals who are at least 40 years of age.

* * *

(c) Bona fide executives or high policymakers

(1) Nothing in this chapter shall be construed to prohibit compulsory retirement of any employee who has attained 65 years of age and who, for the 2-year period immediately before retirement, is employed in a bona fide executive or a high policymaking position, if such employee is entitled to an immediate nonforfeitable annual retirement benefit from a pension, profit-sharing, savings, or deferred compensation plan, or any combination of such plans, of the employer of such employee, which equals, in the aggregate, at least $44,000.

(2) In applying the retirement benefit test of paragraph (1) of this subsection, if any such retirement benefit is in a form other than a straight life annuity (with no ancillary benefits), or if employees contribute to any such plan or make rollover contributions, such benefit shall be adjusted in accordance with regulations prescribed by the Equal Employment Opportunity Commission, after consultation with the Secretary of the Treasury, so that the benefit is the equivalent of a straight life annuity (with no ancillary benefits) under a plan to which employees do not contribute and under which no rollover contributions are made.

A 62-year-old secretary worked for a Tennessee publishing company for over 30 years. She had access to company financial records and made copies of documents when she became concerned that the company would terminate her employment because of her age. The publishing company dismissed the secretary under a workforce reduction plan. She filed a lawsuit against the publisher in the U.S. District Court for the Middle District of Tennessee under the ADEA, seeking backpay and other relief. During the course of pretrial discovery, the publisher learned that the secretary had copied company financial documents. Based on this information, it filed a motion for summary judgment, which the court granted on the basis of the secretary's misconduct. The U.S. Court of Appeals, Sixth Circuit, affirmed the district court decision and the secretary appealed to the U.S. Supreme Court. The Supreme Court rejected the reasoning of the lower courts that the secretary's misconduct constituted proper grounds for termination based on the after-acquired evidence revealed in discovery. The important antidiscrimination objectives of the ADEA precluded the blanket denial of relief to the former secretary. Employee wrongdoing remained relevant and would preclude reinstatement or front pay as an appropriate remedy in this case. However, on remand, the district court could not impose an absolute rule barring the secretary's recovery of backpay. The remedy should calculate backpay from the date of the unlawful discharge to the date the publisher discovered the wrongdoing. The case was remanded for further proceedings. *McKennon v. Nashville Banner Pub. Co.*, 115 S.Ct. 879, 130 L.Ed.2d 852 (1995).

An airline employee was fired when he reached the age of 60 pursuant to company policy. He filed an age discrimination lawsuit against the airline in a federal district court under the ADEA. The parties reached a settlement prior to trial under which the airline paid the employee $145,000. The parties designated half of the payment as backpay and the other half as liquidated damages. The airline did not withhold any payroll or income tax from the liquidated damages portion of the settlement award. The former employee failed to pay any income tax on the liquidated damages portion of the settlement award and the Commissioner of the IRS served him with a deficiency notice, stating that liquidated damages were includable in his gross income. The former employee filed a U.S. Tax Court action asserting that he had properly excluded the liquidated damage award and seeking a refund of tax paid on his backpay. The tax court held that the entire settlement award was excludable from income as damages received on account of personal injury or sickness within the meaning of the IRS Code. The U.S. Court of Appeals, Fifth Circuit, affirmed the tax court decision, and the commissioner appealed to the U.S. Supreme Court.

On appeal, the former employee argued that his settlement was attributable to a personal injury or sickness because it was based upon a tort or tort-type right under the ADEA. The court disagreed, finding that liquidated damages under the ADEA were distinguishable from tort damages for personal injury or sickness and were analogous to back wages which were of an economic character and therefore fully taxable. In order to exclude damage awards from taxation, taxpayers were required to demonstrate that the underlying cause of action was based upon a tort or tort-type right and that the damages were received on account of personal injury or sickness. Because the settlement award in this case failed both parts of the test, the lower court decisions were reversed. *Commissioner of Internal Revenue v. Schleier*, 115 S.Ct. 2159, 132 L.Ed.2d 294 (1995).

A Massachusetts manufacturing employee was terminated when he was 62 years old and a few weeks shy of vesting for his pension benefits. He filed suit in a federal district court alleging violations of the ADEA and ERISA. The jury found for the employee on both violations and further determined that the ADEA violation had been wilful. Thus, the employee was entitled to liquidated damages. The district court granted the employer's motion for judgment notwithstanding the verdict with respect to the finding of wilfulness. Both parties appealed to the U.S. Court of Appeals, First Circuit, which affirmed the jury's finding of a wilful violation of the ADEA. The employer appealed to the U.S. Supreme Court. There were two issues on appeal to the Supreme Court: whether an employer's interference with the vesting of pension benefits was a violation of the ADEA and what standard of wilfulness should be used under the ADEA.

The ADEA was enacted to prevent discrimination based on age and also to "prohibit the problem of inaccurate and stigmatizing stereotypes about productivity and competence declining with age." However, when an employer's decision is wholly motivated by factors other than age, the stigmatizing stereo-types disappear. The court noted that this was true even when the motivating factor was correlated with age (such as pension status). Because age and years of service may be analytically distinct, an employer could take account of one while ignoring the other. Thus, the court reasoned that it was incorrect to say that a decision based on years of service was necessarily "age-based." Next, the Court analyzed the standard for wilfulness under the ADEA. The Court ruled that once a wilful violation had been shown, the employee need not additionally demon-strate that the employer's conduct was outrageous, prove direct evidence of the employer's motivation, or prove that age was the predominant factor in the employment decision. The Supreme Court remanded the case to the court of appeals to determine if the jury had sufficient evidence to find a violation of the ADEA. *Hazen Paper Company v. Biggins*, 113 S.Ct. 1701, 123 L.Ed.2d 338 (1993).

An airline company required all cockpit crew members (pilots, copilots and flight engineers) to retire at the age of 60. An FAA regulation prohibited persons from serving as pilots or copilots after turning 60, but made no similar provision for flight engineers. A group of flight engineers and pilots who wished to become flight engineers sued the airline in a California federal court, contending that the mandatory retirement provision violated the ADEA. The airline defended by arguing that the age 60 limit was a bona fide occupational qualification (BFOQ) which was reasonably necessary to the safe operation of the airline. A jury held for the employees, and the U.S. Court of Appeals, Ninth Circuit, affirmed. The U.S. Supreme Court granted certiorari.

The Court stated that the BFOQ exception to the ADEA's prohibition on age discrimination was intended to be extremely narrow. The BFOQ standard, held the Court, is one of "reasonable necessity," not reasonableness. Thus, even if it was "rational" for the airline to set age 60 as the limit for flight engineers, the airline still had to show that it had reasonable cause to believe that all or substantially all flight engineers over 60 would be unable to safely perform their job duties, or that it would be highly impractical to deal with older employees on an individual basis to determine whether they had the necessary qualifications for the job. Because the airline had not shown this, the Court affirmed the lower court decisions in favor of the employees. *Western Air Lines, Inc. v. Criswell,* 472 U.S. 400, 105 S.Ct. 2743, 86 L.Ed.2d 321 (1985).

A Massachusetts machinist received regular promotions and wage increases based upon excellent performance reviews for 10 years at a machine shop. He was transferred to a different department at the age of 57 and again received high ratings. Later in the year, new management employees instructed their supervi-sors to reevaluate their employees, prompting the machinist's supervisor to comment "these damn people—they want younger people here." The supervisor then gave the machinist a poor evaluation, recommending that he be relieved from his current duties. Five days later the machinist was discharged as part of a reduction in force in which the company's worst employees were discharged. He filed a lawsuit against the employer in the U.S. District Court for the District of Massachusetts, claiming age discrimination in violation of the ADEA. The court granted summary judgment to the employer, and the machinist appealed to the U.S. Court of Appeals, First Circuit. The court determined that the district court had erroneously excluded from evidence the supervisor's hearsay statement concerning management intentions to replace older workers. It had been inappropriate for the district court to grant summary judgment to the employer in view of this evidence, because the statement contained evidence about management attitudes toward older workers. Because exclusion of the statement was an abuse of discretion by the district court that deprived the machinist of an opportunity for a trial, the court of appeals vacated and remanded the case to the district court. *Woodman v. Haemonetics Corp.*, 51 F.3d 1087 (1st Cir.1995).

An insurance brokerage and employee benefits consulting firm employed an executive whose performance came under increasing criticism. After the company forced the executive to resign, he filed an age discrimination complaint against the company with the EEOC, which issued a right to sue letter. The executive filed a lawsuit against his former employer under the ADEA in the U.S. District Court for the District of New Jersey. The court granted the employer's motion for summary judgment. The executive appealed to the U.S. Court of Appeals, Third Circuit, which reviewed the analysis applicable in cases filed under the ADEA. Employees who are at least 40 years old and qualified for the position in question, and who suffer adverse employment decisions can demonstrate an inference of age discrimination when they are replaced by a younger person. The employer stated that the executive's performance had become so poor that his duties were transferred to others, eventually leading to discharge. The executive stated that the reasons stated by the company for discharge were pretextual and that his employment evaluations for more than 20 years indicated satisfactory performance. The court agreed with the executive, stating that long term employment without a record of poor evaluations created an inference of good performance. Because there was a conflict in the evidence, summary judgment was not the appropriate method of resolving the claim, and the district court judgment was reversed and remanded for a jury trial. *Sempier v. Johnson & Higgins*, 45 F.3d 724 (3d Cir.1995).

An electronics corporation transferred a regional sales manager to the position of product marketing manager, a position which the employee felt was a dead-end. The company then terminated his employment, and he filed a lawsuit against it under the ADEA in the U.S. District Court for the District of New Jersey, which granted the employer's summary judgment motion. The employee appealed to the U.S. Court of Appeals, Third Circuit, which determined that the district court had improperly applied the analysis applicable in summary judgment matters. The employee had produced sufficient evidence to present to a jury concerning the company's behavior, including evidence that the position to which he had been transferred was already eliminated at the time of the transfer. There was also evidence that one decisionmaking manager had a bias against older employees. Because the district court's order deprived the employee of the opportunity to present this evidence to a jury, the case was reversed and remanded. *Torre v. Casio, Inc.*, 42 F.3d 825 (3d Cir.1994).

The founder and president of a New Jersey pump and meter company hired a 71-year-old salesman shortly after the business started operating. The salesman credited himself with expanding sales from approximately $100,000 to $13 million per year. The president and salesman then became involved in a bitter dispute about the sales staff. The president fired the salesman, who was then almost 80 years old. The salesman sued the company in a New Jersey trial court, claiming the termination was in violation of the state law against discrimination and the Conscientious Employee Protection Act. He added common law claims for wrongful discharge and emotional distress. The jury awarded the salesman over $1.1 million, which the court reduced to $537,000. The company appealed to the Superior Court of New Jersey, Appellate Division, and the salesman cross appealed. The court rejected the company's argument that the state law against discrimination did not extend to persons over age 70. The law, like the federal ADEA, protected employees who were 40 and over against discrimination. Because the employee had a valid claim under the statute, there was no viable claim for common law employment termination. The court agreed with the company that its policy manual did not protect employees from termination without cause. The trial court judge had improperly instructed the jury concerning testimony attributed to the president, justifying remand for a new trial. *Catalane v. Gilian Instrument Corp.*, 271 N.J.Super. 476, 638 A.2d 1341 (1994).

An employee brought suit against her Texas employer, the owner of an insurance agency, after she was fired. She had worked for the insurance agency for 15 years. The employee's suit against the agency and the insurance company for which he worked alleged age discrimination in violation of Title VII and the ADEA. The trial court dismissed the suit for lack of jurisdiction and the employee appealed to the U.S. Court of Appeals, Seventh Circuit. The court of appeals held that the suit had been properly dismissed. The employee first argued that the insurer was her employer. In rejecting this assertion, the court noted that, in determining whether an employment relationship existed, it would look to the insurer's right to control the employee's conduct. This control component encompasses an employer's right to hire or fire an employee, the right to supervise the employee, and the right to set the employee's work schedule. In this case, the agency was solely responsible for these tasks. Hence the insurer was not the employee's employer. Next, the employee asserted that the agency was acting as an "agent" of the insurer. Title VII and the ADEA define "employer" as a person who has a certain number of employees and any agent of such a person. The court followed other jurisdictions which concluded that an "agent" for the purposes of Title VII and the ADEA is limited to supervisory and managerial employees to whom employment decisions have been delegated by the employer. The insurance agency was solely and independently responsible for all employment related decisions and it was not acting as the insurer's "agent" with respect to employment practices. Further, it did not have enough employees to qualify as an "employer" under Title VII or the ADEA. *Deal v. State Farm County Mut. Ins. Co. of Texas*, 5 F.3d 117 (5th Cir.1993).

After an Illinois retail store determined that an operating manager was dating a subordinate, the operating manager was fired for violating company policy. The manager then sued the store charging age and gender discrimination. He claimed that the store had no policy preventing managers from dating subordinates and protested that he was never warned, on threat of his job, to refrain from dating a coworker. According to him, he was discharged because of his age and because he was male. The district court disagreed and concluded that he did not state a claim under either the ADEA or Title VII. It dismissed the case. The manager then appealed to the U.S. Court of Appeals, Seventh Circuit. The court of appeals noted that there was no uniform policy or practice of prohibiting dating between managers and subordinates and thus it could not serve as a reason for the discharge. However, the store could still discharge the manager if the record showed that he was repeatedly taken aside and warned of the disruptive aspects of his behavior. The determination of this conflict was for a jury.

The manager also contended that the store discriminated against him on the basis of his sex. He alleged that he was fired while the subordinate, a female, was not. However, the court determined that the retail store was entitled to enforce a no-dating policy against supervisors because they are expected to know better. To make out a *prima facie* case of sex discrimination under Title VII, the manager had to show that he was treated differently from a similarly situated female. Since he produced no evidence of similarly situated female managers, the court upheld the grant of summary judgment with respect to the Title VII claim. However, it reversed the trial court's grant of summary judgment with respect to the ADEA claim and remanded the case for trial. *Sarsha v. Sears, Roebuck & Co.*, 3 F.3d 1035 (7th Cir.1993).

A Puerto Rican company decided to downsize its operations and it announced the availability of a Voluntary Separation Program (VSP). The company distributed descriptive documents to all employees regardless of age or years of service. The written materials spelled out the benefits, the method of calculating severance pay and how the program would be implemented. The company encouraged workers to participate, but did not require them to do so. It informed all its employees that if substantially fewer than 26 individuals opted to enter the VSP, others would be reassigned or furloughed in order to reach the required staffing. Two veteran employees were among those who chose to participate in the VSP. In 1990, both men brought separate suits against the company alleging discrimination on the basis of age. They alleged that the company's implementation of the VSP violated the ADEA. The federal district court consolidated the two cases and granted the manufacturer's motion for summary judgment. Both men then appealed to the U.S. Court of Appeals, First Circuit.

The court stated that mere offers for early retirement, even those that include attractive incentives designed to induce employees who might otherwise stay on the job to separate from the employer's service, do not transgress the ADEA. To transform an offer of early retirement into a constructive discharge, the plaintiff must show that the offer was nothing more than a subterfuge disguising the employer's desire to purge the plaintiff from the ranks because of age. The court found that the manufacturer's implementation of the VSP was not this sort of choice. Moreover, the circumstances of the offer were not coercive. The court found that the manufacturer merely asked its employees to choose between immediate severance with its associated benefits or continued work with its inherent risks. Thus, the grant of summary judgment for the employer was affirmed. *Vega v. Kodak Caribbean, Ltd.*, 3 F.3d 476 (1st Cir.1993).

A 75-year-old Missouri man began working in the maintenance department of a concrete company. He allegedly told his supervisor that he went to Florida on vacation two months out of the year, and the supervisor told him that this wouldn't be a problem. However, when he returned from his vacation, he was dismissed. The company had hired a 35-year-old man to work in the maintenance department who testified that the supervisor had expressed concern about the older man's ability to perform the job because of his age. The employee filed an age discrimination suit in a federal district court which found for the employee. He received compensatory damages and attorney's fees. The trial court also doubled the damages for a wilful violation of the ADEA. The employer then appealed to the U.S. Court of Appeals, Eighth Circuit.

The employer argued that the trial court erred by not instructing the jury that additional evidence was needed to find a wilful violation of the ADEA. The U.S. Supreme Court has determined that the standard for wilfulness under the ADEA was simply whether "the employer either knew or showed reckless disregard for the matter of whether its conduct was prohibited by the statute." See *Hazen Paper Co. v. Biggins*, above. Further, the Court held that once a wilful violation has been shown, the employee need not additionally demonstrate that the employer's conduct was outrageous or provide direct evidence of the employer's motivation. The appellate court determined that the evidence indicated a reckless disregard on the part of the employer as to whether its conduct was prohibited and upheld the decision of the district court awarding double damages to the employee. *Brow v. Stites Concrete, Inc.*, 994 F.2d 553 (8th Cir.1993).

A 65-year-old Wyoming man was the field superintendent for an oil and gas company. The company sold its assets to another gas company and all of the former employees began working for the new company. However, after the field superintendent arrived for work, he was offered a position as a tank strapper. He felt that the job was demeaning for a man with 40 years experience and also demanding for a man of his age. After he declined the position, the company discharged him. He then filed this case in a federal district court, asserting that the company had violated the ADEA. The trial court found for the superintendent and awarded him $41,000 for breach of an employment contract, as well as attorney's fees, but it awarded no damages on his ADEA claim. The gas company appealed to the U.S. Court of Appeals, Tenth Circuit. The company asserted that there was no evidence that the worker had been replaced by a worker outside the protected age group. However, the court noted that the new field superintendent was 35 years old. The company also created several supervisory positions to assist the new superintendent with his new and increased duties. However, none of these new positions were offered to the ex-superintendent and all were filled by younger men. Therefore, the ex-superintendent had produced evidence of age discrimination and the issue had been properly submitted to the jury. The company next contended that because the jury had not awarded the ex-superintendent damages on his age discrimination claim, he was not a prevailing party on that claim. The court disagreed and stated that the plaintiff had prevailed on a significant issue in the litigation. *Hall v. Western Production Company,* 988 F.2d 1050 (10th Cir.1993).

A Tennessee administrative employee was dismissed at age 55 pursuant to a reduction in work force. Company management claimed the reduction was to meet a goal of a three to one ratio of manufacturing employees to administrative staff. Three other employees over the age of 50 and two employees under the age of 50 were also dismissed. However, the two younger workers were then rehired. Although the administrative employee requested a transfer to any available position, she was not rehired. She sued the company in a federal district court alleging age discrimination under the ADEA. The jury returned a verdict in her favor for over $120,000. However, the court granted the employer's motion for a judgment notwithstanding the verdict. The employee then appealed to the U.S. Court of Appeals, Sixth Circuit. The court stated that the different treatment of the younger workers did not indicate that age was a determining factor in the actions taken by the employer. One of the workers was rehired by an independent decisionmaker and the other worker's experience was considerably greater than that of the secretary. The court upheld the trial court's grant of a judgment notwithstanding the verdict in favor of the employer. *Phelps v. Yale Security, Inc.,* 986 F.2d 1020 (6th Cir.1993).

A retired Nevada plumber sought to return to work and signed up on the work list at a union hiring hall. The hiring hall sent members out to jobs in the order in which they signed up on the list. However, the hiring hall removed the plumber's name from the list because he was ineligible as a pensioned retiree. The retiree filed a discrimination charge with the EEOC when his name was kept off the list. The EEOC filed an action under the ADEA on behalf of the retiree and similarly situated union members in a federal district court. The district court granted summary judgment in favor of the union. The EEOC then appealed to the U.S. Court of Appeals, Ninth Circuit. The EEOC claimed that the union's policy violated the ADEA because it discriminated against older workers. The union argued that the policy was not discriminatory because the cause of the discrimination was not the retiree's age but his decision to retire. The court concluded that the union's policy was discriminatory. Under the policy only retired, older employees were required to decide whether to remain retired and thus forego the opportunity to work. On the other hand, non-retired workers who received unemployment compensation or who were employed elsewhere would not need to make this choice. Thus, this policy violated the ADEA. The court reversed the grant of summary judgment in favor of the union and granted judgment in favor of the EEOC and the retired workers. *EEOC v. Local 350, Plumbers and Pipefitters*, 982 F.2d 1305 (9th Cir.1992).

A Kansas manufacturer restructured its workforce following drastic reductions in revenues in four consecutive years. The manufacturer hired a consulting firm to analyze its operations and to identify and prioritize job functions. The manufacturer identified employees to be laid off, after first determining whether these employees could be transferred within the company or offered early retirement. Three employees who were laid off filed complaints with the state human rights commission, claiming that the manufacturer had violated a Kansas statute protecting employees aged 40 to 70 from age discrimination. A Kansas trial court vacated a final order of the commission in favor of the employees, and they appealed to the Supreme Court of Kansas. The supreme court found sufficient evidence in the trial court record to substantiate its findings that the manufacturer had not violated the act. Each of the employees had been identified as a poor performer, and two of them were the lowest ranked employees in their respective departments. Two of the employees' job duties had been assigned to other employees who were actually older than each of the complaining parties at the time of the layoffs, and who were also within the protected age group under the statute. Although the third employee's duties were now being performed by a younger employee, his job performance had been unsatisfactory and the layoff did not violate the discrimination statute. The court affirmed the trial court's judgment. *Beech Aircraft Corp. v. Kansas Human Rights Comm.*, 864 P.2d 1148 (Kan.1993).

A 49-year-old Mississippi man worked for a corporation until it closed its plant in the state and let 119 employees go. He was one of the terminated employees. Five other employees were transferred to plants in other states. When the employee became aware that he would not be considered for transfer, he filed a charge of discrimination with the EEOC. The EEOC issued him a letter stating that the evidence did not support a finding of age discrimination, and the employee then brought suit in a federal district court. The court granted summary judgment to the employer, stating that although the employee was in the protected age group when he was terminated, he had not established a *prima facie* case for reduction-in-force age discrimination. The employee appealed to the U.S. Court of Appeals, Fifth Circuit.

On appeal, the court determined that the employee had established a *prima facie* case of age discrimination by showing that he was in the protected age group and that he was discharged. The employer, however, had then articulated a legitimate, nondiscriminatory reason for not transferring him (namely, that the other employees were better qualified). The court then looked to see if the employee had raised a genuine issue of fact regarding whether the employer's reason for terminating him was just a pretext for age discrimination. It determined that the employee had not asserted facts sufficient to raise an issue for trial. Accordingly, the appellate court affirmed the trial court's decision in favor of the employer. *Amburgey v. Corhart Refractories Corp.,* 936 F.2d 805 (5th Cir.1991).

An Ohio man worked for a bank as production control scheduler. At the age of 48, his employment was terminated as a result of a reduction in force. He subsequently brought a lawsuit against the bank, asserting that it had violated Ohio's age discrimination and employment statute. The bank moved for summary judgment, charging that the employee could not prove a *prima facie* case, and that even if he could, there was a legitimate nondiscriminatory reason for his discharge. The Court of Common Pleas of Ohio examined the employee's claim and noted that he was a member of a protected class, he had been discharged, and he was qualified for the position. However, it then noted that he was not replaced by a younger person. Even though some younger employees were retained by the bank, none of them took over his job; his duties were simply distributed among other employees. Further, there was no evidence to indicate that age was even considered as a factor in the employee's discharge. Accordingly, the court granted the bank's motion for summary judgment. *Melms v. Society Bank & Trust,* 579 N.E.2d 797 (Ohio Com.Pl.1990).

A Missouri man worked for an electric company in a managerial capacity and was to supervise the construction of a power plant. Upon completion, his division, as expected, was eliminated. Under these circumstances, the company practice was to either assign the employee to another division or allow him to remain in the position until retirement. Although other positions were available, the employee, who was near retirement age, was not reassigned. The employee sued the electric company for age discrimination under the ADEA. The jury found for the employee and awarded him backpay, as well as front pay after finding that he would have worked until age 70. Punitive damages were also awarded to the employee. The trial court, however, dramatically reduced the amount of front pay. The court reasoned that the employee did not vigorously seek gainful employment in an attempt to mitigate damages. Additionally, the court felt there was insufficient evidence to support the jury's finding that the employee would have remained employed with the company until age 70. Consequently, both parties appealed to the U.S. Court of Appeals, Eighth Circuit.

On appeal, the court noted that there was sufficient evidence to support the jury's findings of age discrimination. The court then examined the front pay award. The basis for the jury's finding was that the employee testified that he planned to work until age 70 and had so informed the company. Also, upon termination, the employee contacted several business associates and contacts regarding employment, sending out 150-200 job application letters. The court noted that there was evidence in the record from which the jury could have found that the employee would have worked until age 70. Therefore, the case was remanded to the district court for reinstatement of the jury's damages award. *Doyne v. Union Elec. Co.,* 953 F.2d 447 (8th Cir.1992).

A corporation hired a Texas man to serve as the manager of one of its divisions. Over the next eleven years, he routinely received merit raises and performance bonuses, eventually achieving the title of vice president of the division. Subsequently, the new division president and the president of the corporation decided that they wanted a younger management team. The employee, now 60 years old, was given three options, the least offensive of which appeared to be as warehouse supervisor at the same salary but with a reduction in benefits. He accepted that position. When he reported for work, however, he was placed in charge of maintenance at the warehouse and spent 75 percent of his working time sweeping floors and cleaning up the employees' cafeteria. He developed numerous physical and psychological problems, and filed an age discrimination charge with the EEOC. Eventually, he brought suit against the company under the ADEA for intentional infliction of emotional distress. He was awarded $3.4 million, and the corporation appealed to the U.S. Court of Appeals, Fifth Circuit.

On appeal, the court noted that there was substantial evidence to support the jury's ADEA verdict. The court also noted that the degrading and humiliating way in which the vice president had been stripped of his duties and demoted to a position with menial and demeaning duties took the case out of the realm of an ordinary employment dispute. Here, the corporation had been unwilling to fire the vice president outright, and instead sought to humiliate him in the hopes that he would quit. This behavior by the corporation was sufficient to support the cause of action for intentional infliction of emotional distress. Accordingly, the appellate court affirmed the district court's decision in favor of the employee. *Wilson v. Monarch Paper Co.,* 939 F.2d 1138 (5th Cir.1991).

A private nonprofit hospital, founded by a congregation of Roman Catholic nuns, operated in accordance with church doctrine. A man worked for the hospital as its director of plant operations for 14 years until his employment was terminated. He had been responsible for overseeing the operation of the physical facilities and the hospital, and for supervising approximately 20 employees. Upon his discharge, he filed suit in a federal district court asserting claims under the ADEA. He maintained that the hospital wanted to save money by replacing him with a younger person who could be paid a lower salary. The hospital argued that the employee was fired because he used racially offensive remarks in the presence of others in violation of Catholic religious tenets.

On the hospital's motion for summary judgment, the court had to determine whether application of the ADEA would violate either the Free Exercise or Establishment Clauses of the First Amendment. The court determined that the ADEA could be interpreted so as to avoid a constitutional violation. This case did not present the problems of excessive entanglement with religion that cases dealing with the National Labor Relations Board's supervision of labor relations presented. Investigation into an ADEA claim was limited in time and scope. Further, since the law was a neutral statute of general applicability, it did not violate the Free Exercise Clause because it was not directed specifically at religious practices. The court thus denied the hospital's motion for summary judgment and allowed the claim to proceed to trial. *Lukaszewski v. Nazareth Hospital,* 764 F.Supp. 57 (E.D.Pa.1991).

The U.S. Supreme Court has held that employers may compel arbitration with respect to an age discrimination claim if the procedures are adequate and the arbitration agreement is not the result of unequal bargaining power. A corporation hired a middle-aged man as its manager of financial services. As required by his employer, he then registered as a securities representative with several stock exchanges, including the New York Stock Exchange (NYSE). In 1987, at the age of 62, the manager was discharged. He filed a claim with the EEOC, then brought suit in a North Carolina federal district court under the ADEA. His employer filed a motion to compel arbitration because NYSE Rule 347 provided for arbitration of any controversy arising out of employment or termination of employment. The district court denied the motion, holding that "Congress intended to protect ADEA claimants from the waiver of a judicial forum." The U.S. Court of Appeals, Fourth Circuit, reversed. The manager appealed to the U.S. Supreme Court.

The Court stated that there was no inconsistency between the public policy behind the ADEA and enforcing agreements to arbitrate age discrimination claims. The ADEA was enacted with the idea of providing a flexible approach to claim resolution. Further, the manager failed to show that the arbitration procedures were inadequate. Since he failed to meet the burden of proving that Congress intended to preclude arbitration of claims under the ADEA, the Court held that the arbitration clause could be enforced. *Gilmer v. Interstate/Johnson Lane Corp.,* 500 U.S. 20, 111 S.Ct. 1647, 114 L.Ed.2d 26 (1991).

A 63-year-old New York man was dismissed from his position as a vice president in the mortgage department of a bank. He filed an age discrimination claim with the EEOC, which referred the matter to the New York State Division of Human Rights. The agency found no probable cause to believe the employee had been discharged due to his age, and the Human Rights Appeal Board affirmed that decision. The employee then brought suit in a federal district court under the ADEA rather than appeal the administrative decision in state court. The district court granted the employer's motion for summary judgment, holding that the agency determination (that no discrimination had occurred) precluded the employee's litigation of his claim in federal court. The U.S. Court of Appeals, Second Circuit, reversed, and further appeal was taken to the U.S. Supreme Court.

The Court noted that the state administrative proceedings did not preclude the ADEA suit in this case because they had not been judicially reviewed. Both § 626(d)(2) and § 633(b) of the ADEA (at Title 29) assume the possibility of federal consideration after state agencies have finished examining the case. If state agency action were given preclusive effect, federal proceedings would be a mere formality. The Court affirmed the reversal of summary judgment and remanded the case. *Astoria Federal Saving and Loan Assn. v. Solimino,* 501 U.S. 104, 111 S.Ct. 2166, 115 L.Ed.2d 96 (1991).

IV. DISCRIMINATION AGAINST PERSONS WITH DISABILITIES

The Americans with Disabilities Act (ADA), 42 U.S.C. § 12101 *et seq.*, is an important federal law that prohibits discrimination against qualified individuals with disabilities with respect to job application procedures, hiring, advancement, discharge, compensation, training, and other terms and conditions of employment. The antidiscrimination principle of the ADA is based upon § 504 of the Rehabilitation Act of 1973, which applies only to programs or activities receiving federal funds. The ADA expands § 504's limited scope to most employers with at least 15 employees. Many states have enacted similar legislation on behalf of individuals with disabilities, and many of these laws are based upon the language of the ADA and § 504.

A. The ADA and the Rehabilitation Act

The Rehabilitation Act of 1973 (29 U.S.C. § 701, *et seq.*) is a comprehensive federal law that encourages equal opportunities in employment, rehabilitative services and education for individuals with disabilities. Section 504 of the Rehabilitation Act (29 U.S.C. § 794) forbids any employer which receives federal funding from discriminating against otherwise qualified individuals with disabilities. Section 504 provides that no otherwise qualified individual with a disability shall, solely by reason of his or her disabilities, be excluded from the participation in, be denied the benefit of, or be subjected to discrimination under any program or activity receiving federal financial assistance.

While the Rehabilitation Act applies only to recipients of federal funds and to federal agencies, the Americans with Disabilities Act (ADA) broadly applies to many public and private institutions. The courts are mandated by law to apply the same legal analysis in ADA cases as that employed in cases filed under the Rehabilitation Act. Case law that has been developed by the courts under the Rehabilitation Act thus forms the legal authority for interpreting the ADA. The following landmark U.S. Supreme Court decision interpreting the Rehabilitation Act is an important precedent for interpreting the ADA. Federal regulations issued under the ADA refer to this case for several ADA definitions.

A Florida school board fired an elementary school teacher after she suffered three relapses of tuberculosis within two years. The disease had been in remission for about 20 years, after the teacher had first been hospitalized in 1957. The teacher sued the school board in a federal district court for discrimination on the basis of disability under § 504 of the Rehabilitation Act. The court held that contagious diseases such as tuberculosis were not disabilities within the meaning of § 504 and determined that the teacher was not a qualified individual with a disability who was entitled to hold her former position. The U.S. Court of Appeals, Eleventh Circuit, reversed the lower court's ruling, and the U.S. Supreme Court agreed to review the case. On appeal, the school board contended that in defining an individual with a disability under § 504, the contagious effects of a disease may be distinguished from the physical effects of the disease. The Court disagreed, and reasoned that the teacher's contagion and her physical impairment both resulted from tuberculosis. Allowing discrimination based on the contagious effects of a physical impairment would be inconsistent with the underlying purpose of § 504, which is to ensure that persons with disabilities are not denied employment opportunities because of social prejudice or ignorance. The Supreme Court noted that society's myths and fears about disability and disease are as disabling as the physical limitations that result from physical impairments, and concluded that contagion cannot remove a person from § 504 coverage.

Because tuberculosis affected the teacher's respiratory system and had required her hospitalization in 1957, she qualified as an individual with a disability within the meaning of § 504. The Court rejected the school board's contention that the contagiousness of the teacher's disability removed her from Rehabilitation Act coverage. The Supreme Court remanded the case to the district court to determine whether the teacher was "otherwise qualified" for her job and whether the school board could reasonably accommodate her as an employee. Whether the teacher was otherwise qualified would depend upon further evidence of how tuberculosis is transmitted, how long carriers remain infectious, the potential for harm to others at the school and the chance of a risk that the teacher could transmit the disease to others in the course of her employment. *School Bd. of Nassau County v. Arline*, 480 U.S. 273, 107 S.Ct. 1123, 94 L.Ed.2d 307 (1987).

The ADA general rule is found at 42 U.S.C. § 12112(a). "No covered entity shall discriminate against a qualified individual with a disability because of the disability of such individual in regard to job application procedures, the hiring, advancement, or discharge of employees, employee compensation, job training, and other terms, conditions, and privileges of employment." A covered entity is an employer engaged in an industry affecting commerce and having 15 or more employees for each working day in each of 20 or more calendar weeks in the current or preceding calendar year. In addition to employers, a covered entity may include the agent of an employer, an employment agency, labor organization or joint labor-management committee.

Although a person's status as a qualified individual with a disability is determined by the courts on a case by case basis, the statute defines qualified individual with a disability as one who, "with or without reasonable accommodation, can perform the essential functions of the employment position that such individual holds or desires." Reasonable accommodation is also a factual issue, but according to the statute may include the making of facilities readily accessible to individuals with disabilities, job restructuring, job-sharing, reassignment to vacant positions, the acquisition or modification of equipment, provision of readers and interpreters and the modification of employment tests. Employers seeking to show that a proposed accommodation is not reasonable must show that providing the accommodation would create an undue hardship.

Undue hardship is defined as "an action requiring significant difficulty or expense," which may in turn involve the nature and cost of the proposed accommodation, the overall size and financial resources of the employment facility and the impact of the accommodation on business operations. Although the statute details several other factors, a court reviewing an employer's perceived undue hardship will make its determination based on the evidence presented by the parties in each individual case. While the ADA may protect some individuals with a history of drug or alcohol abuse, the term qualified individual with a disability specifically excludes current illegal users of drugs from coverage, and employers are specifically permitted to prohibit the illegal use of drugs and alcohol in the workplace. An employer may properly require that employees not be under the influence of drugs and alcohol on the job and may insist that employees conform to the standards of the Drug-Free Workplace Act of 1988 (41 U.S.C. § 701, *et seq.*). Nothing in the ADA is to be construed as encouraging, prohibiting or authorizing the conducting of employee drug tests by covered employers. The text and selected regulations of the ADA, Rehabilitation Act § 504, and the Individuals with Disabilities Education Act are compiled in *Statutes, Regulations and Case Law Protecting Individuals With Disabilities*, available from Data Research, Inc. The book is annotated with many important cases not found in this volume and includes an informative glossary.

The U.S. Court of Appeals, Tenth Circuit, affirmed the summary judgment order of the U.S. District Court for the Western District of Oklahoma in a disability discrimination claim under the ADA by an employee who broke his ankle in a non-work accident. The employee went through a number of medical proceedings and took an extended medical disability leave. When the employee was absent from work for more than one year, the employer terminated his employment stating that it was unable to reasonably accommodate or place him in another job. The court of appeals determined that there was no evidence that the employee could be reasonably accommodated to allow him to perform essential functions of his job. Although the employee had demonstrated that he was an individual with a disability for the purposes of the ADA, there was evidence that he was unable to lift objects weighing more than 15 pounds or to stand for more than four hours, which were essential job duties. There was no evidence that the employer had other available jobs which did not require these abilities. The ADA does not require employers to promote individuals with disabilities in order to reasonably accommodate. Employers were not required to assign employees to occupied positions or to create new ones in order to accommodate them. The failure to prove that an accommodation was possible constituted a failure of proof under the ADA, and the court of appeals affirmed the judgment for the employer. *White v. York International Corp.*, 45 F.3d 357 (10th Cir.1995).

In a case filed in the U.S. District Court for the Southern District of Indiana, a former nursing home worker alleged that she was fired for improper reasons, such as complaining that she had not been paid in a timely fashion for overtime work, filing a worker's compensation complaint and returning to work with physical restrictions. Her refusal to report for work without physical restrictions was the ultimate reason for discharge. The court held that the employee's former supervisor could not be held liable for tortious interference with her employment contract, inasmuch as his actions had been within the course and scope of his duties as a supervisor. The employee's theory conflicted directly with Indiana law that precludes claims for interference with contractual relationships when a supervisor acts within the scope of his own employment. The court rejected the former employee's attempt to expand Indiana's employment-at-will doctrine by creating an exception for violation of statutory rights stated in the ADA. However, the court withheld any judgment on the actual ADA claim itself. *Leslie v. St. Vincent New Hope, Inc.*, 873 F.Supp. 1250 (S.D.Ind.1995).

The U.S. District Court for the Northern District of Ohio dismissed a wrongful discharge complaint filed by an employee who alleged that his former employer violated public policy as stated by the ADA. The former employee filed a motion to reconsider on the basis of a shift in state case law by the Supreme Court of Ohio, citing a recent case in which the court announced a willingness to allow wrongful discharge claims for violation of public policy for reasons other than those specifically listed in state statutes. The court found no reason to apply the state supreme court precedent in this case, stating that Congress was the final word on federal policy preferences. The court stated that failure to dismiss the employee's wrongful discharge complaint based on violations of public policy stated in the ADA and Family Medical Leave Act would circumvent the legislative scheme of enforcing these laws through direct lawsuits filed under those acts. *Gall v. Quaker City Castings, Inc.*, 874 F.Supp. 161 (N.D.Ohio 1995).

The owner and president of a small New Hampshire auto parts distribution company participated in a self-funded medical reimbursement plan administered by a trust. The owner was also an employee of the company. Lifetime benefits under the plan were limited to $1 million per member. The owner/employee then began to develop serious illnesses, many of which were related to the HIV virus. The plan soon limited benefits for HIV-related illnesses to $25,000. The owner/employee died of his illnesses and his estate filed a lawsuit against the plan and trust in a New Hampshire trial court. Although the lawsuit stated only state law claims, the plan and trust removed the case to the U.S. District Court for the District of New Hampshire, arguing that the state law claims were preempted by ERISA. The estate then filed a motion to amend the complaint with ADA claims. The court granted the motion, but then dismissed the claims, finding that the plan and trust were not "employers" under ADA Title I, and that neither entity could be considered a "public accommodation" under ADA Title III. The estate appealed to the U.S. Court of Appeals, First Circuit.

The court found that the district court had erroneously failed to give the estate any notice of its proposed dismissal action, justifying reversal. It also found sufficient uncertainty to warrant reversal on the issue of whether the plan or trust could be considered an employer under the ADA. There was no merit to the district court's finding that Title III's reference to "public accommodation" referred only to physical structures. On the contrary, Congress contemplated "public accommodation" to incorporate service establishments. The case was reversed and remanded. *Carparts Dist. Center, Inc. v. Automotive Wholesaler's Assn. of New England, Inc.*, 37 F.3d 12 (1st Cir.1994).

An Illinois worker contracted multiple sclerosis and his employment was terminated. He filed a discrimination lawsuit against his former employer and three former supervisors in the U.S. District Court for the Northern District of Illinois under the ADA and state laws. The court dismissed all claims except the ADA claim against the former employer. It then considered motions by the former supervisors that would prevent the former employee from amending his original complaint to specifically allege that each of them was a decisionmaking supervisor who might therefore be held liable under the ADA. The court stated that the U.S. Court of Appeals, Seventh Circuit, has upheld personal liability against decisionmaking supervisors in Title VII and ADA cases. Although there can be no general claim of individual liability for discrimination under these acts, some courts have allowed personal liability claims against supervisors who hold decisionmaking authority. The liability must be based on individual acts that are distinct from the institutional policies of the employer. Because the ADA, like Title VII, is a broad remedial statute intended to prohibit employment discrimination, the court determined that the former employee should be permitted to amend his original complaint to allege that the supervisors wielded decisionmaking power. *DeLuca v. Winer Industries, Inc.*, 857 F.Supp. 606 (N.D.Ill.1994).

A Georgia food service worker participated in an employee group welfare benefit plan covered under ERISA. The plan provided health insurance coverage up to a lifetime limit of $1 million. The employee was diagnosed with AIDS and sought benefits under the plan. He claimed that the food service company then discharged him to avoid making future health insurance payments. The company also amended the plan to limit AIDS-related treatment to $10,000 per year with a lifetime maximum limit of $40,000. The employee exhausted the limit, and his former employer refused to pay claims totaling more than $90,000. Shortly before his death, the former employee filed a discrimination complaint with the EEOC, claiming that the plan amendment violated the ADA and ERISA. After receiving a right to sue letter from the EEOC, the former employee's estate filed a lawsuit against the food service company in the U.S. District Court for the Northern District of Georgia. The court noted that Title I of the ADA applied to most private employers as of July 26, 1992 and had no retroactive application. Because the limitation on AIDS-related claims had been made in October 1991, the only time period during which the ADA applied to this case was from July 26, 1992 until the employee's death in September 1992. Since the former employee was not an applicant or employee of the food service company at the time of the alleged violations, the ADA afforded him no protection, and the claim was dismissed. The ERISA portion of the complaint remained viable. *Gonzales v. Garner Food Services, Inc.*, 855 F.Supp. 371 (N.D.Ga.1994).

The vice president of an Illinois medical services corporation advised the corporate president that he had multiple sclerosis and requested that his disability be accommodated by a temporary reduction in his work week to 40 hours. The corporation fired the vice president two days later. He filed a lawsuit against the corporation and its chairman/owner in the U.S. District Court for the Northern District of Illinois. He alleged that the firing violated the ADA, and that the act applied to the chairman/owner. The court considered the chairman/owner's motion for dismissal from the lawsuit. The court observed that "agents" were incorporated within the ADA's definition of employers. The vice president had alleged sufficient facts to implicate the chairman/owner as a decisionmaker of the corporation. Because the ADA applied to agents of an employer, the court refused to dismiss the chairman/owner from the lawsuit. The intention of Congress was apparently to include potential liability for such officers. *Jendusa v. Cancer Treatment Centers of America, Inc.*, 868 F.Supp. 1006 (N.D.Ill.1994).

An Oklahoma warehouse worker suffered an on-the-job injury and took a medical leave of absence. The employer required employees returning from medical leave to obtain doctor statements certifying fitness to resume working. The employee's doctor determined that he was unable to return to his former job, and the employer refused to rehire him. The employee filed a lawsuit in the U.S. District Court for the Western District of Oklahoma, alleging employment discrimination in violation of the ADA and age discrimination in violation of the Age Discrimination in Employment Act (ADEA). The court granted the employer's motion for summary judgment and the employee appealed to the U.S. Court of Appeals, Tenth Circuit. The court determined that the employee had produced insufficient evidence that the employer's reason for failing to rehire him was a pretext. The ADA did not protect employees who alleged that they were unable to perform the duties of a particular job. The ADA definition of qualified individual with a disability encompassed only those employees who were unable to perform a broad class or range of jobs. The employee had failed to make the requisite showing that he was unable to perform other jobs. The employee's ADEA claim also failed, because he failed to demonstrate a nexus between alleged discriminatory statements made by a supervisor and the employer's decision not to rehire him. The court affirmed the district court's summary judgment order. *Bolton v. Scrivner, Inc.*, 36 F.3d 939 (10th Cir.1994).

An Illinois security guard company hired an executive director who was a well-known security industry leader with over 30 years of experience in the field. At the time he was hired, the executive had emphysema and a back injury for which he had received a 20 percent disability rating from the Veteran's Administration. He was then diagnosed with lung cancer, and underwent surgery to remove a lung. After completing treatment and returning to work, the executive was diagnosed with brain tumors, and his doctors advised him that he had only 6 to 12 months to live. The executive returned to work, but because he was frequently absent due to radiation treatments, the company's sole shareholder advised the executive that he would be retired. The executive filed a complaint with the EEOC, which sued the employer under Title I of the ADA and other civil rights laws.

The employer filed a motion for summary judgment, arguing that the executive's performance had been affected by memory loss which required his job responsibilities to be transferred to other employees. It also argued that the executive's prolonged absences interfered with his job performance. The U.S. District Court for the Northern District of Illinois ruled that there were genuine issues of material fact which made a summary judgment motion premature. The court would have to consider further evidence of whether the executive was a "qualified individual with a disability" under the ADA. This could only be determined by examining the facts of whether the executive was able to success-fully perform his job duties at the time he was discharged from employment. The court denied the employer's summary judgment motion. *EEOC v. AIC Security Investigation, Ltd.*, 820 F.Supp. 1060 (N.D.Ill.1993).

The jury found that the defendants discharged the executive because of his terminal cancer, despite the fact that he remained able to perform the essential functions of his position. The jury then awarded him $22,000 in backpay, $50,000 in compensatory damages, $250,000 in punitive damages against the company, and $250,000 in punitive damages against the president and owner. The defen-dants contended that the award of $50,000 in compensatory damages was excessive. The court disagreed and determined that the jury had the right to consider the emotional impact of such a termination on a person who was simultaneously faced with the burden of his own impending death and the resulting inability to continue to provide for those who depended on him. The court concluded that the award of $50,000 was supported by the evidence. Next, the defendants contended that the employee failed to aggregate the sum of the amount of compensatory damages and the amount of punitive damages awarded as required by the statutory caps on such damages pursuant to 42 U.S.C. § 1981a(b)(3). The court agreed with the defendants that the limitations should be applied in the instant case. The statutory language unquestionably provided a limitation on the sum of punitive damages and compensatory damages, by invoking a cap of $200,000. Thus, the punitive damages award was reduced to $150,000. And finally, the court determined that the company and the owner would be held jointly and severally liable for the punitive damages. *EEOC v. AIC Security Investigations, Ltd.*, 823 F.Supp. 571 (N.D.Ill.1993).

A nonprofit Florida club employed a barber who suffered a heart attack and underwent a coronary bypass. The club then terminated his employment. The barber claimed that his employment termination resulted from a disability and that the club refused to reinstate him with an attempt at accommodating him. He filed a lawsuit against the club in the U.S. District Court for the Middle District of Florida. The court converted the club's motion to dismiss into a motion for summary judgment and referred the matter to a magistrate judge. The magistrate judge recommended denial of the summary judgment motion, finding a factual issue concerning whether the club was private within the meaning of the ADA. The court stated that the ADA and Title VII exempted bona fide private membership clubs from classification as employers for the purposes of discrimination lawsuits. To qualify as a bona fide private membership club, the entity must be a club in the ordinary sense of the word; that is, it must be private and impose meaningful limitations on its membership. In this case, the club was a tax exempt organization that qualified as a club under common understanding by limiting its membership and facilities. The barber's evidence of isolated accounts of non-member use of club facilities did not overcome the club's showing that it met the criteria for private club classification under the ADA and Title VII. The court rejected the magistrate judge's recommendation and granted the motion for summary judgment. *Kelsey v. Univ. Club of Orlando, Inc.*, 845 F.Supp. 1526 (M.D.Fla.1994).

A California woman filed a complaint in a state court in 1988. The original complaint alleged retaliation and physical handicap discrimination, among other claims, in violation of California law. The case was moved to a federal district court. The court granted summary judgment for the defendants and the U.S. Court of Appeals, Ninth Circuit, reversed as to the retaliation and physical handicap discrimination claims. After representation by several people, the woman's new counsel filed a motion to amend the complaint on November 9, 1992. The amended complaint requested that the disability discrimination claim be based upon the ADA. The court noted that it would grant leave to amend a pleading when justice so required. Thus, the defendants needed to show that the amendment was futile, that the plaintiff had unduly delayed the amendment, or that the amendment would cause undue prejudice. The employer contended that the ADA was not retroactive. The court noted that the ADA had a delayed effective date which suggested that Congress did not intend it to apply retroactively. Further, the ADA itself and its legislative history mentioned nothing about retroactive application. Thus, retroactive application of the ADA would not be appropriate. The court noted that the amendment would be futile and denied the motion to amend. *Raya v. Maryatt Industries*, 829 F.Supp. 1169 (N.D.Cal.1993).

B. State Laws

A Washington microfilm processor suffered injuries to her hands and arms from repetitive motions on the job. Her supervisor repeatedly denied her requests to rotate shifts and assigned her to a more grueling schedule than that worked by other employees. The employee also claimed that her supervisor subjected her to verbal harassment. After undergoing surgery on both hands and taking a medical leave, she filed an employment discrimination action against the employer in a Washington trial court. The court awarded her damages for disability discrimination and negligent infliction of emotional distress. The Washington Court of Appeals affirmed the trial court judgment. The employer appealed to the Supreme Court of Washington. On appeal, the employer argued that the state workers' compensation act barred an employee from recovering against an employer for physical injuries and negligent infliction of emotional distress. The supreme court stated that because the employee's injuries from discriminatory conduct were of a different nature and arose at a different time in her employment history than her workers' compensation injuries, the discrimination action was not barred by the workers' compensation act. The state law against discrimination was intended to compensate employees injured as a result of discriminatory action, and the compensation act did not bar the claim for emotional distress. The trial court had properly found that the employer had violated its duty to reasonably accommodate the employee's physical condition. *Goodman v. Boeing Co.*, 899 P.2d 1265 (Wash.1995).

The Court of Appeals of New York upheld a finding by the New York City Commission on Human Rights that an employer discriminated against a job applicant with blindness in violation of the New York City Code. The applicant alleged that the employer unlawfully discriminated against him by processing his employment application without considering whether he could be reasonably accommodated in the part-time position conducting public opinion telephone polls. After an administrative delay of almost six years, a hearing was held finding that the employer failed to meet its burden of showing that it was unable to reasonably accommodate the applicant. The employer appealed to a state trial court, claiming that the long delay had caused unreasonable prejudice because it was no longer able to produce necessary witnesses. The court granted enforcement of the commission's order and an appellate division court affirmed. The court of appeals concurred with the lower courts, finding no evidence that the delay had substantially harmed the employer. The commission had not committed error in allocating the burden of proof upon the employer to show undue hardship or inability to reasonably accommodate the employee. *In the Matter of Louis Harris and Associates, Inc. v. deLeon*, 84 N.Y.2d 698, 622 N.Y.S.2d 217, 646 N.E.2d 438 (1994).

A Pennsylvania woman who suffered from epilepsy was hired by a textile processing company as a general laborer. She moved to several different positions in the plant but could only produce 65 percent of the quota set for employees despite company attempts to allow her to become a productive employee. The explanation for her lack of productivity was that the medication she was required to take for her epilepsy caused drowsiness, impaired her ability to remember and concentrate, slowed motor functions and interrupted coordination. After the company fired her, she filed a complaint alleging that she had been discharged because of disability discrimination in violation of the Pennsylvania Human Relations Act (PHRA). The trial court granted the employer's motion for summary judgment and the employee appealed to the Superior Court of Pennsylvania. Under the PHRA, the employee bears the initial burden of establishing a *prima facie* case for discharge on the basis of disability. However, the statute does not prevent the discharge of an employee whose disability substantially interferes with the employee's ability to perform the essential functions of employment. Nevertheless, an employer must make reasonable accommodations to permit the employee to perform the job at hand. A reasonable accommodation is one which does not impose an undue hardship on the employer. The appellate court concluded that the employee's handicap was such that it prevented her from performing the essential functions of her job, despite numerous accommodations provided by the company. Accordingly, the appellate court upheld the decision of the trial court and granted summary judgment in favor of the employer. *Buckno v. Penn Linen & Uniform Service*, 631 A.2d 674 (Pa.Super.1993).

An Illinois woman had been employed as an office manager for a company that employed both smoking and nonsmoking employees. The office manager claimed that she suffered harm because the company allowed cigarette smoking in its facility. She further alleged that the company was notified of the smoking problem through petitions and memos. She then filed suit for damages in an Illinois state court under the state Clean Indoor Air Act. The trial court found for the employer and the employee appealed to the Appellate Court of Illinois. The issue on appeal was whether the act allowed for a private cause of action for damages for § 9 discrimination. Section 9 of the act provides that no individual may be discriminated against in any manner because of the exercise of any right afforded under the act. The court noted that even though the only relief expressly provided for in the act was injunctive relief, the purpose of the act was to protect nonsmoking individuals from the harmful, dangerous and annoying effects of tobacco smoke. It also concluded that providing plaintiffs with a right to damages when they have been discriminated against while exercising their right to breathe clean air in public places was consistent with the underlying purposes of the act. Accordingly, the court reversed the grant of summary judgment and held that an implied private cause of action for damages existed under the act. *Pechan v. Dynapro Inc.*, 622 N.E.2d 108 (Ill.App.1993).

A Texas man worked for a power plant as an auxiliary operator taking instrument readings and monitoring equipment. Eventually, he began training to promote to a higher level operator position. However, he suffered from eczema which caused his skin to itch intensely, split, crack and peel. As a result, he encountered difficulty working in the higher level control room which was cooled by "reheat" air conditioning — a method that removes moisture from the air. His skin condition became so inflamed that he had to peel off layers of skin after each shift. The company subsequently discharged him, claiming that the auxiliary operator position was only a training position for the higher level operator position and that the company required employees to move up to the full-time control room positions. The employee sued the employer in a state trial court, alleging that the power plant had discriminated against him due to his handicap. The trial court found that the employee was a handicapped person as defined by Texas discrimination law, and the power plant appealed to the Court of Appeals of Texas, Corpus Christi.

The issue on appeal was whether the employee's skin condition qualified as a handicap, thus entitling him to the protections against discriminatory employment practices proscribed by Texas law. The employee admitted that his claimed handicap was not based upon mental retardation, hardness of hearing, speech or visual impairment, being crippled, nor upon health impairment requiring special ambulatory devices or services. The court noted that the term "handicap" is generally perceived as "severely limiting one in performing work-related functions in general." Here, because the employee's condition did not require special ambulatory devices or services as contemplated by the language of the statute, he did not meet his burden of proving that he was handicapped. The court reversed the trial court's decision. *Central Power & Light Co. v. Bradbury*, 871 S.W.2d 860 (Tex.App.—Corpus Christi 1994).

A hearing impaired woman began working as a dietary aide at a nursing home. Her duties consisted of cooking, washing dishes, filling trays, preparing food and delivering snacks. Shortly thereafter, the nursing home fired the employee. She then successfully filed an action with the West Virginia Human Rights Commission claiming that she had been illegally discriminated against with regard to her employment because of her hearing impairment. She was given backpay and incidental damages for embarrassment, emotional distress, humiliation and loss of personal dignity. The nursing home then appealed to the Supreme Court of Appeals of West Virginia. An individual with a handicap is otherwise qualified if she is able to perform the job after the employer has made reasonable accommodations. The court noted that the employee was able to perform the job in question. The nursing home contended that it afforded every reasonable accommodation. However, no one spoke with the employee about wearing a hearing aid, and no one asked her if there was anything that could be done to enable her to hear more clearly. The court determined that she was even denied a very simple accommodation for her physical impairment — when communicating, she needed a person to look at her while speaking and to speak loudly. Accordingly, the court determined that the evidence sustained a finding of discrimination and upheld the Human Rights Commission's findings. *Morris Nursing Home v. Human Rights Commission*, 431 S.E.2d 353 (W.Va.1993).

An Arizona job applicant felt that he was denied employment by a manufacturing company due to his age. He filed an age discrimination complaint against the manufacturer with the Arizona Civil Rights Division. The manufacturer's attorney responded that the applicant was not hired because of an ear drainage problem which would preclude the wearing of earplugs. He also stated that the employer had experienced difficulty with hearing-impaired employees becoming disoriented or losing their balance when wearing earplugs. The civil rights division dismissed the age discrimination complaint and instituted a disability discrimination charge. The court granted a summary judgment motion filed by the manufacturer and the applicant appealed to the Court of Appeals of Arizona, Division One. On appeal, the applicant argued that he was not an individual with a disability but had been unlawfully discriminated against because he had been perceived as having a disability. The court stated that the Arizona Civil Rights Act implicitly prohibited discrimination against individuals with perceived disabilities. Therefore, the trial court had erroneously granted summary judgment to the manufacturer. The state law was similar to § 504 of the federal Rehabilitation Act, which expressly protects such individuals. However, because the employer did not necessarily violate the act by simply not hiring the applicant, the case was remanded for a new trial to consider the applicant's general employability and whether he had established a case for disability discrimination. *Bogue v. Better-Bilt Aluminum Co.*, 875 P.2d 1327 (Ariz.App.Div.1 1994).

A Nebraska worker injured her foot and was absent from work for approximately seven weeks. Upon the recommendation of her physician, she was reassigned to an area known as the tool crib. She was not able to work the tool crib fast enough due to her injury and was reassigned to various other tasks. Even with accommodations, she was unable to manage any of the jobs she was assigned. She then went on medical leave. After she was on medical leave for over a year, she was discharged. She filed this suit in a federal district court alleging handicap discrimination under the Nebraska Fair Employment Practice Act (NFEPA). The district court granted summary judgment to the employer, and the employee appealed to the U.S. Court of Appeals, Eighth Circuit.

The NFEPA prohibits discrimination based on an individual's disability. Disability is defined in the statute as any physical condition caused by bodily injury. However, the aggrieved employee has the burden of proving that the condition is unrelated to the ability to perform employment duties and does not adversely affect job performance. The court noted that the worker could not satisfactorily perform any work assignment, even with accommodations. Thus, she did not fall within the protected class under the NFEPA. The appellate court affirmed the decision of the trial court and granted summary judgment to the employer. *Woodyard v. Hover Group, Inc.*, 985 F.2d 421 (8th Cir.1993).

An engineer who worked for a large Washington airplane manufacturer was a biological male at the time of hire (the engineer since changed sexes to become a woman and will be referred to with feminine pronouns). After a number of years, the engineer determined that she was a transsexual. Transexualism is known as gender dysphoria. The engineer then began treatment by a physician to undergo sex reassignment surgery. To qualify, she had to live full-time for a year in the social role of a female. She approached her employer with her intentions and was informed that she could not use the female restrooms or wear feminine attire while she was still an anatomical male. The manufacturer allowed her to wear unisex clothing such as slacks, blouses, flat shoes, nylon stockings, earrings, lipstick, foundation and clear nail polish, but received complaints from other employees regarding the engineer's attire. It then issued the engineer a warning and stated that she would have to report daily to her manager—who would monitor her attire. The manufacturer fired the engineer for wearing an outfit which included pink pearls. She then filed this action in a Washington trial court for handicap discrimination. After the trial court found for the employer, the engineer appealed to the Court of Appeals of Washington, which reversed the trial court's decision. The employer appealed to the Supreme Court of Washington.

The engineer claimed that gender dysphoria was a handicap under state law and that she had been discharged due to her handicap. The issue before the court was whether there was an abnormal condition, and whether the employer discriminated against the employee because of that condition. Gender dysphoria qualified as an abnormal condition. However, the employer discharged the employee because she violated the employer's directives on acceptable attire, not for being gender dysphoric. *Doe v. Boeing Co.*, 846 P.2d 531 (Wash.1993).

A California truck driver began treatment for a kidney disorder, which culminated in a transplant operation. He was left with one functioning kidney, but returned to work and experienced no medical problems. Subsequently, the company added "sleeper runs" which required the driver to sleep in the cab while another person drove the truck. He informed the company that he would be unable to drive "sleeper runs" and supported his position with a medical opinion. He asked to be put on casual runs, but his request was denied. He was then placed on medical leave. Thereafter, he filed this action under the California Fair Employment and Housing Act (FEHA), alleging handicap discrimination. The trial court granted summary judgment for the employer and the driver appealed to the Court of Appeal of California. Under the FEHA, a person is handicapped if he has a condition which "substantially limits one or more major life activities." The court noted that employment is a major life activity. However, the driver could still drive a truck and thus was not substantially limited in a major life activity even though he could not sleep in the cab of a moving vehicle. Thus, being placed on medical leave was not due to a handicap and this did not violate the FEHA. The appellate court upheld the decision of the trial court. *Maloney v. AWR Freight System Inc.*, 20 Cal.Rptr.2d 656 (Cal.App.1993).

A Vermont ski resort hired a woman to work as a chambermaid in 1986. Although she had dentures, she did not wear them to work because they hurt. A year later, the resort hired a new executive housekeeper who indicated to the employee that she had to wear them daily to work. The chambermaid called the executive housekeeper and explained that she was unable to wear the dentures because they did not fit. She asked to be allowed to return to work so that she could earn enough money to purchase a new set. The executive housekeeper told the chambermaid that she could not come back to work without dentures, but that she would hold her job open until December 21. After she did not report to work on that date, the resort fired her. She then sued the resort, claiming it had violated the state Fair Employment Practices Act (FEPA) because it failed to accommodate her handicap. The trial court granted the employer's motion for summary judgment and the chambermaid appealed to the Supreme Court of Vermont.

Under the FEPA, a handicapped individual is defined as a person who: has a physical or mental impairment which substantially limits one or more major life activities; has a record of such impairment; or is regarded as having such an impairment. The supreme court noted that the employee's lack of upper teeth was a physical impairment within the meaning of the FEPA because the lack of teeth is a cosmetic disfigurement and an anatomical loss affecting the muscular, skeletal and digestive systems. Accordingly, the court ruled that she was handicapped and reversed and remanded the case to the trial court to determine if the employer reasonably accommodated her. *Hodgdon v. Mount Mansfield Co., Inc.,* 624 A.2d 1122 (Vt.1992).

A carpenter was hired by a company to do repair work at a nuclear power plant. He was given a psychological evaluation test which revealed alcoholic tendencies. Because of this, he was not granted "unescorted-access" authorization; the company then discharged him. He sued the company in a Michigan trial court, asserting that it had discriminated against him on the basis of a perceived handicap: alcoholism. The court granted summary judgment to the company, and the employer appealed to the Court of Appeals of Michigan. On appeal, the court noted that summary judgment had been improperly granted. There remained a question of whether alcoholism was a handicap under the Michigan Handicappers' Civil Rights Act. Further, the trial court would have to consider whether a person can be considered impaired in ability to perform his job by reason of alcoholism if he does not come to work under the influence and does not demonstrate alcohol-related behavior. The case was reversed and remanded. *Adkerson v. MK-Ferguson Co.,* 477 N.W.2d 465 (Mich.App.1991).

A Maine woman worked as a bank teller for a credit union. A childhood bout with tuberculosis left her lungs damaged and susceptible to infections. However, she worked without difficulty in a smoking environment. After a fire in an adjacent building aggravated her condition and she developed bronchitis, her doctor advised her to avoid smoke and dust during her recovery period. The employer subsequently implemented a smoking policy limited to certain areas of the credit union. The employee resigned after she was reprimanded for leaving her work station to recover from a customer's cigarette smoke. She claimed that she resigned because of an unhealthy working environment. Thereafter, she brought a discrimination claim against the employer. A trial court found in favor of the employer, and the employee appealed.

The Supreme Judicial Court of Maine noted that the pertinent statute defined "discharge" to include situations where the employee has no reasonable alternative to resignation because of intolerable working conditions. It stated that the test was whether a reasonable person under such unpleasant conditions would feel compelled to resign. The court found that the employer had failed to make reasonable accommodation for the employee's bronchial condition. However, the court also found that the employee had failed to show that the employer had refused to consider other accommodations. It found that the employer acted reasonably in its willingness to explore other alternatives at the time the employee resigned. Therefore, the court held that no constructive discharge had occurred, and it affirmed the decision of the trial court. *King v. Bangor Federal Credit Union,* 611 A.2d 80 (Me.1992).

A Texas man was hired by a telephone company in 1976. Ten years later, he was diagnosed as having AIDS and was placed on the corporation's sickness and accident disability benefit plan. This provided benefits for up to 52 weeks. After that time, the employee sought to return to his job. However, his employer required a medical examination and, based on the results, determined that the employee would be subjected to an unacceptable risk of harm if he returned to work. It thus advised him that he could accept long-term disability benefits; he would then be removed from the payroll. The employee did so, but then filed suit against the company, asserting that it had discriminated against him on the basis of his handicap in violation of the Texas Commission on Human Rights Act (TCHRA). The federal district court held that AIDS and its related illnesses were not handicaps under the TCHRA and granted summary judgment to the employer. The employee appealed to the U.S. Court of Appeals, Fifth Circuit.

On appeal, the court examined the statute to find a definition of handicapped. However, the TCHRA provided only a nonexclusive list of physical and mental conditions which were deemed to be handicaps. The common element in the physical conditions was a physiological rather than a pathological condition of health. Since the employee did not suffer any physiological impairments, he was not handicapped within the meaning of the TCHRA. Further, even if he was perceived as handicapped so as to bring him within the protections of the statute, his low platelet count (an AIDS-related illness) would pose a constant risk of instant death if he returned to work. Accordingly, he could not reasonably perform his job duties. The appellate court ruled that the employee was "disabled" and not handicapped under the TCHRA. It therefore affirmed the district court's decision and held that no discrimination had occurred. *Hilton v. Southwestern Bell Telephone Co.*, 936 F.2d 823 (5th Cir.1991).

A New Jersey man began working for a car rental agency as a manager trainee. He attained the position of office manager, becoming responsible for organizing and coordinating the daily activities of his rental office. He received favorable reviews and raises, and also received bonuses for maintaining high levels of sales. The manager learned from an associate that the regional director of the company did not feel the manager could advance his position because of his size and weight. He consulted a weight loss specialist and dropped his weight to approximately 270 pounds. Nevertheless, he was still subjected to allegedly derogatory comments by the regional director. The company discharged the manager for inadequate job performance sometime thereafter, and he then filed a complaint with the New Jersey Division of Civil Rights, asserting that he had been discharged discriminatorily because of his weight. The administrative hearing resulted in a determination for the manager, and the company appealed to the Superior Court of New Jersey, Appellate Division.

The appellate court determined that the factual records supported the conclusion that the manager had been a victim of discrimination because of his obesity. It also stated that obesity could be considered a handicapping condition under New Jersey Law. The statute broadly defined handicapped to include physiological or neurological conditions which were demonstrable, medically or psychologically. Since the manager's obesity existed physiologically and was demonstrable by accepted diagnostic techniques, he was entitled to the full protection of the law. The court thus affirmed the administrative decision in favor of the manager, but modified the damage award. *Gimello v. Agency Rent-A-Car Systems, Inc.,* 594 A.2d 264 (N.J.Super.A.D.1991).

A New Mexico man was hired by a freight company as a truck driver. As a probationary employee, he was bound by the terms of the collective bargaining agreement between the freight company and the union. During this 30-day period, a probationary employee could be terminated for any legal reason, without recourse. As a prerequisite to hiring, the employee was also required to have a physical examination. Based on x-rays taken on the employee's back, it was revealed that he had a back abnormality that would preclude employment as a truck driver. He was fired, and the only reason given was that it was pursuant to the collective bargaining agreement. The employee brought suit against the company and alleged that he was terminated because the freight company perceived that he was handicapped. A state trial court found for the employer, and the employee appealed to the Supreme Court of New Mexico.

On appeal, the court found that the employee had met his initial burden of proof and established a *prima facie* case of discrimination. In so doing, it was the employer's responsibility to articulate a legitimate, nondiscriminatory reason for firing the employee. The employer presented evidence that the employee was slow in taking his employment physical examination, slow in completing his paperwork and was not candid in answering questions on his employment application. At the appellate level, the court noted, it is not appropriate to weigh conflicting evidence or determine the credibility of witnesses. The court found that a reasonable mind could have found that the employer did not fire the employee based on a perceived handicap. As a result, the court affirmed the lower court decision and dismissed the suit. *Martinez v. Yellow Freight System, Inc.,* 826 P.2d 962 (N.M.1992).

V. RELIGIOUS DISCRIMINATION

Religious discrimination in employment is prohibited by Title VII of the Civil Rights Act. Employers who violate the act by intentionally discriminating against employees because of their religion or religious practices may be liable for compensatory and punitive damages, as well as equitable relief. There are, however, some exceptions, such as the one in § 702 of the Civil Rights Act for religious organizations.

The U.S. Supreme Court has held that an employer must make reasonable accommodation for the religious beliefs of employees. However, Title VII does not require accommodations which impose an undue hardship on the employer.

An employee of an airline belonged to a religion known as the Worldwide Church of God. It proscribed work from sunset Friday to sunset Saturday. Because of the employee's seniority, the airline was able to accommodate his religious beliefs until he transferred to a new position with low seniority. The airline agreed to permit the union to seek a change of work assignments, but it was unwilling to violate the seniority system. The airline then rejected a proposal that the employee work only four days a week, stating that this would impair critical functions in its operations. Eventually, the employee was discharged for refusing to work on Saturdays. He sued both the union and the airline under Title VII, claiming religious discrimination. A Missouri federal court ruled in favor of the defendants, and the U.S. Court of Appeals affirmed in part, holding that the airline did not satisfy its duty to accommodate the employee's religious needs. On appeal to the U.S. Supreme Court, it was held that the airline did make reasonable efforts to accommodate the religious beliefs of others. The Court reversed the court of appeals' decision and held in favor of the airline. *Trans World Airlines, Inc. v. Hardison*, 432 U.S. 63, 97 S.Ct. 2264, 53 L.Ed.2d 113 (1977).

A Maryland job applicant was denied employment by a food service when he refused to shave his beard as required by company policy. The applicant was a devout Sikh, whose religion forbade hair cutting. He filed a complaint against the employer with the Maryland Commission on Human Relations, which agreed with the applicant that the employer had engaged in unlawful employment discrimination. At a hearing, the employer justified the no-beard policy based on the need for sanitation, and on two customer surveys which showed a negative consumer attitude toward employees who wore beards. An administrative law judge ruled that the employer had failed to show that it would suffer any undue hardship if it accommodated the applicant by allowing him to wear a net or other beard restraint. A state administrative appeal board reversed the decision, holding that the administrative law judge had misinterpreted evidence in the record. A Maryland trial court affirmed this decision, and the applicant appealed to the Court of Special Appeals of Maryland. The court of special appeals reinstated the administrative law judge's decision, finding that the appeal board and circuit court had failed to give proper deference to her decision. Those entities were not allowed to substitute their judgment on questions of fact as they had done in this case. The court reversed and remanded the case for further consideration by the appeal board. *Kohli v. LOOC, Inc.*, 103 Md.App. 694, 654 A.2d 922 (1995).

A Nebraska telephone company employee wore a button to work that graphically depicted a human fetus. The button caused disruption in the work-place and some employees threatened to walk off their jobs. Her supervisors recommended that she either wear the button only in her cubicle or cover the button. When the employee refused to follow these recommendations on religious grounds, she was sent home and later fired for missing work for three consecutive days without excuse. She filed a lawsuit against the employer alleging discrimi-nation on the basis of religion in the U.S. District Court for the District of Nebraska. The court denied the employer's motion for summary judgment, but conducted a trial which resulted in a judgment for the employer. The employee appealed to the U.S. Court of Appeals, Eighth Circuit. The court of appeals found no error in the district court's findings that the employer had offered to reasonably accommodate the employee's firmly-held religious beliefs, and that her sug-gested accommodations would cause undue hardship to the employer. Title VII does not require an employer to allow an employee to impose personal religious beliefs on other employees. The employer had not opposed the employee's religious beliefs but had sought to protect its other employees from seeing the offensive button. The court affirmed the district court's judgment. *Wilson v. U.S. West Comm.*, 58 F.3d 1337 (8th Cir.1995).

A Wisconsin airline pilot filed a complaint with the EEOC alleging that his labor union discriminated against him on the basis of religion by refusing to allow him to withhold his union dues and pay them to a charity. An EEOC district office issued a determination in favor of the employee, and discovered evidence that four other employees had unsuccessfully sought accommodation from the union concerning their objections to payment of agency fees on the basis of their religious beliefs. The EEOC did not litigate the case, but filed a lawsuit on behalf of a Detroit-based pilot and similarly-situated religious objectors represented by the same union in the U.S. District Court for the District of Columbia. The union filed a motion to dismiss the case on the basis of the Detroit-based pilot's failure to file an EEOC claim. The court denied the motion, holding that the EEOC had standing to challenge policies that constituted ongoing discrimination. The EEOC had attempted to settle the Detroit-based pilot's matter with the union prior to filing suit and the original charge by the Wisconsin pilot had sufficiently notified the union of its discriminatory practices. *EEOC v. Air Line Pilots Assn.*, 885 F.Supp. 289 (D.D.C.1995).

An orthodox Jew answered an advertisement for a commercial real estate position. He alleged that his employment interview was cut short when he revealed his orthodox status. Although the company hired another individual for the position, the selected applicant quit after only a few days on the job, and the company republished an advertisement for the position. When the orthodox Jewish applicant noticed the advertisement, he filed a lawsuit against the company in the U.S. District Court for the Eastern District of New York, alleging violations of Title VII of the Civil Rights Act of 1964. The company filed a summary judgment motion, stating that the applicant had not been hired because of his poor interviewing skills and the perception by the interviewer that he was simply not very bright. The company also noted his lack of pertinent experience. The court disagreed with the applicant's theory that his interview had been cut short upon the disclosure of his religion. This evidence was not sufficient to withstand the company's summary judgment motion. The company had come forth with a sufficient explanation for its refusal to hire the applicant, and he had failed to come forward with contradictory evidence. The court granted summary judgment to the company. *Wechsler v. R D Management Corp.*, 861 F.Supp. 1153 (E.D.N.Y.1994).

A New Mexico truck driver worked for a transportation company whose drivers were unionized. All wages, hours, and terms and conditions of employment were covered under a collective bargaining agreement, including certain rights to bid on hauls between cities by senior employees. Nonsenior drivers were required to take hauling jobs on a first-in, first-out basis. The driver, who was not qualified as a senior driver, was a Seventh-Day Adventist. Because the first-in, first-out job system interfered with his observation of the Sabbath, he attempted to gain an exemption from working between sundown on Friday and sundown on Saturday. The exemptions proposed by the driver would have violated the collective bargaining agreement and were refused. The employee was unavailable for work on a number of Fridays and was fired for repeated unavailability. He sued the transportation company in the U.S. District Court for the District of New Mexico. The court granted summary judgment to the employer on the employee's claim that the failure to accommodate his religious beliefs violated Title VII of the Civil Rights Act of 1964, 42 U.S.C. § 2000e. The employee appealed to the U.S. Court of Appeals, Tenth Circuit.

The court observed that while Title VII makes discrimination on the basis of religion illegal, employers are required to accommodate only those parts of religious observation and practice that they are able to reasonably accommodate without undue hardship. The act does not guarantee employees the accommodation of their choice, and employees are required to cooperate with an employer's attempt at reasonable accommodation. Because Title VII does not require an employer to bear more than a minimal cost to reasonably accommodate an employee's religious beliefs, the transportation company was not required to consent to the employee's demands for special treatment. The act does not require employers to violate collective bargaining agreements. The court of appeals affirmed the district court's decision. *Lee v. ABF Freight System, Inc.*, 22 F.3d 1019 (10th Cir.1994).

A Michigan corporation employed an African-American employee who converted to Islam during the course of his employment. He alleged that he was then harassed by coworkers and that his supervisor attempted to orchestrate his dismissal. Following one incident, the supervisor documented the alleged intentional destruction of company property by the employee. The employee was escorted from the premises and placed on disciplinary leave. The company labor relations manager performed an investigation and concluded that the disciplinary leave should be upgraded to employment termination. The employee then sued the corporation in a Michigan trial court for wrongful discharge, intentional infliction of emotional distress, and fraud and misrepresentation by the supervisor. The court issued a pretrial order limiting the employee's damages because of his refusal to accept a reinstatement offer 13 months after termination. The jury awarded the employee over $61,000 and the court also reinstated him without seniority. The Michigan Court of Appeals affirmed and appeal reached the Supreme Court of Michigan. The supreme court held that the trial court had properly denied the corporation's motion for a directed verdict. However, it had improperly decided to limit the employee's damages prior to a factual determination. The question of the reasonableness of the rejection of the reemployment offer was a question of fact that required consideration by a jury. The court remanded this issue to the trial court but otherwise affirmed its decision. *Rasheed v. Chrysler Corp.*, 445 Mich. 109, 517 N.W.2d 19 (1994).

A Washington man worked for an automobile company for over nine years. He learned of a "new age motivational program" designed to help car dealers increase sales and profits, and he convinced the car dealership to purchase the program for its employees. Upon attending the training program, he became convinced that the program conflicted with his Christian beliefs, and he left the training course prior to its completion. He asked the car dealership to return the remaining program materials and cancel its participation in the program, which it initially did. Shortly, thereafter, the man was fired. He filed a religious discrimination action against the car dealership. The dealership moved for summary judgment, and a trial court granted its motion. On appeal to the state court of appeals, the trial court's decision was reversed. The dealership appealed.

The Supreme Court of Washington reversed the decision of the court of appeals. It stated that to prove a *prima facie* case of religious discrimination, the man was required to establish: 1) that he had a bona fide religious belief that conflicted with an employment requirement; 2) that he informed his employer of the conflict; 3) that he was fired because he refused to comply with the employment requirement. The man failed to present evidence showing that participation in the motivational program was a job requirement. The evidence showed that the dealership did not mandate participation in the training course or in the program. Thus, the man could not prove his *prima facie* case of religious discrimination. The court further held that federal and state laws prohibiting religious discrimination in employment were significantly different, and it declined to decide the legal standard to be applied in determining religious discrimination cases under both federal and state law. The court reinstated the trial court's summary judgment in favor of the dealership. *Hiatt v. Walker Chevrolet Co.*, 837 P.2d 618 (Wash.1992).

A member of the Hawaiian royal family left most of her estate to a private school. The will required that all teachers be Protestant. Although advertisements described the school as "Protestant," the school had never been controlled by or affiliated with any particular denomination. The school did not consider the religion of prospective students and almost all classes were taught from a secular perspective. The stated central mission of the school was to provide "a solid education in traditional secular subjects, instruction in Hawaiian culture and history, and the moral guidance necessary to help students define a system of values." The school turned down an application of a prospective substitute French teacher because she was not Protestant. The applicant filed suit in a U.S. district court alleging Title VII religious discrimination. The district court held for the private school because it fell within certain exceptions for religious educational institutions. The applicant appealed to the U.S. Court of Appeals, Ninth Circuit.

The court noted that a private school could be exempted from the requirements of Title VII if it was deemed a religious school or if its curriculum was "directed toward the propagation of a particular religion." Also, hiring based on religion was permitted if religion was a bona fide occupational qualification (BFOQ) for the position. Here, the school's religious characteristics, including limited religious education, prayer, and occasional references to the Bible, were insufficient to establish that it was a "religious educational institution" for Title VII purposes. The court also noted that given the secular nature of the school and lack of any religious mission, Protestantism was not a BFOQ for teachers. Therefore, the school could not discriminate on the basis of religion. The holding of the district court was reversed. *EEOC v. Kamehameha Schools/Bishop Estate*, 990 F.2d 458 (9th Cir.1993).

After a New Mexico electrician received a poor performance evaluation from his employer, he instituted administrative review proceedings to have the negative evaluation removed from his file. He was unsuccessful, and was placed on conditional employment status. A year later, he was fired. He then sued the employer in a federal district court claiming that his negative evaluation and subsequent termination were motivated by religious discrimination. He claimed that his supervisors, as members of the Mormon church, were biased against non-Mormons. The trial court dismissed the claims and the employee appealed to the U.S. Court of Appeals, Tenth Circuit. In order to prove religious discrimination under Title VII, a plaintiff must demonstrate: that he was subject to an adverse employment action; that, at the time the employment action was taken, the employee's job performance was satisfactory; and that there was additional evidence to support the inference that the employment action was taken because of a discriminatory motive based upon the employee's failure to follow his employer's religious beliefs. The court noted that the employee had failed to present sufficient evidence that the employer's explanations for termination were a pretext for religious discrimination. Accordingly, the appellate court upheld the decision of the trial court and dismissed the suit. *Shapolia v. Los Alamos National Laboratory*, 992 F.2d 1033 (10th Cir.1993).

A Colorado employee instituted a civil rights action against his former employer alleging religious discrimination under Title VII. The employee was a member of the Klu Klux Klan. He asserted that he was discharged because of an Adolph Hitler rally that he organized and in which he participated. The employer moved to dismiss the case in a federal district court. Under Title VII it is an unlawful employment practice for an employer to discharge an employee on the basis of religion. The definition of religion contained in Title VII, however, does not make clear whether the Klu Klux Klan is a religion. The U.S. Court of Appeals, Fourth Circuit, when faced with a similar case, determined that "the proclaimed racist and anti-semitic ideology of the organization takes on a narrow and political character inconsistent with the meaning of religion." The district court also concluded that the Klan was not a religion for the purposes of Title VII, but "rather the Klu Klux Klan was political and social in nature." The court held that the employee had failed to state a claim of religious discrimination under Title VII and dismissed the case. *Slater v. King Soopers, Inc.*, 809 F.Supp. 809 (D.Colo. 1992).

A Michigan man worked for a corporation in an area where other employees displayed photographs of nude women. He allegedly told management on three separate occasions of his religious objections to the pictures. The corporation apparently offered to allow the employee to transfer to a late shift, but the employee refused the offer. He was subsequently discharged because he refused to continue working in the area where the photographs were displayed. He then filed suit against his employer for violations of Title VII and of state law, asserting that he had been discharged because of his religious beliefs. The employer filed a motion for summary judgment in the federal district court where the suit was brought, asserting that the employee had failed to meet the elements of a *prima facie* case of religious discrimination. However, a genuine issue of fact existed as to the sincerity of the employee's religious beliefs. Further, an issue existed over whether the employer had provided a reasonable accommodation to the employee by offering to have him change shifts. Finally, the court noted that the employer could require its employees to take the pictures down without violating their First Amendment rights because the company was not a public entity. Accordingly, the court denied the employer's motion for summary judgment and allowed the case to proceed to trial. *Lambert v. Condor Manufacturing, Inc.,* 768 F.Supp. 600 (E.D.Mich.1991).

A Virginia man worked for a multinational corporation. He was of the Jewish faith, and had previously taken paid leave to observe religious holidays. The company changed its policy regarding time off for religious observances. The employee traveled to Europe on behalf of the company, during which time there was a verbal altercation between the employee and a business associate. When he returned to the U.S., the employee was fired. He filed religious discrimination claims with the County Human Rights Commission and the EEOC, both of which were unsuccessful. He then filed suit in federal district court where his discrimination claim was dismissed. On appeal to the U.S. Court of Appeals, Fourth Circuit, the Court stated that the employee had not established that his job performance was satisfactory, nor had he presented evidence that would support a reasonable inference of discrimination. Accordingly, the court of appeals affirmed the decision of the district court. *Lawrence v. Mars, Inc.,* 955 F.2d 902 (4th Cir.1992).

CHAPTER TWO

EMPLOYER LIABILITY

I. EMPLOYEE INJURIES

An employer may be liable for the tortious acts of its employees to fellow employees. Because state workers' compensation laws are designed to provide the employee's exclusive remedy for job-related injuries, many such claims are preempted. See Chapter Seven, Section I of this volume. Where the injury is not within the course and scope of employment, an employer may be held liable for its negligence in hiring or supervision.

The collective bargaining agreement between an Ohio employer and its workers expired and the parties were unable to reach a new agreement. The workers went on strike. After six weeks, the employer threatened to hire permanent replacement workers. The union called a meeting to discourage employees from capitulating, and a number of workers who contemplated crossing the picket line were threatened by union members. Sixteen of the 800 affected workers returned to work prior to the end of the strike, and the union published their names on a list. Some of the 16 employees who returned to work complained of repeated harassment, verbal threats and vandalism. They filed a lawsuit against the union in an Ohio trial court, which returned substantial damage awards to some of the employees, plus punitive damages. The union appealed to the Court of Appeals of Ohio, Cuyahoga County. The court stated the general rule applicable in emotional distress complaints, which requires proof that the offending party intended to cause emotional distress through extreme and outrageous conduct calculated to cause serious mental anguish. Although some of the threats against the employees in this case had been reprehensible, the employees had failed to produce evidence of severe emotional distress. Threats made by prounion employees were commonplace in labor disputes, and the most frequently used epithet was the federally-protected word "scab." The trial court should have granted the union's dismissal motion and the court of appeals reversed and remanded its decision. *Dickerson v. International United Auto Workers Union*, 98 Ohio App.3d 171, 648 N.E.2d 40 (1994), *cert. den.*, 71 Ohio St.3d 1492, 646 N.E.2d 467 (1995).

A Wyoming natural gas processing company hired a well service to rework some oil wells. The parties had an unwritten working agreement and they assumed that the well service was an independent contractor. Nonetheless, gas company employees routinely exercised control and direction of work performed by employees of the independent contractor well service. An employee of the well service was severely injured in an accident resulting in part from violation of OSHA safety regulations. He filed a lawsuit against the gas processing company in a Wyoming trial court, which conducted a trial that resulted in a damage award of over $1.6 million for the employee. The court denied the gas company's motion for judgment notwithstanding the verdict and the company appealed to the Supreme Court of Wyoming. The supreme court stated that the gas company had performed an active role in supervising and inspecting the well service's work. Therefore, the well service lost its independent contractor status, because it no longer had the ability to manage its own operations and direct its own employees. This resulted in abandonment of the protection of the independent contractor rule, and the gas company became liable for the employee's injuries. The court affirmed the trial court's decision. *Natural Gas Processing Co. v. Hull*, 886 P.2d 1181 (Wyo.1994).

An oil company worker abused drugs and was hospitalized a number of times for paranoid schizophrenia. He was released from the hospital each time with no restrictions on returning to work. The employee occasionally failed to take his medication and skipped meetings with his treating psychologist. The company's physician examined the employee and determined that he was disturbed and depressed. The employee's wife later testified that she was assured by the employee's supervisor that she would be advised if termination was imminent. The company fired the employee for poor job performance without any warning and the employee committed suicide within two weeks. His wife sued the employer in a Texas trial court under the Texas Wrongful Death Statute, claiming negligent and wrongful discharge, intentional and negligent infliction of emotional distress and gross negligence. A jury returned a verdict against the employer for gross negligence and awarded the wife $700,000. The employer appealed the trial court's decision to the Court of Appeals of Texas, Houston.

The court determined that a primary factor in determining employer liability was the foreseeability of the risk of danger to the employee. An employer generally owes no duty of care to employees based on termination decisions. The employer was not negligent in failing to warn the wife of the employee's imminent termination and it had no duty to undertake his medical care. The suicide was not reasonably foreseeable to the employer and it was not under a duty to warn the wife of the impending dismissal. The court of appeals reversed and remanded the trial court's judgment. *Shell Oil Co. v. Humphrey*, 880 S.W.2d 170 (Tex.App.—Houston 1994).

A nurse employed by a Louisiana hospital suffered injuries from a purse-snatching incident outside the hospital entrance as she reported for work. She then complained of severe emotional difficulties and was twice hospitalized for psychiatric problems and related physical symptoms. She stated that she could no longer work and rarely left her home. She filed a lawsuit against the hospital in a Louisiana trial court, claiming that it had negligently failed to provide safe access to the hospital and had failed to implement reasonable security procedures for employees. The trial court held for the hospital and the employee appealed to the Court of Appeal of Louisiana, Second Circuit. The court of appeal noted that when employers assumed the duty to protect others against criminal misconduct by hiring security guards, they could be held liable for injuries resulting from third party violence, if the violence was reasonably foreseeable. In this case, there had been only one similar prior incident nine months earlier, and there was no evidence that the purse-snatching incident was reasonably foreseeable to the hospital. Five security guards were at their stations at the time of the incident and there was no evidence of any breach of the duty to provide protection that had been assumed by the hospital. Because the incident was a random unforeseen violent act, the hospital had no duty to protect the employee. *Rowe v. Schumpert Medical Center*, 647 So.2d 390 (La.App.2d Cir.1994).

An employee of a Texas electronics company served on a jury for four days, believing that her employer would pay her for this time. However, the employer paid her for only two days, pursuant to a Texas statute. When she demanded payment for the other two days, the employer refused and she submitted her resignation. However, she soon rescinded the resignation and was allowed to use sick or personal leave for the two days. The employee's supervisor then stated that he would not accept the employee's rescission of her resignation and escorted her out of the office in view of other employees. A Texas trial court granted summary judgment to the employer on the employee's claims for intentional infliction of emotional distress and fraud, and the employee appealed to the Court of Appeals of Texas, Houston. On appeal, the employee argued that the fact of her termination by itself could be grounds for the emotional distress and fraud claims. The court disagreed, finding that the manner of termination must be extreme and outrageous to support a claim for emotional distress and that the termination action alone did not support this claim. In addition, no claim for fraud could be recognized in an employment at will relationship. The trial court had properly granted summary judgment to the employer. *Sebesta v. Kent Elec. Corp.*, 886 S.W.2d 459 (Tex. App.—Houston 1994).

A South Carolina plant worker was accused of stealing painting equipment from the plant. The company reported the suspected thefts to the local sheriff's department and warrants were issued. The company's human resources manager then advised the employee that the warrants would not be prosecuted. However, two weeks later, just as the employee was leaving for vacation, the manager left a message that he should report to the manager's office when he returned. The employee voluntarily came to the manager's office before the designated time and learned that the theft case had been reopened. He then sued his employer in the U.S. District Court for the District of South Carolina for emotional distress and malicious prosecution. The court held a trial resulting in an award of damages for the employee. The employer appealed to the U.S. Court of Appeals, Fourth Circuit. In reversing the district court's decision, the court of appeals determined that the manager's conduct did not rise to the level of atrocious and intolerable behavior sufficient to support a claim for intentional infliction of emotional distress. However, there had been no probable cause for a warrant to issue, and the claim for malicious prosecution was supported by the evidence. Because the district court had failed to apportion the damage award between the emotional distress and malicious prosecution claims, the damage award was vacated and remanded for a new trial. *Barber v. Whirlpool Corp.*, 34 F.3d 1268 (4th Cir. 1994).

Three female employees of a South Dakota publisher discovered that he was spying on them while they were in the restroom. They quit within one week of learning this and filed a sex discrimination complaint with the South Dakota Division of Human Rights. The action resulted in a settlement that included a letter of apology from the publisher. However, the former employees sought to obtain damage awards for intentional infliction of emotional distress, violation of privacy and punitive damages in a state court. The court granted the publisher's pretrial motion to keep certain facts from the hearing of the jury, including the apology letter, the human rights proceeding itself, and expert testimony from a physician who had treated the former employees. The trial court granted the publisher's motion for a directed verdict on the intentional infliction of emotional distress claim, and awarded punitive damages in excess of $20,000 to the former employees. Both parties appealed unfavorable aspects of the trial court judgment to the Supreme Court of South Dakota.

The supreme court stated that the human rights proceeding did not bar the intentional infliction of emotional distress and invasion of privacy claims. The Division of Human Rights had considered none of these claims and had no power to decide them. There was ample evidence of invasion of privacy and the trial court did not erroneously submit the issue of punitive damages to the jury. However, the trial court should have granted the publisher's motion for a mistrial when the former employees' attorney mentioned the apology letter within the hearing of the jury. It had also committed error by withholding the intentional infliction of emotional distress issue from the jury. The court reversed and remanded the case to the trial court. *Kjerstad v. Ravellette Pub., Inc.*, 517 N.W.2d 419 (S.D.1994).

A Massachusetts woman filed an action in a federal district court under the Racketeer Influenced and Corrupt Organizations Act (RICO) alleging multiple episodes of job-related sexual harassment between November 1990 and May 1991. The employer filed a motion to dismiss. The employer argued that the suit had to be dismissed because the employee could not maintain a claim under RICO. The complaint stated that the employer, through a pattern of racketeering activity, attempted to extort from the employee her civil rights in violation of the Hobbs Act, 18 U.S.C. § 1951. The employer allegedly tried to extort sexual favors from the employee by threatening her financial prospects. The employer argued that the employee could not establish a pattern of racketeering activity because she alleged only one predicate act. To satisfy the pattern requirement of RICO, the employee must demonstrate the existence of two or more predicate acts that are related and that pose at least a threat of continued criminal activity. The court noted that while the employer's acts of harassment all shared one common purpose, his conduct would have been capable of endless repetition. One sexual favor would not have been enough. Thus, the court reasoned that because the object of this scheme was inexhaustible, it was reasonable to view the constituent acts of the scheme as separate predicate acts under RICO. The court also found that the employee might be able to establish the continuity necessary to embrace a RICO claim and denied the employer's motion to dismiss. *Sharp v. Kelley*, 835 F.Supp. 33 (D.Mass.1993).

A food manager aboard a passenger cruise ship was injured when a subordinate crew member threw a bottle of ketchup at him, which resulted in a broken forearm that required surgical repair. The manager sued the shipowner under the Jones Act for his injuries. The complaint alleged negligence, as well as that the vessel was unseaworthy due to the vicious propensity of the crew member's conduct. The shipowner moved for summary judgment. The U.S. District Court for the Southern District of New York held that the shipowner was not negligent because there were no facts to establish that the crew member's violent conduct was foreseeable. It held that the shipowner was not responsible under the doctrine of *respondeat superior* because the alleged attack was committed by a subordinate upon a superior and not by a superior on a subordinate. It was not in furtherance of the employer's business. However, the court upheld the manager's unseaworthiness claim based upon the severity of his injuries as a result of the attack, as well as the apparent sudden and unprovoked nature of the attack. It held that the crew member had a dangerous propensity towards violence so as to have rendered the vessel unseaworthy. *Wiradihardja v. Bermuda Star Line, Inc.*, 802 F.Supp. 989 (S.D.N.Y.1992).

Several migrant farm workers sustained severe injuries in an automobile accident while they traveled to work in a fruit company's van. They received workers' compensation benefits as a result. Subsequently, they filed suit against the fruit company, alleging that their injuries had been caused in part by the company's intentional violations of the Migrant and Seasonal Agricultural Worker Protection Act's motor vehicle safety provisions. The company sought summary judgment which was granted by the Florida federal district court, but the U.S. Court of Appeals reversed. The U.S. Supreme Court granted certiorari. The Supreme Court held that the exclusivity provisions in the state workers' compensation laws did not bar the migrant workers from asserting a claim under the act. Section 1854 of the act established a private right of action which provided for both actual and statutory damages in cases of intentional violations. This federal remedy was not precluded by state law. Thus, even though an award of actual damages under the act could be offset from workers' compensation benefits the claim itself was not precluded. The Court affirmed the court of appeals' decision denying the summary judgment. *Adams Fruit Co. v. Barrett,* 494 U.S. 638, 110 S.Ct. 1384, 108 L.Ed.2d 585 (1990).

A railroad fireman suffered fatal injuries in a collision which was caused by the railroad's negligence. The accident occurred when a locomotive collided with a loaded hopper car which was being stored on a siding track. His estate brought suit under the FELA to recover the damages suffered by his survivors as a result of his death. The jury award was $775,000. The employer appealed because the trial court excluded evidence of the income taxes payable on the decedent's earnings and because the judge refused to tell the jury that the award would not be subject to income taxation. The Appellate Court of Illinois found no error in the court's actions, and the case reached the U.S. Supreme Court.

The Court first noted that the measure of damages in a FELA action is a question that is federal in character. Only after-tax income can provide a realistic measure of a wage earner's ability to support his or her family. Thus, the decedent's income tax was a relevant factor in calculating the loss suffered by his dependents, and it should have been included in the evidence. Next, the Court noted that, since Congress had provided that damages received on account of personal injuries were not taxable income, an instruction should have been given to the jury to that effect. It could do no harm, and it could help prevent overinflated awards made on the erroneous assumption that the judgment would be taxed. The Court thus reversed the lower court's decision and remanded the case. *Norfolk & Western Railway Co. v. Liepelt,* 444 U.S. 490, 100 S.Ct. 755, 62 L.Ed.2d 689 (1980).

A Missouri railroad employee worked 27 years for the railroad. He had never been disciplined or reprimanded for his work performance. A co-worker became his supervisor in 1987, and began a daily campaign of harassment which included verbally attacking him. The worker experienced a tightening in his chest and began to feel ill whenever the supervisor would berate him. He tried to resolve the situation with the supervisor but to no avail. As a result of the encounters with his supervisor, the worker experienced chest pain, muscular aches in his shoulders, and headaches. Ultimately, his doctor determined that he had heart disease and would no longer be able to work. He brought this action against his former employer for damages under the FELA. A Missouri trial court entered judgment in favor of the employee and the railroad appealed to the Missouri Court of Appeals. The employer contended that there was no evidence of employer negligence which caused the injury. The record had established that the worker did not file any formal grievance against the supervisor or advise any other official of the harassment. However, the court noted that supervisory employees are treated as agents of the corporation. Accordingly, the supervisor's knowledge of his own conduct could be imputed to the railroad. Therefore, the jury was entitled to infer that reasonably careful management should have become aware of the supervisor's conduct and taken steps to stop it. The appellate court upheld the decision of the trial court and found for the employee. *Stewart v. Alton and Southern Railway Company*, 849 S.W.2d 119 (Mo.App.1993).

An Alabama railroad employee and his employer became aware that he had significant hearing loss in 1977. In 1983, the employee learned from a physician that he had sustained an untreatable hearing loss due to his working at the railroad. He filed suit under the FELA in 1990. The Alabama trial court granted summary judgment in favor of the employer because the employee's claim was barred by the statute of limitations. The employee then appealed to the Supreme Court of Alabama. The employee contended that the running of the limitations period should be tolled under the continuous tort doctrine. The continuous tort doctrine applies when an employer repeatedly exposes an employee to an occupational hazard over a period of time before the employee can become aware of any injury. However, the statute of limitations began to run when the employee possessed sufficient critical facts from which the injury and its work-relatedness should have been plainly known. The employee admitted that he was aware in 1983 of his hearing loss and its work-relatedness. The court noted that because the employee was aware of his injury and its cause in 1983, but did not sue until 1990, the limitations period applied to bar his original FELA claim for damages based on injuries suffered before 1987. Therefore, the summary judgment in favor of the employer was affirmed. *Chatham v. CSX Transportation Inc.*, 613 So.2d 341 (Ala.1993).

A North Carolina man worked for a railroad and was occupying a line shack when a co-employee threw a cherry bomb into the shack. The incident was intended to be a mere prank, but the employee in the shack claimed that he suffered a hearing loss as a result of the incident. He brought suit against the railroad in a Florida state trial court, alleging that it was vicariously liable for the co-employee's actions and that it was negligent in its own right for failing to provide a safe place to work. Although pranks of this type were prohibited by railroad rules, the employee produced evidence that fireworks explosions in the yard were common. The railroad produced evidence that its supervisors were unaware of any such incidents. The trial court granted the railroad's motion for a directed verdict on the vicarious liability claim, and the jury returned a verdict in favor of the railroad on the negligence claim. The employee appealed.

On appeal to the District Court of Appeal of Florida, the court noted that the trial court had correctly directed a verdict for the railroad on the vicarious liability claim because there was no evidence that the co-employee's actions were in the course and scope of his employment or in furtherance of the railroad's business. The court also found that the jury's verdict was not clearly wrong (as it would need to be for a reversal). Only if the railroad had failed to take reasonable steps to prevent reasonably foreseeable danger would it be held negligent. Here, the jury had not found negligence and the appellate court could not find sufficient reason to overturn that verdict. The ruling for the railroad was affirmed. *Bryant v. CSX Transportation, Inc.*, 577 So.2d 613 (Fla.App.1st Dist.1991).

An Indiana woman worked as a cashier for a large food store chain. She had worked at several of the stores for approximately 14 years and was hired under a contract that entitled her to better pay and benefits than employees hired at a later date. The woman had a history of medical problems which left her with a physical disfigurement and caused her to periodically miss work. On several occasions she had reported the head cashier to union officials for violating union work rules. During a store promotion where eligible participating customers could redeem their store cards for cash after having shopped in the store a certain number of weeks, the woman was accused of theft by exchanging counterfeit cards for cash. She was tried and acquitted by a state trial court. Thereafter, she filed a malicious prosecution action against the store. A trial court found in her favor. The store appealed. The Court of Appeals of Indiana found that there was no probable cause to prosecute the woman; she was never observed to have falsified store cards or to have taken cash. The investigators had relied entirely on the head cashier's explanation of the register tapes without further verification. The court found that malice existed because of the personal animosity toward the woman by the head cashier, and that the store had consciously and intentionally engaged in misconduct which it knew would probably result in injury to the woman. The judgment of the trial court was affirmed. *Kroger Food Stores, Inc. v. Clark,* 598 N.E.2d 1084 (Ind.App.1st Dist.1992).

A Pennsylvania woman was employed as a teacher's aide at a day care center. Her employer continuously harassed her and engaged in unwanted touching, fondling, and spanking. The employee suffered from humiliation, loss of self-esteem, nightmares and insomnia. However, she never sought the help of a physician or psychologist for her problems. Her employer, after spreading rumors about her, eventually fired her. After she was discharged, she filed a complaint in a Pennsylvania trial court seeking damages for various torts, including intentional infliction of emotional distress. The jury found for the employee on the intentional infliction of emotional distress claim. However, the trial court granted the employer's motion for a judgment notwithstanding the verdict. The employee then appealed to the Superior Court of Pennsylvania.

The trial court had granted the motion for judgment notwithstanding the verdict on the ground that the employee had failed to introduce expert medical testimony and had not sustained her burden of proof as to damages. The employee asserted that where there was sufficient evidence of outrageous conduct, expert medical testimony was unnecessary in order for a jury to find liability. The appellate court agreed and stated that the outrageous nature of the defendant's behavior was self-evident; expert medical testimony was not required. Accordingly, the court reversed the decision of the trial court and reinstated the jury's verdict for the employee. *Hackney v. Woodring*, 622 A.2d 286 (Pa.Super.1993).

A hospital contracted with a radiologist and his professional corporation for radiological services. After a series of disputes regarding the radiologist's management practices, the hospital filed an action to determine its rights under the contract to fire him and to withdraw his hospital staff privileges. The radiologist counterclaimed asserting several causes of action, among which were intentional infliction of emotional distress, tortious interference with contractual relationships, and deprivation of due process rights. The hospital moved for summary judgment on all counterclaims, and a trial court denied the motion. The hospital appealed.

The Court of Appeals of Georgia stated that the hospital's conduct toward the radiologist failed to rise to a level of outrageousness and egregiousness required for the claim of intentional infliction of emotional distress. Conflicts between the hospital and the radiologist over the exercise of authority and inconsiderate and unkind remarks did not give rise to this claim. Likewise, the claim for tortious interference failed because the evidence did not establish that the hospital induced adverse actions by third parties. The court stated that no sufficient nexus existed between the hospital's acts and any state action which could give rise to a due process claim. It held that the hospital by-laws alone did not create any contractual right to continuation of staff privileges because of the hospital's authority to establish and revise rules and regulations regarding employees. The court granted summary judgment in favor of the hospital on all these counts. However, it stated that a cause of action in tort existed against the hospital for the failure to follow existing by-laws with regard to termination of the radiologist's staff privileges. *St. Mary's Hosp. v. Radiology Pro. Corp.*, 421 S.E.2d 731 (Ga.App.1992).

II. DEFAMATION

Employers enjoy a limited privilege to communicate necessary information about their employees to the police and prospective employers who require employee information. Courts employ a balancing of interests analysis in determining what information must remain confidential. An employer loses its privilege to communicate information and may become liable for defamation where it communicates false information that damages the employee. Excessive publication may also expose an employer to liability. Many defamation lawsuits arise in the context of drug testing cases. Please see Chapter Six, Section Two for further cases in this area.

A Texas sales manager conducted unorthodox sales meetings that came under the scrutiny of her supervisors. The supervisors conducted an investigation and determined that the manager had acted inappropriately. They eventually fired her for failing to obey their orders. She filed a lawsuit against her former employer and the supervisors in a Texas trial court for emotional distress and slander, claiming that the supervisors had called her a witch, sorceress and satan-worshipper. The jury awarded the former manager $50,000 against one supervisor, and $20,000 against the other, plus $5,000 in punitive damages from both former supervisors. However, it failed to find any liability against the company. The former employee appealed to the Court of Appeals of Texas, Texarkana.

The court stated that in order to hold a party liable for emotional distress, the complained of activity must be extreme and outrageous, beyond all bounds of decency, and atrocious and utterly intolerable in a civilized society. In this case, there was sufficient evidence to support the jury's finding. However, the decision was inconsistent because it awarded judgment against the supervisors, but not against the company, despite the fact that the supervisors had made the comments in the course and scope of their employment. An employer is liable for an employee's illegal acts, even where unauthorized, so long as the act is done while the employee is acting on the employer's behalf. The jury's failure to find liability against the company was contrary to the evidence, and the trial court's judgment was reversed and remanded for a retrial on the issue of the company's potential liability. *Hooper v. Pitney Bowes, Inc.*, 895 S.W.2d 773 (Tex.App.—Texarkana 1995).

The owners of a Montana newspaper filed criminal charges against a former photographer for stealing proof sheets and photographs from their offices. Based on their information, a police officer obtained an arrest warrant leading to criminal charges that were eventually dropped because of the expiration of the applicable statute of limitations. The photographer filed a lawsuit in a Montana trial court for negligent and intentional infliction of emotional distress and defamation by the newspaper owners. The court granted summary judgment motions by the defendants and the photographer appealed to the Supreme Court of Montana. The supreme court recognized an independent cause of action where the complaining party alleges serious or severe emotional distress that was reasonably foreseeable due to a negligent or intentional act or omission. The district court had erroneously ruled that the statements by the newspaper owners were privileged. This was because criminal proceedings had not yet been initiated when they contacted the police. The court had improperly granted summary judgment. The supreme court reversed and remanded the case to the district court. *Sacco v. High Country Indep. Press, Inc.*, 896 P.2d 411 (Mont.1995).

An Indiana food company supervisor learned that an employee was drinking on the job. The supervisor observed the employee drinking something in his parked car in the company parking lot during lunch break. He later went to the employee's unattended car and discovered a cooler containing beer. He approached the employee during the afternoon break, knocked on the car window, smelled beer and confronted the employee. The employee denied drinking beer, but the supervisor opened the car door, reached behind the driver's seat and retrieved an empty beer bottle. The employee was fired for violating the company's alcohol policy. He sued the company and supervisor in an Indiana trial court for trespass, defamation and other claims. The court granted summary judgment to the supervisor and company, and the former employee appealed to the Court of Appeals of Indiana, Second District.

The court first rejected the trial court's finding that the former employee's claims were barred by the state workers' compensation act. The act was inapplicable to the former employee's claims because he had not alleged a physical injury. However, the trial court had properly held that no cause of action exists under Indiana law for tortious breaking and entering or negligent performance of an employment contract. The former employee's claim for trespass was meritless because the supervisor had not substantially impaired his use of the car or caused harm to a legally protected interest. The employee had no absolute right to be free from invasion of privacy on company property, and the court of appeals affirmed the trial court's decision. *Terrell v. Rowsey*, 647 N.E.2d 662 (Ind.App.2d Dist.1995).

A Tennessee automotive parts worker supported the unionization of the plant where he worked. Management employees learned that defective parts were being produced at the plant and the prounion employee was fired for sabotaging the production line. In an alleged attempt to limit further sabotage, the plant manager circulated a memorandum to employees that criticized the union for its unfair tactics and for exploiting the prounion employee's firing. The discharged employee filed a defamation lawsuit against the company in the U.S. District Court for the Eastern District of Tennessee. The court granted summary judgment to the employer, and the employee appealed to the U.S. Court of Appeals, Sixth Circuit. The court stated that while the substantive law of Tennessee applied to this diversity case, the existence of a labor-management dispute called for the application of federal law concerning the degree of fault. Under that standard, the discharged employee was required to show that the memorandum had been published with actual malice, a standard that required the complaining party to show that the defamatory communication was made with reckless disregard for its truth or falsity. Because there was evidence that the manager believed that the employee had engaged in sabotage, the district court had properly granted the company summary judgment.*Holbrook v. Harman Automotive, Inc.*, 58 F.3d 222 (6th Cir.1995).

A Massachusetts car rental manager experienced difficulty with her supervisor during a training conference. On the final day of the conference, she was escorted to a small room and interrogated concerning the theft of an agency automobile. She became hysterical and cried when another employee of the company accused her of lying. The interrogator also stated that the company had strong evidence that she was involved in the theft. The manager sued the rental company in the U.S. District Court for the District of Massachusetts for slander and violation of the Massachusetts Civil Rights Act. Her husband also advanced a claim for loss of consortium. The court held that the only slanderous statement was the one in which the coworker stated that the company had strong evidence that the manager had been involved in the theft. It held that the state act did not afford employees an opportunity to sue employers for the actions of other employees. The manager appealed to the U.S. Court of Appeals, First Circuit.

The court of appeals determined that many of the other statements made by the interrogating employee were slanderous, including the accusation that the manager was a liar. There was no requirement that the defamatory statement be communicated to a large group of people in order to create liability. However, the district court had properly held that the Massachusetts Civil Rights Act did not impose liability on the employer based upon its employee's reckless conduct. The court reversed the district court's decision in part and affirmed in part. *Lyons v. National Car Rental Systems, Inc.*, 30 F.3d 240 (1st Cir.1994).

An Illinois retail salesperson was fired for stealing merchandise. She claimed that her supervisors had failed to conduct an appropriate investigation into the circumstances of the alleged theft and defamed her in the process of terminating her employment. A trial court awarded the former employee $40,000 in compensatory damages and an equal amount in punitive damages on her claims of common law defamation and on a new legal theory of "compelled self-defamation." The employer appealed to the Appellate Court of Illinois, Fifth District.

On appeal, the employee argued that the communication of the termination decision by the assistant store manager to her immediate supervisor constituted defamation. The court disagreed, finding that the statement was protected by a qualified privilege. Otherwise, an employer could never state the reason for taking an employment action. There had been no evidence of malice in the termination, which was a necessary element for liability in a defamation case. Contrary to the former employee's assertions, there had been a thorough investigation into the facts and circumstances of her employment termination and there had been sufficient cause for the employer to believe the employee had stolen merchandise. The former employee would have held the store to a higher standard than that applicable to law enforcement officers conducting criminal searches and seizures. The trial court had also improperly based its decision on the new legal theory of compelled self-defamation. Compelled self-defamation, which might occur when a prospective employer inquired into the reason an employee left her previous employment, could discourage fired employees from mitigating their damages and unduly burden free communication among employers. The court reversed and remanded the case to the trial court. *Harrel v. Dillards Dept. Stores, Inc.*, 644 N.E.2d 448 (Ill.App.5th Dist.1994).

An Indiana employer fired six of its employees for dishonesty. The action took place after an investigation of theft rumors. Because rumors about other terminations persisted after the firings, the company made a slide presentation at a staff meeting that included the names of the discharged employees, with the reasons for dismissal. The slide presentation also reaffirmed "core values" of the company including trust and honesty. Five of the terminated employees filed a lawsuit for defamation in an Indiana trial court. The trial court granted the company's motion for summary judgment and its decision was affirmed in part and reversed in part by the Indiana Court of Appeals. The company appealed to the Supreme Court of Indiana.

On appeal, the supreme court held that intracompany communications concerning employee performance were protected by a qualified privilege. In order to invoke the privilege, the communication must be in good faith, limited in scope to its purpose, and published to appropriate parties only. A communication motivated by ill will that is excessively published, or published with disregard for the truth, is not privileged. In this case, although the statements were made to a large group of employees, and later posted in a place where nonemployees could read them, the company had not excessively published the information. This was because the communication was made to quash rumors and speculation within the company and to reaffirm core values. The court reinstated the trial court's judgment for the company. *Schrader v. Eli Lilly and Co.*, 639 N.E.2d 258 (Ind.1994).

An Illinois manufacturer became aware of increasing substance abuse by on-duty employees. It hired a consulting firm to formulate a drug and alcohol policy and the consultant placed investigators within the plant to observe employees. As a consequence, 41 employees were fired for substance abuse. The employees were escorted off the premises by security guards. Four employees who were terminated in this manner filed a lawsuit against the employer in an Illinois trial court, claiming that the company had violated its own four-step progressive disciplinary policy and defamed them by using the security guard escort and calling their names over the loudspeaker. The court held for the employer, and the employees appealed to the Appellate Court of Illinois, First District.

The appellate court determined that the trial court could have properly found from conflicting evidence in the record that no employment contract existed in the form of a termination policy contained in an employee handbook. No handbook was produced at trial, the former employees gave conflicting testimony, and the employer presented evidence that no such handbook even existed. The trial court had properly held that there was no defamatory action by the employer in using security guards to escort the former employees from the premises. There was no evidence that any statement was made to publicize the employment termination or that any false statement had been made in reckless disregard of the truth. The court affirmed the judgment for the employer. *Davis v. John Crane, Inc.*, 633 N.E.2d 929 (Ill.App.1st Dist.1994).

Two flight attendants informed their employer that a pilot made unwanted sexual advances to them. The pilot complained that the airline failed to properly investigate the charges, resulting in defamatory statements about him circulating throughout the airline. The pilot sued the airline for defamation in a Colorado trial court. The airline made pretrial requests for documents and written interrogatories in which it requested specific information about the pilot's prior sexual contacts and relationships during the past five years. It also sought the name, address, phone number, age and other information about each individual that the pilot had dated or attempted to have relations with during the previous five years. The pilot objected to the discovery requests. The trial court granted the airline's motion to compel answers to the discovery requests, and the pilot appealed to the Supreme Court of Colorado.

The supreme court agreed with the trial court's ruling that the discovery requests were reasonably calculated to produce admissible evidence. However, the trial court had abused its discretion by failing to balance the airline's need for this information against the privacy interests of the pilot and the persons with whom he had relations. Courts are required to balance competing interests of parties through the use of a three-part analysis: whether the party seeking to prevent disclosure has a legitimate expectation that the information will not be disclosed, whether there is a sufficiently compelling state interest that exceeds the asserted privacy interest, and whether the disclosure can be made in a less intrusive manner. The supreme court vacated the trial court's discovery order and remanded the case for application of the balancing standard. *Williams v. Dist. Court, Second Judicial Dist.*, 866 P.2d 908 (Colo.1993).

The president of a Massachusetts company suspected employees of taking cash for merchandise and diverting company proceeds. When the company's shipping manager was fired, another employee quit. Shortly thereafter, the company president discussed the thefts with the police, who began an investigation that never resulted in criminal proceedings. In response to a request for a reference, the president told the potential employer that he would not rehire the employee who had quit. The former employee sued the company, its president, and some police officers in a Massachusetts trial court for defamation, malicious prosecution, tortious interference with advantageous business relationships and intentional infliction of emotional distress. After a jury verdict for the company on the defamation claim, the court granted judgment notwithstanding the verdict for the company on the malicious prosecution, tortious interference and intentional infliction of emotional distress claims. The court allowed a single claim for tortious interference with business relationships to stand against some defendants. Appeal was made to the Appeals Court of Massachusetts, Essex.

The court of appeals found that the company president could not be charged with malicious prosecution for reporting a crime to the police. There was no evidence that the president had tortiously interfered with the former employee's business relations by responding to the potential employer's request for information. There was no evidence of extreme or outrageous conduct by the company to support the intentional infliction of emotional distress claim. The company prevailed on all issues that were appealed. *Conway v. Smerling*, 37 Mass.App.Ct. 1, 625 N.E.2d 268 (1994).

A West Virginia grocery store fired an employee for poor work performance and for stealing a box of cough drops. The employee sued the store in a West Virginia trial court for lost wages, defamation and punitive damages. He alleged that the grocery store defamed his character by disseminating the information that he was fired for stealing the cough drops. The trial court returned a verdict for the employee. The grocery store appealed to the Supreme Court of Appeals of West Virginia. The court held that no evidence was presented that any grocery store employee told anyone about the discharge. On the other hand, the man had told many others that he had been discharged for stealing. Accordingly, there had been no nonprivileged communication of the information by the store to any third party, and it could not be found to have defamed the former employee. Therefore, the appellate court reversed the finding of defamation by the lower court and entered judgment for the store. *Stalnaker v. One Dollar, Inc.*, 426 S.E.2d 536 (W.Va.1992).

An Ohio man worked for an insurance company. As a result of irregularities in the handling of transactions, a question arose as to whether the employee was a cocaine user. The employee later resigned his position and applied for an agent position with another insurer. A former fellow employee was asked what he knew about the man, and he told the prospective employer that he had heard about the possibility of cocaine use by the applicant. The man then found work with a third insurer who was also told about the possibility that he used cocaine. The agent sued the first insurer, alleging that he had been slandered. The court ruled for the insurer, and the agent appealed to the Court of Appeals of Ohio. On appeal, the court noted that the allegedly slanderous statements were qualifiedly privileged. Thus, the agent had to show that the statements were false and that they were made with actual malice (with the knowledge that they were false or with reckless disregard as to the truth or falsity of the statements). Since the statements were made in the context of hiring recommendations, and since they did not actually accuse the agent of cocaine usage, they were not actionable slander. The court of appeals affirmed the trial court's ruling in favor of the insurer. *Lyons v. Farmers Ins. Group of Companies*, 587 N.E.2d 362 (Ohio App.1990).

A Louisiana man supervised nine dispatchers at a gas company. The company decided to conduct an attitude survey designed to determine how conditions could be improved for its employees. During the survey and feedback sessions, several of the nine dispatchers complained about the supervisor's use of indecent language and his treatment of female employees. The company's human resources manager met with three women dispatchers who related incidents in which the supervisor had improperly touched employees, used profanity, and made improper sexual comments. After the vice president concluded that the allegations were true, he offered the supervisor voluntary resignation or termination. The supervisor chose resignation, and then brought suit in a Louisiana trial court against the company and his subordinates for defamation and invasion of privacy. The trial court entered judgment in favor of the supervisor, and the defendants appealed to the Court of Appeal of Louisiana.

The company asserted the affirmative defense of privilege. Liability for defamation does not attach to privileged communications. The court determined that the company conducted an appropriate and reasonable investigation after learning of possible sexual harassment. The company took individual employees aside without indicating what the subject matter was in an attempt to keep the inquiry confidential. Thus, the court found that the company's communication enjoyed a qualified privilege. The appellate court reversed the decision of the trial court and found for the company and its employees. *Hines v. Arkansas Louisiana Gas Company,* 613 So.2d 646 (La.App.2d Cir.1993).

An Alabama hotel manager concluded that an employee had violated several written policies of the hotel. The employee resigned when the manager confronted him with the violations. The employee sued the hotel and two other employees, alleging claims for wrongful termination and defamation. The hotel and the employees moved for summary judgment, which was granted by a trial court. The employee appealed. The Supreme Court of Alabama held that the employee was not wrongfully terminated because there had been no employment contract with the hotel. Therefore, the state's long-standing "employee at will" doctrine prevailed. This doctrine provided that the hotel could fire employees at its discretion absent an employment contract for a specific term or absent conditions or terms for dismissal. The court found that the defamation claim failed because there had been no publication to a third party of the allegedly defamatory communications. The communications in question were published only to a few of the hotel's employees and only to the extent reasonably necessary to investigate the employee's behavior. These employees were acting in the scope of their duties with the hotel, and thus they were not considered third parties. Because publication to a third party is a necessary element of a defamation claim, the hotel and the employees were not liable for defamation. Accordingly, the court affirmed the decision of the trial court. *Burks v. Pickwick Hotel,* 607 So.2d 187 (Ala.1992).

An Indiana telephone company employee was placed on authorized disability leave. His division's manager came across a newspaper article which stated that the employee was a principal and an active manager and partner in an Indiana business. The manager sent the newspaper article to the company's medical director, who was responsible for maintenance and supervision of the employee disability leave programs. The medical director then wrote a memorandum to three company employees. It stated, "this disturbs me, and I am wondering if ... we would consider that this is fraud since he has been on disability for some time." The secretary of the benefit committee, the assistant vice president of personnel and a company attorney involved in labor matters received the memo and a copy of the article. The employee discovered that the memo had been circulated and brought suit against the company's medical director for defamation. The trial court granted summary judgment to the medical director, and the employee appealed to the Court of Appeals of Indiana.

On appeal, the court noted that the basic elements for a defamation claim are a defamatory imputation, publication, malice, and damages. There was a question in this case as to whether publication had occurred. The plaintiff employee acknowledged that two of the employees, the secretary of the benefit committee, and the assistant vice president of personnel, had responsibility to act on the information provided by the medical director. Therefore, the memorandum was not published when it was sent to them. The court then determined that the attorney had some managerial responsibility to act upon the information provided by the medical director. Accordingly, it determined that the attorney was an appropriate party to receive the communication and that no publication had been made. The court further stated that even if the attorney was not an appropriate party to receive the memo, the attorney's relationship with the company and the medical director was such that a qualified privilege was established. The court thus affirmed the grant of summary judgment for the medical director. *Burks v. Rushmore*, 569 N.E.2d 714 (Ind.App.1st Dist.1991).

A transportation company conducted regular meetings to discuss general problems and concerns within the company. The meetings were part of the company's effort to promote open communication. After one meeting a memorandum was posted about an employee (who had not been present) which read: FAVORITISM, * * *, SICK, MOVE-UPS, BROWN NOSE, SHIT HEADS. When the employee asked the company to remove the memorandum, it did so. Nevertheless, several other employees circulated copies of the memo which the company eventually removed. The employee was subjected to verbal and physical harassment following the memorandum's posting, and he claimed that these resulted in emotional and physical problems. He sued the company for defamation and infliction of emotional distress in a Minnesota trial court. The court granted the company's motion for summary judgment, and the employee appealed to the Court of Appeals of Minnesota.

On appeal, the court noted that a defamatory statement must be communicated to someone other than the plaintiff, it must be false, and it must tend to harm the plaintiff's reputation in the community. The court further held that, under the U.S. Supreme Court decision in *Milkovich v. Lorain Journal Co.*, expressions of opinion are constitutionally protected as nondefamatory only if the statements cannot reasonably be interpreted as stating actual facts. The court then agreed with the trial court that the statements made in the memorandum were clearly opinion and were too imprecise to be actionable. The court said, "[a]lthough uncomplimentary, 'shit heads' does not suggest verifiably false facts about [the employee]." The court thus held the statements in the memorandum to be constitutionally protected. It then analyzed the emotional distress claim and found that the employee's claim could not stand. The words were not sufficiently severe to be shocking or egregious. The court of appeals therefore affirmed the grant of summary judgment in favor of the company. *Lund v. Chicago and Northwestern Transportation Co.*, 467 N.W.2d 366 (Minn.App.1991).

The labor relations coordinator at an auto manufacturing plant was informed by police that company-owned equipment had been pawned at a local pawnshop. The coordinator called the employee whose name was on the ticket and asked him to come to her office. After the employee denied any knowledge of the equipment or the pawn ticket, he was temporarily suspended pending an investigation. A security guard escorted him out of the building in accordance with company policy on suspensions. Five days later, after the investigation, the employee returned to work, receiving pay for the period of his suspension. He did not file a grievance under the collective bargaining agreement regarding either the meeting or the suspension. Instead, he sued the company for defamation and infliction of emotional distress. A Texas federal district court granted summary judgment to the employer, and the employee appealed.

On appeal to the U.S. Court of Appeals, Fifth Circuit, the court agreed with the district court that the employee's state law claims were preempted by the Labor Management Relations Act, and that the employee could not pursue his claims because he had failed to use the grievance procedure described in the collective bargaining agreement. Further, the employee had made no showing that the employer's action involved malice (a necessary element of a defamation claim). The court affirmed the district court's decision against the employee. *Bagby v. General Motors Corp.,* 976 F.2d 919 (5th Cir.1992).

An Indiana man worked for a steel company until he was fired as a result of unsatisfactory evaluation reports written by his supervisor. The employee brought suit against his supervisor for defamation and tortious interference with his employment relationship. A trial court found in favor of the supervisor on both claims. The employee appealed the defamation action, and the court of appeals affirmed. He then appealed to the state supreme court.

The Supreme Court of Indiana noted that an action for defamation must show that the defamatory matter was "published," or communicated to a third person or persons. It held that the evaluation reports communicated within the company were "published" for purposes of the defamation action. While personnel evaluation reports communicated in good faith within a company are protected by qualified privilege, the privilege may be overcome by a showing of abuse. Here, the evidence did not show that the supervisor was primarily motivated by ill will in making the statements, or that there was excessive publication of the alleged defamatory statements. More particularly, it had not been shown that the statements were made without grounds for belief in the truth of their contents. Because of the absence of substantial evidence or reasonable inferences showing abuse of the privilege, the court affirmed the decision of the trial court. *Bals v. Verduzco,* 600 N.E.2d 1353 (Ind.1992).

III. AUTOMOBILE INCIDENTS

Generally, when an employee is involved in an automobile accident, an employer will only be held liable if the employee was acting in furtherance of the employer's business or if the employee's actions were authorized by the employer.

A Wisconsin man worked for a company as an over-the-road truck driver. He and his wife discussed the possibility of her riding as a passenger with him. However, before she could accompany her husband, the company required her to sign a form entitled "Passenger Authorization." In addition to providing authorization to the wife, the form served as a general release of all claims she might have against the company. Subsequently, the wife was injured while accompanying her husband on one of his trips. She sued the company to recover for her injuries and a state trial court dismissed her complaint, finding that she had signed an exculpatory contract which foreclosed her claim as a matter of law. The state court of appeals affirmed that decision and she appealed to the Supreme Court of Wisconsin.

The issue before the supreme court was whether the wife's signed form constituted a valid exculpatory contract releasing her claims against the company. The court held that the contract was void as against public policy. The court listed three factors that led to its conclusion. First, the release should have been conspicuously labeled to put the wife on notice that she was releasing the company from liability. Since it was labeled as a "Passenger Authorization," it did not do so. Second, the release was extremely broad and all-inclusive. It excused intentional, reckless and negligent conduct. Third, the contract was a standardized agreement on the company's printed form which offered little or no opportunity for negotiation or free and voluntary bargaining. The court reversed the lower court decisions and held that the lawsuit against the company could proceed. *Richards v. Richards*, 513 N.W.2d 118 (Wis.1994).

A 16-year-old Virginia resident attempted to reach a service station in a car that was almost out of gas. He operated the vehicle in the left lane of a busy highway and was killed when a dump truck struck the rear of his vehicle. The deceased's estate sued the truck driver and his employer in a Virginia trial court for wrongful death. Following a four day trial, a jury found the driver and his employer liable for a damage award of $670,000. The court granted motions for judgment notwithstanding the verdict, ruling as a matter of law that the deceased was guilty of negligence that was the proximate cause of his death. It ruled that violation of a Virginia traffic statute (governing stopping and impeding traffic on highways) created negligence as a matter of law. The estate appealed to the Supreme Court of Virginia. The supreme court held that the question of proximate cause should have been answered by the jury, not the court. The trial court had also given erroneous jury instructions by holding the 16-year-old driver to a different standard of care than other drivers. He should have been held to the same duty of care as a reasonable person in similar circumstances. Because the error was harmful, a new trial would be required at which the jury should evaluate the deceased by adult standards. The case was remanded for a new trial upon all issues including negligence, proximate cause and damages. *Thomas v. Settle*, 439 S.E.2d 360 (Va.1994).

A North Carolina publishing company held a retirement party for its editor at the home of its publisher and president. The publisher hired a catering service and alcoholic beverages were served. An employee who had consumed three or four alcoholic drinks at the party was involved in a traffic accident after leaving. The employee admitted driving while intoxicated and running a red light in criminal proceedings which followed. The driver of the other vehicle died nine months after the collision. His estate sued the employee, publisher and publishing company in a North Carolina trial court for wrongful death. All parties moved for summary judgment, and the court dismissed the newspaper and publisher from the lawsuit while granting the estate's summary judgment motion against the employee. The case was appealed to the Court of Appeals of North Carolina.

According to the court of appeals, the publisher and publishing company were social hosts in this matter, and business or employer liability was not an issue. Social hosts could only be held liable for the acts of a guest if they had knowledge of the guest's intoxicated or impaired condition prior to serving alcohol. The trial court had properly granted summary judgment because of a lack of evidence in the record of any such knowledge by the publisher or publishing company. The employee's high blood alcohol content after leaving the party did not raise any inference that the social hosts had knowledge of his condition at the time drinks were served. The trial court had also properly granted summary judgment to the estate against the employee and had properly dismissed the employee's motion for summary judgment based upon alleged contributory negligence by the deceased. *Camalier v. Jeffries*, 438 S.E.2d 427 (N.C.App.1994).

A Texas employee left work for the day and drove to a friend's house to pick up her briefcase, which she had left accidentally. On her way home, she was involved in an accident in which another woman was killed. Her estate sued the employer for injuries arising out of the accident. The trial court entered summary judgment in favor of the employer and the estate appealed to the Court of Appeals of Texas. Under Texas law, an employee generally is not in the course or scope of employment while driving a vehicle to and from his or her place of work. However, an exception to this general rule exists where an employee has undertaken a special mission at the direction of the employer. To be on a special mission, an employee must be under the control of or acting to further the interests of the employer. No evidence showed that the trip was a special mission undertaken at the direction of the employer. Instead, the testimony established that the employee's trip to retrieve her briefcase was not initiated by the employer, but instead by the fact that she had left her briefcase at her friend's home that morning. Accordingly, the appellate court upheld the decision of the trial court. *Direkly v. ARA Devcon, Inc.*, 866 S.W.2d 652 (Tex.App.1993).

A major oil company sponsored a Christmas party for its Alaska employees. The company contracted with a hotel to provide all the services associated with the party, including alcohol service. Shortly after midnight, a few employees decided to go to a local tavern. An intoxicated employee was driven to the tavern and back home again by a concerned co-employee. After he arrived home, he left his residence and drove out of town where he was involved in an accident. The personal representatives of the accident victims sued the oil company and the co-employee who had driven the intoxicated employee home. The court granted summary judgment in favor of the oil company and the co-employee. The personal representatives appealed to the Supreme Court of Alaska. The court held that since the oil company did not hold a liquor license, it was not liable as a social host for the injuries resulting from the employee's intoxication. The personal representatives also argued that the oil company, if not liable as a host, might be liable as the employer of an intoxicated person who caused injuries. The court declined to impose a duty upon the employer not only of getting the employee safely home, but of securing the keys or setting up an all night vigil to make sure the employee didn't leave again. Also, the co-employee had conscientiously discharged his duty by driving the employee home. Accordingly, the supreme court upheld summary judgment in favor of the oil company and the co-employee. *Mulvihill v. Union Oil Co.*, 859 P.2d 1310 (Alaska 1993).

A British corporation hired a consultant to visit the United States and observe the operation of a cable company. While in the United States, the consultant was in an accident in which another man was killed. The deceased man's estate brought an action in a Georgia trial court against the corporation under the theory of *respondeat superior (*holding the employer responsible for the negligence of the employee who is acting within the scope of employment). The trial court found that the consultant was an independent contractor and ruled for the corporation. The estate appealed to the Court of Appeals of Georgia. The estate claimed that the consultant was an employee of the corporation. An employer-employee relationship exists when the employer assumes the right to control the time and manner of executing the work. The corporation had set forth specific facts showing that the consultant was employed as an independent contractor. The corporation did not furnish the consultant with any health benefits or pay taxes on his behalf, nor did it pay for his rental car. Further, the corporation exerted no control over the cable operation. Therefore, the court concluded that he was an independent contractor and upheld the decision of the trial court. *McDaniel v. Peterborough Cable Vision, Ltd.*, 425 S.E.2d 424 (Ga.App.1992).

A salesman for a pharmaceutical company, while driving to the post office to mail some paperwork, apparently cut off another motorist, causing a fight. The other motorist was injured in the fight; he brought suit against the salesman's employer for negligent hiring and further asserted a claim based upon *respondeat superior* (holding the employer liable for the acts of its employee). The case was brought in federal court, and the employer moved for summary judgment. The court first determined that the salesman was not acting in the scope of his employment when he assaulted the other motorist. Neither did his employer authorize his actions in any way. Next, the court found that the company could not be liable for negligent hiring because it was not shown that the salesman had a propensity for violence. Accordingly, the court granted summary judgment to the company. *Thatcher v. Brennan*, 657 F.Supp. 6 (S.D.Miss.1986).

A woman sustained personal injuries as a result of an automobile collision caused by the negligence of a man who was driving an automobile for a car dealership. He was one of several people driving cars from Raleigh to Fayetteville. The woman brought suit against the car dealership claiming that the man was acting within the scope and course of his employment with the car dealership when the accident occurred. Both the man and the car dealership denied the existence of an employer-employee relationship. A jury found in favor of the woman, and the car dealership appealed. The Court of Appeals of North Carolina affirmed the decision of the trial court. The car dealership argued that the man was acting as an independent contractor at the time of the accident, and thus the car dealership was not liable for injuries to the woman. The court, however, found that there was sufficient evidence of the existence of an employer-employee relationship. The car dealership could terminate the man's employment at any time and exercised control over the time and manner in which the tasks were to be performed. The man testified that he was assigned a vehicle to drive, and that he was instructed to follow the lead vehicle on a route designated by the car dealership. Thus, the court found that the car dealership was liable to the woman as a result of injuries sustained in the automobile collision caused by the negligence of its operator. *Brewer v. Spivey*, 423 S.E.2d 95 (N.C.App.1992).

A corporation which provided security services stationed a guard at an apartment complex. The guard borrowed a tenant's vehicle with permission, and returned the keys to the front desk. Later, without permission, he obtained the keys and again borrowed the car. On this occasion he was involved in an automobile accident. The other driver sued him and the security corporation. The trial court granted summary judgment to the corporation, and appeal was taken to the Supreme Court of Nevada. The supreme court first stated that *respondeat superior* liability could attach only when the employee is under the control of the employer, and when the act is within the scope of employment. The employee was clearly acting outside the scope of his employment and was not furthering the business interests of the corporation when he took the tenant's car. The court found that the corporation had conducted a reasonable background check on the employee and had turned up nothing which might indicate he would use his position to misappropriate a vehicle. Accordingly, the court affirmed the trial court's decision in favor of the corporation. *Burnett v. C.B.A. Security Service, Inc.*, 820 P.2d 750 (Nev.1991).

A New York engineer trainee attended company training sessions from 8:00 - 4:30 each day. He was free to stay late or return to the plant to use its laboratories. One day, after staying late, the employee went to a local restaurant for dinner. On his way back to the plant he was involved in an accident. The other driver sued him for negligence and also sued the corporation under the doctrine of *respondeat superior*. The injured party asserted that the employee had been acting within the course and scope of his employment and that the corporation was thus responsible for the employee's negligent acts. The corporation moved to dismiss the complaint against it, but the trial court denied the motion. The corporation appealed to the New York Supreme Court, Appellate Division.

The appellate division court noted that the question of *respondeat superior* was normally one of fact for the jury. However, in this case, there were no disputed facts. It was clear that the corporation did not have the power to control its employee's actions after 4:30 on the day of the accident and the employee could do as he pleased. He was not, therefore, acting within the course and scope of his employment at the time of the accident, and no liability could attach to the corporation. The appellate court reversed the trial court's decision and dismissed the complaint against the corporation. *Tenczar v. Richmond*, 568 N.Y.S.2d 232 (A.D.3d Dept.1991).

A company which operated cafeterias sponsored, funded, and conducted Christmas parties as a fringe benefit for its employees and to improve employer-employee relations. Attendance at the parties was voluntary. During a Christmas party, one employee became intoxicated. He left the party with another group of employees and guests intending to go to another party not hosted by the company. He lost control of his car on the way to the other party and struck the other group's vehicle. A passenger in that vehicle was severely injured and brought suit against the company, claiming that it was vicariously liable for the negligent driving of its employee. After judgment for the company, the passenger appealed to the Supreme Court of Virginia. On appeal, the passenger argued that the employee was acting within the scope of his employment while attending the company's party, and that when he first began to drive his car in an intoxicated condition while on the company premises, he committed a negligent act within the scope of his employment. The court, however, noted that at the time of the injury, there was no master-servant relationship in existence. Since the employee was not acting for the company when he hit the other car, the employer could not be held vicariously liable. *Sayles v. Piccadilly Cafeterias, Inc.*, 410 S.E.2d 632 (Va.1991).

A South Carolina corporation held a Christmas party for its employees as a social event with voluntary attendance. At the party, an employee and guest became intoxicated from alcohol and cocaine. Subsequently, the employee left the party and drove her vehicle into another vehicle, seriously injuring her guest passenger. The representatives of the injured guest filed a complaint against the corporation for providing the alcohol and for the negligent and reckless action of its employee. The district court held the corporation not liable and granted it summary judgment. The court found that the corporation was a "social host" and therefore was not liable. The attendance by guests and the consumption of alcoholic beverages were voluntary. Additionally, neither the employee nor her guest were in a helpless position at the party so as to invoke a duty by the employer. Moreover, the employee's conduct was not within the scope of employment. *Hill v. Honey's Inc.*, 786 F.Supp. 549 (D.S.C.1992).

A bank created an educational assistance program by which it agreed to reimburse employees for tuition and book expenses as long as the employees pursued job related degrees. One of the bank's employees, who had already been pursuing a business administration degree, entered into the bank's program. After completing her work shift, and while on the way to the university, the employee struck and seriously injured a motorcyclist. He brought suit against the bank, seeking to hold it liable for the injuries he had incurred. The bank moved for summary judgment which the trial court granted, and the motorcyclist appealed to the California Court of Appeal, Fourth District.

The court of appeal noted that the going-and-coming doctrine normally will not make an employer liable for actions by its employees while engaged in the ordinary commute to the place of work. However, if the employee was engaged in a special errand at the request of her employer, the bank would be vicariously liable. In this case, since the employee had been under no specific order or direct request to attend college classes, the special errand exception did not apply to the going-and-coming rule. Even though the bank was benefiting from the employee's college course work, her schooling had no direct impact on day-to-day banking operations. Accordingly, the court affirmed the trial court's grant of summary judgment to the employer. *Blackman v. Great American First Savings Bank*, 284 Cal.Rptr. 491 (Cal.App.4th Dist.1991).

A part-owner of a painting company took a group of employees from Oahu to Kauai for a job that was scheduled to last approximately one month. The company rented two cars for use by its employees. The part-owner entrusted one of the cars to an employee who was attending a party. Another employee went along. When the employee who had been given the car became intoxicated, he entrusted the car to his co-employee. That employee, who was also intoxicated, was then involved in a collision in which a third party was injured. She brought a lawsuit against the company and the part-owner under theories of *respondeat superior* and negligent entrustment. Upon the grant of summary judgment to the employer, the injured woman appealed to the Supreme Court of Hawaii.

The supreme court first noted that neither of the two employees who attended the party had been acting within the scope of their employment. Thus, the employer could not be vicariously liable for their acts. The court then looked at the negligent entrustment claim and determined that also must fail. Here, the part-owner did not lend the car to the employee who was involved in the accident, but to another employee. Further, it had not been shown that lending the car to the employee would pose an unreasonable risk of harm. Accordingly, the grant of summary judgment was affirmed. *Henderson v. Professional Coatings Corp.*, 819 P.2d 84 (Hawaii 1991).

An Illinois employee finished work one day and drove to a store to purchase a carpenter's square which he intended to use at work and also at home. On the way to the store, his vehicle struck a five-year-old child, causing severe injuries to the child. The child's father brought a lawsuit against the driver's employer on a theory of *respondeat superior.* He asserted that the driver was in the course of his employment at the time of the incident since he was driving to a store to purchase the square for use in his employment. The employer contended that the employee was on a personal trip at the time of the accident. The jury ruled in favor of the employer, and the father appealed to the Appellate Court of Illinois, First District. On appeal, the court noted that it had not been error to allow the employee to state that he intended to use the square for personal as well as business use. Further, it had not been error for the employer's attorney to state in his opening and closing arguments that the employee was on a personal trip and that he needed the carpenter's square for his own personal use. The court affirmed the verdict in favor of the employer. *Fakhoury v. Vapor Corp.*, 578 N.E.2d 121 (Ill.App.1st Dist.1991).

A Florida man worked as a parts employee/mechanic for a company that serviced county vehicles. The man was killed when the fuel truck he was driving overturned and exploded. As the personal representative of his son's estate, the employee's father brought an action for wrongful death against the company and several of its supervising employees. He claimed that his son operated the fuel truck without a chauffeur's license and without any experience in driving such a truck. He also alleged that the truck was allowed to be used in an unsafe manner. The company filed a motion for summary judgment, asserting its immunity under the Workers' Compensation Act. A circuit court granted the company's motion and the employee's representative appealed. The District Court of Appeal of Florida, Second District, found that genuine issues of material fact existed as to whether the conduct of the supervising employees amounted to gross negligence or wilful and wanton disregard for the employee. Specifically, the court found conflicting evidence regarding the supervisors' knowledge about safety problems with the truck, the employee's willingness or inability to drive the truck, and whether the supervising employees had knowledge of the employee's experience and ability or lack thereof. Consequently, the court reversed the summary judgment in favor of the employer and remanded the case to the circuit court. *Madaffer v. Managed Logistic Systems*, 601 So.2d 1328 (Fla.App.2d Dist.1992).

An Ohio woman was injured in an automobile accident due to the negligence of an uninsured driver. She was insured by her employer's group health plan and all her medical expenses were paid. The employer's self-insured plan provided benefits on the condition that the covered person would agree to reimburse the plan immediately upon collection of damages. There was no recovery from the uninsured driver. However, the employee received $50,000 as a result of her uninsured motorist coverage provided by her automobile insurance carrier. The employer demanded payment of the medical insurance proceeds, asserting that because of the terms of the subrogation clause it was entitled to the funds received from her automobile insurer. When the employee refused to reimburse her employer, it sued for the funds. The trial court granted summary judgment in favor of the employer and the employee appealed to the Court of Appeals of Ohio.

The employee contended that the employer was only allowed subrogation for third party recoveries and not for a first party recovery. The court noted that the term "damages" was not defined in the policy. Therefore, the rules of construction dictated that the court give the word its plain and ordinary meaning. Damages are defined as compensation imposed by law for loss. Therefore, the court concluded that the definition of damages necessitated that there be a tortious activity and that the driver be liable to the injured party. Here, the monies that the employee received from her own insurer were not damages subject to reimbursement to the employer because she did not receive the money from a tortfeasor. The appellate court reversed the decision of the trial court and found for the employee. *Allied Moulded Products Inc. v. Keegan,* 611 N.E.2d 377 (Ohio App.1992).

IV. DANGEROUS CONDITIONS AND DEFECTIVE EQUIPMENT

Liability for dangerous workplace conditions and equipment often involves consideration of whether an employer-employee relationship exists between the parties, and may depend upon an employer's ownership of equipment or property. Where an employer fails to provide a safe working environment, liability may also depend on state and federal labor laws, like the Occupational Safety and Health Act (also discussed in Chapter Five). There is no common law duty to provide employees with a safe workplace. Many state laws have modified this rule. Employer liability may, however, be foreclosed by the exclusivity of remedies doctrine of workers' compensation laws. See Chapter Eight, Section One.

An oil company hired a contractor to repair an offshore drilling platform. Most of the handrails on the second level of the platform were in disrepair and a welder employed by the contractor was assigned the repair job. He had previously repaired handrails with two assistants to hold the rails, but in this case used only one. The rail fell and the assistant was unable to stop it from landing on the welder's back. He underwent surgery for herniated discs and was assigned a ten to 15 percent whole body impairment by his treating physician. He was advised not to return to welding work and filed a lawsuit against the oil company and two employees, asserting strict liability and negligence under Louisiana law. The court conducted a trial and awarded the welder damages for lost wages and medical expenses. The Louisiana Court of Appeal, Third Circuit, reversed the trial court decision and the welder appealed to the Supreme Court of Louisiana. The supreme court stated that an employer was not liable for premises liability under strict liability principles unless the premises presented an unreasonable risk of harm to others. In this case, there had been no showing that the premises presented an unreasonable risk of harm. The injury was attributable to the manner of repairing the rail with the help of only one assistant rather than to exposure to an unreasonable risk of harm. Although the status of being a welder had a bearing on the determination of the reasonableness of the risk, the court refused to adopt a repairman exception to strict liability. The court affirmed the decision of the court of appeal. *Celestine v. Union Oil Co. of California,* 652 So.2d 1299 (La.1995).

A group of Colorado activists submitted a proposed amendment to the state constitution that was intended to promote safe working environments. The amendment proposed that nongovernment employers who knowingly or recklessly maintain an unsafe work environment should be stripped of immunity in lawsuits filed by injured workers as a result of unsafe conditions. The amendment also provided for the setoff of damages in such lawsuits of benefits paid to employees under the state workers' compensation act. The activists claimed that the state Title Setting Review Board had inappropriately phrased the proposed amendment by inaccurately drafting the title and had violated another state constitutional provision requiring the approval of only single subject initiatives. The Colorado Supreme Court denied the activists' petition, ruling that the board's action had been proper. Because the title sufficiently advised the electorate of the purpose of the amendment, the ballot title was affirmed. *In the Matter of the Title, Ballot Title and Submission Clause*, 898 P.2d 1071 (Colo.1995).

A Louisiana nurse tested positive for HIV after being splashed with blood from an HIV positive patient who was being shaved for surgery. She claimed that a coworker and supervisor either negligently or intentionally failed to advise her of the patient's condition, causing her injury. A Louisiana trial court denied her claim under state law and the Court of Appeal of Louisiana, Third Circuit, reviewed her appeal. The court determined that genuine issues of fact existed concerning the actual notice given to the nurse by her supervisor concerning the hazards presented by the patient and the need to take adequate protective measures. The motives and intent of the supervising employee were also in dispute, making the trial court order for summary judgment inappropriate. The case was reversed and remanded. *Juneau v. Humana, Inc.*, 657 So.2d 457 (La.App.3d Cir.1995).

The Court of Appeals of Georgia reversed a judgment in favor of the employer of a worker who was injured when he fell 30 feet from an icy steel beam on a building under construction. He claimed that the building's general contractors were negligent as a matter of law for failing to provide safety nets as required by OSHA and that the builder was liable to him for his injuries under Georgia law. The court of appeals reversed a summary judgment order for the builder by a state trial court, disagreeing with the lower court's ruling that the employee knew of the icy conditions but assumed the risk of injury by walking on the beam. The court of appeals ruled that there was sufficient evidence concerning the conditions under which the employee worked to avoid summary judgment and require a trial. The employee had presented evidence that he had been threatened with employment termination should he refuse to walk on the icy beams without a safety net. *Styles v. Mobil Oil Corp.*, 459 S.E.2d 578 (Ga.App.1995).

A South Carolina factory worker injured herself while cleaning a machine at the factory. Her employer had modified certain safety features on the machine, and a number of employees, including the injured worker, had previously fallen as a result. The employee received workers' compensation benefits, but was then fired for excessive unexcused absences. She filed a lawsuit against the employer for breach of contract and wrongful discharge, a products liability action against the manufacturer of the machine, and a tortious interference with contract claim against her supervisors. The court conducted a trial and granted post-trial motions for the manufacturer based on evidence that the machine had been substantially modified after delivery and that the employee was aware of the cleaning risks. The court also granted directed verdicts for the supervisors. The jury returned a verdict for the employer on the contract and wrongful discharge claims, and the employee appealed to the Supreme Court of South Carolina.

The court reversed the trial court's decision concerning the manufacturer's liability for producing a defective machine. Although the equipment had been modified by the employer after installation, a question remained concerning whether the modification had been foreseeable by the manufacturer. The jury was entitled to decide this issue and it was remanded to the trial court for reconsideration. However, the trial court had made appropriate rulings concerning dismissal of the claims against the supervisors and the breach of contract issues. In this case, the employee handbook contained a disclaimer that it created any employment contract. The trial court had appropriately found that the disclaimer was conspicuous as a matter of law. The supreme court affirmed those parts of the trial court's decision. *Fleming v. Borden, Inc.*, 450 S.E.2d 589 (S.C.1994).

A New York railway supply company leased property to a service that maintained rail cars. An employee of the service company was injured when he fell from a ladder while sandblasting a rail car. The ladder tipped, causing the employee to fall, and the hand-held sandblaster continued to spray sand, possibly due to a defect. The employee sued the supply company and rail car owner in a New York trial court alleging violation of New York Labor Law § 240(1), which requires contractors who clean buildings and structures to furnish workers with proper scaffolding, ladders and safety devices. The trial court denied cross motions for summary judgment by the parties and appeal was made to the New York Supreme Court, Appellate Division, which held that the supply company was an owner under the Labor Law. It rejected the supply company's argument that it should not be liable under the Labor Law because it allegedly instructed the employee to use a scaffold rather than a ladder, and therefore the employee was a recalcitrant worker who refused to use available and appropriate equipment. The supply company and car owner appealed to the Court of Appeals of New York.

According to the court, the rail car was a structure within the meaning of the Labor Law, and the supply company qualified as an owner. The Labor Law imposed absolute liability on owners to provide safe working conditions where there were risks related to elevation differences. Because the ladder did not prevent the employee from falling, the supply company did not meet the objectives of the Labor Law. Its failure to provide a safe scaffold or ladder was a substantial cause leading to the fall and injury, irrespective of the allegedly defective sandblaster. Evidence that the employee had been instructed to use a scaffold rather than a ladder did not create a sufficient fact issue to support the supply company's argument that the employee was a recalcitrant worker who had refused to use appropriate safety devices, and there should be no trial on that issue. The court of appeals affirmed the appellate division's decision in favor of the employee. *Gordon v. Eastern Railway Supp. Inc.*, 82 N.Y.2d 555, 606 N.Y.S.2d 127, 626 N.E.2d 912 (1993).

A teenage service station employee died due to injuries from a gunshot wound which he suffered during a robbery attempt at the station. The teenager's mother sued the oil company which leased the station to the teenager's employer for failing to maintain a safe workplace. Following a trial in a Texas district court, the mother was awarded over $382,000 plus interest. The Court of Appeals of Texas reversed the part of the judgment awarding mental anguish damages to the mother, but otherwise affirmed the trial court decision. The company appealed to the Supreme Court of Texas.

The supreme court observed that the legal standard in oil company liability cases involving injuries to customers and employees on leased premises was a combination of landlord-tenant and agency law. Under landlord-tenant law, landowners have no duty to prevent criminal acts of third persons not under their control and have a duty only to advise tenants of latent dangerous conditions. Under agency law, employers are responsible to provide a safe workplace for their employees and ordinary principles of negligence apply. In this case, the hybrid form of landlord-tenant and agency law was insufficient to impose liability. In reversing and remanding the case, the court announced a new standard of law to apply in injury cases involving premises leased by oil companies. On remand, the trial court was to scrutinize whether the tenant had specific control over the safety and security of the premises, rather than to reconsider general rights of control over operations. The broader question of the oil company's right to control general operations at the service station was irrelevant to the analysis of liability, and on remand the court was to determine if it had the specific right to control the alleged security defects which had led to the teenager's death. *Exxon Corp. v. Tidwell*, 867 S.W.2d 19 (Tex.1993).

A Missouri worker was killed while operating a machine at a wire rope factory. The worker's survivors sued employees of the company including its vice president, managers, foremen and engineers. The survivors claimed that the employees had failed to respond to requests for safety systems and switches on the machine. A Missouri trial court granted the employees' motion to dismiss the lawsuit. The survivors appealed to the Missouri Court of Appeals, Western District. The court of appeals stated that an employer has a duty to provide a safe work environment, and that the state workers' compensation act gave employers immunity from common law liability for breaches of the duty. Employer immunity under the workers' compensation act extended to employees carrying out company duties, and a coworker's failure to perform a delegated duty did not create liability unless the coworker took some affirmative action that increased the risk of injury. Because the survivors had merely rephrased an invalid common law complaint for breach of the duty to provide a safe work environment, the employees were immune from their claims. *Felling v. Ritter*, 876 S.W.2d 2 (Mo.App.W.D.1994).

An employee of a Michigan manufacturing company witnessed the death of a coworker from only a few feet away. The coworker was killed when struck by a metal bar from a defective machine. The employee alleged that he was struck by the victim's flesh and a piece of metal that he had been holding. However, he did not allege that he had been cut or bruised. Even though the employee was unrelated to the victim and not a close friend, he alleged that the incident caused him emotional distress with physical injuries, including aggravation of his asthma and high blood pressure. He stated that the emotional shock of the incident caused him to suffer a stroke more than one year later. He sued the company in the U.S. District Court for the Eastern District of Michigan, which considered the company's motion for summary judgment. The court held that under Michigan law, no recovery could be made by a party alleging negligent infliction of harm to a third person, unless the party was a member of the victim's immediate family. Further, the employee had submitted no medical evidence that he himself was injured by a machine malfunction. Because the law did not provide a remedy for third party bystanders who were not immediate family members, the court granted summary judgment to the employer. *Maldonado v. National Acme Co.*, 849 F.Supp. 1175 (E.D.Mich.1994).

A Wisconsin woman was injured when her hand was drawn into a box-making machine. The president and primary owner of the plant had purchased the box-making machine and leased it to the plant. The employee filed a liability suit against the president. The trial court entered summary judgment in favor of the president and the employee appealed to the Court of Appeals of Wisconsin. The exclusive remedy provision of the Worker's Compensation Act provides that the right to the recovery of compensation shall be the exclusive remedy against the employer. Nevertheless, under the doctrine of dual capacity, an employer may be liable in tort to an employee where the employer acts as a third person rather than as an employer. The question, therefore, was whether the president, as the owner and lessor of the machine and as president and owner of the corporation, was two separate legal persons. The court concluded that the president, by personally purchasing and leasing the machine, could not escape potential tort liability because he created a separate legal entity and accepted the personal advantages derived from such an arrangement. Thus, the appellate court reversed the trial court's decision.*Rauch v. Officine Curioni, S.P.A.*, 508 N.W.2d 12 (Wis.App.1993).

A New York railroad worker was directed to secure a metal grating to prevent homeless people from getting into the trainmen's room. In order to secure the window, the worker was required to remove a pile of debris. While wearing heavy duty work gloves, he reached into the pile and felt a sharp pain. When he withdrew his hand, he observed a hypodermic needle which had penetrated his glove and embedded in his hand. He removed the needle and went immediately to a hospital. He was advised to have an HIV blood test. It takes up to six months for the virus to incubate and he was advised to use a condom during sexual intercourse and have another HIV-blood test in six months. The worker complained of sleeplessness, disruption of family bonds and fear on the part of coworkers. He then filed this negligence action in a federal district court under the Federal Employers' Liability Act (FELA).

He alleged that the railroad was negligent in failing to provide him with a safe place to work and that its negligence caused his physical and psychological injuries. The railroad moved for partial summary judgment. Specifically, the railroad asked the court to dismiss all claims relating to the alleged fear of contracting AIDS. The railroad claimed that there was no proof that the worker was exposed to the AIDS virus (HIV). The court noted that the worker's claim of a fear of contracting AIDS was essentially a claim for negligent infliction of emotional distress leading to posttraumatic stress. The court ruled that summary judgment would be inappropriate in this case. The finder of fact could conclude that the worker had sustained sufficient injury to support an award for mental anguish even if subsequent medical diagnoses failed to reveal any other physical injury. *Marchica v. Long Island R.R.*, 810 F.Supp. 445 (E.D.N.Y.1993).

An Ohio industrial employee's position required him to periodically test a sulfuric acid solution and to add the correct amount of concentrated sulfuric acid when necessary. After a number of years, the plant decided to install a meter in the sulfuric supply line. The plant supervisor called an equipment supplier and asked for a meter suitable for use with sulfuric acid. After he was told that no such meter existed he asked for a meter for use with water. The supplier said that he had a meter but warned the supervisor that it was not intended for use with sulfuric acid. The supervisor installed the meter without performing any tests. When the employee went to use the sulfuric acid line, it burst—drenching him with concentrated sulfuric acid. He sustained severe and debilitating injuries which ultimately forced his retirement from the company. He sued his employer for an intentional tort. An Ohio court granted the employer's motion for a directed verdict and the employee appealed to the Court of Appeals of Ohio.

An action brought by an employee for an intentional tort requires proof that the employer either specifically desired to injure the employee or knew that injury to the employee was substantially certain to result from the employer's act. In this case, the employer had been warned that the meter was unsuitable for its intended use in a process which was already known to be dangerous. The employer installed the device despite this knowledge. Therefore, the court determined that the employer could be treated as if it desired the harm which resulted from its conduct. The employee had alleged facts which could convince reasonable minds that the defendant knew that injury was substantially certain to occur. Thus, the trial court erred in granting the motion for a directed verdict. The appellate court reversed the decision and remanded the case. *Howard v. Columbus Products Company*, 611 N.E.2d 480 (Ohio App.1992).

In 1981, the U.S. Occupational Safety and Health Administration (OSHA) instituted a rule controlling occupational exposure to bloodborne pathogens. The rule was designed to protect health care workers from viruses, particularly those causing hepatitis B and AIDS which can be transmitted in the blood of patients. OSHA's role reflects the public health philosophy of universal precautions, which means treating the blood of every patient to be a carrier of the hepatitis B virus or the AIDS virus. OSHA estimated that the rule would save the lives of approximately 350 health care workers and cost $820 million annually. Employer groups representing dental workers, the home health care industry, and the medical staffing industry petitioned the U.S. Court of Appeals, Seventh Circuit, for review of the rule. The employer groups argued that OSHA had not determined that a significant risk to workers existed. However, the court noted that OSHA need not quantify significant risk to a scientific certainty, but rather it need only establish the existence of a significant risk. OSHA had shown that if a worker was exposed to blood, there was a significant risk of infection from a potentially fatal disease. Thus, the court determined that the rule was rational and upheld it with respect to the dental care industry. However, the rule was not rational as applied to the home health and medical staffing industries. *American Dental Association v. Martin*, 984 F.2d 823 (7th Cir.1993).

A North Carolina construction company was hired to perform services at a manufacturing plant. It delivered a welding machine to the job site to be used by its employees. The standard practice was for the construction company to deliver the welding machine without a male-end plug. At the site, the plug was then wired and grounded by an employee of the manufacturer. The manufacturing employees used the welding machine for projects totally unrelated to the construction project. A manufacturing employee was electrocuted when he touched both the welding machine and another piece of grounded equipment. A safety compliance officer issued the construction company a citation for failure to train employees and properly inspect equipment, but the Safety Health and Review Board dismissed the citation. A North Carolina trial court reinstated the citation and the construction company appealed to the Court of Appeals of North Carolina.

The construction company argued that its reliance on the manufacturer's electrician was sufficient. The general rule was that each employer was responsible for the safety of its own employees. The company argued that it was not its own employee who was injured and that the manufacturer's electrician had caused the accident. Although it was not a construction company employee who was injured, the construction company employees were exposed to the same conditions as the manufacturer's employees with respect to the welding machine. Thus, if a hazard existed, the construction company would have a duty to provide for the safety of its employees. The standard for determining if a hazard existed was whether a reasonably prudent person would recognize it as a hazard. The construction company was aware that the welding machine utilized high voltages of electricity. It also knew that if improperly grounded, the welding machine was dangerous. The company had a nondelegable duty to inspect the grounding of its welding machine and properly train all employees. The appellate court upheld the decision of the trial court and reinstated the citation. *Brooks v BCF Piping, Inc.*, 426 S.E.2d 282 (N.C.App.1993).

A New York man, employed as a supervisor by a subcontractor, was required to inspect a construction site. The employee was inspecting bolts when he was knocked from the beam through an unguarded opening in the third floor to the second floor some 28 feet below. The supervisor filed suit in a state court against the contractor and filed a motion for partial summary judgment based upon the violation of the scaffolding statute. The trial court denied the summary judgment motion and the supervisor appealed to the Supreme Court of New York, Appellate

Division. The supervisor claimed that the scaffolding statute was applicable and that the contractor had a nondelegable duty to furnish safety devices. The court noted that there was no evidence indicating there were any safety devices in place to prevent the supervisor from falling from the third floor to the second floor. The contractor, however, contended that it was not the absence of safety devices but rather the actions of another worker that had caused the supervisor's injuries. The court noted that there was an absolute nondelegable duty set forth in the scaffolding law, and contributory negligence on the part of the injured worker or coworker was of no consequence. Accordingly, the appellate court awarded the supervisor partial summary judgment on the issue of liability under the scaffolding law. *Ianelli v. Olympia & York Battery Park*, 593 N.Y.S.2d 553 (A.D.1993).

A Florida hotel hired a general contractor to remodel rooms. The general hired a subcontractor to replace the existing patio doors. While working for the subcontractor, an employee tripped in a service entryway to the main lobby (an area of the hotel which was not under construction). The general maintained workers' compensation insurance covering employees of the subcontractors involved in the remodeling. The injured employee sued the hotel owner, alleging that a flooring defect caused his injury. The hotel owner claimed that it was immune from suit because it was the worker's statutory employer under Florida workers' compensation law. A trial court granted summary judgment to the hotel owner, and the worker appealed. On appeal to the District Court of Appeal of Florida, the court noted that the hotel owner did not have any statutory duty to provide workers' compensation coverage. Further, the owner owed the worker, as well as others who were legitimately on the premises, an independent duty of care to maintain the premises in a reasonably safe condition. Accordingly, the hotel owner was not entitled to immunity from suit, and the trial court decision had to be reversed. *Hogan v. Deerfield 21 Corp.*, 605 So.2d 979 (Fla.App.4th Dist.1992).

A welder worked for a construction company which was hired by a corporation to dismantle an elevator and reduce its height. The elevator was old and had been patched several times by the corporation. The welder's superiors calculated the best way to perform the dismantling. However, during the operation, the elevator collapsed. The welder was injured as a result. He brought suit against the corporation, asserting that it was negligent in failing to disclose that the elevator was unsafe. A Georgia trial court granted summary judgment to the corporation, and the welder appealed to the Court of Appeals of Georgia.

On appeal, the court noted that the welder had failed to show that there was a defect in the elevator which caused it to collapse, and of which the corporation had superior knowledge. The Mine Safety Health Administration (which investigated the accident) concluded that the collapse was triggered by the dismantling operation, not by structural deterioration alone. Further, the dismantling of the elevator was not "inherently dangerous work regardless of how carefully performed." The use of additional cranes and structural bracing would have made the dismantling safe. Accordingly, the corporation could not be held liable for the welder's injuries, and the lower court's grant of summary judgment had been proper. *Brooks v. Oil-Dri Corporation of Georgia,* 422 S.E.2d 22 (Ga.App.1992).

A New York employee, working for a radio company, attempted to install a radio antenna on top of the roof of a building. The employee mounted a ladder which broke, causing him to fall. The ladder was brought to the work site by the employee and was owned by either the employee or the employer. Subsequently, the employee filed suit against the building owner for negligence and various violations of state labor law. The building owner then joined the employer to become a party in the lawsuit. The supreme court dismissed the complaint, holding the building owner and employer not liable. On appeal, the New York Supreme Court, Appellate Division, upheld the dismissal. The court found that the employee failed to present sufficient evidence that the building owner or the employer had "actual constructive notice of the defect of the ladder." Moreover, the employee provided no evidence that his injuries were "occasioned by his use of either defendants' plant, tools or methods." Therefore, the employee's allegation of an unsafe workplace was rejected. The court also deemed the claims under the labor law to be misplaced. *Kesselbach v. Liberty College Inc.,* 583 N.Y.S.2d 739 (A.D.2d Dept.1992).

An Alabama man worked in a coal mine which was leased by his employer. He worked as a "trip rider," which involved loading and unloading supplies and materials that were transported through the mine on material cars. While material was being hauled through the mine and the employee was positioned at the back of the car, protruding material from the car hit a low-ceiling, striking the roof and causing it to fall on the employee, severely injuring him. He brought a claim against the coal mine owner and its agent, alleging negligence for unsafe working conditions. A trial court entered summary judgment in favor of the owner and its agent. The employee appealed.

On appeal, the Supreme Court of Alabama stated that in order to prove negligence, the employee had to prove that the company and its agent owed him a duty, breached that duty, and injured him as a result of that breach. Here, the court found that the agreement between the owner and the lessee gave the owner no right to control mining operations. In fact, the agreement specifically stated that the lessee was an independent contractor. The employee argued that the owner and its agent were liable for the negligence of the lessee because a master-servant relationship had been created between them. He claimed that employees of the owner's agent had attended safety meetings and issued safety reports, thereby evidencing a reserved right to control mining operations. The court held that this evidence was insufficient to show that a master-servant relationship existed between the employee and the owner or its agent. It affirmed the trial court's decision in favor of the owner and its agent, holding that the employee failed to present substantial evidence that the owner or its agent owed a duty to the lessee's employee. *Kendrick v. Alabama Power Co.,* 601 So.2d 912 (Ala.1992).

A company hired a janitorial service to clean its manufacturing plant. Subsequently, a janitor who worked for the service was found curled up in the bottom of a degreasing machine. A plant security guard attempted to remove the janitor from the degreaser, but was unsuccessful due to the heavy amount of toxic chemicals that were in the machine. The janitor was eventually removed from the machine, but died four days later without regaining consciousness. His parents then brought a wrongful death action against the company, claiming that it was negligent. The company maintained that Nevada's workers' compensation laws provided the exclusive remedy and that the lawsuit was barred by their provisions. The trial court granted summary judgment to the company, and the parents appealed to the Supreme Court of Nevada.

The supreme court first noted that the company had a duty to warn the janitor of the dangers of the degreaser machine and to insure that the work area was safe. A question of fact existed as to whether the company had breached its duty to the janitor. Further, since the janitor had been employed by the service (which had been hired by the company), a question of fact existed as to whether the janitor was an employee of the company. If not, workers' compensation would not bar the parents' claim. The lower court's decision was reversed. *Sims v. General Telephone & Electronics*, 815 P.2d 151 (Nev.1991).

A female convenience store employee was sexually assaulted by a male customer while working the graveyard shift. She was the sole employee on duty at that time. Although the inside of the store was well-lit, the lighting fixtures outside the store were all inoperable. Store personnel had asked that the fixtures be replaced up to a week before the incident, but no repairs were made. The employee brought a personal injury action against the company. A jury found for the employee. The trial court vacated the jury verdict and found for the company. The employee appealed. The Court of Appeal of Louisiana, First Circuit, stated that although the employee proved that the company did not maintain lighting or provide adequate security, this was not sufficient to hold the company liable for an intentional tort. To escape employer immunity from liability under the Workers' Compensation Act in a claim for intentional tort, the employee had to prove that the injury was inevitable or substantially certain to occur. This she failed to do. Additionally, the doctrine of *respondeat superior*, imposing liability on a principal for the acts of its agent, had no basis here because there was no employer-employee relationship between the store and the assailant. The court of appeal affirmed the trial court judgment in favor of the store. *Knight v. Cracker Barrel Stores Inc.*, 597 So.2d 52 (La.App.1st Cir.1992).

An Alabama employee of a subcontractor was installing plasterboard in a house under construction. In hanging the plasterboard, the employee fell through a temporary staircase constructed by the general contractor. The employee sought compensation for his injuries from the general contractor. The trial court granted summary judgment against the employee. On appeal to the Supreme Court of Alabama, the court affirmed the lower court's decision. The court found that the employee's knowledge and awareness of the dangers surrounding the use of the temporary staircase prevented recovery. Additionally, the employee was found to have appreciated the danger. *Harvell v. Johnson,* 598 So.2d 881 (Ala.1992).

An Ohio manufacturer contracted with an industrial gas company for the purposes of purchasing liquid nitrogen and leasing two liquid nitrogen storage tanks. As part of the contract, the gas company furnished and installed the tanks, and was responsible for their maintenance. A gas company employee was injured while attempting to pump 1,300 gallons of liquid nitrogen into a 550 gallon tank. He subsequently filed suit against the manufacturer in an Ohio trial court alleging breach of duty to provide a safe workplace. The court granted summary judgment to the manufacturer and the gas company employee appealed to the Court of Appeals of Ohio. The issue was whether the manufacturer breached a duty owed to the employee. The court noted that Ohio law requires a landowner to provide a safe place of employment for an independent contractor and its employees for areas in the landowner's control. However, the positioning of the tanks and their storage lines was the responsibility of the gas company. Thus, the court found, as a matter of law, that the manufacturer owed no duty to the employee regarding the safe placement of the tank's pipes. The appellate court affirmed the decision of the trial court and granted summary judgment to the manufacturer. *Zink v. Owens Corning Fiberglass Corp.*, 584 N.E.2d 1303 (Ohio App.6th Dist.1989).

A New Mexico man worked at a dairy. His duties included cleaning cows and milking machines, driving cows to and from the milking area, and attaching machines to the cows. While attaching a milking machine to a cow that had never been milked before, he was kicked in the shoulder and injured. He was off work for several months. Upon his return, while attempting to prevent a cow from doubling back out of the pen area, he stepped in an uncovered drain and injured his foot. He then brought suit against the dairy for negligence. The trial court granted summary judgment to the dairy, and the employee appealed to the Court of Appeals of New Mexico. On appeal, he asserted that the dairy knew that certain cows are known to be restless, and that it should have provided proper equipment for milking such cows. He further contended that inadequate lighting was responsible for his foot injury, asserting that he wouldn't have fallen in the open drain if the lighting had been better. The court of appeals determined that the employee had raised sufficient issues of material fact, and concluded that summary judgment had been improper. The trial court's decision was reversed, and the court remanded the case for trial. *Diaz v. McMahon*, 819 P.2d 1346 (N.M.App.1991).

An Oregon man worked as a truck driver, and delivered logs to sawmills. One mill used a boom to lift logs from delivery trucks and placed them in a river for storage. The driver arrived at the mill with a truckload of logs, but there was another truck on the unloading dock. While he waited, the driver helped the other driver and boom operator prepare the load for removal, as was the customary procedure. While the operator was lifting the logs, the driver was injured. He filed a lawsuit in an Oregon trial court, alleging a violation of the Employer Liability

Law (ELL). The jury found for the driver and the mill appealed to the Oregon Court of Appeals. On appeal, the mill claimed that the driver was contributorily negligent. The driver indicated that drivers customarily help each other prepare their loads. The evidence, however, was silent as to what drivers ordinarily do in these situations. The court noted that the jury could reasonably have concluded it was unsafe to be outside while the boom was lifting logs. The court therefore ruled that the trial court erred in granting the driver's directed verdict motion on the issue of contributory negligence. The court noted that the jury had found the mill liable under the ELL, and awarded damages. The court did not disturb these findings, but remanded the case to the jury on the contributory negligence issue. *Hardt v. Columbia Plywood*, 826 P.2d 85 (Or.App.1992).

A Florida manufacturing employee brought suit against a pesticide manufacturer seeking damages for injuries sustained from exposure to pesticides. The complaint alleged liability based on negligence, strict liability, and breach of implied warranty of merchantability. Each claim based liability on the inadequate labeling of the alleged dangers arising from exposure to the pesticides. The case went to the U.S. Supreme Court which remanded it for further consideration in light of *Cipollone v. Liggett Group, Inc.*, 112 S.Ct. 2608 (1992). In *Cipollone*, the court found that the Federal Cigarette Labeling and Advertising Act contained an express preemption provision which was controlling. Thus, the state claims were preempted. The appellate court noted that the Federal Insecticide, Fungicide, and Rodenticide Act (FIFRA) contained a similar provision: "State[s] shall not impose ... any requirements for labeling or packaging in addition to or different from those required under this subchapter." Thus, FIFRA forbids any inquiry under state law standards to determine the adequacy of labeling. Therefore, the claims were preempted by FIFRA and the court granted summary judgment to the manufacturer. *Papas v. Upjohn*, 985 F.2d 516 (11th Cir.1993).

V. EMPLOYEE TO THIRD PARTY INJURY

Where an employee injures a third party, the exclusivity of remedies component of state workers' compensation laws does not bar recovery in a lawsuit against the employer. However, if the employee was not acting in furtherance of the employer's business, the injured party will not be able to recover from the employer on a theory of vicarious liability or *respondeat superior*.

An engineering director at a Utah laboratory became romantically involved with his secretary. He promoted her, authorized her to record unworked overtime hours and awarded her substantial bonuses and personal gifts. The secretary nonetheless terminated the relationship and began a sexual relationship with another employee. She then filed for divorce and her husband filed a lawsuit in a Utah trial court against the employer and two employees for intentional infliction of emotional and physical injury and for intentionally interfering with his marital contract. The court denied the employees' summary judgment motions, but awarded summary judgment to the employer. The husband appealed to the Supreme Court of Utah, which agreed to hear only the appeal concerning the employer's liability.

The court noted that an employer may be vicariously liable for wrongful actions of its employees if they are committed within the scope of their employment. The acts must occur during work hours, must be of the general kind the employee is required to perform, and be motivated by service to the employer. Here, employees' actions were outside the scope of their employment as neither had been hired to engage in romantic relationships with coworkers. An employee's conduct may be outside the scope of employment even when it takes place on the job, if motivated by personal interest. The husband was also unable to state a claim for negligent supervision because the employer had no duty to determine the marital status of its employees or to monitor workplace romances. Refusing to impose a duty on employers to control employee relationships, the court affirmed the trial court decision. *Jackson v. Righter*, 891 P.2d 1387 (Utah 1995).

Two New Jersey corporations were held by the same ownership. Each hired workers from different unions to utilize labor from another union that they could not otherwise use. One of the corporations loaned an employee to drive a dump truck for the other as its special employee. The driver backed over an employee of the special employer, killing him. The deceased employee's widow filed a personal injury lawsuit against the special employee (driver) and his regular employer in a New Jersey trial court. She also obtained workers' compensation benefits from the husband's former employer. The trial court granted the driver's summary judgment motion and also awarded summary judgment to his employer. The estate appealed to the Supreme Court of New Jersey. The court reiterated the basic rule that workers cannot sue coworkers for negligence in workplace accidents. The workers' compensation act thus prohibited the estate's lawsuit against the coworker. However, employers who lent special employees to other employers did not derivatively obtain immunity from liability through their special employees. The deceased worker had no employment relationship with the special employee's regular employer, and the employer enjoyed no benefit of immunity under the workers' compensation act. This was consistent with general agency principles in which the principal may be liable for an agent's negligent act, even though the agent has personal immunity. The court reversed and remanded the case to the trial court. *Volb v. G.E. Capital Corp.*, 139 N.J. 110, 651 A.2d 1002 (1995).

In 1964, a real estate partnership hired an ex-convict who had been convicted of manslaughter nine years earlier. The employee worked as a porter and lived in the building for over 20 years. During that time, he developed a relationship with a woman in the building and became the godfather of her daughter. The woman then discovered that the employee was sexually molesting her daughter. She sued the real estate partnership and its successor in a New York trial court alleging negligent hiring. The court denied a motion for summary judgment filed by the successor landlords and they appealed to the New York Supreme Court, Appellate

Division, First Department. The appellate division court held that the real estate partnership's hiring of the employee could not be considered the proximate cause of an injury years later. His development of a close relationship with the family was an independent and unforeseeable intervening event that severed any connection between the hiring and the molestation. The family's claim was based on a theory that would violate an important public policy of the state, which was to encourage employment of ex-convicts. The court reversed the trial court's judgment with instructions to grant the motion for summary judgment. *Ford v. Gildin*, 613 N.Y.S.2d 139 (A.D.1st Dept.1994).

A New York tractor-trailer operator was assaulted while making a delivery to a grocery store. The man who assaulted the operator worked as a laborer for the grocery store as well as other surrounding businesses only as needed. The grocery store owner informed the laborers of their duties but did not actively direct them in executing these duties. The grocery store owner considered the laborer to be an independent contractor. The operator filed suit against the grocery store seeking compensation for his injuries. A New York trial court denied the owner's motion for summary judgment and he appealed to the New York Supreme Court, Appellate Division. The operator contended that the laborer was an employee, not an independent contractor, and that the owner was therefore liable for his employee's tortious acts. The appellate division disagreed, ruling that the laborer was an independent contractor. The court noted that employers of independent contractors are generally not liable for injuries caused to a third party. Here, the grocery store owner's minimal supervisory authority over the independent contractor was not sufficient to impose liability on the store. The holding of the trial court was affirmed. *Lazo v. Mak's Trading Co.*, 605 N.Y.S.2d 272 (A.D.1st Dept.1993).

A security guard firm in Illinois hired an applicant as a security guard. The guard later resigned, stating that he had found a better paying job. A year later, the guard reapplied for a job with the firm. His supervisor remembered that he had left the firm in "good standing," and was eligible to be rehired. As a result, the firm neglected to conduct the detailed investigation and background check which would ordinarily be conducted and which was required by Illinois law. Thus, it was never discovered that the guard had several misdemeanor convictions and an arrest warrant outstanding. The guard was sent to work at a gas station, where he completed three shifts. A few days later, he arrived at the gas station and stated that he was not scheduled to work there that day. He asked a cashier to give him a ride to his work assignment if she was going in the same direction. She agreed to give him a ride and they left together in her car. Her body was discovered the next morning, and the guard was convicted of rape and murder. The cashier's estate sued the firm, alleging that it was negligent in hiring the guard and that the negligent hiring was a proximate cause of the kidnap, rape and murder of the cashier. A jury ruled in favor of the estate, and the firm appealed to the Appellate Court of Illinois.

On appeal, the firm did not contest that it was negligent in hiring the guard, but it maintained that the negligent hiring was not a proximate cause of the cashier's injuries and death as a matter of law. The court agreed. There must be a tangible connection between the employee's violent tendencies, the particular job he is hired to do, and the harm to the plaintiff. No such connection was present here. Here, it was not the fact that the guard was a security guard that got him into the cashier's car and proximately caused her injuries and death; it was the fact that she trusted him because she knew him from work where he happened to be employed as a security guard. The court reversed the decision in favor of the estate and held that the firm was not liable. *Carter v. Skokie Valley Detective Agency*, 628 N.E.2d 602 (Ill.App.1st Dist.1993).

After experiencing back pain and bladder problems, a Washington man went to a clinic for examination and treatment. During the exam, the doctor told him that certain tests were necessary because of irregularities in the prostate exam. He was then told that a sperm sample was required and that the normal procedure was for the doctor to manually obtain it. The doctor manually stimulated the patient to ejaculation. Approximately two and a half years later, another patient complained to the director of the clinic about inappropriate sexual behavior by the doctor. The clinic acted immediately and determined that the doctor had engaged in improper sexual conduct with over one hundred patients during a period of two and a half years with the clinic. The patient then filed suit against the clinic. The trial court granted summary judgment in favor of the clinic and the patient appealed to the Court of Appeals of Washington.

In order to hold an employer vicariously liable for the acts of its employees, it must be established that the employee was acting in furtherance of the employer's business and that he was acting within the scope of employment. The patient argued that the doctor's sexual assault happened in conjunction with an authorized examination and therefore, the clinic should be held liable. The court disagreed and determined that the tortious sexual assault should not be attributable to the clinic. The assault emanated from the doctor's personal motives for sexual gratification. There was no evidence that the act was done in furtherance of the clinic's business. Accordingly, the court upheld the trial court's grant of summary judgment to the clinic. *Thompson v. Everett Clinic*, 860 P.2d 1054 (Wash.App.1993).

Twelve women worked as models in a fashion show at the St. Louis Convention Center. At the same time, a company contracted with the city to provide guards at the center. A number of television surveillance cameras were scattered around the center to allow the guards to videotape suspicious activities. The guards were told to practice taping on the VCR. A makeshift curtain dressing area was set up near the stage for the models, but was in a location that could be monitored by one of the cameras. While the models were changing clothes in the dressing area, some guards videotaped them. The tape was later given to a television anchorman, who aired an edited version of it on the news. The models brought suit against the guards' employer for invasion of privacy. They recovered

$1,000 each in actual damages and $35,000 each in punitive damages. The guards' employer appealed to the U.S. Court of Appeals, Eighth Circuit.

The appellate court noted that in this case the employees of the company had been told to practice taping with the VCR. Thus, there had been a jury question as to whether the employer could be held liable for the guards' action in taping the models. Further, there was evidence that guards of a supervisory rank were aware of the taping. Accordingly, even though the taping had been done partly to satisfy the personal interests of the employees, it was possible for the jury to have found that the guards were acting at their employer's direction. The court affirmed the award of compensatory damages, but remanded the case for further review of the punitive damages award. *Doe by Doe v. B.P.S. Guard Services, Inc.*, 945 F.2d 1422 (8th Cir.1991).

A trucking company hired a man as a long-haul driver. The company contacted the man's former employers to verify his work record, and it was given good recommendations. Although the man had prior criminal convictions, he stated that he had none on his application. After his hiring, he was informed that he was expected to sleep in the truck and to stop only for food and vehicle servicing. He was to sleep at rest stops along the highway. After making several trips without incident, the driver exited the highway during a trip, and sexually assaulted a female night clerk at a hotel. She then sued the trucking company, asserting negligent hiring, among other claims. The trial court granted summary judgment to the company, and the night clerk appealed to the Colorado Court of Appeals. On appeal, the clerk argued that the company breached a duty of care to the general public by failing to investigate the driver's nonvehicular criminal record. The court disagreed. Harm of this nature was not reasonably foreseeable from the company's point of view. Normally, drivers have only incidental contact with the public. Further, assuming that such criminal records could be obtained, an employer is entitled to depend to some extent on the criminal justice system's determination that the individual is again ready to become an active member of society. The court affirmed the ruling for the trucking company. *Connes v. Molalla Transport Systems, Inc.,* 817 P.2d 567 (Colo.App.1991).

A Florida furniture company hired a man to deliver furniture without conducting an interview, obtaining employment references, or requiring a job application form to be filled out. The delivery man had previously worked as a laborer on construction projects for a company owned by a managing agent of the furniture company. Unknown to the company, the employee had an extensive criminal record. He also suffered from various psychiatric problems. The employee delivered a couch to a university student who lived alone. Sometime thereafter, he returned to her apartment and savagely attacked her. She then brought suit against the furniture company, asserting, among other claims, that it had been negligent in hiring and retaining the man. A jury awarded her $2.5 million in compensatory and punitive damages, and the company appealed to the District Court of Appeal of Florida.

On appeal, the company argued first that it had no legal duty to investigate the employee's background because the job involved only incidental contact with customers. The court rejected this argument. It found that an employee who delivers furniture cannot be said to have only incidental public contact as a matter of law. The company next argued that it met its duty to evaluate the employee based on its prior experience with him in similar jobs. The court also rejected this argument, noting that the delivery man's prior employment as a laborer where there was extremely limited customer contact was not sufficient to give the company notice of the employee's fitness for the deliveryman job. The question of the employer's negligence in hiring or retaining the employee had properly gone to the jury. Further, the evidence was such that the jury could reasonably have determined that the company's conduct showed a reckless disregard of human life or of safety and, thus, the punitive damages award was also justified. *Tallahassee Furniture Co. v. Harrison*, 583 So.2d 744 (Fla.App.1st Dist.1991).

Four patrons visited a New Jersey amusement park. Because many of the park's attractions were water rides, the patrons placed their property in a coin-operated locker. When they returned one hour later, they found that the locker had been broken into and that their property was missing. Upon inquiry at the courtesy desk about their property, the attendant stated that nothing had been turned in. One of the patrons believed he saw his property behind the desk counter and attempted to retrieve it by going behind the counter. At that point a park attendant stopped him, and a fight broke out. The patrons' property was subsequently recovered from behind the counter, except for money and jewelry which had apparently been stolen. The patrons brought an action against the park for conversion and assault. A federal district court ruled in their favor. The park appealed.

The U.S. Court of Appeals, Second District, stated that under New Jersey law, the question of whether the employees were acting within the scope of their employment when they allegedly assaulted the patrons was a question of fact for the jury. The court stated that the district court's refusal to submit this issue to the jury was error. It further held that the evidence was unclear as to the condition of the lock and the manner in which entry into the locker had been accomplished. This also should have been submitted to the jury. The court vacated the judgment and remanded the case to the district court. *Gray v. Great American Recreation Assn., Inc.*, 970 F.2d 1081 (2d Cir.1992).

A phone company sent an employee to a woman's residence to reestablish her telephone service. The woman alleged that after completing his work, the employee raped her. She brought an action against the company under the theories of *respondeat superior* and negligent hiring and retention of the employee. A trial court granted summary judgment for the phone company. The woman appealed. The Court of Appeals of Georgia stated that the doctrine of *respondeat superior* would apply if the employee was acting within the scope of his employment at the time of the injury. It held that the alleged rape was not employment related and did not further the phone company's business. It was a purely personal act for which the phone company could not be held liable. The evidence showed that the work performed did not require the employee's presence inside the woman's home, and that the employee had completed the job when the rape allegedly occurred. The court found that although the phone company was aware of the employee's absences and work-related injuries, it was not aware of the employee's alcoholism or of any dangerous or violent propensities. There was never any unusual behavior exhibited at work, nor was there any use of alcohol so as to put the company on notice of the possible impairment of judgment by the employee. The company was not aware of any complaints by customers about the employee. Accordingly, the court affirmed the judgment of the trial court. *Mountain v. Southern Bell Tel. & Tel.,* 421 S.E.2d 284 (Ga.App.1992).

CHAPTER THREE

TERMINATION OF EMPLOYMENT

I. AT-WILL EMPLOYMENT

Employment contracts are presumed to be terminable at the will of either the employer or the employee, unless expressly agreed otherwise. The at-will presumption has some exceptions, including an employee discharge that violates an important public policy or forces an employee to choose between employment and personal legal rights.

A South Carolina employer hired a sales representative with oral assurances of job security and a guarantee that he would not be fired without just cause. The parties agreed in writing that the sales representative would receive copies of written reprimands and that three or more reprimands could be considered cause for termination. Several years later, company sales representatives were required to sign a new employment agreement establishing a new commission formula and

123

reciting that the representatives were employees at will. The representative's performance became the subject of two meetings at which he was told to improve his performance or be fired. He received only one written reprimand which was never placed in his personnel file, and was then fired without further warning. He filed a lawsuit against the company in the South Carolina Circuit Court, Horry County, which entered judgment for the sales representatives of over $70,000, including an amount for severance pay. The employer appealed to the Supreme Court of South Carolina.

On appeal, the company argued that the employee could not rely upon his original employment agreement and that it no longer created a binding contract. The supreme court held that the employer could not deviate from its promise to follow its own employment procedures. The employer had breached its employment contract by failing to give the representative three written warnings and failing to place them in his personnel file. The court observed that even if the employer made a valid change in the employment contract, it had modified that contract by providing a first written warning as required by the original contract. The court affirmed judgment for the employee. *King v. PYA/Monarch, Inc.*, 453 S.E.2d 885 (S.C.1995).

A vice president of the manufacturing division of a Massachusetts elevator service company became involved in a corporate power struggle with other officer/shareholders. He owned stock pursuant to a buyback agreement that allowed the company to repurchase stock at the end of his tenure. Before the vice president was forced out of his position, he joined in a shareholder derivative suit concerning the buyback agreement. After being fired, he sued the company in a Massachusetts trial court, claiming that the discharge had been in violation of public policy because it was in retaliation for participating in the derivative action. The court agreed with the employee, and also held that the manufacturer had breached the covenant of good faith and fair dealing implied in at-will employment contracts. Some of the officer/shareholders who had forced the vice president from his position were held in breach of the duty of good faith and loyalty owed to other shareholders. Appeal was made to the Supreme Judicial Court of Massachusetts, Middlesex.

The supreme judicial court reversed the trial court's decision concerning wrongful termination. The buyback program was an internal company matter that did not concern a public policy exception to the general rule of at-will employment. There was no public policy preventing an employer from firing an employee for participating in a shareholder derivative action. The court affirmed the trial court's judgment concerning the good faith and loyalty issues, but reversed the trial court ruling that the other shareholders had interfered with the vice president's contractual relations. The case was remanded for further action. *King v. Driscoll*, 418 Mass. 576, 638 N.E.2d 488 (1994).

Since at least 1947, Goodyear Tire & Rubber Company enforced an anti-nepotism policy precluding any store manager from supervising a family member. One of the company's Texas stores nonetheless hired the brother of an employee, then trained and promoted him to store manager. The company's management was aware of the family relationship, but no attempt was made to enforce the anti-nepotism policy. Approximately 17 years after the brother was employed at his sister's store as her supervisor, the company determined that the arrangement was in violation of the anti-nepotism policy. After offering the sister a transfer, which she refused for personal reasons, the company fired her. She filed a lawsuit against the company in a Texas trial court for wrongful termination. The court found that the company had expressly waived its anti-nepotism policy by not enforcing it and had unlawfully discharged the sister. The Court of Appeals of Texas affirmed, and the company appealed to the Supreme Court of Texas.

The supreme court determined that although Texas law presumes employment to be at will, the at-will doctrine is subject to agreements to the contrary. In this case, the company had fired the employee for the only reason it could not lawfully fire her. It had expressly waived the anti-nepotism policy as it applied to the sister. The court of appeals affirmed the lower court decisions in favor of the sister. *Goodyear Tire & Rubber Company v. Portilla*, 879 S.W.2d 47 (Tex.1994).

A not-for-profit corporation in Tennessee hired an executive director under a contract which provided that either party could terminate the agreement without cause on 60 days' written notice. The board of directors subsequently gave the executive director the required notice and discharged him. He was an at-will employee at the time of his discharge. He sued the corporation and two members of the board of directors for, among other claims, breach of contract and procurement of breach of contract. The trial court awarded him compensatory damages against the corporation and compensatory and punitive damages against the two board members. The court of appeals sustained only the compensatory damage awards against the board members. They appealed to the Supreme Court of Tennessee. The supreme court noted that the only way the executive director could prevail was to show that the two board members intentionally interfered with his employment by the corporation and that they were not acting in furtherance of the corporation's interest when they did so. The executive director had shown that the board members had interfered with his employment by making statements about his performance at board meetings. However, he had been unable to show that they were acting for any purpose other than their perceived best interest for the corporation. Accordingly, the judgments against the board members were reversed and the suit was dismissed. *Forrester v. Stockstill*, 869 S.W.2d 328 (Tenn.1994).

A Missouri woman worked as a bank employee for 18 years. She was fired because of consistent problems with the teller section which was under her supervision. These problems included excessive cash shortages, poor teller training, and complaints about customer service. She filed a claim against her former supervisors for tortious interference with contract or business expectancy. A trial court found in her favor, and the bank appealed. The Missouri Court of Appeals stated that there was nothing unjustified about removing or terminating a supervisory employee whose department was not performing acceptably or satisfactorily. The court stated that the bank supervisory personnel had the authority to recommend the woman's termination, and they had ample justification to do so. The woman was an employee at will, and to support a cause of action for intentional interference with a contract by a supervising employee over an at-will employee requires evidence eliminating any business justification at all for the termination. The court found that the evidence presented did not meet that requirement. There was no evidence that the termination was for other than legitimate business reasons. The court reversed the judgment of the trial court and upheld the discharge of the employee. *Eggleston v. Phillips,* 838 S.W.2d 80 (Mo.App.1992).

A New York employee was terminated from employment and brought suit against the employer for wrongful discharge. The Supreme Court dismissed the complaint. On appeal, the Supreme Court, Appellate Division, affirmed the dismissal. The court held that absent an express agreement limiting an employer's right to terminate at-will employees, the employer's right would not be limited by either oral assurances or the employee manual. The court also noted that even though the employer "was subject to state and local regulation and funding it did not reach the level of state action" to invoke due process protections. *Paolucci v. Adult Retardants Center, Inc.,* 582 N.Y.S.2d 452 (A.D.2d Dept.1992).

An Illinois department store manager informed her district manager that she was in the process of obtaining a divorce, and asked him about the possibility of moving to Tupelo, Mississippi, to be near her adult daughter. She later requested of the district manager, and of the store manager in Tupelo, that a letter be prepared for the judge presiding over her divorce as to her ability to retain her health insurance. Both managers wrote letters which guaranteed the employee 30 hours per week. She moved to Tupelo three months later, but did not contact the store manager to inform him of her anticipated moving date. When she suddenly presented herself at the store for employment, there were no job openings. She was not hired. She sued for breach of contract, but a federal district court granted summary judgment to the employer.

On appeal to the U.S. Court of Appeals, Fifth Circuit, the court noted that despite the letters written by the two managers, the employment was only at will. The letters did not modify her at-will status because they did not specify a "definite length of term of employment." A guarantee of 30 hours per week does not establish a definite term of employment. Nor did the employee handbook modify the at-will nature of the employment. It contained no promises of tenure. Finally, the court determined that the employee's estoppel argument (that she had detrimentally changed her position in reliance on the letters) did not stand up because the employee's decision to leave Illinois was motivated by her divorce, not by the promise of a job in Tupelo. Accordingly, the court affirmed the lower court's decision in favor of the employer. *Solomon v. Walgreen Co.,* 975 F.2d 1086 (5th Cir.1992).

An Ohio man worked for a restaurant without a written contract for twelve years. During the employment relationship, he advanced in the company and eventually became part of the administrative staff. On at least two occasions, the employee prepared to leave his job to begin a business of his own, but was asked to remain. Subsequently, the restaurant advised him that his employment was being terminated. The employee brought suit alleging breach of contract, misrepresentation, and infliction of emotional distress. The trial court granted the employer's motion for summary judgment and the employee appealed to the Ohio Court of Appeals. On appeal, the court noted that Ohio adheres to the employment-at-will doctrine, which states that employment agreements with no term of duration are terminable at the will of either party for any reason not contrary to law. In this case, there was no evidence that the employer was ever dissatisfied with the employee's work performance. In fact, only two weeks before being fired, the employee was told that his services would be continually retained. The employee had then detrimentally relied on the employer's promises, an exception to the at-will doctrine. The court stated that such evidence could not be resolved in a summary judgment motion. It remanded the case for a trial on the merits. *Ganim v. Brown Derby, Inc.*, 585 N.E.2d 982 (Ohio App.8th Dist.1990).

A man worked as a store manager under an employment-at-will contract. When the man was fired, he brought suit against his supervisor and the store owner for unlawful termination and breach of an employment contract, among other claims. He argued that his supervisor altered inventory records and then used them as an excuse for his discharge. A district court dismissed his claims. The man appealed. The Court of Appeals of North Carolina noted that a claim for wrongful discharge of an at-will employee may exist if the contract is terminated for an unlawful reason or a purpose that contravenes public policy. However, it then noted that the state had not yet recognized a public policy exception to the employment-at-will doctrine for bad faith discharge of an employee. Even though the evidence supported a showing of bad faith on the supervisor's part for altering records, which was not to be condoned, the court stated that there existed no bad faith exception under state law to provide relief to the employee. It held that such behavior does not rise to the level of a public policy concern. Therefore, it affirmed the decision of the trial court. *Tompkins v. Allen,* 421 S.E.2d 176 (N.C.App.1992).

After a New York woman had been employed by an insurance company for several years, she applied for a position with another insurer as a claims examiner. During an interview with the supervisor, she was informed that certain training courses would be given and that tests would be administered on the training materials. The applicant advised the supervisor that she did not test well and would not be interested in the job if passing the test was a requirement. The supervisor allegedly told her there was no need to worry about the tests because they were not important. She then left her former job and began training. Subsequently, she failed three tests and was discharged. She then commenced this action in a New York trial court averring fraudulent representation for the purpose of inducing her to terminate her previous employment. After the trial court denied summary judgment, the insurance company appealed to the Supreme Court, Appellate Division.

The insurance company asserted that the complaint should be dismissed because the applicant was an at-will employee. The applicant, however, argued that she was not suing based on breach of an employment contract but on a tort claim: that the insurance company's agent fraudulently misrepresented the facts to induce her into entering into employment. The applicant asserted that she would not have left her former position if the supervisor had told her the truth about the job requirements. The court noted that if she prevailed, she could recover for the loss of benefits and salary connected with her former employment. Since the allegations sufficiently asserted tortious conduct on the part of the insurer, the court concluded that the insurance company's motion for summary judgment was appropriately denied. *Navaretta v. Group Health Inc.*, 595 N.Y.S.2d 839 (A.D.3d Dept.1993).

II. EMPLOYEE HANDBOOKS

Employee handbooks and manuals are usually only a guide for both employer and employee. Yet, these documents can modify at-will employment if they do not clearly state that they are nothing more than a guide.

A New Mexico bank fired a branch manager, stating that she had repeatedly failed to timely submit employee performance reviews and failed to improve her work performance. The former branch manager denied these charges, and stated that the bank's action had been motivated by its desire to reduce overhead costs by discharging her under the pretext of bad performance. She filed a lawsuit against the bank in a New Mexico trial court, claiming that the bank's employee handbook contained a progressive disciplinary procedure which created an employment contract. She asserted that the bank had breached the contract by firing her without following handbook procedures. The court granted summary judgment to the bank, and the former manager appealed to the Court of Appeals of New Mexico. The court of appeals noted that factual issues existed concerning whether the handbook created an expectation of an implied contract that might limit the bank's right to terminate the employee. Factual issues also abounded concerning the motivation for the discharge. However, the trial court had correctly granted summary judgment to the bank concerning whether additional written memoranda concerning disciplinary action created contractual rights for the former manager. The court reversed and remanded the trial court's summary judgment concerning the handbook claims. *Kiedrowski v. Citizens Bank*, 893 P.2d 468 (N.M.App.1995), *rev. den.*, 890 P.2d 1321 (N.M.1995).

A South Carolina manufacturing company issued an employee handbook containing seniority provisions with a procedure for reductions in employment within job classifications on the basis of seniority. When the company purchased new equipment that made some job classifications obsolete, employees occupying those jobs were placed in lower-skilled jobs and forced to take a pay cut. The company followed the seniority provisions in doing so. Nevertheless, the employees filed a lawsuit in a South Carolina trial court, claiming that language in the employee handbook prohibited the employer from taking this action. The court granted summary judgment to the employer, and the employees appealed to the Court of Appeals of South Carolina.

On appeal, the employees argued that the following language vested them with contractual rights and privileges: "if something beyond the control of the company occurs and it becomes necessary to reduce the number of persons within a job classification, the movement backward will be made in the reverse order of the movement forward." The employees argued that replacing their jobs with machinery was within the control of the company and that demotion could only occur when something beyond the control of the company occurred. The court of appeals refused to allow the seniority clause to bind the company in the manner claimed by the employees. The employee handbook simply described the employer's commitment to the seniority system when something beyond the control of the company occurred and it became necessary to reduce the number of persons within a job classification. It did not state that the only time the company could demote employees was when something beyond its control happened. In this case, the employer had followed the procedures outlined in the handbook. The trial court had properly granted summary judgment to the employer. *Holden v. Alice Mfg., Inc.*, 452 S.E.2d 628 (S.C.App.1994).

An Ohio accounting firm hired an employee under an agreement that she would have to work overtime during the tax season. She verbally agreed to work overtime so long as she was compensated, but upon hire, she was issued a personnel manual that limited "comp time" to extra half or full days worked on Saturdays. Extra hours worked during the week were not considered comp time under the manual. When asked to perform more work, the employee requested compensation for overtime according to the pre-hire agreement. The employee was told to resign. She alleged that she suffered severe emotional distress as a result of her employment termination. She also claimed that her former employer failed to reimburse her for medical expenses as set forth in the personnel manual. An Ohio trial court granted summary judgment to the employer, and the employee appealed to the Court of Appeals of Ohio. The court found no support for the employee's argument that the personnel manual created an employment contract. On the contrary, the employment-at-will relationship presumed by Ohio law was applicable in this situation, and the employer could lawfully discharge her. There was no merit to the employee's argument that she had relied upon statements by the partners that her employment situation was not at will. The trial court had improperly granted summary judgment concerning the denial of reimbursement of medical expenses. However, the appellate court otherwise affirmed its judgment. *Juergens v. Strang, Klubnik and Assoc., Inc.*, 96 Ohio App.3d 223, 644 N.E.2d 1066 (1994).

A manager employed by a national restaurant chain was in charge of hiring, firing, training and managing employees at an Illinois restaurant. The manager hired a disabled individual to work at the front counter, and was contacted within four days by his supervisor to remove the individual because of her appearance. The manager refused to take action, and was fired for insubordination. He filed an employment discrimination complaint with the Equal Employment Opportunity Commission (EEOC), which issued a right to sue letter. The manager then filed a lawsuit against his former employer in the U.S. District Court for the Northern District of Illinois, claiming violations of the Americans with Disabilities Act (ADA), and state law claims including breach of contract, retaliatory discharge and intentional infliction of emotional distress. The company filed a motion to dismiss the contract-based claims, and the court considered the motion.

The employee alleged that he reasonably believed the company's handbook required him to refrain from discriminating against disabled individuals because of the following statement: "Your discriminatory treatment of others will result in disciplinary action up to and including losing your job." The court agreed that this statement created legal consideration for a promise and did not merely restate the employer's preexisting legal duty to refrain from discrimination. However, the employment handbook also contained a disclaimer advising employees that employment could be terminated at will by either party. It expressly disclaimed that the handbook created an employment contract. Because the handbook did not modify the at-will status of the employment relationship, the court granted the company's motion to dismiss the contract-based claims. *Talanda v. KFC Natl. Mgmt. Co.*, 863 F.Supp. 664 (N.D.Ill.1994).

A New Jersey maintenance mechanic worked for a large manufacturing company which had distributed an employment manual containing a four-step disciplinary policy. The company found some of its property in the mechanic's locker and discharged him for theft, one of several grounds listed for immediate dismissal. The mechanic filed a lawsuit against the employer in a New Jersey trial court, claiming that the employer violated the disciplinary procedure in the employment manual. The court granted the employer's summary judgment motion, finding that the manual did not create an implied employment contract. The New Jersey Superior Court, Appellate Division, reversed the trial court's decision and the employer appealed to the Supreme Court of New Jersey.

The supreme court stated that an employment manual which fails to include a clear and prominent disclaimer may create an enforceable contract even when the employment is otherwise terminable at will. If the manual is sufficiently definite to raise the reasonable expectations of employees concerning job security provisions, the provisions may be construed as contractual promises. The case was reversed and remanded to the trial court to decide whether the manual created a reasonable expectation of job security that formed an implied employment contract. The jury was then to determine whether the mechanic was guilty of stealing or unauthorized possession of company property. *Witkowski v. Thomas J. Lipton*, Inc., 136 N.J. 385, 643 A.2d 546 (N.J.1994).

In a companion case, the New Jersey supreme court affirmed lower court decisions in favor of an employee fired under similar circumstances. The employee was a supervisor with over 18 years of service for a food distributor. The company found that he had permitted the stealing of merchandise from his area and, after firing him also determined that he had converted merchandise to his own use. The employer published a 160-page manual containing eleven pages of disciplinary procedures which it had circulated to about 300 of its 3,000 employees. The disciplinary procedures called for three steps, including counseling and written warnings prior to discharge for cause. Theft of company property was grounds for immediate discharge. However, the supreme court determined that the eleven-page discharge procedure section must be construed in light of the entire 160-page document, which failed to conspicuously disclaim that the manual formed a contract. Employers seeking to avoid a finding that a manual created a contract were required to display a disclaimer in a very prominent position using layman's terms. The trial court had properly held that an employment contract existed and appropriately refused to consider evidence acquired after the termination action. *Nicosia v. Wakefern Food Corp.*, 136 N.J. 401, 643 A.2d 554 (N.J.1994).

A security contractor assigned an employee to work at a Wyoming oil refinery. The contractor required the employee to follow its chain of command instructions in dealing with work problems. When the employee repeatedly violated the chain of command instructions, the contractor terminated her employment. She then sued the contractor in a Wyoming district court for breach of employment contract, alleging that the contractor had failed to follow its own disciplinary procedures as outlined in an employee handbook. The court granted the contractor's summary judgment motion, and the employee appealed to the Supreme Court of Wyoming. On appeal, the employee argued that the contractor had breached an employment contract that had been created by the disciplinary procedure contained in the employee handbook. The employer argued that a disclaimer contained on the first page of the handbook preserved the employment at will relationship. The court stated that employment at will is presumed under Wyoming law. This presumption may be overcome when systematic disciplinary procedures or other language of an employee handbook unambiguously create an employment contract. However, a disclaimer may prevent the modification of at will status if it is conspicuous and unambiguous. In this case, the employer's handbook conspicuously placed (on the first page) a disclaimer containing the following language: "the company retains the absolute right to terminate any employee, at any time, with or without good cause." The disclaimer appeared in bold type and capital letters. Because the employee was sufficiently notified not to rely on any terms of the handbook, she remained an at-will employee and the handbook did not create an employment contract. The summary judgment ruling for the employer was affirmed. *Lincoln v. Wackenhut Corp.*, 867 P.2d 701 (Wyo.1994).

A Utah metallurgical engineer worked for over 15 years for a mining company in several different positions. He generally received favorable evaluations, but eventually got a substandard rating and was told that he had one last chance to redeem himself. The mining company then terminated the engineer's employment for inadequate performance without providing progressive discipline, notice, hearing or other protections. The engineer claimed that the company policy in effect at the time of his hiring was applicable and required a written warning and a suspension or hearing for disciplinary purposes. He claimed that the policy constituted a contract of employment that replaced the presumption of at-will employment. He sued the mining company in a Utah trial court, which held for the company. The engineer appealed to the Court of Appeals of Utah.

The court of appeals observed that employment in Utah is presumed to be at-will and that overcoming this presumption requires showing a definite communication by the employer to the employee that a contract exists under different terms. The company policy referred to by the engineer had been replaced with a policy that did not call for progressive discipline or other protections. The most recent employee policy was applicable, not the original one. The current employee handbook language called for hearings for disciplinary offenses, but not in cases of insufficient performance, which was the cause of termination in this case. The court of appeals affirmed the trial court decision for the employer. *Sorenson v. Kennecott-Utah Copper Corp.*, 873 P.2d 1141 (Utah App.1994).

An Iowa grocery store's management received reports that the night stock crew was eating food without paying for it. The management then hired a private investigator who interviewed the employees on the night crew. During an interview, the leader of the night crew wrote out a statement indicating that during his employment he had eaten about $20 worth of food and would be willing to pay for it. He was fired despite his willingness to pay for the food. The night crew leader then filed a breach of employment contract claim in an Iowa trial court. The trial court granted summary judgment to the grocery store, and the employee appealed to the Supreme Court of Iowa.

The employee claimed that the employment handbook created an express contract of employment. The grocery store argued that the employee was an at-will employee and was subject to discharge at any time for any reason, or for no reason at all. The court noted that the question was whether the terms of the employee handbook were sufficiently definite to constitute an offer of continued employment. Throughout the handbook, the employer had placed clauses that retained its right to terminate the employment relationship at any time. Further, the night crew leader had signed a receipt for a copy of the handbook which stated: "I recognize that either [the store] or I may terminate the employment relationship at any time for any reason." Thus, the court reasoned that the employment handbook did not create a contract of employment and it upheld the grant of summary judgment for the grocery store. *French v. Foods, Inc.*, 495 N.W.2d 768 (Iowa 1993).

A South Carolina man was employed by a telephone company for 16 years. He had received a copy of the company booklet entitled "Your Special Duties" which was incorporated by reference into the employee handbook. The booklet provided for a multistep disciplinary process. After he admitted that he received a gift from a vendor in violation of company policy, he was fired. The policy stated that an employee may not accept gifts that may appear to influence a company decision. The employee then brought a breach of contract action in a South Carolina trial court asserting wrongful discharge and violation of the disciplinary proceedings set forth in the employee handbook. The jury returned a verdict for the employee and the telephone company appealed to the Court of Appeals of South Carolina.

The telephone company contended that no employment contract was established because the handbook and booklet did not alter the at-will employment relationship. However, the court found sufficient evidence to support the jury's finding that the book altered the otherwise at-will employment relationship. Thus, the company's promulgation of policies detailing the mechanics of discharging employees prevented it from discharging such employees without compliance with the stated policies. The company next alleged that there was no evidence of a breach of contract. The court noted that after the employee was discharged, the company changed its policies to require a total ban on vendors giving gifts under any circumstance. This was relevant to the issue of ambiguity concerning the conflict of interest provision, and therefore was admissible. Accordingly, the appellate court upheld the decision of the trial court and ruled for the employee. *Kumpf v. United Telephone Company,* 429 S.E.2d 869 (S.C.App.1993).

A Michigan "wage roll" employee was discharged from his job for sleeping during working hours in violation of company rules. He filed suit against the company for wrongful discharge, contending that a "just cause" employment contract existed between them. He stated that the company had represented to him that he could not be fired without just cause, and that the company maintained a progressive discipline policy which was not followed. The company argued that no just cause employment contract existed, and, if there was one, the employee's admission of sleeping on the job constituted just cause for termination. Upon the company's motion for summary judgment, the district court found that questions existed as to an implied "for cause" termination policy and it denied the motion. The company filed a motion for reconsideration.

The U.S. District Court for the Eastern District of Michigan ruled in favor of the company. The court noted that state law presumed employment relationships to be at will, and that the employee's admission of violating a rule specifically articulated in the policy manual justified his discharge. The company's representations to the employee that he could be discharged only for a good reason constituted a policy rather than establishing that policy as a contract. Notwithstanding that the employee's discharge notice read, "willfully sleeping during working hours," and that the employee questioned the interpretation of "willful," the court found that the company expressly reserved the right to discharge the employee for "sleeping during working hours," as written in its policy statement. *Bolen v. E.I. Dupont Nemours & Co.,* 793 F.Supp. 140 (E.D.Mich.1991).

A man began his employment with a parcel service company as a package car driver. He was later promoted to a managerial position. The company had a written antifraternization policy that discouraged fraternization between supervisors or managers and employees. After the man began a relationship with a female employee, he was confronted by company officials and asked to resign or be terminated for violation of the antifraternization rule. He refused to resign and was subsequently fired. He brought several claims against the company, among which were breach of contract, violation of public policy, tortious invasion of privacy and intentional infliction of mental and emotional distress. The company brought a motion for summary judgment.

The U.S. District Court for the Southern District of Mississippi held that the policy book distributed to managerial employees did not create an express or implied contract of employment because of its aspirational language and lack of specific employee directives. It held that the man's employment was one of "at will." That is, the employer could terminate an employee hired for an indefinite term for any or no reason. It found that the state recognized no public policy exception to the at-will termination rule. The court found that the company had not been shown to have acted in bad faith or to have recklessly pried into the man's privacy, and that its actions were not so extreme, outrageous or repulsive as to establish a claim for intentional infliction of mental and emotional distress. Because the man knew of the policy and its possible repercussions before beginning his prohibited relationship, the court granted summary judgment in favor of the company. *Watkins v. United Parcel Service, Inc.,* 797 F.Supp. 1349 (S.D.Miss.1992).

A mine worker in Wyoming signed an application which stated that the employment was at will and terminable by either party. He then received an employee handbook containing guides for the employer's policies and procedures, with a disclaimer stating that the handbook was not intended to be an employment contract. When the mine worker was subsequently discharged, he brought a lawsuit against the employer for breach of contract based on the employee handbook. The trial court granted summary judgment to the employer, and the mine worker appealed to the Supreme Court of Wyoming. The mine worker argued on appeal that the handbook created an employment contract with respect to the employer's policies, and that the employer had breached that contract. The supreme court held that an issue of fact existed as to whether that was the case. It was unclear whether the employer intended to modify the at-will employment. Further, the disclaimer in the handbook was not sufficiently set off from the rest of the material contained therein. Accordingly, the grant of summary judgment was reversed. *McDonald v. Mobil Coal Producing, Inc.,* 820 P.2d 986 (Wyo.1991).

A Washington woman was employed by a railroad for 18 years. She held a number of administrative clerical positions. In 1986, in anticipation of taking a medical leave of absence, she requested a copy of the policy manual. The medical leave policy called for the reinstatement of employees upon submission of a physician's statement if there was available work for which the employee was qualified. The employee submitted an application for medical leave which contained the same policy statement. She fulfilled all requirements as stated in the medical leave claim form and was granted the medical leave. While the employee was on medical leave, the railroad eliminated her position. She then sued the railroad in a Washington trial court alleging breach of contract. The jury found for the employee and awarded her $170,000 for past and future damages. The company appealed to the Court of Appeals of Washington. The court noted that the question of whether the employee handbook provisions were part of the contract was a question of fact to be decided by the jury. Here, there were at least two separate written policies with respect to reinstatement of an employee after medical leave. There was ample evidence to support a finding that the employer had a contractual obligation to reinstate the employee. Therefore, the appellate court affirmed the decision of the trial court. *Kohn v. Georgia Pacific Corporation*, 850 P.2d 517 (Wash.App.1993).

A New York woman worked for a bank as a security analyst for 13 years. During her employment, she had been provided with two employee handbooks. Both handbooks stated that since there was no contractual arrangement between the bank and its employees, an employee could resign her position at any time for any reason. Similarly, an employee could be terminated at any time for reasons determined solely by the bank's management. Subsequently, the bank underwent restructuring, and an investment firm was formed to manage securities portfolios for institutional clients. The analyst left the bank to join this newly formed corporation but was fired for an antagonistic attitude, substandard research, and lack of contribution. The employee appealed to the Appellate Division of the Supreme Court of New York. On appeal, the court noted that it was well settled that absent an agreement establishing a fixed duration, an employment relationship was presumed to be terminable at any time, by either party. The employment policies established for the newly created investment firm were the same as the parent bank, and were known by the employee. The court accordingly dismissed the claims. *Feeney v. Marine Midland Banks, Inc.*, 579 N.Y.S.2d 670 (A.D.1st Dept.1992).

A Utah man worked as a process inspector for a corporation for nine years, but never entered into an express contract with the employer regarding its ability to terminate his employment. He was given an employee handbook which noted the corporation's procedures for certain actions, but the handbook contained conspicuous language stating that its provisions were not intended to be an employment contract. In the employee's ninth year with the corporation, he verified that he had completed an inspection at which he had in fact only glanced. When a space shuttle rocket motor was subsequently damaged because certain hoses had been improperly installed, the employee was fired. He then sued the corporation, claiming breach of an implied-in-fact contract provision. The trial court granted summary judgment to the employer, and the employee appealed to the Supreme Court of Utah. The court first stated that an employee manual can be an implied-in-fact contract if it is sufficiently definite to show that the employer is making an offer of employment which is other than employment at will. In this case, the handbook contained clear language which disclaimed any contractual liability and the employee did not show that the employer intended to modify the at-will relationship. Accordingly, no implied contract existed and the trial court had been correct in granting summary judgment to the employer. *Johnson v. Morton Thiokol, Inc.*, 818 P.2d 997 (Utah 1991).

A Texas man worked for a grocery company for 36 years. Shortly after being hired, he was given an employee handbook which described termination procedures. However, the employee signed an agreement which stated that the handbook did not constitute an employment contract. After the employee was discharged, he filed a breach of contract lawsuit in a U.S. district court. The district court awarded damages, finding that the handbook created a written contract for lifetime employment. The company appealed. On appeal to the U.S. Court of Appeals, Fifth Circuit, the company asserted that the employee had been an at-will employee. The court stated that Texas traditionally held employment contracts to be terminable at will by either party, absent a specific contract term to the contrary. In this case, the procedures in the employee handbook had not been expressly agreed to by both parties. The handbook had been intended more as a guideline for the employer to follow. The court then looked at the oral agreement to provide lifetime employment. It found that, under Texas law, an oral promise of lifetime employment is barred by the statute of frauds and had to be in writing to be enforceable. The court thus reversed the district court's decision and held that no breach of contract had occurred.*Zimmerman v. H.E. Butt Grocery Co.*, 932 F.2d 469 (5th Cir.1991).

A Mississippi nurse received a manual from her employer outlining its policies, procedures and purposes, including guidelines for employee conduct and procedures for administering corrective disciplinary action. The manual stated that employee dismissal would be viewed as a last resort. Following an exchange with her supervisor over a problem in serving lunch, the employee was dismissed for insubordination. She brought an action against the employer for wrongful termination, claiming that the employer completely disregarded its disciplinary procedures contained in the manual by discharging her. The employer argued that the employment contract was terminable at will. A trial court agreed and granted summary judgment in favor of the employer. The employee appealed. On appeal, the Supreme Court of Mississippi held that where an employer distributes manuals to all its employees stating its rules of employment and setting forth specific procedures for employee disciplinary action, the manual becomes a binding part of the contract. The court found that the manual contained no express disclaimer or provision stating that it did not affect the employer's right to terminate the employee at will. The employer was obligated to follow its own provisions for disciplining the employee. *Bobbitt v. The Orchard, Ltd.,* 603 So.2d 356 (Miss.1992).

A group of dental claim approvers at an insurance company worked as at-will employees for the company. They were sent to an out-of-state office to help with some work there, and were given money for travel expenses. However, the company's policy was not clearly explained to them. When they returned to their home office, a dispute arose as to the money they had spent while traveling. The company fired them for "gross insubordination." They sued the company, claiming that the employee handbook created an employment contract. The court entered judgment in their favor, and the court of appeals affirmed. The employer appealed to the Supreme Court of Minnesota. On appeal, the supreme court noted that the employer handbook created a binding unilateral contract by providing a definite offer on job security and dismissal policy. The handbook clearly stated that no employee would be dismissed without previous warning and a probationary period unless the dismissal was for serious misconduct. Here, the employer had breached its contractual obligations as created by the handbook, and could be liable for breach of contract. The court affirmed this part of the decision in favor of the employees. *Lewis v. Equitable Life Assurance Society,* 389 N.W.2d 876 (Minn.1986).

An Ohio man worked as a salaried employee for a company in the area of quality control. Although he initially received satisfactory annual reviews, his performance was later rated as "below acceptable." Subsequently, he received a written warning from his supervisor, reprimanding him for taking unscheduled vacation time without prior approval. Shortly thereafter, he was fired. He sued the company for wrongful discharge, claiming that an employment policy manual altered his at-will employment and that the company had not followed its promised procedures when it fired him. A state trial court granted summary judgment to the company, and the employee appealed to the Court of Appeals of Ohio. On appeal, the court noted that the possible penalties listed in the manual were not intended to be a sequence ranging from reprimand through suspension to termination. Rather, the company maintained discretion as to which penalty would be used in which situation. Accordingly, the policy manual did not alter the at-will employment relationship between the parties. The court next determined that the employee could not succeed on his argument that the policy manual created an implied contract. The company and the employee never manifested mutual assent to the terms of the manual as a condition of their employment agreement. The court affirmed the trial court's decision for the company. *Gargasz v. Nordson Corp.,* 587 N.E.2d 475 (Ohio App.9th Dist.1991).

A Kansas man was hired as a security guard by a nursing home and was given the nursing home's personnel policies manual which addressed disciplinary procedures and employee benefits. He signed a receipt for the manual and agreed to abide by its provisions. Five months later, the employment manual was revised to clarify that the nursing home was an at-will employer and that employees could be terminated by it without cause. However, the addition of the at-will clause did not change the stated policy of the nursing home that it would not discharge an employee except for cause. The security guard suffered a hernia during the course of his employment at the nursing home. He filed for workers' compensation benefits, and was placed on a leave of absence. When he attempted to return to work, he discovered that his job had been filled by a part-time security guard. He apparently was supposed to take over a part-time position at the nursing home, but he did not report for work on either day that he was scheduled. He was then fired by the nursing home.

He filed suit against the nursing home for breach of contract, among other claims, and a jury ruled in his favor. Appeal was taken to the Supreme Court of Kansas. That court had to determine whether the nursing home's stated policy of prohibiting discharges without cause served to create an implied contract between the nursing home and the security guard. Although the evidence supporting the existence of an implied contract was not overwhelming, the court determined that the employer's philosophy of treating employees fairly was enough to support the jury's verdict in favor of the employee. The court thus affirmed the jury's verdict and determined that the employer had breached an implied contract with its employee. *Brown v. United Methodist Homes*, 815 P.2d 72 (Kan.1991).

III. BREACH OF CONTRACT

Breach of contract complaints arise under both oral and written employment contracts, typically where the employee claims that an oral promise or language contained in an employee handbook has modified the presumption of employment at will. Resolution of these cases involves the examination of the agreement of the parties.

A. Written Contracts

A Missouri employee resigned from his job of 30 years under a written agreement calling for a retirement benefit package and an assurance that the former employee was "welcome to approach" the company as a vendor or buyer in the future. The agreement also provided monetary benefits in exchange for dismissal of age discrimination and retaliation claims. The former employee then negotiated a $1.7 million sale involving his former employer. After the former employee arranged the details of the sale, the former employer canceled it, and he filed a lawsuit against it in a Missouri trial court for breach of the resignation agreement and other claims. The court granted the former employer's summary judgment motion and the employee appealed to the Missouri Court of Appeals, Western District.

The court held that the settlement agreement foreclosed the former employee's claim for an additional $330 per month in further retirement benefits. The trial court had correctly granted summary judgment on that claim, and on the former employee's claim for tortious interference with a business expectancy. However, the trial court had improperly granted summary judgment on the former employee's claim for breach of contract and fraud because of evidence in the record that the sale had been rejected in violation of the negotiated agreement. The "welcome to approach" language was not insufficiently vague and uncertain to be unenforceable and the former employee should have received an opportunity to show whether the former employer had breached its contract and defrauded him in the process of negotiating the agreement. *Maupin v. Hallmark Cards, Inc.*, 894 S.W.2d 688 (Mo.App.W.D.1995).

Two account executives abruptly resigned from a stock brokerage firm to work for a competitor and solicited business from former customers. The firm brought federal district court actions in Illinois and Kentucky to enjoin the former account executives from further use of its records pending arbitration. The account executives filed a lawsuit in a New York trial court for an order compelling the firm to submit to expedited arbitration under New York law. The court ordered the parties to proceed to expedited arbitration, even though their employment contracts contained arbitration clauses employing New York Stock Exchange rules. These rules required arbitration but did not call for expedited proceedings. The New York Supreme Court, Appellate Division, affirmed the trial court order and the brokerage firm appealed to the Court of Appeals of New York. The court determined that the arbitration of employment disputes in the securities industry was governed by the Federal Arbitration Act and not by New York law. The order for expedited arbitration was improper because the arbitration agreement of the parties did not require expedited proceedings. The Federal Arbitration Act encouraged private agreements to arbitrate and did not require expedited arbitration absent an agreement of the parties. Accordingly, the trial court order was vacated and the parties were directed to submit arbitration claims to a panel of New York Stock Exchange Arbitrators in accordance with exchange rules. *Salvano v. Merrill Lynch, Pierce, Fenner & Smith, Inc.*, 85 N.Y.2d 173, 623 N.Y.S.2d 790, 647 N.E.2d 1298 (1995).

A Pennsylvania man received a letter from a company offering him employment as a plant manager and stating his salary, his job duties, and the benefits to which he would be entitled. The letter stated that each year he would be participating in the benefits program on a full-year basis. However, the position became unavailable when the company closed the plant and the company then offered the manager a different position in another letter. This letter provided that his participation in any future profit sharing would remain the same as in the earlier letter. The manager accepted the offer by signing and returning the letter. He began working, but was discharged five months later. He then brought this action in an Illinois trial court alleging breach of employment contract. The trial court dismissed the complaint and the manager appealed to the Appellate Court of Illinois. The manager alleged that the second letter incorporated the first letter by reference and that these two documents constituted an employment contract for a term of one year. The company contended that the employment relationship was terminable at will and could not give rise to a cause of action for breach of contract. The court agreed with the manager that the second letter incorporated by reference the first letter. However, the mere fact that the manager's profit sharing was to be calculated yearly did not indicate an intention to establish an employment term of one year. Thus, the presumption of an at-will employment relationship existed and the court affirmed the trial court's dismissal of the suit. *Jago v. Miller Fluid Power Corp.*, 615 N.E.2d 80 (Ill.App.1993).

A Nebraska employee agreed to leave his employment as an accountant and tax specialist to accept employment by a major corporation as a vice president. He was given a written contract which contained two separate policies governing termination. The first allowed the employee to be terminated "for cause" consisting of "gross negligence or willful misconduct" without further compensation. The second provision addressed termination "without cause," allowing the employee to receive compensation to the date of termination if he breached. On the other hand, his regular compensation would be paid until the expiration of the five-year employment term if the employer breached. After two years of employment, the employee was discharged. He sued the company for breach of contract to recover the salary compensation for termination without cause as outlined in the contract. A Nebraska district court found for the employee.

The Supreme Court of Nebraska affirmed the judgment for the employee even though he had found employment after his dismissal. The court found that the compensation clause constituted an enforceable agreement. The unambiguous stipulation of damages provision in the contract would not be reduced by the employee's post-termination employment because the contract did not state or suggest such a reduction. The court further upheld the clause as reasonable and enforceable because during the formation of the contract, the employer and employee were attempting to protect the employee from early termination and loss of clientele and opportunities in his previous position as an accountant. The stipulated damages served to offset possible permanent injury to the employee's professional reputation and career development, and the clause was enforceable. *Kozlik v. Emelco Inc.*, 483 N.W.2d 114 (Neb.1992).

A man was hired under a preincorporation agreement to be the president of a corporation with its principal office in Alabama. The employment agreement provided that the man would serve as an officer and would also serve as a director of the company if he was requested to do so. He subsequently resigned from his position as a director. He was then allegedly told to clean out his desk and go home; he did not return to work after that. He later brought a lawsuit for breach of contract. The company asserted that the employee had breached the employment agreement when he unilaterally resigned from the board of directors, and it moved for summary judgment. The trial court granted its motion, and the employee appealed to the Supreme Court of Alabama.

On appeal, the court noted that the agreement did not provide with any degree of specificity whether the employee was obligated to serve on the company's board of directors. It appeared that the employee's obligation to serve was incidental to his primary obligation to serve as president and chief operating officer of the corporation. Accordingly, the employee was not barred from bringing suit to enforce the employment agreement. The supreme court held that the trial court had erred in granting summary judgment to the company because issues of material fact existed for a jury to   consider. *McDonald v. U.S. Die Casting Co.*, 585 So.2d 853 (Ala.1991).

An Illinois man worked as an executive for a company which was later acquired by an international corporation. Under his contract of employment with the company, he was paid approximately double what executives of the international corporation were paid. When executives of the corporation informed him of the salary discrepancy, he indicated that he was not willing to renegotiate. His contract required a three-year notice of termination, unless he was guilty of some misconduct or breach of contract. The corporation orally informed the man of its intent to give him a three-year notice of termination. While the written notice of termination was being prepared, allegations of sexual harassment by the employee against coworkers surfaced. Upon further investigation, he was fired for "misconduct" pursuant to his contract provisions. He brought suit against the corporation for breach of contract. Both parties moved for summary judgment, and a federal district court granted summary judgment for the corporation. The employee appealed. The U.S. Court of Appeals, Seventh Circuit, held that the corporation had not breached the man's employment contract because there was detailed evidence of sexually harassing behavior which was serious enough to be "misconduct" under the contract provisions. Although he argued that the corporation manufactured these allegations to avoid the three-year notice of termination, he did not present sufficient evidence from which a jury could determine that the alleged sexual harassment did not actually occur. Therefore, the court affirmed the summary judgment in favor of the corporation. *Scherer v. Rockwell Intern. Corp.*, 975 F.2d 356 (7th Cir.1992).

A company which provided marketing services to retail outlets hired a South Carolina man as a vice president with responsibility for sales and marketing. He signed an employment contract which provided for periodic reviews, but did not state a specified term of duration for the contract. Several months later, the company discharged him for poor sales performance. He then filed suit in a New York federal district court, alleging wrongful discharge. The court granted the company's motion for summary judgment, and the employee appealed to the U.S. Court of Appeals, Second Circuit. The court of appeals applied New York law to the controversy and noted that if the employment agreement did not state a fixed duration, the employment was presumed to be at will. The employee's assertion that he had been hired as an independent contractor did not take the employment out of the at-will arena. Further, the provision for periodic reviews was not enough to show that the parties intended a review to precede termination. The court thus affirmed the grant of summary judgment to the employer. *Arledge v. Stratmar Systems, Inc.*, 948 F.2d 845 (2d Cir.1991).

B. Oral Contracts

A California chemist accepted employment with a Connecticut pharmaceutical company. He believed that the new job precluded employment termination without just cause, based on oral promises made by company employees and an employment manual containing a management open-door policy. The company later updated its manual, removing restrictions on employment termination without just cause. The employee made specific recommendations for safety equipment that management personnel rejected, and relations became strained. The employee was sent to a training seminar which he felt was unnecessary. His claim for seminar expenses included some personal and undocumented items, and the company fired him for falsifying company documents. The employee denied falsifying documents, stating that he misunderstood company policy. He was denied the opportunity to appeal the decision under the open-door policy. He obtained a damage award against the company in a Connecticut trial court, and the employer appealed to the Supreme Court of Connecticut.

The supreme court determined that there was sufficient evidence that the contract was terminable only for cause and that it included the employee's right to speak to an executive officer prior to any termination action. The company was in breach of contract and the trial court had properly awarded damages for the breach. It had also been appropriate for the trial court to award damages for defamation, because the company had created a memorandum concerning the expense report that included false information. The court rejected the employer's argument that intracorporate communications were privileged in any defamation complaint. The court affirmed the trial court judgment for the employee.*Torosyan v. Boehringer Ingelheim Pharmaceuticals, Inc.*, 234 Conn. 1, 662 A.2d 89 (1995).

A Washington company contracted with two hospitals for the services of a nuclear medical technologist, for which it was billed by one of the hospitals. The company solicited the technologist to leave the hospital and work for the company for five years at the same pay. The parties failed to sign a contract but the technologist nonetheless accepted the employment offer. The company lost its contract with the other hospital, and the technologist was replaced by a company employee with more seniority. He filed a lawsuit in a Washington trial court against the company, alleging wrongful termination, breach of contract and defamation. The court dismissed the case, finding that the employment contract was void because it was not in writing and could not be performed within one year. The Washington Court of Appeals reversed the summary judgment ruling and the employer appealed to the Supreme Court of Washington. The supreme court recited the general rule that a contract for personal services which by its own terms cannot be performed within a year must be in writing. The employee was not entitled to any exception to the rule under equitable theories of estoppel. Under such equitable theories, courts may require a party to perform duties imposed by an otherwise nonbinding agreement to avoid injustice. The supreme court declined to adopt the doctrine of promissory estoppel in this case and affirmed the trial court's summary judgment for the company. *Greaves v. Medical Imaging Systems, Inc.*, 879 P.2d 276 (Wash.1994).

An Indiana newspaper employee was granted sick leave of up to five months on three separate occasions for knee surgery. He was then advised by his physician that he required a total knee replacement. He told his supervisor that he would be unable to work for approximately three months. He allegedly obtained a promise from his supervisor that he could have leave for as long as he needed. However, after the employee underwent surgery, he notified the employer that he would require more than three months leave. The supervisor then advised him that he would be fired if he did not return to work at the expiration of the three-month period. The employee did not receive a release from his physician to return to work until six months after the surgery and the employer fired him. The employee filed a lawsuit against the employer in an Indiana trial court, which granted summary judgment to the employer, finding that the alleged oral employment contract was unenforceable and that the employer was not legally prevented from firing the employee for failing to return to work as first promised. The Indiana Court of Appeals affirmed the oral contract ruling but reversed summary judgment on the employee's reasonable reliance claim.

On appeal to the Supreme Court of Indiana, the court affirmed the lower court dismissal of the oral contract claim. However, the court of appeals had disregarded Indiana law that limited relief to at-will employees bringing claims against employers for their reliance damages. Because the court of appeals' decision contemplated expectation damages, its decision was reversed and remanded. Any lost wage claim by the employee would be limited to those wages accruing between the date of actual termination and the date of the employee's release to return to work, less the amount of any disability benefits received. He was not entitled to be restored to his job, nor to receive damages for the period following the date of his medical release to return to work. *Jarboe v. Landmark Comm. Newspapers of Indiana, Inc.*, 644 N.E.2d 118 (Ind.1994).

An Illinois insurance executive met with representatives of a competitor and considered an offer which included a salary increase and better benefits. He then discussed the matter with two officers of his employer and decided not to change jobs. Within a short time, however, the company fired the executive, and he filed a wrongful discharge lawsuit against it in an Illinois trial court. A jury returned a verdict of $260,000 for the executive, but the trial court granted the company's motion for judgment notwithstanding the verdict. The Appellate Court of Illinois reversed the trial court order, finding that when an employee gave up an employment offer in exchange for and in reliance upon his employer's promise of permanent employment, the contract was enforceable. The case returned to the trial court, which granted summary judgment to the company. The appellate court reversed the matter again, finding that the trial court had improperly relied upon a new argument not previously raised by the company concerning the state insurance code. On remand, the court conducted a second trial and awarded the executive damages as found by the jury. For the third time, appeal was taken to the Appellate Court of Illinois. The court determined that there was evidence of a clear and definite promise of permanent employment to the executive and that a reasonable jury could have concluded that the officers had authority to make the offer of permanent employment. Accordingly, the judgment for the executive was affirmed. *Martin v. Federal Life Ins. Co.*, 644 N.E.2d 42 (Ill.App.1st Dist.1994).

The vice president and general manager of a Connecticut manufacturing company occasionally walked through the plant speaking to employees to boost morale. On several occasions, he allegedly assured individual employees of their job security. The company had a policy set forth in a personnel manual that described a progressive disciplinary procedure for employee violations of company rules. An employee who alleged that he had been assured of his job security by the vice president made a disparaging comment to a plant inspector concerning a company product in the presence of a customer. The company fired the employee the following day without notice and without following company disciplinary procedures. The employee filed a lawsuit against the employer in a Connecticut trial court. The jury awarded him damages of over $400,000 under various causes of action. The court set aside the verdict concerning intentional infliction of emotional distress and negligent misrepresentation and the parties appealed to the Appellate Court of Connecticut.

The court found sufficient evidence for the jury to have determined that the employee had been assured that he would not be fired except for cause and pursuant to the employer's personnel manual. However, the trial court had committed error by awarding "front pay" because front pay was equitable in nature and the employee's claim was contractual. The court of appeals affirmed the trial court's decision to disallow the intentional infliction of emotional distress award because of a lack of evidence that the employer intended to inflict emotional harm or should have known it would result. The court of appeals reversed the trial court decision in part and remanded several issues for a new trial. *Barry v. Posi-Seal International, Inc.*, 36 Conn.App. 1, 647 A.2d 1031 (1994).

An industrial supply company employee planned to start a new business to sell specialized equipment. The employee, another individual and the president of a sheet metal company signed a contract under which the employee and the individual would become employees of the sheet metal company during the start-up period of the new business. When sales reached a certain point, the two individuals would own 90 percent of the business, but the sheet metal company would initially own the entire business. The business did not become profitable, and the sheet metal company insisted that the employee relocate from Indianapolis to New York. When the employee stated that he would not move, the sheet metal company terminated his employment. The employee sued the company in the U.S. District Court for the Western District of New York.

The court granted the sheet metal company's summary judgment motion concerning breach of contract, agreeing that the employee had been employed at will. However, the court conducted a trial on the employee's claim of a breached oral agreement concerning relocation. It instructed the jury to award damages if the employee's refusal to relocate was the only reason for employment termination. The court awarded nominal damages and the employee appealed to the U.S. Court of Appeals, Second Circuit. The court of appeals agreed with the employee that he was entitled to a jury trial on the question of his status as an at-will or contractual employee. It also agreed with the employee that the trial court had unfairly instructed the jury concerning the proper legal standard to employ. It was unfair for the court to require him to prove that refusal to relocate was the only cause of employment termination. The court reversed and remanded the district court's decision and remanded the case for a new trial. *Jones v. Dunkirk Radiator Corp.*, 21 F.3d 18 (2d Cir.1994).

A plastics manufacturer hired an executive under an oral agreement for a fixed first year salary and bonus, with bonuses in future years to be based on company profits. The parties did not discuss the duration of employment, nor did they discuss what constituted just cause for dismissal. Within four months, the relationship between the executive and the owner became so bad that the executive was fired. He sued the company in a Washington trial court for breach of contract, wrongful discharge, negligent misrepresentation and several other claims. Some claims were dismissed or voluntarily dropped, and the court held a trial on the breach of contract complaint. The court awarded over $400,000 for breach of contract and promissory estoppel, a legal doctrine used in the absence of a contract but where the complaining party allegedly relies on promises by the defendant. The Washington Court of Appeals reversed and remanded the case and the employee appealed to the Supreme Court of Washington. The supreme court found insufficient evidence to support the executive's claim that the company had promised him employment beyond one year. Statements made during the interview process did not constitute clear or definite promises of permanent employment or guarantee against dismissal except for just cause. The executive was, however, entitled to damages for breach of contract and severance pay of approximately $92,000. *Havens v. C & D Plastics, Inc.*, 124 Wash.2d 158, 876 P.2d 435 (Wash.1994).

A New Mexico healthcare facility hired a nursing coordinator for a 90-day probationary period. Four months later, the employee was promoted to the director of nursing position at another facility owned by the same company. She began a new 90-day probationary period as director of nursing. Although the employee later stated that she had been assured that her job performance was good, the healthcare facility asked for her resignation within 90 days. The employee sued the healthcare corporation and its individual officers in a New Mexico trial court for emotional distress and breach of contract, among other claims. A trial was held on the breach of contract complaint and a jury returned a damage award of $2,500 for economic loss as well as $63,500 for emotional distress. The court entered judgment for $2,500 plus interest and costs, but refused to enter judgment on the emotional distress claim. The employee appealed to the Supreme Court of New Mexico. The court determined that there was no substantial evidence to justify damages for emotional distress. The trial court had erroneously granted a motion for a directed verdict on the employee's breach of implied covenant of good faith and fair dealing claim, but there was no reason to grant a new trial because the employee had already recovered on her breach of contract claim. The supreme court affirmed the judgments on all issues.*Bourgeous v. Horizon Healthcare Corp.*, 872 P.2d 852 (N.M.1994).

A motion picture production employee alleged that an agent for a film production manager offered him a 14-week employment contract. The employee stated that upon arriving at the worksite, he was advised that another person had already been hired for the job. The employee sued the film production company and agent in a North Carolina trial court for breach of contract, fraud and unfair and deceptive trade practices under state law. He claimed that he gave up two other employment offers and moved from Florida to North Carolina in order to accept the job. The court granted the production company's dismissal motion and the employee appealed to the Court of Appeals of North Carolina.

The court of appeals held that the complaint alleged facts supporting the claim for breach of contract that were sufficient to avoid pretrial dismissal. Because the employee had stated specific facts that supported the fraud claim, the trial court had also improperly dismissed that portion of the complaint. However, dismissal of the claim under the North Carolina Unfair and Deceptive Trade Practices Act was appropriate because the act did not extend to employment cases. The court of appeals remanded the case to the trial court. *Brandis v. Lightmotive Fatman, Inc.*, 443 S.E.2d 887 (N.C.App.1994).

The principal shareholder of a California raceway corporation interviewed candidates for a new general manager. The shareholder was not able to obtain the most desirable candidate for the job. He then held two interviews with an applicant during which the applicant expressed a desire for job security. The shareholder allegedly told the applicant that he had a long-term commitment to his employees and that she would be a permanent employee so long as she did a good job. The applicant then turned down a better paying job close to her home to work at the raceway. Within six months, her employment was terminated, and the shareholder's first choice was brought in at a higher salary. The manager sued the corporation for breach of contract, damage to her reputation and violation of a California statute. A jury returned a verdict including awards of $3,000 for violation of the statute, $65,000 for breach of contract and $476,250 for negligent misrepresentation. The court then reduced the judgment because the damages for breach of contract duplicated the award for misrepresentation. Both parties appealed to the California Court of Appeal, First District.

On appeal, the raceway corporation argued that the evidence was insufficient to establish intentional misrepresentation in violation of the statute. The court disagreed, stating that the manager had proven a knowingly false representation concerning the length of her prospective employment. The shareholder had made repeated assurances that the employment was to be permanent, yet replaced the manager as soon as his first choice for the position became available. However, the trial court had incorrectly attempted to segregate the manager's damages by allocating damages on each theory of recovery. The jury should have been instructed to award damages under any single theory of recovery because all damages flowed from the same conduct. The court reversed the part of the judgment concerning damages and remanded it for reconsideration. *Finch v. Brenda Raceway Corp.*, 27 Cal.Rptr.2d 531 (Cal.App.lst Dist.1994).

A Texas man worked for an aircraft company, eventually rising to the position of field office manager. The company experienced a sharp decline in the volume of its business in the early 1980's, however, and decided to close the field office where he was employed. The company told the employee that it would assist him in finding another position within the company or provide him with out-placement assistance if he did not want to retire. The company was not able to find him another position within its divisions because of the downturn in the industry. The employee elected not to accept out-placement assistance and retired. He then filed suit against the company alleging that it had made fraudulent misrepresentations to him and that it had breached its oral contract to employ him until the age of 65. A federal district court granted summary judgment to the company, and the employee appealed to the U.S. Court of Appeals, Fifth Circuit.

On appeal, the court noted that Texas did not recognize oral promises of permanent employment. Consequently, the employee was employed at will and subject to termination at any time. Further, since the company did not promise to get the employee another job, its statement that it would attempt to get another job for him within the company was not fraudulent misrepresentation. Thus, the court affirmed the district court's grant of summary judgment to the company, and remanded the case for a determination as to whether it would be entitled to collect attorney's fees from the employee. *Crenshaw v. General Dynamics Corp.*, 940 F.2d 125 (5th Cir.1991).

IV. WRONGFUL DISCHARGE

Employers may not discharge employees for engaging in protected activity or asserting rights to which they are legally entitled, such as the filing of a workers' compensation claim. Even if the employment relationship is at will, actions which violate an explicit public policy may create liability.

A. Refusal to Commit Unlawful Acts

A former employee of a Texas asbestos disposal company claimed that he had been fired for refusing to participate in a plan to defraud an internal auditor who was preparing financial reports to be filed with the SEC. The former employee claimed that management employees prepared rehearsed answers and reports that artificially inflated earnings by $1.5 million. He sued his former employer in a Texas trial court for wrongful termination, intentional infliction of emotional distress and negligent misrepresentation. The court granted summary judgment to the employer, and the former employee appealed to the Court of Appeals of Texas, Houston. On appeal, the employer argued that the former employee had been discharged because of a personality conflict, for making threats against other employees and disloyalty. The court held that the trial court had improperly granted summary judgment to the employer because factual disputes existed concerning the reason for dismissal, as demonstrated by conflicting testimony. The court had also improperly granted summary judgment on the intentional infliction of emotional distress claim despite the absence of evidence that the former employee sought medical treatment. The court reversed and remanded the trial court's judgment. *Higginbotham v. Allwaste, Inc.*, 889 S.W.2d 411 (Tex.App.—Houston 1994).

The District Court of Appeal of Florida, Fifth District, affirmed the dismissal of a lawsuit filed by a former employee who claimed that she had been fired for refusing to generate excessive client billings in violation of state law. The applicable Florida statute required an actual reporting of wrongdoing to the appropriate state or federal agency, and not mere disclosure to a supervisor. Because the trial court had noted an absence of the statutorily-required disclosure of wrongdoing, the case had been properly dismissed. *Kelder v. ACT Corp.*, 650 So.2d 647 (Fla.App.5th Dist.1995).

The Court of Appeals of Michigan affirmed the dismissal of a whistleblower lawsuit filed by a discharged airline ticket agent who asserted that she had been fired in violation of Michigan law for attempting to report information about suspicious passengers to the U.S. Drug Enforcement Administration. The court of appeals held that the trial court had properly granted the employer's dismissal motion because the state whistleblowers' protection act was intended to protect employees who reported violations of law arising out of company business. In this case, the employee had been discharged for violating her supervisor's instructions to make such reports only through management personnel. That claim had nothing to do with company business and was not protected by the act. *Dolan v. Continental Airlines*, 526 N.W.2d 922 (Mich.App.1995).

A Pennsylvania woman worked as the bookkeeper-accountant for a home-health service. The service was a nonprofit corporation which provided skilled nursing care, home health aids, and other services to individuals, some of whom were covered by the federal Medicare program. The bookkeeper's duties included providing information and documents used to prepare cost reports to be submitted to a Medicare intermediary. In 1991, the service received a letter from the intermediary requesting additional information concerning the 1990 fiscal year cost report. The service requested the bookkeeper to recreate documents to provide a fictitious account of the services provided by the home health aid service. After she refused, she was discharged. She then filed suit against the employer in a federal district court for a violation of the federal False Claims Act.

The court noted that the False Claims Act makes it unlawful for an employer to discharge an employee because the employee refuses to participate in submitting false claims under the Medicare program. The court found for the bookkeeper and determined that she was entitled to relief. The Act provides for reinstatement with the same seniority status the employee would have had but for the discrimination, two times the amount of backpay, and interest on the backpay. Therefore, the bookkeeper was entitled to receive twice her lost wages, reinstatement, and attorney's fees. *Godwin v. Visiting Nurse Assoc. Home Health Service*, 831 F.Supp. 449 (E.D.Pa.1993).

A West Virginia truck driver was instructed to transport a load of lumber to Norfolk, Virginia, where the lumber was to be loaded onto a cargo ship and transported overseas. While testing the brakes on his trailer, he discovered that they were defective. After an unsuccessful repair attempt, the driver decided not to take the lumber to Norfolk because the trailer was unsafe. He contacted a manager who agreed that the truck should not leave the lot. Because of the driver's failure to take the lumber to Norfolk, the cargo ship left without it. His supervisor was angry and six weeks later, used a radar gun to clock the driver's truck speed at 70-71 miles per hour. The company policy provided that any driver operating a truck at 70 or more miles per hour would be fired. The driver was fired. However, he claimed that he had filed a written report two weeks earlier indicating that his speedometer was giving false readings. He sued his former employer for breach of contract and wrongful discharge in a federal district court. The court granted the employer's motion for summary judgment and the driver appealed to the U.S. Court of Appeals, Fourth Circuit.

The driver first claimed that the employment handbook created a contract and that the company had violated its terms. However, the court noted that the handbook contained clear language indicating that the handbook was not a contract. Next, the driver contended that the company's reasons for discharging him were pretextual. He asserted that the company had discharged him in retaliation for his refusal to drive a truck with defective brakes. He argued that the discharge violated the West Virginia faulty brake statutes. The court agreed that the discharge may have been retaliatory, and determined that summary judgment was inappropriate. The court remanded the case to the trial court to determine if the discharge was in retaliation for refusing to violate the faulty brake statutes. *Lilly v. Overnite Transportation Co.*, 995 F.2d 521 (4th Cir.1993).

After a waitress at a Texas restaurant counseled another waitress not to have an abortion, she was fired. Supposedly, the manager was the father of the baby and was angered that the waitress had discussed the abortion issue. She filed suit in a Texas trial court for wrongful discharge. The court determined that she was an at-will employee and dismissed the action. The employee then appealed to the Court of Appeals of Texas. The waitress alleged that her termination was in retaliation for her actions in counseling a fellow waitress. She argued that it was unlawful suppression of her right to discuss the issue of abortion. The court of appeals noted that the Texas Supreme Court has carved out only one exception to the general rule of at-will employment: it allows a cause of action for wrongful termination when the employee has been discharged for refusing to perform an illegal act. Numerous other exceptions have been created by the legislature. However, the court noted that the employee's public policy argument (suppression of her right to discuss abortion) did not fall within these exceptions and it affirmed the trial court's dismissal. *Amador v. Tan*, 855 S.W.2d 131 (Tex.App.1993).

B. Statutory Rights

1. Workers' Compensation

A Kentucky steelworker claimed that he was laid off by his employer because of his workers' compensation claims history with previous employers. The employer justified the layoff on economic grounds and the employee filed a lawsuit against it in a state trial court. The court granted summary judgment to the employer, but the state court of appeals reversed and remanded the case. The employer appealed to the Supreme Court of Kentucky, which analyzed the case under state workers' compensation law, which prohibited the retaliatory discharge of an employee for filing a valid workers' compensation claim. The court distinguished the discharge in this case from retaliatory discharge complaints based on firings motivated by the desire to punish an employee for exercising legal rights. In this case, the discharge was not retaliatory in nature, but had an economic basis in reducing the employer's cost of workers' compensation insurance premiums. The court rejected the employee's argument that it should adopt case law from Michigan and Illinois which expanded retaliatory discharge claims to include discharges based on claims filed against prior employers. The court reinstated the summary judgment order of the trial court. *Nelson Steel Corp. v. McDaniel*, 898 S.W.2d 66 (Ky.1995).

A Michigan employee injured her wrist on the job and claimed that her employer fired her before the end of her probationary period in retaliation for filing a workers' compensation claim. A Michigan trial court awarded her damages despite the employer's argument that her at-will employment status barred the claim. The Michigan Court of Appeals ruled on appeal that the employee was not entitled to punitive damages or damages for mental or emotional distress, but that she was entitled to nominal damages. The employee appealed to the Supreme Court of Michigan, which stated that despite the at-will status of the employment relationship of the parties, the employer had a duty not to retaliate against the employee for filing a workers' compensation claim. The cause of action for violating the workers' compensation act was independent of the employment contract. Although the court had previously declined to recognize a cause of action for bad faith breach of an employment contract, it authorized a cause of action for mental and emotional distress apart from the breach of contract in appropriate cases. In this case, the employee was entitled to recover her lost wages because she had a reasonable expectation that she would not be fired for filing a workers' compensation claim. An award of nominal damages would not compensate the employee for the employer's violation of public policy and the case was therefore reversed and remanded. *Phillips v. Butterball Farms Co., Inc.*, 531 N.W.2d 144 (Mich.1995).

A Texas company utilized a number of employee incentive awards to discourage absences for work-related injuries, including cash awards, dinners, and other financial incentives. A welder injured his back in a work-related accident. He worked for several days before advising his supervisor that he could not continue working and that he was considering the filing of a workers' compensation claim. The supervisor stood to receive an award if his employees worked for 1,000 days without any work-related injuries. He selected the welder for layoff, although the company later denied that he had any discretion to select individuals for layoff. The company laid off approximately one-third of its employees during the next year. The welder sued the company in a Texas trial court for wrongful discharge and violation of Texas law. The court conducted a trial resulting in a $125,000 damage award for the employee, plus $100,000 in exemplary damages and prejudgment interest of over $67,000. The Texas Court of Appeals, Amarillo, affirmed the trial court action, finding no lack of evidence to support the damage award. Evidence indicated that the company had no formal policy for layoffs. The jury was entitled to infer an improper motive due to the proximity in time between the layoff and the welder's statements concerning a workers' compensation claim. The court reduced the damage award but otherwise affirmed the trial court decision. *Gifford Hill American, Inc. v. Whittington*, 899 S.W.2d 760 (Tex.App.—Amarillo 1995).

A Tennessee airline employee had a poor attendance record and became subject to disciplinary action under the applicable collective bargaining agreement. The airline offered him a "last chance agreement" allowing him up to three absences or tardies over a 24-month period in order to preserve his employment. The employee was absent or tardy eight times during the next year, and twice suffered on-the-job injuries. The airline fired the employee under the last chance agreement, and he filed a grievance. An arbitrator ruled for the airline. Following an unsuccessful appeal to the System Board of Adjustment, the worker filed a lawsuit in a Tennessee trial court, alleging that he had been discharged in retaliation for filing a workers' compensation claim. The court granted the airline's summary judgment motion. On appeal, the Court of Appeals of Tennessee, Western Section, held that the lawsuit was preempted by the Railway Labor Act, because it was a minor dispute; in other words, a dispute arising from the interpretation of a collective bargaining agreement. The court held that alternatively, the trial court had properly granted summary judgment because the employee had not actually filed a claim for workers' compensation benefits at the time of the discharge. Therefore, the termination could not have been retaliatory as there was no causal relationship between the claim for benefits and the discharge. *Rutherford v. Northwest Airlines, Inc.,* 880 S.W.2d 947 (Tenn.App.1994).

A Missouri Court reached a different result in a case concerning a Missouri employer's discharge of an employee who suffered an injury to a finger and missed many months of work. Prior to being laid off she was temporarily placed in a clerical position off the assembly line, but claimed that she was not hired or promoted internally according to company policy. She alleged that 16 employees were recalled from layoff status despite having less seniority than she had, and that 29 new employees were hired during the period under consideration. She also alleged that a supervisory employee had told her that she was not being rehired because of her workers' compensation claim. Since fact issues existed concerning whether the company had discriminated against the employee because of her workers' compensation claim or her disability, the trial court had improperly granted summary judgment to the employer, and the Missouri Court of Appeals, Western District, reversed and remanded the case. *Peregoy v. Libby Corp.*, 879 S.W.2d 746 (Mo.App.W.D.1994).

An employee of an Oklahoma oil field service was injured when a customer of the service dropped a pipe on his foot. The employee received workers' compensation benefits from his employer, and he filed a third-party claim for work-related injuries against the customer. When the customer notified the service of the lawsuit, it demanded that the employee dismiss the lawsuit immediately. When he refused to do so, the service fired the employee. He filed a lawsuit against his employer in an Oklahoma trial court for wrongful termination. The trial court dismissed the lawsuit, and its decision was affirmed by the Oklahoma Court of Appeals. The Supreme Court of Oklahoma granted the employee's petition for review. The supreme court stated that Oklahoma recognized only a narrow class of exceptions to the presumption of employment-at-will. An employer may be held liable for wrongful dismissal of an employee where the termination is for the exercise of a legal right or interest. In this case, the third-party job-related injury lawsuit was similar to a workers' compensation claim. Like the pursuit of a workers' compensation claim, the worker's third-party job-related injury lawsuit constituted the exercise of a legal right. Accordingly, the termination had been in violation of Oklahoma public policy because it forced the employee to choose between keeping his job and pursuing a legal right. The court vacated and remanded the lower court decisions. *Groce v. Foster*, 880 P.2d 902 (Okl.1994).

Three Oklahoma painters received subpoenas to testify in a workers' compensation case filed by a coworker. The painters then alleged that they were constructively discharged by the painting contractor because of their anticipated testimony in the workers' compensation case. They sued the contractor in an Oklahoma trial court, which gave instructions to the jury concerning constructive discharge, actual damages and punitive damages. The jury returned verdicts for the painters including actual damages of less than $4,000 in each case, and $50,000 in punitive damages in each case. The trial court granted the contractor's motion for remittitur under an Oklahoma statute that required a court to make special findings concerning wilful conduct in order to make an award of punitive damages in excess of actual damages. Accordingly, the painters received punitive damage awards equal only to their actual damage awards. All parties appealed to the Supreme Court of Oklahoma.

On appeal, the painters argued that a workers' compensation statute allowing punitive damages of up to $100,000 applied in their cases. The contractor argued that the statute did not apply, and that the trial court had improperly instructed the jury concerning constructive discharge. The court ruled that the Oklahoma Workers' Compensation Act was not in conflict with the remittitur statute and that the trial court had correctly reduced the punitive damage awards. There was also no error in the trial court's jury instructions concerning constructive discharge, which called for determining whether reasonable persons would feel that working conditions were so intolerable that they compelled resignation. The supreme court affirmed the trial court's decision. *Wilson v. Hess-Sweitzer & Brant, Inc.*, 864 P.2d 1279 (Okl.1993).

Two Kansas workers injured in job-related incidents were later fired by their employers for refusing to return to work or perform assigned duties. Both employees claimed that the firings came in retaliation for filing workers' compensation claims. They filed lawsuits against their employers in the U.S. District Court for the District of Kansas which certified a question to the Supreme Court of Kansas regarding the proper standard of proof in claims for retaliatory discharge. The employer argued that employees advancing claims for retaliatory discharge were required to prove their cases by clear and convincing evidence. The employees argued that the lower preponderance of evidence standard applied because of the difficulty in proving retaliatory motive.

The supreme court observed that Kansas employment law presumed employment to be at will. The exceptions to the at-will presumption included violations of public policy, such as retaliatory discharge for whistleblowing. Although the general standard for proof in Kansas was a preponderance of the evidence, the state's courts had previously imposed a burden of clear and convincing evidence in retaliatory discharge claims for whistleblowing. The court determined that the same standard of proof should be required in retaliatory discharge actions arising from workers' compensation claims. Employees attempting to prove retaliatory discharge in workers' compensation matters would be required to establish the claim by a preponderance of evidence, but the quality of the evidence must be clear and convincing in nature. *Ortega v. IBP, Inc.*, 874 P.2d 1188 (Kan.1994).

An Illinois woman was apparently injured in the course of her employment. She notified her employer, and requested compensation for her medical expenses under the Illinois Workers' Compensation Act. Shortly thereafter, her employer discharged her for filing a "false" workers' compensation claim. Her union filed a grievance under the collective bargaining agreement (CBA) and an arbitrator found in the employee's favor and ordered her reinstated with full backpay. Meanwhile, she brought a retaliatory discharge claim against her employer in a state trial court. The employer removed the case to federal court, then sought dismissal, which the court granted. The U.S. Court of Appeals, Seventh Circuit, affirmed. The employee petitioned the U.S. Supreme Court for review.

At issue was whether the employee's claim was preempted by § 301 of the Labor Management Relations Act. The Supreme Court held that it was not.

Therefore, if the employee could show that she had been discharged, and that the employer's motive was to deter her from exercising her rights under the workers' compensation act, she could win her suit. No interpretation of the CBA would have to be made. Since the inquiries were purely factual, the claim was independent of the CBA and § 301 did not preempt it. The Court reversed the court of appeals' decision and held that the employee could continue her claim. *Lingle v. Norge Division of Magic Chef, Inc.*, 486 U.S. 399, 108 S.Ct. 1877, 100 L.Ed.2d 410 (1988).

A West Virginia company employed a production worker for over 20 years. The company then discharged him because of excessive absenteeism. He filed a grievance against the company, and an arbitration board ruled against him. He next filed an action against the company claiming discriminatory discharge because he had filed a claim for workers' compensation benefits. Both parties filed motions for summary judgment, and a trial court denied both motions. Upon renewal of the worker's motion for summary judgment, a trial court granted his motion on the issue of liability and awarded him damages. The company appealed. The Supreme Court of Appeals of West Virginia reversed the decision of the trial court. It found that there was a genuine issue of material fact as to whether the employee's discharge was prompted by his claim for workers' compensation benefits or by his absenteeism and overall work record. It was also unclear as to whether he would ever be able to return to work due to the severity of his injuries. These factual issues precluded the granting of a motion for summary judgment. The case was remanded for further proceedings. *Pannell v. Inco Alloys Intern., Inc.*, 422 S.E.2d 643 (W.Va.1992).

An Indiana legal secretary began experiencing numbness and tingling in her hands and fingers. She told her employer of the condition of her hands, and informed him that she intended to file a workers' compensation claim so that she could pay for the treatment she needed. Her employer fired her at the end of the meeting. She then brought suit, alleging that she had been fired because of her intent to file a workers' compensation claim. A jury awarded her $15,000, and her employer appealed to the Court of Appeals of Indiana. He contended on appeal that a claim could be maintained only where an employee is discharged after filing a workers' compensation claim. Since he had fired his secretary for stating her intent to file a claim, he asserted that no cause of action existed. The court disagreed with his analysis. There were strong public policy reasons for disallowing such retaliatory discharges. It is important that employees not feel they will lose their jobs for exercising their statutory right to workers' compensation benefits. The court affirmed the damage award to the secretary. *Stivers v. Stevens*, 581 N.E.2d 1253 (Ind.App.4th Dist.1991).

An employee of a corporation incurred a work-related injury to his right elbow and neck. He received temporary disability benefits, and eventually returned to work. His condition, however, was such that he missed further work.

He was again examined by several doctors who released him to work with a lifting restriction of 30 pounds. Since a 60-pound restriction was the lowest available for positions for which the employee was qualified, he had a meeting with management to determine his status. The managers apparently told him that if any work came open which he could perform, they would get in touch with him. When he did not communicate further with the company, he was fired under a provision which required employees to report continued absences from work within three working days. In an arbitration, the firing was determined to be a legitimate exercise of the company's prerogative. The employee sued the company in a Kentucky trial court, asserting that it had discharged him in retaliation for pursuing workers' compensation benefits. At the end of the trial, the court directed a verdict for the employer, and did not allow the jury to rule on the case. The employee appealed to the Court of Appeals of Kentucky.

The court noted that the burden was on the employee to show that "he was engaged in a statutorily protected activity, that he was discharged, and that there was a connection between the protected activity and the discharge." It then stated that he had clearly been engaged in a protected activity at the time of the discharge. Further, he had presented evidence that his employer had possessed a hostile attitude toward him and that the reason for firing him had been pretextual. Therefore, the case should have gone to the jury so that it could decide if the discharge had been retaliatory and wrongful. The court reversed the trial court's decision and remanded the case for a retrial. *Willoughby v. Gencorp, Inc.*, 809 S.W.2d 858 (Ky.App.1991).

A West Virginia man worked as an installer for a cable company for several years. He was injured when a utility pole that he climbed began to fall and he had to jump for safety. He then sought and received temporary total disability benefits as workers' compensation. Approximately four months after his injury, when it was still unclear as to when he would be able to return to work, the cable company removed him from its payroll records. The employee was released for work approximately one year after the injury; however, his employer refused to rehire him. He then sued claiming that he had been fired in retaliation for filing a workers' compensation claim. A jury awarded him damages, and the employer appealed to the Supreme Court of Appeals of West Virginia.

On appeal, the court noted that an at-will employee could seek damages from his employer if he was discharged in contravention of public policy. The court then determined that to succeed in a claim for retaliation, the worker had to show that he was injured on the job, that he filed for benefits, and that the filing was a significant factor in the employer's decision to discharge him. If the employee had not been able to perform his job duties, the employer would have been justified in discharging him. However, in this case the jury had determined that the employer violated West Virginia law by discharging the employee just four months after the injury. Since there was sufficient evidence to support the jury's finding the court affirmed its decision. *Powell v. Wyoming Cablevision, Inc.*, 403 S.E.2d 717 (W.Va.1991).

An Oklahoma truck driver was driving a truck filled with carbon dioxide to an oil well site. While searching for a site entrance in the dark, he attempted to cross a narrow wooden bridge on an unfamiliar, obscure country road. The wheels gave way, and the truck tumbled down the embankment, injuring the driver. A week later, he filed a claim for workers' compensation benefits. He was then discharged from his job because of his involvement in a "major preventable" accident. This was grounds for termination under a collective bargaining agreement. The claimant subsequently sued his employer for retaliatory discharge, and a jury awarded him approximately $360,000. The employer appealed to the Court of Appeals of Oklahoma.

On appeal, the court noted that the claimant had established a *prima facie* case for retaliatory discharge. He showed that he had been fired after instituting a good faith claim for a work-related injury. Further, even if the employer had other legitimate reasons for firing the employee, the discharge would be considered violative of Oklahoma law if retaliatory motivations comprised a "significant factor" in the decision to fire him. Here, the circumstantial evidence (employee testimony of employer dissatisfaction with the filing of workers' compensation claims) was sufficient to allow a jury finding of retaliatory discharge. The court affirmed the award to the claimant. *Mantha v. Liquid Carbonic Industries, Inc.,* 839 P.2d 200 (Okl.App.1992).

An Illinois man worked as a warehouseman for a company until he sustained a work-related back injury. He was then placed on temporary total disability and was paid workers' compensation benefits. While he was receiving those benefits, an investigator employed by the company photographed and videotaped the employee carrying furniture from his old home to a new residence. Shortly thereafter, the employee was confronted with this evidence, and discharged. He filed an unsuccessful unemployment compensation claim with the Illinois Department of Employment Security (DES). His appeal was dismissed. The employee then filed a claim against the company for retaliatory discharge in an Illinois trial court, and the company moved to dismiss the claim. After the trial court granted the motion, the employee appealed to the Appellate Court of Illinois. The appellate court noted that the employee must prove that his discharge was causally related to the filing of the claim for workers' compensation to successfully assert a retaliatory discharge claim. Here, it had been established that the employee's discharge was unrelated to the filing of the claim, and was rather a result of the wilful actions by the employee in violation of the company's rights. The court thus affirmed the trial court's dismissal of the case. *Colvett v. L. Karp & Sons, Inc.,* 570 N.E.2d 611 (Ill.App.1st Dist.1991).

2. Whistleblowing Activities

An engineering consulting firm provided technical support services to federal defense agencies. A program manager for the firm wrote an anonymous letter to a corporate officer detailing many incidents of improper conduct by a department head at the manager's facility. The letter claimed that the department head had engaged in illegal, immoral and unethical activities including theft of government documents and security violations. The manager later sent a letter to a federal agency informing it of the improprieties. Following an internal investigation, the program manager admitted writing the letter. Because most of the charges could not be substantiated, the company fired the manager on the basis of recklessly defaming a coworker. The manager filed a complaint against the employer in a Connecticut trial court for violation of the state whistleblower protection statute, which requires a discharged employee to show that his employment termination is caused by retaliation for engaging in a protected activity. This includes reporting violations to state or federal agencies. The company removed the matter to a federal district court, which granted the company's summary judgment motion. The employee appealed to the U.S. Court of Appeals, Second Circuit.

The court of appeals determined that the district court had improperly made inferences from the evidence in favor of the employer, rather than leaving issues of fact for resolution by a jury. The former manager had set forth a *prima facie* case that the employer had violated the whistleblower protection act, and was entitled to a jury trial for a resolution of factual disputes. The company had undertaken its own investigation without any threat of extortion by the employee (as the employer alleged) because the department head's violations had already been reported to the appropriate agency. *LaFond v. General Physics Services Corp.*, 50 F.3d 165 (2d.Cir.1995).

A Florida carpenter worked for a contractor at a nuclear power plant. He was transferred to a crew working on a temporary project and began experiencing disagreements with his foreman concerning safety procedures for contaminated tools. The foreman learned that the carpenter went over his head to make a complaint concerning the handling of contaminated tools. The carpenter was soon laid off, before the layoff of less experienced crew members. Within 30 days, the entire crew was laid off. The carpenter filed an administrative complaint with the U.S. Department of Labor, claiming that the employer had violated the whistleblower protection provision of the Energy Reorganization Act. An administrative law judge held that the carpenter had not been engaged in a protected activity. The secretary of labor reversed the decision, finding that it was not supported by the evidence, and remanded the case to the administrative law judge, who determined that the carpenter was entitled only to back wages for one month and not to reinstatement. The secretary affirmed the final administrative decision and the contractor appealed to the U.S. Court of Appeals, Eleventh Circuit.

The court of appeals agreed with the secretary that the carpenter had made out a valid claim for discrimination by showing that the Energy Reorganization Act applied and that he had been engaged in protected activity which adversely affected the terms and conditions of his employment. The carpenter's initiation of an internal complaint constituted a protected activity. Because the secretary's decision was supported by substantial evidence, the court of appeals affirmed the decision for the carpenter. *Bechtel Construction Co. v. Secretary of Labor*, 50 F.3d 926 (11th Cir.1995).

A television cable installation manager injured his back while unloading a 65-pound reel of cable. Although the manager had not asked coworkers for help, he had previously requested the company to provide safety equipment to prevent injury. The manager became unable to work because of the injury and workers' compensation coverage was not available to him. He filed a negligence lawsuit in a Texas trial court against the cable company and its officers. A jury returned a verdict of almost $700,000 for the manager and the court found the corporate officers jointly and severably liable in their individual capacities. The company and officers appealed to the Court of Appeals of Texas, San Antonio. On appeal, the defendants argued that the factual basis for the damage award was insufficient because it was not an industry practice to furnish cable installers with safety equipment. The court rejected this argument, observing that an employer has a nondelegable and continuous duty to provide a safe workplace and adequate help for employees to complete their job assignments. This duty extended to the obligation to provide safe tools and equipment. The trial court had properly apportioned damages against the officers for having knowledge and participating in the negligent conduct because in their individual capacities they had directly participated in the operations that had resulted in the injury. The court of appeals affirmed the trial court's decision.*Leitch v. Hornsby*, 885 S.W.2d 243 (Tex.App.— San Antonio 1994).

An Ohio atomic plant employee was injured when he was exposed to the release of some hazardous materials. He underwent surgery for removal of polyps and suffered sinus and gastrointestinal problems. Although he obtained a letter from his doctor indicating work restrictions that would prevent him from further exposure to hazardous substances, the plant physician ordered the employee to return to work without restrictions. The employee was fired when he refused to work and instead went to a hospital for an independent test. He filed a lawsuit in an Ohio county court, asserting intentional tort and wrongful discharge claims. The court granted dismissal and the matter was appealed to the state supreme court, which reversed and remanded the case. The trial court then conducted a trial resulting in a $100,000 compensatory damage award. The employer appealed to the Court of Appeals of Ohio.

On appeal, the employer argued that its knowledge that employees were being exposed to hazardous materials was insufficient to create liability. The court observed that in order to hold an employer liable for intentional conduct, the employee must establish the employer's knowledge of the existence of a danger and knowledge of a substantial certainty of harm to an employee. Simple knowledge of a risk was insufficient to establish intent. In this case, there was substantial evidence of the employer's knowledge of needed safety measures. The jury could have properly found damages in the amount of $100,000 even though the employee's present medical expenses totaled less than $50,000. The court affirmed the judgment for the employee. *Tulloh v. Goodyear Atomic Corp.*, 93 Ohio App.3d 740, 639 N.E.2d 1203 (1994).

A New York woman was hired by a corporation to fill the position of accounts payable supervisor. Her desk was located near the employee smoking lounge. She complained to several managerial employees that smoke drifting from the lounge irritated her allergies and asked that her work area be relocated. Her supervisors refused her request. She later made a complaint to the Suffolk County Department of Health which sent an inspector to the premises. The employee was then fired for poor attendance or excessive absenteeism during her probationary period. She sued the corporation under New York's whistleblower law, claiming that the termination of her employment was in retaliation for her complaint to the department of health. The corporation moved for summary judgment.

The supreme court denied the corporation's motion, noting that the whistleblower law created a statutory remedy for employees fired or otherwise penalized for having reported to a public body a legal violation which "creates and presents a substantial and specific danger to the public health or safety." Here, the employee claimed that the corporation had violated both state and county laws regulating smoking in the workplace. The court rejected the corporation's claim that the employee would have been discharged because of an after-discovered misrepresentation on the employee's application. Even though after-acquired evidence of a discharged employee's misrepresentation on an application can be a defense to a wrongful discharge claim, the court found that the misinformation supplied by the employee on the application was not material, was not made to induce employment, and was not relied upon by the corporation in hiring her. The court allowed the case against the corporation to continue. *Bompane v. Enzolabs, Inc.*, 608 N.Y.S.2d 989 (Sup.1994).

A Massachusetts company employed an African-American who claimed that a group of white employees harassed him after he gave testimony on behalf of another African-American employee at an arbitration hearing. He claimed that the white employees engaged in a retaliatory campaign by forming as a group and staring at him while he worked. His complaint to the company resulted in warnings that his "unfounded allegations" constituted failure to cooperate with management. When the employee appeared for work late one day, his supervisor confronted him and after an argument, fired him for insubordination. He filed a lawsuit against the employer in the U.S. District Court for the District of Massachusetts for race discrimination, breach of contract and violations of Massachusetts and federal law. He abandoned the race discrimination complaint, and the district court granted the employer's summary judgment motion on the other claims. The employee appealed the dismissal of the retaliatory discharge claims under Massachusetts law to the U.S. Court of Appeals, First Circuit.

The court of appeals noted the lack of evidence produced by the employee to indicate a causal connection between his testimony before the arbitration hearing and the alleged harassment. There was evidence that some of the alleged harassers were not even aware of his testimony. There was also no connection between his appearance before the arbitration hearing and his discharge more than two years later. The court affirmed the district court's award of summary judgment. *Lewis v. Gillette, Co.*, 22 F.3d 22 (1st Cir.1994).

An Iowa woman worked for a supermarket as a part-time grocery checker. The 39-year-old employee perceived an inclination by management to assign more work hours to younger employees. She complained about the alleged disparity, and subsequently filed an age discrimination claim with the Iowa Civil Rights Commission. In an unrelated matter, the employee alleged that a new smoking ban was implemented solely to aggravate her. In her vehement opposition to the smoking policy, she defiantly told management they would have to fire her to get rid of her, which they promptly did. After a lower court found for the employer in an age discrimination and retaliatory discharge suit, the employee appealed to the Iowa Supreme Court. On appeal, the court noted that in order to establish a *prima facie* case of retaliatory discharge, the employee needed to show a causal link between her civil rights claim and her ultimate discharge. The court found no such correlation, and pointed out that filing a discrimination claim does not immunize the employee from discharge for past or present inadequacies, unsatisfactory performance, or insubordination. Consequently, the court affirmed the decision of the district court for the employer. *Hulme v. Barrett*, 480 N.W.2d 40 (Iowa 1992).

A black customer service representative for a Kansas City cable company was promoted to a supervisory position. She complained to the director of human relations concerning an office note written about her that she claimed was racially derogatory. The author of the note was disciplined, and later apologized to the representative both orally and in writing. The representative was later evaluated by her supervisor in her new position. Although the review was below average, it was encouraging and noted that she was still learning her full job responsibilities. The representative quit. Several of her supervisors tried to contact her to reconsider, but she never returned their calls. She filed a race discrimination and retaliatory discharge claim under Title VII against the company.

The U.S. District Court for the Western District of Missouri noted that since the representative had quit her job, she would have to prove that she was constructively discharged in order to succeed on either claim. Constructive discharge occurs when an employer deliberately renders the employee's working conditions intolerable and by its actions intends to force the employee to quit. The court found that the lack of training that the representative experienced in her new position was a common shortcoming in employment training and did not render her work environment intolerable. Likewise, although her performance review was less than glowing, it did not create an intolerable work environment. The fact that several of her supervisors tried to contact her to get her to reconsider leaving the company indicated that the company had not forced her to quit. The court held that no constructive discharge had occurred, and it ruled against the representative on her claims of race discrimination and retaliatory discharge. *Ross v. Kansas City Cable Partners*, 798 F.Supp. 577 (W.D.Mo.1992).

3. Statutory Rights — Generally

An Ohio physician formed a pension plan for which he served as administrator and trustee on behalf of himself and his employees. He made investment decisions through a friend who was a financial planner and insurance salesman. Some plan funds were invested with a commodities investor who embezzled the funds, resulting in a substantial loss of plan assets. An employee whose lost share of plan funds was almost $20,000 demanded reimbursement and rejected the physician's offer to repay the amount in the form of taxable bonuses. The employee filed a lawsuit seeking reimbursement despite the physician's threats of discharge or reduced work hours. Within one month, the physician terminated her employment, stating that he was reducing the extent of his practice. The U.S. District Court for the Northern District of Ohio awarded the employee the entire amount of claimed plan benefits with interest. It also awarded over $100,000 in backpay and front pay for wrongful discharge in violation of the Employee Retirement Income Security Act (ERISA), plus $33,000 for attorney's fees.

The physician appealed to the U.S. Court of Appeals, Sixth Circuit, which found no error in the district court decision. ERISA creates a statutory cause of action for retaliation against an employee for asserting rights under a pension plan and prohibits interference with the attainment of benefits by employees. Although ERISA prohibits damage awards that are characterized as legal damages, the award of backpay in this case was considered an equitable remedy because it was restitutionary. The front pay award was also an equitable remedy that was not prohibited by ERISA. The court rejected the physician's argument that he should not be liable for plan losses that had been suffered long before the employee's discharge. It affirmed the district court judgment. *Schwartz v. Gregori*, 45 F.3d 1017 (6th Cir.1995).

A trucking company hired an assistant supervisor at an Ohio garage facility. He signed a document agreeing that his employment was "subject to termination without recourse at any time for any or no reason." During an annual performance review two years later, the garage manager allegedly told the assistant supervisor that he had a secure job at the garage for as long as he wanted. The assistant later reported to his supervisors that certain required safety inspections were not being performed. A subsequent business decline forced a personnel reduction, and the assistant supervisor was discharged. Because the action took place just prior to the vesting of his company pension benefits, he filed a lawsuit in the U.S. District Court for the Southern District of Ohio, claiming that the discharge violated ERISA. The employee also filed state law claims including breach of contract. The court held that the discharge had been for legitimate economic reasons and granted the employer's summary judgment motion. It also refused to exercise jurisdiction over the state law claims and dismissed them without prejudice.

The employee then filed a state court action against the employer, which was also summarily dismissed. The employee appealed to the Court of Appeals of Ohio. The court held that the employee was legally prevented from relitigating the state law claims for breach of contract and retaliatory discharge in violation of the state whistleblower's act. In the process of dismissing the ERISA claim, the federal court had expressly ruled that the discharge had been for economic reasons. This determination legally precluded the state court from reconsidering the reasons for discharge. The court further determined that the garage manager's statements to the assistant supervisor did not bind the company to a permanent employment contract because it was a one-time oral assurance made by an employee who was not an immediate supervisor. The trial court had properly dismissed the case. *McIntosh v. Roadway Express, Inc.*, 94 Ohio App.3d 195, 640 N.E.2d 570 (1994).

A Missouri employee worked for a corporation for five months and was fired the same day his employer received a court order to withhold $450 per month from his wages for delinquent child support. He filed a lawsuit against the corporation in a Missouri trial court, claiming that the discharge violated the state statute providing for wage withholding. The court granted the corporation's motion to dismiss the lawsuit for failure to state a claim, but the Missouri Court of Appeals reversed the decision. The corporation appealed to the Supreme Court of Missouri. The supreme court observed that the wage withholding statute set forth a procedure under which only the state division of child support enforcement was authorized to bring a circuit court action to determine whether an employer had violated the statute. Under this procedure, courts were permitted to reinstate employees with back wages, costs, attorney's fees and the amount of child support that should have been withheld and paid during the time an employee was wrongfully discharged. However, there was no express authorization in the statute of a private cause of action for individuals to seek and obtain statutory enforcement remedies. Because the employee had failed to avail himself of the statutory procedures through the child support enforcement agency, and there was no evidence of any legislative intent to create a private cause of action, the trial court had properly dismissed the matter. *Johnson v. Kraft General Foods, Inc.*, 885 S.W.2d 334 (Mo.1994).

An employee of a West Virginia oil company was looking for a used car. He looked first at a dealership that was principally owned by his employer. The employee later decided to buy a car from a competitor of the dealership, and was fired four days later. The employer stated that he had been disloyal for purchasing the car from the competitor. The employee sued the employer in a West Virginia trial court for wrongful discharge, claiming that the action had been retaliatory and violative of his right to engage in commercial transactions. The court dismissed the lawsuit, finding that the employee had no statutory or constitutional protection against the employer's action. The employee appealed to the Supreme Court of Appeals of West Virginia. The court stated that whether the discharge was wrongful depended on the existence of a substantial public policy against such actions. A West Virginia statute prohibiting coal mining companies from requiring miners to purchase their goods at company stores stated a substantial public policy against employer-coerced purchases. The policy applied in this case because the statute intended to prevent employment practices that threatened job security. In this case, the automobile purchase had nothing to do with employment at the oil company. A claim for wrongful discharge might exist if the action was in retaliation for purchasing the car from the competing dealership. The court reversed and remanded the case for a determination of whether the discharge had been retaliatory. *Roberts v. Adkins*, 444 S.E.2d 725 (W.Va.1994).

A Hawaii condominium association hired an assistant manager. After working for several months, the assistant manager submitted a medical bill incurred by his wife that he believed was covered by the association's insurance carrier. The association deducted $141 from the assistant manager's next paycheck, and when he questioned the deduction, he was referred to the association's managing agent. The agent advised the assistant manager that the association had erroneously failed to deduct $141 from each of his previous paychecks for insurance coverage, and that similar deductions would be made in the future. The assistant manager advised the agent to reimburse him for the amount deducted and canceled his coverage. Within ten days, the association fired him. He sued the association and agent in a Hawaii trial court, alleging that he had been fired in retaliation for inquiring into the payroll deduction. The court granted summary judgment motions filed by the association and agent, and the assistant manager appealed to the Intermediate Court of Appeals of Hawaii.

On appeal, the employee argued that his firing violated a public policy encompassed in a state statute that required employers to furnish employees with accurate information concerning their payroll deductions and to maintain accurate records for six years. The association and agent argued that the employee was terminable at will and had been fired for misconduct, insubordination and unsatisfactory work performance. The court of appeals observed that the Hawaii statute did not create a cause of action under which employees could sue employers, but did state a public policy protecting at-will employees from being discharged for asserting their rights under the statute. The discharge of an employee requesting further information into a payroll deduction violated a clear public policy. Because a genuine issue of fact existed, the lower court had erroneously granted summary judgment to the association and agent, and the decision was vacated and remanded. *Smith v. Chaney Brooks Realty, Inc.*, 865 P.2d 170 (Hawaii App.1994).

A discharged employee filed a complaint against his former employer in a Pennsylvania trial court stating that it had violated government contracts by overbilling for work actually performed, and that his job was terminated as a result of his telling authorities of the unlawful business practices. The trial court entered judgment for the employer and the employee appealed to the Superior Court of Pennsylvania. The employee argued that there were two reasons for claims of wrongful discharge in an at-will employment relationship: first, when the termination threatened clear mandates of public policy; and second, when the discharge was based on a specific intent to harm. The court noted, however, that the discharge must threaten or violate a clear mandate of public policy to be actionable. A review of the cases regarding this cause of action revealed that courts have found a clear mandate of public policy threatened on only three occasions— 1) discharge for reporting nuclear safety violations; 2) discharge of an employee who had been convicted and pardoned; and 3) discharge for serving jury duty. The employee failed to show how his case would fit into these three categories. Here, the employee alleged that the employer's conduct violated a clear mandate of public policy pursuant to Pennsylvania's whistleblower law. However, the act's scope was limited to employees discharged from governmental entities or any other body which was created or funded by the government. The court was not prepared to expand the coverage of the act to include the private arena. Therefore, the court upheld the judgment of the trial court and found for the employer. *Krajsa v. Keypunch Inc.*, 622 A.2d 355 (Pa.Super.1993).

A corporation which produced, marketed and sold recorded products hired a man who rose to the position of West Coast Regional Manager. The corporation had a practice of shipping products at no charge for promotional purposes. These promotional products were not labeled as such and could thus be sold in the retail market. When the manager noticed that certain recipients of the material did not ordinarily handle such products, he became suspicious of criminal conduct. After he reported his suspicions to higher management he was fired, allegedly for poor job performance. The manager brought suit against the corporation, claiming that the reason for his discharge was pretextual and that he was actually fired in retaliation for attempting to prevent criminal behavior. The trial court granted the corporation's motion to dismiss the complaint, and the manager appealed to the California Court of Appeal, Second District. The court noted that the employment contract was one of indefinite duration and was generally terminable at the will of either party. However, the corporation's right to discharge the manager was subject to limits imposed by public policy. Because the public had a fundamental interest in a workplace free from crime, the discharge was wrongful only if the corporation had discharged the manager in retaliation for his reporting suspicions of illegal conduct. The court of appeal reversed the dismissal and allowed the manager's claim to proceed to trial. *Collier v. Superior Court*, 279 Cal.Rptr. 453 (Cal.App.2d Dist.1991).

A secretary at a Texas company was selected as a juror and served on a jury for six working days. Three days after her selection, she was discharged. She filed suit in a state trial court, and the action was removed to a federal district court in Texas. Five days before trial, the employee attempted to add two more claims against the company arising from her termination, but the court refused to allow the amendment. At trial, it awarded her six months' compensation which was the maximum amount allowed under the Texas Juror Reemployment Statute (TJRS). She appealed to the U.S. Court of Appeals, Fifth Circuit, asserting that she should have received punitive damages in excess of the compensatory damages allowed by the statute. The court of appeals noted that the TJRS did not seem to contemplate punitive damages. However, by analogizing the statute to the Texas Workers' Compensation Retaliation Statute, the court found that the term "damages" allowed punitive damages according to the Texas Supreme Court. Nevertheless, even though punitive damages could be recovered, the maximum amount of actual and punitive damages recoverable was six months' worth of the employee's compensation. *Fuchs v. Lifetime Doors, Inc.*, 939 F.2d 1275 (5th Cir.1991).

An Oklahoma customer service supervisor received a jury summons from a county district court which required her to report for jury duty for one week of service. She gave her supervisor a copy of the summons, and reported for jury duty. She was not selected for a jury on either Monday or Tuesday, being released for the afternoon. However, she did not return to work in the afternoon on those days. On Wednesday, the regional supervisor met with her after jury duty had concluded for the day and requested that she obtain a statement from the court that she was not allowed to be on call for jury duty at work. She did not obtain the statement and was fired. She received juror compensation for the entire week, then sued the employer for wrongful discharge. A jury awarded her $175,000 in actual damages and $350,000 in punitive damages. The company appealed to the Oklahoma Court of Appeals. On appeal, the court noted that to establish a *prima facie* case of wrongful discharge under the Oklahoma statute, the employee needed to show that she had been absent from work because of the requirement that she serve as a juror, and that she had been discharged because of this absence. Here, the court determined that there had been sufficient evidence presented from which the jury could conclude that the discharge had been retaliatory in nature. The court affirmed the jury's verdict, but lowered the punitive damages award to $175,000. *Brown v. MFC Finance Company of Oklahoma*, 838 P.2d 524 (Okl.App.1992).

A South Carolina employee alleged that his employer violated the Fair Labor Standards Act (FLSA) by requiring him and other employees to work excessively long hours without compensation. Shortly after he reported the employer's conduct to the U.S. Department of Labor, he was fired. The employee sued in state court, alleging that he was discharged in retaliation for filing the complaint with the federal agency. The employer filed a summary judgment motion, and asserted that the FLSA precluded any claim the employee had under state tort law. The motion was granted and the employee appealed to the Supreme Court of South Carolina. The supreme court noted that the FLSA provides that it is illegal to discharge or discriminate against an employee because the employee has filed a complaint under the Act. When a statute like the FLSA creates a substantive right and provides a remedy for infringement of that right, the employee is limited to that statutory remedy. The court held that this was applicable whether the right is created by federal or state law. The employee, therefore, was limited to his remedy under the FLSA. Since it appeared the employee may have had a valid claim under the FLSA, the case was remanded to the trial court for further consideration. *Dockins v. Ingles Marliet, Inc.*, 413 S.E.2d 18 (S.C.1992).

A Massachusetts assistant director of nursing employed under an at-will employment contract was discharged following remarks made during an internal survey. A former assistant sent a letter regarding her concerns about the medical staff and administration to the organization headquarters. The headquarters sent a survey team to evaluate the situation. The hospital administrator was very upset and inquired about the source of the letter. The director of nursing denied involvement, although she did not respond to his inquiry regarding the current assistant director of nursing's involvement. During the survey, the assistant director of nursing discussed communication problems, providing detailed examples of patient care problems and problems with the assistant chief of staff. The assistant director of nursing's comments were acknowledged in reports from the survey team. After receipt of the reports, the hospital administrator became upset and blamed the nursing department for the survey team's recommendation to make another visit specifically exploring the communication problems. Subsequently, the hospital administrator stopped speaking to the assistant director of nursing and ordered her employment terminated for "patient care issues." The nurse filed a wrongful termination claim, asserting that her firing violated public policy. The Superior Court entered judgment in favor of the assistant director of nursing. The hospital appealed.

On appeal, the Supreme Judicial Court of Massachusetts noted that the termination did not violate public policy, and it therefore reversed the superior court holding. Even though the assistant director of nursing occupied a role affecting the public interest in health, she was still an at-will employee making her subject to "without cause, without notice" termination. Status as health care employees does not make employees immune to termination even regarding issues "they feel are detrimental to health care." The court held that the public interest in good medical care would not be violated. Additionally, the court noted that the assistant director's claim for intentional interference with contractual relations failed for lack of evidence showing that the hospital director's purpose for discharging her was not legitimate. *Wright v. Shriners Hospital for Crippled Children et al.*, 589 N.E.2d 1241 (Mass.1992).

C. Performing Statutory Obligations

Two Tennessee truck drivers alleged that they were fired by their employer because they refused to operate a truck which they had not had time to inspect before driving. They filed a lawsuit against the employer in a Tennessee trial court, which refused to award the employer a directed verdict and allowed the case to proceed to the jury. The jury held for the drivers and the employer appealed the judgment to the Tennessee Court of Appeals, which reversed the trial court decision, finding that the state Motor Carriers Act did not create a cause of action for retaliatory discharge. The drivers appealed to the Supreme Court of Tennessee, which observed that the Motor Carriers Act declared it the public policy of Tennessee to protect the safety and welfare of the public by imposing a number of requirements upon motor vehicle operators. Tolerating the retaliatory discharge of these employees for observing the safety provisions of the act would impair the legislature's declared policy of protecting the public. Because the firing of employees who sought to uphold the motor carrier act violated a clear public policy, the trial court had properly allowed the jury verdict to stand and the court reinstated its judgment. *Reynolds v. Ozark Motor Lines, Inc.*, 887 S.W.2d 822 (Tenn.1994).

A Missouri shoe company employee was exposed to a chemical spray used in the operation of one of the company's machines. The employee questioned the safety of the chemical and inquired about safety protection methods. She made a complaint to the local Occupational Safety and Health Administration (OSHA) office, then filed a formal complaint alleging hazardous conditions at her workplace. An OSHA compliance officer conducted an on-site investigation, which infuriated the company president. Within five weeks of the investigation, the company fired the complaining employee under a relatively new employee tardiness policy. The employee was the first person ever prosecuted under the policy, and there was evidence that other employees had similar or worse attendance records. The discharged employee filed a lawsuit against the employer in the U.S. District Court for the Eastern District of Missouri, which granted the employer's motion for summary judgment. The employee appealed to the U.S. Court of Appeals, Eighth Circuit.

The court of appeals held that the district court had incorrectly required the employee to prove that the manufacturer had actual knowledge of her identity as the complaining employee. Even though the OSHA inspector had not revealed the employee's identity, evidence indicated that the president was aware of it. The appropriate standard for avoiding summary judgment in a retaliatory discharge case was a showing that the employee had engaged in a protected activity and that a causal connection between the protected activity and the adverse employment action existed. Because the district court had applied a higher standard of inquiry that ignored evidence of the causal connection between the protected activity and the adverse action, summary judgment was inappropriate and the district court decision was reversed. *Reich v. Hoy Shoe Co., Inc.*, 32 F.3d 361 (8th Cir.1994).

A national insurance company consolidated its automobile insurance business in the state of New Jersey into a single subsidiary pursuant to a consent order with the state commissioner of insurance. It also agreed to withdraw its other subsidiaries from New Jersey. The consent order imposed certain minimal capitalization requirements and substantial deposits with the commissioner's office to guarantee the ability to satisfy liabilities. The company hired an executive officer to lead the subsidiary under a written employment contract of five and one-half years' duration. The executive disagreed with the company's handling of matters related to the order, and he was fired after two years of employment. He alleged that the company engaged in fraudulent conduct, including falsified reports to reduce its payment obligations under the consent order. The former executive filed a lawsuit in the New Jersey court system under the state whistleblower's statute. The company filed a motion to stay the action and compel arbitration as required by the employment contract.

The Superior Court of New Jersey, Law Division, rejected the employee's argument that his employment involved only intrastate commerce and was therefore not governed by the Federal Arbitration Act (FAA). Even though the claim was based on violations of a state law protecting conscientious employees, these matters were subject to private arbitration in accordance with the employment agreement. The arbitrator would be required to consider the alleged statutory violations, and the arbitration clause did not deprive the executive of an opportunity to raise these issues. The court granted the company's motion to compel arbitration and stay the state court action. *Bleumer v. Parkway Ins. Co.*, 277 N.J.Super. 378, 649 A.2d 913 (1994).

An Oregon pharmacy technician noted inaccuracies in the monthly inventory of drugs in her employer's pharmacy department. When she advised her immediate supervisor of the inaccuracies, and advised him that the drug inventory recordkeeping violated state standards, he allegedly did nothing. The employee further alleged that during the course of the next two years, the supervisor retaliated against her by refusing to speak to her and imposing a strict absenteeism policy upon her. The supervisor accused the employee of stealing cocaine from the pharmacy and called the sheriff's department to investigate his claim. The sheriff's department refused to arrest the employee upon the supervisor's request, and within two months the employee quit. She sued the employer in an Oregon trial court for retaliatory discharge and intentional infliction of emotional distress. The court dismissed the complaint, and the employee appealed to the Court of Appeals of Oregon. The court determined that false accusations of theft and the involvement of the sheriff's department on false pretenses, if proven, could constitute grounds for either retaliatory discharge or intentional infliction of emotional distress. Employers could not discharge employees who performed important societal obligations, in this case the obligation to comply with a statute or administrative rule. Although employment termination by itself did not constitute grounds for intentional infliction of emotional distress, the reporting of the incident to the sheriff's department could constitute grounds for extreme emotional distress. The court reversed and remanded the case to the trial court. *Dalby v. Sisters of Providence in Oregon*, 865 P.2d 391 (Or.App.1993).

An attorney worked for a company which distributed kidney dialysis equipment. When notified that certain machines did not comply with FDA regulations, he advised the company not to accept the machines for distribution. He later discovered that the company planned to accept the machines anyway. He told the president of the company that he would do whatever was necessary to stop the sale of the machines. Shortly thereafter he was fired. He sued the company for retaliatory discharge, and the trial court granted summary judgment to the company. He appealed to the state appellate court which reversed and remanded. Further appeal was taken to the Supreme Court of Illinois.

The supreme court looked at the special relationship between attorneys and clients, concluding that in-house counsel generally do not have a cause of action for retaliatory discharge. Here, the attorney had a duty to report the information about the dialysis machines; he had no choice in the matter. Thus, he did not have the dilemma of choosing between reporting the violation and staying quiet to protect his job. Further, if information obtained by attorneys could be used in retaliatory discharge suits, employers might be hesitant to turn to in-house counsel for advice on potentially questionable corporate conduct. The court reversed the appellate court's decision, and held that the retaliatory discharge claim could not stand. *Balla v. Gambro, Inc.,* 584 N.E.2d 104 (Ill.1991).

After a Missouri hospital nurse made the diagnosis that a patient's condition was toxic shock syndrome, she anticipated immediate doctor's orders for antibiotics to combat the life-threatening infection. After time passed with no such orders, she was instructed by her supervisor to "document, report the facts and stay out of it." The treating doctor never gave the orders that she expected for the proper care of the patient. When protocol allowed, she discussed the patient's condition with another doctor. Nevertheless, the patient later died of massive internal infection. The nurse indicated to the family that she would obtain the medical records and made several disparaging statements concerning the treatment of the patient. She was then fired and received a letter which stated that the cause for her dismissal was that she made certain statements concerning the hospital, its staff or employees which were "untrue and detrimental to the hospital." The nurse then filed a wrongful discharge claim in a Missouri trial court. The trial court granted the hospital's motion for summary judgment and the nurse appealed to the Missouri Court of Appeals.

The nurse contended that the trial court erroneously determined that there was no public policy exception to the employment-at-will doctrine. The appellate court agreed, citing numerous cases which found a public policy exception to the employment-at-will doctrine. The hospital argued that the Nursing Practices Act on which the nurse relied did not constitute a clear mandate of law in which a cause of action for wrongful discharge could be based. The court noted that the Nursing Practices Act set forth a clear mandate of public policy that the nurse "not stay out of a dying patient's improper treatment." The constant and immediate involvement in seeking proper treatment for the patient was her absolute duty. Therefore, the court reversed the grant of summary judgment to the hospital, remanding the case for a trial at which the nurse could establish that her discharge resulted from retaliation for her performance of a mandated lawful act. *Kirk v. Mercy Hospital, Tri-County,* 851 S.W.2d 617 (Mo.App.1993).

A Missouri man worked as a licensed veterinarian for a private university for approximately four years. He then claimed that he was discharged in retaliation for reporting his employer's infractions of the Animal Welfare Act (AWA). He brought suit for wrongful discharge, and his employer filed a motion to dismiss. A trial court granted the employer's motion, and the veterinarian appealed. The Missouri Court of Appeals held that the veterinarian was an at-will employee, despite the evidence presented by the employer that the veterinarian was a contract employee. The court noted that the state recognized a public policy exception for wrongful discharge to an employee hired at will. That exception existed where the employer's act of discharge violated a statute, a regulation based on a statute, or a constitutional provision. The court found that federal regulations based on the AWA created a non-retaliation requirement for reporting violations. It held that the veterinarian had stated a cause of action for wrongful discharge under the state public policy exception to the employment-at-will doctrine, and it reversed the decision of the trial court. *Luethans v. Washington University,* 838 S.W.2d 117 (Mo.App.E.D.1992).

V. COLLECTIVE BARGAINING AGREEMENTS

Where a collective bargaining agreement exists, cases may become more complicated as an employee could potentially have claims against both the employer and the union. For further cases involving union and employer obligations under federal law, see Chapter Five.

A Louisiana man worked for a company as a machine operator on a hazardous machine. Company rules provided that the use or bringing of controlled substances on to the premises would result in discharge. Police officers found the employee in another person's vehicle on company premises where marijuana was present. They also found marijuana gleanings in the employee's car. The company learned of the first incident and fired the employee. He contested his discharge and filed a grievance seeking arbitration under the collective bargaining agreement. Shortly before the arbitration hearing, the company learned of the marijuana found in the employee's car. However, the arbitrator then held for the employee because there was insufficient proof that the employee had used marijuana on the premises. The company appealed to a federal district court, which overturned the arbitrator's decision. The U.S. Court of Appeals, Fifth Circuit, affirmed, and the case reached the U.S. Supreme Court.

The Supreme Court noted that the lower courts had erred in overturning the arbitrator's decision because of public policy concerns. Here, the arbitrator's refusal to consider the later evidence was not bad faith or affirmative misconduct. Further, arbitrators have wide discretion in formulating remedies, and it was error for the courts to overturn this arbitrator's decision because they viewed discharge as the proper remedy. The Court reversed the lower courts' holdings and upheld the arbitrator's decision. *United Paperworkers International Union v. Misco, Inc.,* 484 U.S. 29, 108 S.Ct. 364, 98 L.Ed.2d 286 (1987).

Caterpillar Tractor Company hired a group of employees to work at a California facility. Each position was covered by the collective bargaining agreement (CBA). These employees all reached managerial or weekly salaried positions, outside the coverage of the CBA. They held their positions for a number of years, and alleged that the employer made oral and written representations that "they could look forward to indefinite and lasting employment." The company then downgraded them to unionized positions which were supposedly only temporary. Thereafter, the company notified them that it was closing the California facility and that they would be laid off. The employees sued the employer in state court, contending that it had breached the individual employment contracts between them. The employer removed the case to a federal district court, and the case was dismissed for failure of the employees to state a claim under § 301 of the

Labor Management Relations Act. The U.S. Court of Appeals, Ninth Circuit, reversed, holding that the case must be heard in state court, and the case came before the U.S. Supreme Court.

The Supreme Court agreed with the court of appeals that the state law contract claims were not preempted by § 301. Here, even though the employees could have brought suit under § 301, they chose to sue under state law on their individual contracts. No interpretation or application of the CBA was necessary to decide their claims. Further, even though the employees were covered by the CBA, their individual contracts were not necessarily subsumed into the CBA. The Court thus affirmed the judgment of the court of appeals, and held that the state law claims should be heard in state court. *Caterpillar Inc. v. Williams*, 482 U.S. 386, 107 S.Ct. 2425, 96 L.Ed.2d 318 (1987).

A Wisconsin car manufacturer discharged an employee after he sexually assaulted a female coworker by grabbing her breasts. The union filed a grievance which the manufacturer denied and the matter proceeded to arbitration. The arbitrator refused to consider the evidence of other sexual harassment by the employee that the manufacturer had uncovered after the discharge. The arbitrator determined that the discharge based on one incident was too severe and ordered the manufacturer to reinstate the employee. The manufacturer reinstated the employee for one day and then discharged him for the other incidents of harassment that it had uncovered after his initial discharge. The union asked the court to find the manufacturer in contempt. After the court denied the contempt motion, the union appealed to the U.S. Court of Appeals, Seventh Circuit. The court noted that the manufacturer had "fresh evidence" upon which to base its second discharge of the employee. Accordingly, the court held that it had complied with the order and that it was not in contempt. *Chrysler Motors Corp. v. International Union, Allied Industrial Workers of America, AFL-CIO*, 2 F.3d 760 (7th Cir.1993).

A Missouri employee of a power company was discharged for reasons based on his entire work record, which included his work attitude, failure to follow instructions, and careless performance of his duties. He filed a grievance pursuant to provisions of the collective bargaining agreement, and the matter was submitted to an arbitrator. The arbitrator found that the employee had been unjustly discharged and ordered his reinstatement. The company then brought an action to vacate the arbitration award, claiming that the arbitrator's decision was based in part on a posthearing communication with a union official which deprived the company of a fair hearing. It also alleged misconduct on the arbitrator's part for his participation in the posthearing contact. The union filed a counterclaim for enforcement of the arbitration award. Both parties made cross motions for summary judgment. A district court granted the union's motion for summary judgment and denied the company's motion. The company appealed.

The U.S. Court of Appeals, Eighth Circuit, affirmed the decision of the district court. It held that although the arbitrator violated procedural regulations by conducting a posthearing consultation, his conduct neither deprived the company of a fair hearing nor influenced the outcome of the arbitration. The court found that although the arbitrator's conduct constituted misbehavior, his decision was based upon the testimony and other evidence presented at the hearing. It found that the arbitrator had not acted in bad faith since he voluntarily disclosed his posthearing consultation to both parties. The result of the posthearing consultation supported evidence of which the arbitrator had previous knowledge. *M & A Elec. Power v. Local Union No. 702*, 977 F.2d 1235 (8th Cir.1992).

A truck driver left to deliver a load, but called while en route to inform his employer he was unable to finish the trip because he had been drinking and needed rehabilitation. The employer agreed to allow the truck driver a leave of absence conditioned on his completion of an alcohol rehabilitation program. The truck driver asked to return to work prior to completion of the rehabilitation program. Consequently, the employer discharged him "for failing to complete a job and failing to meet the conditions of his leave of absence." The union pursued a grievance hearing under the CBA alleging that the termination was not "for cause." However, the discharge was affirmed. The truck driver then filed a complaint with the National Labor Relations Board (NLRB) claiming that his discharge was the result of his union and protected concerted activities including invoking a right provided for in the CBA. The claim was denied because of insufficient evidence. Finally, the truck driver instituted an action in a U.S. district court seeking "reinstatement, backpay, and punitive damages because [his employer] violated California statutory and common law by discharging him in retaliation" for his protected activities. The Missouri federal district court granted summary judgment in favor of the employer holding the claims were preempted by the National Labor Relations Act (NLRA) and Labor Management Relations Act (LMRA). The employee appealed the preemption claims.

On appeal, the U.S. Court of Appeals, Eighth Circuit, affirmed the district court's holding in favor of the employer. The court reiterated that union activities protected under the NLRA would be addressed by the NLRB, not state or federal courts. In particular, a right under an employee's CBA would fall under the NLRA protection and jurisdiction. Additionally, the truck driver did not present a compelling local interest as an exception to the NLRA standard. In fact, the claims brought by the truck driver could have been properly brought before the NLRB. Moreover, the truck driver was unsuccessful in the grievance process and in bringing the suit to the NLRB. *Platt v. Jack Cooper Transport Co., Inc.,* 959 F.2d 91 (8th Cir.1992).

VI. OTHER TERMINATION CASES

Discharge of an employee can lead to lawsuits in a wide range of areas. There can be severance pay problems, allegations of misconduct or abandonment, and challenges to various employment practices.

A field service representative installed and serviced medical instruments in three midwestern states. Although he was based in Illinois, his supervisor was headquartered in Massachusetts. The supervisor fired the representative for mismanagement and insubordination. Despite obtaining a higher-paying job, the representative filed a lawsuit against the manufacturer and his former supervisor in the U.S. District Court for the Northern District of Illinois, alleging retaliatory discharge, defamation and tortious interference with advantageous business relations. The court conducted a trial resulting in a $100,000 damage award for the representative, consisting of $10,000 in actual and $50,000 in punitive damages against the manufacturer and $40,000 in punitive damages against the supervisor. The manufacturer and supervisor appealed to the U.S. Court of Appeals, Seventh Circuit.

The court of appeals observed that the defendants had failed to challenge personal jurisdiction at the district court level, and had thereby forfeited their right to do so. The court also observed the inconsistency of awarding punitive damages against the supervisor even though no general damages were attributed to him. Despite this inconsistency, the court refused to turn aside the district court's decision. Punitive damages were justifiable because there was sufficient evidence in the record to sustain the award based on a showing of "actual malice." The finding of actual malice was supported by evidence of indifference by the defendents to the truth or falsity of statements made about the representative. *Rice v. Nova Biomedical Corp.*, 38 F.3d 909 (7th Cir.1994).

A management employee at a West Virginia steel company was suspected of wrongful conduct involving an outside contractor, including the approval of falsified invoices, acceptance of gratuities, and use of subcontractor employees for personal reasons. The company suspended the manager with pay while investigating the charges. The investigation revealed that he had accepted gratuities but that he was not guilty of any criminal wrongdoing. The company nonetheless discharged the manager, stating that the allegations of impropriety compromised his ability to function effectively. The manager filed a complaint in a West Virginia trial court, alleging wrongful discharge, breach of the duty of good faith and fair dealing, defamation, negligent investigation, violation of public policy and punitive damages. The trial court granted the company's motion for a directed verdict on most of the manager's claims, but denied its motion for a directed verdict on the claim for outrage and intentional infliction of emotional distress. The jury returned a $500,000 compensatory damage award plus $150,000 in punitive damages on those claims. The trial court struck down the punitive damage award, but allowed the manager to recover compensatory damages. The company appealed to the Supreme Court of Appeals of West Virginia.

The supreme court of appeals observed that in many wrongful discharge actions, claims for emotional distress and outrage cannot stand. This occurs when the emotional distress results from the discharge itself; for example, where embarrassment and financial loss result from the discharge. In other cases, outrage or emotional distress result from the manner of the discharge; for example, where the employer's motivation for the discharge is improper. Although it was possible for an outrage complaint to survive in a wrongful discharge, there was no such conduct in this case. The company had acted appropriately in investigating the manager's conduct. The distress he allegedly suffered resulted from the discharge itself. The court reversed and remanded the trial court's decision. *Dzinglski v. Weirton Steel Corp.*, 445 S.E.2d 219 (W.Va.1994).

An industrial relations manager resumed working for a brewery after a three-year absence. Prior to his leave, a voluntary resignation, the manager had achieved six years of experience with the brewery. The manager received one "needs improvement" rating at the end of his first year of reemployment, and thereafter received good ratings. After a second "needs improvement" rating about four years after resuming work, the manager quit again, and filed a lawsuit against the brewery in a California trial court. The court dismissed the manager's claims for age discrimination, constructive wrongful discharge, violation of public policy, breach of contract, and intentional and negligent infliction of emotional distress. It then awarded summary judgment to the brewery on the breach of contract and public policy claims. The California Court of Appeal reversed the public policy claim, and the brewery appealed to the Supreme Court of California.

The supreme court stated that constructive discharge is an employer-coerced involuntary action that requires proof that the employer either intentionally created or knowingly permitted conditions that were so intolerable that an employer would realize that a reasonable person would feel compelled to resign. In this case, regardless of whether the employee had been constructively discharged, there was no wrongful termination because the employee had relied upon incidents that had occurred up to four years prior to his voluntary termination. The remoteness in time and lack of aggravated circumstances indicated that the termination was not wrongful. Because the employee had failed to demonstrate the violation of a fundamental public policy, his claim should have been dismissed and the court of appeal's decision was reversed. *Turner v. Anheuser-Busch, Inc.*, 32 Cal.Rptr.2d 223, 876 P.2d 1022 (Cal.1994).

A manager in the electronics department of a Texas retail store was indirectly involved in a transaction after which a customer left the store without paying for merchandise. The store manager investigated the matter and told the electronics manager that he would probably be fired despite his 29 years of store employment. He made this statement even though the company had a policy of not firing persons with more than 25 years of employment without approval of regional management. The store manager kept the electronics manager waiting for several days, and the electronics manager offered to take a demotion. The store accepted the offer and within a year, the demoted manager accepted early retirement as part of a reduction in force. The retirement offer included a waiver of all claims and damages against the store.

The demoted manager sued the store in a Texas trial court, alleging that the early retirement agreement had been fraudulently induced and that the store was guilty of duress, coercion and fraud. The court awarded the manager almost $600,000 for lost salary, mental anguish and punitive damages. The Texas Court of Appeals affirmed the judgment and the store appealed to the Supreme Court of

Texas. The supreme court agreed with the store that the trial court had improperly instructed the jury concerning the elements of fraud. The jury instructions should have included the element of intent to cause the consequences of the allegedly fraudulent misrepresentation. The trial court had merely stated that it was sufficient to find that the store intended to mislead the former electronics manager. Accordingly, the court reversed and remanded the case for a new trial. *Sears, Roebuck & Co. v. Meadows*, 877 S.W.2d 281 (Tex.1994).

A route supervisor at a Maryland bakery scheduled his vacation so that he could participate in a golf tournament. Because of a late, unexpected shortage of help at that time, his superior ordered him to report to work even though the superior was aware of the conflict. When he failed to show up, he was fired. He sued the bakery for wrongful discharge and intentional infliction of emotional distress. The bakery removed the case to federal district court and moved for summary judgment, claiming that the supervisor was an at-will employee and that the discharge was not so outrageous as to sustain a claim for intentional infliction of emotional distress. The district court agreed, and the supervisor appealed only the latter ruling to the U.S. Court of Appeals, Fourth Circuit. The supervisor argued on appeal that the bakery knew of his plans, knew of the importance of the job to him because of his need to support his family, and knew of the stress that would result if he were fired. He asserted that the bakery's actions were extreme and outrageous, going beyond all possible bounds of decency. The court disagreed. It noted that the bakery was doing nothing more than making certain its offices were sufficiently staffed during a period of shortage. In placing its own needs above those of the supervisor, the bakery did not exceed the bounds usually tolerated by society. The court affirmed the district court's decision. *Lewis v. Schmidt Baking Co.*, 16 F.3d 614 (4th Cir.1994).

A hotel in Hawaii adopted a policy which provided that two direct relatives could not work in the same department together. If they married after being hired, one of the two would be asked to transfer or resign. A couple who had been cohabiting got married shortly after the husband was hired. A year later, the new owner of the hotel sought to enforce the rule. When neither husband nor wife transferred, the husband was discharged. He sued the hotel in a Hawaii court, claiming a violation of a Hawaii law against discrimination based on marital status. The trial court granted summary judgment to the hotel, and appeal was taken to the Supreme Court of Hawaii. The supreme court determined that it was the fact of marriage which caused the discharge. It then stated that the policy of firing persons who marry others working in the same department violated Hawaii law unless a statutory exception could be shown. The court vacated the decision and remanded the case so that the hotel could attempt to show that its policy fell within one of the statutory exceptions. *Ross v. Stouffer Hotel Co.*, 816 P.2d 302 (Hawaii 1991).

A trucking company discharged one of its drivers, alleging that he had disabled several lights on his assigned truck in order to obtain extra pay while awaiting repairs. The driver filed a grievance, asserting that the discharge had been in retaliation for having complained of safety violations. He also filed a complaint with the Department of Labor, alleging that his firing violated § 405 of the federal Surface Transportation Assistance Act, which forbids such an action. A field investigator obtained statements substantiating the driver's claim, offered the company the opportunity to submit a written statement detailing the basis for the employee's discharge, but it was not allowed to examine the substance of the investigator's evidence. A preliminary administrative order called for the employee's reinstatement and the company filed suit in a Georgia federal court, arguing that reinstatement prior to an evidentiary hearing violated its due process rights. The court ruled for the company, and appeal was taken directly to the U.S. Supreme Court. The Supreme Court affirmed in part and reversed in part the district court's decision. It stated that due process required prereinstatement notice of the employee's allegations, notice of the substance of the relevant supporting evidence, an opportunity to submit a written response, and an opportunity to meet with the investigator and present statements from rebuttal witnesses. Due process did not require employer confrontation and cross-examination before preliminary reinstatement if a prompt post-reinstatement evidentiary hearing was available. *Brock v. Roadway Express, Inc.,* 481 U.S. 252, 107 S.Ct. 1740, 95 L.Ed.2d 239 (1987).

An employee of a chain of New England retail stores managed a clothing department at a location in Connecticut. Although the store was closed by law on Sundays, when state law allowed, it began to keep Sunday hours. After working occasional Sundays for two years, the employee notified his employer that he would no longer work on that day because it was his Sabbath. A Connecticut law stated that employers could not require their employees to work on their Sabbath days, nor was refusal to work on the Sabbath to be deemed grounds for dismissal. The employer demoted the employee to a clerical position. He then resigned and filed a grievance administratively. He was found to have been discharged in violation of the statute, and a state trial court upheld that decision. The Connecticut Supreme Court reversed, and the case came before the U.S. Supreme Court.

The Court held that the Connecticut law violated the Establishment Clause of the First Amendment. Essentially, it imposed on employers an absolute duty to conform their business practices to the particular religious practices of the employees. Under this law, Sabbath religious concerns automatically controlled over all secular interests at the workplace. The primary effect of this law, then, was the advancement of religion, which is forbidden by the Establishment Clause. The Court affirmed the state supreme court's decision in favor of the employer. *Estate of Thornton v. Caldor, Inc.,* 472 U.S. 703, 105 S.Ct. 2914, 86 L.Ed.2d 557 (1985).

CHAPTER FOUR

EMPLOYEE BENEFITS

I. RETIREMENT BENEFITS

ERISA, the Employee Retirement Income Security Act of 1974, 29 U.S.C. § 1001, *et seq.*, is a comprehensive federal statute that imposes uniform rules and standards upon private pension and welfare benefit plans. It describes the fiduciary responsibilities of plan administrators and specifies rules for pension participation, funding, vesting and financial reporting. ERISA preempts all state laws "as they may now or hereafter relate to any employee benefit plan described in section 1003(a) of this title . . . ." Because the question of ERISA applicability frequently determines the outcome of pension litigation, a substantial body of law has developed concerning whether a particular state law "relates to" a plan described by ERISA.

A. ERISA in General

The U.S. Supreme Court ruled that the guaranteed benefit policy exclusion in ERISA does not cover funds, administered by an insurer, that bear no fixed rate of return and have yet to be converted into guaranteed funds. At issue were the funds of a group annuity contract (GAC). The contract was between the insurer and a bank acting as trustee for a corporate retirement plan. Under the contract, the deposits to secure retirement benefits were not immediately applied to the purchase of annuities. Instead, these "free funds" were commingled with the insurer's general corporate assets. In this manner, the deposit account balances reflected the insurer's overall investment experience. During the life of the contract, amounts credited to the deposit account could be converted into a stream of guaranteed benefits for individual employees. The trustee asserted that the insurer was managing "plan assets" and was therefore subject to fiduciary responsibility as mandated by ERISA. The insurer countered that its actions fell within the statutory exclusion for "guaranteed benefit policies."

The Court recited the general rule that ERISA preempted state insurance law. Though the Court agreed with the insurer that the McCarran-Ferguson Act (M-F Act) reserved to the states primary responsibility for regulation of the insurance industry, it noted that ERISA did not order an unqualified deferral to state law. The M-F Act mandates that only laws specifically relating to the business of insurance may supersede state insurance laws. The Court then noted that ERISA, both in general and in guaranteed benefit policy provisions in particular, specifically relates to the business of insurance. ERISA controlled in this instance and it specifically preempted "all state laws" insofar as they related to any employee benefit plan. A statutory exception excludes from the scope of ERISA's fiduciary requirements assets held pursuant to "an insurance policy or contract to the extent that such policy or contract provides for benefits the amount of which are guaranteed by the insurer." The Court determined that GAC fit this exception only in part. Problematic was the insurer's responsibility for administration of the "free funds." The Court concluded that the insurer's fiduciary responsibility applied to the extent that it engaged in the discretionary management of assets attributable to that phase of the contract which provided no guarantee of benefit payments or fixed rates of return. ERISA exempts "an insurance policy or contract to the extent that such policy or contract" provides for guaranteed benefits. In applying this to GAC, the Court determined that GAC annuities would be exempt but that the "free funds" would not be. Hence, each component of the contract had to be examined to determine its exemption and in this instance the insurer had a fiduciary responsibility with respect to the "free funds" until they became guaranteed benefits. *John Hancock Mut. Life Ins. Co., v. Harris Trust and Savings Bank*, 114 S.Ct. 517, 126 L.Ed.2d 524 (1993).

A class of former employees of the Kaiser Steel Corporation who participated in the company's retirement plan brought suit for the plan's losses against an actuary employed by the company who they alleged had knowingly participated in misfeasance by plan fiduciaries. The plan was qualified under ERISA. The actuary was employed in 1980 when Kaiser began to phase out its steel making operations, prompting early retirement by a large number of plan participants. The actuary had failed to change the plan's actuarial assumptions to reflect the additional costs imposed by the retirements. As a result, Kaiser did not adequately fund the plan. Eventually the plan's assets became insufficient to satisfy its obligations, and was terminated. The former employees then began receiving only the benefits guaranteed by ERISA which were substantially lower than the fully vested pensions due them under the plan. After a California federal district court and the U.S. Court of Appeals, Ninth Circuit, dismissed the complaint, the former employees appealed to the U.S. Supreme Court.

ERISA § 502(a)(3) permits plan participants to bring civil actions to obtain "appropriate equitable relief" to redress violations of the plan. The Court determined that requiring the actuary to make the plan whole for the losses it sustained would not constitute "appropriate equitable relief." What the employees were seeking here was compensatory damages, not "equitable relief." The Supreme Court determined that the text of ERISA indicated that Congress intended equitable relief to include only those types of relief that were typically available in equity, such as injunction, mandamus, and restitution. Accordingly, the Supreme Court affirmed the lower court decisions and dismissed the complaint. *Mertens v. Hewitt Associates*, 113 S.Ct. 2063, 124 L.Ed.2d 161 (1993).

A Texas man worked for a company as a salesman and distributor of construction equipment. Four months before his pension would have vested, the employee was fired during a reduction in force. He sued the company in state court for wrongful discharge. The trial court granted summary judgment to the employer, the Texas Court of Appeals affirmed, and the case reached the Texas Supreme Court. That court reversed, finding that ERISA did not preempt the employee's lawsuit. The company then sought review from the U.S. Supreme Court. The Supreme Court found that the employee's claim was expressly preempted by ERISA. Here, for the employee to prevail on his claim, the court below would have to find that an ERISA plan existed and that the employer had a pension-defeating motive in terminating the employment. Since this "related" to an ERISA plan, it was preempted. Only federal courts could hear this type of case. The Supreme Court reversed the Texas Supreme Court's decision. *Ingersoll-Rand Co. v. McClendon*, 498 U.S. 133, 111 S.Ct. 478, 112 L.Ed.2d 474 (1990).

One of the trustees of a sheet metal workers' pension fund embezzled over $375,000 from the union. Two pension plans contended that the trustee had forfeited his right to receive benefits as a result of his criminal misconduct. They also asserted that even if he had not forfeited his benefits, those benefits should be paid to the union and not to him. A Colorado federal district court held that because there was a judgment against the trustee for $275,000, a constructive trust should be imposed on the trustee's benefits until the judgment was paid off. The U.S. Court of Appeals, Tenth Circuit, affirmed, and certiorari was granted by the U.S. Supreme Court. The Court held that the constructive trust violated the prohibition on assignment or alienation of pension benefits called for by ERISA. Here, although the trustee had stolen money from the union, he had not stolen money from the pension funds. Even if the Labor-Management Reporting and Disclosure Act authorized the imposition of a constructive trust when a union officer breached his fiduciary duties, that did not override ERISA's anti-alienation provision. ERISA reflected a congressional policy choice to safeguard a stream of income for pensioners even if that prevented others from obtaining relief for the wrongs done them. The Court reversed the lower courts' decisions and remanded the case. *Guidry v. Sheet Metal Workers National Pension Fund,* 493 U.S. 365, 110 S.Ct. 680, 107 L.Ed.2d 782 (1990).

During the course of the remand proceedings, the union and the trustee agreed that the trustee's monthly pension payments would be made to a bank account opened by the trustee specifically to receive his pension funds, and that the funds would then be subject to garnishment by the union. The issue which then came before the court of appeals was whether the union was entitled under ERISA to garnish bank accounts designated as containing only the proceeds of the pension payments. The U.S. Court of Appeals, Tenth Circuit, noted that the text of § 206(d)(1) was ambiguous. It stated that "benefits provided under the plan may not be assigned or alienated," but it did not define "benefits under the plan." The court noted that this phrase could mean the right to future payment or the actual money paid by the plan and received by the beneficiary. If the term "benefits" meant the actual money paid to the trustee, then the funds would be protected by this statute. The court then looked to the legislative history and the intent of the statute and concluded that § 206(d)(1) protection did not extend to the funds once the plan participant asserted dominion over them. Since the garnishment action was not "against the plan," the court held that it was not prohibited by ERISA. *Guidry v. Sheet Metal Workers Local No. 9,* 10 F.3d 700 (10th Cir.1993).

An interstate truck driver retired with over 25 years of participation in a multiemployer pension fund. He received increased retirement benefits by contributing $3,359 to the plan, which qualified him for benefits available to participants having 30 years of service. Several months after the commencement of benefits, the driver accepted a job as a mail carrier with the U.S. Postal Service. The plan review committee held that the reemployment violated plan rules and voted to suspend his benefits. The plan claims appeal committee affirmed the decision, and the driver sued the plan in the U.S. District Court for the Southern District of Ohio. The court held that the plan had arbitrarily suspended the driver's benefits in violation of ERISA and U.S. Department of Labor regulations. The plan appealed to the U.S. Court of Appeals, Sixth Circuit.

The court found the plan's suspension of benefits provision in conformity with ERISA and its regulations. ERISA did not protect the suspension of benefits of multiemployer plan participants who were not yet at their normal retirement age and took other jobs in the same industry, trade or craft and same geographical region. The suspension of benefits provision actually exceeded the minimum standards of ERISA and its regulations by providing additional protections against forfeiture of benefits by reemployed participants prior to normal retirement age. Because the driver had engaged in prohibited reemployment, the plan had not arbitrarily suspended his benefits, and the court of appeals reversed and remanded the district court decision. *Whisman v. Robbins,* 55 F.3d 1140 (6th Cir.1995).

General Motors Corporation offered certain salaried employees participation in a stock purchase program that allowed them to transfer assets among seven categories semiannually. A number of employees used backdated asset transfer forms to take advantage of market fluctuations. When General Motors learned of the intentional backdating, it fired the employees. One of the employees filed a lawsuit against GM in a Michigan trial court for breach of contract, wrongful discharge, ERISA violations, conversion of assets and intentional infliction of emotional distress. GM removed the action to the U.S. District Court for the Eastern District of Michigan, which granted GM summary judgment on a number of state law claims and dismissed the ERISA claims. The U.S. Court of Appeals, Sixth Circuit, reversed and remanded the case, affirming the district court decision that the employee had no wrongful discharge claim under Michigan law but reversing dismissal of the ERISA claims. After ruling on a number of pretrial motions by the parties, the court conducted a trial.

The court found that the former employee had intentionally backdated documents to take advantage of market activity including the stock market crash of 1987. The plan did not authorize the backdating of asset transfer forms and the employee was aware that his actions were not legitimate. The backdating of asset transfers impoverished the plan by the same amount which the employee gained, and GM was entitled to freeze his assets and subtract any gains resulting from backdating. GM had not ratified the employee's actions by failing to immediately discover them, and its reconciliation of his account had not been arbitrary or capricious. The employee was not entitled to equitable relief under ERISA, and his employment termination had been in good faith. The court entered judgment for GM. *Richards v. General Motors Corp.*, 876 F.Supp. 1492 (E.D.Mich.1995).

A Pennsylvania clinic employed a secretary as its sole clerical worker. It offered her a defined contribution retirement plan which paid a percentage of gross clinic receipts. The clinic later eliminated the gross receipts percentage component and converted the plan to a defined benefit plan without telling the employee. After retiring, the employee sued the clinic in the U.S. District Court for the Eastern District of Pennsylvania, claiming that it had violated her rights under ERISA. The court held that the clinic had acted as a fiduciary in reducing her compensation, and breached its fiduciary duty by failing to explain changes to her pension. The court fined the clinic $100 per day for failing to respond to a letter sent by the employee's attorney prior to the litigation, which it deemed to be a statutory request for an explanation of benefits. This resulted in a penalty of $191,300 and a total judgment for the employee of $614,000. The clinic appealed to the U.S. Court of Appeals, Third Circuit.

The court of appeals held that the clinic was an employer, not a fiduciary under ERISA. Accordingly, there could be no fiduciary duty to the employee. ERISA does not prohibit employers from making legitimate business decisions. The elimination of part of the employee's compensation and replacement of the defined contribution plan with the defined benefit plan were permissible management decisions. The lower court had misconstrued ERISA § 502(a)(1)(B) as authorizing a private right of action even though there was no discriminatory employment action taken against the employee. The attorney's letter did not meet statutory requirements for a request for explanation of benefits and the penalty was vacated. The court reversed and remanded the case. *Haberern v. Kaupp Vascular Surgeons Pension Plan*, 24 F.3d 1491 (3d Cir.1994).

B.   Vesting Rights and Plan Amendment Issues

An Alabama credit union offered three retirement plans to its employees. It posted notices and sent copies of a memo to employees about a number of amendments that significantly altered the plans. An employee who retired after 20 years of service stood to lose a five percent contribution from the employer due to the amendments. He filed a lawsuit in the U.S. District Court for the Northern District of Alabama, alleging that the employer and its insurer violated ERISA by amending the plans in a manner that retroactively decreased his benefits. The court granted a motion for summary judgment by the employer and insurer, and the employee appealed to the U.S. Court of Appeals, Eleventh Circuit. The court determined that the posting and distribution of the memo did not protect employee interests in their pension assets and violated essential policy goals of ERISA. Although the employer announced the amendments to the plans at the time they were approved, it failed to satisfy the requirements of ERISA when it did not give any formal written notice for more than two years. The employee was entitled to benefits that had accrued until the day of his employment termination, and other employees covered under the plans were entitled to benefits under terms that existed before the amendments. There was no merit to the employee's argument that the insurer was a fiduciary under ERISA because of its knowledge of the amendments. The court affirmed the district court's decision in part, reversed it in part and remanded the case. *Smith v. National Credit Union Admin. Bd.*, 36 F.3d 1077 (11th Cir.1994).

Executive employees of a bottling company participated in one of two retirement plans. They also received corporate stock having a zero value at the time of award, which increased to fair market value upon vesting. In connection with a hostile takeover, the stock compensation plan was amended so that participants received market value stock. However, such payments were not includible as earnings for the purposes of the retirement plans. Executives participating in the stock compensation plan filed a lawsuit in the U.S. District Court for the Southern District of New York, seeking a declaratory order that the stock payments should be considered earnings for purposes of their pension plans. The court denied summary judgment motions by both parties and following a trial, dismissed the complaint. The executives appealed to the U.S. Court of Appeals, Second Circuit. The court of appeals observed that the deferred vesting and valuation components of the stock compensation plan prevented characterization of the stock compensation as earnings. It was not arbitrary or capricious to disqualify the stock compensation from classification as earnings because failure to do so might risk disqualifying the plans by causing them to discriminate in favor of highly-compensated individuals. The district court had properly dismissed the lawsuit. *O'Neil v. Ret. Plan for Salaried Employees of RKO Gen., Inc.*, 37 F.3d 55 (2d Cir.1994).

Former employees of a Pennsylvania steel manufacturer sued the manufacturer, claiming it refused to rehire them to avoid pension liability. Under the pension plan, an employee earned credit towards a pension based on the number of years of continuous service. The former employees applied for, and alleged that they were qualified for, positions with the manufacturer. However, the manufacturer refused to rehire them. A federal district court granted the manufacturer's motion to dismiss the lawsuit, holding that the former employees did not have standing to file a lawsuit under ERISA. Both parties agreed that in order to state a claim under ERISA, the former employees had to be participants in the plan. ERISA defines a participant as "any employee, or former employee ... who is or may become eligible to receive a benefit of any type from an employee benefit plan." However, the court noted that the claimant may become eligible for a benefit if the claimant has a reasonable claim that he or she will prevail in a suit for benefits. The former employees did not have a reasonable expectation of reemployment, and therefore, did not have a reasonable claim for benefits. The court affirmed the judgment of the district court and dismissed the suit. *Shawley v. Bethlehem Steel Corp.,* 989 F.2d 652 (3d Cir.1993).

An employee who worked for a service company participated in its profit sharing plan and became fully vested. During this time, the plan offered several forms of payments, including a lump sum payment. Upon terminating his employment, the employee requested that his retirement benefits be paid in a lump sum. The plan had been amended in 1990 to delete the lump sum option and provide only for benefits in installments. The employee then commenced a lawsuit in a Wyoming federal district court claiming a violation of ERISA. The court found that the pension plan was lawfully amended to eliminate the option of lump sum payments and the employee appealed to the U.S. Court of Appeals, Tenth Circuit. The employee contended that the company had violated § 1054(G)(2) of ERISA by eliminating the lump sum payment option. Section 1054(G)(2) prohibits the amendment of a pension plan to eliminate accrued benefits, including an optional form of payment. A limited exception to the statute was created in 1988. Because the company failed to comply with the statute by selecting a form of benefit prior to the statutory deadline, its subsequent plan amendment did not qualify for the exception. Thus, the company was not entitled to formally amend its plan to eliminate the lump sum option for those whose rights had already accrued. The court reversed the decision of the district court and remanded the case with directions to enter judgment for the employee. *Counts v. Kissack Water & Oil Service, Inc.,* 986 F.2d 1322 (10th Cir.1993).

A company maintained a retirement benefits plan in which it retained the corporate authority to adopt, amend, modify or terminate the plan. In 1986, the company's board of directors amended the plan to provide early retirement benefits to eligible participants at specified locations. When the company announced the termination of its local operations, a group of employees, who were otherwise eligible for retirement benefits, were denied special benefits because they had not worked at a location where such benefits were available. The employees sued the company, alleging that the selective administration of the special benefits plan violated several provisions of ERISA. An Illinois federal district court granted summary judgment to the employer, and the employees appealed to the U.S. Court of Appeals, Seventh Circuit.

On appeal, the employees argued that the company had violated its fiduciary duties to them by creating special benefits to other employees. The court of appeals disagreed. It noted that ERISA permits employers to wear two hats; they assume fiduciary status only when they function as plan administrators. Employers who amend, terminate or establish benefit plans are not acting as fiduciaries by those actions. Only when they are managing plan assets and administering the plan are they to be judged by the higher duty of loyalty. The court affirmed the district court's decision in favor of the company. *Fletcher v. Kroger Co.,* 942 F.2d 1137 (7th Cir.1991).

A West Virginia man worked as a coal miner for various companies. For approximately 15 years, his employment was "credited service" under the United Mine Workers of America Pension Plan. He then took a salaried position with a different employer which was not credited service. He remained in salaried positions until his retirement in 1984. When the pension plan rejected his application for benefits, he brought suit in a West Virginia federal district court, asserting that the denial was arbitrary and inconsistent with ERISA. The court granted summary judgment to the pension plan, and the retiree appealed to the U.S. Court of Appeals, Fourth Circuit. The court of appeals looked to the regulation promulgated by the Department of Labor which addressed covered service vesting. The regulation allowed for vesting when an employee moved to a new employer while remaining in covered service or when an employee moved into noncovered service with the same employer. Here, the worker had gone from covered to noncovered service and had switched employers. Accordingly, he was not covered under the pension plan and the district court had correctly ruled in favor of the plan. *Gauer v. Conners,* 953 F.2d 97 (4th Cir.1991).

Two men worked as hourly employees for a company for approximately 30 years, although there were brief periods of time where neither was in the company's employ. The company phased down its operations and eventually closed the plant where the employees worked. Because of work time spent outside of the company, the employees' total years of service plus years of age made them ineligible for the full pension and benefits plan. A company supervisor informed them that the break-in-service rule enabled them to bridge the time they did not work for the company, thus qualifying them for a particular plan. Later, the employees were informed that the supervisor had misinterpreted the rule, but they qualified under a plan that provided for less benefits. The employees filed a complaint against the company in a federal district court for breach of fiduciary duty, failure to remedy fiduciary breaches, and for negligent misrepresentation. The company brought a motion for summary judgment.

The U.S. District Court for the District of New Jersey first addressed the negligent misrepresentation claim. It held that the claim was preempted by

ERISA. The court stated that ERISA superseded all state laws insofar as they relate to an employee benefit plan. Here the claim specifically referred to the ERISA plan, thus falling within ERISA jurisdiction. Further, since the employees had neither alleged nor presented evidence of any bad faith conduct by the company, no claim of breach of fiduciary duty was established. The court granted the company's motion for summary judgment on the negligent misrepresentation claim and dismissed all of the employees' claims. *Bernatowicz v. Colgate-Palmolive Co.,* 785 F.Supp. 488 (D.N.J.1992).

An insurance company agreed to enroll an agent in a company retirement plan. In accordance with the terms of the contract, the agent agreed to sell insurance policies of that company exclusively. Additionally, the contract terms stated that the agent would forfeit his retirement benefits if, within a year of his termination and 25 miles of his prior business location, he sold insurance for competitors of the insurance company. The company exercised its contractual right to terminate its relationship with the agent. Within a month, the agent sold insurance policies for several competitors from his old office. The company reacted with the charge that his new business activities disqualified the agent from receiving his retirement plan benefits. The agent sued the company under ERISA. A North Carolina federal district court found for the agent and the U.S. Court of Appeals affirmed. The insurance company appealed to the U.S. Supreme Court.

On appeal, the Court noted that the agent's ERISA claim could succeed only if he was an employee. ERISA's definition of "employee" is "any individual employed by an employer," a definition the Court found circular and unhelpful. Consequently, the Court suggested assessing and weighing all the elements of an employment relationship, including: the location of the work, the duration of the relationship between the parties, the method of payment, and the provision of employee benefits, among others. The Court reversed and remanded the case for a determination of whether the agent qualified as an employee under traditional agency law. *Nationwide Mutual Insurance Co. v. Darden*, 503 U.S. 318, 112 S.Ct. 1344, 117 L.Ed.2d 581 (1992).

A California man worked as a laborer for just over 14 years in "covered employment" under a pension plan. However, he needed to work 15 years for his pension rights to fully vest. For the next five years, the man could not find covered employment. Eventually, he was able to find such work, and then put in over five years of credited service. Upon the worker's death, his widow sought survivor benefits to which she would have been entitled if her husband's rights had vested. The pension committee determined that the worker's rights were not vested because of the break in service. A U.S. district court affirmed the order and the widow appealed to the U.S. Court of Appeals, Ninth Circuit.

The appellate court looked at the issue of whether the break in service rule was invalid for pension plan participants who incurred a break due to involuntary unemployment and who later worked in sufficient covered employment to vest themselves if pre-break employment was considered. The court then stated that the plan had acted arbitrarily in applying the break in service rule to cancel the worker's credits without ascertaining whether the break was due to involuntary unemployment. The court held that if the widow could show that the break was due to involuntary employment, she would be entitled to the pension benefits. The court reversed and remanded the case. *Bolton v. Construction Laborers' Pension Trust*, 954 F.2d 1437 (9th Cir.1991).

A Kansas company hired an executive officer and told him that it maintained a salary continuation plan. The plan contained no provision for vesting of benefits and did not comply with ERISA disclosure requirements. When the employee learned that the company was being sold, he prepared a backdated document which recited that his benefits were vested. The employee left the company and it refused to pay him benefits, claiming that the backdated document constituted fraud. The U.S. District Court for the District of Kansas held that the company had not promised any vested benefits and that none were payable. It dismissed the company's counterclaim that the employee was required to refund other compensation under the Kansas faithless servant doctrine. Both parties appealed to the U.S. Court of Appeals, Tenth Circuit.

On appeal, the employee argued that he was entitled to vested benefits due to the company's failure to comply with ERISA disclosure requirements. The court determined that an employer must first promise to pay vested benefits before any ERISA claim existed. Because the company had made no promise of vesting, no benefits had actually vested. The company was not entitled to a refund of salary and other benefits under the faithless servant doctrine. The trial court had correctly found that the employee's submission of a backdated document was in the good faith belief that he was entitled to benefits. Because of the employee's honest belief that he was entitled to benefits, the district court could have found an absence of fraud. The court affirmed the district court's decision. *Hein v. TechAmerica Group, Inc.*, 17 F.3d 1278 (10th Cir.1994).

C.   Coordination of Benefits

Three Maryland steelworkers were laid off when a mill was permanently closed. Each of the employees had over 35 years of service and elected to retire and collect pension benefits rather than accept lower paying jobs or go on layoff status. The company pension plan called for payment of a special payment equal to 13 weeks of vacation pay, less any regular vacation pay disbursed during the year of retirement. The state Department of Economic and Employment Development (DEED) denied the retirees' claims for unemployment benefits under a statute that disallowed benefits where monthly pension benefits exceeded the amount of unemployment benefits claimed. The DEED board of appeals held that the special payment was not a lump sum payment and thus disqualified the applicants from benefits during the first 13 weeks of unemployment. The board allowed compensation only to the extent that the special payment represented vacation pay (four weeks in the case of one employee and three weeks for the other two). A Maryland trial court disallowed benefits entirely, and the claimants appealed to the Court of Special Appeals of Maryland.

The court of special appeals held that the board and circuit court had correctly characterized the special payment as part of a periodic pension compensation package and not a lump sum, because it was an advance on the first three months of retirement compensation. Accordingly, the special payments did not constitute a lump sum due to a plant closing or layoff that would be exempt from the deductibility provisions of state unemployment compensation law. The trial court had correctly refused to deduct the amount of vacation pay from the gross value of the special payment and the court of special appeals affirmed its decision. *Facello v. Dept. of Economic and Employment Development*, 104 Md.App. 575, 657 A.2d 363 (1995).

A 59-year-old employee accepted early retirement after suffering a back injury on the job. The employer assumed liability for the injury and paid the employee benefits for total incapacity. The employer tendered a check for the balance of the employee's pension account. The following day, the employee deposited the funds into his IRA account to defer taxation. The applicable Maine statute reduced the employer's obligation to pay compensation benefits by the amount of after tax payments received under an employment benefit plan. The employer accordingly filed a petition with the state workers' compensation commission to coordinate benefits by reducing its obligation by the amount of pension funds that had been rolled over into the IRA. The commission determined that the employee had not "received" payment of his pension benefits under state law and denied the petition. The employer appealed to the Supreme Judicial Court of Maine. On appeal, the employer argued that the state workers' compensation act was designed to provide income to injured employees during periods of incapacity and prevented double recovery of retirement and compensation benefits. The employee argued that he had not received duplicate benefits because he had no access to his IRA funds until he withdrew them, which he planned to do after the age of 70. The supreme judicial court found the employee's argument consistent with the legislative purpose of the act and with Internal Revenue Code provisions and regulations governing IRAs. Because the legislature did not intend to allow immediate coordination of benefits in the case of IRA rollovers, the decision of the state compensation commission was affirmed. *Jordan v. Sears, Roebuck & Co.*, 651 A.2d 358 (Me.1994).

Two retired Indiana coal miners filed separate claims for benefits under the federal Black Lung Benefits Act. After an initial determination of eligibility, both received benefits, but were notified that if it was determined in later proceedings that they were not eligible for benefits under the act, any payment made would be an overpayment and subject to recovery. In subsequent appeals by the employer, they were found ineligible for benefits. The Director of the Office of Workers' Compensation Programs (OWCP) in the Department of Labor sought to recover the benefits paid. The retirees requested waivers of recovery. They were both denied waivers and the Benefits Review Board affirmed the denial. The retirees petitioned the U.S. Court of Appeals, Seventh Circuit, for review of the board's order. The court of appeals noted that under the act, after an initial determination of eligibility for benefits, the responsible coal mine operator may challenge the determination of eligibility. If the claimant is subsequently found ineligible, the OWCP may demand recoupment of all benefits paid. The court rejected the retirees' argument that an interim benefits award is unaffected by the later determination of ineligibility for benefits. The regulations which implement the Black Lung Benefits Act anticipate that a decision to award benefits can be reversed at any point before the award becomes final. Payments made prior to the determination of eligibility may be recovered if the claimant is found ineligible. Also, the court noted that the retirees were not entitled to a waiver of repayment because the interim determination of eligibility did not constitute "erroneous information" within the meaning of the regulations which allowed waiver. Even though requiring the retirees to pay back the money seemed to be a harsh result, none of the grounds raised on appeal had merit. The retirees' petition was denied. *Bracher v. Director, OWCP*, 14 F.3d 1157 (7th Cir.1994).

A garbage collector worked for the same company for 26 years until he retired. He received pension benefits of $968 per month. Later he applied for permanent disability benefits with the California State Workers' Compensation Appeals Board for a job-related shoulder injury. The collector received a $14,500 settlement award. However, the pension plan administrator reduced the collector's monthly pension benefits by $559 per month to offset for the settlement award. This reduction was effective for two years and was based upon a plan provision that allowed the deduction of workers' compensation benefits. The collector filed a formal challenge, and a federal district court held for the collector. The company appealed to the U.S. Court of Appeals, Ninth Circuit.

The company argued that workers' compensation benefits may be offset whether they are considered wage replacement or disability compensation under § 203 of ERISA. Section 203 provides that "[e]ach pension plan shall provide that an employee's right to his normal retirement benefit is nonforfeitable upon his attainment of normal retirement age." The court of appeals noted that it must first be determined whether the benefits at issue were wage replacement or disability compensation before the application of the integration method of calculating pension benefits. The court further held that state law determines the character of the benefits. The integration of workers' compensation benefits depends on how they are treated under state law—those relating to income replacement may be offset, those relating to injury may not. Because the injury occurred after retirement, the settlement was considered compensation for bodily injury. The pension payment could not be offset. *Losada v. Golden Gate Disposal Co.*, 950 F.2d 1395 (9th Cir.1991).

A company implemented a voluntary, discretionary retirement plan which set maximum benefits at $225 per month. Later, the company was sold, and the new company instituted a new lump sum profit sharing plan. The two plans were integrated following the adoption of ERISA, and an offset mechanism was established. Subsequently, an employee retired and received a lump sum payment of $50,000. The employee was never to receive a monthly payment of $225 because the payment he had already received would allow monthly interest income exceeding that amount. Although he was allowed to purchase postretirement medical insurance, the company did not pay for such benefits. He brought suit against the company for violating ERISA. A Wisconsin federal district court granted summary judgment to the company, but refused to award it attorney's fees. Both parties appealed. The U.S. Court of Appeals, Seventh Circuit, noted that the integration of the two retirement plans did not violate the nonforfeiture provisions of ERISA. Congress provided that pension benefits could be offset by other retirement benefits. The court stated that the employee had failed to show that the employer had in place a postretirement medical benefits plan to which he had been denied access. Finally, the court determined that the denial of attorney's fees was not an abuse of discretion, and affirmed the district court's decision. *Pritchard v. Rainfair, Inc.*, 945 F.2d 185 (7th Cir.1991).

II. WELFARE AND HEALTH BENEFIT PLANS

ERISA also covers employee welfare benefit plans. These include plans to provide "medical, sickness, accident, disability and death benefits, training programs, day care centers, scholarship funds, and legal services" as well as plans to provide severance benefits and certain vacation benefit plans. ERISA participation, vesting and funding requirements do not apply to welfare benefit plans, but such plans may create vested rights by an agreement of the parties.

A. ERISA Applicability and Compliance

ERISA, at 29 U.S.C. § 1002(1), defines an employee welfare benefit plan as:

"[A]ny plan, fund, or program which was heretofore or is hereafter established or maintained by an employer or by an employee organization, or by both, to the extent that such plan, fund, or program was established or is maintained for the purpose of providing for its participants or their beneficiaries, through the purchase of insurance or otherwise, (A) medical, surgical, or hospital care or benefits, or benefits in the event of sickness, accident, disability, death or unemployment, or vacation benefits, apprenticeship or other training programs, or day care centers, scholarship funds, or prepaid legal services, or (B) any benefit described in section 186(c) of this title (other than pensions on retirement or death, and insurance to provide such pensions)."

ERISA applies to an employee benefits plan if it is established or maintained by an employer or an employee organization engaged in commerce or in any industry or activity affecting commerce, 29 U.S.C. § 1003(a). This section applies to both pension benefit plans and welfare benefit plans. However, group or group-type insurance programs offered by an insurer under which the employer does not contribute any funds, where participation is voluntary, where the employer does not endorse the program but merely collects premiums, and where the employer receives no compensation in connection with the program are not employee welfare benefit plans for purposes of ERISA. See 29 CFR § 2510.3-1 (j).

A corporation maintained and administered a single-employer health plan for its employees. In response to rising health care costs, it discontinued coverage for retirees upon the termination of operations at the facility from which they had retired. After closing a New Jersey facility, the corporation's executive vice president notified retirees of the facility by letter that their post-retirement health benefits were being terminated. The retirees filed a lawsuit against the corporation in the U.S. District Court for the District of New Jersey, alleging that the termination of benefits violated § 402(b)(3) of ERISA, 29 U.S.C. § 1102(b)(3). Section 402(b)(3) required employee benefit plans to have "a procedure for amending such plan, and for identifying the persons who have authority to amend the plan." The retirees claimed that the company's summary plan description lacked a valid amendment procedure and that its action constituted a plan amendment. The district court agreed with the retirees, and ordered the corporation to pay them over $2.6 million in benefits. The U.S. Court of Appeals, Third Circuit, affirmed the district court's decision and the corporation appealed to the U.S. Supreme Court.

The Supreme Court agreed with the corporation that the minimal language in its summary plan description satisfied the amendment procedure requirement of ERISA § 402(b)(3). Under the plan description, the corporation "reserve[d] the right at any time to amend the plan...." ERISA created no substantive entitlement to employer-provided welfare benefits and employers were allowed to freely modify, amend or terminate welfare plans under most circumstances. The Court reasoned that a plan that simply identified the person or persons having authority to amend a plan necessarily indicated the amendment procedure. The reservation clause contained in the corporation's summary plan description identified "the company" as the person having amendment authority. It was then only necessary to apply corporate law principles to identify the particular individual or corporate committee with decisionmaking authority. It was unnecessary to further specify the names of individuals or committees within a corporation to satisfy ERISA, and for single-employer health plans it was sufficient to identify the employer as the entity having amendment authority. Other ERISA sections required plan administrators to furnish beneficiaries with the names and addresses of the plan administrator and other fiduciaries, but ERISA did not require the provision of names and addresses of individuals with amendment authority. The court reversed and remanded the court of appeals' decision, directing the court to consider on remand whether the corporation had complied with its valid amendment procedure. Under this fact inquiry, the court was to apply corporate law principles to determine whether the appropriate corporate officials had actually approved the amendments contained in the revised summary plan description. *Curtiss-Wright Corp. v. Schoonejongen*, 115 S.Ct. 1223, 131 L.Ed.2d 94 (1995).

A corporation operated a self-funded health care plan under which plan members agreed to reimburse it for benefits paid if the member recovered on a claim in a liability action against a third party. The daughter of a plan member was seriously injured in an automobile accident, and the plan paid part of her medical expenses. A negligence action against the driver of the vehicle in which the daughter was injured settled. The plan member refused to reimburse the plan, asserting that Pennsylvania law precluded subrogation by the plan. The member sought and obtained a declaratory judgment that the state statute prohibited the plan from enforcing the subrogation provision. The U.S. Court of Appeals affirmed, and the case came before the U.S. Supreme Court.

The Court stated that ERISA preempted the application of the Pennsylvania law, and that the plan could seek subrogation. Since Congress clearly intended to exempt from state regulation ERISA employee benefit plans, the state statute could not stand here. State laws that directly regulate insurance are "saved" from preemption, but this does not apply to self-funded employee benefit plans because they are not insurance for purposes of such laws. *FMC Corp. v. Holliday*, 498 U.S. 52, 111 S.Ct. 403, 112 L.Ed.2d 356 (1990).

A District of Columbia workers' compensation statute required employers who provided health insurance for their employees to also furnish equivalent health insurance coverage for injured employees eligible for workers' compensation benefits. An employer filed an action in the U.S. District Court for the District of Columbia against the district and its mayor, claiming that the act was preempted by ERISA. The court granted the district's motion to dismiss. On appeal, the U.S. Court of Appeals reversed, holding that preemption was within ERISA's structure and plain meaning. The district appealed.

The U.S. Supreme Court affirmed the judgment of the court of appeals. It stated that a law "relates to" a covered employee benefit plan if it has a connection with or reference to such a plan. ERISA preempts any state law that refers to or has a connection with covered benefit plans that do not fall within its exceptions — even if the law is not specifically designed to affect such plans, the effect is only indirect, and the law is consistent with ERISA's substantive requirements. The Court held that employer-sponsored health insurance programs are subject to ERISA regulation, and any state law imposing requirements by reference to such covered programs is preempted by ERISA. ERISA's exemptions do not limit its preemptive sweep once it is determined that a law "relates to" a covered plan. The court held that ERISA superseded the workers' compensation act because the act related to a covered plan. The district could not require employers to provide equivalent health insurance coverage for injured employees who were eligible for workers' compensation. *District of Columbia v. Greater Washington Board of Trade*, 113 S.Ct. 580, 121 L.Ed.2d 513 (1992).

A claims examiner for a life insurance company was a beneficiary under two employee benefit plans administered by her employer. After becoming disabled with a back ailment, she received plan benefits for five months until an orthopedic surgeon's report caused the benefits committee to terminate her benefits. She requested a review of that decision, and five months later had her benefits reinstated with retroactive benefits paid in full. Even though she was paid all the benefits to which she was contractually entitled, she sued her employer for improper refusal to pay benefits. After removal to a California federal district court, summary judgment was granted to the employer on the ground that ERISA barred any claims for extracontractual damages arising out of the original denial of her claim for benefits. The U.S. Court of Appeals reversed in part, holding that the 132 days which the employer took to process the worker's claim violated the fiduciary's obligation to process claims in good faith.

On further appeal, the U.S. Supreme Court observed that § 409(a) of ERISA provides that fiduciaries who breach their duties or obligations are personally liable to make good any losses that result from their breach. The Court held that § 409(a) did not provide a cause of action for extracontractual damages to a beneficiary caused by improper or untimely processing of benefit claims. The fiduciary's liability was to the employee benefit plan, and the plan's liability was to the beneficiary. There was no extracontractual cause of action available between the beneficiary and the fiduciary. Accordingly, the Court reversed the lower court's decision, holding that the employee was not entitled to compensatory or punitive damages from her employer. *Massachusetts Mutual Life Ins. Co. v. Russell,* 473 U.S. 134, 105 S.Ct. 3085, 87 L.Ed.2d 96 (1985).

Two large, multiemployer ERISA benefit plans with thousands of participating employers operated under trust agreements for the purpose of providing health, welfare and pension benefits to employees performing work which was covered by collective bargaining agreements between a union and various employers. Under the agreements, each employer was required to make weekly contributions to the plans. Because of their size, the plans relied on employer self-reporting to determine the extent of an employer's contribution liability, and they policed this system by conducting random audits of the participating employers' records. However, when certain new signatories refused to allow the plans to conduct audits, the plans sued them in a Michigan federal court. The district court ruled for the plans, but the U.S. Court of Appeals reversed.

On further appeal, the U.S. Supreme Court held that the employers had to allow the plans to conduct audits. The trustees of the plans had the power under the trust agreements to demand and examine pertinent employer records, and the interpretation of the agreements as authorizing the audits was not inconsistent with ERISA. Under ERISA, trustees had the same powers they enjoyed under the common law—"all such powers as are necessary or appropriate for the carrying out of the trust purposes." Since the employers had agreed to be bound by the trust agreements, the Court reversed the court of appeals' decision, and held in favor of the plans. *Central States, Southeast and Southwest Areas Pension Fund v. Central Transport, Inc.,* 472 U.S. 559, 105 S.Ct. 2833, 86 L.Ed.2d 447 (1985).

A company sponsored a postretirement employee medical plan which it represented as providing lifetime benefits. Although one clause in the policy stated that coverage continued for the lifetime of the employee, a reservation of rights clause in a different section of the policy declared the right of the company to terminate the plan for any reason. For several years, the company represented to employees at meetings and in written communications that benefits were for life, but it later asserted the right to terminate the plan under the reservation of rights clause. Retirees filed a class action suit against the company and plan administrator in the U.S. District Court for the Eastern District of Pennsylvania, which held for the employer on the retirees' breach of contract and equitable claims. On reconsideration, the court held for the retirees on the breach of fiduciary duty claim, and the company appealed to the U.S. Court of Appeals, Third Circuit. The court found substantial evidence in the record that the employer had misled many of its employees to whom it owed a duty of loyalty under ERISA. Because the employer had repeatedly asserted that the plan provided lifetime benefits, the retirees had advanced a valid ERISA claim for breach of fiduciary duty, and were entitled to equitable relief. The court affirmed the district court decision and remanded the case. *In re Unisys Corp. Retiree Medical Benefit ERISA Litigation,* 57 F.3d 1255 (3d Cir.1995).

A Texas employee was covered under his employer's group medical and hospitalization insurance plan. He became totally disabled from an automobile accident. The employer changed policies within five months of the accident, and the employee was not covered under the new policy because it contained an exclusion for preexisting conditions. The employer continued to pay benefits to the former employee for a six-year period. When the payments were discontinued, the former employee's guardian filed a lawsuit against the employer and insurer in the U.S. District Court for the Northern District of Texas, claiming ERISA violations. The court granted summary judgment to the employer and insurer, claiming that their actions did not violate ERISA. The guardian appealed to the U.S. Court of Appeals, Fifth Circuit. On appeal, the guardian argued that the change in insurance policies discriminated against the former employee and unlawfully interfered with his rights under ERISA. The court of appeals disagreed, finding no direct evidence of a specific intent by the employer to discriminate against the former employee. The employee had no rights under the terminated insurance policy, and he had no vested benefits at the time of the change in policies. ERISA allows employers to amend or terminate a medical policy at any time, so long as employee rights are not vested. Accordingly, the court affirmed the district court's order for summary judgment. *Hines v. Massachusetts Mut. Life Ins. Co.,* 43 F.3d 207 (5th Cir.1995).

A medical health and welfare trust sold group medical, dental, and life insurance policies to small, unrelated employers in Massachusetts. The employers established employee welfare benefit plans under ERISA, for which the trust controlled assets and paid benefits. The U.S. Secretary of Labor brought a number of ERISA claims against the trust, stating that it had falsely represented that it was tax-exempt and exempt from state insurance regulation. The complaint stated that the trust failed to pay over $2 million in medical benefits and that officers of the trust breached their fiduciary obligations under ERISA. The alleged fiduciary breaches included engaging in prohibited transactions, mismanagement of funds, misrepresentation to employers and state regulators, and operating an illegal insurance company. The trust became insolvent and its officers defaulted in the lawsuit. The U.S. District Court for the District of Massachusetts dismissed the secretary's ERISA complaint against a financial consultant for a major accounting firm who had provided professional advice to the trust. The secretary appealed dismissal of this claim to the U.S. Court of Appeals, First Circuit.

The court of appeals stated that the section of ERISA under which the secretary had advanced this claim authorized actions against fiduciaries who violated ERISA. It also permitted equitable remedies for prohibited acts and practices, but did not authorize or expand the reach of ERISA to new parties or transactions not otherwise covered. The advisor's alleged participation in fraudulent activities by trust officers was not a fiduciary breach that violated ERISA as he was not a party to any prohibited transaction, nor the recipient of any plan assets. The secretary's argument that the advisor should be barred from future potential abuses was speculative. The court affirmed dismissal of the claim against the advisor. *Reich v. Rowe*, 20 F.3d 25 (1st Cir.1994).

A Georgia insurance statute requires insurers to provide at least ten days written notice prior to canceling insurance policies for failure to pay premiums. One exception to ERISA preemption of state laws permits the states to regulate insurance. A Georgia commission agent for a nationwide insurer participated in a group medical policy paid for by his employer. The policy provided dependent medical coverage at the expense of employees. The employee's wife was covered under this feature. She suffered a severe accident that resulted in ongoing medical expenses until her death nine years later. During this time period, the employee's compensation account became insufficient to cover his deduction for dependent coverage. When the employee's compensation account became insufficient a second time, the employer terminated the wife's coverage without prior notice. The employee and his wife sued the employer in a Georgia trial court, claiming that coverage had been terminated in violation of the Georgia statute. The employer removed the case to the U.S. District Court for the Middle District of Georgia. The court ruled for the employee and his wife, and the employer appealed to the U.S. Court of Appeals, Eleventh Circuit.

The court of appeals observed that ERISA welfare benefit plans were programs established or maintained by employers to provide medical benefits to participants or their beneficiaries. The plan at issue clearly met those requirements. The Georgia statute regulated only the administration of policies, not their substantive terms. Accordingly, the statute did not regulate the business of insurance within the meaning of federal law. Application of the Georgia notice statute would be contrary to ERISA's goal of establishing a uniform regulatory system for employee benefit plans. The court of appeals reversed and remanded the district court's decision. *Smith v. Jefferson Pilot Life Ins. Co.*, 14 F.3d 562 (11th Cir.1994).

A pension fund administered a multi-employer, labor-management trust fund which provided medical, dental, and other health care services to workers and their dependents. The fund was an ERISA welfare benefit plan. The state of New York imposed a tax on the gross receipts from patient care services and general operations of all state hospitals. The pension fund complied with the law and paid assessments for one year, but then discontinued paying them. It filed a lawsuit in the U.S. District Court for the Southern District of New York, claiming that ERISA preempted the state tax. The district court found that the state tax was one of general application that was not preempted by ERISA. Because it had only an incidental impact on the plan, it was not preempted and the court granted summary judgment for the state commissioner of health. The plan trustees appealed to the U.S. Court of Appeals, Second Circuit. The court of appeals disagreed with the district court's analysis. The state tax was directly related to the pension fund because it depleted plan assets. Therefore, it was not remote and had a direct affect on the plan. The statute was not one of general application, but was one that targeted the health care industry and affected the fund in its principal role as an employee welfare benefit plan. The fact that the tax was insignificant did not reduce its direct relationship to the plan. The court reversed the district court's decision. *NYSA-ILA Medical and Clinical Services Fund v. Axelrod*, 27 F.3d 823 (2d Cir.1994).

A Michigan manufacturer provided health insurance coverage to its salaried nonunion employees, retirees and their dependents from 1968 to 1984, but there was no written agreement requiring it to do so. In 1984, the manufacturer sold one of its divisions to another company. The new company continued to provide insurance coverage to nonunion employees and retirees. The insurer's handbook stated that it was merely a guide to benefits and not a contract. A retirement agreement was also provided which stated that "this addendum may be canceled ... following 30 days written notice." Subsequently, the new manufacturer sent a letter to all nonunion retirees and all spouses of deceased retirees that their health insurance coverage would be terminated. The retirees filed a complaint in a federal district court seeking a restraining order preventing the termination as a violation of ERISA. The court ordered a permanent injunction prohibiting the employer from terminating health insurance coverage to retirees and their spouses, and the employer appealed to the U.S. Court of Appeals, Sixth Circuit.

ERISA divides employee benefits into two types: pension plans and welfare benefit plans. A retiree health insurance benefit plan is a welfare benefit plan and is not subject to mandatory participation, vesting, and funding requirements. However, the parties may agree to vest a welfare benefit plan. To determine whether the parties have agreed to vest the welfare benefit plan, the court applied the federal common law of contract to ascertain the parties' intent. The retirees claimed that several high-level officials told them that their health insurance benefits would continue for the rest of their lives. However, the court explained that the written terms of the plan documents could not be modified or superseded by the employer's oral statements unless the documents were ambiguous. The court noted that the retirement agreement and health insurance handbook stated that coverage could be terminated on 30 days' notice. Therefore, it concluded that the written provisions were unambiguous and the employer's oral statements did not modify the written statements. The court held that the district court erred in concluding that the plaintiffs' benefits had vested. *Boyer v. Douglas Components Corp.*, 986 F.2d 999 (6th Cir.1993).

A retired Michigan man's former employer gave notice that it intended to discontinue health insurance for its retirees. The retiree then filed this action in a federal district court alleging that the discontinuance of health insurance benefits for retirees violated the employer's fiduciary duties under ERISA. He claimed that his right to health insurance had vested, and that the employer could not terminate benefits. The district court found for the employer and the retiree appealed to the U.S. Court of Appeals, Sixth Circuit. ERISA distinguishes between employee pension plans and employee welfare benefit plans. Health insurance plans are considered welfare benefit plans, for which there is no vesting requirement under ERISA. However, the parties may agree to a vesting of welfare plan rights. Courts must look to the intent of the parties and apply the federal common law of contract to determine whether benefits have vested. The court concluded that the insurance policy unambiguously provided that the plan could be terminated by the employer upon 30 days' written notice. It determined that the insurance plan did not vest and upheld the district court's decision that the employer had a right to discontinue it. *Gill v. Moco Thermal Industries, Inc.*, 981 F.2d 858 (6th Cir.1992).

A Florida printing business was a wholly owned subsidiary of another company. It distributed handbooks to its employees which contained a severance pay policy. The policy stated that if employees were discharged for reasons other than cause, the company would pay them one week's pay in lieu of notice for each six months of service. This policy was governed by ERISA. The handbook provided to the employees was the parent company's handbook. The parent company sold substantially all of the assets of the subsidiary to a new owner. The new owner retained the former employees of the subsidiary in their same jobs at the same salary levels. However, it did not give them credit for their years of service for purposes of accruing and calculating severance pay benefits. Thus, many employees who had been with the subsidiary for a long time lost substantial severance benefits. A group of employees brought a class action lawsuit against the former owner of the company in a federal district court, seeking to recover severance benefits. The court ruled against the employees and they appealed to the U.S. Court of Appeals, Eleventh Circuit.

On appeal, the court noted that the lower court had improperly determined that no severance benefits were due despite the fact that none of the employees were ever unemployed. Here, the employees had been discharged by the parent company and its subsidiary for reasons other than cause when the business was sold. Regardless of whether the employees were employed by the entity that purchased the subsidiary's assets, they were entitled to severance pay. The court also noted that the employees had not been given the option to remain with either the parent or the subsidiary; they had to choose between either resignation or employment with the new owner. An individual need not suffer a period of unemployment to qualify for severance benefits under ERISA. The court reversed and remanded the case. *Bedinghaus v. Modern Graphic Arts*, 15 F.3d 1027 (11th Cir.1994).

B. Coverage Issues

An employee welfare benefits plan paid for the medical expenses of a covered employee's daughter after she was seriously disabled in a train accident. When the employee's plant was sold to another company, the successor company promised the plant employees insurance benefits under the same terms as the predecessor's plan. It continued paying medical expenses on behalf of the employee's daughter. When the plan administrator learned that the family had obtained a $7 million settlement from the railroad and engineer, it sought reimbursement for benefits paid on her behalf under the plan's third-party exclusion, which required covered persons who received third party judgments or settlements to reimburse the plan for any amounts advanced. The employee refused to reimburse the plan and filed a lawsuit against it and the successor company in the U.S. District Court for the Northern District of Illinois. The court granted summary judgment to the company and plan, and the employee appealed to the U.S. Court of Appeals, Seventh Circuit.

The court agreed with the plan administrator that it should be dismissed from the lawsuit because it was not a fiduciary as defined by ERISA. The company, not the administrator, made all significant decisions concerning the plan. The family argued that continuation coverage existed under the successor's plan and that the third-party recovery provision was not a part of the plan when the family first became covered by the successor's plan. The court rejected this argument, finding that the family knew about the third-party clause and successor company's right to reimbursement. The successor was entitled to restitution for amounts it had advanced under the third-party exclusion provision. *Harris Trust and Savings Bank v. Provident Life and Accident Ins. Co.*, 57 F.3d 608 (7th Cir.1995).

A retail company administered an ERISA health benefits plan that had a one-year exclusion period for preexisting conditions. It rehired a former employee who had elected to take COBRA continuation coverage under the plan. He failed to make his final COBRA payment when his payments by payroll deduction resumed. The payroll deduction did not pertain to the same period of coverage as the unpaid COBRA payment. Several months later, the employee suffered a heart attack that was attributable to preexisting conditions. The health plan refused to pay the employee's medical bills, stating that the lapse in coverage due to failure to make the final COBRA payment triggered the preexisting condition exclusion. The employee sued the company as administrator of the plan in the U.S. District Court for the Eastern District of Texas, which ordered the plan to accept a late payment submitted by the employee to prevent a lapse in coverage. The plan appealed to the U.S. Court of Appeals, Fifth Circuit.

The court of appeals disagreed with the district court's determination that the retailer had voluntarily assumed a duty to inform the employee of the impending lapse of COBRA coverage. The employee had received an adequate written notice advising him that his coverage would be canceled if not paid by a specified date. Although ERISA authorizes courts to award equitable relief in certain cases, the district court had abused its discretion by awarding judgment to the employee. The plan was not legally bound to inform the employee that his payment was delinquent and the court of appeals reversed and remanded the district court judgment. *Switzer v. Wal-Mart Stores, Inc.*, 52 F.3d 1294 (5th Cir.1995).

An Alabama telecommunications worker became addicted to painkillers following a sinus operation and hysterectomy. Her physician diagnosed her as having a major depressive disorder and her psychiatrist found that she was too depressed to return to work. Her employer authorized disability benefits for several months, but insisted that she return to work. After an unsuccessful attempt to resume working, the employee resigned, and the employer refused to award her benefits under its employee disability plan. The employee appealed the denial of her claim to the U.S. District Court for the Northern District of Alabama, which determined that she was totally disabled and entitled to benefits. It also certified a class action on behalf of similarly situated employees. The employer appealed to the U.S. Court of Appeals, Eleventh Circuit, which agreed that the employer had erroneously determined that the employee was not totally disabled. She had submitted a number of medical opinions that she was affected by drugs and could not make rational decisions at the time of her employment termination. The employer's determination had been based on factors other than the medical record including the employee's job performance and rate of absenteeism. Her final attempt to resume her job did not bar her from collecting disability benefits. The court affirmed the district court's judgment for the employee and also affirmed the decision to certify a class of employees who might be entitled to benefits under the plan. *Marecek v. BellSouth Services, Inc.*, 49 F.3d 702 (11th Cir.1995).

A California hospital information specialist was employed in a demanding position that required frequent travel and overtime work. He began suffering from physical symptoms including an umbilical hernia, abdominal cramps, diarrhea, rectal bleeding, headaches, and ulcerative colitis. He became severely fatigued and unable to work and was fired for unsatisfactory work performance. After undergoing treatment by several doctors and applying for workers' compensation benefits, his application for long-term disability benefits was approved for two years. The disability plan limited the award to two years because it was caused by a "mental illness" or "functional nervous disorder," and not by a physical disability. The employee appealed to the U.S. District Court for the Central District of California, which awarded summary judgment to the plan. He then obtained a diagnosis of chronic fatigue syndrome from an immunologist and sought to present the new diagnosis to the court. The court refused to consider it and the employee appealed to the U.S. Court of Appeals, Ninth Circuit.

The court agreed with the former employee's argument that the lack of a definition of the terms "mental illness" and "functional nervous disorder" in the plan created an ambiguity that had to be construed against the plan. The court stated that the district court should have considered factual disputes in the record and should not have summarily dismissed the case. The court of appeals characterized the diagnosis as a new explanation for the disability and not a new claim. It reversed and remanded the case to the district court with directions to use the chronic fatigue syndrome diagnosis to determine whether the former employee suffered from a disability not caused by mental illness or functional nervous disorder. *Mongeluzo v. Baxter Travenol Long Term Disability Benefit Plan*, 46 F.3d 938 (9th Cir.1995).

An Oregon employer maintained a group cancer insurance policy but failed to notify an employee of its availability. The employee was diagnosed with cancer, and submitted an application for coverage five days later. The insurer rejected the application when it discovered the cancer diagnosis. The employee then filed a lawsuit against the employer and insurer in the U.S. District Court for the District of Oregon, seeking compensatory damages and other relief under ERISA. The court granted summary judgment motions filed by the employer and insurer, and the employee appealed to the U.S. Court of Appeals, Ninth Circuit. The court of appeals reversed the district court's ruling that the employee had no standing to bring an ERISA lawsuit. ERISA permitted lawsuits by individuals wishing to clarify future rights and benefits under a plan, and the employee's status as an employee made her a plan participant under statutory language. However, she had no viable private claim against the employer and insurer for breach of fiduciary duty because ERISA only permitted beneficiaries to sue on behalf of the entire plan. The employee was suing solely on her own behalf. The court disallowed the employee's claim for compensatory damages as not available under ERISA, but reversed and remanded the question of her entitlement to statutory damages because of the plan administrator's failure to provide her with plan documents upon request. If proven, the employee was entitled to a penalty of up to $100 per day from the date of the refusal as statutory damages. *McLeod v. Oregon Lithoprint Inc.*, 46 F.3d 956 (9th Cir.1995).

A Texas research worker participated in an ERISA-regulated health benefits plan furnished through her employer. After she developed cancer, the healthcare provider refused to pay for certain requested treatments. The employee filed a lawsuit against the provider in the U.S. District Court for the Southern District of Texas, which granted the provider's summary judgment motion based on ERISA preemption. The employee appealed to the U.S. Court of Appeals, Fifth Circuit. On appeal, the employee argued that the healthcare provider had fraudulently induced her to purchase its coverage by representing that it was an honest company that never engaged in deceptive trade practices. She also alleged that the company had "secret guidelines" that it employed to defeat her claims for coverage. The court agreed with the employee that the allegations of false advertising did not pertain to an ERISA plan, and accordingly, this claim was not preempted. However, her claim that the company maintained secret policy guidelines that precluded coverage was inextricably involved with the interpretation and administration of an ERISA plan. Accordingly, any state law claim based on that argument was preempted by ERISA, and the district court had properly dismissed any such claims. The court reversed and remanded the remaining issues for further consideration. *Hubbard v. Blue Cross & Blue Shield Assn.*, 42 F.3d 942 (5th Cir.1995).

A claims adjuster worked for 19 years in a capacity that required her to perform inspections by climbing ladders and crawling under houses. Her medical condition then prevented her from performing these duties and she applied for benefits under her employer's long term disability plan. The plan paid benefits for two years for occupational sicknesses and accidents that prevented the claimant from performing any occupation. The plan's claims reviewer had difficulty obtaining physician statements from the employee's doctor, and plan doctors determined that the claim was unsubstantiated. The employee alleged that the denial of her claim violated ERISA and she filed a lawsuit against the employer and its insurer in the U.S. District Court for the Western District of Louisiana. The court entered judgment for the plan administrator and the employee appealed to the U.S. Court of Appeals, Fifth Circuit. The court of appeals rejected the employee's contention that the insurer abused its discretion in determining that she was not totally disabled. Medical records supported the plan's determination. The employee was also unable to demonstrate that she was entitled to a presumption of total disability or that she had been deprived of a full and fair review because of alleged bias in the insurer's review procedures. The court affirmed the district court's judgment for the plan administrator. *Sweatman v. Commercial Union Ins. Co.*, 39 F.3d 594 (5th Cir.1994).

A small Oregon employer hoped to furnish its employees with health insurance and contacted a broker to obtain coverage. Employees submitted the necessary applications and the broker forwarded them to an insurer. The broker assured the employer that coverage would commence on the desired date. After the applications were submitted, but before preliminary approval by the insurer, an employee was diagnosed HIV-positive. The insurer then requested updated employee records and soon denied the application. The employee sued the employer, broker and insurer in an Oregon trial court for negligence, breach of contract and breach of fiduciary duty. The employee and employer settled prior to trial, and the court granted the insurer's summary judgment motion on the grounds that the claims were preempted by ERISA. It then conducted a trial and awarded judgment to the broker. The employee appealed to the Court of Appeals of Oregon. On appeal, the employee argued that because no ERISA plan had been established, there could be no preemption of state law claims by ERISA. The court agreed, finding that the insurer had defeated the employer's attempt to purchase insurance by declining the application and that the state law claims were unrelated to an ERISA plan. Accordingly, the court reversed the trial court's summary judgment order concerning the insurer. However, it affirmed the trial court's judgment for the broker. *Shaw v. PACC Health Plan, Inc.*, 130 Or.App. 32, 881 P.2d 143 (1994).

A Georgia clinic provided group health insurance to its employees without cost. The employer then purchased a different policy that excluded coverage for preexisting employee medical conditions which were evident during the 12 months immediately preceding the date of coverage. An employee of the clinic who was unaware of the exclusionary clause had surgery on her knee shortly after the change in policies, and both carriers denied coverage. When the hospital sued her for nonpayment of her treatment costs, the employee filed a third-party complaint against her employer, alleging that it had breached her employment contract by failing to inform her of the effective termination of her coverage when it changed insurance policies. A Georgia trial court granted summary judgment to the employer, and the employee appealed to the Court of Appeals of Georgia. The court noted that in Georgia, an employer acts as the agent of its employees when changing group insurance policies and has a duty to notify employees of the differences between old and new policies. Employers were required to advise employees of their rights to continuation coverage under existing policies when they purchased new insurance policies. In this case, factual issues remained concerning whether anyone had notified the employee of the change in coverage. This and other fact questions made pretrial dismissal of the lawsuit inappropriate, and the court of appeals reversed and remanded the case. *Brandon v. Mayfield*, 452 S.E.2d 181 (Ga.App.1994).

A Colorado employee, covered under a qualified ERISA plan, went into premature labor with twins. The local hospital could not accommodate her neonatal needs and she was flown by helicopter to a regional hospital. She delivered one child by natural birth and the other by cesarean section. The administrator of the plan denied the employee's request for the amount beyond the $2,500 maximum benefit for cesarean sections. It also denied her expenses for the helicopter transport. The employee challenged these denials in a U.S. district court. The court granted the employee the requested benefits and reasonable attorney's fees. The health care administrator appealed to the U.S. Court of Appeals, Tenth Circuit. The health care administrator first contended that the maternity expense benefit provision mandated only one maximum payment pursuant to the schedule of benefits. The court of appeals agreed, ruling that women were entitled to only one maximum benefit payment per pregnancy. The plan did not provide for a maximum benefit payment for each birth. Second, the court determined that premature labor with twins constituted an "emergency." Consequently, hospital expense benefits covered the necessary helicopter transport. Finally, the district court's decision to award the employee attorney's fees was not clearly erroneous. The holding of the district court was affirmed in part and reversed in part. *Rademacher v. Colo. Assn. of Soil Conservation Med. Plan*, 11 F.3d 1567 (10th Cir.1993).

A legal secretary employed by an Illinois financial services corporation experienced frequent headaches, fatigue, extreme sensitivity to smoke and other substances, and allergies. She submitted a claim for disability benefits under the corporation's employee benefits plan. She submitted proof of being hypersensitive to common environmental chemicals and was awarded benefits. The plan underwriter then submitted the employee's medical records to an independent medical consulting agency, which determined that the records were not based upon accepted medical information, having been generated by a physician describing himself as a specialist in clinical ecology. Based on the independent evaluation, the underwriter recommended termination of benefits. The employee sued the plan administrator in the U.S. District Court for the Northern District of Illinois, which granted the administrator's summary judgment motion and counterclaim for overpaid disability benefits. The employee appealed to the U.S. Court of Appeals, Seventh Circuit.

The court of appeals determined that the plan's decision to terminate benefits was not unreasonable, arbitrary or capricious because the employee's proof of disability was based upon clinical ecology, an area which was not accepted by the AMA or other recognized medical body. The employee had also failed to submit medical proof of a psychiatric disability, which she had claimed as an alternate ground for obtaining benefits. The independent evaluation gave the employee a later opportunity to review the decision, satisfying minimal due process requirements. The district court had properly granted summary judgment to the plan administrator. *Donato v. Metropolitan Life Ins. Co.*, 19 F.3d 375 (7th Cir.1994).

A Massachusetts man went on full disability leave. He received full salary and employment benefits, including Blue Cross group plan coverage for himself and his wife. More than a year later he terminated his employment. His former employer then informed him of his statutory right to continue group coverage for up to 18 months at his own expense. He elected for continuation coverage. The next year he became eligible for Medicare. Although Medicare eligibility would make him ineligible for continuation coverage, it would also serve as a new qualifying event and make his wife eligible for three years of continuation coverage. At the same time, however, the company terminated his group plan coverage and adopted a self-funded insurance plan. As the new plan would not be convertible to individual coverage at the end of his wife's continuation coverage period, the man decided to exercise his conversion option on the Blue Cross group plan. Prior to the changeover, he asked the group to convert his wife's group coverage to individual coverage under the Blue Cross managed major medical plan. Blue Cross returned certain medical bills unpaid. After several unsuccessful efforts to obtain satisfactory coverage, the couple sued the company. A federal district court ruled that the wife was entitled to three years of continuation coverage. The employer appealed to the U.S. Court of Appeals, First Circuit.

Under the Consolidated Omnibus Budget Reconciliation Act (COBRA), an employer that sponsors a group health insurance plan must offer continuation benefits to employees and qualified beneficiaries for at least 18 months after the occurrence of a qualifying event. The employer contended that the qualifying event was the date of the employee's disability. The court noted that the statutory language offered no explicit guidance in determining the relevant qualifying event. Here, the employee's termination did not coincide with the loss of coverage under the employer's plan. The court of appeals determined that continuation coverage ran from the date of the event which triggered the loss of benefits under the terms of the group insurance plan, and not from when the company ceased its voluntary provision of employer-paid group plan insurance. The court remanded the case to determine the terms of the plan. *Gaskell v. Harvard Co-op Society*, 3 F.3d 495 (1st Cir.1993).

An employee covered under an ERISA plan was denied healthcare coverage for his newborn daughter who experienced medical complications. The plan administrator denied coverage. The plan gave discretionary authority to construe the plan to the administrator. The employee brought this action in a federal district court alleging abuse of discretion. The district court awarded the employee coverage and attorney's fees and the company appealed to the U.S. Court of Appeals, Eighth Circuit. The employee alleged that his daughter was covered under his preexisting dependent coverage plan. The court agreed with the district court that the plan in effect when the child was born clearly and unambiguously provided newborns with coverage from birth. Although the plan summary was at odds with the plan, the summary stated that the plan controlled when the summary and the plan conflicted. Further, the appellate court concluded that the district court did not abuse its decretion in awarding attorney's fees. *Sturges v. Hy-Vee Employee Benefit Plan and Trust*, 991 F.2d 479 (8th Cir.1993).

A Georgia retail furniture chain employed 160 persons full-time. In 1988, the chain sponsored an employee welfare benefit plan within the meaning of ERISA. The plan provided group hospital and medical benefits up to a lifetime maximum of $1 million per employee. An employee who participated in the plan tested HIV-positive. Shortly thereafter, the chain's insurer notified the chain of its intent to cancel the policy because of the high incidence of HIV in the retail industry generally and among the chain's plan members in particular. At the time, five employees had HIV. Its insurance broker advised the chain that it could insure its plan only by placing a maximum lifetime limit on coverage of HIV-related illnesses. The chain then modified its plan to include a $25,000 cap on all HIV-related medical claims. The modification was made pursuant to the plan's express terms, which stated that the chain had an absolute right to modify the plan at any time. The employee then filed suit in a federal district court alleging that the modification violated § 510 of ERISA. The federal district court granted summary judgment for the employer, and the employee appealed to the U.S. Court of Appeals, Eleventh Circuit.

The court noted that the primary purpose of § 510 was to prevent employers from "discharging or harassing employees to prevent them from obtaining vested rights." Therefore, absent evidence of retaliation or interference with rights under the plan, ERISA provides no right to permanent health insurance. The court further noted that Congress' express intent was that employers be free to fashion medical benefit plans as costs, technology, and the marketplace dictate. Congress intended flexibility in employer modification of employee benefit plans. Therefore, the court of appeals upheld the decision in favor of the employer. *Owens v. Storehouse, Inc.*, 984 F.2d 394 (11th Cir.1993).

A Colorado man began working as a commercial real estate division manager for a real estate company in Denver. He was HIV-positive but kept his condition a secret and spoke of his disease as a diminished lymphoma, a term he made up. His supervisors then met with him and discharged him. He indicated that he was HIV-positive and that terminating his job would also terminate his insurance benefits. The supervisors indicated that they had not been aware that he had HIV and suggested that he stay on as a real estate agent so that he could continue his insurance at his own expense. The manager declined to do so and filed a federal district court action for violation of ERISA § 510. The district court found for the real estate company and the manager appealed to the U.S. Court of Appeals, Tenth Circuit. Under ERISA § 510, it is unlawful to discharge a person for the purpose of interfering with the attainment of pension rights under an ERISA plan. Therefore, the manager was required to prove that his discharge had been motivated by an intent to interfere with employee benefits protected by ERISA. The court noted that there was ample evidence concerning the possible effect of an HIV victim on benefit plans. However, there was no evidence that anyone in the real estate company had made such calculations. The appellate court upheld the decision of the district court and concluded that the manager failed to prove the intent required by ERISA. *Phelps v. Field Real Estate Co.,* 991 F.2d 645 (10th Cir.1993).

An employee of a music company, which had in effect a group medical plan, discovered that he was HIV-positive. The employee met with company officials to discuss his illness. At that time, the group plan provided for lifetime medical benefits of up to $1 million for all employees. Seven months after this incident, the company became self-insured under a new plan which limited benefits payable for HIV-related claims to a lifetime maximum of $5,000. Shortly thereafter, the employee exhausted his $5,000 limit. He then sued the company, asserting that it had violated § 510 of ERISA. That section prohibits discrimination against employees who exercise rights to which they are entitled under employee benefit plans. The company moved for summary judgment, asserting that it had the right to change its group medical plan to avoid the expense of paying for treatment. A Texas federal district court granted summary judgment to the employer, and the employee appealed to the U.S. Court of Appeals, Fifth Circuit. On appeal, the court noted that the employee would have to prove that the company intended to specifically discriminate against him to win on his claim. Here, the reduction in benefits would apply equally to all employees filing for such claims. Section 510 of ERISA only disallows discrimination which is motivated by a desire to retaliate against an employee or to deprive an employee of an existing right to which he may become entitled. It does not prohibit the kind of discrimination of which the employee had accused the employer. Thus, the district court's decision was affirmed. *McGann v. H & H Music Co.*, 946 F.2d 401 (5th Cir.1991).

A Pennsylvania man filed a claim for black lung benefits which was denied under U.S. Department of Labor (DOL) interim regulations because his employer had met its burden of showing that pneumoconiosis was not a contributing factor in his disability, and thus his disability did not "arise in whole or in part out of coal mine employment." Two other claimants from other states were also initially denied benefits and the cases were consolidated before the U.S. Court of Appeals, Third Circuit. The court determined that the DOL interim regulations violated the Black Lung Benefits Reform Act because they were more restrictive than earlier regulations of the Department of Health, Education, and Welfare. The U.S. Supreme Court agreed to hear the cases to decide the validity of the DOL regulations. The Court held that the labor secretary's decision was reasonable and was entitled to deference. Accordingly, the regulations were valid and enforceable. The Court affirmed in part and reversed in part the lower court decisions, holding that none of the three claimants were entitled to benefits. *Pauley v. Bethenergy Mines, Inc.*, 501 U.S. 680, 111 S.Ct. 2524, 115 L.Ed.2d 604 (1991).

III. EMPLOYER LIABILITY AND RECOUPMENT

A plan may incur liability not only by failing to pay benefits which are due participants, but also by withdrawing from a multiemployer plan. However, it may also recoup excess funds from terminated plans if the funds do not have to be paid out as accrued benefits (nonforfeitable benefits) or as other benefits under the plans.

The Multiemployer Pension Plan Amendments Act of 1980 (MPPAA), 29 U.S.C. §§ 1381-1461, requires employers who withdraw from underfunded multiemployer pension plans to pay a fair share of the plan's unfunded liabilities. The MPPAA gives withdrawing employers the option to pay their withdrawal liability in a lump sum, or to amortize the amount in level annual payments "calculated as if the first payment were made on the first day of the plan year following the plan year in which the withdrawal occurs and as if each subsequent payment were made on the first day of each subsequent plan year." A brewing company withdrew from an underfunded plan with a withdrawal charge of $23.3 million. Prior to withdrawing, it had typically made annual payments of approximately $4 million to the fund, and the relevant annual interest rate was seven percent. Although the plan and the brewery agreed on the amount of withdrawal liability, the parties disagreed on the amount of interest that had accrued during the withdrawal year. The plan claimed that interest began accruing on the last day of the plan year preceding withdrawal, while the brewery argued that accrual began on the first day of the plan year following withdrawal. The difference in sums was in excess of $2.6 million. An arbitrator agreed with the brewery, but the

U.S. District Court for the Eastern District of Wisconsin reversed. The U.S. Court of Appeals, Seventh Circuit, reversed the district court's decision, and the plan appealed to the U.S. Supreme Court.

On appeal, the plan argued that the brewery's interpretation undermined a basic congressional policy objective of the MPPAA that required withdrawing employers to pay their fair share of underfunding. The Court disagreed, noting that nothing in the MPPAA required withdrawing employers to pay an actuarially perfect fair share of withdrawal liability. It also stated that the MPPAA provision describing withdrawing employer liability did not cause interest to start accruing during the withdrawal year itself. Rather it called for calculation as if the first payment were made on the first day of the plan year following the plan year in which withdrawal occurs. Because a withdrawing employer owed nothing to a plan until the plan demanded payment as set forth by the MPPAA, the employer was unable to determine its liability until sometime after the beginning of the withdrawal year. Another reason supporting the brewery's position was MPPAA language concerning amortized withdrawal charges. The amount of annual payment was fixed at a level that equated the withdrawing employer's typical contribution in prior years at an interest rate equal to the plan's normal assumptions. Charging the withdrawing employer a full year of interest would constitute an overcharge and a windfall to employers remaining in the plan. The court affirmed the court of appeals' decision for the brewery. *Milwaukee Brewery Workers' Pension Plan v. Jos. Schlitz Brewing Co.*, 115 S.Ct. 981, 130 L.Ed.2d 932 (1995).

Two shipping companies entered into a joint venture by establishing a third company to operate their ships. The two original companies then withdrew from shipping operations and maintained no relationship with their former unionized employees. The multi-employer pension plan in which the unionized employees had participated calculated withdrawal liability for the two companies in excess of $1.6 million. The companies resisted payment of their withdrawal liability, and an arbitrator affirmed the determination of liability. The U.S. District Court for the Southern District of New York confirmed the arbitration award and the companies appealed to the U.S. Court of Appeals, Second Circuit. The court of appeals observed that ERISA expressly exempted joint ventures from withdrawal liability where they changed their identity or form by reorganization, merger, consolidation or division. In this case, the legal consequence of the companies' action was the creation of a distinct third entity. The creation of the new entity was entirely different from a merger, division, or consolidation as defined by ERISA. The creation of the third company was not within the group of events that Congress intended to exempt from withdrawal liability. The two original companies no longer maintained a relationship with their former employees and retained only secondary liability to the fund. The arbitrator and the district court had properly found that the formation of the joint venture triggered employer withdrawal liability under ERISA. *Bowers v. Andrew Weir Shipping, Ltd.*, 27 F.3d 800 (2d Cir.1994).

A corporation sold a subsidiary and terminated the ERISA retirement plan which was funded by the employer. As a single-employer plan, all accrued benefits automatically vested. The corporation paid out the benefits which had vested, including unreduced early retirement benefits to those employees who met both the age (62) and years of service (30) requirements. A group of employees who did not meet both requirements sued the corporation because it recouped nearly $11 million. They maintained that it was first required to distribute contingent early retirement benefits, even if unaccrued, before recouping plan assets. A Virginia federal district court ruled for the corporation, and the U.S. Court of Appeals, Fourth Circuit, reversed. The case came before the U.S. Supreme Court, which held that the section of ERISA under which this lawsuit was brought did not create benefit entitlements, but merely provided for the orderly distribution of plan assets. However, since there were two alternative sections of ERISA which could potentially lead to a recovery by the employees, the Court remanded the case. *Mead Corp. v. Tilley,* 490 U.S. 714, 109 S.Ct. 2156, 104 L.Ed.2d 796 (1989).

After becoming concerned that a significant number of multiemployer pension plans were experiencing extreme financial hardship, and that the future implementation of mandatory guarantees might result in the termination of several large plans, Congress enacted the Multiemployer Pension Plan Amendments Act of 1980 (MPPAA). This required employers withdrawing from a multiemployer pension plan to pay a fixed and certain debt to the plan amounting to the employer's proportionate share of the plan's "unfunded vested benefits."

The trustees of a multiemployer pension fund brought an action challenging the constitutionality of the withdrawal liability provisions of the MPPAA. After summary judgment was entered in favor of the government by a California federal court, the trustees appealed to the U.S. Supreme Court. The Court determined that the imposition of withdrawal liability on employers did not violate the constitutional prohibition against taking property without just compensation. The Court affirmed the lower court's decision against the trustees. *Connolly v. Pension Benefit Guaranty Corp.,* 475 U.S. 211, 106 S.Ct. 1018, 89 L.Ed.2d 166 (1986).

A New York corporation filed a petition for reorganization under Chapter 11 of the U.S. Bankruptcy Code. At that time, it was the sponsor of three defined benefit pension plans covered by Title IV of ERISA that were chronically underfunded. At the corporation's request, the Pension Benefit Guaranty Corporation (PBGC) terminated the plans. The corporation and its employees then negotiated new pension arrangements which provided substantially the same benefits as before. The PBGC then issued a notice of restoration to undo the termination because the new "follow-on" plans were abusive of the insurance program. When the corporation refused to comply with the restoration, a lawsuit followed. A U.S. district court held for the corporation, and the U.S. Court of Appeals, Second Circuit, affirmed.

On appeal, the U.S. Supreme Court reversed the lower courts. It found that the PBGC's restoration decision was not arbitrary or capricious. It did not matter that the PBGC had not considered all the potentially relevant areas of the law before making its decision. Section 4047 of ERISA gave the PBGC the power to restore terminated plans in any case where it determined such action to be appropriate under Title IV of ERISA. Further, the PBGC had complied with the requirements of § 555 of the Administrative Procedure Act. As such, the agency decision was valid and the corporation had to restore the plans which had been terminated. *Pension Benefit Guaranty Corp. v. LTV Corp.,* 496 U.S. 633, 110 S.Ct. 2668, 110 L.Ed.2d 579 (1990).

A Texas corporation maintained several tax-qualified deferred pension benefit plans which were subject to the minimum funding requirements of ERISA. In 1983 and 1984, the company contributed unencumbered property to the pension trust and credited that value against its minimum funding obligation. The Commissioner of Internal Revenue ruled that the company's transfers were prohibited sales or exchanges under § 4975(c)(1)(A) of the Internal Revenue Code. This ruling resulted in a determination that the company owed an excise tax liability. The company appealed to the tax court which entered summary judgment in its favor. After the U.S. Court of Appeals, Fifth Circuit, upheld the decision of the tax court, the commissioner appealed to the U.S. Supreme Court.

The issue on appeal was whether the contribution of unencumbered property was a prohibited sale or exchange under § 4975(c)(1)(A). The Court noted that for income tax purposes the transfer of property in satisfaction of a monetary obligation is usually considered a sale or exchange. Section 4975 prohibits any direct or indirect sale or exchange of property in satisfaction of a debt between a plan and a disqualified entity such as the company. Since Congress was aware when it enacted § 4975 that the phrase "sale or exchange" had been construed to include the transfer of property in satisfaction of a monetary obligation, it intended to prohibit such transfers by the passage of this section. Further, Congress' goal in enacting ERISA was to bar a transaction that was likely to injure the pension plan. Since a transfer of unencumbered property to satisfy a monetary obligation had the potential to burden a plan, the Supreme Court upheld the decision of the commissioner to levy taxes on the corporation and reversed the court of appeals' decision. *Commissioner of Internal Revenue v. Keystone Consolidated Industries, Inc.,* 113 S.Ct. 2006, 124 L.Ed.2d 71 (1993).

An Illinois trucking company used the services of drivers who owned their own rigs. Between May 1984 and August 1986, the company treated the truckers as employees for purposes of pension and health coverage. Subsequently, the trucking company decided that the drivers were independent contractors who were ineligible to participate in the plans. It then sent letters asking for refunds. The pension fund filed an interpleader action, offering to pay the money to its rightful owners. The employer made a claim and also brought its own suit against the welfare fund, asking for a refund of premiums. The district court awarded the pension money to the drivers and concluded that, because the company was not entitled to a refund, it lacked standing to sue the fund. The employer then appealed to the U.S. Court of Appeals, Seventh Circuit.

The court of appeals determined that the company had standing to sue the fund. It had paid the fund a large sum of money, which it wanted back. The appellate court determined that just because a litigant is doomed to lose does not indicate that it lacks standing to sue. The company claimed that it should receive its part of the pension plan contributions. The company pointed out that the pension plan was noncontributory — meaning that the funds sent to the pension plan were not treated as part of the drivers' gross income for tax purposes — and contended that it was entitled to the return of its money. The court, however, disagreed and stated that the company pension was a form of deferred compensation, received after retirement. Accordingly, the court upheld the district court's decision and awarded the money to the drivers. The court also awarded reasonable attorney's fees to the funds because the company's position was not substantially justified. *Construction Industry Retirement Fund of Rockford v. Kasper Trucking, Inc.*, 10 F.3d 465 (7th Cir.1993).

A Massachusetts photographic company provided a profit sharing retirement plan and an employee bonus plan. The company received a $925 million settlement for patent infringement from a competitor. The infringement took place over the course of 10 years. A former employee brought this breach of contract action in a federal district court. He claimed that the employer contributions over the 10 years of infringement were under-subscribed. After the court granted summary judgment to the company, the former employee appealed to the U.S. Court of Appeals, First Circuit. The employee contended that the settlement payment should be applied to the profits over the course of the 10 years of infringement which in turn would provide additional benefits and bonuses to retirees and employees that would have been received from these additional receipts. The court looked to the common law of contract to determine if the settlement payment should be applied to the years in question. The plans stated that "net profit" would be computed in accordance with standard accounting practices. Standard accounting practices required that litigation settlements be recognized as income in the year received. Thus, the $925 million should have been recognized as income in 1991, the year received. The appellate court upheld the decision of the trial court and granted summary judgment to the company. *Pizzuti v. Polaroid Corp.*, 985 F.2d 13 (1st Cir.1993).

A company acquired the assets and liabilities of two other companies in 1981. Part of the acquisition was an hourly benefit plan which each acquired corporation had set up. The benefit plans were in accordance with ERISA. The company closed down one of the subsidiaries and purchased fixed annuities for the employees who qualified under the plan. It then transferred to itself nearly $7,000,000 in surplus plan assets. A class action suit was brought against the employer, alleging that by distributing the money to itself, it had violated its fiduciary duties under ERISA. Section 4044(d)(1) of ERISA permits distribution of excess assets to employers if all the liabilities of the plan have been satisfied, if the distribution does not contravene the law, and if the plan provides for such a distribution. In this case, the plan did not provide for reversion of excess assets to the employer. The employer had attempted to amend the plan to allow reversion; however, the language of the plan, in conjunction with the collective bargaining agreement between the union and the employer, stated that such an amendment could not be made on a unilateral basis. The federal district court thus held that the distribution of excess assets to the employer violated the provisions of ERISA. The court granted summary judgment to the plaintiff class. *International Union of Electronic Workers, AFL-CIO v. Murata Erie North America, Inc.,* 772 F.Supp. 870 (W.D.Pa.1991).

A trucking company operated a terminal in Chicago, Illinois, until the spring of 1984. It made contributions to a pension fund pursuant to its collective bargaining agreement with a union. As a result of a 1984 strike, the company terminated its operations, laid off employees, and discontinued its contributions to the fund. Shortly thereafter, the fund assessed withdrawal liability against the company (and two other companies). The fund brought suit against the companies to compel payment of the withdrawal liability. A federal district court entered summary judgment in favor of the pension fund. While an appeal was pending, the employer met with one of the fund's trustees to negotiate a settlement agreement. They apparently agreed on a settlement. Later, the employer sued the pension fund for failing to abide by the terms of the settlement agreement. The district court held for the pension fund, and the employer appealed to the U.S. Court of Appeals, Seventh Circuit.

On appeal, the court noted that the fund was controlled by more than one trustee, and that ERISA provided for joint management and control in such a case. This would require the action of all the trustees to bind the fund unless the trustees had delegated authority to the one trustee to enter into the settlement with the employer. Here, the trustees had not delegated such power to the one trustee. Further, there was no "apparent authority" on the part of the one trustee to make the deal because the employer had received a letter prior to the negotiations which stated that all the trustees had to agree to the settlement for the fund to be bound. The court of appeals affirmed the decision in favor of the pension fund, holding that it was not bound by the terms of the alleged oral settlement. *Mason & Dixon Lines, Inc. v. Glover,* 975 F.2d 1298 (7th Cir.1992).

An Oklahoma man worked for a freight company from 1955 to 1984, when it closed. In 1973, the company began contributing to a pension plan on its employees' behalf. In 1982, when the employees voted to change unions (and opted for the new union's pension plan), the company ceased contributing to the plan. In 1984, the old pension plan began transferring the accrued assets and liabilities to the new union's pension plan. Under a forfeiture provision, the old plan cancelled nine years of credit earned by the employee for years that he worked prior to the date the company began making payments under the plan. The employee later brought suit against the old plan, claiming that the forfeiture provision violated ERISA. A federal district court ruled for the plan. The employee appealed to the U.S. Court of Appeals, Tenth Circuit.

On appeal, the court noted that § 1415(b) of ERISA does not forbid a reduction in accrued benefits in a transfer which occurs as a result of a change in the employee's collective bargaining representative. A plan may provide for a forfeiture of accrued benefits for service for years before the year in which the employer was required to contribute to a plan. Accordingly, since there was no violation of ERISA, the court affirmed the district court's decision in favor of the plan, and held that the employee was not entitled to the nine years of service credit which had been lost. *Walter v. International Assn. of Machinists Pension Fund*, 949 F.2d 310 (10th Cir.1991).

IV. SEVERANCE BENEFITS

Employee severance pay or retirement incentive plans may be qualified under ERISA, if they are part of a written employee benefit plan that creates a reasonable expectation for the payment of benefits. One-time-only lump sum payments that are not subject to an ongoing administrative program are typically not covered by ERISA.

An employer sold its plastics division as a going concern to another corporation. Most of its employees were rehired by the corporation and continued in their same positions. At the time of sale, the employer maintained, and was the plan administrator and fiduciary of, a termination pay plan covered by ERISA. Certain former employees brought suit against the employer after it denied their requests for severance benefits and for information about their benefits. A Pennsylvania federal district court granted summary judgment to the employer, and the U.S. Court of Appeals, Third Circuit, affirmed in part and reversed in part. Appeal was taken to the U.S. Supreme Court. The Court first held that the correct standard of review for the denial of benefits was the de novo standard which allowed for greater review and gave less deference to the plan administrator. The Court then defined "participant entitled to disclosure." A participant is either an employee in (or reasonably expected to be in) currently covered employment, or a former employee who has a reasonable expectation of returning to covered employment (or a covered claim to vested benefits). Because the court of appeals did not attempt to determine whether these former employees were participants, the case had to be remanded for such a determination. *Firestone Tire and Rubber Co. v. Bruch*, 489 U.S. 101, 109 S.Ct. 948, 103 L.Ed.2d 80 (1989).

A packaging and processing company discontinued operations at a plant, laying off almost all its employees. Some of them then filed suit against the company seeking severance pay under Maine law. The company asserted that ERISA preempted the plant-closing statute (which required the company to provide severance pay). The Supreme Judicial Court of Maine held that the company was liable for severance pay under the statute because ERISA only preempted state laws that relate to benefit plans created by employers or employee organizations. The company sought further review from the U.S. Supreme Court.

The Court held that the Maine statute was not subject to preemption by ERISA. Here, the state law merely required a one-time lump-sum payment which was triggered by a single event (the plant closing). There was no ongoing administrative program which the employer had to meet. Thus, there was no potential problem of multiple regulation by state and federal statutes. Further, the Maine statute was not preempted by the NLRA because it did not impermissibly intrude upon the collective bargaining process. *Fort Halifax Packing Co. v. Coyne*, 482 U.S. 1, 107 S.Ct. 2211, 96 L.Ed.2d 1 (1987).

When two banks merged, the State of Washington required one of them to sell part of its business as a condition of state approval. The bank adopted a merger transition program (MTP) which offered severance benefits to employees who were not retained by divested bank units. The MTP required the purchaser to retain employees who had been affected by the divestiture in appropriate positions. These employees were not entitled to the benefit package. Former employees of the merging bank, and who had been retained by the buyers of the divested units, claimed that they had not been "appropriately employed" and that they were entitled to benefits. The bank's benefits committee denied their claims, and the employees filed a lawsuit against their former employer under ERISA. The U.S. District Court for the Western District of Washington granted summary judgment to the former employer as administrator of the benefits plan, and the former employees appealed to the U.S. Court of Appeals, Ninth Circuit.

The court held that the former employees had failed to show any breach of the MTP. Evidence indicated that the benefits committee had not abused its discretion in denying benefits to employees who were reemployed by the divested bank units under the MTP. The court distinguished these former employees from a group of displaced employees who had obtained employment with the divested bank units through their own efforts. Because these employees were not similarly situated, the claim for wrongful denial of benefits was meritless. The district court had properly granted summary judgment to the former employer, and the court of appeals affirmed its decision. *Parker v. BankAmerica Corp.*, 50 F.3d 757 (9th Cir.1995).

An Illinois employer amended its employee stock option plan in an attempt to guard against hostile takeovers. The amendment granted employees stock options that were exercisable in return for the employee's agreement to remain working for at least one year. The amendment made all outstanding options immediately exercisable in the event of a change in the control of the company and did not clearly specify that the option holder's right was exercisable at the time of separation. Instead, it stated that the option could be exercised within three months of separation. Two employees who were terminated due to a corporate reorganization received only the portion of their stock options that was vested at the time of separation. They asserted a right to receive all shares covered by their options at the time of termination, whether the options were fully vested or not. They sued the former employer in the U.S. District Court for the District of

Connecticut, which held in their favor. The employer appealed to the U.S. Court of Appeals, Second Circuit.

On appeal, the employer argued that its practice of canceling unvested portions of terminated employee stock options was appropriate and complied with the IRS Code. It also claimed that the retention of payments by the former employees indicated their acceptance of the amount paid. The court of appeals disagreed, construing the ambiguity in the plan amendment language against the employer. The option rights extended to all unvested portions of options that were outstanding at the time of separation, and the fact that the former employees had cashed their checks did not indicate that they accepted a lesser amount. The court affirmed the district court's judgment. *Lamb v. Emhart Corp.*, 47 F.3d 551 (2d Cir.1995).

An employer administered a defined benefit pension plan. When the company merged with another corporation, it offered a voluntary program to selected employees to encourage early retirement. The program was not offered to employees whom the new corporation sought to retain. Employees who did not receive an offer filed a lawsuit against the corporation in the U.S. District Court for the Southern District of New York, claiming violations of the fiduciary sections of ERISA. They argued that the employer violated its duty to act solely for the benefit of plan participants. The court granted summary judgment to the employees and enlarged its relief to a potential class of over 1,600 individuals, creating potential liability for the corporation of $55 million. It appealed to the U.S. Court of Appeals, Second Circuit.

The court rejected the employees' argument that trustees of a single employer were bound to the same fiduciary standard as the administrators of multiemployer plans, who are barred from acting on an employer's behalf. Single employer plan trustees, who are also corporate officers, take actions on behalf of both plan participants and the employer. Their fiduciary duties extend to the corporation as well as to employees. The corporation had the right to exclude selected employees from the early retirement plan in furtherance of its business objectives. Single employer plans could be amended without being subjected to fiduciary review, because in amending the plans, their trustees were not within the ERISA definition of fiduciary. The court reversed and remanded the district court's judgment. *Siskind v. Sperry Retirement Program, Unisys*, 47 F.3d 498 (2d Cir.1995).

General Motors closed an Ohio stamping plant and placed laid-off employees in a program under which they continued to receive salary and benefits while performing community service. GM then presented laid-off employees with two options, a lump sum payment or permanent layoff with temporary benefits such as health insurance, unemployment benefits and a guaranteed income stream plan. Employees were advised that the programs were mutually exclusive, and all of them chose the lump sum payment. Eight months later, GM withdrew the mutual exclusivity provision and offered another group of laid-off workers both temporary and lump sum benefits. Employees who were in the group that had been laid off earlier filed a lawsuit against GM in the U.S. District Court for the Southern District of Ohio, which dismissed the lawsuit. The employees appealed to the U.S. Court of Appeals, Sixth Circuit.

GM argued that the former employees could no longer be considered participants in an ERISA plan. The court rejected this argument, stating that so long as the former employees would have been eligible to receive benefits except for the alleged wrongdoing, they were participants for ERISA purposes. However, the court disagreed with the former employees' argument that GM was not permitted to alter benefits according to changed circumstances. GM had truthfully represented that the packages were mutually exclusive at the time they were first offered. GM had not breached any fiduciary duty under ERISA. The representation was true at the time it was made and the district court had properly dismissed the case. *Swinney v. General Motors Corp.*, 46 F.3d 512 (6th Cir.1995).

A computer systems, software and service corporation maintained a self-administered severance pay package that awarded severance benefits to employees who lost their jobs due to economic reasons including the closing of a plant. The company eliminated over one fourth of its workforce due to economic factors and sold a plant in South Carolina to another corporation. The plant remained in operation and no jobs were lost. The company made efforts to preserve employee seniority rights and was required to reimburse the buyer for severance benefits in the event of further layoffs. Nonetheless, a group of employees filed an ERISA action against the selling corporation in the U.S. District Court for the District of South Carolina, claiming entitlement to severance pay. The court remanded the case to the plan's benefits claim appeal committee, which determined that the employees had not been severed due to the sale of the plant. The district court affirmed the committee's ruling, and the employees appealed to the U.S. Court of Appeals, Fourth Circuit.

On appeal, the employees argued that the committee's decision was subject to strict judicial scrutiny because the committee was composed of corporate executives who had a conflict of interest. The court agreed, but determined that even under strict judicial scrutiny, the committee had made a correct decision. The plant never closed and there was no interruption of production or employment. An award of severance benefits would result in a windfall to the employees and would contravene plan goals of limiting severance benefits to those who actually lost their jobs. The court affirmed the district court's judgment. *Hickey v. Digital Equipment Corp.*, 43 F.3d 941 (4th Cir.1995).

A manufacturer consolidated several of its product lines which had steeply declining sales into a new subsidiary with the intent of improving its financial statements and eliminating liability for employee benefits in these lines. The manufacturer, however, made assurances that employment benefits and job security would remain the same. The new entity went into receivership within two years and its employees and retirees lost their welfare benefits. The former employees filed a lawsuit in the U.S. District Court for the Southern District of

Iowa, claiming fraudulent misrepresentation, breach of contract, interference with their rights under ERISA and breach of fiduciary duty. A jury returned verdicts of $10 million in benefits and severance pay, and $36 million in punitive damages. The court granted the manufacturer's motion to set aside the entire punitive damage award and part of the general damage award. All parties appealed to the U.S. Court of Appeals, Eighth Circuit.

The court of appeals held that the district court had properly disallowed the claim for severance pay. The company's personnel manual created no reasonable expectation of an entitlement to severance pay. The order to set aside the punitive damage award was correct, because ERISA did not empower a court to award monetary damages. Although the district court had properly dismissed the fraudulent misrepresentation claim as preempted by ERISA, the parent corporation and its subsidiary had violated their ERISA fiduciary duties. While the former employees were not entitled to monetary damages, they were entitled to alternative relief in the form of restitution and an order reinstating them to full participation in the manufacturer's employee welfare benefit plan. *Howe v. Varity Corp.*, 36 F.3d 746 (8th Cir.1994).

The U.S. District Court for the District of Massachusetts consolidated separate actions filed by employees who alleged that their employers misrepresented information about the availability of early retirement plans. In both cases, employees who were considering retiring inquired about the financial condition of their employers and sought information on the availability of improved pension or severance plans. The employees retired after receiving no positive response from their respective employers. However, within a few months of retiring, they learned that both employers were offering enhanced early retirement benefits to employees who had not yet retired. The retirees filed claims against their former employers under ERISA for breach of fiduciary duty and discrimination. The court considered dismissal motions filed by the employers.

Because ERISA does not limit an employer's discretion to amend, create or terminate retirement benefit plans, the employers did not violate ERISA by refusing to disclose their internal deliberations about their business activities. However, employers were forbidden from making material misrepresentations concerning prospective ERISA plans under serious consideration. The court granted the dismissal motions concerning the breach of fiduciary duty claims, ruling that the employers were not required to disclose their business plans. It refused to dismiss misrepresentation claims filed by employees who had made specific allegations that they had directly inquired about impending changes in pension benefits. It was proper to dismiss the claims of employees who based their claims on policy statements in a company newsletter because they failed to make a direct inquiry into benefits. The court refused to dismiss the discriminatory conduct claims, but rejected the former employees' request for a jury trial, because this was not a guaranteed right under ERISA. *Vartanian v. Monsanto Co.*, 880 F.Supp. 63 (D.Mass.1995).

A Connecticut corporation employed an electrical engineer for approximately six years. It then began restructuring its operations because of financial problems. The corporation placed the engineer on a paid leave of absence and advised him that it was terminating his employment two months later. It advised him by letter that he could remain on paid leave of absence for three more months to give him the option of exercising company stock options with a value of approximately $167,000. The engineer exercised these options and enjoyed other severance benefits pursuant to a written agreement. Seventeen months later, the engineer sued the corporation in a Connecticut trial court, claiming that he had been coerced into accepting the severance agreement. The jury returned a verdict for the engineer and awarded him $413,000 in damages. However, the trial court set aside the verdict, and the engineer appealed to the Supreme Court of Connecticut. The supreme court stated that the retention of contractual benefits over a considerable time period constituted contract ratification. In this case, the engineer had retained the benefits of the severance package for 17 months before claiming that he had been coerced into accepting the package. The court rejected the engineer's argument that the severance agreement was a threat by the corporation to preclude him from exercising his stock options. The argument could not succeed where the engineer had been able to exercise his options. The trial court had properly granted the corporation's motion for a directed verdict against the engineer. *Young v. Data Switch Corp.*, 231 Conn. 95, 646 A.2d 852 (1994).

Sears advised a number of its employees working at an Alabama retail distribution center that the facility was being converted to a home delivery center and that they would lose their jobs as a result. The employees were offered a severance incentive package that required their signatures on a release that recited the waiver of any right to sue Sears for wrongful employment termination. The delivery center was converted, but the job reduction was not as severe as first indicated. However, Sears refused to rehire the severed employees and they filed age discrimination charges with the EEOC, claiming that they had been forced to accept the severance benefits under duress and through misrepresentations. None of the former employees paid back any of their retirement benefits, and Sears filed a motion for summary judgment in the U.S. District Court for the Northern District of Alabama. The court granted summary judgment to Sears on the employee claims of fraud, but denied the motion concerning retention of pension benefits. Sears appealed to the U.S. Court of Appeals, Eleventh Circuit.

The court held that ADEA plaintiffs were not required to tender back retirement benefits as a prerequisite to challenging the release/waiver in court. Retention of benefits during the pendency of the lawsuit did not constitute ratification of the releases. The court affirmed denial of the motion for summary judgment as it concerned retention of benefits. Although the employees had been employed at will until the employer's offer of severance pay, the offer converted this status as an offer of a "supplemental contract." The retirees stated a valid claim for fraud and misrepresentation in the offer of the supplemental contracts, and the summary judgment ruling on the fraud claims was reversed. *Forbus v.*

Sears Roebuck & Co., 958 F.2d 1036 (11th Cir.1992). *cert. den.,* — U.S. —, 113 S.Ct. 412, 121 L.Ed.2d 336 (1993). (*Forbus I*).

On remand, the district court granted Sears' motion to amend its claim to assert preemption of the state law fraud claims under ERISA. The court also granted Sears' motion for partial summary judgment on these claims. The former employees appealed to the court of appeals, which found no error in the district court's order to allow the amended answer. However, the court had erroneously determined that the claims were preempted by ERISA. This was because the claims were for improper job termination, rather than fraud involving the pensions. The state laws in question made no reference to pension plans and the ERISA preemption ruling was reversed. *Forbus v. Sears Roebuck & Co.*, 30 F.3d 1402 (11th Cir.1994). (*Forbus II*).

A Maryland employer laid off a programmer-analyst with 27 years of experience. She agreed to sign a release that waived any and all employment related claims against the company, including claims based on age discrimination. The release/waiver allowed only five days for her signature, subject to the complete loss of her retirement benefits. Although very upset by the layoff notice, the employee agreed to sign the waiver. She soon read a newspaper advertisement for an analyst position in her former department, and sued the company. However, she delayed filing suit until the severance benefits were actually paid. She retained the benefits after receiving them and filed an ADEA complaint against the employer in the U.S. District Court for the District of Maryland. The court held that the release was valid, and the former employee appealed to the U.S. Court of Appeals, Fourth Circuit.

According to the Court of Appeals, employee waivers of their ADEA rights are valid, so long as they are knowing and voluntary. Applying ordinary contract principles, the court found the former employee's decision "voluntary, deliberate and informed." The company had committed no fraud in offering the severance benefits at the time of the layoff. The retention of severance benefits by the former employee had the legal effect of contract ratification. She could not repudiate the contract because she had ratified it, and summary judgment for the company was appropriate. *O'Shea v. Commercial Credit Corp.*, 930 F.2d 358 (4th Cir.1992).

Several employees of a Texas refinery were discharged following the closure of one of its offices. The employees were given the option of releasing their claims under the ADEA in return for weekly cash payments pursuant to a termination pay plan. The release-of-claims agreement expressly provided that the employees had 45 days to consider the agreement as required by the Older Workers Benefit Protection Act (OWBPA). However, the employees alleged that they were pressured to sign the agreement as soon as possible. The employees eventually agreed to receive the weekly cash payments in consideration for the release of their claims. In spite of the agreement, the employees filed ADEA claims in a U.S. district court. The employees did not offer to "tender back" the cash payments already received. The district court dismissed the claims and the employees appealed to the U.S. Court of Appeals, Fifth Circuit. The court noted that the

OWBPA provided that employees who enter release agreements without being given 45 days to consider the releases can avoid the releases at their own election. However, the court determined that the employees ratified the release agreements by failing to tender back the consideration (the cash payments) after learning that the release was avoidable. The court expressly refused to analogize ADEA cases to U.S. Supreme Court Federal Employers' Liability Act cases which permitted suits even absent a return of consideration. Thus, the court held that even assuming an OWBPA violation, the employees' failure to "tender back" consideration paid by the employer ratified the release agreements. The holding of the district court was affirmed. *Wamsley v. Champlin Refining and Chemicals*, 11 F.3d 534 (5th Cir.1993).

A Colorado employer discharged employees in a workforce reduction, and offered them a lump-sum payment based upon the length of time each employee had been employed. The payments were made pursuant to a written agreement and were made only to those employees who were willing to sign the agreement. The agreement contained a release for any and all claims against the employer or its officers, directors or agents. The only two benefits excepted from the broad release of rights and claims were those arising under the employer's pension plan or under the workers' compensation act. Unemployment compensation benefits were not excepted from the release, nor were they otherwise referred to in the agreement. Two employees who accepted the terms of the agreement and were paid the lump-sum amounts applied for unemployment compensation benefits. The employer insisted that the payments made to them under the written agreement constituted a severance allowance which would cause their unemployment compensation to be reduced. A hearing referee held that, because the purpose of the written agreement was to obtain the release of the employees' claims against the employer, the payments made by the employer could not be considered a severance allowance. The Industrial Claim Appeals Panel reversed the referee's decision, concluding that the payments met the criteria for severance pay. The claimants appealed to the Colorado Court of Appeals.

On appeal, the court noted that the payments made by the employer were based upon the length of time each employee had been employed. However, not every payment by an employer based upon the length of an employee's service is to be considered severance pay. Rather, the purpose of the payment has to be considered. Here, the written agreement between the parties demonstrated that the employer's primary purpose in making the lump-sum payment was to benefit the employer. Accordingly, since the payment was not for services rendered, but to settle any claims asserted by employees, the payments could not be considered a severance allowance under Colorado law. *Moore v. Digital Equipment Corp.*, 868 P.2d 1170 (Colo.App.1994).

A group of New Mexico employees worked for a mine that was sold to another corporation. The new owners allowed the employees to continue employment at their same positions. Under the previous employer's policy manual, the employees could receive severance pay where permanent jobs were eliminated unless the employees had been offered comparable jobs. The employees brought a claim against their previous employer to receive severance pay. The district court granted a summary judgment in favor of the previous employer. On appeal, the U.S. Court of Appeals, Tenth Circuit, affirmed the lower court's decision against the employees. The court held that the provision regarding a comparable job offer did not exclude an offer of employment from another employer. Additionally, the court held that in order for a job to be comparable, it did not have to be identical. Here, the employees continued to work without interruption. Accordingly, they were not entitled to severance pay. *H.W. Awbrey v. Pennzoil Co.,* 961 F.2d 928 (10th Cir.1992).

An Idaho creamery notified a supervisory employee that it would eliminate his position in two weeks due to a reduction in its workforce. It offered him continued employment as a salesman or cooler employee at approximately half his present pay rate. The employee requested two weeks of severance pay that he claimed was due under the employee handbook. The handbook stated that severance pay was not due in cases of employment termination for cause. Alternatively, where termination was without cause, the employee was entitled to the equivalent of two weeks pay. The employer refused the employee's request and he filed a lawsuit in an Idaho trial court for severance pay plus treble damages and attorney fees under an Idaho statute. The court granted summary judgment to the employee and the employer appealed to the Court of Appeals of Idaho.

The court determined that the references to termination for cause and without cause in the employee handbook were not explained and were ambiguous. It was reasonable for the employee to believe that termination resulting from a reduction in force was not a termination for cause. The court affirmed that portion of the trial court's summary judgment order. However, the court should not have ruled that the employee was entitled to severance pay and attorney's fees without a factual determination of the circumstances surrounding the employer's offer of continued employment. The court remanded the case to the trial court. *Farnsworth v. Dairymen's Creamery Assn.,* 876 P.2d 148 (Idaho App.1994).

V. VACATION AND SICK BENEFITS

Vacation and sick benefits are generally a matter of contract interpretation and require an examination of the employment contract. The U.S. Supreme Court has held that a policy of paying discharged employees a lump sum out of corporate general assets does not constitute an employee welfare benefit plan under ERISA.

A Massachusetts bank discharged two vice presidents and allegedly failed to compensate them for vacation time they had accrued but not used. The state charged the bank president with criminal violation of a state law which prohibited this. The bank president moved to dismiss the case against him on the ground that ERISA preempted all state laws relating to an "employee welfare benefit plan."

The question of whether payments for unused vacation time constitutes an employee welfare benefit plan came before the U.S. Supreme Court.

The Court noted that the creation of a separate fund to pay employees vacation benefits would bring the plan under ERISA coverage. However, the employer here had a policy of paying vacation benefits out of its general assets. Because ERISA had been enacted to prevent mismanagement of accumulated plan funds and to prevent failure to pay benefits from such funds, it did not apply to the situation involved here. The vacation pay owed in this case was fixed, payable from general assets, and not dependent on contingencies outside the employee's control. Accordingly, the criminal action against the bank president was not preempted by ERISA. *Massachusetts v. Morash*, 490 U.S. 107, 109 S.Ct. 1668, 104 L.Ed.2d 98 (1989).

A collection agency obtained money judgments against 25 people who were participants in an employee welfare benefit plan covered by ERISA. The covered workers drew their vacation benefits from the plan annually. The collection agency sought to garnish the debtors' plan benefits to collect the money judgments. A Georgia trial court allowed the garnishment, but the state court of appeals reversed, holding that a Georgia statute barred the garnishment of funds of an employee benefit plan which was subject to ERISA. The Georgia Supreme Court reversed, deciding that ERISA preempted the Georgia statute. The case reached the U.S. Supreme Court. The Court first noted that ERISA preempted the state law because it related to a pension plan described under ERISA. It then stated that Congress did not intend to preempt state-law garnishment of ERISA welfare benefit plans, even where the purpose was to collect judgments against plan participants. ERISA only placed a ban on alienation or assignment of *pension* benefits. Here, the vacation benefits could be garnished because they were not part of a pension plan. The Court affirmed the Georgia Supreme Court's decision in favor of the collection agency. *Mackey v. Lanier Collections Agency & Service,* 486 U.S. 825, 108 S.Ct. 2182, 100 L.Ed.2d 836 (1988).

A California management employee lost his job when his position was eliminated. He filed a claim against his former employer with the state labor commissioner, seeking pay for unused vacation time and for overtime worked on weekends and holidays during his twelve years of employment. The commissioner ordered the employer to pay the employee $6,000 for claims arising during the four years immediately prior to termination, but ruled that all earlier claims were precluded by California's four-year statute of limitations which is applicable to written contracts. A state trial court substantially confirmed the commissioner's decision, and the employee appealed to the California Court of Appeal, Second District. The court stated that a claim for unused vacation pay was considered as a claim for additional wages. The right to take vacation vested annually and the employee could have asserted his right to take vacation time when it accrued under the contract. There was no evidence that the employer had refused to award vacation time during the employee's employment term, and accordingly, he had suffered no forfeiture justifying the tolling of the statute of limitations. It would be inappropriate not to apply the statute of limitations in a case such as this, where the employee himself had an unclear memory of the contested time period. The court affirmed the trial court's judgment for the employer. *Sequeira v. Rincon-Vitova Insectaries, Inc.*, 38 Cal.Rptr.2d 264 (Cal.App.2d Dist.1995).

A Maine mill employee worked substantial overtime hours for several years during a mill modernization project. Because of the project, the employee and several others were unable to use their earned vacation time or receive cash compensation for accrued vacation time upon retirement or resignation. The mill was bought by another corporation and the employee was required to forfeit 70 weeks of unused, accumulated vacation time. The new owner instituted an "employee protection plan" providing for severance benefits in the event of a material reduction in responsibilities, authority or salary due to the takeover. The employee quit and stated that he had suffered a material reduction in responsibilities, salary or benefits as defined in the employee protection plan. He sought compensation for vacation benefits, but the plan denied his request. He filed a lawsuit against the plan, its administrator and the two companies in the U.S. District Court for the District of Maine, which considered summary judgment motions by the parties. The court noted the existence of several issues of material fact that precluded pretrial dismissal of the lawsuit. It rejected the plan administrator's argument that its decision was entitled to deference, ruling that it had the authority to review evidence that had not been considered by the administrator. It also rejected dismissal motions by the companies because there was evidence that they controlled the plan and were proper parties. The issue of the employee's entitlement to a cash payment for overtime compensation also could not be resolved prior to trial. *McLaughlin v. Reynolds*, 886 F.Supp. 902 (D.Me.1995).

A group of Pennsylvania newspaper employees filed a lawsuit against their employer and plan administrator in a federal district court following the sale of the newspaper, claiming that they had been denied vacation pay and bonuses in violation of ERISA and Pennsylvania wage law. The dispute concerned interpretation of the newspaper's dismissal and death benefits policy. A clause in the policy stated that employee pension benefits were severable from the dismissal and death benefits policy. The U.S. District Court for the Western District of Pennsylvania agreed with the employees that the clause was ambiguous and denied a summary judgment motion filed by the newspaper. The employees were entitled to vacation benefits and bonuses because under the terms of the applicable collective bargaining agreement, they had left their employment with the newspaper when the business was sold. Accordingly, the newspaper's argument that they had not been separated failed. Because fact issues existed concerning the employer's good faith in denying benefits and wages, the question of violation of state law would require a trial. *Anderson v. Pittsburgh Press Co.*, 880 F.Supp. 407 (W.D.Pa.1995).

A Louisiana attorney quit his job after six years of employment and demanded a full year's worth of vacation pay, consisting of 15 days. He asserted that his right to vacation pay vested upon the start of a new work year. The former employer contended that the attorney was entitled only to his earned prorated share of annual vacation time, and paid him for ten days. The attorney filed a lawsuit against his former employer in a Louisiana trial court for additional wages, penalties and attorney's fees. The court ruled for the employer and the attorney appealed to the Court of Appeal of Louisiana, Fifth Circuit. On appeal, the court affirmed the principle that accrued, unused vacation time is considered wages under Louisiana law. The employer's manual stated that vacation time was awarded pro rata throughout the year and that the attorney had already received his share of payment. There was no merit to the attorney's argument that his former employer had failed to comply with his statutory demand for payment, and the court of appeal affirmed the trial court decision for the former employer. *Lambert v. Usry & Weeks*, 643 So.2d 1280 (La.App.5th Cir.1994).

A Louisiana company fired a customer service representative who had worked for the company for over three years. It refused to pay her for one week of accrued vacation time that she had not taken at the time of her discharge and for a bonus that had been earned but not paid. The employee filed a lawsuit against the employer in a Louisiana trial court, which awarded her $275 for the unused vacation pay plus a penalty of $4,950 under a Louisiana statute. The court denied the employee's claimed bonus, but awarded attorney's fees. The employer appealed to the Court of Appeal of Louisiana, Third Circuit. The court of appeal stated that unused vacation pay was clearly to be considered "wages" under the statute. Contrary to the employer's argument, the statute required no showing of bad faith by the employer in order to qualify for the penalty wage award. Additionally, there was substantial evidence in the record that the employer did not act in good faith in denying payment for the vacation time. The attorney's fee award was appropriate and an additional amount was awarded on appeal. The court affirmed the trial court's judgment. *Domite v. Imperial Trading Co., Inc.*, 641 So.2d 715 (La.App.3d Cir.1994).

A Minnesota-based company was purchased by a corporation that decided to close all Minnesota operations. The company's written vacation policy provided that separating employees were entitled to pay in lieu of unused vacation time in described circumstances, including "involuntary separation for other than cause." Two employees lost their jobs as a result of the closing and sought compensation for their accrued, unused vacation days. The company refused the requests, stating that the employees, who had been terminated on December 31 of the prior year, had failed to earn their vacation because they did not work into the new year. A Minnesota trial court granted summary judgment to the employees, and the company appealed to the Court of Appeals of Minnesota. The court of appeals stated that an employer's liability for vacation pay is a purely contractual matter. In this case, the employer had obligated itself to pay the employees for any unused vacation time by setting forth the vacation policy. The employees had performed contractually by working throughout the year. The employer had received the benefit of their work and was obligated to pay them for their accumulated vacation time. The trial court order for summary judgment had been correct and the court affirmed it. *Brown v. Tonka Corporation*, 519 N.W.2d 474 (Minn.App.1994).

The Louisiana Court of Appeal, Fifth Circuit, held that an employer could refuse to pay an involuntarily terminated employee for unused, accrued vacation pay. The employer, a Louisiana department store, learned that an employee had lied on his job application by stating that he had not been convicted of a crime. In reality, he had pled guilty to drug-distribution charges only two weeks prior to filling out the job application. The store fired the employee for dishonesty when it learned of the falsification. It paid all wages then due, but refused to pay the employee for 34 hours of accrued, unused vacation time claimed by the employee. A Louisiana trial court awarded summary judgment to the employer, and the employee appealed to the Louisiana Court of Appeal, Fifth Circuit.

On appeal, the employee maintained that Louisiana statutes governing forfeiture of vested rights required the employer to pay for the accrued vacation time. The court stated that although unused vacation may be considered as wages under the statutes, a contrary policy established by an employer may preclude this construction. In this case, the employer's handbook explicitly stated that "vacation is a benefit and not an earned wage." The handbook further limited the payment of unused, accrued vacation pay to employees whose employment became terminated by death, retirement or voluntary separation. Because the employee was involuntarily separated, he was ineligible to receive pay for unused vacation. Accordingly, the trial court had properly granted the employer's summary judgment motion. The court reemphasized that the employee was fired due to his own misrepresentation, and that under the employer's handbook "the right to be paid for unused vacation does not vest in the employee until such time that the appropriate conditions prior to separation from employment are met...." *Huddleston v. Dillard Dept. Store, Inc.*, 638 So.2d 383 (La.App.5th Cir.1994).

A veteran telephone company employee experienced poor health after 25 years of work and took extended sick leave. The company then gave her a "final warning," stating that she would be fired and lose her pension if she took any more sick leave. She was then offered a lump sum payment of over $115,000 and other inducements for early retirement. The employee accepted the retirement package after some consideration, fearing that she would lose all her retirement benefits. The company later alleged that it had miscalculated the lump sum, and attempted to recoup over $31,000. The retiree filed a lawsuit against the company in an Illinois trial court, alleging violations of ERISA and state law, and the company removed the action to the U.S. District Court for the Northern District of Illinois. The court dismissed the state law claims as preempted by ERISA, as well as her claims of fraud and estoppel. However, the court found that the company might be liable under ERISA § 510 (29 U.S.C. § 1140) for interfering with the employee's claim to pension rights by threatening her with the final warning and deprivation of her pension. Because the company induced the early retirement through threats of loss of benefits, it violated ERISA § 510 by interfering with the employment relationship. The court denied the company's motion to dismiss this part of the complaint. *Weatherly v. Illinois Bell Telephone*, 856 F.Supp. 1301 (N.D.Ill.1994).

I. WAGE AND HOUR LAWS

The **Fair Labor Standards Act of 1938 (FLSA), 29 U.S.C. § 201** *et seq.*, is a comprehensive federal statute which mandates the payment of minimum wage and overtime compensation to covered employees. States also have laws that are similar to the FLSA. Most employees are covered under these laws, but there are some exceptions (such as seamen, executives, and bona fide administrative employees, among others). The FLSA prohibits employment of any covered employee in excess of 40 hours per week unless the employee is paid at least time-and-a-half. The FLSA also requires employers to pay at least minimum wage. The state laws generally provide similar requirements.

A. The Fair Labor Standards Act

A group of employees who worked on a barge which processed fish sued their employer to recover overtime benefits under the Fair Labor Standards Act. A Washington federal district court held that they were not entitled to protection under the FLSA because they were "seamen" and thus exempted from the provisions of the act. The U.S. Court of Appeals, Ninth Circuit, reversed, holding that the employees were not seamen, and appeal was taken to the U.S. Supreme Court. The Court held that the court of appeals had improperly arrived at its judgment. Accordingly, it vacated the decision and remanded the case. *Icicle Seafoods, Inc. v. Worthington*, 475 U.S. 709, 106 S.Ct. 1527, 89 L.Ed.2d 739 (1986).

A corporation acquired a security interest in a Tennessee manufacturer's inventory. When the manufacturer began to fail financially, the corporation took possession. However, because some of the inventory had been manufactured during a period in which employees were not paid, the Department of Labor sought to prohibit the sale or transportation of the "hot goods" in interstate commerce. The case came before the U.S. Supreme Court which held that § 15(a)(1) of the FLSA, which prohibits "any person" from introducing into interstate commerce goods produced in violation of the minimum wage or overtime provisions of the act, applied to the corporation here. Even though the corporation was just a secured creditor, it was still subject to the restrictions set forth by the act. *Citicorp Industrial Credit, Inc. v. Brock*, 483 U.S. 27, 107 S.Ct. 2694, 97 L.Ed.2d 23 (1987).

A shoe manufacturer employed seven mechanics to maintain and repair its equipment. In 1984, the Secretary of Labor filed a complaint against the company, alleging that it had failed to pay those employees overtime compensation as required by the FLSA. The company asserted that the two-year statute of limitations precluded the action, but the secretary maintained that the three-year statute (for wilful violations of the FLSA) applied. A Pennsylvania federal district court agreed with the secretary, but the U.S. Court of Appeals, Third Circuit, vacated its decision, holding that only where the employer knew or showed reckless disregard for the matter of whether its conduct was prohibited by the FLSA would the three-year statute of limitations apply. On further appeal to the U.S. Supreme Court, this standard was upheld. *McLaughlin v. Richland Shoe Co.*, 486 U.S. 128, 108 S.Ct. 1677, 100 L.Ed.2d 115 (1988).

A nonprofit religious organization derived most of its income from the operation of commercial businesses staffed by its "associates." These people, former drug addicts and criminals, received no cash salaries, but were provided with food, clothing, shelter and other benefits. The Secretary of Labor filed an action in federal court against the organization and its officers, alleging violations of the FLSA. An Arkansas federal district court held that the organization was an "enterprise" within the meaning of the FLSA. Further, under the economic reality test of employment, the associates were employees of the organization protected by the FLSA. The U.S. Court of Appeals affirmed the finding of liability by the district court, and the case reached the U.S. Supreme Court.

The Court noted that the FLSA contained no express or implied exception for commercial activities conducted by religious or other nonprofit organizations. Further, even though the associates claimed that they were not employees, they did expect compensation of a sort for their work; thus, the economic reality was that they were employees under the FLSA. Finally, the Court held that application of the FLSA did not violate the Free Exercise Clause or the Establishment Clause of the First Amendment. The FLSA did not require the payment of cash wages, so the employees could still be paid in the form of benefits. Also, they could return any payments made to them if they so wished, and provided it was voluntary, this would not violate the FLSA. Nor did the FLSA's recordkeeping requirements inhibit religious activities undertaken with a business purpose. The Court therefore determined that the FLSA applied to the organization, and affirmed the lower court's decision. *Tony & Susan Alamo Foundation v. Secretary of Labor,* 471 U.S. 290, 105 S.Ct. 1953, 85 L.Ed.2d 278 (1985).

Truck drivers employed by a freight company were required to conduct safety inspections of their trucks, and transport them to a repair facility if they failed the inspections. They were not paid for doing this. Their union filed a grievance on their behalf, but a joint committee rejected the grievance. The drivers then filed suit against the employer in an Arkansas federal district court, asserting that their time was compensable under the FLSA. They also claimed that the union had breached its duty of fair representation. The court addressed only the fair representation claim, holding against the drivers. The U.S. Court of Appeals, Eighth Circuit, affirmed, and the case came before the U.S. Supreme Court.

The Court held that the drivers' claims under the FLSA were not barred by the submission of their grievance to the joint committee. Here, the rights at issue arose out of a federal statute, not out of the collective bargaining agreement. The district court should have addressed their claims under the FLSA. The collective bargaining process applies to members of a collective organization, but the rights asserted here were individual rights protected by Congress. They could not be waived. FLSA rights are best protected in a judicial forum, not by an arbitrator. The Court reversed the court of appeals' decision. *Barrentine v. Arkansas-Best Freight System,* 450 U.S. 728, 101 S.Ct. 1437, 67 L.Ed.2d 641 (1981).

Employees of an award-winning New Hampshire daily newspaper claimed that their supervisors discouraged them from reporting overtime and falsified time records to avoid payment for overtime work. The U.S. Secretary of Labor brought an administrative action on behalf of the employees, claiming that the newspaper wilfully violated FLSA overtime and recordkeeping provisions. Federal regulations issued under the FLSA classify most newspaper employees as entitled to overtime compensation, unless they primarily perform duties that require them to use invention, imagination, or talent. The FLSA requires employers to pay not less than one and one-half times the regular rate of pay for work in excess of 40 hours in a single work week, with exceptions for executive, administrative and professional employees. The secretary sought a permanent injunction on behalf of the newspaper employees against further FLSA violations by the newspaper plus an award of backpay, interest and liquidated damages.

The U.S. District Court for the District of New Hampshire held that while the employees were entitled to overtime compensation because they were not engaged in primarily artistic or creative endeavors, the court refused to grant an injunction against future FLSA violations and refused to award compensation for a wilful violation of the FLSA. On appeal, the U.S. Court of Appeals, First Circuit, affirmed this decision, finding no merit to the newspaper's argument that the regulations relied upon by the secretary were obsolete. There was no evidence that the newspaper industry had changed substantially since the publishing of the regulations in 1949. There was also no evidence that the newspaper's violations had been wilful and it was within the discretion of the district court to deny an injunction against future violations. *Reich v. Newspapers of New England, Inc.*, 44 F.3d 1060 (1st Cir.1995).

The U.S. District Court for the District of Columbia reached a different result in the case of a prominent *Washington Post* reporter who covered Washington, D.C. political news. The court considered evidence that distinguished the investigative reporting done by reporters at the *Post* from the work done by small town newspapers, such as that in the above case, which called for less discretion and creativity on the job. The court refused to rely upon the Department of Labor regulations analyzed by the First Circuit in the case above. It characterized the regulations as agency interpretations that had merely been included in the Code of Federal Regulations. The court was not bound by the interpretations and did not apply them in distinguishing the *Post* reporter's duties from those of small town journalists. It denied the reporter's claim for overtime compensation based on strong evidence that his work required invention, imagination and talent. The court entered judgment for the *Post*. *Sherwood v. Washington Post*, 871 F.Supp. 1471 (D.D.C.1994).

Meat packing employees of a nationwide packer were classed in two general categories, the first consisting of those who used knives and other cutting utensils, and the second consisting of those who did not. The first class of employees wore heavy and cumbersome protective gear, while the second category wore lighter gear with hard hats, safety footwear and safety eyewear. The U.S. Secretary of Labor brought an action on behalf of employees in both classes under the FLSA, seeking enforcement of the act's overtime and recordkeeping provisions. The secretary argued that employees in both classes should be paid for taking off, cleaning and putting on safety and sanitary equipment before and after shifts. The U.S. District Court for the District of Kansas determined that workers equipped with knives were entitled to be paid for time spent dressing and undressing. However, the second category of employees was not entitled to be paid for this time. The court initially granted an injunction awarding the employees restitution, but then set aside the injunction. Appeal was brought to the U.S. Court of Appeals, Tenth Circuit.

The court of appeals agreed with the district court's decision concerning the two classes of employees, but disagreed with the court's reasoning. It held that the different treatment of the knife-equipped workers could be justified because of the physical labor and time involved in equipping themselves for work and undressing afterward. In addition to being essential to work, the putting on and taking off of the special protective equipment was itself work. The same could not be said for the other workers, who were relatively lightly equipped. The court affirmed this part of the district court decision, but ordered that the restitutionary injunction be reinstated. *Reich v. IBP, Inc.*, 38 F.3d 1123 (10th Cir.1994).

Employees of a New York food corporation participated in a voluntary uniform wearing program for almost 40 years. The parties then negotiated a collective bargaining agreement which made the use of work uniforms mandatory. Although the union bargained for employee compensation at overtime rates for changing time, this demand was dropped and the final collective bargaining agreement did not include pay for changing time. Local employees then filed a grievance over the issue, which was denied, and the employees filed a lawsuit against the employer in the U.S. District Court for the Northern District of New York, alleging violations of the FLSA. The court granted the employer's summary judgment motion and the employees appealed to the U.S. Court of Appeals, Second Circuit. The court of appeals determined that the FLSA excluded changing time from coverage unless expressly included in a collective bargaining agreement or where it was acknowledged by custom or practice. In this case, the collective bargaining agreement contained no express terms for changing time. Although the mandatory uniform policy was relatively new, it established a "practice" grounded upon the parties' collective bargaining negotiations. The parties to a collective bargaining agreement were deemed to have established a practice if they negotiated over an issue and came to an understanding that resolved it without including it in the final contract. Accordingly, the grievance had been properly denied and the court affirmed the district court's summary judgment order. *Arcadi v. Nestle Food Corp.*, 38 F.3d 672 (2d Cir.1994).

A corporation operated six gas and convenience stores in Tennessee. A wage and hour compliance officer with the U.S. Department of Labor conducted an investigation which revealed past and present violations of the minimum wage, overtime and recordkeeping provisions of the FLSA. The U.S. Secretary of Labor filed a lawsuit against the corporation in the U.S. District Court for the Western District of Tennessee, which held that the corporation had routinely deducted losses including uncollectible credit card sales and cash register shortages from the wages of its hourly employees. It also determined that some employees were not paid at all for some work. The court awarded backpay and liquidated damages to some former employees, but denied a prospective injunction requested by the secretary. It also refused to award backpay and liquidated damages to 25 employees who were not fully identified by corporate payroll records. The secretary appealed to the U.S. Court of Appeals, Sixth Circuit.

The court of appeals observed that the district court had denied injunctive relief in part because FLSA penalties were severe and any repetitious violations would be dealt with more harshly. However, prospective injunctions under the FLSA served a remedial rather than a punitive purpose. Since the corporation had not demonstrated a likelihood that it would comply with the FLSA in the future, the district court should have awarded the injunctive relief requested by the secretary. The 25 unidentified employees should have received backpay and liquidated damages even if the award would be paid to the U.S. Treasury on their behalf, assuming their claims were valid. The court reversed and remanded the case for a determination of whether back wages for the unidentified employees could be calculated. *Reich v. Petroleum Sales, Inc.*, 30 F.3d 654 (6th Cir.1994).

Two convenience store employees were promoted to store manager positions after hiring on as manager trainees. They screened and interviewed job applicants, trained new employees and made minor employment decisions. They also had some authority over ordering and stocking groceries and were on call to remedy problems such as equipment failures. Although the store chain limited their supervisory duties, they had the first hand duty of notifying employees upon termination. The management employees filed a lawsuit against the chain in the U.S. District Court for the Middle District of Georgia, claiming that the store's failure to pay them for working overtime violated the FLSA. The court considered the employer's summary judgment motion. The court evaluated the case under the "short test" found in federal labor regulations. The test requires an employer to show that an employee who is exempt from the FLSA as an executive is primarily employed in management duties by regularly and customarily directing the work of two or more employees. The employees under consideration in this case met the short test requirements despite limitations put on their authority by the store chain. The managers still performed management functions as their primary duties. The court explicitly rejected an argument by the managers that they performed clerical duties more than 50 percent of the time. The time percentage test had no relevance where the short test applied. The court granted the employer's summary judgment motion. *Sturm v. TOC Retail, Inc.*, 864 F.Supp. 1346 (M.D.Ga.1994).

Members of a Texas family controlled two small businesses that operated from the same building. One provided general contractor services for refineries, and the other provided labor under subcontract. The general contractor accounted for at least 90 percent of the subcontractor's business. Through the subcontractor, the contractor hired welders who owned their own equipment and paid them an hourly amount for equipment rental. However, it reduced the hourly equipment rental rate when welders worked overtime. The effect of this practice was to offset the increased wage rate for overtime work by the welders. The subcontractor folded shortly after the U.S. Secretary of Labor filed a lawsuit in the U.S. District Court for the Southern District of Texas for violating the FLSA. The secretary sued both organizations under the theory that they constituted a single enterprise performing related activities for a common business purpose. The court granted summary judgment to the secretary, awarding over $150,000 in overtime compensation on behalf of the welders. An appeal was brought to the U.S. Court of Appeals, Fifth Circuit.

The court of appeals agreed with the district court concerning the relationship of the subcontractor and contractor, which the district court characterized as "mutually parasitic." They constituted a single enterprise for FLSA purposes. The subcontractor and contractor were unable to substantiate any economic reason for offsetting overtime compensation with the lower rental rate for equipment supplied by workers. The district court had properly found that the compensation method employed by the contractor and subcontractor impermissibly circumvented the FLSA. *Reich v. Bay, Inc.*, 23 F.3d 110 (5th Cir.1994).

The U.S. Secretary of Labor sued the publisher of 19 community newspapers serving the Pittsburgh area, claiming that it had violated the minimum wage, overtime, and records requirements of the FLSA with respect to the wages it paid its reporters. The publisher asserted that the FLSA did not cover its actions because all but six of its newspapers fell within the scope of the small newspaper exemption to the act (newspapers with circulations below 4,000) and that, in any event, its reporters were exempt as professional employees. A federal district court determined that the publisher had violated the FLSA with respect to six of the publisher's newspapers. It held that 13 of the 19 newspapers were exempt from the FLSA under the small newspaper exemption. It also stated that none of the reporters were exempt as professional employees. Both parties appealed to the U.S. Court of Appeals, Third Circuit.

The Third Circuit first noted that it was the first court of appeals to construe the small newspaper exemption in the 55 years since its enactment. It then held that the district court had erred in its application of the exemption to the publisher's newspapers. It stated that the lower court should have used an inquiry similar to the one required to determine "enterprise" liability under the FLSA. In other words, the court should have determined whether the papers were engaged in related activities, if they were under unified operation or common control, and if they had a common business purpose. If so, they would be considered a single entity for applying the FLSA. Using this approach, the court held that the newspapers were not exempt from the FLSA. Their aggregate circulation was more than 4,000. Further, the lower court had correctly ruled that the reporters were not exempted as professional employees under the FLSA. The publisher was held liable for violating the FLSA, but the case was remanded for a determination of backpay owed. *Reich v. Gateway Press, Inc.*, 13 F.3d 685 (3d Cir.1994).

A Washington pump mill operated 24 hours a day, seven days a week. Rather than employing separate maintenance repair persons during the evening and night shifts, it developed an ongoing policy of telephoning its regular daytime mechanics at home after hours to return to the plant to fix equipment. Lists were developed according to expertise. The employees were required to accept their "fair share" of call-ins. Their collective bargaining agreement provided for call-in time compensation, but not for nonwork periods when the employees were subject to call-ins. They filed suit in a federal district court, seeking overtime compensation for the hours they were required to be available for on-call requests. The district court granted summary judgment to the employees. The employer appealed.

The U.S. Court of Appeals, Ninth Circuit, examined the general applicability of the FLSA to call-in time. It noted that the U.S. Supreme Court has held that time spent waiting for work is compensable if waiting time is spent "primarily for the benefit of the employer and his business," and that the determination is based on the degree to which the employee is free to engage in personal activities and on the agreement between the parties. The court concluded that the employees were not restricted during their on-call hours. They were not subject to an on-premises living requirement, not required to stay at home, not required to accept all call-ins, and could accept at a time most convenient to them. The court of appeals reversed the district court's judgment. *Owens v. Local No. 169,* 971 F.2d 347 (9th Cir.1992).

An electric supply company employed approximately 120 people, including inside sales persons, purchasing agents and computer operators. In 1987, the Department of Labor conducted an investigation of the company's payment practices. It then filed an action in a New Jersey federal district court, alleging that the company had violated the overtime and record-keeping provisions of the FLSA. The department sought to have the company pay unpaid overtime compensation and to prevent the company from further violating the FLSA. It also requested that the company pay liquidated damages or prejudgment interest to compensate the employees who had been underpaid. The company argued that its inside sales persons and purchasing agents were "bona fide administrative employees" and were exempt from the FLSA's overtime pay requirements. The district court ruled that the employees were entitled to the overtime pay required by the FLSA, and it awarded unpaid overtime wages and prejudgment interest to them. The company appealed to the U.S. Court of Appeals, Third Circuit.

On appeal, the court agreed with the district court that the company's employees were not bona fide administrative employees because their primary duties did not consist of work which was directly related to management policies or general business operations. The underlying reality of the company's business was the production of wholesale sales. Since the employees' duties were to produce and increase those sales, they could not be considered to be administrative employees. The court then noted that the FLSA provides not only for payment of unpaid wages, but also for an equivalent amount of mandatory liquidated damages. Unless the employer is able to show that its violation of the act is in good faith and on reasonable grounds, the liquidated damages must be awarded. Here, the court determined that the company did not take the affirmative steps necessary to allow a finding of reasonable good faith. The court awarded liquidated damages as well as unpaid overtime wages, but it vacated the award of prejudgment interest. *Martin v. Cooper Electric Supply Co.,* 940 F.2d 896 (3d Cir.1991).

An Ohio employer engaged in the operation of three amusement parks. The parks employed numerous 14- and 15-year-old children. A previous investigation conducted by the Department of Labor revealed that the employer violated several child labor provisions of the FLSA. These provisions involved the specific number of hours and times that these children were allowed to work under the child labor laws. The employer was assessed a fine. Five years later, another investigation revealed the occurrence of several hundred additional violations. These violations were ascertained directly from the employer's own records. The Secretary of the Department of Labor then filed an action seeking to enjoin the employer from violating the wage and hour provisions of the child labor laws related to 14- and 15-year-old children.

A federal district court noted that the employer's business activities constituted an enterprise engaged in commerce or in the production of goods for commerce, and was thus subject to the provisions of the FLSA. Despite the employer's arguments that the violations were unintentional and that serious efforts were made to reduce the number of violations, the court found that the employer's past and continued violations were wilful and that they appeared likely to continue. Accordingly, the court granted the injunction restraining the employer from violating the wage and hour provisions of the child labor laws. *Martin v. Funtime, Inc.*, 792 F.Supp. 539 (N.D.Ohio 1991).

B. State Laws

The New York Supreme Court, Appellate Division, Third Department, reinstated an order of the state industrial board of appeals which had ruled that a manufacturer did not violate New York wage law by requiring its route salespersons to make reimbursements to the manufacturer for product shortages. The manufacturer's practice was to charge route salespersons for shortages in a transaction separate from the payment of wages. Salespersons received their wages regardless of any shortage, but the manufacturer's policy called for suspension and eventual termination in the event of failure to pay for shortages. The appellate division court observed that while the state labor law forbade charges against wages or payments as a separate transaction that would otherwise not be permissible as a deduction, the reimbursements in this case were permissible because they were unrelated and independent transactions from the payment of wages. Because a collective bargaining agreement governed the relationship between the manufacturer and route salespersons, a finding of violation of the state wage law might also violate the superseding provisions of federal labor law. The court reinstated the board's order in favor of the manufacturer. *Hudacs v. Frito-Lay, Inc.*, 625 N.Y.S.2d 722 (A.D.3d Dept.1995).

The collective bargaining agreement between a group of Hawaii hotels and hotel bellhops fixed an hourly wage and allowed them to keep all tips and porterage fees. Porterage was a fixed service charge for handling baggage from tours and groups. When the state minimum wage was raised from $3.85 to $4.75 in 1992, the bellhops claimed that their current wages were beneath the minimum wage because porterage fees should not be considered a component of their wages. A Hawaii circuit court rejected their argument, ruling that the fees could be used to satisfy the minimum wage requirement. The bellhops' union appealed to the Supreme Court of Hawaii. The supreme court observed that while the federal Fair Labor Standards Act permits employers to include tip income of up to 50 percent of the minimum wage for determining compliance with the minimum wage law, Hawaii law permitted only a 20 cent tip credit, or less than four percent of the minimum wage. The legislative history of the state minimum wage act indicated that employers were largely prohibited from relying on outside sources to satisfy their obligation to pay the minimum wage. The court agreed with the union's assertion that porterage fees could be considered as gratuities for the purposes of the minimum wage statute, as these fees were designed to replace tips lost by the handling of large tour groups. The hotels were not entitled to summary judgment because the union had raised a genuine factual issue concerning the correct computation of their wages. The circuit court decision was vacated and remanded. *Heatherly v. Hilton Hawaiian Village Joint Venture*, 893 P.2d 779 (Hawaii 1995).

A temporary labor service placed workers at a California manufacturing plant where they were required to remain on the premises during their lunch break. The workers had no duties during their 30-minute break, but were required to use an on-site cafeteria. A number of temporary employees filed a complaint with the state labor commissioner, claiming entitlement to wages for restricted lunch periods. The temporary service succeeded in overturning the commissioner's ruling for the employees in a state municipal court, and this judgment was affirmed by a California superior court. However, this ruling pertained only to the plant in question, and the employment service's state court action against the commissioner to prevent enforcement of the policy statewide resulted in a ruling for the commissioner. The service appealed to the California Court of Appeal, Fifth District.

The court of appeal stated that the definition of "hours worked" contained in California Industrial Welfare Commission regulations included all times during which an employee was "subject to the control of an employer," including the times employees were required to remain on the worksite. The court rejected the service's argument that the regulation was too vague to be legally valid. It also rejected an argument that the regulation should not be enforced because it was inconsistent with federal regulations that did not require employees to be paid for on-site lunch periods. The state was permitted to adopt more protective regulations for California workers and the court affirmed the judgment for the commissioner. *Bono Enterprises, Inc. v. Labor Comm., State of California*, 38 Cal.Rptr.2d 549 (Cal.App.5th Dist.1995).

A Washington placement agency employed a staffing coordinator who received pay at straight time rates for work in excess of 40 hours per week. She also received incentive bonuses. After resigning from her position, the former coordinator claimed that the agency failed to pay her overtime wages as required by Washington's Minimum Wage Act (MWA). She filed a complaint against the agency in a Washington trial court, which found that the coordinator was an administrative employee who was exempt from the overtime provisions of the MWA. The former coordinator appealed to the Court of Appeals of Washington, Division One. The court stated that an employer must generally pay all employees overtime compensation for work in excess of 40 hours per week. The MWA relieved employers of this obligation for employees who were engaged in executive, administrative or professional capacities. In this case, although the company designated the employee as an administration worker, it paid her additional amounts at straight pay rates for her work in excess of 40 hours per week. This was evidence that the parties contemplated that she was an hourly employee. Accordingly, the court held that the employee was entitled to overtime wages and it reversed and remanded the trial court's decision. *Tift v. Professional Nursing Serv., Inc.*, 886 P.2d 1158 (Wash.App.Div.1 1995).

Employees of a Washington rubbish disposal company were paid for 40 hours of work per week regardless of their actual work time. Some routes could be completed in 40 hours or less, but some routinely required more than 40 hours of work to complete. When employees learned that they were entitled to overtime pay under a Washington state law, they began to record their work hours. The state department of labor and industries began investigating unpaid overtime complaints by drivers. The company then installed time clocks and imposed stricter schedules. A number of drivers then claimed that the employer verbally abused and threatened them when they requested overtime pay, and three of them later testified that their routes were enlarged after complaining. Six drivers quit the company, and five of them filed a lawsuit in a Washington trial court, alleging wrongful harassment and constructive discharge. The court awarded the drivers $141,000 for their wrongful harassment claims, plus attorney's fees and costs in excess of $215,000. The Washington Supreme Court agreed to review the case.

On appeal, the employer argued that the claims for overtime pay were preempted by federal labor law and subject to review only by the National Labor Relations Board (NLRB). The supreme court determined that the overtime wage claim did not come within the coverage of the NLRA, which afforded employees protection for collective bargaining rights. The alleged employer retaliation in this case concerned local law and did not come under the coverage of the NLRA. The court substantially affirmed the trial court's decision, but remanded the case to the trial court for recalculation of the attorney's fees and costs award. *Hume v. American Disposal Co.*, 880 P.2d 988 (Wash.1994).

Pennsylvania's Prevailing Wage Act required employers engaged in public contracts to pay their employees the prevailing minimum wage and benefits for each craft or classification of worker and to keep accurate employee records. Employers could pay wages in excess of the prevailing minimum, and any shortfall in the prevailing level of benefits could be paid in cash. In response to complaints from contractors, the state Prevailing Wage Appeals Board made a declaratory order using a line-item approach for the consideration of employee benefits that singled out ERISA plan benefits as a separate category. Contractors and interested parties filed a lawsuit in the U.S. District Court for the Middle District of Pennsylvania, seeking an order to declare both the order and the wage act preempted by ERISA. The court granted the requested order and appeal reached the U.S. Court of Appeals, Third Circuit.

The court of appeals agreed that the board's declaratory order violated ERISA by singling out ERISA plan benefits for special treatment. However, the prevailing wage act did not violate ERISA because it had no direct relationship to an ERISA plan and primarily required employers to pay a minimum cash wage if they sought to participate in public projects. Employers could comply with the law without making any adjustment to their ERISA plans by paying cash wages in an amount that satisfied the act's total wage requirements. Because the act neither encouraged nor constrained any employer action concerning ERISA plans, it was not preempted, and the court of appeals reversed the declaratory order. *Keystone Chapter, Associated Builders and Contractors, Inc. v. Foley*, 37 F.3d 945 (3d Cir.1994).

A Montana disposal company paid its employees for overtime work by using a fluctuating pay scale that amounted to less than time and one-half of the regular wage for work in excess of 40 hours per week. Five employees and former employees of the disposal company filed claims in a Montana trial court for overtime pay. The court ordered the disposal company to pay overtime wages at the time and one-half rate required by state law, a statutory penalty under a Montana wage law, attorney's fees and costs, and interest on the unpaid wages. The disposal company appealed to the Supreme Court of Montana. The supreme court noted that the Montana wage law employed a strict mathematical formula that was applicable except in cases where a clear mutual understanding existed for an alternative salary arrangement, including a fixed salary. Because the employees had never consented to fixed salaries that could result in less than time and one-half of their regular wage rate for overtime work, there was no mutual understanding of the parties for an alternate wage rate, and the disposal company had violated the state wage law. The trial court had properly assessed a misdemeanor penalty against the employer, and did not commit error by awarding attorney's fees and interest as provided by the statute. *Craver v. Waste Management Partners of Bozeman*, 874 P.2d 1 (Mont.1994).

II. THE NATIONAL LABOR RELATIONS ACT

The National Labor Relations Act (NLRA) guarantees employees "the right to self-organization, to form, join, or assist labor organizations," 29 U.S.C. § 157. The NLRA also makes it an unfair labor practice for an employer "to interfere with, restrain, or coerce employees" in the exercise of their § 157 rights, 29 U.S.C. § 158(a)(1). This comprehensive federal statute regulates almost all aspects of labor relations. For additional cases involving

employment termination under collective bargaining agreements, see Chapter Three, Section Five.

The NLRA grants employees the right to organize and engage in collective bargaining free from employer interference. Employees are considered "supervisors" and thus are not covered under the NLRA if they have the authority to use independent judgment to "hire, transfer, suspend, lay off, recall, promote, discharge, assign, reward, or discipline other employees, or responsibly to direct them, or to adjust their grievances, or effectively to recommend such action," and they hold that authority "in the interest of the employer." The National Labor Relations Board (NLRB) issued a complaint against the owner and operator of an Ohio nursing home, alleging that unfair labor practices had been committed in the disciplining of four licensed practical nurses. An administrative law judge found that the nurses were not supervisors and a NLRB panel affirmed that decision. The U.S. Court of Appeals, Sixth Circuit, reversed the administrative decision, and the case came before the U.S. Supreme Court.

The Supreme Court held that the NLRB's test for determining whether nurses were supervisors was inconsistent with the NLRA. Here, the NLRB had erroneously concluded that the nurses were not supervisors because their focus was on the well-being of the nursing home residents, not on the interests of the employer. The Supreme Court noted that because patient care is a nursing home's business, attending to the needs of the residents is in the employer's interests. The Court rejected the argument that granting organizational rights to nurses whose supervisory authority concerns patient care would not threaten the conflicting loyalties that the supervisor exception was designed to avoid. The NLRA had to be enforced according to its own terms. The Court affirmed the court of appeals' decision finding the four nurses to be supervisors outside the protections of the NLRA. *NLRB v. Health Care & Retirement Corp.*, 114 S.Ct. 1778, 128 L.Ed.2d 586 (1994).

The Rules on Containers required certain containers which would otherwise be loaded or unloaded within the local port area of New York to be loaded or unloaded by longshoremen at the pier. When an objection was filed to the rules, the NLRB held that, with two exceptions (shortstopping truckers and traditional warehousers), the rules were valid and enforceable. On cross appeals to the U.S. Court of Appeals, the appellate court held that the rules were lawful in their entirety. The U.S. Supreme Court granted limited review.

The Supreme Court noted that Congress had not intended to prohibit agreements directed toward work preservation. The central inquiry in these claims of work preservation was whether the union's objective in making the agreements was to preserve work or whether the agreements were tactically calculated to satisfy union objectives elsewhere. So long as the union had no forbidden secondary purpose to disrupt the business relations of a neutral employer, such effects were "incidental to primary activity." Here, the clear primary objective of the rules was the preservation of work in the face of a threat to jobs. Even if the Rules were economically inefficient it was not the Court's place to outlaw such collective bargaining. That decision had to be left to Congress. The Court affirmed the court of appeals' decision upholding the rules as lawful. *NLRB v. International Longshoremen's Assn.*, 473 U.S. 61, 105 S.Ct. 3045, 87 L.Ed.2d 47 (1985).

An Alabama man worked for a stevedoring company as a ship superintendent, an immediate superior of the longshoremen working for the company. However, the ship superintendents generally made less money than the longshoremen. As a result, there was an attempt at unionization. A union official allegedly assured the superintendents that the union would get them their jobs back if they were discharged for participating in union-related activities. After being fired, the ship superintendent sued the union, alleging fraud and misrepresentation under state law. A jury entered a verdict in his favor for $75,000. The union then sought to overturn the verdict on the grounds that the NLRA preempted state law, but the court denied the motion. The Alabama Supreme Court affirmed, and the case came before the U.S. Supreme Court.

Before the Court, the union maintained that the NLRB had not clearly determined the superintendent to be a "supervisor." Thus, it charged that he was an "employee" covered by the NLRA. However, the Court noted that the union had not pointed to any evidence to support its assertion that the superintendent was an "employee." Because the NLRA does not apply to "supervisors," and because the union had not demonstrated that the superintendent was not a "supervisor," the Court held that the NLRA did not preempt the state law. The Court affirmed the verdict in favor of the superintendent. *International Longshoremen's Assn. AFL-CIO v. Davis,* 476 U.S. 380, 106 S.Ct. 1904, 90 L.Ed.2d 389 (1986).

A.   Striking, Picketing and Handbilling

A food and commercial workers union attempted to organize employees at a Connecticut retail store. The employer refused to allow the union on store property to distribute handbills. The union then filed a complaint with the NLRB alleging that the employer had violated the NLRA by barring the union organizers from its property. The NLRB ordered the employer to cease and desist barring the union from the parking lot. The employer then sought review in the U.S. Court of Appeals, Fifth Circuit, which affirmed the NLRB's decision. The employer appealed to the U.S. Supreme Court.

The Court noted that § 7 of the NLRA provides that "employees shall have the right to self-organization, to form, join, or assist labor organizations." Further, the NLRA also makes it an unfair labor practice for an employer "to interfere with, restrain, or coerce employees in the exercise of [these] rights." The Court determined that these sections gave *employees* rights, not unions or their organizers (nonemployees). Thus, the Court reasoned, "the right to distribute is not absolute, but must be accommodated to the circumstances." If it is unreasonable for a union to distribute literature to employees entirely off the employer's premises, distribution in parking lots or other common areas may be warranted. The Court concluded that there were no "unique obstacles" hindering the union from reaching the employees, because it had access to the list of names and addresses. Therefore, the Supreme Court reversed the appellate court's decision and determined that the employer did not violate the NLRA by preventing union organizers from distributing handbills in the parking lot. *Lechmere, Inc. v. NLRB,* 502 U.S. 527, 112 S.Ct. 841, 117 L.Ed.2d 79 (1992).

A company hired a contractor to build a department store for it in a Florida mall. A union believed that the contractor was paying substandard wages and fringe benefits. It thus engaged in peaceful handbilling of the businesses in the mall, asking customers not to shop there until the mall's owner publicly promised that all construction at the mall would be done using contractors who paid fair wages. The mall owner, after failing to convince the union to alter the handbills to state that the dispute was not with the owner, filed a complaint with the NLRB, charging the union with engaging in unfair labor practices under § 8(b)(4) of the NLRA. The NLRB dismissed the complaint, concluding that the handbilling was protected by § 8(b)(4)'s proviso exempting nonpicketing publicity which is intended to truthfully advise the public that products are produced by an employer with whom the union is involved in a labor dispute. The U.S. Court of Appeals affirmed, but the U.S. Supreme Court reversed on the ground that the mall owner and its other tenants did not distribute the contractor's products. The Court then remanded for a determination of whether § 8(b)(4) had been violated. *Edward J. DeBartolo Corp. v. NLRB,* 463 U.S. 147, 103 S.Ct. 2926, 77 L.Ed.2d 535 (1983).

On remand, the NLRB ordered the union to stop distributing the handbills because the handbilling was an attempt to inflict economic harm on secondary employers. This constituted economic retaliation and was therefore a form of coercion prohibited by § 8(b)(4)(ii)(B). The U.S. Court of Appeals denied enforcement of the NLRB's order, holding that there was no clear congressional intent to proscribe such handbilling in the NLRA. The U.S. Supreme Court again granted certiorari. The Supreme Court held that § 8(b)(4) did not contain any clear expression of congressional intent to prohibit this kind of handbilling. Further, since there were serious constitutional problems, including First Amendment free speech concerns, with the board's construction, a clear expression that that was Congress' purpose would be required before such an interpretation would be adopted. Accordingly, the peaceful handbilling, which was unaccompanied by picketing, did not have to be considered coercive even though it was outside the protection of § 8(b)(4)'s publicity proviso. The Court affirmed the court of appeals' decision denying enforcement of the NLRB's order. *Edward J. DeBartolo Corp. v. Florida Gulf Coast Building & Construction Trades Council,* 485 U.S. 568, 108 S.Ct. 1392, 99 L.Ed.2d 645 (1988).

After contract negotiations between a title insurance company and its employees' union reached an impasse, the employees went on strike. They also picketed five local title companies who derived over 90 percent of their gross incomes from the sale of the insurer's policies. The U.S. Supreme Court held that the secondary picketing amounted to coercion of neutral parties with the object of forcing them to cease dealing in the primary party's product. Successful secondary picketing would force the local title companies to choose between survival and cutting their ties with the insurer. Section 8(b)(4)(ii)(B) of the NLRA barred such coercive activity. Further, application of this section of the NLRA to the picketing involved here did not violate the First Amendment. The NLRB's order to stop the picketing had to be enforced, held the Court. *NLRB v. Retail Store Employees Union, Local 1001,* 447 U.S. 607, 100 S.Ct. 2372, 65 L.Ed.2d 377 (1980).

A union had a dispute with a railroad over the renewal of a collective bargaining agreement. The union struck the railroad, then extended its picketing to other railroads which interchanged traffic with the struck railroad. These railroads filed suit to enjoin the picketing, and an Illinois federal district court issued an injunction against the picketing. In finding that the case did not "grow out of a labor dispute" as defined by the Norris-LaGuardia Act, and that none of the picketed railroads were "substantially aligned" with the struck railroad, the court determined that the injunction could issue. The U.S. Court of Appeals reversed, and the U.S. Supreme Court granted review.

The Court held that the district court did not have jurisdiction to enjoin the secondary picketing in the railway labor dispute. The Norris-LaGuardia Act was enacted to preclude courts from enjoining secondary as well as primary activity. Railroads were to be treated no differently than other industries in this regard. Because the definition of "labor dispute" is broad, the adoption of the "substantial alignment" test (which would narrow that definition) would defeat Congress' intent by requiring courts to second-guess which activities are truly in the union's interest. Further, there was nothing in the Railway Labor Act to indicate that Congress intended to permit federal courts to enjoin secondary activity as a means of settling strikes and avoiding interruptions to commerce. The Court affirmed the appellate court's decision. *Burlington Northern Railroad Co. v. Brotherhood of Maintenance of Way Employees,* 481 U.S. 429, 107 S.Ct. 1841, 95 L.Ed.2d 381 (1987).

Some local labor unions engaged in a number of unauthorized, "wildcat" strikes at a company's coal mines in violation of the collective bargaining agreements in place between the employer and the international union. The regional subdivision of the international was unsuccessful in attempting to persuade the miners not to strike and to return to work. The employer then sued the international, the regional subdivision, and the local unions under § 301 of the Labor Management Relations Act. The West Virginia federal district court granted injunctive relief and damages against all the defendants, but the U.S. Court of Appeals reversed as to the international and the regional subdivision because they did not instigate, support, ratify, or encourage the strikes.

On further appeal, the U.S. Supreme Court held that neither the international nor the regional subdivision could be held liable for the unauthorized strikes. There was no obligation implied in law on their part to use all reasonable means to prevent and end unauthorized strikes. If the strike had been authorized (and in violation of the collective bargaining agreements), then the international would have been liable under § 301, but such was not the case here. Further, it was clear from the agreements that the parties decided not to impose on the international an obligation to take disciplinary action against unauthorized strikers to get them back to work. Accordingly, the Court affirmed the appellate court's decision in favor of the international and the regional subdivision. *Carbon Fuel Co. v. United Mine Workers of America,* 444 U.S. 212, 100 S.Ct. 410, 62 L.Ed.2d 394 (1979).

Four employees of a meat packing company in Kentucky were known union supporters and were members of an organizing committee which distributed union handbills outside the plant. They also complained about working conditions, including the temperature of their work area. The employees staged a work slowdown which forced some of their coworkers to work harder. After several warnings, and continued observation of the slowdown, the company fired the workers. The former employees filed an administrative complaint against the company for violation of the NLRA which declares it an unfair labor practice to interfere with, restrain or coerce employees engaged in protected union activity. An administrative law judge held that the company violated the NLRA and directed it to cease and desist from retaliating against prounion employees. He also ordered the company to reinstate the employees. An NLRB panel affirmed the administrative decision, and the NLRB applied to the U.S. Court of Appeals, Sixth Circuit, for enforcement of the panel's order. The court disagreed with the administrative law judge's factual findings, stating that overwhelming evidence existed that the employees had caused a work slowdown. It also found no evidence of anti-union bias by the company for firing the employees two days after they had been observed circulating union petitions, and after they had recently complained about the air conditioning in their work area. The court denied the NLRB's petition for enforcement. *NLRB v. Cook Family Foods, Ltd.,* 47 F.3d 809 (6th Cir.1995).

A labor organization sought permission from an Indiana employer to post notices concerning union meetings on a bulletin board that had primarily been used by employees to announce items for sale. When the employer denied permission to use the board, the union filed a complaint with the NLRB, which ordered the employer to allow the union to post notices on the board. It also ordered the employer to cease and desist from threatening prounion employees with unemployment. The latter charge was advanced when a prounion employee was told by a supervisor that "if we got a union in there we'd be in the unemployment line." The employer petitioned the U.S. Court of Appeals, Seventh Circuit, for review and the NLRB sought enforcement of its order.

The court rejected the NLRB's argument that when the employer authorized the use of the bulletin board by employees to announce used auto sales and other items, it also had to allow them to use the board for union announcements. There was no evidence that the employer had ever allowed access to the board to announce meetings for any other organizations. Because the union had not been singled out by the employer for exclusion from the board, the policy did not violate the NLRA. In other cases in which violations had been found, the employer had opened its bulletin board to notices about meetings. The court denied enforcement of the NLRB's order concerning the bulletin board, but affirmed its order to stop threatening union advocates with unemployment. *Guardian Industries Corp. v. NLRB*, 49 F.3d 317 (7th Cir.1995).

Washington's "Little Norris LaGuardia Act," patterned after federal labor law, protects workers who engage in "self organization or in other concerted activities for the purpose of collective bargaining or for mutual aid or protections." Ten unrepresented dairy workers claimed that their employer retaliated against them for attempting to negotiate better wages, medical coverage and working conditions. The workers went on strike, and shortly thereafter, managers advised them that if they did not return to work they would be fired. Managers also videotaped employees on the picket line and eventually fired those who participated in the strike. The former employees filed a lawsuit against the employer in a Washington trial court, claiming that it violated their rights to engage in concerted activities for the purpose of collective bargaining and constituted wrongful discharge in violation of the public policy as set forth by the state labor act. The court granted the employer's motion to dismiss the lawsuit, and this decision was affirmed by the state court of appeals. The former employees appealed to the Supreme Court of Washington.

On appeal, the employer argued that the state law did not create rights for non-unionized workers. The former employees argued that they had been engaged in activity that required the protection of the act. The supreme court agreed with the former employees, finding no language in the statute that limited its application to unionized workers. The state legislature had explicitly intended to protect the rights of individual workers, including those not represented by a labor organization. In making its decision, the court observed that federal courts interpreting the National Labor Relations Act did not require union membership to establish claims. Because the state labor act was not limited to unionized workers, the former employees had also stated a claim for wrongful discharge in violation of public policy. The court reversed and remanded the case for trial. *Bravo v. Dolsen Companies*, 888 P.2d 147 (Wash.1995).

Members of a Pennsylvania grocery workers' union called a strike and began picketing grocery stores. The workers allegedly engaged in mass picketing, violence, harassment and intimidation against customers and employees who failed to respect the picket line. On the second day of the strike, the grocery store applied to a state court for an injunction against mass picketing, violence and harassment. The court granted the requested order, based on the testimony of several witnesses that union officers had organized, participated and abetted mass picketing with the intention of intimidating customers, vendors and employees. The parties settled the labor dispute within six weeks and the strike was ended. However, the union appealed the trial court's decision, claiming that it was entitled to its reasonable costs and attorney's fees under Pennsylvania labor law. The Pennsylvania Superior Court determined that the injunction had been granted erroneously, and remanded the case for an award of attorney's fees and costs. The employer appealed to the Supreme Court of Pennsylvania.

The supreme court held that reasonable cause existed for granting an injunction against mass picketing and violence. The state Labor Anti-Injunction Act generally prohibited courts from issuing injunctions involving labor disputes, but allowed courts to issue injunctions where striking employees "seized" an employer's property. Mass picketing constituted a seizure under the act when it forcibly denied free access to the employer's property. Since the trial court had found a consistent pattern of forcible denial of access to the employer's property, a seizure had occurred. Accordingly, it was irrelevant that union representatives were not directly involved in the violence or harassment, and that the acts committed were not in furtherance of express union policies. The court reinstated the preliminary injunction of the trial court. *Giant Eagle Markets Co. v. United Food and Comm. Workers Union, Local Union No. 23*, 652 A.2d 1286 (Pa.1995).

A small Ohio city had three grocery stores, two of which were unionized. Labor organizers attempted to call attention to the fact that employees at the third supermarket were not represented by passing out prounion literature in front of the store. The store manager asked the union agents to leave, and called police when they refused. A few days later, the store filed a civil trespass action against the union in a state court, which issued a temporary restraining order against trespassing by the organizers. The union filed a dismissal motion based on preemption grounds under the NLRA, which was denied. It then filed an unfair labor practices charge against the store with the NLRB. The NLRB determined that the store had committed unfair labor practices and ordered it to cease and desist from preventing the picketing. The store appealed to the U.S. Court of Appeals, Sixth Circuit. The court of appeals observed that the NLRA protected employees by guaranteeing their rights to self-organize and bargain collectively. In this case, the picketing was directed at store customers, and was not directly aimed at union organization. Accordingly, it was not a core activity that was protected by the NLRA. The store had rightfully asked the union organizers to leave its property and had appropriately requested the assistance of the police and state courts. The court vacated the NLRB's order and denied enforcement. *NLRB v. Great Scot, Inc.*, 39 F.3d 678 (6th Cir.1994).

A general contractor hired eight subcontractors at a Seattle worksite, including a nonunion mechanical subcontractor. A local plumbers and pipefitters union began picketing the site and the nonunion subcontractor recognized a "sweetheart union" as the representative of its employees. The subcontractor then voluntarily withdrew recognition of the sweetheart union when the regional director of the NLRB advised it that the arrangement violated the NLRA. The subcontractor entered a settlement agreement with the NLRB and plumbers and pipefitters local to discontinue recognition of the sweetheart union. However, the union resumed picketing when it observed a solitary worker entering the worksite through a neutral gate. The general contractor filed a complaint with the regional director against the union for picketing the worksite despite the settlement. The U.S.

District Court for the Western District of Washington granted the NLRB's petition for an injunction to prohibit picketing, and the union appealed to the U.S. Court of Appeals, Ninth Circuit. The court of appeals affirmed the district court's order, finding that picketing was not necessary to counterbalance the influence of an entrenched sweetheart union. Recognitional picketing was inappropriate because the nonunion subcontractor had ceased recognizing the sweetheart union. This was squarely within an exception to the general right of employees to picket. *Nelson v. Plumbers and Pipefitters Local No. 32*, 35 F.3d 491 (9th Cir.1994).

B. Strike Replacements

In a Texas case, after the expiration of a collective bargaining agreement, employees called an economic strike. The employer hired permanent replacement employees. When the union attempted to accept the employer's previous offer, the employer informed it that the offer was no longer available and it then withdrew recognition from the union, refusing to further bargain with it. The employer felt that the union was no longer supported by a majority of the employees in the unit. The union then filed an unfair labor practice charge with the NLRB, asserting that the employer had violated the NLRA. Using a case-by-case approach, the NLRB found that the employer's evidence of its replacements' union sentiments was not sufficient to rebut the presumption of the union's majority support. The U.S. Court of Appeals, Fifth Circuit, held that the NLRB had to presume that strike replacements opposed the union. The case then came before the U.S. Supreme Court, which held that the NLRB did not have to presume opposition to the union by the replacements. A replacement who otherwise supports the union may be forced by economic concerns to work for a struck employer. The Court thus reversed the court of appeals' ruling and remanded the case. *NLRB v. Curtin Matheson Scientific, Inc.*, 494 U.S. 775, 110 S.Ct. 1542, 108 L.Ed.2d 801 (1990).

A Massachusetts linen supply company was a member of an association formed to negotiate collective bargaining agreements with a truckdrivers' union as a multiemployer unit. During negotiations for a proposed agreement, an impasse was reached, and the union began a selective strike against the company. The company hired permanent replacements and notified both the union and the association that it was withdrawing from the association. When a collective bargaining agreement was later executed, the company refused to sign it. The U.S. Supreme Court held that the bargaining impasse did not justify the company's withdrawal from the multiemployer bargaining unit. Here, there was no unusual circumstance to justify the unilateral withdrawal by the employer. To permit withdrawal at an impasse would undermine the utility of multiemployer bargaining as a practical matter. The Court required the company to implement the new collective bargaining agreement. *Charles D. Bonanno Linen Service v. NLRB*, 454 U.S. 404, 102 S.Ct. 720, 70 L.Ed.2d 656 (1982).

A corporation produced ammunition from depleted uranium at a Tennessee plant. The manufacturing process produced carcinogenic and toxic materials, and the plant was regulated by the U.S. Nuclear Regulatory Commission and a Tennessee health agency. A labor dispute arose between the corporation and plant employees when state inspections revealed significant noncompliance with state regulations. The corporation instituted full-time respirators for employees in some sections of the plant. Employee unrest continued and bargaining unit employees began a work stoppage as soon as the applicable collective bargaining agreement expired. Later state agency inspections revealed that while exposure levels exceeded industry norms, they were within legal limits. After closing operations for some time, the corporation hired permanent replacement employees. The labor union representing bargaining unit employees filed an unfair labor practice charge with the NLRB, alleging that the employees should not be considered economic strikers because they were engaged in a good faith work stoppage due to abnormally dangerous work conditions. Under federal law, such employees were not deemed to be strikers, and employers could not permanently replace them without violating federal law. An administrative law judge held for the union, but the NLRB reversed the decision. The union appealed to the U.S. Court of Appeals, District of Columbia Circuit.

The court held that the NLRB had failed to decide the case on correct legal grounds. Two members of the board had found that the employees did not reasonably believe that working conditions were abnormally dangerous at the time of the strike. A concurring board member had held that a work stoppage due to abnormally dangerous conditions could not be justified where economic factors were also present. The court stated that the NLRB's decision was entitled to little deference because of its failure to properly apply federal labor law. It reversed and remanded the case to the NLRB for reconsideration. *Oil, Chemical and Atomic Workers Intl. Union, AFL-CIO v. NLRB*, 46 F.3d 82 (D.C.Cir.1995).

An Oregon steel mill refused to reemploy economic strikers despite their qualification to hold vacant positions at the mill. An administrative law judge held that this action violated the NLRA, and this decision was affirmed by an NLRB panel. The steel mill appealed this finding to the U.S. Court of Appeals, Ninth Circuit, and the NLRB cross-appealed for enforcement of the administrative decision. The court observed that the steel mill had failed to meet its burden of showing that it had not rehired the former strikers for economic reasons. Despite evidence that the mill kept such records, it failed to produce them and therefore could not show that it had refused to rehire the employees for lawful reasons. Because the employer also failed to show that the former strikers had found regular and substantially equivalent employment or had refused a prior offer of substantially equivalent employment, the court granted the NLRB's petition for enforcement. *NLRB v. Oregon Steel Mills, Inc.*, 47 F.3d 1536 (9th Cir.1995).

A strike occurred at a Minnesota transportation company and the employer instituted a declaratory judgment action requesting a holding that the Minnesota Striker Replacement Act was unconstitutional because it violated the Supremacy Clause of the U.S. Constitution. The act provided that it was an unfair labor practice for an employer to replace striking employees with permanent hires. The state of Minnesota and the union opposed the lawsuit, claiming that the statute had been enacted to prevent strike violence and was therefore excepted from federal preemption. A Minnesota trial court agreed and also held that preemption was not required because the NLRA merely permitted an employer to hire permanent replacements; it did not state in unmistakably clear language that Congress intended this area to be free of state regulation. The court ruled in favor of the union and the state. The Court of Appeals of Minnesota affirmed.

On further appeal, the Minnesota Supreme Court reversed the lower court decisions. It cited a 1938 U.S. Supreme Court case, *NLRB v. Mackay Radio & Telegraph Co.*, 304 U.S. 333, in which the Supreme Court stated that it was not an unfair labor practice to replace striking employees with others in an effort to carry on the employer's business. The Minnesota court noted that the state statute had trespassed on territory preempted by Congress. It noted that the right to hire permanent replacements was at least arguably protected by the NLRA. Further, the court noted that the Supreme Court has held that self-help is the prerogative of the employer because it must be allowed to employ economic weapons, just like the union and employees. This was an area Congress meant to be unregulable. The court held that the state statute was preempted by the NLRA. *Midwest Motor Express v. IBT, Local 120*, 512 N.W.2d 881 (Minn.1994).

After a company refused to pay the final cost of living adjustment under a collective bargaining agreement, the union led its employees out on strike and filed an unfair labor practice charge with the NLRB. Thereafter, the company reversed its position and made the payment. However, because it was considering discharging certain strikers for misconduct, the picketing continued. Eventually, some of the strikers were rehired by the company and the dispute was ended. The NLRB determined that the strike, which had begun as an unfair labor practices strike, had ended as an economic strike. Accordingly, permanent replacement by new hires was a risk the strikers took after the company had relented on the cost of living issue. The union appealed to the U.S. Court of Appeals, District of Columbia Circuit. On appeal, the court noted that the evidence supported the finding that the strike was prolonged for reasons entirely unrelated to the company's unfair labor practices. Further, the discharge of a striking employee who had thrown rocks at a job applicant's vehicle was justified by the employee's misconduct. The court thus upheld the NLRB's determination that the company had lawfully replaced certain striking employees with permanent hires. The union's petition for review was denied. *General Industrial Employees Union, Local 42 v. NLRB*, 951 F.2d 1308 (D.C.Cir.1991).

A hospital in Connecticut employed approximately 600 nurses. When their collective bargaining agreement ended without a new agreement having been reached, they went on strike. The hospital hired new nurses and some who crossed over the picket line. The hospital gave them their choice of positions and shifts as well. When the strike ended, the new agreement did not guarantee that striking nurses would be reinstated to their prior positions. The union pursued unfair labor practice charges against the hospital with the NLRB, which found that the hospital had violated the NLRA. The hospital appealed to, and the NLRB sought enforcement from, the U.S. Court of Appeals, Second Circuit. On appeal, the court noted that the replacements could be deemed permanent where they filled positions during the strike and continued to fill them afterwards. However, for departments which had been closed during the strike, the replacements could not be considered permanent. This ruling conformed to the NLRB's decisions. The court then noted that the right to hire permanent replacements was a limited one, and the burden was on the hospital to show that its guarantees to the nonstrikers were justified by legitimate and substantial business necessity. The hospital had done so only for some of the positions. The court granted enforcement of the NLRB's order. *Waterbury Hospital v. NLRB*, 950 F.2d 849 (2d Cir.1991).

Production employees for a Chicago bakery went on an economic strike upon failure to reach a new collective bargaining agreement. The bakery hired replacement employees. The union subsequently sent the bakery a notification that the employees wished to return unconditionally and another notification of a request to attempt negotiations again. The bakery questioned the unconditional aspect of the return and reinstated only one employee. The union sought reinstatement for the remaining employees. An administrative law judge (ALJ) entered judgment against the bakery. The NLRB affirmed the ALJ's decision and ordered reinstatement. The bakery appealed. On appeal, the U.S. Court of Appeals, Seventh Circuit, ordered enforcement of the NLRB's petition to reinstate the employees. The court found that the employees' agreement to return to work was unconditional. It also held that the bakery lacked a "legitimate and substantial business justification" to preclude reinstatement. Specifically, it found that the replacement workers were not permanent. The fact that some employees had applied for pension benefits did not constitute abandonment of employment. *NLRB v. Augusta Bakery Corp.*, 957 F.2d 1467 (7th Cir.1992).

C. Employer Violations of the NLRA

A grocery store chain discharged the managers of its meat departments because they had joined a local union. The union then filed unfair labor practice charges with the NLRB. However, the charges were dismissed on the ground that the NLRA did not extend its protection to "supervisors" like the managers. The managers subsequently brought suit in state court under a right-to-work law. Summary judgment was granted to the grocery store chain. The North Carolina Supreme Court upheld that ruling, and appeal was taken to the U.S. Supreme Court. It was conceded before the Court that the second clause of § 14(a) of the NLRA excluded the managers from the protection of the federal statute. The Court went on to hold, however, that the second clause of § 14(a) also applied to state laws like the right-to-work law at issue here. The national policy against compulsion upon employers from either federal or state authorities to treat supervisors as employees would be flouted if the state statute were enforced. Accordingly, the lower court decisions were affirmed, and the managers' lawsuit for damages could stand. *Beasley v. Food Fair of North Carolina, Inc.,* 416 U.S. 653, 94 S.Ct. 2023, 40 L.Ed.2d 443 (1974).

A New Mexico trucking company employed a casual dockworker under a contract that required him to be available prior to a shift in case he was needed. The company fired the employee in a dispute over the contract provision, but he was reinstated after filing a grievance and an unfair labor practice charge. He was fired a second time for allegedly failing to respond to a call under a more stringent verification procedure imposed by the company. The employee was again reinstated pursuant to a successful grievance. The company then instituted a new policy calling for discharge of employees who were late for work twice without good cause. The employee was late for work twice within six days, and on the second occasion called to explain that his car had broken down. The company investigated the incident and determined that he had been lying. He was then fired on the grounds of tardiness under the new policy. The employee filed a second unfair labor practice charge against the company, and repeated his false story about car trouble at a hearing. An administrative law judge determined that the company had illegally discharged the employee on the second occasion. However, he determined that the third discharge had been based upon good cause. The NLRB affirmed the ALJ's finding in the second discharge matter, but reversed the third discharge ruling. Even though the employee had lied about his reason for being late, the company had not actually discharged him for lying. The company had instituted a retroactive policy and had used it as a pretext to discharge him. Accordingly, the discharge was unlawful and the board reinstated the employee with backpay. The U.S. Court of Appeals, Tenth Circuit, affirmed the board's order and the company appealed to the U.S. Supreme Court.

The Supreme Court addressed the narrow issue of whether the board was required to decide the case by imposing a rule that automatically disqualified employees from benefiting from any proceeding in which they lied. Although false testimony in any formal proceeding was intolerable, the Congressional delegation of powers to the NLRB expressly authorized it to take affirmative action to effectuate federal law. Because the statute did not restrict the NLRB's authority to order reinstatement, it was not required to adopt a strict rule barring reinstatement with backpay for an employee who falsely testified. Because the NLRB had acted within its discretion, its decision was affirmed. *ABF Freight System, Inc. v. NLRB,* 114 S.Ct. 835, 127 L.Ed.2d 152 (1994).

A maintenance company obtained a contract for cleaning services at a federal government building in New York. A building official urged the company to retain as many employees of the former contractor as possible, but the newly-selected company refused to hire more than 10 of them after its president observed two employees sleeping on the job. The company filled remaining positions with a few of its present employees, some of whom had poor work records, and others who were not previously employed by either firm. It recognized the union local representing its work force at another building, even though the majority of employees at the government building were already represented by another union. The local representing former government building workers filed an unfair labor practice charge against the maintenance company, and an administrative law judge found that the company had committed an unfair labor practice. The company appealed to the U.S. Court of Appeals, District of Columbia Circuit. The court stated that although a successor employer is not obligated to hire its predecessor's employees, it may not refuse to hire employees of a predecessor solely because of their union affiliation. The court rejected the company's explanation that it would have made the same personnel choices regardless of union status. There was sufficient evidence in the administrative record that the company's stated reasons for its personnel actions had been pretextual. The court affirmed the administrative decision. *Laro Maintenance Corp. v. NLRB*, 56 F.3d 224 (D.C.Cir.1995).

A Michigan hospital experienced severe financial losses and projected a $3 million loss for the upcoming year. It proposed several cost cutting measures and advised the union representing its registered nurses of the likelihood of layoffs. A number of reforms were implemented without consulting the union. It discontinued the longstanding practice of purchasing and laundering surgical scrub suits for employees, requiring them to buy and clean their own uniforms. It also discontinued a night shift staffing program that had effectively enhanced salaries by 19 percent. The union challenged the termination of these practices in an unfair labor practice complaint filed with the NLRB. An administrative law judge held for the union and the NLRB adopted the decision in full. The hospital appealed to the U.S. Court of Appeals, Sixth Circuit.

According to the court of appeals, an employer violates the National Labor Relations Act by unilaterally changing any term or condition of employment that is subject to mandatory bargaining. The practice of providing surgical scrubs was a mandatory subject of bargaining for which the hospital was required to provide notice and an opportunity to bargain. The court affirmed the NLRB's decision concerning that issue. However, the collective bargaining agreement vested the hospital's management with the power to make assignments for the night shift by giving the director of nursing complete authority to determine night shift assignments. The court denied enforcement of the NLRB's order on the night shift issue. *Gratiot Community Hospital v. NLRB*, 51 F.3d 1255 (6th Cir.1995).

A Virginia corporation and the union representing its production and maintenance employees.negotiated six consecutive three-year contracts that included a Christmas bonus provision. Although the method of calculating the bonus was not stated in the agreements, the bonus was paid based upon a formula that multiplied an employee's hourly pay rate by the number of weeks worked by the employee during the year. The Christmas bonus provision was included in a seventh collective bargaining agreement and paid according to the formula during the first year of the contract. However, the employer substantially reduced the Christmas bonus to only $100 per employee, over the union's objection. The union then filed a grievance, which the company refused to arbitrate. The NLRB determined that the employer had violated the NLRA by unilaterally reducing the bonuses. The employer appealed to the U.S. Court of Appeals, Fourth Circuit.

The court observed that the NLRA required an employer to bargain with a duly elected representative regarding wages, hours and other employment terms and conditions. In this case, the Christmas bonus had been computed by an established method that became an implicit term of the collective bargaining agreement. The contract stated that the Christmas bonus "shall remain in full force and effect during the term of this agreement," indicating that the parties had contemplated that the bonus computation should remain unchanged. A clearly established employment term could not be altered except by mutual consent of the parties. Accordingly, the employer's petition was denied and the NLRB's cross appeal for enforcement was granted. *Bonnell/Tredegar Industries, Inc. v. NLRB*, 46 F.3d 339 (4th Cir.1995).

Several food processing employees met with union representatives to discuss organizing a Mississippi plant. The NLRB conducted a representation hearing and planned an election. However, the election was canceled and the union filed an NLRB complaint, alleging that the company had engaged in numerous unfair labor practices, including interrogating employees about union activities, threatening discharge, reducing wages, delaying a wage increase and engaging in other reprisals for union support. An administrative law judge held that the company had violated the NLRA. He also determined that a supervisor who refused to engage in anti-union intimidation was entitled to backpay in his termination matter, despite sexual misconduct by the supervisor. The NLRB affirmed most of the ALJ's conclusions, finding that the company had violated the NLRA. The company appealed to the U.S. Court of Appeals, Fifth Circuit.

The court of appeals determined that there was credible evidence that the discharged supervisor was entitled to backpay because he had been unlawfully fired for refusing to engage in anti-union activities. Backpay was properly limited to the date the employer discovered his sexual misconduct. The court also affirmed the unfair labor practice charges based on evidence of interrogation, threats, reduction in working hours and pretextual disciplinary practices against pro-union workers. However, the court disagreed with the NLRB's decision that the delayed wage increase had been unlawfully motivated. The wage increase was not regularly scheduled and there was evidence that the employer had permissibly delayed it to avoid the risk of another unfair labor practice charge. The court affirmed and reversed parts of the NLRB's decision and remanded the case. *Marshall Durbin Poultry Co. v. NLRB*, 39 F.3d 1312 (5th Cir.1994).

A canning company maintained a New Jersey plant which was one of only two of its 32 nationwide plants with a nonunion workforce. It installed a costly new production line to take advantage of relatively low wages at the plant. A union that represented workers at 12 of the company's other plants campaigned to represent workers at the New Jersey plant. The unionization experience at three other plants had included the termination of employee participation in a retirement thrift plan. The New Jersey plant manager made statements to employees concerning the threat of layoffs and loss of the thrift plan should unionization take place. The manager also wrote a letter reminding employees that the union could not guarantee job security and that the company's customers would seek alternatives if costs rose substantially. The union filed an unfair labor practices charge against the company with the NLRB, claiming unlawful threats of plant closure, layoffs and elimination of the retirement thrift plan. The board issued a bargaining order and the company appealed to the U.S. Court of Appeals, District of Columbia Circuit. The court of appeals determined that the NLRB had improperly analyzed the manager's letter and statements as illegal threats. Federal labor law did not inhibit an employer's freedom of speech so long as the communication did not contain a threat of reprisal or promise of benefits. Contrary to the NLRB's findings, the letter merely expressed an opinion. Nothing in the letter or manager's statements threatened reprisal. The court vacated the NLRB's order. *Crown Cork & Seal Co. v. NLRB*, 36 F.3d 1130 (D.C.Cir.1994).

A manufacturing company in Ohio sold components to manufacturers of foreign automobiles. It was the sole source supplier of products for three such companies. A labor organization began an organization campaign and obtained 59 union authorization cards from approximately 75 affected employees. The organization then filed an election petition rather than demanding collective bargaining. The company president wrote a four page letter to his employees stating that if the company unionized, sole source business would be reduced by 50 percent. He wrote that because domestic auto companies typically required unionized suppliers to build up a 90-day inventory to guard against strikes, and that layoffs were inevitable. Management employees also expressed anti-union sentiments, and the labor organization lost the election by one vote. The company implemented a wage increase within a week of the election, and the labor organization filed an unfair labor practice charge with the NLRB. The board issued an order to bargain and the company appealed to the U.S. Court of Appeals, Sixth Circuit. The court of appeals found insufficient evidence to support the order to bargain—a drastic remedy. The president's letter had constituted an opinion and not a threat. The labor organization had failed to identify any substantial violations of the NLRA. The proposed bargaining unit had increased from approximately 75 employees to almost 250 during the five years following the election and this change in circumstances militated against enforcing the bargaining order. The court accordingly denied enforcement of the order. *DTR Industries, Inc. v. NLRB*, 39 F.3d 106 (6th Cir.1994).

A California power company unilaterally implemented a drug testing program for employees working in the nuclear reactor section of a generating station. It claimed the right to do so under the applicable collective bargaining agreement, which contained a reservation of company rights to implement safety rules and procedures and limited the union's role to submission of suggestions on plant safety conditions. The union instituted an unfair labor practice charge with the regional director of the NLRB. The regional director set aside the charge pending resolution of a grievance under the contract. An arbitrator determined that the power company had properly relied upon the reservation of rights in the contract and had not violated the collective bargaining agreement. The NLRB affirmed the arbitrator's decision, and the union appealed to the U.S. Court of Appeals, District of Columbia Circuit. On appeal, the union argued that the arbitrator's decision was palpably wrong as a matter of national labor law because it was inconsistent with the NLRA. The court of appeals disagreed, finding the arbitrator's reliance upon the contractual safety clause to be appropriate and consistent with national labor policy. The power station was a safety-critical environment and institution of the drug testing policy had been appropriate. Because the arbitrator had not abused his discretion, the court affirmed the decision for the company. *Utility Workers Union of America, Local 246, AFL-CIO v. NLRB*, 39 F.3d 1210 (D.C.Cir.1994).

A Mississippi electrical contractor was adamantly anti-union. Its employee handbook clearly explained that the company position on solving personnel problems was preferably without interference from union outsiders. In 1990, an international union began an active organizing campaign among the employees. A union representative made first contact with a foreman who had been with the electrical contractor for one year. A few weeks later the union sent a letter to the contractor indicating that the union and employees were engaging in organizing activity. The letter also listed nine employees who wished to be identified as members of the organizing committee. The list included the name of the foreman. Three days later, the company fired the foreman and his termination slip stated that he was fired "for solicitation." The union filed unfair labor practice charges against the company. The case was heard by an administrative law judge who found against the company on all issues. The company then appealed to the U.S. Court of Appeals, Fifth Circuit.

The company contended that the foreman was a supervisor and thus not protected from retaliatory discharge under the NLRA. Section 8(a)(3) of the NLRA makes it an unlawful labor practice for an employer to discriminate "in regard to hire or tenure of employment or any term or condition of employment to encourage or discourage membership in any labor organization." However, supervisors are not entitled to protection under the NLRA. The contractor contended that as a job foreman, the employee was a supervisor and not a covered employee. The court noted that the controlling factor was the employee's supervisory authority. After reviewing the record, the court found substantial evidence supporting the NLRB's finding that the employee's status was that of a skilled craftsman guiding less experienced employees, and not that of a statutory supervisor. Accordingly, the court upheld the NLRB's order against the company for committing unfair labor practices. *NLRB v. Adco Electric Inc.*, 6 F.3d 1110 (5th Cir.1993).

A mining corporation operated five locations which employed both union and nonunion workers. It occasionally paid bonuses or "appreciation payments" to all employees. However, payments to union-represented employees were halted near the time of a union decertification vote at one mine in New Mexico.

The unionized employees filed a complaint with the NLRB, claiming that the corporation had committed an unfair labor practice, discouraged union membership and interfered with the exercise of labor rights guaranteed by the NLRA. The NLRB held for the unions and employees, and the corporation appealed to the U.S. Court of Appeals, Tenth Circuit. The court of appeals held that employees had no reasonable expectation of receiving bonuses. Therefore, the additional compensation did not constitute wages or terms and conditions of employment under the NLRA. There was no merit to the employees' argument that the change in bonus policy violated the act. The NLRB had mistakenly inferred a discriminatory intent on behalf of the corporation without clear evidence of an unlawful motive. The granting of benefits to unrepresented employees but not to unionized employees was not prohibited without further proof of motive. Because there was no evidence that the corporation encouraged employees to abandon their unions or otherwise interfere with their rights, the court set aside the NLRB's order. *Phelps Dodge Mining Co., Tyrone Branch v. NLRB*, 22 F.3d 1493 (10th Cir. 1994).

A driver employed by a small Illinois trucking company began to organize employees by obtaining their signatures on union authorization cards. The company's president allegedly threatened to close the company or fire all the drivers rather than tolerate the union. When employees held an organizational meeting, the company ran a newspaper advertisement for new drivers. However, the company's vice president then announced a pay increase and other inducements. The union-organizing driver arranged for delivery of cards for eight of the company's eleven proposed bargaining unit employees. A few days later, three union supporters, including the organizer, were fired. When the union wrote to the company to demand recognition, the company refused to respond and the union filed a complaint with the NLRB, claiming unfair labor practices. The NLRB issued an order requiring the company to bargain with the union, and the company appealed to the U.S. Court of Appeals, Seventh Circuit.

On appeal, the company argued that it had fired the employees for poor performance. The court observed that the administrative law judge in the proceedings below had found the drivers more credible than company witnesses concerning this issue. There was substantial evidence in the record that the company had violated the NLRA by interfering with employee rights to organize, join a labor organization, and bargain collectively. Because the record demonstrated that the employees were fired for union activities, the NLRB's order was appropriate and was properly enforced. *NLRB v. Q-1 Motor Express, Inc.*, 25 F.3d 473 (7th Cir. 1994).

A union initiated an organizational drive at a textile printing company in North Carolina. The drive ended with the union's defeat in a representation election. Following the election, the company allegedly engaged in a variety of unfair labor practices, including the discharge of employees who had vocally supported the union. An administrative law judge determined that the company had violated several provisions of the NLRA. Shortly thereafter, as a result of a business downturn, the company was forced to lay off employees. The company decided to base the layoffs on employee performance rather than on seniority, as had been done in the past. Four print finishing department employees were discharged under this policy and they alleged that the company had violated the NLRA by its actions. The NLRB affirmed an administrative law judge's decision that the company had violated the NLRA, and appeal was taken to the U.S. Court of Appeals, Fourth Circuit.

The court of appeals held that, with respect to three of the four employees, the NLRB had failed to demonstrate the most basic element of an unlawful discharge—namely, that the employer was even aware of the discharged employees' protected activities. With respect to the last employee, the court determined that there was sufficient evidence to show that the company had acted with improper motivation in discharging him. He was the most senior employee in the department, his immediate supervisor believed the discharge to be a big mistake, and he was a vocal union activist whose views were well known to the company's management. However, the court noted that it could not assume that the company had acted in violation of the NLRA with respect to all the discharged employees just because it did so with respect to one of them. The court ordered enforcement of the NLRB's order in part and denied enforcement in part. *Goldtex, Inc. v. NLRB*, 14 F.3d 1008 (4th Cir.1994).

When an Atlantic City casino opened in 1990, it employed eight full-time entertainment technicians and frequently used the services of a group of on-call technicians. These on-call technicians performed substantially the same tasks as the full-time technicians. One year later, the casino increased its full-time entertainment technician staff from eight to 28, and also took on ten regular part-time employees. The International Alliance of Theatrical Stage Employees (union) submitted a representation petition to the NLRB, seeking to represent the entertainment technicians. The NLRB conducted a representation proceeding. At the proceeding, the casino argued that the appropriate collective bargaining unit should exclude all on-call technicians. In support of its claim, the casino argued that, given the recent and dramatic increase in full-time and regular part-time workers, the on-call technicians could not reasonably expect to receive sufficient future employment to place them in a community of interest with the full-time and regular part-time technicians who properly belonged in the unit. The regional director held that the bargaining unit should include both full-time and regular part-time technicians, defining the latter category to include those on-call technicians who had worked an average of four hours a week during the preceding quarter. The NLRB affirmed the director's decision and the casino appealed to the U.S. Court of Appeals, Third Circuit.

The court noted that workers who have no reasonable expectation of working in the same workplace in the future could not share a community of interest. In resolving the issue of whether less than full-time technicians share a community of interest with full-time technicians, the court determined that the part-time employees did the same work as the full-time technicians and were employed with sufficient regularity to have interests similar to those of full-time employees. Therefore, the court upheld the NLRB's decision to include the on-call technicians in the bargaining unit. *NLRB v. Trump Taj Mahal Associates*, 2 F.3d 35 (3d Cir.1993).

An Ohio union represented nonprofessional service and maintenance employees of nonprofit healthcare facilities. In 1989, the facilities' board of trustees adopted a resolution that all facilities would be smoke-free by April 1, 1990. The assistant administrator formed a Smoke-Free Facilities task force, and requested members of the union to participate. The union president designated a union steward to represent the union at the task force meetings. The task force presented the final draft of the no-smoking policy at its March 7 meeting. The assistant administrator then held a courtesy meeting with the union president to explain the policy. After the meeting, the union president made a bargaining demand which was ignored. The union then filed an unfair labor practice charge claiming that the facilities' operator had refused to bargain with respect to the ban on smoking. The NLRB determined that the union had made a timely demand to bargain after it was formally and fully appraised of the intent to implement the no-smoking ban. The employer appealed to the U.S. Court of Appeals, Sixth Circuit. The court determined that the NLRB applied an erroneous legal standard in determining that the date on which the union was given sufficient notice was the courtesy meeting. The court ruled that although the union received formal and full notice at this meeting, it had received actual notice much earlier. The union steward had attended some of the meetings and a final draft of the policy was presented in early March. The court further found that the union did not file a timely demand to bargain and thus waived its right to bargain. The court set aside the NLRB's order to require bargaining. *YHA, Inc. v. NLRB*, 2 F.3d 168 (6th Cir.1993).

After a union organizational campaign which ended in a tied representation election, a manufacturer of coal mining supplies laid off several of the union's principal supporters and subcontracted the construction of electroconnectors. An administrative law judge determined that this reflected antiunion motivation. The NLRB agreed and ordered the firm to reinstate the workers with backpay. Further, the NLRB ordered the manufacturer to undo the subcontract and resume the manufacture of these parts at its premises. The NLRB petitioned the U.S. Court of Appeals, Seventh Circuit, for enforcement of its order. The court noted that the NLRB's usual practice in cases involving discriminatory relocation of operations was to require the employer to restore the operation in question unless the employer could demonstrate that restoration of the status quo was inappropriate. The employer alleged that the NLRB did not review the evidence or make any findings with regard to the financial burden to restore the relocated operation. The appellate court agreed and determined that the NLRB did not adequately explain its decision to restore the operation. The court enforced the NLRB's order in part. *NLRB v. Special Mine Services, Inc.*, 11 F.3d 88 (7th Cir.1993).

A Virginia manufacturing company negotiated an agreement with a supplier which would significantly improve its quality control process and assure it of a reliable source of material. To celebrate the agreement, the company issued a ticket to each employee for a free ice cream cone in the lunchroom. Some employees voiced ridicule toward the free ice cream cones, and two employees worked together on a sarcastic letter which was posted on the premises. A handwritten note at the bottom of one of the copies of the letter referenced a union meeting. The employer decided to fire the two employees who had written the letter. After the discharge, the NLRB found that the employer had dismissed them for engaging in concerted activities, a violation of the NLRA.

On petition for review to the U.S. Court of Appeals, Fourth Circuit, the court found that the actions of the employees in preparing the mocking letter were not protected concerted activities. The letter was not intended to enlist the support and assistance of other workers to correct inadequate working conditions. It was instead a mere lark, prepared to belittle the company's gesture of appreciation. Although the discharges may have been a harsh response by the employer, they were not in violation of the NLRA. Further, since the decision to fire the employees was made before management saw the copy referencing the union meeting, it was not made in the context of union activity. *New River Industries, Inc. v. NLRB*, 945 F.2d 1290 (4th Cir.1991).

An Indiana manufacturer of hospital beds sought to reorganize its quality control system, shifting work from union bargaining unit employees to nonunion positions. The manufacturer and union met regarding the change, but the union rejected the transfer. The manufacturer then made the change, filling the new positions mostly with former inspectors. The union filed an unfair labor practices claim alleging that the nonunion classification violated the collective bargaining agreement. An arbitrator found in favor of the manufacturer, but the NLRB rejected the arbitrator's findings. The NLRB held a hearing where an administrative law judge (ALJ) found against the manufacturer. The NLRB affirmed the ALJ's judgment. The manufacturer sought review while the NLRB sought enforcement. On appeal, the U.S. Court of Appeals, Seventh Circuit, rejected the NLRB's order for enforcement. The court held that the manufacturer's transfer met the requirements of a lawful transfer. Specifically, the transfer was not prohibited by the collective bargaining agreement and the manufacturer attempted to bargain in good faith with the union. The court found that the manufacturer was motivated to improve its quality, not by an antiunion sentiment. Hence, the manufacturer was found not to have "unlawfully altered the scope of the bargaining unit." *Hill-Rom Co. v. NLRB,* 957 F.2d 454 (7th Cir.1992).

An employee for a Missouri company which provided decorating services for conventions and expositions was regularly assigned to act as a supervisor for out of town work projects even though he was a union employee covered by a collective bargaining agreement. The union called a twelve-day economic strike. The employee was then no longer assigned to out-of-town work projects. He initiated an unfair labor practice complaint against the company. The NLRB agreed with the administrative law judge that the failure to assign out of town work was in retaliation for protected strike activities. The company appealed to the U.S. Court of Appeals, Eighth Circuit, and the NLRB petitioned for enforcement of its order granting backpay and requiring reassignment to out of town work. The court of appeals affirmed the NLRB's order, finding that the employee was not an unprotected supervisor under the NLRA. He was instead a protected employee who was given supervisory appointments as part of his work. The company thus could not take action against him because of his protected activity. *United Exposition Service Co. v. NLRB,* 945 F.2d 1057 (8th Cir.1991).

A Massachusetts corporation which operated a textile dyeing and finishing plant laid off all its employees and went out of business. One of its officers then teamed up with a former customer, acquired the plant, and began to operate a similar business. The new company hired many ex-employees of the old corporation. The union which had represented those employees requested the new company to recognize it as the collective bargaining agent for the new company's employees. The company refused. The union then filed an unfair labor practice charge with the NLRB. An ALJ found that the new company was a "successor" to the old corporation and that its refusal to bargain was an unfair labor practice. The U.S. Court of Appeals enforced the order, and the case was appealed to the U.S. Supreme Court. The Court held that there was "substantial continuity" between the two enterprises since the employees' jobs remained essentially unaltered. Further, at the time one full shift of workers had been hired, a majority were ex-employees of the old corporation. Accordingly, even though the union's demand for bargaining had been premature, the new company was under an obligation to bargain once it had a "substantial and representative complement" of its work force in place. The Court affirmed the lower court's ruling. *Fall River Dyeing & Finishing Corp. v. NLRB,* 482 U.S. 27, 107 S.Ct. 2225, 96 L.Ed.2d 22 (1987).

A large unionized newspaper company implemented drug tests and a strict absenteeism policy without negotiating with the union. The union filed an unfair labor practice charge with the NLRB. The NLRB ruled in favor of both the company and the union on different issues, and both petitioned for judicial review. The U.S. Court of Appeals, Seventh Circuit, stated that the management rights clause of the collective bargaining agreement gave the company the exclusive right to establish and enforce reasonable rules and regulations relating to employee conduct. It found that the company's regulation requiring an employee to undergo a medical evaluation and to take an alcohol or drug test where there is an "articulable belief" that he may be under the influence of a drug was a reasonable rule of employee conduct. This even applied to an employee's off-duty conduct, so long as company regulations were "reasonable." The court then found that the progressive discipline regulation for absenteeism and related infractions resulting in the discharge of an employee who committed eleven violations within a one-year period did not violate the collective bargaining agreement. The employer could discipline employees for absenteeism regardless of whether substitute employees were available. Accordingly, the court granted the company's petition for review and denied the union's petition. *Chicago Tribune Co. v. NLRB,* 974 F.2d 933 (7th Cir.1992).

D. Union Certification and Decertification Elections

The NLRB certified a local union in Washington as the collective bargaining representative of a bank's employees. Eight years later, in an election in which only union members were allowed to vote, the local voted to affiliate with an international labor organization. It then petitioned the NLRB to amend its certification to reflect this change. The NLRB initially granted the petition, finding that the bank had committed an unfair labor practice by refusing to bargain with the new entity, but eventually decided that, because nonunion employees had not been allowed to vote in the affiliation election, the election did not meet minimal due process standards. It found the affiliation invalid. On appeal to a U.S. circuit court of appeals, the court remanded the case because it deemed the NLRB's requirement that nonunion employees be allowed to vote on affiliation questions inconsistent with the NLRA. The case then reached the U.S. Supreme Court. The Supreme Court held that the NLRB had exceeded its authority under the NLRA in requiring that nonunion employees be allowed to vote for affiliation before it would order the employer to bargain with the affiliated union. Here, even though there was not a question of representation which would allow for decertification the NLRB had effectively circumvented the decertification procedures, and exceeded its statutory authority. This was exactly the type of outside interference in union decisionmaking that Congress intended to abolish by enactment of the NLRA. Accordingly, the Court affirmed the appellate court's decision to remand the case. *NLRB v. Financial Institution Employees of America Local 1182,* 475 U.S. 192, 106 S.Ct. 1007, 89 L.Ed.2d 151 (1986).

A union was elected as the collective bargaining representative of the employees of two small Illinois leather processing firms which made up a single integrated employer for purposes of the NLRA. The firms then challenged the election on the ground that six of the seven eligible voters were illegal aliens. After the NLRB denied the challenge, the firms sent a letter to the Immigration and Naturalization Service (INS), asking it to check into the status of a number of employees. Subsequently, the NLRB determined that the firms had committed an unfair labor practice by reporting their employees to the INS in retaliation for the employees' union activities. The NLRB ordered reinstatement with backpay. The U.S. Court of Appeals, Seventh Circuit, modified the NLRB's order, keeping the reinstatement offers open for four years, and requiring the offers to be written in Spanish. It also held that even though the employees were not entitled to backpay when they were not legally entitled to be present in the United States, an award of six months' backpay would be appropriate.

On further appeal, the U.S. Supreme Court held that the NLRA did apply to undocumented aliens with respect to unfair labor practices committed against them. Accordingly, the court of appeals had properly determined that the firms had committed an unfair labor practice against the illegal aliens by constructively discharging them (through reporting them to the INS). However, it had not been proper to award a minimum backpay amount without regard to the employees' actual economic losses. Backpay can only reimburse for actual, not speculative, consequences of an unfair labor practice. The court of appeals had also exceeded its authority by keeping the offers open for four years, and by requiring them to be written in Spanish. The Court affirmed in part the court of appeals' decision, holding that a remand to the NLRB was necessary so that appropriate relief could be determined. *Sure-Tan, Inc. v. NLRB,* 467 U.S. 883, 104 S.Ct. 2803, 81 L.Ed.2d 732 (1984).

A food processing company negotiated the purchase of a controlling interest in a North Carolina poultry farming company. While the purchase was still pending, a labor organization campaigned to represent three separate units of unrepresented poultry company employees. Although the union won the election and was certified to represent employees, the farming company refused to enter into a collective bargaining agreement, and no agreement existed when the stock purchase was consummated. The food processing company then offered employees of the newly-acquired business jobs under substantially different terms than before the stock purchase and stated that the union no longer represented the employees. Forty-seven employees refused the jobs and the union filed an unfair labor practice complaint with the NLRB. The NLRB held for the union and the companies appealed to the U.S. Court of Appeals, Fourth Circuit.

The court of appeals stated that the National Labor Relations Act requires employers to bargain with duly elected labor organizations and that certified unions are presumed to enjoy majority support for one year. A change of ownership does not affect certification and a new employer is generally obligated to recognize and bargain with a certified union. Because there were no circumstances that relieved it from the general rule, the food processing company was required to recognize the union and the NLRB was entitled to enforcement of its order for collective bargaining. The court rejected the argument of the companies that many of the affected employees were agricultural laborers not covered under the NLRA. *Holly Farms Corp. v. NLRB,* 48 F.3d 1360 (4th Cir.1995).

A union sought to represent production and maintenance employees at a California ice cream plant and scheduled an election. A few days before the election, the union's national president appeared at the plant and promised to vigorously pursue back wage claims against the employer, allegedly estimated at $35,000 per employee. A union attorney also stated that the union had already filed a lawsuit against the employer for backpay. The lawsuit was eventually dismissed by stipulation of the parties. The union won the election by a substantial margin, and the employer refused to bargain with it even though the NLRB certified it as the employees' bargaining agent. The union filed an unfair labor practice charge against the employer, and the NLRB ordered the company to bargain. The employer appealed to the U.S. Court of Appeals, Sixth Circuit. On appeal, the employer argued that the election should be set aside because the union had made a preelection promise of benefits. The court of appeals agreed, observing that the promise of legal representation for the employees was a financial enticement that promised to confer a tangible and substantial financial benefit on them prior to an election. The union had no right to use preelection benefits to obtain employee support, and the court reversed the NLRB's finding that the employer had committed an unfair labor practice by not bargaining with the union. *Nestle Ice Cream Co. v. NLRB,* 46 F.3d 578 (6th Cir.1995).

A union sought to represent truck drivers working at a Pennsylvania terminal. The parties agreed to conduct an election, and the twelve votes cast were equally divided. The union challenged the vote of the terminal's sole part-time driver, claiming that he had worked too few hours to have a sufficient community of interest in the bargaining unit. The NLRB regional director referred the matter for a hearing that resulted in a recommendation that the part-time driver's ballot be stricken and the union certified. The employer refused to bargain with the union, claiming that the ballot should have been counted, and the union filed an unfair labor practice charge with the NLRB. The union obtained a favorable order, and the employer appealed to the U.S. Court of Appeals, District of Columbia Circuit.

The court of appeals stated that the NLRB's general rule disqualified part-time employees from voting unless they averaged four or more hours of work per week during the quarter preceding the election. However, this rule was not inflexible and the NLRB had previously recognized a responsibility to protect the voting rights of all employees having a reasonable expectancy of further employment. A mechanical application of the four-hour rule was inconsistent with this standard, and the NLRB's reliance on it in this case was arbitrary. The part-time driver had been hired to fill a position that consistently required more than four hours of work per week and had his quarterly work record been projected forward from the time of his hire until the election, he would have been deemed eligible under the four-hour rule. The court reversed the NLRB's decision and denied its cross-petition for enforcement of its order. *B B & L, Inc. v. NLRB,* 52 F.3d 366 (D.C.Cir.1995).

A Massachusetts printing plant closed, resulting in the loss of 365 jobs held by employees who constituted the majority of two small locals. Employees at another printing company whose employees were represented by the locals sought representation by another union because of the loss of union leadership by former employees at the closed plant. The other union made an administrative transfer of the locals pursuant to a vote. However, the printer refused to recognized the new union, stating that the transfer altered previously negotiated terms and conditions of employment. The union filed an unfair labor practice charge with the NLRB for refusing to bargain with it and allegedly changing terms and conditions of employment. The NLRB petitioned the U.S. District Court for the District of Massachusetts for an order that would require the printer to recognize and bargain with the local. The court denied injunctive relief and the NLRB appealed to the U.S. Court of Appeals, First Circuit. The court of appeals identified a number of factors to consider in administrative transfer matters. These included the continuity of union leadership, changes in the rights and duties of local members and other contractual matters. Courts must also consider minimal due process circumstances in the transfer vote. In this case, there was a lack of continuity in union leadership due to significant changes in the structure of the union, and because of contractual and procedural changes. Accordingly, the district court had not abused its discretion in denying the NLRB's petition for recognition. *Pye on Behalf of NLRB v. Sullivan Brothers Printers, Inc.*, 38 F.3d 58 (1st Cir.1994).

A corporation operated a hotel and restaurant complex in Connecticut. A labor organization began campaigning to be the representative of its employees and obtained authorization cards from a majority of the workers. However, it lost a union election. It then filed an unfair labor practices complaint with the NLRB, claiming that the employer had threatened union supporters and encouraged anti-union feelings. The union claimed that the employer had fired one local union supporter and reduced the hours of several others. An administrative law judge determined that the employer had committed unfair labor practices. However, it denied the NLRB general counsel's request for a bargaining order, instead directing a second election. The NLRB determined that a bargaining order was appropriate and the employer petitioned the U.S. Court of Appeals, Second Circuit, for review.

The court determined that the administrative finding of unfair labor practices was supported by substantial evidence. However, a bargaining order was an extraordinary and drastic remedy that was unfavored at law and imposed only when traditional remedies could not eliminate the effects of the employer's unfair labor practices. In this case, three years had passed from the time of the election until the NLRB's final order. There had been a high turnover rate in the hotel workforce and the passage of time militated against the imposition of a bargaining order. The employer was properly required to bargain with the union, but a bargaining order was inappropriate. On remand, the board was to consider whether a new election should take place. *JLM, Inc. v. NLRB*, 31 F.3d 79 (2d Cir.1994).

A labor organization successfully unionized a Mississippi food processing plant after employees narrowly voted in favor of the union. However, the employer claimed that prounion employees had disrupted the election by threatening antiunion or undecided voters on the day of the election. One prounion employee threatened another employee by waving his finger in his face, and another solicited prounion votes by positioning himself near the voting room and actively campaigning for a prounion vote. The company refused to recognize the union, asserting that the election was tainted. It refused to bargain with the union. The NLRB's regional director filed an unfair labor practices complaint and ordered the company to cease and desist the unfair practices. It then petitioned the U.S. Court of Appeals, Fifth Circuit, for enforcement of its order. The court disagreed with the board's findings, determining that the coercive and threatening conduct in the voting area required remanding the case for an evidentiary hearing to determine if there had been an atmosphere of free choice in the election. *NLRB v. McCarty Farms, Inc.*, 24 F.3d 725 (5th Cir.1994).

After a Minnesota hotel opened its doors in 1987, a number of unions solicited new employees to sign union authorization cards. The hotel agreed voluntarily to recognize and bargain with the unions if a card check established that they represented a majority of employees. A card check found that a majority of the employees had signed valid cards and the hotel commenced contract negotiations. The unions proposed that the parties adopt the terms of an area agreement, which was a contract between the unions and four other hotels. Management rejected the proposal, canceled numerous meetings, and notified the unions that because employees had filed a decertification petition, the company had a good faith doubt concerning the unions' majority status. It declined to bargain further at that time. The unions filed charges with the NLRB alleging numerous violations of the NLRA. The NLRB found that the hotel had violated several sections of the act. The hotel then appealed to the U.S. Court of Appeals, Eighth Circuit.

The hotel contended that the record did not contain substantial evidence to support a finding that the hotel had failed to bargain in good faith. The court noted that the hotel had unlawfully refused to bargain with the union concerning changes in employee working conditions, job assignments, and wage rates. Further, there was substantial evidence that management continuously canceled meetings with union representatives which stifled negotiations. Next, the hotel contended that the NLRB erred in finding that its conduct had tainted the employees' decertification petition. The court found that the combination of unfair labor practices away from the bargaining table, together with tactics at the negotiating sessions, foreseeably caused employee dissatisfaction with their union representatives. Consequently, the NLRB's conclusion was supported by substantial evidence and the court affirmed its decision against the hotel. *Radisson Plaza Minneapolis v. NLRB,* 987 F.2d 1376 (8th Cir.1993).

An Indiana corporation adopted a bylaw in 1979 which stated that the corporation would be dissolved in the event of unionization of its employees. In 1988, approximately two months before a vote on unionization, the employer read to its employees that corporate bylaw. The employees then rejected unionization. The NLRB determined that the announcement was a threat in violation of the NLRA. It ordered the employer to expunge the bylaw, to cease further coercive activity, and to post a notice to employees indicating that it had violated the law and would cease such violations. The employer sought review of the NLRB's order before the U.S. Court of Appeals, Seventh Circuit. The court of appeals noted that a delicate balance existed between the company's right to freely express itself, and the employees' right to freedom of association. If the bylaw was a sufficiently definite and binding policy which was to be carried out should the employees decide to unionize, then the employer's announcement of the possible closure would be permissible. However, in this case, the company had presented no evidence that it in fact intended to close should the employees decide to unionize. The announcement seemed to be nothing more than a threat. Accordingly, the court determined that the employer had attempted to coerce its employees and that the NLRB's order was proper. *Wiljef Transportation, Inc. v. NLRB,* 946 F.2d 1308 (7th Cir.1991).

A number of employees of a Connecticut corporation became dissatisfied with their collective bargaining representative, and contacted a rival union. An election resulted in the new union being elected. However, the corporation challenged the vote, forcing another election. The second election resulted in a vote for no union representation, but this election was set aside after a lawsuit was initiated. An ALJ tried the case and determined that the corporation had manipulated its attendance policy to encourage its employees to vote against union representation. The ALJ further found that the corporation had selectively enforced its attendance policy so as to discipline only those employees who had engaged in pro-union activity. The ALJ concluded that this was a violation of federal labor law, but held that the corporation had not discriminated against pro-union employees. The NLRB reviewed the ALJ's decision and found that the corporation's activities had been discriminatory. As a result, it ordered three employees reinstated with backpay. The corporation appealed to the U.S. Court of Appeals, Second Circuit. On appeal, the court noted that the holding by the ALJ that the corporation had violated federal labor law was supported by substantial evidence. The court then noted that the corporation's discharge of the three employees came about because of illegally issued warnings relating to the elections. The court thus upheld the NLRB's decision and ordered the employees reinstated with backpay. *NLRB v. Fermont*, 928 F.2d 609 (2d Cir.1991).

E.   Arbitration Requirements

A California grocery clerk was employed under a collective bargaining agreement which called for binding arbitration to resolve disputes arising from employment termination or suspension. After the employer fired the grocery clerk, it refused to comply with her demand for the immediate payment of the wages owed her. Full payment was made by mail three days later. The clerk filed a claim for a penalty in an amount equal to three days wages under a California statute allowing such claims where an employer wilfully fails to pay wages owed to a discharged employee. The California Division of Labor Standards Enforcement (DLSE) refused to take action to enforce the claim, advising her by letter that it did not resolve disputes arising from collective bargaining agreements that contained arbitration clauses. The clerk filed a lawsuit in the U.S. District Court for the Northern District of California under 42 U.S.C. § 1983, claiming that the DLSE's policy violated her rights under the NLRA. The court granted the clerk's summary judgment motion. The U.S. Court of Appeals, Ninth Circuit, reversed the district court's decision and the U.S. Supreme Court granted review.

On appeal, the DLSE argued that its policy was compelled by federal labor law, which required the application of contractual grievance procedures and preempted nonnegotiable matters of state law. The Court disagreed, finding that the issue of whether the employer had wilfully failed to pay the clerk's wages was independent of the collective bargaining agreement and was a matter of state law. It was unnecessary to look to the collective bargaining agreement except to compute damages. Therefore, there was no basis for federal preemption of the state law claim. The employee was entitled to relief under 42 U.S.C. § 1983 for violation of her rights under the NLRA. The NLRA did not automatically preempt all state law. The Court reversed the court of appeals' judgment. *Livadas v. Bradshaw*, 114 S.Ct. 2068, 129 L.Ed.2d 93 (1994).

On remand, the district court reinstated its original order and ordered the DLSE to take remedial action to bring its policies into compliance with federal law. Temporary procedures ordered by the court included evaluation of each incoming claim by the DLSE to assess jurisdiction. The order included an explicit directive to the DLSE to avoid rejecting claims solely on the basis of the existance of a collective bargaining agreement. *Livadas v. Bradshaw*, 865 F.Supp. 642 (N.D.Cal.1994).

A corporation operated a check-printing plant in California. After the expiration of the collective bargaining agreement (CBA) between the corporation and the union, ten employees were laid off. The union filed grievances, claiming a violation of the CBA. The corporation refused to process the grievances or submit to arbitration. The NLRB determined that the corporation had violated the NLRA and ordered it to process the grievances and to bargain with the union over the layoffs, but it refused to order arbitration. The U.S. Court of Appeals, Ninth Circuit, enforced the NLRB's order except that it found the layoff grievance arbitrable, and the corporation petitioned for a writ of certiorari from the U.S. Supreme Court. The Court held that the layoff dispute was not arbitrable. It refused to impose a statutory duty on the corporation to arbitrate a post-expiration dispute. Arbitration will not be imposed if to do so would go beyond the scope of the parties' consent. Further, since the layoff dispute did not arise under the CBA, the arbitration provisions of the CBA could not be used to force arbitration. *Litton Financial Printing v. NLRB*, 501 U.S. 190, 111 S.Ct. 2215, 115 L.Ed.2d 177 (1991).

From 1941 to 1981, a printers' union for a Cincinnati newspaper bargained for and obtained the right to reproduce pre-set advertising copy without being laid off. Pre-set work consisted of reproducing advertising copy that was not to be published, but was nonetheless reproduced to prevent a lack of work attributable to new technology. The 1981 collective bargaining agreement between the printers' union and publisher limited pre-set reproduction work to printers who were employed full time as of a particular date and prohibited overtime compensation for this work. When the agreement expired in 1984, the parties reached a bargaining impasse and the publisher imposed unilateral terms and conditions of employment. It laid off three printers eligible to do pre-set reproduction work and refused to arbitrate their grievances. It later fired another printer and refused to arbitrate his grievance. The union filed a complaint against the publisher in the U.S. District Court for the Southern District of Ohio, which granted the publisher's summary judgment motion. The union appealed to the U.S. Court of Appeals, Sixth Circuit. The court observed that parties to collective bargaining agreements may include clauses to enforce the agreements even after expiration. A postexpiration grievance could arise when it involved facts and circumstances arising prior to contract expiration. In this case, however, the union was unable to show that the parties intended to vest the printers with the right to do pre-set reproduction work following expiration of the contract. Unlike severance and vacation pay, pre-set reproduction work was not considered a vested or accrued right and the district court had properly granted the publisher summary judgment. *Cincinnati Typographical Union No. 3, Local 14519 v. Gannett Satellite Information Network, Inc.*, 17 F.3d 906 (6th Cir.1994).

A Pennsylvania manufacturer and the union representing its workers agreed to a three year contract containing an arbitration clause. The contract included an ambiguous wage clause which stated that upon expiration of the agreement and until a new agreement was negotiated, wages must be retroactive to the contract expiration date, or until the agreement, upon 60 days written notice, was terminated. When the parties were unable to reach a new agreement after expiration of the contract, the union requested arbitration. The manufacturer claimed that the dispute concerning retroactive wages was not arbitrable and filed a lawsuit in the U.S. District Court for the Eastern District of Pennsylvania for an order to enjoin arbitration. The court awarded relief to the manufacturer and the union appealed to the U.S. Court of Appeals, Third Circuit.

The court stated that under general contract principles, the terms of a lapsed contract may survive unless one of the parties manifestly indicates through words or conduct that it no longer wishes to be bound by contractual terms, and the parties continue to act as though they are performing under the contract. In this case, neither party had clearly notified the other that it was repudiating the arbitration clause. There was no evidence that either party was dissatisfied with the arbitration process. The court vacated the district court injunction and remanded the case with instructions to proceed with arbitration to resolve the retroactive wage grievance. *Luden's Inc. v. Local Union No. 6 of Bakery, Confectionery and Tobacco Workers' Int. Union of America*, 28 F.3d 347 (3d Cir.1994).

A Texas oil company process technician's duties included working with volatile gases and liquids at high temperatures. He was a member of an industrial workers' union subject to a collective bargaining agreement. The collective bargaining agreement authorized the oil company to discipline its employees for just cause, but provided for final and binding arbitration of unsettled employee grievances. The oil company also had a comprehensive alcohol and drug policy which required workers who completed programs for substance abuse to participate in a mandatory five-year after-care program. The after-care program also provided for random tests for drugs and alcohol throughout the five-year period. Less than two months into the after-care program, the employee tested positive for cocaine. He was immediately fired and the union filed a grievance contesting the termination. The arbitrator held that the discharge was unjustified and directed the oil company to reinstate the employee.

When the company informed the union that it would not abide by the award, the union instituted this suit in a federal district court. The court granted summary judgment to the company, and the union appealed to the U.S. Court of Appeals,

Fifth Circuit. The company sought to have the arbitrator's award vacated because it allegedly violated public policy. The court agreed and determined that the employee's position was rightly characterized as safety sensitive. It would be against public policy to force employers to reinstate known drug users into safety sensitive positions. The court of appeals affirmed the decision of the district court in favor of the company. *Gulf Coast Industrial Workers Union v. Exxon Company*, 991 F.2d 244 (5th Cir.1993).

An Illinois truck driver's vision fell short of Department of Transportation (DOT) regulations, and his employer fired him. The driver challenged his dismissal by filing a grievance with the union. Eventually, pursuant to the collective bargaining agreement, he filed for arbitration. He underwent four eye examinations, two of which determined that his vision fell below the DOT requirements and two of which concluded that his vision satisfied the DOT requirements. The arbitrator issued an opinion in which he concluded that the driver was to undergo another examination by a neutral opthamologist who was to submit a binding opinion. The opthamologist determined that the driver's right eye was correctable to 20-20 vision, but that he could not see every letter in the 20-40 line. Based on a review of the DOT regulations, the arbitrator determined that the driver was visually qualified to perform his duties. He ordered the company to reinstate the driver. The company refused and filed this lawsuit challenging the arbitrator's award. The district court granted the union's motion for summary judgment and the company appealed to the U.S. Court of Appeals, Seventh Circuit.

The company claimed that the award forced it to violate federal law. In order for a federal court to vacate an arbitration award for manifest disregard of the law, the party challenging the award must demonstrate that the arbitrator deliberately disregarded what the arbitrator knew to be the law in order to reach a particular result. However, the court noted that it was clear that the arbitrator's award did not reflect a manifest disregard for the law. He reviewed the DOT's regulations regarding vision requirements and determined that the driver met those requirements. Accordingly, the court upheld the arbitrator's decision to reinstate the driver. *National Wrecking Company v. International Brotherhood of Teamsters, Local 731*, 990 F.2d 957 (7th Cir.1993).

A nurses' union was granted an award by an arbitrator that required the employer to reimburse union members who suffered monetary losses as a result of the employer's reduction in sick leave payments made after the enactment of a state statute which reduced the percentage of regular compensation supplementing workers' compensation benefits. The state law decreased the amount payable as a supplement to workers' compensation, but the collective bargaining agreement in place prior to the statute's enactment allowed sick leave payments up to 100 percent of regular compensation when added to workers' compensation. The union made a motion to confirm the award, and the employer moved to vacate it. A trial court denied the union's motion. The union appealed.

The Supreme Court of Rhode Island affirmed the decision of the arbitrator. It held that the statute in question applied to the collective bargaining agreement negotiated after the effective date of the statute, but not to the agreement negotiated before the law's enactment and that the arbitrator did not exceed her authority with respect to the applicable agreement. It noted that the general legal principle is to give statutes and their amendments prospective application, and that courts have given statutes retroactive application only by the legislature's express language or by necessary implication. Here there was no evidence that the statute was to be retroactively applied. Accordingly, the court reversed the decision of the trial court and upheld the arbitrator's award. *National Assn. of Nurses v. State of Rhode Island,* 614 A.2d 782 (R.I.1992).

An Ohio employee was discharged and the employer refused to submit his grievance to arbitration. The union argued that the employee was entitled to arbitration under the old collective bargaining agreement, an implied agreement, or under the new CBA. A federal district court held that the employer's refusal to arbitrate was valid because no enforceable CBA existed at the time of the employee's dismissal. Thus, the judge granted summary judgment in favor of the employer. The U.S. Court of Appeals, Sixth Circuit, adopted the district court's decision. First, the court rejected the union's claim that the dispute arose out of the old CBA. Because the events leading to the discharge and the discharge itself occurred after expiration of the old CBA, the employer had no obligation to arbitrate. Regarding existence of an implied agreement to arbitrate, the district court determined that the union could not have reasonably believed there existed an implied agreement. There lacked an express indication from the employer recognizing the grievance provision, and the employer only implemented selected portions. Moreover, the strike called by the union demonstrated that the union did not believe an implied agreement reflecting the old agreement existed because the old agreement contained a no strike clause. Finally, the new CBA would not be applicable because the employee's discharge occurred prior to the new agreement becoming effective. The employer, therefore, had no contractual duty to reinstate the employee. *International Brotherhood of Teamsters, Chauffeurs, Warehousemen and Helpers of America, Local Union 1199 v. Pepsi-Cola General Bottlers, Inc.,* 958 F.2d 1331 (6th Cir.1992).

F.   Other NLRA Cases

Skilled maintenance and engineering employees of a New York hospital elected a collective bargaining organization as their representative. The hospital refused to bargain with the organization, claiming that the election had been improper because the maintenance and engineering employees did not constitute an appropriate unit for representation. The NLRB charged the hospital with refusing to bargain in violation of the NLRA. Due to administrative delays, the NLRB did not issue a final order for more than 12 years after the complaint was filed and more than 15 years after the election. An administrative law judge determined that the maintenance and engineering department constituted an appropriate bargaining unit and that the hospital must comply with the bargaining order. The NLRB then petitioned the U.S. Court of Appeals, Second Circuit, for an enforcement order.

The court of appeals observed that while the NLRB had procrastinated and was not deserving of the normal deference granted to administrative agencies, there had been a genuine question concerning the appropriate legal standard to apply during the course of administrative proceedings. It was within the board's discretion to apply the community of interests test rather than the disparity of interests test to determine whether the employees constituted an appropriate bargaining unit. The community of interests shared by the employees included common supervision, separation from other employees, a high degree of skill, a distinct wage rate and minimal interchange with other employees. The court denied enforcement of the bargaining order due to the long delay since the election and employee turnover during the administrative review period. An order for a new election was the appropriate remedy. *NLRB v. Long Island Coll. Hosp.*, 20 F.3d 76 (2d Cir.1994).

The Oregon Labor Commissioner promulgated rules which required employers to grant ten-minute rest periods to employees for each four-hour period worked. The rules excluded from their coverage employees covered by a collective bargaining agreement. A class of union employees sued the labor commissioner under 42 U.S.C. § 1983, claiming that excluding them from benefits on the basis of their union membership interfered with their collective bargaining rights under the NLRA. A federal district court held that the NLRA did not preempt the Oregon regulations, and appeal was taken to the U.S. Court of Appeals, Ninth Circuit. The court of appeals noted that a state may establish statewide minimum labor standards, even though the standards would have the effect of dictating some terms of collective bargaining agreements, so long as the standards affect union and nonunion employees equally. The problem here was that the Oregon regulations applied only to nonunion workers. Despite the attempt by the state to avoid interfering in the collective bargaining process by excluding union employees from the rules, union employees' rights under the rules were infringed. The court of appeals determined that the state could have provided rest periods to all Oregon employees without running afoul of the NLRA. The district court's decision was reversed, and the rules were held to be preempted by the NLRA. *McCollum v. Roberts*, 17 F.3d 1219 (9th Cir.1994).

A company with a seafood cannery in Puerto Rico decided to close the plant. It notified the union with which it had entered into a collective bargaining agreement (CBA) of the closing. The union had five days to begin the arbitration-grievance procedure according to the CBA, but it waited a month before objecting to the proposed closing. At that time, rather than seeking arbitration, the union filed suit in a federal district court, seeking a temporary restraining order to prevent the company from closing the plant. The court refused to order injunctive relief, and the plant closed as scheduled. The union appealed to the U.S. Court of Appeals, First Circuit. On appeal, the court noted that the Norris-LaGuardia Act prohibits federal courts from issuing injunctions in cases involving labor disputes. Even though a narrow exception exists in cases where a party seeks injunctive relief "in aid of arbitration," such was not the case here because the union had not sought arbitration. It simply hoped to forbid an act by the company (closing its plant) which it believed was improper. Since the request for injunctive relief fell outside the exception, the district court had properly refused to issue the injunction. The court of appeals affirmed the district court's decision. *Congreso Di Uniones Industriales De Puerto Rico v. V.C.S. National Packing Co.*, 953 F.2d 1 (1st Cir.1991).

III. LABOR ASSOCIATIONS AND COLLECTIVE BARGAINING AGREEMENTS

Labor associations may be liable to their members for unfair labor practices under the NLRA, and may also be liable for violating the Labor Management Relations Act (LMRA), which requires labor associations (unions) to act toward their members in good faith and to fairly represent them. A labor association that engages in conduct which is "arbitrary, discriminatory, or in bad faith" may be liable for breach of the duty of good faith and fair representation of its membership. Unions also have a duty, when collecting fees from nonmembers, to use those fees only for collective bargaining.

A. Agency Fees and Union Security Agreements

Under a collective bargaining agreement, employees of a Maryland company who chose not to become union members were required to pay the union agency fees to be represented by it in collective bargaining. A group of these employees initiated a lawsuit against the union, challenging its use of agency fees for purposes other than collective bargaining. A federal district court found that such expenditures violated the First Amendment rights of nonmembers, and enjoined the collection of fees for purposes other than collective bargaining. The U.S. Court of Appeals agreed that the agency fees could not be used for nonrepresentational purposes, but based its ruling on § 8(a)(3) of the NLRA. The case reached the U.S. Supreme Court. The Court affirmed the court of appeals' decision, finding that § 8(a)(3) did not permit a union to expend funds collected from nonmember employees, over objection, on activities unrelated to collective bargaining. *Communications Workers of America v. Beck*, 487 U.S. 735, 108 S.Ct. 2641, 101 L.Ed.2d 634 (1988).

The president of a local bargaining unit at a California cement company proposed the conversion of 17 jobs into supervisory positions, then supported a proposal to eliminate the bargaining unit. The union sanctioned the president and three other employees by barring them from office and from attending most union meetings. The president then quit paying union dues. The employer advised him that he would be fired under the union security agreement for failure to pay dues.

He filed an unfair labor practice charge against the union with the NLRB, claiming that the threat of employment termination violated the NLRA. An administrative law judge determined that the union had the right to protect itself against the proposed elimination and that the discipline did not violate the NLRA. The NLRB affirmed the decision, and the president appealed to the U.S. Court of Appeals, District of Columbia Circuit. The court of appeals determined that the union had imposed routine discipline ón the president that was permitted by the NLRA. The union had not deprived him of any membership rights and its action could be characterized as enforcement of the union security agreement. This was an available remedy that was not inconsistent with prior decisions of the NLRB prohibiting the enforcement of union security clauses to coerce employees who were rightfully exercising their NLRA rights. The discipline in this case was lawful and the court denied the president's petition. *Gilbert v. NLRB*, 56 F.3d 1438 (D.C.Cir.1995).

The NLRA authorizes union security agreements between employers and unions that require employees to become members of a bargaining unit and maintain membership in a union. However, employees are required only to pay union initiation fees and dues and cannot be compelled to participate further in the activities of a labor union. An employee who worked in a unionized facility complained that the union security agreement applicable in his workplace violated the NLRA by ambiguously requiring bargaining unit employees to become union members "in good standing." The National Labor Relations Board agreed with the employee, stating that the union's failure to disclose the lack of any employee requirement to participate in a union beyond the payment of dues and fees constituted an unfair labor practice. The union appealed to the U.S. Court of Appeals, District of Columbia Circuit, and the NLRB cross-petitioned for enforcement of its order.

The court of appeals observed that the NLRB's decision had reversed a longstanding policy of tolerating such ambiguous notices to employees. There was also a complete lack of evidence that the union had acted in bad faith, which was a requirement of any unfair labor practice charge. Although the NLRB was free to adopt a new policy, it could only have prospective application and could not constitute grounds to support the unfair representation complaint in this case. The court granted the union's petition and denied the NLRB's cross-petition for enforcement. *Int. Union of Electronic, Electrical, Salaried, Machine and Furniture Workers, AFL-CIO v. NLRB*, 41 F.3d 1532 (D.C.Cir.1994).

A clerical worker in Virginia was employed by a company that withheld union dues and initiation fees from his paycheck without his authorization. The applicable CBA required employees to become and remain union members in good standing under a security clause that required full union membership. When the worker requested a breakdown of how his union dues were being spent, he was not told that he could object to the withholding of fees for nonrepresentational activities and could only be compelled to pay the amount spent on representational activities. He was instead threatened with employment termination if he failed to become a union member. He filed an unfair labor practices charge against the employer and union with the NLRB. The employer and union settled the matter with the NLRB, but the employee opposed the settlement and appealed to the U.S. Court of Appeals, Eighth Circuit.

The court of appeals held that the NLRB should not have approved the settlement because the security clause was unlawful and should have been expunged. No security clause could require full union membership as a condition of employment. The only aspect of union membership that could be required as a condition of employment was the payment of union dues. This requirement was further limited to representational activities. Since the security clause in the CBA implied that full union membership was required as a condition of employment, it was void and should have been stricken. An underlying policy of the NLRA is voluntary unionism, and nonunion employees cannot be coerced to contribute to union activities beyond collective bargaining, contract administration and grievance adjustment. *Bloom v. NLRB*, 30 F.3d 1001 (8th Cir.1994).

B.   Union Representation Duties

A labor union fined two of its members, who worked as supervisors, for violating its constitution by working for employers who did not have collective bargaining agreements with the union. The employers then filed unfair labor practice charges with the National Labor Relations Board, alleging that the union had violated § 8(b)(1)(B) of the NLRA by restraining or coercing an employer in the selection of its representatives for the purposes of collective bargaining or the adjustment of grievances. An administrative law judge agreed with the employers, and the board entered an order against the union. However, the U.S. Court of Appeals reversed. The case then came before the U.S. Supreme Court.

The Court held that discipline of a supervisor union member is prohibited under § 8(b)(1)(B) only when that member is engaged in § 8(b)(1)(B) activities, like collective bargaining and grievance adjustment, or some other closely related activity. Since neither supervisor had such responsibilities, the union discipline was not an unfair labor practice. Further, the Court noted that the absence of a collective bargaining relationship between the union and the employers made the possibility of employer coercion too attenuated to form the basis of an unfair labor practice charge. Finally, the Court noted that the employers were not coerced by reason of the supervisors being fined by the union. Accordingly, the Court affirmed the circuit court's decision in favor of the union. *NLRB v. International Brotherhood of Electrical Workers, Local 340,* 481 U.S. 573, 107 S.Ct. 2002, 95 L.Ed.2d 557 (1987).

A national union amended its constitution to provide that resignations or withdrawals from the national or its locals would not be permitted during a strike or lockout, or at a time when either appeared imminent. Ten Illinois union members violated this provision by resigning during a strike and returning to work. After the strike ended and a new collective bargaining agreement was signed, the union fined the ten employees. The employers' representative then filed charges with the National Labor Relations Board against the union, claiming that the imposition of fines was an unfair labor practice. The board agreed that it was unfair—in violation of § 8(b)(1)(A) of the NLRA—and the U.S. Court of Appeals affirmed. On further appeal, the U.S. Supreme Court held that the levying of fines against the employees here violated their § 7 rights because it coerced or restrained them from choosing not to engage in "concerted activities." Further, the Court stated that the board had justifiably concluded that by restricting the right of employees to resign from the union, the provision in question impaired the policy of voluntary unionism implicit in § 8(a)(3) of the NLRA. Finally, the Court noted that Congress' intent to preserve for unions the control over their own "internal affairs" did not suggest an intent to authorize restrictions on the right to resign. The Court affirmed the board's decision against the union. *Pattern Makers' League of North America v. NLRB,* 473 U.S. 95, 105 S.Ct. 3064, 87 L.Ed.2d 68 (1985).

A meat packing company and the union representing workers at a Kansas packing plant negotiated a master agreement restricting the company's rights to close the plant. The company closed the Kansas plant three years later, but to facilitate negotiations at a South Dakota plant, the union entered into two secret side letter agreements with the company that would allow reopening of the Kansas plant without the master agreement restrictions. The union failed to notify its membership of the side letter agreements and the plant reopened as a nonunion facility. Union members filed a lawsuit against the union for breach of the duty of fair representation and against the company for unfair labor practices. The U.S. District Court for the District of Kansas conducted an eight week trial resulting in findings of breach of contract by the company and bad faith by the union. The union members and company reached a settlement and the court awarded the union members $4.7 million against the union. The U.S. Court of Appeals, Tenth Circuit, reversed and remanded the case for inclusion of additional damages, holding that the district court should have awarded damages until the date of the settlement between the workers and the company. The U.S. Supreme Court denied an appeal by the union, and the case was remanded to the district court.

On remand, the district court rejected an argument by the union that the company would have been forced by market factors to lay off the entire group of workers. Instead, it held that the plant would have employed a similar number to that employed by the nonunionized facility, and that less senior employees would have been laid off at various times. It approved a $13.7 million damage award based on this analysis. The union appealed again to the Tenth Circuit, which found no error in the district court's damage calculation. It had been based on reasonable findings of fact that all class members would have been retained for some time at a higher wage than that which was actually paid when the facility was nonunionized. The court granted a $1 million reduction for damages that should have been set off for pension benefit netting. *Aguinaga v. United Food and Commercial Workers Intern. Union,* 58 F.3d 513 (10th Cir.1995).

A California plumbing contractor operated two companies, one represented by a union and the other nonunion. The unionized company was shut down after five years. The unionized employees claimed that the contractor transferred work to the nonunion company and breached the applicable collective bargaining agreement by failing to extend its terms and conditions to the nonunion company. The union filed a lawsuit against the contractor in the U.S. District Court for the Northern District of California, claiming violations of the LMRA and ERISA. The court awarded the union members $2.5 million in fringe benefit contributions, liquidated damages, interest, and attorney's fees, plus $2 million in punitive damages. The contractor appealed to the U.S. Court of Appeals, Ninth Circuit.

The court stated that the general rule applicable in "double breasted operations" was that the collective bargaining agreement of the unionized company did not apply to the nonunion firm. Employees seeking to find federal labor law violations under the alter ego theory were required to show that a single employer owned and managed both entities, that the operations were interrelated and were centrally controlled, and were required to demonstrate fraudulent intent by the employer. The employees in this case had attempted to show that the contractor's nonunionized company was the alter ego of the unionized company. The district court had properly granted summary judgment on the issue of whether the contractor was a single employer, but had erroneously ruled that no factual dispute existed concerning fraudulent intent. Accordingly, the district court decision was vacated and remanded. *UA Local 343 v. Nor-Cal Plumbing, Inc.*, 48 F.3d 1465 (9th Cir.1995).

A lamp manufacturer began laying off its union employees at a Brooklyn plant. After reducing the number of employees from over 150 to less than 50, the manufacturer closed the plant. Several employees claimed that they were laid off prior to junior employees in violation of the applicable collective bargaining agreement. They claimed that their union steward and business agent refused to take action, and filed a lawsuit against the union and employer in the U.S. District Court for the Eastern District of New York, claiming breach of the duty of fair representation against the union and violation of the WARN Act against the employer. The court dismissed the claim concerning the union's failure to inform employees of the upcoming layoffs, but retained a claim for failing to respond to the seniority grievances. The employer and employees reached a settlement concerning the claim against the employer. The court conducted a jury trial which resulted in an award of backpay for the employees on the seniority claims. It then granted a motion to set aside the verdicts as speculative and reduced the damage award to $1 per employee. The court also drastically reduced the attorney's fee award. Both parties appealed to the U.S. Court of Appeals, Second Circuit.

On appeal, the union claimed that it was not required to prosecute the seniority claims because the employees had failed to make a formal written complaint or to identify employees with less seniority than themselves. It also claimed that the employees had failed to exhaust their union remedies. The court of appeals disagreed, finding no duty of employees to produce seniority information, and that resort to the courts was required by the futility of available union remedies. The court of appeals reversed the damage award reduction, finding sufficient evidence in the record to determine the amount of the lost wage claim. The court also remanded the attorney's fees and interest issues to the district court for recalculation. *Cruz v. Local Union No. 3*, 34 F.3d 1148 (2d Cir.1994).

A Texas worker had a history of absenteeism which led to probationary employment negotiations between his union steward and an employer's supervisor. The parties agreed upon an attendance probation agreement (APA) that conditioned his further employment upon meeting minimum attendance requirements. The employee suffered an on-the-job injury that resulted in a three month absence. He filed a workers' compensation claim, but was fired for violating the APA, having exceeded the minimum permitted absences. The employee filed a grievance through the collective bargaining association, resulting in another APA settlement allowing him to return to work. However, the worker rejected the settlement and filed a lawsuit against the employer in the U.S. District Court for the Northern District of Texas. The court granted summary judgment to the employer, and the employee appealed to the U.S. Court of Appeals, Fifth Circuit. The court determined that the employee's claims were preempted by LMRA § 301. This was because they required reference to a collective bargaining agreement. The APA was subsumed by the collective bargaining agreement and was not independent of it. The district court had properly granted the employer's summary judgment motion for the breach of contract and tort claims advanced by the employee. *Thomas v. LTV Corp.*, 39 F.3d 611 (5th Cir.1994).

The president of a New York dairy negotiated the purchase of a smaller dairy. He secretly advised the president of the dairy workers' union about the purchase. The dairy agreed to purchase the smaller dairy's facilities and to indemnify the owner for its unfunded ERISA pension liability. After the sale, a plant was closed and many employees of the purchased dairy lost their jobs. Others lost seniority, and an employee demanded that the union president merge the seniority lists of the two dairies as set forth under the applicable collective bargaining agreement (CBA). When the union president refused to take action, the employee and other union members filed a lawsuit in the U.S. District Court for the Southern District of New York against the purchasing dairy for breach of contract, and against the union for breach of its duty of fair representation. The court held for the employees, but this decision was vacated and remanded by the U.S. Court of Appeals, Second Circuit. On remand, the district court again held for the employees, and the dairy and union appealed again.

The court of appeals held that the union had breached its duty of fair representation because of the union president's secret agreement with the dairy not to enforce the requirement for merging seniority lists. It had not been shown that the agreement was necessary for the sale to be consummated and the unfunded ERISA liability to be paid. Even though the union president had acted in bad faith by concealing the agreement from employees, the court again remanded the case for a determination of whether the dairy had breached the

CBA. On remand, the district court was to consider the dairy's argument that the CBA had been modified by the oral agreement between the dairy and union presidents. The court affirmed the district court's decision concerning the liability of the union for breach of its duty of fair representation. *Lewis v. Tuscan Dairy Farms, Inc.*, 25 F.3d 1138 (2d Cir.1994).

The business manager of a Michigan ironworkers' local chartered a bus and took a group of union members to a Minnesota worksite where many nonunion employees were working. A number of Michigan union members were apprehended and ultimately pled guilty to criminal charges for rioting, violence, physical attacks and property damage occurring at the worksite. The union official then arranged for a $30,000 loan to finance bail and attorney's fees for the rioting workers. The nonunion contractor filed an unfair labor practices charge against the Michigan local for threatening, coercing and restraining its employees by trespassing, assault, battery, property destruction and arson in violation of the NLRA. An administrative law judge determined that the local did not engage in any unfair labor practices and this decision was affirmed by the NLRB. The contractor appealed to the U.S. Court of Appeals, Eighth Circuit.

The court found clear evidence that the local had failed to disavow the antiunion activities and had thereby ratified, condoned and adopted the unlawful conduct of its members. The court had little difficulty finding that local members were aware of the antiunion force that was mobilized and transported over 400 miles. Applying agency principles, the union was liable for the unlawful acts of its members under the doctrine of ratification by its failure to repudiate the unlawful actions. Accordingly, the local committed an unfair labor practice in failing to disavow the unlawful acts. The union's argument that it was protecting the rights of its members to exercise their constitutional rights was unconvincing as there was no evidence of any business being carried on in Minnesota by the Michigan local. The local was guilty of the unfair labor practice charges and the court reversed and remanded the NLRB's decision. *BE & K Construction Co. v. NLRB,* 23 F.3d 1459 (8th Cir.1994).

A North Carolina food distributor claimed that a union election by its employees violated the NLRA. The union offered to waive the employees' initiation fees if they elected the union on its first election attempt. If the election failed, the employees would not be offered a fee waiver in any future attempt to organize. The distributor refused to bargain with the union after it had been duly elected. The union filed an unfair labor practices charge against the distributor with the NLRB. A hearing board determined that the distributor had violated the NLRA by refusing to bargain with the union and ordered it to cease and desist from interfering with, restraining, or coercing its employees. The distributor appealed to the U.S. Court of Appeals, Fourth Circuit. The court determined that the presumption of validity in union elections could only be overcome by specific evidence of interference that inhibited employee free choice. The court distinguished the union's offer to waive initiation fees from the invalid fee waiver scheme at issue in *NLRB v. Savair Mfg. Co.,* 414 U.S. 270, 94 S.Ct. 495, 38

L.Ed.2d 495 (1973). In that case, the U.S. Supreme Court invalidated a union's offer to waive fees for only those employees voting for the union. There was no impermissible behavior by the union in this case because the union could lawfully promise free representation as long as it did so evenhandedly. The across-the-board fee waiver did not violate employee free choice and the court held for the union. *NLRB v. VSA, Inc.*, 24 F.3d 588 (4th Cir.1994).

Numerous employees contracted silicosis after being exposed to silica products manufactured by various manufacturers. The employees sued several defendants including the manufacturers. One manufacturer filed a third party demand naming several other defendants including a labor union. The manufacturer claimed that the union had voluntarily enforced safety programs and that the officers of the union knew of the hazards associated with the inhalation of crystal-free silica and failed to notify its membership. The union filed a summary judgment motion and the trial court granted it. The manufacturer then appealed to the Court of Appeal of Louisiana. The court noted that a union can only exert influence; it cannot control or direct management. Therefore, the union had no direct control or direct responsibility for the processes creating the hazards which might result from inhalation of crystal-free silica. Even assuming that the union had a duty under tort law to inform its membership of the alleged hazards, breach of its duty did not exculpate the manufacturer. Therefore, the duties owed by the union and the manufacturer were independently owed. Accordingly, the court of appeals upheld the district court judgment and dismissed the manufacturer's third party complaint against the union. *Doiron v. Southern Silica of Louisiana*, 613 So.2d 1064 (La.App.1993).

Continental Airlines filed a petition for reorganization under Chapter 11 of the Bankruptcy Code. It then repudiated its collective bargaining agreement with the pilots' union and cut pilots' salaries and benefits by more than half. This resulted in a strike that lasted for more than two years. During the strike, Continental set up a system of bidding for vacancies, and assigned all the positions to working pilots. This effectively ended the strike. The union then entered into an agreement with Continental whereby striking pilots were allowed to participate in the bidding allocation. Thereafter, a group of pilots sued their union, alleging that it had breached its duty of fair representation by negotiating an agreement that arbitrarily discriminated against striking pilots. A Texas federal district court ruled for the union. The U.S. Court of Appeals, Fifth Circuit, reversed, and the case came before the U.S. Supreme Court.

The Court held that the rule announced in *Vaca v. Sipes*, 386 U.S. 171, 87 S.Ct. 903, 17 L.Ed.2d 842 (1967)—that a union breaches its duty of fair representation if its actions are either "arbitrary, discriminatory, or in bad faith"— applies to *all* union activity, including contract negotiation. The court then stated that a union's actions would be arbitrary only if the union's behavior was so far outside a "wide range of reasonableness" as to be irrational. This had to be determined in light of the factual and legal landscape at the time of the union's actions. Here, even if the union made a bad settlement, its actions at the time of the settlement were not irrational. Thus, it did not breach its duty to the pilots. The Court reversed the court of appeals' decision. *Air Line Pilots Assn. International v. O'Neill*, 499 U.S. 65, 111 S.Ct. 1127, 113 L.Ed.2d 51 (1991).

After an underground fire at an Idaho mine, the survivors of four miners filed a state-law wrongful death action against the miners' union, alleging that, based on a collective bargaining agreement, it had negligently conducted safety inspections. The Idaho Supreme Court eventually determined that the survivors had stated a valid claim under state law that was not preempted by § 301 of the LMRA. The U.S. Supreme Court agreed to review the case. The Supreme Court first held that the survivors' claims that the union had been negligent in its safety inspections were not independent of the collective bargaining agreement. Here, the union's representatives were participating in the inspection process according to the provisions of the agreement. Thus, any duty owed the miners arose out of the agreement, and the state-law tort claim was preempted by § 301. Next, the Court held that the § 301 claim could not succeed against the union because only negligence had been alleged by the survivors. More than mere negligence was needed for liability under § 301. Also, there was no more far-reaching duty owed by the union to the miners by virtue of the agreement. That contract was merely between the union and the employer. Accordingly, the Court reversed the state supreme court's decision, finding that the state-law tort action could not be maintained. *United Steelworkers of America v. Rawson*, 495 U.S. 362, 110 S.Ct. 1904, 109 L.Ed.2d 362 (1990).

An electrical apprentice, and member of a union, worked for a Florida power company. She was assigned to a job in an electrical substation, and was injured when she came into contact with some highly energized components. Two years later, she sued her union, alleging that it had a duty to ensure that she was provided safety in her work place, and that she not be required to take undue risks while performing her duties—risks which were beyond her training and experience. She claimed that the tasks she had been performing at the time of her injury were beyond the scope of her training and experience. The union removed the case to a federal court which dismissed the suit as untimely, but the U.S. Court of Appeals reversed. The U.S. Supreme Court granted review. The Supreme Court noted that the Labor Management Relations Act preempted any state-law action she might have had because interpretation of the collective bargaining agreement would be necessary. Under federal law, the court of appeals would be required to determine whether the apprentice's claim was time-barred by the six month limitations period of the NLRA, or whether some other period should be used. The Court vacated the court of appeals' decision and remanded the case. *International Brotherhood of Electrical Workers, AFL-CIO v. Hechler,* 481 U.S. 851, 107 S.Ct. 2161, 95 L.Ed.2d 791 (1987).

A Michigan company discharged two employees for "just cause," and the employees disputed this. They believed there had been no just cause, which was required by the collective bargaining agreement (CBA). They invoked the grievance procedures of the CBA without success, and then filed suit against the company under § 301 of the LMRA. A federal district court granted summary judgment to the company and the U.S. Court of Appeals, Sixth Circuit, affirmed, holding that a strike or other job action is the proper remedy for failure to successfully resolve a grievance where arbitration is not required. The employees sought review from the U.S. Supreme Court.

The Court reversed the appellate court's ruling. It noted that § 301 provides a federal remedy for breach of a CBA, and that there was a strong presumption that the federal courts would provide access for the peaceful resolution of labor disputes. Here, since the parties had not agreed to a different method of resolving disputes (e.g., arbitration), a neutral forum would be provided. Even though the CBA allowed strikes or lockouts upon exhaustion of the grievance process, this did not mean that the employees had to resort to such economic weapons as strikes. The Court remanded the case for further proceedings. *Groves v. Ring Screw Works*, 498 U.S. 168, 111 S.Ct. 498, 112 L.Ed.2d 508 (1990).

A United Mine Workers local district office conducted an election for assistant compensation director. The assistant compensation director was also to serve as a member of the union board of directors. The director who was elected began serving a four-year term during which board members established a layoff procedure to reduce costs. Under the procedure, the director was laid off for a substantial part of his term, and he was laid off at the time his term expired. Although the director had voted in favor of the layoff procedure, he sued the union and some of its officials in a West Virginia trial court. The court conducted a trial resulting in an award of $50,000 to the director. It denied post-trial motions to dismiss the union officials' federal law preemption claim. The officials appealed to the Supreme Court of Appeals of West Virginia.

On appeal, the union officials argued that § 301 of the LMRA established federal court jurisdiction in any lawsuit involving the violation of a contract between labor organizations, and that a union constitution is a contract between labor organizations. The court agreed that union constitutions were contracts under § 301, resulting in federal jurisdiction. The federal LMRA applied when a suit involved any contract between an employer and a labor organization or between labor organizations. Because collective bargaining unit members were the beneficiaries of such contracts, they were entitled to bring a lawsuit under § 301. Section 301(a) controlled whenever a union member sued either the local or international union in a dispute involving a local constitution. Section 301 preempted state law. The court reversed and remanded the trial court's decision. *Satterfield v. Claypole*, 438 S.E.2d 564 (W.Va.1993).

A Montana grocery employee was discharged after 25 years of employment for allegedly violating work rules regarding the proper procedure for recording customer sales. After meeting with two security personnel during an investigation, the employee signed a letter in which she admitted that she failed on occasion to record customer transactions. She was then fired. She filed a grievance with the union, but when the company denied the grievance, the union did not seek arbitration as provided for in the collective bargaining agreement. The employee later sued the company and the two security officers, alleging that she had been coerced into writing the confession. A state trial court granted summary judgment to the defendants, finding that the claims brought by the employee were pre-empted by § 301 of the LMRA.

On appeal to the Supreme Court of Montana, the court noted that § 301 preempts state law claims which are founded on rights created by a collective bargaining agreement or which are "substantially dependent on analysis of a collective bargaining agreement." In this case, the court determined that a decision could be reached without reference to or interpretation of the collective bargaining agreement because the employee was suing for damages resulting from false imprisonment, emotional distress, unlawful restraint, intimidation, employer misconduct, and slander. Accordingly, the trial court's decision had to be reversed, and the case remanded for further proceedings. *Hanley v. Safeway Stores, Inc.,* 838 P.2d 408 (Mont.1992).

C.   The Labor-Management Reporting and Disclosure Act

A member of a local electrical union sued both it and its officers in an Ohio federal district court. He asserted that, because of his opposition to proposed union actions, they had discriminated against him with respect to certain job referrals. This would be a violation of the Labor-Management Reporting and Disclosure Act (LMRDA). He also alleged that their conduct breached § 301 of the LMRA by violating the union's constitution and bylaws. The district court dismissed all the claims, and the U.S. Court of Appeals affirmed in part, reversing the dismissal of the LMRDA claim. The U.S. Supreme Court then agreed to hear the case. The Court first held that the union member was entitled to a jury trial on the LMRDA action. Even though he sought injunctive relief as well as damages, the court compared a LMRDA action to a personal injury action for which a jury trial right existed. Further, the federal courts had jurisdiction to hear suits brought under the LMRA against unions by individual members. Here, even though the union member's suit under the LMRA was a third party suit seeking to enforce a contract between the local and international union, § 301 of the LMRA did not limit itself to suits by the contracting parties. His suit was governed by federal law. The Court reversed the court of appeals' decision and remanded the case. *Wooddell v. International Brotherhood of Electrical Workers, Local 71,* 502 U.S. 93, 112 S.Ct. 494, 116 L.Ed.2d 419 (1991).

An Ohio labor union member was called before the Senate Committee on Labor and Human Resources to testify about employment referral discrimination in the construction trade. During this time, the editor of the local's newsletter published an article informing members that a "notorious anti-union senator" had presided over hearings that were "neither fair nor impartial." The union member interpreted this article as attacking him and responded with a letter to the editor. The editor refused to print the letter because he disagreed with its content. The member then sued the editor and the union in a federal district court alleging that the refusal to publish the letter violated his free speech rights embodied in the LMRDA § 411(a)(2). The trial court entered judgment for the union holding that the union had not opened the newsletter to the opinions of its members. The union member then appealed to the U.S. Court of Appeals, Sixth Circuit.

In order to determine if the editor's refusal to publish the letter violated the LMRDA, the court had to ascertain whether the newsletter was a "protected, open and exclusive form of communication" and whether the editor was prohibited from "unreasonably refusing to allow co-owners access to that forum based solely on the content of their expression." After a thorough review of the record, the court concluded that the newsletter was open to the public. The record showed that on occasion the editor used the publication to express his personal views. In addition, the newsletter regularly ran articles offered by the Ohio governor that were favorable to organized labor. Moreover, the newsletter printed an anonymous letter from "a brother engineer" denouncing the reform efforts of union rebels. Accordingly, the court concluded that the newsletter was an open forum for the discussion of union issues. The member should have been permitted to respond to the article criticizing his actions and speaking out against union management. Thus, the court reversed the decision of the district court and held that the refusal to publish the letter violated the free speech provision of the LMRDA. *Shimman v. Miller*, 995 F.2d 651 (6th Cir.1993).

A local union in the midst of a financial crisis asked its international union for help. A trustee was sent to put the local back on sound economic ground. At a special meeting set up to vote on a dues increase, one of the local's officials voiced opposition to the increase because the trustee would not commit to lowering expenditures. After the vote for a dues increase failed, the trustee removed the elected official because of his outspoken opposition to the increase in union dues. In a California federal court, the official challenged his removal as violative of his free speech rights under the LMRDA. The court ruled for the international, but the U.S. Court of Appeals reversed. On further appeal, the U.S. Supreme Court held that the removal of the elected union official, in retaliation for the statements he made at the dues meeting, violated the LMRDA. It not only interfered with his Title I rights—which protected him if he spoke out against the union leadership—but it also denied the members who voted for him the representative of their choice, chilling their Title I free speech rights as well. The Court affirmed the court of appeals' decision, holding that the official's statements were entitled to protection. His removal was invalid even though it was carried out during a trusteeship that was lawfully imposed. *Sheet Metal Workers' International Assn. v. Lynn,* 488 U.S. 347, 109 S.Ct. 639, 102 L.Ed.2d 700 (1989).

A local union operated a hiring hall through which it referred both members and nonmembers for construction work. A union member brought suit against the union for violating its duty of fair representation by passing him over in making job referrals and in refusing to honor employer requests for his services—all because he supported a rival business manager candidate. He also alleged that the union violated the LMRDA by its actions. An Ohio federal district court dismissed the suit as outside its jurisdiction, and the U.S. Court of Appeals, Sixth Circuit, affirmed. The U.S. Supreme Court granted review. The Court first held that the district court did not lack jurisdiction over the suit. Further, the union member had stated a valid claim for breach of the duty of fair representation. However, the failure of the business manager and business agent to refer him for employment could not be attributed to the union for the purpose of maintaining a claim under § § 101(a)(5) and 609 of the LMRDA. Here, the union was not attempting to discipline the member for his political convictions; it was only individual officers who allegedly did so. Also, the Court noted that the fair representation claim did not require a concomitant claim against an employer for breach of contract; whatever an employer's liability, the union member would still have a legal claim against the union. The Court reversed in part the lower courts and remanded the case. *Breininger v. Sheet Metal Workers International Assn. Local Union No. 6,* 493 U.S. 67, 110 S.Ct. 424, 107 L.Ed.2d 388 (1989).

IV. OSHA AND OTHER SAFETY REGULATIONS

The Occupational Safety and Health Act of 1970, 29 U.S.C. § 651 *et seq.*, (OSH Act), requires employers to provide a place of employment which is "free from recognized hazards that are causing or are likely to cause death or serious physical harm." Employers' duties are of two kinds: first is the general duty to provide a safe work environment, and second is the specific duty to conform to specific health and safety standards which are promulgated by the Secretary of Labor and the Occupational Safety and Health Administration (OSHA).

A Colorado steel corporation equipped 28 of its employees with respirators that failed an "atmospheric test" designed to ascertain whether such respirators were sufficiently tight so as to protect the wearers from carcinogenic emissions. As a result, some employees were exposed to coke-oven emissions exceeding the regulatory limit. A compliance officer, under the direction of the U.S. Secretary of Labor, issued a citation to the steel company for violating an OSH Act regulation. The company contested the citation, and the Occupational Safety and Health Review Commission vacated the citation because the officer had cited the wrong regulation. The secretary appealed to the U.S. Court of Appeals, Tenth Circuit, which affirmed the commission's order. The secretary then sought review from the U.S. Supreme Court.

The question before the Court was to whom should a reviewing court defer when the secretary and the commission have reasonable but conflicting interpretations of an ambiguous Department of Labor regulation. The Court decided that it would defer to the labor secretary, who is more likely to develop the expertise relevant to assessing the effect of a particular regulatory interpretation. The Court thus reversed the court of appeals' decision and remanded the case for a determination of whether the secretary's interpretation was reasonable. *Martin v. OSHRC,* 499 U.S. 144, 111 S.Ct. 1171, 113 L.Ed.2d 117 (1991).

The federal Mine Safety Health Amendments Act of 1977, 30 U.S.C. § 801 *et seq.*, was enacted to protect the health and safety of coal miners. Under the act, the Secretary of Labor must conduct unannounced health and safety inspections of mines. Mine operators are authorized to accompany the secretary's agent during inspections. Miners may designate their own representatives under the act. A Wyoming surface coal mine that was subject to the act employed about 500 nonunion miners. The miners selected two nonemployees as their representatives for the walk around inspection. The representatives worked for the United Mine Workers of America (UMWA). The mining company refused to post information concerning the representatives as required by federal regulations under the mine act. The company complained to the Mine Safety Health Administration (MSHA) that posting notice compromised its rights to exclude union organizers from its property under the NLRA and violated principles of collective bargaining. The U.S. District Court for the District of Wyoming granted the company's request for a preliminary injunction preventing the MSHA from enforcing the regulation. The U.S. Court of Appeals, Tenth Circuit, reversed the district court decision, finding that the district court had no jurisdiction over the dispute. The mining company appealed to the U.S. Supreme Court.

The Supreme Court determined that the mine act imposed a detailed structure for reviewing violations and specified a 30-day period during which citations could be challenged. Appeals could be brought before an administrative law judge with the possibility of review by the federal Mine Safety and Health Review Commission, which had the actual authority to impose the civil penalties proposed by the secretary. Only then could mine operators resort to the federal court system by bringing an appeal to the court of appeals with the possibility of Supreme Court review. Accordingly, the court of appeals had correctly ruled that the district court was without jurisdiction to review the matter. The mining company's argument that the presence of UMWA designees at the mine presented a risk of irreparable harm was speculative. *Thunder Basin Coal Co. v. Reich*, 114 S.Ct. 771, 127 L.Ed.2d 29 (1994).

Two employees of an Ohio corporation refused to perform their usual maintenance duties on a suspended wire-mesh screen which hung about 20 feet above the plant floor. They believed the screen was unsafe (and, in fact, one fatality had already resulted from an employee's fall through an old part of the screen). The corporation suspended the employees, and placed written reprimands in their files. The U.S. Secretary of Labor then brought suit against the corporation for discriminating against its employees in violation of the OSH Act. A federal district court held for the corporation, but the U.S. Court of Appeals, Sixth Circuit, reversed. The case reached the U.S. Supreme Court.

The Court held that the regulation which allowed an employee to choose not to perform an assigned task because of a reasonable apprehension of death or serious injury (coupled with a reasonable belief that no less drastic alternative was available) was valid. Here, the employees had exercised their rights under the OSH Act, and the corporation had taken adverse actions against them. The regulation helped effectuate the general duty clause of the act which requires employers to provide a place of employment free from recognized hazards which are likely to cause serious injury or death. The Court affirmed the court of appeals' decision, requiring the corporation to pay the employees for the period of time they were suspended, and to remove the reprimands from their files. *Whirlpool Corp. v. Marshall,* 445 U.S. 1, 100 S.Ct. 883, 63 L.Ed.2d 154 (1980).

The OSH Act gives the U.S. Secretary of Labor broad authority to establish standards to ensure safe and healthy working conditions. With respect to carcinogens, the position was taken that no safe exposure level could be determined, and that the OSH Act required the exposure limit to be set at the lowest technologically feasible level that would not impair the viability of the industries regulated. The secretary then lowered the benzene exposure limit to one part per million, causing Texas benzene producers to challenge the standard. The U.S. Court of Appeals, Fifth Circuit, held the standard to be invalid, and the U.S. Supreme Court granted certiorari. The Court determined that the court of appeals had correctly refused to enforce the exposure limit because it was not supported by appropriate findings. Here, the secretary had not made a finding that the workplace was "unsafe" before creating the standard. The Court noted that "safe" is not the equivalent of "risk-free." There must be a significant risk of harm before a workplace can be termed "unsafe." Even though certain assumptions indicated that the number of leukemia cases might be reduced by lowering the exposure level, there had never been a finding that leukemia was caused by exposure to low levels of benzene. The Court affirmed the court of appeals' decision, holding that the secretary had exceeded his power in setting the new standard. *Industrial Union Dept. v. American Petroleum Institute,* 448 U.S. 607, 100 S.Ct. 2844, 65 L.Ed.2d 1010 (1980).

An Illinois boat manufacturer applied a highly combustible compound to its boat hulls. Regulations published by the U.S. Department of Labor under the OSH Act required all manufacturers who sprayed the compound to use a booth equipped with a sprinkler system because of its extreme volatility. The department of labor cited the manufacturer after an inspection determined that it was not equipped with a booth and sprinkler system. The company ignored further citations and warnings for several years until the Occupational Safety and Health Administration obtained an order from the U.S. Court of Appeals, Seventh Circuit, enforcing a $135,000 penalty. The department of labor then determined that the company continued to violate its regulations and sought a contempt citation from the U.S. District Court for the Central District of Illinois. During these proceedings, it was learned that the company's sole shareholder had drained the company of its assets and transferred them to a new corporation.

The secretary then sought to include the shareholder and his new corporation in the original complaint. A court-appointed special master recommended imposing a $1,000 per day penalty on the manufacturer, as permitted by the statute. However, the special master refused to allow the labor secretary to amend the pleadings to include the shareholder and new corporation. On appeal, the court of appeals found sufficient evidence that the shareholder was the alter ego of both companies and had refused to observe corporate formalities. Therefore, it was appropriate to allow the secretary to pursue collection against him individually and against his new corporate form. It also doubled the penalty for contempt to $1,452,000 plus interest, in addition to the original $135,000 fine. *Reich v. Sea Sprite Boat Co., Inc.*, 50 F.3d 413 (7th Cir.1995).

The Maryland Commission of Labor and Industry issued a citation to an employer under the state Occupational Safety and Health Act after the death of an employee. The employee was killed when he was drawn into a lathe he was attempting to polish. A state inspector issued a citation charging that no machine guard was provided to protect operators from the lathe's moving parts, even though the employee was wearing gloves in violation of the company's safety code. In an administrative review hearing before the state commissioner of labor, the employer argued that machine guards required by federal regulations could not have protected the worker from the fatal injury. The commissioner allocated the burden of proving this point to the employer and upheld the citation. A state trial court reversed the commissioner's decision, but the state Court of Special Appeals reversed the trial court decision. The employer appealed to the Court of Appeals of Maryland, which determined that federal regulations could be considered in interpreting the state OSH act. The commissioner had correctly interpreted federal regulations as imposing the burden of proof upon the employer to show the impossibility of protecting machine operators from hazards caused by rotating parts. The court affirmed the judgment for the commissioner. *Bethlehem Steel Corp. v. Comm. of Labor and Industry*, 339 Md. 323, 662 A.2d 256 (1995).

An employee of a North Carolina contractor was killed when a trench caved in during an inspection. The walls of the trench were vertical, rather than sloped as required by federal regulations. Another employee had been covered to his knees when a part of the trench caved in one month prior to the fatality. The state labor commissioner cited the company for violating OSH standards and imposed an $8,000 fine for violating state safety and training requirements. It added an additional penalty for a wilful or serious violation of federal regulations. The contractor contested the safety citation and the finding of wilfulness, but the state safety and health review board sustained the penalties. A state trial court affirmed the board's decision and the contractor appealed to the Court of Appeals of North Carolina. The court of appeals determined that the commissioner's findings supported the conclusion that the company had committed a safety violation. However, the findings did not support a conclusion that the violation was serious or wilful. A serious violation could be sustained by proof that the employer had knowledge of a violating condition, which was absent in this case. The court disagreed with the board's finding that the employee's death established a case of substantial probability that the employer should have known that a violation existed. The court reversed and remanded the case to the trial court for an order designating the safety violation as nonserious and reversing the finding of wilfulness. *Associated Mechanical Contractors, Inc. v. Payne*, 453 S.E.2d 545 (N.C.App.1995).

OSHA inspected a California cabinet company workshop and issued several citations for serious violations of workplace safety standards under the OSH Act. Two days before an abatement date set by the administration, the company's employees formed a partnership and entered into a contract to manufacture cabinets exclusively for the company in exchange for 75 percent of net profits from sales. The administration inspected the shop again and issued a notification of failure to abate the violations. It issued more citations, which the company contested, claiming that it was no longer an employer under the OSH Act. The Occupational Safety and Health Review Commission (OSHRC) affirmed the citations and the penalty, determining that the workers were "employees" under the act. The company appealed a penalty of over $43,000 to the U.S. Court of Appeals, Ninth Circuit.

The court of appeals employed an economic reality test to determine whether the workers were considered employees under the OSH Act. In this case, the company conducted negotiations with suppliers and customers, provided designs, specifications, tools and equipment, scheduled work, controlled pricing, chose materials and marketing, provided accounting and administrative services, and made personnel decisions. The workers provided only their labor and were not allowed to work for other cabinet makers. Accordingly, the workers were "employees" under the OSH Act definition. The company failed to show that compliance with the statute was impossible or alternatively that the violations were legally insignificant. The court rejected the company's assertions that it could better make safety determinations than could the administration, or that the hazards of OSH Act compliance were greater than noncompliance. The court affirmed the decision of the OSHRC. *Loomis Cabinet Co. v. OSHRC,* 20 F.3d 938 (9th Cir.1994).

A building subcontractor's employee was injured when he fell from the second floor of a building that was under construction. He filed a lawsuit against another subcontractor at the worksite, claiming that it was liable for his injuries because it had control of the unfinished staircase from which he had fallen. He also alleged that state and federal OSHA standards imposed a duty of care upon the subcontractor and added claims based on alternate theories. A Delaware trial court granted the subcontractor's oral motion for summary judgment, but then ordered the parties to file additional documents for reconsideration of the matter.

Upon reconsideration, the court determined that state OSH standards were inapplicable because they were preempted by the federal OSH Act inasmuch as they concerned identical areas of workplace safety regulation. Federal OSHA standards did not create a private cause of action for injured workers by establishing a duty of care on the part of subcontractors. Even though the employee was deprived of this cause of action, OSHA workplace regulations served as a guide for a standard of conduct that bound the subcontractor. Because a fact issue remained concerning breach of this standard of conduct by the subcontractor, summary judgment was inappropriate. There was also a fact question concerning the subcontractor's liability based on simple negligence principles. The court granted the subcontractor summary judgment concerning the statutory claims of OSHA violations and denied summary judgment on the question of negligence. *Figgs v. Bellevue Holding Co.*, 652 A.2d 1084 (Del.Super.1994).

OSHA received a two-sentence-long written complaint from an employee regarding working conditions in the employer's plant. OSHA attempted to obtain consent to inspect the plant, but consent was refused because the employer would not allow the inspectors to use video cameras. OSHA then obtained a search warrant based on the complaint, but its compliance officers were again denied permission to enter the plant because the warrant was based on an employee complaint that failed to satisfy the statutory requirement of "reasonable particularity." OSHA withdrew its application for the warrant, interviewed the complaining employee, and obtained additional information tending to support the complaint that unsafe conditions were present in the plant. OSHA then obtained another warrant which would allow it to videotape plant employees at their work stations. The warrant was granted but the employer again denied access to the plant. A federal district court then held the employer in contempt of court and imposed fines on it. Eventually, the employer permitted the OSHA inspectors to begin their investigation with video cameras. It then challenged the contempt holding in the U.S. Court of Appeals, Seventh Circuit.

The court of appeals first noted that allowing videotaping of the workplace would not impose an unreasonable intrusion on the employer. Thus, even though the regulations did not expressly authorize videotaping, such activity was authorized under the regulation which permitted photographing and other reasonable investigative techniques. Next, the court determined that the inspection warrant was supported by probable cause. Here, even though the employee complaint did not allege a violation of some specific standard, it was permissible for courts to authorize OSHA searches under the general duty clause when OSHA had not yet promulgated a specific standard addressing the complained of harm. Finally, the court held that the fines for civil contempt were permissible because the warrant was valid and because it was within the lower court's authority to impose a monetary penalty to secure compliance with its ruling. The court affirmed the lower court's ruling. *Matter of Kelly-Springfield Tire Co.*, 13 F.3d 1160 (7th Cir.1994).

The U.S. Secretary of Labor issued a citation to a manufacturing company in Georgia for violation of the permissible exposure limits of cotton dust. The standard was contained in an OSHA regulation. The secretary termed the violation a "serious violation." The Occupational Safety and Health Review Commission vacated the citation and the secretary appealed this decision to the U.S. Court of Appeals, Eleventh Circuit. On appeal, the court noted that the commission had properly determined that the secretary had failed to meet her burden of proving that the company could have known of the impermissible exposure by exercising reasonable diligence. Under § 666(k) of the OSH Act, there can be no "serious violation" unless the company could have reasonably discovered the impermissible exposure. Since the secretary failed to meet her burden, the court of appeals affirmed the commission's decision. *Martin v. OSHRC*, 947 F.2d 1483 (11th Cir.1991).

A Louisiana construction company was hired to put metal roofing and siding over the skeletal structure of five aircraft hangars. One of the iron workers was on his knees shaking out insulation when a gust of wind caught the insulation he was holding and pulled him forward. He lost his balance and fell 60 feet to his death through an open structure of steel to the concrete below. The next day an OSHA compliance officer inspected the hangar and assessed a $1,000 citation for failing to install a safety net under the roof. After the citation was given, the company installed the safety net but filed a notice of contest with the Department of Labor and a hearing was conducted before an administrative law judge. At the hearing, the construction company demonstrated that the customary practice was that iron workers did not use safety nets while working on flat rooftops. The ALJ disagreed and affirmed the citation. The construction company appealed to the U.S. Court of Appeals, Fifth Circuit.

The construction company contended that the violation was for a general regulation and that because the custom in the industry was not to use safety nets, the secretary of labor was required to show that the company had actual knowledge that it was required to furnish a safety net. The court determined that the sufficiency of notice required under the due process clause is reasonableness. If, for example, an OSHA regulation instructs an employer to provide safety equipment for its workers, an employer cannot be cited if a reasonable person in the employer's position would not have recognized that a hazard existed. The court determined that OSHA's consistent holdings requiring an employer to install safety nets, even if the roof on which the employee was working was flat, sufficiently notified the employer of its duty. Thus, the court held that the company's right to due process was not violated. *Corbesco, Inc. v. Dole*, 926 F.2d 422 (5th Cir.1991).

A laboratory technician at a nuclear fuels production facility complained to management and to the Nuclear Regulatory Commission about perceived violations of nuclear safety standards. When the company did not adequately address her concerns, she deliberately failed to clean some contamination left by a previous work shift. She outlined the contaminated areas with red tape, then pointed them out to her supervisor a few days later (when they still had not been cleaned). Her employer then discharged her for her knowing failure to clean up radioactive contamination. After unsuccessfully pursuing an administrative remedy, the technician sued her employer in a North Carolina federal district court for intentional infliction of emotional distress. The court dismissed her claim as conflicting with § 210 of the Energy Reorganization Act. The U.S. Court of Appeals, Fourth Circuit, affirmed, and the case reached the U.S. Supreme Court. The Supreme Court held that the technician's claim was not preempted by § 210. This section was primarily intended to protect employees even though it did bear some relation to the field of nuclear safety. Accordingly, not all state law claims arising from the section were included in the field (nuclear safety) which

Congress intended to preempt. The Court reversed the court of appeals' decision and remanded the case for a trial on the merits. *English v. General Electric Co.*, 496 U.S. 72, 110 S.Ct. 2270, 110 L.Ed.2d 65 (1990).

State administrative rules published by the Oregon Occupational Safety and Health Division required employers to maintain written hazard communication program records. The records must describe hazardous chemicals used in the workplace, the method the employer will use to advise employees of hazards, and employee training for hazardous chemicals. Violation of the rules results in civil penalties and citations. A retail plumbing and electrical supply store used a lubricant that irritated skin and produced gases that could result in dizziness, headache, respiratory irritation and unconsciousness. When a state safety compliance officer inspected the store, he found no written hazard communication program record. He issued a citation and a $75 penalty. The store requested a hearing at which the hearing officer determined that although the store demonstrated high safety standards and was generally conscientious, it had violated the administrative rule by failing to have a single, written hazard communication document. The store appealed to the Court of Appeals of Oregon. The court determined that the hearing officer had correctly interpreted the safety regulations as requiring a single integrated document explaining how the employer complied with the hazardous materials communication program and communicated necessary information to employees. Because the employer had published no single document as required by administrative rules, the court affirmed the finding of a violation. However, the court reversed the penalty because the violation was minimal. *G & G Electric and Plumbing Dist., Inc. v. Oregon Occupational Safety & Health Div.*, 126 Or.App. 437, 869 P.2d 378 (1994).

A steel manufacturer engaged its own employees in modifying a mechanical shop to house certain new equipment. The Michigan Bureau of Safety and Regulation inspected the work site and issued citations for violations of the construction safety standards embodied in the Michigan Occupational Safety and Health Act. The company sought to dismiss the citations because it was a manufacturer and not in the construction business. After two administrative hearings, a state trial court dismissed the citations because the company was not primarily engaged in construction operations. Appeal was taken to the Court of Appeals of Michigan. The appellate court agreed that the company was not "primarily engaged" in construction. However, it then stated that the Michigan statute clearly applied construction safety standards to all construction activities without regard to the employer's classification. It thus reversed the trial court's decision, but remanded the case to the lower court for consideration of other issues unresolved at the trial court level. *Great Lakes Steel Div. v. Bureau of Safety*, 477 N.W.2d 124 (Mich.App.1991).

A safety officer with the North Carolina Department of Labor inspected a metal fabrication plant and observed three unguarded press brakes. He recommended that the company be issued citations for occupational safety and health violations. The citations were issued, and the company filed a notice of protest. A hearing was conducted in which the company asserted that it was impossible with existing technology to guard the points of operation of the press brakes because of the numerous sizes of metal pieces used and the number of bends required. The company asserted that its business was basically custom in nature and that no available alternative, protective measures existed. The hearing officer found for the company. A review board and a trial court both reversed this decision, and the company appealed to the Court of Appeals of North Carolina.

On appeal, the court noted that to prove impossibility the company had to show that compliance with the standard was not possible or would preclude work performance, and that alternative means of protection were not available. Here, there had been conflicting testimony as to whether alternatives existed. Further, the company admitted that it had not looked into alternative measures of prevention even though it had been told that no existing safety guards could be used. The court determined that there had been substantial evidence that it was feasible to guard the press brakes. It thus affirmed the lower court's decision and upheld the citations against the company. *Brooks v. Austin Berryhill Fabricators, Inc.*, 401 S.E.2d 795 (N.C.App.1991).

V. OTHER LABOR REGULATIONS

There are a great many federal and state statutes and regulations which affect labor relations and employment. The FLSA, the NLRA and the OSH Act are among the most litigated. The cases below involve some of the other labor statutes and regulations with which employers must contend.

A. The Railway Labor Act

The Railway Labor Act (RLA) governs labor relations in the railroad and airline industries by imposing a comprehensive scheme for dispute resolution. The federal goal of keeping labor disputes in these areas out of lengthy court proceedings is reflected in the relegation of "minor disputes" to compulsory arbitration. "Minor disputes" are defined as those arising out of the interpretation of collective bargaining agreements concerning rates of pay, rules, or working conditions.

A Hawaii aircraft mechanic had a Federal Aviation Administration (FAA) license that authorized him to service and approve aircraft for flight. The FAA could revoke or suspend the license if he failed to perform required repairs. The mechanic recommended replacement of a part during an inspection of an aircraft. His supervisor refused to replace the part, and at the end of the shift, the mechanic refused to sign a maintenance record approving the plane for flight. The supervisor suspended the mechanic pending a termination hearing and the mechanic reported the incident to the FAA. The mechanic filed a grievance under the collective bargaining agreement between his employer and his labor union. The agreement prohibited discharge without just cause and prohibited discipline for refusing to perform work in violation of safety laws. The hearing officer recommended termination for insubordination and the employee filed a lawsuit in a Hawaii circuit court for violation of the Hawaii Whistleblower Protection Act. He also claimed that the airline had breached the collective bargaining agreement. The airline removed the action to the U.S. District Court for the District of Hawaii, which dismissed the breach of contract claim as preempted by the Railway Labor Act (the RLA, which covers the airline industry as well as railways). The federal court also remanded the state claims to the state trial court. The trial court dismissed the mechanic's claimed public policy violation as preempted by the RLA. The mechanic filed a second lawsuit in state court, which held that his state law claims were preempted by the RLA.

The Supreme Court of Hawaii held that the state tort actions were not preempted by the RLA. The U.S. Supreme Court granted the airline's petition for review. The Supreme Court reviewed the history of the RLA and other federal labor statutes that applied preemption analyses. It held that such statutes promoted stability in labor-management relations by offering comprehensive frameworks for resolving labor disputes. Although the RLA preempted minor disputes under collective bargaining agreements, it did not preempt substantive protections under state laws. In this case, the mechanic alleged that the airline had a state law obligation not to fire him in violation of public policy or in retaliation for whistleblowing. The RLA and other similar federal labor statutes did not preempt such state law claims. The Supreme Court affirmed the decision of the Supreme Court of Hawaii. *Hawaiian Airlines, Inc. v. Norris*, 114 S.Ct. 2239, 129 L.Ed.2d 203 (1994).

A crew dispatcher for a New York commuter railroad claimed that her supervisor falsely accused her of drug use in front of other employees. She filed a lawsuit for slander in a New York trial court, alleging mental anguish and physical injury. The court denied a motion by the supervisor that the court had no jurisdiction to hear the case because of the mandatory arbitration provisions of the RLA. The jury awarded the employee $1.2 million in compensatory and punitive damages and the supervisor appealed to the New York Supreme Court, Appellate Division, which reversed the trial court order. The employee appealed to the Court of Appeals of New York. The court of appeals observed that the congressional goal of resolving labor disputes under federal law could only be accomplished by granting final authority to arbitration boards. To prevent aggrieved employees from avoiding the RLA, the courts have defined minor disputes as those that require some interpretation of a contract. Under this expansive definition, the employee's complaint was an attempt to circumvent the RLA, thereby avoiding arbitration and getting an opportunity for a jury verdict. Because resolution of the employee's state law claim required reference to conduct governed by the collective bargaining agreement, the state court was without jurisdiction and the matter was properly before the labor adjustment board. The court of appeals affirmed the appellate division court's order reversing the trial court decision. *Harris v. Hirsh*, 83 N.Y.2d 734, 613 N.Y.S.2d 842, 636 N.E.2d 1375 (1994).

A railroad with operations in Pennsylvania agreed to sell its assets to a newly formed subsidiary of another railroad (buyer). The buyer did not intend to assume the seller's collective bargaining contracts, needing only 250 of the 750 employees then working for the seller. The Railway Labor Executives' Association then sought a federal district court order to determine the seller's obligations under the RLA, and to enjoin the sale until those obligations could be met. The unions filed RLA § 156 notices proposing extensive changes in existing agreements, and went on strike. Subsequently, the buyer obtained an exemption from the ICC which essentially amounted to an approval of the sale, and a federal district court enjoined the work stoppage. The court also issued an injunction against the sale, and the U.S. Court of Appeals, Third Circuit, affirmed the order in part but set aside the injunction against the strike. The U.S. Supreme Court granted review.

The Court held that the RLA did not require or authorize an injunction against the sale of the seller's assets to the buyer. Also, the § 156 notices did not obligate the seller to postpone the sale beyond the approval date set by the ICC. However, the seller did have a limited duty to bargain regarding the effects of the sale. This obligation ceased on the date for closing the sale. Next, the Court decided that the case had to be remanded for a determination as to whether the RLA created a duty not to strike while its dispute resolution mechanisms were underway. The court reversed the injunction against the sale, and vacated the judgment setting aside the injunction against the strike, remanding the case for further proceedings. *Pittsburgh & Lake Erie Railroad Co. v. RLEA,* 491 U.S. 490, 109 S.Ct. 2584, 105 L.Ed.2d 415 (1989).

A union representing flight attendants declared a strike after reaching a collective bargaining impasse over wages and working conditions, and after pursuing the required dispute resolution mechanisms of the RLA. The airline continued its operations by hiring permanent replacements along with those who had not gone out on strike or who had abandoned the strike. After the strike ended, an agreement was entered into whereby strikers who returned to work would be reinstated with their seniority rights intact. The union then filed an action in a federal district court, contending that even if the strike was economic, the full-term strikers were entitled to displace junior crossover attendants. A Missouri federal district court denied relief to the union, but the U.S. Court of Appeals, Eighth Circuit, held that the less senior crossovers could be displaced. Further appeal was taken to the U.S. Supreme Court, which held that the RLA did not require the airline to lay off the junior crossovers. Since new hires could not be displaced after an economic strike, it would be unfair to differentiate between them and junior crossovers. The airline had lawfully exercised its economic power during the strike. *Trans World Airlines v. Independent Federation of Flight Attendants,* 489 U.S. 426, 109 S.Ct. 1225, 103 L.Ed.2d 456 (1989).

A carman, employed by a railroad, brought a lawsuit against his employer under the FELA. He claimed that fellow employees had harassed, threatened and intimidated him, and that the railroad condoned these acts. The railroad answered by asserting that the employee's sole remedy was through the National Railroad

Adjustment Board, according to the Railway Labor Act (RLA). It claimed that the RLA set forth binding arbitration procedures which the employee was forced to follow. A California federal district court granted summary judgment to the railroad, and the U.S. Court of Appeals, Ninth Circuit, reversed and remanded. Further appeal was taken to the U.S. Supreme Court.

The Court first noted that the FELA was enacted to provide a federal remedy for railroad workers who were injured as a result of employer or co-employee negligence. Employers may not limit their FELA liability in any way. The RLA, on the other hand, was set up to provide elaborate procedures for the resolution of labor disputes. Here, although the injury at issue might have been subject to arbitration under the RLA (a dispute arising out of workplace conditions which was similar to a "minor" labor dispute), it was also possibly the type of injury which the FELA was enacted to address. The Court remanded the case for a determination of whether emotional injury was cognizable under the FELA. *Atchison, Topeka and Santa Fe Ry Co. v. Buell,* 480 U.S. 557, 107 S.Ct. 1410, 94 L.Ed.2d 563 (1987).

An engineer employed by a railroad in Massachusetts belonged to the United Transportation Union (UTU). However, the collective bargaining agent for railroad engineers was another union. When the engineer was charged with a violation of company work rules, he requested that the UTU be allowed to represent him at the internal disciplinary hearing. The request was denied. He then represented himself and received a 30-day suspension. Following that, he sued the railroad and the majority union, contending that his rights under the Railway Labor Act had been violated because the UTU was not allowed to represent him. A federal district court and the U.S. Court of Appeals ruled against him, and the case then reached the U.S. Supreme Court. The Court held that the engineer was not entitled to have the UTU represent him at company-level proceedings. The other union could adequately represent him. Further, if the dispute was not resolved at that level, the UTU could represent the engineer in an appeal to the National Railroad Adjustment Board. The Court affirmed the lower courts' decisions. *Landers v. National Railroad Passengers Corp.*, 485 U.S. 652, 108 S.Ct. 1440, 99 L.Ed.2d 745 (1988).

An association was certified as the representative of the flight attendants of an airline with operations in Oregon. However, over a year and a half later, negotiations between the union and the airline were still unproductive, despite the intervention of the National Mediation Board. The union filed suit against the airline under the RLA, asserting that it had violated its statutory duty to "exert every reasonable effort" to reach an agreement with the union. A federal district court held that the airline had violated the RLA. The airline appealed to the U.S. Court of Appeals, Ninth Circuit. On appeal, the court noted that it is proper for federal courts to consult NLRA cases for assistance in construing the RLA. The U.S. Supreme Court has held that "the duty to exert every reasonable effort imposed by the RLA requires at least the avoidance of bad faith as defined under the NLRA, that is, going through the motions with a desire not to reach an agreement." Here, the district court had relied on the NLRA cases solely to impose on the airline the duty which the Supreme Court had held to be common to both statutes. Since the district court had merely ordered the airline to perform its existing duty under the RLA (without imposing upon it any duties derived from the NLRA) the court of appeals affirmed the district court's decision. However, the court reversed the award of attorney's fees against the airline. *Assn. of Flight Attendants v. Horizon Air Industries, Inc.,* 976 F.2d 541 (9th Cir.1992).

B. The Worker Adjustment and Retraining Notification Act

The Worker Adjustment and Retraining Notification (WARN) Act, 29 U.S.C. § 2101 *et seq.*, requires covered employers to serve written notice upon employees or their representatives 60 days in advance of a plant closing or mass layoff. Violation of the notice requirement may result in civil liability and employees may collect backpay for each day of the violation. The statute does not contain a limitation on actions.

A manufacturing company laid off 85 employees at a plant without giving the required 60-day notice. The employees sued the company in a federal district court in Pennsylvania, which denied the employer's summary judgment motion on the basis of a state statute of limitations. The court decided that the case was not barred because the limitations period from the most appropriate analogous state law did not bar the lawsuit. Another Pennsylvania federal district court determined that the sixth-month limitations period from the National Labor Relations Act was more analogous to WARN than any state statute of limitations. Accordingly, it applied the federal statute in barring another WARN claim. The U.S. Court of Appeals, Third Circuit, consolidated the cases and determined that the applicable statute of limitations was that found in Pennsylvania law. Because this decision conflicted with the decisions of federal appeals courts in the Second, Fifth and Sixth Circuits, the U.S. Supreme Court agreed to consider the cases.

The Court observed the general rule that where Congress fails to specify a limitations period in a federal law, the appropriate statute of limitations is drawn from the state in which the case is venued. Since 1830, state laws have supplied the appropriate limitations period for such claims under federal law, except where to do so would frustrate an important Congressional purpose. In this case, it was entirely appropriate to apply Pennsylvania law as the limitations period for WARN actions. The employers had set forth no reason to deviate from the general rule, and the court of appeals' decision was affirmed. *North Star Steel Co. v. Thomas,* 115 S.Ct. 1927, 132 L.Ed.2d 27 (1995).

The WARN Act requires covered employers to give their employees 60 days notice before a plant closing or mass layoff. The notice requirement applies where more than 50 full-time employees suffer an employment loss, defined as employment termination, a layoff exceeding six months, or a 50 percent reduction in work hours for a six-month period. A California videotape business was acquired by a holding company, with only a few days notice to employees. Most of the company's employees accepted employment with the new entity, but many suffered a pay cut and loss of fringe benefits under collectively bargained for union health and pension plans. The new employer refused to recognize the union's representation of approximately one-third of the transferred employees, and the union filed a lawsuit against the selling company for damages under WARN. A federal district court held that there had been no employment loss under WARN because fewer than 50 employees lost their jobs. The union appealed to the U.S. Court of Appeals, Ninth Circuit.

The union argued that the definition of "employment loss" under WARN should encompass a reduction in pay and benefits resulting from a business sale. It also claimed that the sale had been a sham and that the new entity was the alter ego of the former employer. The court found no WARN violation, accepting the U.S. Department of Labor's interpretation that a business seller is liable for violations of WARN only up to the date of sale. The buyer is responsible thereafter. It held that WARN applied only to employees who actually experienced a covered employment loss, and not a technical termination through sale. The WARN Act did not apply to modifications of the terms of employment, such as compensation and benefits. The sale in this case was not an event that triggered the coverage of WARN, and the district court had properly held for the former employer. *International Alliance v. Compact Video Services, Inc.*, 50 F.3d 1464 (9th Cir.1995).

A nuclear chemical processing plant in Oklahoma was shut down for routine maintenance. During the shutdown, soil contamination was discovered and the Nuclear Regulatory Commission (NRC) ordered that the facility remain closed. The shutdown lasted approximately nine months, and no employees were laid off during this time. However, shortly after the NRC terminated its shutdown order, a cloud of hazardous and potentially lethal gas escaped from the facility. This resulted in another shutdown and because the parent company of the plant decided not to provide any additional funds, it determined not to restart operations. The parent company sent notices to employees that they were being discharged in five days. Some of the employees sued the company in the U.S. District Court for the Eastern District of Oklahoma, alleging violations of the WARN Act. The court noted that the plant could be excused from giving 60 days' notice if the plant closing was caused by circumstances that were not reasonably foreseeable to the company as of the date notice was required under the WARN Act. In this case, the release of toxic gas was sudden and unforeseeable, and acted as a triggering mechanism for the shutdown. This in turn created an inability to generate revenue, causing the refusal of the parent company to provide additional financing. Accordingly, the facility had exercised sound business judgment in terminating plant operations, and the failure to provide the required WARN Act notice was excused. The court granted judgment to the company. *Bradley v. Sequoyah Fuels Corp.*, 847 F.Supp. 863 (E.D.Okl.1994).

A corporation manufactured outdoor lawn furniture at a plant that lost money for several years. A bank which held a lien on corporate assets insisted that it either find a buyer for the lawn furniture division or increase its retail sales accounts. The corporation was unable to comply with this demand, and the bank suspended further loans. Three days later, the furniture division notified its workers by a letter to their bargaining representative that their jobs would be terminated the following day. The letter stated that performance in the division was disappointing and that "the substandard working capital required of business does not make it a viable entity." A number of employees claimed that the short notice violated the WARN Act, 29 U.S.C. §§ 2101-2109. They filed a lawsuit against the corporation in the U.S. District Court for the Eastern District of California, which granted the corporation's summary judgment motion. The employees appealed to the U.S. Court of Appeals, Ninth Circuit.

The court of appeals stated that the WARN Act, with certain exceptions, requires covered employers to give affected workers 60 days' written notice of any plant closure or mass layoff. The employees claimed that the vaguely-worded notice was insufficient to serve as the required "brief statement of the reason for reducing the notice period." The court of appeals disagreed, finding that the notice was sufficient to notify employees that the division had lost its financing and could not continue operations. Although the notice was somewhat unclear, it was not false or misleading, and the court of appeals affirmed the judgment of the district court. *Alarcon v. Keller Industries, Inc.*, 27 F.3d 386 (9th Cir.1994).

An industrial products manufacturer created a consolidated parts department within one of its divisions to help the facility run more efficiently and to help reduce certain overhead costs. When the department failed to achieve the expected reduction in costs, the manufacturer decided to decentralize the department's work. It closed the department and laid off 41 employees affiliated with the department. It also laid off 15 employees who worked in the division in departments related to the one which had been dissolved. The discharged employees filed a lawsuit under the WARN Act. A federal magistrate judge found that the corporation did not order a "mass layoff" under the statute but that it had ordered a "plant closing" without providing the required 60-day notice. The corporation objected to the magistrate's recommendation, and a Rhode Island federal district judge reviewed the magistrate's report.

The district court first found that the department was an "operating unit" for purposes of the WARN Act. Here, the corporation had set up the department with its own managers, its own separate budget, and its own separate workforce. Next, the court held that the evidence was clear that the corporation considered the department to be a separate organizational unit, and that it planned and executed a shutdown of that unit. Even though some of the department's work was picked up by other departments, the department was a distinct organizational and production entity that was closed by the corporation. Also, more than 50 employees lost their jobs within a 30-day period. Even though the general downturn in the economy was the reason the additional 15 employees who lost their jobs were not reassigned to other groups, the employment loss was caused by the closure of the department. Finally, the court noted that the layoffs resulted from a "plant closing" within the meaning of the WARN Act because the department was an operating unit within a single site of employment. The court affirmed the magistrate's recommendations. *Pavao v. Brown & Sharpe Mfg. Co.*, 844 F.Supp. 890 (D.R.I.1994).

Employers who violate the WARN Act may become liable for employee backpay for each day of violation. A publishing corporation closed its Arkansas plant without giving its employees 60 days' notice. As a consequence, the employer had to comply with the penalty provision of WARN by paying its former workers for the 60 days after the plant closed. The employer paid the affected employees for the equivalent of the time each former employee would have worked in the ensuing 60 days—approximately 42.5 days. Ninety-five former employees filed suit against the employer seeking a full 60 days pay for each employee, not merely wages for those days each employee would have worked in the 60-day period following the closing of the plant.

The U.S. District Court for the Eastern District of Arkansas considered motions for summary judgment with respect to the employer's liability. The court determined that the statute was unambiguous on its face as to the compensation to be paid to salaried workers. Each salaried worker had to be paid backpay for each day of violation. The court then determined that there was no reason to differentiate between salaried and hourly workers. Accordingly, backpay was required for each day of violation up to a maximum of 60 days. If the employer had given 59 days notice and the 60th day had fallen on a legal holiday or a Sunday, the employer would nevertheless have been required to pay each worker for that day. The violation is the failure to give employees adequate opportunity to find employment elsewhere. Accordingly, the employer was required to pay all the employees for every day of the violation. *Joshlin v. Gannett River States Publishing Corp.*, 840 F.Supp. 660 (E.D.Ark.1993).

The U.S. Court of Appeals, Fifth Circuit, in a similar case to the one above, interpreted the WARN Act differently than the Arkansas federal district court. The Fifth Circuit held that an employer that had failed to give the required notice had to pay damages for each day the aggrieved employees would have worked but for the violation, rather than each day of violation. The court determined that this approach more closely matched the intent of Congress when it passed the WARN Act. Also, this approach would not lead to anomalous results by paying part-time workers who work longer shifts more than full-time employees who work only eight-hour shifts. *Carpenters District Council of New Orleans & Vicinity v. Dillard Department Stores*, 15 F.3d 1275 (5th Cir.1994).

A mining company owned two mines, at which it employed 107 and 39 employees respectively. The company then decided to combine its activities at the larger mine for efficiency. As a result, 57 positions at the mine were eliminated. However, 14 employees were able to "bump" employees at the smaller mine. The company did not give 60 days' notice to its employees of its decision to consolidate. The mine workers' union then sued the company in a federal district court under the WARN Act for violating the act's 60-day notice period for plant closings or mass layoffs. Both sides moved for summary judgment. The court held that under the act, "mass layoff" is a reduction in force at a single site of employment where 33 percent of the employees and at least 50 employees are discharged. A "plant closing" is a shutdown which results in an employment loss of 50 or more employees at a single site. Here, the court noted that only 43 employees at the larger mine actually lost their jobs because 14 workers were able to bump less senior workers at the smaller mine. Accordingly, the layoffs did not require the 60-day notice necessary for plant closings and mass layoffs. The court granted the company's motion for summary judgment. *United Mine Workers International v. Harman Mining Corp.*, 780 F.Supp. 375 (W.D.Va.1991).

A hotel owner in Connecticut contracted with a hotel management firm to operate the hotel. There was a collective bargaining agreement in effect between the employees and the management firm. When the decision was made to close the hotel, the firm notified the employees and the group health insurer. The hotel owner was supposed to continue to fund insurance, but it failed to do so. As a result, coverage terminated with the closing of the hotel. Some former employees discovered the cancellation of their insurance and sought a preliminary injunction to force the management firm to provide medical care to the laid off employees. The suit was based on the WARN Act, and the Consolidated Omnibus Budget Reconciliation Act (COBRA) which requires group health plan sponsors to provide continuation coverage for laid off employees. A federal district court denied the relief sought, and appeal was taken.

The U.S. Court of Appeals, Second Circuit, noted that even though the hotel owner had made the decision to close the hotel, the management firm was covered under WARN. WARN provides an exclusive remedy of money damages for violations. Thus, the preliminary injunction was beyond the scope of the relief which could be provided. Next, the court noted that the obligation to provide continuation coverage ceases when the group health plan ceases. If there is no longer a group health plan in existence, it would not make sense to require a continuation of group coverage. Only where the plan remains in effect must continuation coverage be provided under COBRA. The court affirmed the lower court's decision denying injunctive relief to the former employees. *Local 217, Hotel & Restaurant Employees Union v. MHM, Inc.*, 976 F.2d 805 (2d Cir.1992).

C. Other Statutes

A welder employed by a New York railroad company worked in an area reputed to be a center for illegal drugs. While working in an enclosed area that had been broken into by vagrants, the welder was stabbed by a discarded hypodermic needle hidden in some debris. The piercing caused the welder's hand to bleed, and blood was observed in the hypodermic needle. The employee immediately went to a hospital where he was told to get an HIV test and to take other precautions. The welder never developed HIV, but he continued to undergo testing. He developed post-traumatic stress symptoms and lost 30 pounds after the incident. He sued the employer in the U.S. District Court for the Eastern District of New York under the Federal Employers' Liability Act (FELA) for emotional distress and received a $126,000 damage award. The railroad appealed to the U.S. Court of Appeals, Second Circuit. The court of appeals stated that FELA created liability for railroads under a lower standard of proximate cause than was generally applicable in employment cases and that any causal relation between the injury and the railroad's conduct could create potential employer liability. FELA plaintiffs were only required to show that the employer played a part in bringing about the injury. In this case, the welder was entitled to past, present and future damages as there was evidence that he would suffer from post-traumatic stress disorder for the rest of his life. The court of appeals affirmed the district court's judgment. *Marchica v. Long Island Railroad Co.*, 31 F.3d 1197 (2d Cir.1994).

An international union and its employees challenged the validity of certain Nevada gaming control laws in a federal district court. The laws in question required labor organizations to report and disclose the names and backgrounds of key employees and required the disqualification for union employment of anyone who had a criminal record or an unsavory background. Several union employees refused to provide the required background information. After the district court dismissed the action, the employees and the union appealed to the U.S. Court of Appeals, Ninth Circuit. The employees and the union claimed that the regulations were invalid because they were preempted by federal law. The court determined that Nevada had a substantial state interest in controlling gaming. Further, the court explained that the NLRA indicated that states may restrict employees in their designation of union representatives and adopt different and more stringent qualification requirements for union officials. States may enact these restrictions if they are confronted with the public evils of crime, corruption and racketeering. The federal laws did not preempt the state laws and the Nevada gaming control laws were found to be valid. The court of appeals affirmed the district court decision and dismissed the action. *Hotel Employees v. Nevada Gaming Comm'n*, 984 F.2d 1507 (9th Cir.1993).

A production supervisor for a Texas manufacturer was an active member of the United States Marine Corps Reserve. He notified the manufacturer of his imminent mobilization as a result of the war in the Persian Gulf. Two weeks later, the manufacturer notified him, in writing, that due to economic pressures, he would be laid off. The employee was then called to military duty and requested that he be allowed to return to his job when his tour of duty was completed. The company informed him that he would not be guaranteed a job upon his return from active duty and that he would not be granted a military leave of absence. Upon his return from duty, he visited the company's offices to reapply for his former job under the Veteran's Reemployment Rights Act (VRRA). He was told that no positions were available and he was not rehired. He then brought suit against his former employer alleging violations of the VRRA in a United States district court.

The court noted that the VRRA requires employers to reinstate employees who have temporarily left their employment to serve in a military reserve unit to the positions they formerly held. The company maintained that the employee held only a temporary position when he reported for active duty. The district court agreed. At the time he left to report for active duty, he was no longer working for the company. Although he was still receiving paychecks, this compensation was merely in lieu of the notice the company would normally have given him prior to terminating his employment and did not constitute a position of employment within the meaning of the VRRA. Thus, the court ruled that the employer did not violate the VRRA and it granted the employer's summary judgment motion. *Greene v. Advanced Micro Devices Inc.*, 824 F.Supp. 653 (W.D.Tex.1993).

The Immigration Reform and Control Act (IRCA) generally provides that employers must verify the legal immigration status of their employees. The employer must examine documents which evidence identity and work authorization, and failure to comply with IRCA can result in civil and criminal sanctions. A Quaker organization did not comply with the act because it believed that to do so would violate the religious beliefs and practices of its members. The organization thus brought a lawsuit for injunctive and declaratory relief in a California federal district court, asserting that its free exercise of religion was violated by the "employer sanction" provisions of IRCA. The district court granted the government's motion to dismiss the claim, and the organization appealed to the U.S. Court of Appeals, Ninth Circuit. On appeal, the court noted that a recent U.S. Supreme Court decision dramatically changed the manner in which it had to evaluate free exercise complaints like the one before it. Here, as in the recent Supreme Court case, there was no allegation that IRCA's employer sanction provisions were directed at religious belief or at the free exercise of religion. Since IRCA was not aimed at suppressing the free exercise of religion, the court rejected the organization's free exercise claim and affirmed the district court's decision. *American Friends Service Committee Corp. v. Thornburgh*, 941 F.2d 808 (9th Cir.1991).

CHAPTER SIX

EMPLOYMENT PRACTICES

I.   HIRING PRACTICES

Generally, employers may use various preemployment measures to insure that applicants will be suited for the positions available. However, employers may not discriminate or otherwise refuse to hire applicants for reasons which violate public policy.

A New Jersey law firm contacted an employment agency to obtain secretarial candidates. The agency forwarded its fee schedule and arranged for the firm to interview six or seven applicants. After identifying a top candidate, the firm notified the agency that it would not hire her unless there was a possibility of negotiating the placement fee down. The agency declined and the firm placed an advertisement in a newspaper for a secretary. The previously selected candidate then reapplied for employment, and the firm hired her. When the agency learned of the hiring, it billed the firm $7,800, which the firm refused to pay. The firm then discharged the secretary, and the agency sued the firm in a New Jersey trial court, which held for the agency. The law firm appealed to the Superior Court of New Jersey, Appellate Division. The appellate division court likened the employment agency fee to a real estate broker's claim for a commission. An agency, like a broker, must establish that it was a producing cause of the placement. The fact that the law firm had dismissed the employee within 45 days of hiring her bolstered the agency's argument that the firm's action violated the agency agreement. The court affirmed the trial court's judgment. *Michele Matthews, Inc. v. Kroll & Tract*, 275 N.J.Super. 101, 645 A.2d 798 (1994).

A corporation which hired security officers for its retail stores required all applicants to take a psychological test called a psychscreen. The psychscreen was designed to screen out applicants who were emotionally unstable, who might put customers or employees in jeopardy, or who would not take direction and follow procedures. Three applicants who were required to take the test brought lawsuits against the corporation, asserting constitutional and statutory claims. They sought a preliminary injunction to prohibit the corporation from using the psychscreen during the action. They claimed that the test asked inappropriate questions about an applicant's religious attitudes and sexual orientation which were irrelevant to a determination of whether an applicant would be a successful security officer. A California trial court found that the corporation had demonstrated a legitimate interest in psychologically screening its applicants, and found that the test was not unreasonable. The court denied the request for a preliminary injunction, and the applicants appealed to the Court of Appeal, First District.

On appeal, the corporation conceded that the psychscreen constituted an invasion of the privacy rights of its applicants, but it maintained that the intrusion was justified. The court of appeal noted that unless there was a compelling interest for allowing the test, a preliminary injunction ought to be granted. The court then stated that the questions in the psychscreen were overbroad and did not further the corporation's interest in employing emotionally stable persons. It thus granted the preliminary injunction to the applicants and remanded the case for trial. *Soroka v. Dayton Hudson Corp.*, 1 Cal.Rptr.2d 77 (Cal.App.1st Dist.1991).

A prospective employee inquired of one of her previous employers about the possibility of a position in New York City. The prospective employee had several telephone conversations with representatives and had an interview at the headquarters. During this time the prospective employee was also pursuing other job opportunities and was offered a position with another firm. Upon informing her previous employer of the offer, an executive vice president allegedly advised her to seek a salary package from the vice president of marketing, and further assured her that if the vice president did not offer her a job that the president of one of the other divisions would present her with an offer. As a result, the woman declined the offer from the other firm. Ultimately, the two employment proposals prepared by her previous employer did not materialize. The woman sued the employer for breach of contract and negligent misrepresentation. The trial court granted summary judgment to the employer on the breach of contract claim, and appeal was taken to the New York Supreme Court, Appellate Division.

On appeal, the appellate court affirmed the dismissal of the breach of contract claim based on the lack of an employment contract and because the employer made no offer of employment. Additionally, even if the employer's representations could be construed as an offer there was no agreement regarding duration; therefore, she could have been terminated at any time and for any reason or no reason without eliciting a breach of contract action. The appellate court also indicated that the negligent misrepresentation claim should be dismissed. The court stated that the employer's assurance was not false information, but rather an expression of future expectation. Furthermore, the woman's reliance was not reasonable because as an at-will employee she could be fired without cause anytime. *Bower v. Atlis Systems, Inc.*, 582 N.Y.S.2d 542 (A.D.3d Dept.1992).

A Minnesota company engaged in taconite mining required prospective employees to participate in a preemployment physical examination because the applicants needed to perform heavy, physically demanding work. The company relied upon the medical recommendation of the doctors performing the physicals to reject or disqualify the applicants. A group of prospective employees, rejected because their back conditions indicated their unemployability, filed a complaint with the Department of Human Rights. The company again consulted with the doctors regarding the accuracy of the preemployment examinations, particularly the back x-rays. Obtaining reassurance from the doctors, the company continued its policy of preemployment screening. When the applicants' discrimination claims were heard, the administrative law judge (ALJ) concluded that prospective employees who were rejected were within the meaning of the Minnesota Human Rights Act and, based on contradictory testimony from the Department of Human Rights experts, were unlawfully discriminated against. The employer appealed to the Minnesota Court of Appeals. On appeal, the court held that "an employer who has relied upon competent medical advice that there existed a reasonably probable risk of serious harm should be allowed some discretion in determining whether an individual should be disqualified from employment." The court upheld the employer's policy of relying on medical advice before hiring applicants. *State of Minnesota, Dep't of Human Rights v. Hibbing Taconite Co.*, 482 N.W.2d 504 (Minn.App.1992).

A South Carolina doctor applied for reappointment with a hospital system. He had previously been on the staff at one of the system's hospitals. In his application, the doctor stated that he had not voluntarily relinquished his staff privileges (nor had them revoked) at any member hospital. The system's administrators wrote to the hospital he had worked at, inquiring about his status. They were informed that the doctor's privileges had been terminated for failure to follow regulations regarding recordkeeping. The hospital also indicated that the doctor may have given inadequate care to a patient. The hospital system convened a hearing at the doctor's request. The hearing committee recommended that the doctor's application be denied. The system's medical staff council then recommended to the board of trustees that the application be denied, that the doctor not be allowed to reapply for one year, and that the doctor undergo psychiatric evaluation before being allowed to reapply. The doctor brought suit against the hospital system, asserting that its actions deprived him of his due process rights.

The trial court held for the system, and the doctor appealed to the Court of Appeals of South Carolina.

The appeals court noted that the doctor's interest in being reappointed was a property interest which required due process before it could be denied. The court then held that the hospital system had afforded the doctor due process because it had given him adequate notice and opportunity for the hearing, and had allowed him to present evidence and cross-examine witnesses. Further, the system had not excluded the doctor from practice for arbitrary, capricious or discriminatory reasons. However, the court did note that it had been improper to force the doctor into psychiatric evaluation because the system did not afford him due process before doing so. It thus affirmed in part the trial court's holding in favor of the hospital system. *Huellmantel v. Greenville Hospital System,* 402 S.E.2d 489 (S.C.App.1991).

An electric company was a member of a multiemployer bargaining unit represented by the Minneapolis chapter of the National Electrical Contractors Association (NECA). Under a collective bargaining agreement between NECA and a local union, the electric company was only allowed to hire electricians from applicants referred to it by the union hiring hall. However, to balance this power, the company could hire or reject any applicant. After an applicant was twice referred and twice rejected, he complained to the union which asked why the company had refused to hire him. The company cited "past problems" without elaborating. An unfair labor practice charge was filed with the National Labor Relations Board, in which it was alleged that the nonhiring was discriminatory in nature because of the union member's past service as a job steward, but an administrative law judge (ALJ) found that the language of the collective bargaining agreement precluded the union from inquiring into the reasons for the rejection of the applicant. The board reversed the ALJ's decision, and the company appealed to the U.S. Court of Appeals, Eighth Circuit.

On appeal, the court noted that the information request could not be enforced here because the information sought was not relevant to the union's duties. The union would have no authority to bring a grievance because of the employer's refusal to hire the applicant. The company had the right to decide not to employ the applicant (even as discrimination against him for his prior performance of duties as a job steward). Accordingly, the union was not entitled to obtain the information it sought. The court reversed the board's order. *Parsons Electric Co. v. NLRB,* 976 F.2d 1167 (8th Cir.1992).

II.   DRUG TESTING

Challenges to drug testing in the private sector are less likely to succeed than their counterparts in the public sector. For one thing, the Fourth Amendment argument fails due to the lack of government involvement. (The Fourth Amendment only prohibits unreasonable searches and seizures by the government.) So even though drug testing is a search and seizure,

employees cannot utilize the "reasonableness" standard of the Fourth Amendment to strike down such policies.

A railroad corporation had in place a policy which required its employees to undergo periodic physical examinations as well as examinations upon return from leave. Occasionally, drug screening was a part of the exams. The railroad then announced a policy of including drug screening in all exams. The union challenged this policy in a federal district court which held that the case involved a "minor dispute" under the Railway Labor Act. The U.S. Court of Appeals reversed, holding that the dispute was major, and an appeal was taken to the U.S. Supreme Court. The Court noted that "major disputes seek to create contractual rights," while minor disputes seek to enforce them. Here, the employer was asserting a contractual right to take a contested action which was arguably justified by the terms of the parties' collective bargaining agreement. Thus, it was a minor dispute under the RLA. Since the railroad's arguments were not obviously insubstantial, the minor dispute came within the exclusive jurisdiction of an adjustment board. The Court reversed the court of appeals' decision, and allowed the case to go before the board. *Consolidated Rail Corp. v. Railway Labor Executives' Ass'n,* 491 U.S. 299, 109 S.Ct. 2477, 105 L.Ed.2d 250 (1989).

A Texas employer required its employees to participate in random drug testing. The testing laboratory informed the employer's vice-president that one employee tested positive for drug use, and the vice-president told the employee's supervisors not to assign him to hazardous work. The confirming test result was negative, and the supervisors apologized to the employee for telling him he had failed the drug test. The employee was fired the next year for an unrelated matter, and he sued the employer in a Texas trial court for negligent infliction of emotional distress, slander, breach of contract, defamation, invasion of privacy and intentional infliction of emotional distress. The court granted the employer's summary judgment motion, and the employee appealed to the Court of Appeals of Texas, Houston. The court agreed with the employee that the employer had breached its own policy of confidentiality in reporting lab results, but that its report was not false. The employer's truthfulness was a complete defense to the slander cause of action. The employee's breach of contract claim also failed, because the employment relationship was at will. The employee was unable to show that the employer's conduct had been intentional, reckless, extreme or outrageous. Accordingly it did not support a claim for emotional distress. The trial court had appropriately granted summary judgment to the employer. *Washington v. Naylor Industrial Serv., Inc.,* 893 S.W.2d 309 (Tex.App.—Houston 1995).

A Massachusetts woman worked for a manufacturer as a tool grinder. She received regular raises and bonuses, was never reprimanded, and was never under any reasonable suspicion that she ingested illegal drugs. Work at the company required employees to be well trained, constantly alert, and extremely careful. The tools manufactured by the company were razor sharp and had to be handled with great care. One of the company's owners became concerned about drug use by employees and decided to initiate a drug testing policy. The tool grinder refused to take the test because she found the testing procedure degrading. The company discharged her. She brought suit in a state trial court alleging, among other claims, a violation of her statutory right to privacy and wrongful termination in violation of public policy. The court ruled for the employer, and she appealed to the Supreme Judicial Court of Massachusetts.

The supreme court noted that submission to urinalysis involves a significant invasion of privacy, especially when employees are required to submit to a visual inspection to ensure that they are not concealing vials of urine. However, the company had a legitimate business interest in protecting its employees and customers, and the owner had a strong basis for suspecting that employees were using drugs. Further, the owner had promised that anyone who tested positive would not be fired, but would be retested in 30 days and given an opportunity to undergo counseling at company expense. Thus, the drug testing policy was reasonable and did not violate the tool grinder's right to privacy. Accordingly, the discharge was not a wrongful termination in violation of public policy. The trial court's decision was affirmed. *Folmsbee v. Tech Tool Grinding & Supply, Inc.*, 630 N.E.2d 586 (Mass.1994).

Three groups of railroad employees were discharged or disciplined for violating their employer's drug and alcohol policies. They claimed that the Iowa Code prohibited the drug testing policies used by the employer to detect substance abuse. They filed a lawsuit against the employer in an Iowa trial court, which granted summary judgment to the employer. The employees appealed to the Supreme Court of Iowa, which held that the regulations promulgated by the U.S. Department of Transportation preempted the field of employee drug testing by railroads. The employees in this case were maintenance of way employees, who were classified as safety-sensitive by the transportation department. The state legislation at issue was not a railroad safety regulation and was in conflict with federal employee drug testing policy. The court therefore affirmed the trial court's summary judgment ruling. *Brotherhood of Maintenance of Way Employees v. Chicago and North Western Trans. Co.*, 514 N.W.2d 90 (Iowa 1994).

An electronic equipment manufacturer conducted a drug testing program which required employees to give a urine specimen. Although employees produced specimens in private, they were closely monitored, with a technician standing outside to listen. Two employees who protested the program filed a lawsuit against the manufacturer in a Massachusetts trial court. They left their jobs after commencing the action. They sought declaratory and injunctive relief, costs and attorney's fees. The court denied their motion for a preliminary injunction that would prohibit enforcement of the policy, and granted the manufacturer's summary judgment motions, except that it ruled for one of the employees on his Privacy Act claim. The former employees and the manufacturer appealed unfavorable aspects of the trial court decision to the Supreme Judicial Court of Massachusetts.

The court stated that employee urinalysis programs significantly invaded privacy rights and required a balancing of interests between the employer's legitimate business needs and employee privacy. Because of the differing duties of the employees in this case, a different result applied to each. One of the employees was an account executive who was required to drive a company-owned vehicle more than 20,000 miles per year. He had a privacy interest that was outweighed by the manufacturer's interest in protecting public safety during use of its vehicle. Accordingly, summary judgment was appropriate in his case. However, a technical editor (the other employee) whose work was checked by others and could not result in any harm to public health and safety had a privacy interest that exceeded the employer's legitimate business interests. Accordingly, the balancing formula required a different ruling for this employee. The supreme judicial court affirmed the trial court's decision. *Webster v. Motorola, Inc.*, 418 Mass. 425, 637 N.E.2d 203 (1994).

A contractor which did work for the Washington Public Power Supply System implemented a mandatory urinalysis drug testing program for prospective employees. The was done in response to a proposed rule published by the Nuclear Regulatory Commission as a means of ensuring public safety. Several applicants of the contractor brought a lawsuit in a state trial court to challenge the testing policy. The court granted summary judgment to the contractor and the state. Subsequently, the applicants appealed to the Supreme Court of Washington. The supreme court looked to the Fourth Amendment of the U.S. Constitution (which prohibits unreasonable searches and seizures), noting that urinalysis is a search and seizure. However, the court then stated that the administrative search exception made the urinalysis valid even without a warrant because the industry of nuclear power was a pervasively regulated industry. The public safety interests outweighed the privacy concerns of the individuals to be tested. Accordingly, the drug testing was not violative of the Fourth Amendment, and the program was upheld. *Alverado v. Washington Public Power Supply System,* 759 P.2d 427 (Wash.1988).

Mercury is a toxic substance subject to the standards and regulations promulgated by the Occupational Safety and Health Administration (OSHA). Pursuant to OSHA's recommendations, a company which manufactured products that required the handling of mercury adopted a policy which required urinalysis on employees who worked with open mercury. Subsequently, an employee who worked with mercury tubes refused to submit to urinalysis. The company discharged her. She then sued for money damages, reinstatement, backpay and other relief, asserting various claims against the company, including invasion of privacy. The company removed the case to an Illinois federal district court, then moved for summary judgment, claiming that the employee's claims were pre-empted by § 301 of the Labor Management Relations Act (LMRA).

The federal court noted that even though the collective bargaining agreement had expired, it provided for automatic renewal from year to year. Accordingly, the employee's claims were preempted by § 301 because they implicated and arose under the agreement. The employee's claims required an interpretation of the collective bargaining agreement. Further, since the employee had not exhausted her grievance or arbitration remedies before bringing suit, her action could not be maintained as a § 301 action. Next, the court noted that there could be no Fourth Amendment search and seizure violation here because there was insufficient government action for such a claim to lie. The court granted summary judgment to the company on all the claims, and assessed Rule 11 sanctions (of attorney's fees and costs) against the employee on her Fourth Amendment argument. *Kelly v. Mercoid Corp.,* 776 F.Supp. 1246 (N.D.Ill.1991).

A Louisiana man worked for an oil company as an oil field pumper and was subject to drug testing to determine "fitness for duty." After an unannounced examination of employees at a job site, the worker failed an initial screening test which involved the ability to track a moving point of light with his eyes. He was then required to provide a urine sample which tested positive for marijuana. The worker's father, a long-time employee of the company, asked for a further investigation, so the laboratory which had performed the urinalysis sent a sample to a doctor who had it tested at another laboratory. The doctor confirmed the positive result, and the worker was fired. He sued the oil company, the laboratories and the doctor in federal court, alleging violations of the Fair Credit Reporting Act (15 U.S.C. § 1681 *et seq.*). The court dismissed the action, and the worker appealed to the U.S. Court of Appeals, Fifth Circuit.

While the court of appeals admitted that the FCRA did not seem to have been enacted with drug-screening reports in mind, the language of the statute was broad. Under the FCRA, consumer reporting agencies must follow certain procedures when releasing consumer reports (including not only credit reports, but reports of consumers' employment eligibility). The worker maintained that the urinalysis reports were consumer reports because they were used to determine his eligibility for employment. The court stated that while drug test reports might be included in FCRA coverage, a statutory exception made the FCRA inapplicable here because the reports here came from the testing of the urine sample that the worker himself had provided. The reports thus were not "based on information from an outside source." Accordingly, the FCRA did not apply in this instance, and the lower court decision was affirmed. *Hodge v. Texaco, Inc.,* 975 F.2d 1093 (5th Cir.1992).

An oil company operated a refinery in New Jersey, where it employed 330 people. After discovering evidence of on-the-job marijuana usage, the company implemented a random urine testing program. The program required an observer to be present when the samples were obtained so that fake samples could not be submitted. An employee was selected for a random test. He tested positive for two drugs and was discharged. He then brought suit against the company, asserting that it had wrongfully discharged him. The trial court held that the termination was "contrary to a clear mandate of public policy of the State of New Jersey," and granted summary judgment to the employee. The oil company appealed to the Superior Court of New Jersey, Appellate Division. On appeal, the court found that the drug testing policy enacted by the private sector employer did not give rise to constitutional prohibitions. The Fourth Amendment proscription against unreasonable searches and seizures was meant to limit the exercise of government power. It did not apply to drug testing by private employers. The court further noted that even if an employer's violation of an employee's right to privacy might transgress public policy, the employee would still have no cause of action. This was because there was no right to use controlled dangerous substances even in the privacy of the home. Accordingly, the appellate court determined that there had been no violation of a "clear mandate of public policy." It reversed the summary judgment and remanded the case to the trial court. *Hennessey v. Coastal Eagle Point Oil Co.*, 589 A.2d 170 (N.J.Super.A.D.1991).

An Alaska drilling company established a drug testing program for its employees. Two men who worked on drilling rigs on the North Slope refused to submit to urinalysis and were discharged. They then brought suit challenging the drug testing policy. They claimed that the policy violated their right to privacy under the Alaska Constitution and that the policy was a breach of the covenant of good faith and fair dealing implied in all employment contracts. The trial court held for the company, and the employees appealed to the Supreme Court of Alaska. The supreme court noted that, unlike California's Constitution (which has been construed to apply to nongovernmental invasions of privacy) the Alaska Constitution's right to privacy clause extended only to governmental action. Next, the court found that the workers here were at-will employees and that the public concerns for employee safety outweighed any violation of the implied covenant of good faith and fair dealing, and also outweighed any privacy expectations the workers may have had. The court affirmed the trial courts' decision in relevant part. *Luedtke v. Nabors Alaska Drilling, Inc.,* 768 P.2d 1123 (Alaska 1989).

After the Federal Railroad Administration (FRA) set forth random drug testing regulations, the Railway Labor Executives' Association (RLEA) brought a lawsuit against the Secretary of Transportation, challenging the regulations by asserting that they required unreasonable searches in violation of the Fourth Amendment to the U.S. Constitution. The RLEA also asserted that the regulations violated the separation of powers doctrine because they did not fall within the FRA's statutory authority. Further, it contended that the FRA could not delegate to private railroads the power to conduct random drug testing. A federal district court judge granted summary judgment to the Secretary of Transportation, and the RLEA appealed to the U.S. Court of Appeals, Ninth Circuit.

On appeal, the court noted that the random drug testing only applied to employees in safety-sensitive positions. Because the public's safety interests outweighed the privacy interests of the railroad employees, the regulations were valid. The court then stated that Congress had generally authorized the FRA to promulgate random drug testing as a safety measure. Thus, the FRA's random drug testing regulations did not violate the separation of powers doctrine. Finally, the court stated that the FRA had the power to delegate to private railroads the authority to conduct random drug testing of employees. The court therefore affirmed the district court's decision. *Railway Labor Executives' Ass'n v. Skinner*, 934 F.2d 1096 (9th Cir.1991).

A transportation company hired a Washington woman to fill an office position in June 1986. She became a terminable-at-will employee. In August 1988, the company expanded its drug testing policy to include all employees. Even though the office worker had performed at or above company expectations, and the company never suspected that she used drugs, she was required to submit to random drug testing as a condition of employment. She protested the policy verbally and in writing, finally refusing to submit to drug testing. The company fired her. She then sued the company for wrongful discharge. A state trial court dismissed the case, and the office worker appealed to the Court of Appeals of Washington. On appeal, she contended that a clear mandate of public policy existed which prohibited a private employer from terminating an at-will employee for refusing to submit to drug testing. The court, however, found no "clear mandate" which favored employee privacy over employer drug testing. Accordingly, it affirmed the trial court's decision dismissing the case. *Roe v. Quality Transportation Services,* 838 P.2d 128 (Wash.App.Div.3 1992).

An Oklahoma delivery business instituted a drug testing policy as required by the federal government. One of its truck drivers signed a consent form in which he agreed to random drug tests as a condition of employment. After he tested positive for drug use, he was discharged. He sought unemployment compensation from the state Commission for Benefits. The commission awarded him unemployment benefits and determined that a positive drug screen absent any impairment or strange behavior did not amount to misconduct connected with his work. The commission's board of review affirmed the decision. The delivery business further appealed. The Oklahoma Supreme Court stated that the commission improperly added the requirement of proof of impairment or strange behavior to the delivery business's burden of proof. A strong federal public policy existed to insure that the operators of commercial vehicles do not use drugs, either on or off duty. The clear purpose of this policy was to protect the motoring public. When an employer fires a commercial driver because the driver has tested positive for drug use, the commission may not impose additional requirements of proof on the employer before denying unemployment benefits. Therefore, the supreme court ordered the commission to deny unemployment compensation to the driver. *Farm Fresh Dairy Inc. v. Blackburn*, 841 P.2d 1150 (Okl.1992).

III. NONCOMPETITION AGREEMENTS AND TRADE SECRETS

Restrictive covenants and covenants not to compete must be reasonable or courts will not uphold them. Courts look to the scope, duration and geographic limitations of "no compete" clauses to test their validity. Trade secrets must be subject to efforts that are reasonable to maintain their secrecy. If information is readily available, or if the employer does not take

reasonable steps to protect it, the information will not be given trade secret protection.

A. Noncompete Agreements

Several employees of a Texas paper supply company resigned and set up a competing venture. The new venture obtained the customer list of the former employer and actively solicited its customers. Each former sales employee had been employed under an agreement prohibiting the use of customer lists and the soliciting of business from customers after leaving the company. The former employer filed a lawsuit against its former employees in a Texas trial court, seeking a temporary injunction which would prohibit them from violating their non-compete agreements, using confidential information and trade secrets and soliciting customers. The court granted the injunction and the former employees appealed to the Court of Appeals of Texas, Amarillo. The court determined that the former employees had been employed at will and that the agreements not to compete were illusory because they were not part of an enforceable employment agreement. The trial court had erroneously granted the order to prohibit solicitation of customers under the agreement. However, there was no error in the prohibition against use of the former employer's confidential information. The former employer was entitled to enforcement of that part of the trial court order. *Miller Paper Co. v. Roberts Paper Co.*, 901 S.W.2d 593 (Tex.App.—Amarillo 1995).

The Georgia Court of Appeals reversed a trial court order in favor of two former employees of a computer software company who resigned and took a customer order for their own purposes. The former employees allegedly intended to compete directly with their former employer by developing capital asset tracking software systems. The court determined that the trial court order amounted to an inappropriate order for summary judgment where fact issues existed. The trial court had also erroneously determined that one of the former employees had not violated a covenant not to compete with her former employer. This was a factual issue for which the former employer was entitled to further consideration by the trial court.*Electronic Data Systems Corp. v. Heinemann*, 459 S.E.2d 457 (Ga.App.1995).

A cellular communications company hired a sales representative to sell pagers and required her to execute a covenant not to compete. The employment was at will, subject to the employer's agreement to train the sales representative and the representative's agreement to give a 14-day notice prior to quitting and to furnish an inventory of company property in her possession upon her termination. The representative sought to avoid the covenant not to compete after several years of work, and the company refused. She filed a lawsuit in a Texas trial court, which held the covenant unenforceable. The Court of Appeals of Texas reversed the trial court decision, and the employee appealed to the Supreme Court of Texas. The supreme court determined that an at-will employment contract may contain other agreements as long as they do not hamper the ability of either party to terminate the employment relationship at will. An agreement not to compete could be enforceable if it was ancillary to an otherwise enforceable agreement and permissible in scope, duration and geographical area. Because the covenant not to compete in this case was not designed to enforce any promise by the employee — for example, a promise not to disclose confidential proprietary information — it was not ancillary to the agreement, and was therefore unenforceable. The court reversed and remanded the case to the court of appeals. *Light v. Centel Cellular Company of Texas*, 883 S.W.2d 642 (Tex.1994).

A Louisiana brokerage office employed a branch manager whose duties included recruiting brokers. He executed annual employment agreements that prohibited him from soliciting other employees in the event that his own employment was terminated. The prohibition on solicitation applied to other branch offices within a 50-mile radius. When the branch manager quit to work for another brokerage firm, he refused to return a $7,000 incentive advance and also solicited employees of his former office in violation of the employment agreement. The brokerage firm filed for arbitration against the former branch manager and his new employer. It also filed a lawsuit in the U.S. District Court for the Eastern District of Louisiana for restraining orders against the former branch manager. The former branch manager counterclaimed for a permanent injunction prohibiting his former employer from proceeding with arbitration, and claiming that the nonsolicitation clause was not specific enough to be legally enforceable under Louisiana law. The court granted the brokerage firm its request for an order preventing further solicitation of employees for one year after the date of the hearing. The court also dismissed the former branch manager's counterclaim, and he appealed to the U.S. Court of Appeals, Fifth Circuit.

The court of appeals observed that Louisiana law did not prohibit an employment contract such as the one at issue in this case, because it did not unlawfully restrain the branch manager from engaging in his profession. The employment contract merely prohibited the former branch manager from soliciting a small group of former coworkers. The court rejected the former branch manager's argument that he should not be required to refund the $7,000 incentive advance because there was a failure of consideration supporting the employment contract. There was no failure of consideration here. The district court had correctly dismissed the former branch manager's counterclaim and the court of appeals affirmed that decision. *Smith, Barney, Harris Upham & Co., Inc. v. Robinson*, 12 F.3d 515 (5th Cir.1994).

A founding shareholder, officer and employee of a corporation in Illinois entered into a capital stock repurchase agreement whereby he sold his interest in the company back to the corporation. As part of the agreement, he agreed that for a period of two years he would not engage directly or indirectly in the solicitation of any client of the corporation for business that was being actively performed for that particular client as of March 26, 1990. Subsequently, the corporation filed a motion in a state trial court, seeking a temporary restraining order against the ex-employee, alleging that he was violating the nonsolicitation agreement. The court granted the injunction against the former employee, prohibiting his solicitation of clients of the corporation. The ex-employee appealed to the Appellate Court of Illinois.

The appellate court noted that the corporation had a legitimate, protectable interest which warranted protection. Here, the ex-employee had client knowledge that he would not have had but for his employment with the corporation. Since it would be difficult to assess the damages with any degree of accuracy, injunctive relief was warranted. The restrictive covenant was reasonable because the ex-employee received almost $150,000 for his stock, the covenant only prohibited contact and solicitation of the corporation's clients for a two-year period, and the covenant did not preclude the ex-employee from operating a competing business. Accordingly, the court affirmed the trial court's decision to grant the injunction. *A-Tech Computer Services, Inc. v. Soo Hoo*, 627 N.E.2d 21 (Ill.App.1st Dist.1993).

A New York chiropractor maintained an office where he employed another chiropractor. The contract between the parties stated that the employee, in the event of his termination from employment, would not establish a competitive business within a seven-mile radius of the employer's office for a period of two years. Subsequently, the employer sold his practice to another chiropractor, but remained as a consultant, entitled to a share of the profits. Eight months later, the employee resigned and opened his own chiropractic office five blocks away. His former employer sued him for damages. The supreme court dismissed the complaint and appeal was taken to the Supreme Court, Appellate Division. On appeal, the court noted that the former employer had no interest to be protected in the chiropractic office because he had sold it prior to the employee's resignation and alleged breach of the restrictive covenant. Even though the former employer was still working out of the office and purportedly sharing in the profits, he was doing so as a consultant and not as an owner. Accordingly, he had no interest in the business which could be protected by the restrictive covenant. The court affirmed the dismissal of the complaint. *Pascal v. Beigel*, 609 N.Y.S.2d 72 (A.D.2d Dept.1994).

A longtime employee of an Illinois lumber company signed an employment agreement stating that the company would retain him as an employee in exchange for promises not to compete with the company for one year following employment termination, and to safeguard confidential business information. The agreement recited the company's right to terminate his employment at any time. The employee was elevated to executive vice president of a division of the company, but was later demoted to general manager of a plant. A competitor offered the employee a job as its vice president of operations. The employee then obtained the lumber company's customer lists and a comprehensive list of its suppliers. The following day, the lumber company and employee signed an agreement outlining termination conditions, including a salary allowance and other benefits. In return, the employee agreed not to disclose trade secrets. The document expressly incorporated the earlier employment agreement. Nonetheless, the employee accepted employment with the competitor, and the lumber company obtained a preliminary injunction against its former employee to enforce the restrictive covenants of the employment and termination agreements. The former employee appealed to the Court of Appeals of Indiana, First District.

The court determined that the employment agreements were supported by valid consideration and were therefore enforceable. The parties had exchanged promises, on the one hand not to divulge confidential information, and on the other hand to continue at-will employment. The information obtained shortly before employment termination included customer and supplier lists and pricing information that were considered trade secrets. Although restrictive covenants beyond the geographic area of employment are generally unenforceable, the trade secret covenant was enforceable regardless of geographic considerations. The trial court had correctly held that the employee had a duty to maintain secrecy concerning trade secrets and it had properly granted the lumber company's request for injunctive relief. *Ackerman v. Kimball International, Inc.*, 634 N.E.2d 778 (Ind.App.1st Dist.1994).

A certified public accountant was employed by a Missouri accounting firm. He developed a specialty in the area of not-for-profit corporations. After he made an attempt to leave the firm's service, the firm offered him the opportunity to become a director. He accepted the offer, but a few years later he resigned. In his letter of resignation, he had indicated the number of work hours left to finish up business with the firm's clients. Shortly after receiving the resignation letter, the firm had a directors meeting and discussed the resignation and the possibility that clients would leave the firm. While completing the work for the firm's clients, the accountant formed another accounting firm and advised former clients that he was leaving. He also sent notices to the other clients he had served indicating his willingness to do their accounting work. Many of these clients employed the new accounting firm. The former corporation sued the accountant for breach of fiduciary duty. The jury awarded actual and punitive damages to the firm and the accountant appealed to the Missouri Court of Appeals.

The firm argued that the accountant breached his fiduciary duty as a director by entering into a competing business before the date of his resignation. The court noted that the accountant indicated by a dated letter the number of hours he was going to need to finish up business with the firm's clients. The court ruled that the date of the letter was the date of his resignation, rather than the date the accountant actually left. The court noted that clients were absolutely privileged to pick their own professional accountants. Therefore, unless the firm had a binding contract with the clients, they could have chosen any accounting firm they wished. Further, the remaining directors had known that clients of the corporation might follow the accountant. There was no showing of misrepresentation or concealment by the accountant. Therefore, the appellate court reversed the decision of the trial court and awarded judgment for the accountant. *Dwyer, Costello and Knox v. Diak*, 846 S.W.2d 742 (Mo.App.1993).

An Arizona woman worked for a commercial property management firm for two years. Subsequently, she submitted her resignation and stated that she intended to start her own commercial property management firm. On the day that she submitted her resignation, the employee notified her commercial clients that she was resigning, and gave the effective date. She expressly stated that she was not soliciting their business for her new firm, but only thanked them for their kindness and support during their business relationship. Her employer sued and alleged, among other things, a breach of fiduciary duty. The trial court entered summary judgment for the former employee, and the employer appealed to the Arizona Court of Appeals. On appeal, the court stated that before the end of the employment relationship, an employee can properly purchase a rival business and upon termination of employment immediately compete. The employee is not, however, entitled to solicit customers before the end of her employment, nor can she do other similar acts in direct competition with the employer's business. The court found that no evidence existed to indicate that the employee acted improperly. An employee making preparations to compete after termination of her employment is permitted to advise current customers that she is leaving. The court, therefore, affirmed the trial court's granting of summary judgment. *McCallister Co. v. Kastella,* 825 P.2d 980 (Ariz.App.1992).

A corporation purchased a computer software product line from another corporation and then hired two of its employees. A third employee proceeded to establish a new business. The business started by the third employee received investments from the two employees who continued to work for the new owner. The third employee's new business provided professional consulting services to clients using the computer software product line produced by his old employer. Later, the other two employees left the corporation to join the new business. The corporation which owned the computer software product line filed a breach of contract claim against the two employees under their employment agreements and sued the third employee under the terms of his old contract with the previous owner of the software line. The superior court granted summary judgment in favor of the employees. The corporation appealed.

The Court of Appeals of Georgia concluded that when the new owner purchased the computer software line, the employment contract with the third employee was assigned to it. The new employer could enforce any violation of the nondisclosure and nonsolicitation clause. The appellate court held that the superior court erred in granting the third employee summary judgment because he breached the nondisclosure clause (which was effective for two years after employment) by disclosing information about the system. Additionally, the third employee violated the nonsolicitation clause by encouraging the two other employees to leave the corporation. The two other employees who signed new contracts with the corporation were not in violation of the nondisclosure clause. The lack of a time limit on the nondisclosure clause made the clause unenforceable. The nonsolicitation clause, on the other hand, was enforceable because of the two-year time limit. Therefore, the court erred in granting summary judgment in favor of the employees. *U.S. Corp. of America v. Parker*, 414 S.E.2d 513 (Ga.App.1991).

An Illinois fastener manufacturer entered into an employment agreement with one of its salesmen. The employment agreement had two sections. The first section stated that for a period of one year after his employment had terminated for any reason, the employee could not directly or indirectly solicit, accept orders, or interfere with any business of the employer. The second section stated that the employee had to protect all trade secrets and confidential information of the employer. The salesman voluntarily terminated his employment and the employer brought an action against the salesman for violation of the agreement. The trial court granted the salesman's motion for judgment on the pleadings, finding that the nonsolicitation clause in the agreement was overly broad because it contained no geographic limitations. The court further refused to sever that provision from the remainder of the agreement. The fastener manufacturer appealed to the Appellate Court of Illinois.

The appellate court noted that the reasonableness of a noncompetition agreement is measured by its hardship to the employee, its effect upon the general public, and the reasonableness of the time, territory, and activity restrictions. Thus, it was more difficult for an employer to justify prohibiting its former employees from accepting orders from the employer's clients than merely prohibiting its employees from soliciting such clients. The appellate court held that fact issues existed regarding the reasonableness of the nonsolicitation clause. Thus, the trial court had erred in granting summary judgment. The case was remanded to the trial court for a factual determination as to whether the noncompetition agreement was enforceable. Next, the court ruled that the parties intended the nonsolicitation and nondisclosure provisions to be severable, and the equities were in favor of enforcing those provisions in the agreement that were valid unless they were closely connected with unenforceable provisions. Accordingly, the appellate court reversed the grant of summary judgment and remanded for further proceedings in conformity with its decision. *Abbott-Interfast Corp. v. Harkabus*, 619 N.E.2d 1337 (Ill.App.1993).

A Georgia woman worked as a hair stylist in a barber shop. The employment agreement contained a covenant not to compete, which stated that she could not compete with the barber shop for a period of one year and within a radius of two miles from the barber shop upon her termination of employment. It stated that she was not to engage in any duty or responsibility that she had performed as a hair stylist for the barber shop. The barber shop brought a claim against the woman for violation of this covenant not to compete when her employment was terminated and she went to work for a competitor. A trial court found that the covenant not to compete was enforceable and held the woman in violation of the terms of the covenant. An injunction was issued, and the woman appealed to the Supreme Court of Georgia. On appeal, the court reversed the decision of the trial court. It held that the covenant not to compete was unreasonable because the hair stylist was prohibited from working in any capacity for a competitor. The covenant also failed to specify with any particularity the activities that the woman was prohibited from performing. The court found that the covenant imposed a greater limitation upon the woman than was necessary for the protection of the barber shop. *Fleury v. Afab, Inc.*, 423 S.E.2d 49 (Ga.App.1992).

A Virginia disc jockey was fired February 3, 1992. On that date, the radio station and the disc jockey entered into a written, noncompetition agreement. The agreement provided that $2,000 be paid to the disc jockey in return for his promise not to compete for a period of twelve months within 60 air miles of the broadcast station. On February 17, he obtained employment at another radio station within the 60-mile radius. He then returned the check. However, the radio station filed suit to enjoin him from working at the competing radio station. The disc jockey filed a cross complaint alleging that the agreement was void and unenforceable. The jury returned a verdict in favor of the disc jockey and the radio station appealed to the Supreme Court of Virginia.

The court ruled that the 60-mile, twelve-month limit was not unduly harsh and oppressive in diminishing the disc jockey's legitimate efforts to earn a living. Nor would the enforcement of the agreement be unreasonable from a public policy standpoint. Further, the radio station had invested substantial time and money in promoting the disc jockey as an on-air personality. The agreement was reasonable and was no greater than necessary to protect the legitimate business interests of the radio station. Accordingly, the court reversed the trial court's decision and remanded the case to the trial court: 1) to enter a judgment for the radio station enjoining the disc jockey from violating the noncompetition agreement for a period of twelve months and 2) directing the radio station to pay the disc jockey the $2,000. *New River Media Group, Inc. v. Knighton*, 429 S.E.2d 25 (Va.1993).

An Indiana promotional corporation raised funds for various police organizations nationwide. The president and owner hired an employee to solicit and market the corporation's services to various police organizations. The employment agreement contained a covenant not to compete which stated that for a period of one year after termination, the employee would not contact any client, customer or sponsor of the corporation. After a few years, the employee quit and formed his own company. He solicited over 15 customers of the corporation and entered into contracts with five. The corporation brought suit in a federal district court for breach of contract. The corporation moved for a preliminary injunction to enforce the covenant not to compete. The trial court granted the preliminary injunction and the employee appealed to the U.S. Court of Appeals, Seventh Circuit.

Courts will grant injunctive relief where the noncompete covenant is reasonably necessary for the protection of the employer's business, not unreasonably restrictive of the employee's rights, and not against public policy. The trial court had upheld the covenant not to compete but had modified it, only prohibiting the employee from communicating with current customers of the organization. The appellate court agreed and found that the covenant was necessary to protect the employer's business, as the business relied on customer relations. Since there were numerous other possible clients available this was not an unreasonable restriction on the employee's rights. Thus, the corporation sufficiently proved the inadequacy of any legal remedy and the irreparable harm involved. The appellate court affirmed the grant of a preliminary injunction to the corporation restricting the former employee from contacting current clients. *JAK Productions, Inc. v. Wiza*, 986 F.2d 1080 (7th Cir.1993).

A custom tailoring company hired a Texas man and had him sign two noncompete agreements which limited his activities in a related business in the same counties for at least two years after termination. Four years after being hired, the employee opened his own custom tailoring business in competition with his former employer. The employer brought suit, seeking a temporary injunction to prevent the employee from competing until a court could construe the noncompete clause. The trial court denied relief to the company, and it appealed to the Court of Appeals of Texas. The appellate court first noted that the company would have to show that without injunctive relief it would suffer an irreparable injury for which it had no adequate legal remedy. Here, the company could not do so. Next, the court noted that the methods and tools used by the employer were not unique. In fact, the employee had used some of his own developed techniques rather than those of his employer. Accordingly, the trial court's judgment was affirmed, and the request for a temporary injunction was denied. *Tom James Co. v. Mendrop*, 819 S.W.2d 251 (Tex.App.1991).

Two New York employees worked for a multi-media producing company as "project managers." They also served as liaisons with clients. Upon consolidation of the sales and production departments, the two managers were required to sign a restrictive employment covenant because of their increased interaction with the clients. The covenant restricted the employees from competing with the company for two years, even if they were fired. After the two employees were fired, they and another person formed a business to compete with their former employer. During the two years after termination, the former employees proceeded to interact with the former employer's clients. The company sought an injunction to stop the former employees from soliciting the clients. A lower court ruled in favor of the employer and denied the former employees' motion to dismiss. The former employees appealed. On appeal, the Supreme Court, Appellate Division, affirmed the lower court's judgment in favor of the employer. The court found both the content and the duration of the restrictive convenant to be reasonable. The covenant did not prohibit working with clients whom the employees had not previously serviced and did not confine them to a specific geographic area. *Contempo Communications, Inc. v. MJM Creative Services, Inc.*, 582 N.Y.S.2d 667 (A.D.1st Dept.1992).

A Texas woman worked as a travel agent and signed an "Employee Noncompetition Agreement." The agreement prohibited solicitation for services to the employer's customers for two years after her departure. Further, the woman was restricted from disclosing names of customers or other information. Additionally, the employee was an at-will employee who could be terminated without cause or notice. The woman left her employment and then became president of a competing travel agency. The former employer sought and was granted temporary injunctive relief prohibiting her solicitations pending trial for a breach of contract. The trial court held for the employee, finding the covenant was unenforceable. The appellate court reversed and the woman appealed.

The Supreme Court of Texas reversed the appellate court and reinstated the trial court's decision. The Supreme Court held that the enforceability of a covenant required the covenant to be ancillary to an enforceable agreement. The court found that an at-will employment relationship does not constitute an enforceable agreement because the relationship may be terminated at any time. Thus, the covenant could not be enforced. *Travel Masters, Inc. v. Star Tours, Inc.,* 827 S.W.2d 830 (Tex.1991).

A company engaged in the business of selling high quality hand-finished shopping bags employed four people to run its operation. Subsequently, the president informed the company's principal of his immediate resignation. He left the company to form a competing business, taking his fellow employees with him. The company then sued, alleging that the employees had secretly formed the competing business while they were still full-time employees of the company, thereby breaching their duty of loyalty to the company. A New York trial court granted a preliminary injunction to the plaintiff company, barring the former employees from soliciting or engaging in any business activity with the company's customers. They appealed to the New York Supreme Court, Appellate Division.

On appeal, the court noted that a preliminary injunction could not be granted unless there was a prospect of irreparable injury if the injunction was withheld. Here, the former employees had conceded that they diverted at least twelve orders to the competing business prior to their departure from the company. However, the company had failed to show that an award of money damages would not make it whole. The former employees, now that they had left the company's employment, were free to engage in a competing business and solicit customers of the former employer. There were no trade secrets or noncompete covenants at issue here. Accordingly, the court reversed the lower court's grant of a preliminary injunction. *Elpac Ltd. v. Keenpac North America Ltd.,* 588 N.Y.S.2d 667 (A.D.3d Dept.1992).

B. Trade Secrets

The Supreme Court of Georgia affirmed a trial court order permitting a former employee of a Georgia newspaper to use the employer's proposed name for a new publication. She obtained a trademark for the name devised by her former employer and began publishing her own newspaper under the name. The supreme court stated that the Georgia Trade Secrets Act did not protect information that was not a trade secret. In this case, the former employer had failed to obtain a trademark for the publication. Its written customer list was readily ascertainable by consulting the telephone directory and did not qualify for protection as a trade secret. *Leo Publications, Inc. v. Reid,* 458 S.E.2d 651 (Ga.1995).

A company which was engaged in the business of brokering transactions in a variety of money market instruments, like mortgage-backed securities and repurchase agreements, hired three employees who all signed a "Proprietary Rights and Non-Disclosure Agreement." The agreement covered confidential and proprietary information, including all data, customer lists and other information submitted to the employees. They agreed to maintain confidentiality and not to make any unauthorized use of the information. Subsequently, the three employees resigned and immediately began working for a competitor. The company then sought a temporary restraining order to preliminarily enjoin the individuals from using confidential information or trade secrets of the company in any way. Specifically, the company was concerned about the ex-employees' knowledge of approaching "off dates." The off date is the fixed future date at which time money "borrowed" by means of selling securities, is repaid by buying the securities back. At the time of the off date, a transaction can be continued (rolled over) or negotiated into a new deal. Thus, off dates are an important piece of knowledge because that is the time when deals are made.

Before a New York trial court, the defendant ex-employees had argued that the off date information did not meet the trade secret test because the off date was known to the buyer, the seller and the broker; the element of secrecy was lacking. The court, however, disagreed with this argument. Even though individual buyers, sellers and brokers knew the off dates for the transactions they had entered into, the extensive compilation of numerous off dates by the company could be considered protected confidential information. The court held that this amounted to a trade secret. Accordingly, it granted the company a preliminary injunction against its former employees. *Garvin Guybutler Corp. v. Cowen & Co.,* 588 N.Y.S.2d 56 (Sup.1992).

An Illinois salesman quit his job when he learned that his employer was advertising for a new salesman to take over his territory. He was employed at will, but had signed an employment agreement containing a covenant not to compete with the company for two years by refraining from contacting any person or company in the territory to sell a competitor's product. The agreement was not supported by any legal consideration such as money or guaranteed employment. The salesman accepted employment with a competitor and began to solicit current and former customers of his former employer. The company filed a lawsuit in the U.S. District Court for the Central District of Illinois for an order to enforce the covenant. The court denied the company's motion for a preliminary injunction, and the company appealed to the U.S. Court of Appeals, Seventh Circuit. The court found that the company had no trade secrets to protect because it had made no effort to keep its customer lists secret. Under Illinois law, the company had failed to protect its interests and was not entitled to a preliminary injunction. The court of appeals affirmed the district court's judgment. *Curtis 1000, Inc. v. Suess,* 24 F.3d 941 (7th Cir.1994).

Several employees of an industrial supply company, all holding managerial positions, began discussing leaving the company and forming their own industrial supply business. While still employed by the company, they took a number of steps toward forming their own business, including speaking with customers, vendors, and employees. They all resigned on the same date. The company then brought suit against them alleging that they had breached their fiduciary duties to the company and misappropriated confidential documents which it characterized as trade secrets. The trial court granted partial summary judgment in favor of the employees, and both parties appealed to the Supreme Court of Alabama.

On appeal, the court first noted that the employees had been hired at will. They did not sign employment contracts, nor did they sign noncompetition agreements. Accordingly, the employees had been under no duty to give their employer advanced notice of their resignations. There was, however, a question as to whether the employees had breached their fiduciary duty by soliciting employees, customers, and vendors of the company while still employed there. The court remanded on this question. The court then turned to the allegedly misappropriated customer and vendor lists. To constitute a trade secret, the employer would have to show that the lists were "the subject of efforts that were reasonable under the circumstances to maintain [their] secrecy." Here, the company failed to show that it had taken reasonable steps to insure that the lists remained a trade secret. The court affirmed in part and reversed in part the trial court's decision. *Allied Supply Co., Inc. v. Brown*, 585 So.2d 33 (Ala.1991).

A research scientist with a Ph.D. in physical biochemistry accepted employment with a corporation, signing an agreement with a noncompete covenant in which he agreed not to render services to a competitor for one year after the termination of employment. Subsequently, the scientist left the corporation and went to work for a competitor. The corporation sued for injunctive relief, seeking to stop the scientist from misappropriating trade secrets, and asking for enforcement of the one-year noncompete provision. A federal district court entered an order enjoining the scientist from disclosing the corporation's trade secrets for a period of one year. However, the court refused to enforce the noncompete clause. The corporation appealed to the U.S. Court of Appeals, Eighth Circuit.

On appeal, the court decided that the noncompete clause was unenforceable as a matter of Illinois law. In Illinois, restrictive covenants are enforceable only if reasonably necessary to protect legitimate business interests of employers. Since the goal of the noncompete clause in this case was the protection of trade secrets, and since the scientist was able to work for the competitor without disclosing the corporation's trade secrets, the noncompete clause was overbroad and unreasonable. Accordingly, the court affirmed the district court's order. *Baxter International, Inc. v. Morris*, 976 F.2d 1189 (8th Cir.1992).

A Virginia man began to operate a hair replacement business. He sold hair replacement units to customers, and his employees attached the units to the customers' hair. Two employees who sold hair replacement units terminated their employment without giving prior notice. They had never entered into a covenant not to compete. When they left, they did not take any supplies, equipment, or products with them; nor did they take any written customer lists or documents.

They then began to operate a competing business and solicited 100 of the former employer's customers by telephone, utilizing a list they had compiled solely from their memories. The former employer filed a bill of complaint against the employees alleging that they had tortiously interfered with his contracts with his customers. The trial court entered judgment in favor of the employer and the employees appealed to the Supreme Court of Virginia.

The employees argued that they were entitled to rely upon their memories to compile a list of former customers and solicit their business, and that these acts did not constitute "improper methods." The court determined that they did not employ improper methods by utilizing their memories to compile a list of the names of former customers and soliciting business from these customers. It is not unusual for an employee to leave his or her employment and start a competing business. When this occurs, inevitably customers of the former employer will desire to deal with the former employee in the new business. Therefore, the court determined that if the former employer wished to prevent the employees from soliciting his customers, he should have required them to execute a covenant not to compete. The court reversed the judgment of the trial court and remanded the case with instructions to enter judgment on behalf of the former employees. *Peace v. Conway*, 435 S.E.2d 133 (Va.1993).

A bovine embryo transfer company hired two men to perform nonsurgical ova or embryo transfers on superior cows. The animals were selected by ranchers who hired the company to genetically improve their stock. A couple of years after their employment began, the two men were asked to sign an employment contract which contained trade secret protection provisions and certain restrictions in the event either employee left the company. The employees signed the contract. However, neither employee was a veterinarian at the time, and the process of embryo transfer they used was considered by Montana law to be the practice of veterinary medicine. As such, they were in violation of a Montana misdemeanor statute. When the two employees subsequently left the company to form their own company, performing the same services, their former employer filed suit against them for breach of contract, among other claims. The trial court ruled for the company, and the two ex-employees appealed to the Supreme Court of Montana.

On appeal, the court found that the underlying and primary object of the employment contracts was to perform embryo transfers on livestock in Montana. Therefore, since neither employee was a veterinarian, and since their work was the illegal practice of veterinary medicine, the object of the contract was unlawful at the time the contract was entered into and performed. The supreme court held that the company could not use the courts to enforce the illegal contract. It thus reversed the trial court's decision and ruled in favor of the two ex-employees. *Portable Embryonics v. J.P. Genetics, Inc.*, 810 P.2d 1197 (Mont.1991).

An Alabama technician worked for an automatic door company, providing service, installation and some public relations. The company required him to sign an employment contract restricting disclosure of any trade secrets learned during employment for one year after termination. Moreover, the contract prohibited the technician from soliciting, diverting, or taking away any of the company's customers from a specific list of states. Upon the technician's resignation, he became employed by a competing automatic door company. The technician's former employer sought an injunction to prohibit the solicitation of its customers. At the first hearing, the trial court denied a preliminary injunction. The second hearing resulted in a permanent injunction restricting the technician from soliciting. He appealed.

On appeal, the Supreme Court of Alabama reversed the lower court's decision because it might have been erroneously based on misuse of confidential information, which the former employer could not show. The court held, however, that the solicitation provision was enforceable because it was limited to a specific area and customers. The court awarded damages, noting that the former employer was entitled to nominal damages for the mere breach. However, the court held that the former employer must prove actual monetary losses to receive compensatory damages. The court remanded the case so that the trial court could calculate the measure of damages according to the amount the company lost. *Corson v. Universal Door Systems, Inc.,* 596 So.2d 565 (Ala.1991).

IV. SALARY AND BENEFIT DISPUTES

The following cases deal with lawsuits which have arisen out of wage or benefit disputes. For other similar cases, see Chapter Four which deals with employee benefits.

A manufacturing company hired a sales representative under an oral agreement calling for commissions on all sales in the representative's territory based on a percentage of gross profits. The company failed to forward sales reports to the representative, and he discovered that company products had been sold in his territory through a freight handler. When he requested a commission for the sales, the company refused payment and he resigned. The representative filed a lawsuit against his former employer in an Alabama trial court for breach of contract and fraud. The court conducted a jury trial resulting in a general damage award of $31,000, plus punitive damages of $160,000, the estimated profit made by the company from the disputed sales. The manufacturer appealed to the Supreme Court of Alabama, which noted that the trial court's decision was based upon sufficient evidence that the manufacturer had no intention of honoring the oral promise to pay the representative commissions on all products shipped to his area. The supreme court affirmed the trial court's judgment. *Sealing Equipment Products Co., Inc. v. Velarde,* 644 So.2d 904 (Ala.1994).

A Montana corporation hired a manager under an agreement to pay him 20 percent of net corporate profits, subject to a minimum of $5,000 monthly. The manager soon expressed discomfort with the corporation's practices and stated his willingness to quit working rather than comply with them. Instead, the corporation fired him near the end of his third month of employment. It paid the manager $15,000 for the three months, even though profits warranted payment of a higher amount. The former manager demanded additional wages and a penalty under a Montana wage statute in a lawsuit filed in a Montana district court. The court dismissed the matter for lack of jurisdiction, and the former manager appealed to the Supreme Court of Montana. On appeal, the court rejected the corporation's argument that the state department of labor's administrative procedure was the only remedy available for unpaid wage claims. A Montana statute conferred jurisdiction on state trial courts, in addition to creating an administrative regime for employees who could not afford an attorney. The supreme court reversed and remanded the matter for further proceedings. *Stanley v. Holms*, 883 P.2d 837 (Mont.1994).

A discharged Georgia restaurant employee filed a lawsuit against his former employer in a state trial court, seeking payment of unpaid annual bonuses. The former employer filed an unsuccessful motion for a directed verdict based on its argument that the claim was unenforceable. A jury awarded damages to the employee, and the Georgia Court of Appeals affirmed, holding that the promise to pay the bonuses was enforceable because it had been made at the beginning of the employment term. The employer appealed to the Supreme Court of Georgia, which observed that in order to be enforceable, a claim of future compensation must not only be made at the beginning of the employment, it must be for an exact amount or based upon a formula or method of determining the exact amount of the bonus. A promise to pay a certain percentage of a company's net earnings was sufficiently definite to be enforceable, but a promise to pay an amount within a certain range was not enforceable. In this case, the bonuses were to be based in part on a formula but there was evidence that the company president retained discretion to set the amount. A bonus that was only partially tied to a definite formula was insufficient to be objectively ascertainable and was unenforceable at law. Because the parties had never agreed upon a sufficiently definite form of computing the bonus, the lower courts had erroneously ruled for the former employee, and the supreme court reversed their judgments. *Arby's, Inc. v. Cooper*, 454 S.E.2d 488 (Ga.1995).

In another Georgia case, a discharged employee sued her former employer, alleging that its chief operating officer fraudulently induced her to accept an offer of employment, and denied her $40,000 in promised bonuses, by waiting several days after her departure before declaring bonuses. The trial court held for the employer, and the former employee appealed to the Georgia Court of Appeals. The court considered a letter from the chief operating officer to the former employee written at the time she accepted employment that promised a bonus of not less than $20,000 during her first year of employment. The former employee argued that the statement created a vested right to a bonus in her second year of employment. The court of appeals found evidence that the promise to pay a bonus in the second year was merely implied and that the chief operating officer had not told her how any bonus would be computed. Accordingly, the trial court had properly entered summary judgment for the former employer as there had been no false representation. *Bandy v. Mills*, 454 S.E.2d 610 (Ga.App.1995).

A Maryland statute requires employers to pay their employees at regular intervals. A separate section applicable in cases of employment termination requires an employer to pay all amounts to a separated employee on or before the day on which the employee would have been paid had the employment continued. A medical technician signed a one-year contract with a hospital service provider, but was fired after only one month of employment. She received two weeks' severance pay, but nonetheless prosecuted her former employer for breach of contract. A state trial court awarded damages in the form of unpaid wages for the rest of the one-year employment term, but granted the employer a judgment notwithstanding the verdict as to the claim that the employer had violated the statute. The employee appealed to the Court of Appeals of Maryland. The court recited the common law prohibition against a damage award for "constructive services," a doctrine under which a separated employee asserts a claim for wages simply by remaining available to perform work under a terminated contract. The provisions of the wage act were not to be construed as replacing the common law. The court affirmed the trial court decision awarding a single year's unpaid wages and affirmed its judgment notwithstanding the verdict prohibiting an additional award under the wage act. *Battaglia v. Clinical Perfusionists, Inc.*, 338 Md. 352, 658 A.2d 680 (1995).

The president of a Connecticut real estate corporation promised a full commission to the first person on his staff to locate a new office for the company. After the president left the company, three salespersons claimed to have located the same corporate office and sought shares of the $24,000 commission. The corporation paid only $2,400 of the claimed commissions, reserving the balance for legal fees resulting from problems with the property. Two salespersons filed complaints with the state commissioner of labor, seeking payment of the commissions. The commissioner filed a successful complaint on behalf of the salespersons in a Connecticut trial court, and the corporation appealed to the Supreme Court of Connecticut. The corporation argued on appeal that the salespersons were independent contractors rather than employees, and that they were thus not covered by the state wage act. The court observed that the fundamental distinction between employees and independent contractors was the right or the absence of right to control the means and methods of work. The real estate corporation exerted great control over its sales staff, including the right to fire salespersons. This level of control was sufficient for the trial court to have found that the salespersons were covered under the act. Accordingly, the supreme court affirmed the trial court's judgment for the salespersons. *Tianti v. William Raveis Real Estate, Inc.*, 231 Conn. 690, 651 A.2d 1286 (1995).

A New York company hired a senior vice president under terms that included an annual salary, a signing bonus and an annual incentive bonus package totaling $200,000. The vice president expected to report directly to the president of the corporation's professional products group. However, on the first day of her employment, she was advised that the professional products group had been merged into another division and that the vice president's position had been eliminated. She was assigned to a position in the new division which did not report to the president. The vice president immediately resigned and filed a lawsuit against the corporation in a New York trial court, claiming violation of the state Labor Law's wage payment provisions. She claimed payment for one day of work, plus bonuses totaling $45,000, a severance package of $150,000 and termination benefits of $100,000, in addition to her attorney's fees and an added amount for wilful violation of the statute. The New York Supreme Court, Appellate Division, dismissed the complaint, ruling that the trial court had improperly denied the employer's dismissal motion for failure to state a cause of action. Although the vice president retained her right to sue the former employer for breach of contract, her claim did not involve the failure to pay wages and she could not bring a complaint under the wage provisions of the state labor law. *Parker v. Revlon, Inc.*, 621 N.Y.S.2d 306 (A.D.1st Dept.1995).

A South Carolina radio advertising salesman was employed under a contract that called for the payment of sales commissions for separating employees only when the advertisements were actually broadcast. When his employment was terminated, the employer refused to pay commissions on seven contracts under which no advertisements had been broadcast. A South Carolina trial court directed a verdict in favor of the employer for three contracts, but allowed a jury to consider the remaining contract claims, which related to the employee's work for a division of the employer. This resulted in an award of damages for the employee plus attorney's fees. Both parties appealed to the Supreme Court of South Carolina. On appeal, the employee argued that he was entitled to treble damages under the state wage act. The employer argued that it was entitled to a directed verdict on all of the contracts in dispute and that it could not be liable for treble damages in a good faith wage dispute. The court held that treble damages are not payable where a good faith wage dispute exists between the employer and employee. The trial court had properly withheld an award of treble damages and allowed the question of the four contracts to appear before the jury. It had also made an appropriate partial award of attorney's fees. The supreme court affirmed the trial court's judgment. *Rice v. Multimedia, Inc.*, 456 S.E.2d 381 (S.C.1995).

A California department store imposed a wage deduction on its sales personnel that represented a prorated share of commissions on returned items for which the salesperson could not be identified. The store justified the policy as a response to employee abuse for failing to follow procedures that would allow the identification of the affected salesperson. A sales employee filed a lawsuit against the store in state court, claiming that it had violated a California law prohibiting employers from recapturing wages already paid by an employer to an employee. The San Francisco County Superior Court granted summary judgment to the store and the employee appealed to the California Court of Appeal, First District.

The court of appeal observed that California had a strong public policy against deductions from employee wages for cash shortages, breakages, and other business losses resulting from simple negligence by employees. Employers were not allowed to make their employees insurers against business losses. The store's policy penalized conscientious employees who accurately reported their returns by charging a portion of the returns of dishonest employees against their wages. The store had other options to prevent employee fraud that did not violate California law. The court reversed and remanded the trial court decision. *Hudgins v. Neiman Marcus Group, Inc.*, 41 Cal.Rptr.2d 46 (Cal.App.1st Dist.1995).

A Louisiana farmer instructed an employee that he would withhold the replacement cost of damaged equipment from his wages if the employee continued to be careless in maintaining equipment. The farmer later deducted $61.25 from the employee's pay for damaging cultivator parts when the employee ran a tractor over an area known to contain tree stumps. The employee quit immediately and filed a lawsuit against the farmer in a Louisiana trial court for the wage withholding and a statutory penalty, plus attorney's fees. The court ruled for the farmer and the employee appealed to the Court of Appeal of Louisiana, Second Circuit. The court of appeal stated that in order to recover under the Louisiana Wage Statute, the employer must have acted arbitrarily, unreasonably or in bad faith. When a legitimate dispute exists concerning the amount owed an employee upon employment termination, courts should avoid the award of penalties. In this case, the employee admitted that he knew there were tree stumps in the area over which he had attempted to drive the tractor. He also admitted that he had been warned that he would be liable for future damage caused by his carelessness. The wage withholding did not violate the statute and the trial court decision was affirmed. *Cupp v. Banks*, 637 So.2d 678 (La.App.2d Cir.1994).

An Oregon general contractor obtained contracts to perform five public works projects. It subcontracted with an excavating company that failed to pay its employees the prevailing wage in the area for the type of work being performed. Several employees of the subcontractor filed a lawsuit in an Oregon trial court against the general contractor, seeking to recover the difference between their actual wages and the prevailing wage under an Oregon statute that was modeled after the federal Davis-Bacon Act, 40 U.S.C. § 276a *et seq.* Both acts require workers on government projects to be paid a minimum wage equivalent to the prevailing wage for similar work in the area. The court awarded the general contractor summary judgment, and this result was affirmed by the Oregon Court of Appeals. The workers appealed to the Supreme Court of Oregon.

On appeal, the workers argued that the state law created a private right of action for them to collect unpaid wages from the general contractor. They also claimed that they were entitled to collect unpaid wages from the general contractor as the intended third-party beneficiaries of existing contracts between the public agencies and the general contractor. The supreme court rejected both theories. The statute only authorized the state commissioner of labor and industries to bring a civil action to compel a public agency to withhold from a contractor the equivalent of double the wages in dispute if the contractor refuses to pay the prevailing wage. The subcontractor's employees were under contract only with the subcontractor and could not be third-party beneficiaries of a contract with the general contractor.

There was no private right of action under the statute and the court affirmed the lower court decisions. *Stockton v. Silco Construction Co.*, 319 Or. 365, 877 P.2d 71 (1994).

A Louisiana company paid its sales staff strictly by commissions after an initial period of salary plus expenses. When a sales employee left the company, it refused to pay his commissions for orders that were placed but not delivered. The employee sued the company in a Louisiana trial court, which held that there was no contractual agreement between the parties concerning commissions in the event of employment termination. The employee appealed to the Court of Appeal of Louisiana, Third Circuit. The court of appeal determined that despite the absence of a definite contract, the employee might still recover commissions under the equitable doctrine of unjust enrichment. The court of appeal determined that the employer had been enriched by its retention of commissions earned by the employee, and conversely, that the employee had been impoverished without justification. Because the employee had no alternate remedy at law, he was entitled to $18,000 in unpaid commissions under the theory of unjust enrichment. The court reversed and remanded the trial court's decision. *Fogleman v. Cajun Bag & Supply Co.*, 638 So.2d 706 (La.App.3d Cir.1994).

A Wisconsin convenience store manager was paid a fixed salary and also received a commission based on a percentage of store sales. The company's policy was to hold store managers responsible for cash and merchandise shortages, returned checks, bad credit card charges and damaged or unreturned videos. During a period of five years, the manager claimed that he lost over $26,000 due to the company policy. He sued the company in a Wisconsin trial court seeking twice the amount of the deductions under a state wage statute. The court determined that the store manager's commissions were not wages and dismissed the lawsuit. The Wisconsin Court of Appeals affirmed the trial court decision, and the manager appealed to the Supreme Court of Wisconsin. The supreme court determined that the statute's definition of wages encompassed many types of compensation. The statute did not operate as a minimum wage law or fairness guarantee as the court of appeals had ruled. The statute was intended to protect employees from arbitrary salary reductions attributable to performance. The court ruled that commissions were included in the statutory definition of wages. The supreme court reversed and remanded the case. *Erdman v. Jovoco, Inc.*, 512 N.W.2d 487 (Wis.1994).

A Michigan man worked for a company as a service technician at $8.00 an hour. He was subsequently transferred to another division of the company, and was apparently notified in writing that his wage would be increased to almost $13.00 an hour. Upon his transfer, he received a raise of only $.75 an hour. He then brought an action against his employer, alleging that it had breached its agreement to pay him a particular hourly wage upon his transfer. The trial court granted summary disposition for the employer after finding that it lacked jurisdiction because the employee had failed to exhaust his administrative remedies as provided in the Michigan Wages and Fringe Benefits Act. The employee appealed to the Court of Appeals of Michigan.

On appeal, he asserted that the language of the act was permissive, and that it did not provide the exclusive remedy for employees with wage complaints. The act states: "An employee who believes that his or her employer has violated this act may file a written complaint with the department within twelve months after the violation." The appellate court determined that the statutory remedy was merely cumulative. Since the employee was seeking an enforcement of a contract, and had an action at common law against his employer, the statutory remedy was cumulative and not exclusive. The court thus reversed the trial court's decision and remanded the case. *Murphy v. Sears, Roebuck & Co.,* 476 N.W.2d 639 (Mich.App.1991).

In 1981, Congress enacted the Economic Recovery Tax Act under which certain individuals employed overseas were not required to pay federal income tax on all or part of their wages. A company which employed an engineer outside the United States enacted a tax equalization plan which provided for a cut in salary to these employees in the amount they would be taxed—as a way of equalizing compensation among all its workers. Several years later, the company notified the engineer that it had overpaid him erroneously and that he was required to refund it over $34,000. The engineer refused to do so, and the company sued for breach of contract, among other claims. The New York Supreme Court granted summary judgment to the company, and the engineer appealed to the Appellate Division.

The court ruled that the engineer had to repay the overpaid compensation because he knew of the plan's implementation and further knew that it was a condition of his employment. His at-will employment was modified by the terms of the plan; thus, the company could enforce those terms against the engineer. Further, the refund owed to the company was not a deduction from wages or an assignment of income, both of which require written authorization. Accordingly, the lack of a writing was not fatal to the company's demand for a refund. *General Electric Technical Services Co. v. Clinton,* 577 N.Y.S.2d 719 (A.D.3d Dept.1991).

A Minnesota hospital provided free parking to its registered nurses represented by the Minnesota Nurses Association. This policy was in effect from the hospital's inception in 1965 until 1989, when the hospital constructed a new parking garage to accommodate an expansion in its facilities. The hospital decided to charge its employees twelve cents per hour for parking to recoup some of the expenses of the construction. However, the association objected to the proposal and after discussions failed, it filed a grievance. The dispute was submitted to an arbitrator, who concluded that free parking was not a benefit protected by the collective bargaining agreement, but that it nevertheless could not be unilaterally terminated outside the context of collective bargaining negotiations. A federal district court upheld the arbitrator's decision, and the hospital appealed to the U.S. Court of Appeals, Eighth Circuit.

On appeal, the hospital contended that since free parking was not listed in the agreement, it could unilaterally revoke the benefit. The association contended that article 32 of the agreement applied. The article stated that nurses who enjoyed greater benefits than the minimums set forth in the agreement would not have those benefits reduced as long as they remained in the hospital's employ. The appellate court noted that the arbitrator had found the language of the agreement unclear, and looked beyond the agreement to past practices to determine the essence of the agreement. Since the court found his determination to be reasonable, it affirmed the district court's decision upholding the arbitrator's determination. *Fairview Southdale Hospital v. Minnesota Nurses Ass'n*, 943 F.2d 809 (8th Cir.1991).

A Massachusetts businessman began employment with a major corporation as a vice president in charge of sales and marketing. He entered an employment agreement to purchase stock. The stock provision stated the executive would have to resell his stock on leaving employment pursuant to the terms of the Management Ownership Agreement (MOA) making the repurchase of stock conditional on a legally available surplus of funds. The employment agreement also included a provision for a minimum purchase price if the resale took place as a result of the employee's death or the employee made a written request on or before July 1, 1991. Before the executive's employment ended, the chairman and a major stockholder of the corporation sought the executive's retirement. He sued for breach of the employment contract, and also charged that the company wrongfully refused to repurchase his stock. The trial court judge found a breach of contract and ordered the employer to pay salary and benefits, but refused to order the corporation to repurchase the stock. The judge reasoned that the executive failed to make a written request before the specified time. Further, the MOA provision restricted the repurchase of stock to only when a surplus was available. The executive appealed the decision on repurchasing the stock.

On appeal to the Appeals Court of Massachusetts, the court stated that the minimum purchase price was an exception to the general requirement that any stock be sold pursuant to the terms of the MOA. In essence, the executive's failure to make a request in writing by the specified date was excused because the obligation arose from the breach of contract. Thus, the corporation was required to repurchase the stock. *Nedder v. Knapp Shoes, Inc.*, 590 N.E.2d 713 (Mass.App.1992).

A doctor worked for a Miami medical center under a one-year employment contract. The contract provided for a salary plus bonus (based on performance) and stated that it would be automatically renewed unless either party gave notice of termination by June 1989, two months before the contract expired. Neither party gave notice of termination. An effort to renegotiate the terms of the employment contract failed, and the doctor resigned five days after the start of the second year. The medical center then sued for breach of the employment contract, seeking to recover the $28,000 bonus it had paid the doctor. It alleged that it would not have paid the bonus if the doctor had given notice of termination. A state trial court ruled for the medical center and the doctor appealed.

On appeal to the Florida District Court of Appeal, the trial court's decision was reversed. The medical center was not entitled to a return of the bonus earned for the first year's work. Since the employee had worked the full year, and since the bonus was attributable to the first year of the contract, the employee did not have to give the bonus back. The breach here occurred in the second year when the doctor failed to give notice prior to the resignation. The case was remanded so that the trial court could enter judgment in favor of the doctor. *Diaz v. Dr. Bertram P. Shapiro, P.A.*, 605 So.2d 966 (Fla.App.3d Dist.1992).

V. THE FAMILY AND MEDICAL LEAVE ACT OF 1993

The Family and Medical Leave Act of 1993, 29 U.S.C. §§ 2601-2654, grants eligible employees the statutory right to take up to twelve weeks of unpaid leave per year under specified circumstances related to family health care and childbirth. Eligible employees are expressly authorized by the act to take leave upon the birth of a child by the employee or the employee's spouse, or by the placement of a child for adoption or foster care with the employee. The act also applies when the employee is needed to care for a child, spouse or parent who has a serious health condition, and when the employee is unable to perform employment duties because of a serious health condition.

For an employee to be eligible for coverage under the act, the employee must have worked for the employer for at least twelve months and must have worked at least 1,250 hours during the twelve-month period preceding the leave. Spouses who are employed by the same employer are limited to a total of twelve weeks of leave for childbirth, adoption, or the care of a sick parent. The act establishes special rules governing the availability of employee leaves for local educational agency employees who are principally employed as instructors. The special rules apply to the scheduling of intermittent leave based upon planned medical treatment and leaves beginning or ending during the five-week period prior to the end of an academic period. Employees who receive paid leave from their employers may elect to (and certain employers may require their employees to) substitute accrued paid leave for the twelve-week statutory minimum.

Employees are obligated under the act to provide their employers with reasonable prior notice when leave is foreseeable. They must also prove that they have a serious health condition within the meaning of the act by documenting the condition with sufficient certification from a health care provider. Employers are expressly entitled to obtain a second opinion on the employee or employee family member's health condition when the validity of the certification is in doubt. Small employers are exempt from coverage under the act, as its coverage is limited to private employers with 50 or more employees for each working day during 20 or more calendar weeks in a current or preceding calendar year. Employers who employ less than 50 people within a 75-mile radius of the worksite are also not within the coverage of the act. Employers may also require eligible employees to periodically report their status and intentions during leave periods.

The taking of a family or medical leave by an eligible employee shall not result in the loss of any employment benefit accrued prior to the commencement date of the leave, but the act does not entitle employees to accrue seniority rights or employment benefits during leave periods. Although eligible employees who take leaves for purposes described in the act are entitled to be reinstated to equivalent positions upon their return from leave, restored employees are not entitled to rights, benefits or positions other than those to which they would have been entitled had they not taken leave. It is unlawful for employers to restrain employees from exercising their rights under the act. The rights established under the act are enforceable in civil actions for damages in the amount of lost wages, employment benefits, interest and attorney's fees and costs.

The U.S. Department of Labor Wage and Hour Division has published final regulations for the FMLA, 29 U.S.C. § 2601, et seq. The regulations interpret the act and provide guidance to employers for compliance, including many definitional sections. They also explain that the FMLA is intended to benefit employers by encouraging high performance and stability while reassuring employees that they do not have to choose between continued employment and family obligations. The regulations define "serious health condition" and "medical necessity," among other important FMLA terms. They clarify how much leave an employee may take and specify that FMLA leave may be taken intermittently or on a reduced leave schedule in certain circumstances. The regulations state that an employee needing intermittent leave may be placed in an "alternative position" to accommodate the leave. Such a transfer must comply with any applicable collective bargaining agreement, such federal statutes as the Americans with Disabilities Act, and state laws.

The regulations include a section on the effect of employee rights under the FMLA where other laws, employment practices and collective bargaining agreements apply. Generally, employers must observe any employment benefit program or plan that provides greater family or medical leave rights than those conferred by the FMLA. The regulations specify that no such employment benefit program, plan or agreement may reduce FMLA rights. The FMLA does not affect federal and state antidiscrimination laws including Title VII of the Civil Rights Act of 1964, the Pregnancy Discrimination Act or the ADA. Nothing in the FMLA supersedes state and local laws that provide greater protection or family leave than that guaranteed by the FMLA. 29 CFR Part 825. 60 Fed.Reg. 2180.

The FMLA, 29 U.S.C. § 2601 et seq., permits eligible employees to take a total of twelve weeks of leave during a twelve-month period for specified circumstances including "a serious health condition" of the employee or immediate family member. A Pennsylvania employee missed four days of work due to her child's ear infection and fever. Upon her return to work, the employer fired the employee for excessive absenteeism. She filed a lawsuit against the employer, claiming that the action violated the FMLA. The court considered the parties' cross motions for summary judgment. It held that the act pertained only to serious health conditions existing at the time of the employee's absence, not to minor conditions that were only potentially serious. The child's ear infection was a minor illness that did not require the continuing supervision of a physician nor require the employee to miss more than three days of work. Accordingly, the parent's argument that the ear infection had potentially serious consequences was unavailing. Under FMLA regulations, there was no serious health condition requiring the employee to be absent from work for the minimum specified period. The parent's motion for summary judgment was denied, and the employer's motion for summary judgment was granted. *Seidle v. Provident Mut. Life Ins. Co.*, 871 F.Supp. 238 (E.D.Pa.1994).

VI. OTHER EMPLOYMENT PRACTICES CASES

The manager of a Louisiana store placed a hidden microphone in the employee break room to hear employee conversations. Employees complained that the manager did so to eavesdrop on their personal conversations and that he also routinely monitored personal telephone calls. The manager stated that he was attempting to deter and warn an employee suspected of stealing. The manager's supervisor disciplined him for unprofessional conduct and for failing to obtain approval of the surveillance plan. The employees filed a lawsuit against the manager and store in a Louisiana trial court, claiming violations of state and federal privacy acts. The court granted summary judgment to the store. The employees appealed to the Louisiana Court of Appeal, Third Circuit.

On appeal, the employees argued that the Louisiana Electronic Surveillance Act and the federal statute upon which it was based protected against invasions of privacy by authorizing civil damage awards against the recipients of communications that have been intercepted, disclosed or used in violation of law. The store argued that it could not be held vicariously liable for the manager's unlawful surveillance activities without proof of the store's criminal wilfulness to violate state or federal law. The court of appeal stated that the trial court should not have granted pretrial summary judgment on the question of employer liability. Because fact issues existed concerning liability for the interception of the private communications, the court reversed and remanded the case. *Benoit v. Roche*, 657 So.2d 574 (La.App.3d Cir.1995).

A New York shipping company relied upon subsidies from the U.S. Maritime Administration to meet its day-to-day expenses including wages and withholding taxes. The subsidies supported American merchant vessels by equalizing some of their operating costs with foreign competitors. In this case, the subsidies amounted to more than $800,000 for the completion of each round trip voyage. As the company's financial condition declined, the maritime administration extended over $8.7 million in working capital loans to the company and guaranteed other bank loans. During the first quarter of 1986, despite receiving over $14 million in customer payments and $3.3 million in government subsidies, the company was unable to pay over $559,000 in withholding taxes. The following month, the maritime administration was called upon to satisfy its loan guarantees. The administration imposed a cash plan on the company, then withheld subsidy payments. Within four months, an involuntary petition of bankruptcy was filed and two of the company's officers lost control of company management. The IRS filed a claim against the officers for unpaid taxes of over $1.7 million, including the unpaid withholding taxes.

The former officers filed a claim for a refund of small amounts of tax they had paid, and the U.S. counterclaimed for penalties in the U.S. District Court for the Southern District of New York. The officers argued that their failure to pay withholding taxes was not wilful because the maritime administration's actions were unexpected. The court stated that the IRS Code makes corporate officers liable for failing to forward withholding taxes. Payment of other obligations during a relevant time period indicates wilfulness. In this case, the company had paid approximately $10 million to creditors other than the IRS during the relevant time period. The withholding of subsidies had not occurred until over one month after the taxes were due. The failure to pay withholding taxes was wilful, and the court granted the U.S.'s motion for summary judgment. *Skouras v. U.S.*, 854 F.Supp. 962 (S.D.N.Y.1993). The former officers appealed to the U.S. Court of Appeals, Second Circuit, which affirmed the district court's decision. The U.S. was entitled to the penalties assessed against the former officers. 26 F.3d 13 (2d Cir.1994).

In a similar case, a former officer of an Illinois limousine manufacturer was unable to pay withholding taxes after paying his employees and incurring a setoff of funds by a bank. The company agreed to sell its assets to a corporation which agreed to assume the unpaid withholding taxes. When the IRS and the purchasing corporation could not agree on the withholding taxes, the transaction fell through and the officer sued for a refund of a small portion of the assessed penalty he had paid. The U.S. counterclaimed for unpaid withholding taxes of $117,000. The U.S. District Court for the Northern District of Illinois stated that the liability for withholding taxes attaches upon the day they are withheld from wages and not upon the date of filing for a return. An employer's wilfulness in failing to pay withholding tax is determined at the moment withheld funds are paid to creditors other than the U.S. This is because employers act as government trustees of withholding taxes prior to paying them. Accordingly, the agreement between buyer and seller was irrevelant to the issue of liability. The U.S. was entitled to the withholding taxes. *Anderson v. U.S.*, 855 F.Supp. 236 (N.D.Ill.1994).

A former employee of a New York container corporation died of a rare form of leukemia. When another employee of the corporation was diagnosed with the same disease, he filed a workers' compensation claim. The corporation sought the deceased employee's medical records to defend itself in the workers' compensation claim. The deceased employee's widow refused to consent to release of the records, but the company and its insurer obtained them through the use of medical expense claim reimbursement forms submitted during the employee's treatment period. It then used the records in defense of the workers' compensation claim. The deceased employee's widow filed a lawsuit against the corporation and its insurer in a New York trial court, claiming fraud, conversion of the records, invasion of privacy and other complaints. The court granted summary judgment to the defendants, and the widow appealed to the New York Supreme Court, Appellate Division. The appellate division court stated that the medical records were the property of the doctors, and that the widow had no possessory interest in them. She had also failed to make out a proper claim for fraud because the corporation never advised her that it was ceasing its effort to obtain the records. There was also no invasion of privacy claim available to the widow, as the applicable New York statute merely prohibited the use of a person's name or picture for advertising or trade purposes. The court affirmed the trial court's judgment. *Waldron v. Ball Corp.*, 619 N.Y.S.2d 841 (A.D.3d Dept.1994).

A Maryland employer authorized an employee to make bank deposits of checks payable to its accounts receivable. One of the company owners instructed the employee to endorse checks with a stamp bearing the company name and to also stamp each check "for deposit only." The owner then discovered that the employee had failed to stamp checks with the "for deposit only" stamp and that she had deposited some checks into her own account. The employer fired her and sought recourse against the bank for negligent payment of the wrongfully deposited checks. A Maryland trial court determined that the lack of a "for deposit only" stamp did not make the endorsements forgeries. The court held that the bank was not liable for the items, and the employer appealed to the Maryland Court of Special Appeals. The court of special appeals reversed and remanded the trial court decision, finding the bank liable for conversion by paying the checks. The bank appealed to the Court of Appeals of Maryland.

The court distinguished the matter of the employee's lack of authority to deposit checks into her own personal account from her improper endorsement of the checks. The later misappropriation of funds did not convert authorized endorsements into forgeries for which the bank might be liable. In reaching this conclusion, the court followed the decisions of courts in New York, Colorado and Pennsylvania, and rejected the contrary reasoning of Kansas and Louisiana courts. The unauthorized omission of the "for deposit only" stamp by the employee only made her endorsements unauthorized, and did not render them forgeries. The court vacated the appellate court decision and remanded the case to the trial court. *Citizens Bank of Maryland v. Maryland Industrial Finishing Co., Inc.*, 338 Md. 448, 659 A.2d 313 (1995).

The husband of a Florida insurance company employee went to her office with a concealed baseball bat. He approached a coworker of his wife and questioned him about an alleged extramarital affair. After 45 minutes, the coworker persuaded the husband to leave peacefully. The wife then told her employer that her husband owned a gun and had injured another person in a prior incident. The insurance company sought a temporary injunction from a Florida trial court to restrain the husband from coming onto its property. The court denied the requested order, holding that it had no jurisdiction to issue an injunction against the commission of a crime. The company appealed to the District Court of Appeal of Florida, Fifth District. The court of appeal observed that the insurance company had been forced to hire security guards and was under the threat of interruption of its normal business. Because a number of employees were in imminent danger of harm, the trial court had jurisdiction to issue injunctive relief. The company had demonstrated a probability of irreparable injury. The court vacated the trial court's decision and remanded it for reconsideration. *Travelers Ins. Co. v. Conley*, 637 So.2d 373 (Fla.App.5th Dist.1994).

The Vietnam Era Veterans' Readjustment Assistance Act, 38 U.S.C. §§ 2021, 2024, guarantees the right of military reservists to return to their jobs with their rights of seniority, status, pay and other benefits as if they had not been absent due to reserve obligations. It also prohibits denials of hiring, retention and promotion because of reserve obligations. A commercial airline employed an Air National Guard reservist as a flight engineer. He violated the airline's employment scheduling policy by indicating his availability to work on days that conflicted with his reserve obligations. Because of failure to notify the airline in advance of his National Guard commitments, replacement crewmembers had to be located at the last minute. The airline fired the engineer, but he was rehired several months later under an agreement by which he received no backpay and his employment file indicated only a leave of absence without pay. The engineer was upgraded to co-pilot, but did not complete the final requirement for training by flying as an observer for a day. Instead, he called the airline to ask for a day off on the day he was scheduled to observe. After his request was denied, he called in sick. The airline fired the employee after determining that he had abused its sick leave policy. The engineer challenged the discharge as discrimination based on his military reserve status. The Illinois Department of Employment Security affirmed the termination, as did the U.S. District Court for the Northern District of Illinois. The employee appealed to the U.S. Court of Appeals, Seventh Circuit. The court found sufficient evidence in the record to justify all the employer's actions. The employee's first termination matter had been settled and could not be considered by the court now. The airline's reason for finally terminating the employee's employment was nondiscriminatory and did not violate the readjustment assistance statute. The court affirmed the district court's decision for the employer. *Pignato v. American Trans Air Inc.*, 14 F.3d 342 (7th Cir.1994).

CHAPTER SEVEN

WORKERS' COMPENSATION

I. EXCLUSIVE REMEDY

Workers' compensation is a system designed to protect both employer and employee. Generally, an employee gives up the right to sue his or her employer in exchange for the security of obtaining workers' compensation benefits for accidental injuries which arise out of and occur in the course of employment. However, where the injury is not sufficiently work-related, or where the injury is caused by an intentional tort, employer liability may result. See also Chapter Two, Section I.

An accounting supervisor at a Wisconsin company experienced difficulty with a subordinate employee. The supervisor missed several days of work, met with a psychotherapist, and requested a short-term leave. She was diagnosed as suffering from major depression, and after failing to return on her expected return date, the company advised the supervisor that it considered her employment to be voluntarily terminated. Her claim for unemployment compensation benefits was denied initially, but later approved. She also received a lump sum payment in settlement of a workers' compensation claim. However, the supervisor advanced claims for handicap discrimination and violation of Wisconsin's Family and Medical Leave Act before the State Department of Industry, Labor and Human Relations (DILHR). The DILHR dismissed these complaints, finding that the workers' compensation act constituted the exclusive remedy for the supervisor's claims. The supervisor appealed to the Court of Appeals of Wisconsin. The court determined that the medical leave provisions of the FMLA did not apply to cases of temporary disability. In such cases, the sole remedy was the workers' compensation act. There was no ground for the supervisor to recover on a theory that she had been fired at a time when she should have been allowed to take medical leave. Accordingly, the DILHR had properly dismissed the claims. *Finnell v. Dept. of Industry, Labor & Human Relations, Equal Rights Div.*, 519 N.W.2d 731 (Wis.App.1994).

Oregon workers' compensation law provides the exclusive remedy for compensable injuries to workers and their beneficiaries. The definition of "compensable injury" excludes injuries or diseases from being compensable if they are not the major contributing cause of disability. An Oregon steelworker had a preexisting sinus condition that was aggravated by substances inhaled on the job. His claim for workers' compensation benefits was denied because work exposure was not the major cause of his condition. The denial was upheld by a hearing referee and the state workers' compensation board. Instead of appealing the decision further, the employee filed a lawsuit against the employer in a state trial court for violations of other state laws. The court granted summary judgment to the employer, ruling that the employee's exclusive remedy was workers' compensation. The Oregon Court of Appeals affirmed, and the employee appealed to the Supreme Court of Oregon.

The employee argued that the exclusivity provisions of the workers' compensation act were inapplicable because his injury was not compensable as defined by the law. The employer argued that the exclusivity provision barred all other civil claims of potential liability of an employer for an employee's work-related injury. Noting the ambiguity in the statutory language, the court considered the 1990 amendments to the compensation act, which indicated that state representatives sought to narrow the scope of applicability of the workers' compensation act and leave room for other civil actions where injuries were noncompensable under the act. Because the employee's injury fell outside the act's definition of compensable injury, the law did not bar his negligence lawsuit, and the supreme court reversed and remanded the case. *Errand v. Cascade Steel Rolling Mills, Inc.*, 320 Or. 509, 888 P.2d 544 (1995).

A Pennsylvania YMCA camp counselor was injured while riding in an automobile driven by a coworker when both were on work-related business. The counselor received workers' compensation benefits for her injuries, but two years later filed a personal injury lawsuit against the driver. The driver claimed immunity under the workers' compensation statute, and a Pennsylvania trial court granted her motion for summary judgment. The Pennsylvania Superior Court initially reversed and remanded the case, but upon reargument, affirmed the trial court judgment. The passenger appealed to the Pennsylvania Supreme Court, where she argued that the state workers' compensation act did not bar an award of uninsured motorist benefits under the Pennsylvania Motor Vehicle Financial Responsibility Law. The driver argued that the financial responsibility law did not supersede the exclusivity provisions of the workers' compensation act. The court examined case law that supported the driver's argument, agreeing with the superior court's statement that recent changes in the law affirmed the principle that injured employees could not obtain a double recovery for work-related injuries. The state workers' compensation act was intended to be the injured worker's exclusive remedy for employment-related injuries that were not intentionally inflicted. The summary judgment in the driver's favor was affirmed. *Ducaji v. Dennis*, 656 A.2d 102 (Pa.1995).

An Indiana restaurant employee was attacked and stabbed by a coworker during an incident in which two other coworkers were murdered. The surviving employee sued the restaurant for misconduct in staffing the restaurant with inexperienced and untrained management personnel. An Indiana trial court granted the employer's motion for judgment on the pleadings, ruling that the state workers' compensation act was the employee's exclusive remedy. The Supreme Court of Indiana held that the workers' compensation act applied where an employee's injury arose out of employment and was caused by an accident. In order to avoid application of the act, the complained of injury must have been caused by an employer's intentional act, with actual knowledge that injury was certain to occur. Because the employee had failed to show that the restaurant intended her injury, her exclusive remedy was in the state workers' compensation system. The court remanded the case for dismissal because of lack of subject matter jurisdiction. *Foshee v. Shoney's Inc.*, 637 N.E.2d 1277 (Ind.1994).

In a companion case, the Supreme Court of Indiana reversed a summary judgment ruling against an African-American auto salesman who claimed that his supervisors assaulted and slandered him and forced him to quit. The court found no evidence that the auto dealership intended to discriminate against him, inasmuch as only the supervisory employees had engaged in the conduct alleged. However, because the employee had not claimed a physical injury, but had only claimed embarrassment and humiliation, the lawsuit was not barred by the exclusivity provisions of the workers' compensation act. The injuries alleged were not covered under the act and the employee had potentially viable claims under the state Employer's Liability Act. The court reversed the summary judgment order on those alternative grounds. *Perry v. Stitzer Buick GMC, Inc.*, 637 N.E.2d 1282 (Ind.1994).

In a third companion case, the Supreme Court of Indiana answered certified questions from the U.S. District Court for the Southern District of Indiana concerning the applicability of the workers' compensation act to cases of intentional conduct. The court held that the intentional torts of an employer were beyond the scope of the act, because the act pertained only to personal injury or death arising out of employment which occurred by accident. An injury occurred "by accident" only when neither the injured party nor the employer intended the injury to result. The employer itself must have intended the injury and it was insufficient that the supervisors, managers, or foremen had acted intentionally. However, the state Occupational Diseases Act made no exception for diseases intentionally caused by an employer, and was applicable to disablement or death suffered in the course of employment. *Baker v. Westinghouse Electric Corp.*, 637 N.E.2d 1271 (Ind.1994).

A California jewelry sales clerk was accused of stealing a small amount of cash. She was detained by several store employees, including two security officers. The sales clerk was escorted to a waiting room where the store's personnel manager stated that witnesses were waiting in the next room and that she must confess. The store's loss prevention manager allegedly used profanity and the clerk was detained for over one hour. When she became hysterical and broke into tears, the interrogators admitted that no witnesses were waiting and they released her. She sued the store for false imprisonment, and intentional and negligent infliction of emotional distress. She stated that the false imprisonment resulted from an approved company policy. A California trial court agreed with the store that the state workers' compensation act was the exclusive remedy for her injuries. This result was affirmed by the state court of appeal, and the employee appealed to the Supreme Court of California.

The supreme court reviewed the history of California's workers' compensation law, observing that intentional torts by employers constitute an exception to the exclusivity of the workers' compensation act as an employee remedy. Accordingly, a claim alleging an intentional assault upon an employee by an employer could not be barred by the defense that workers' compensation was the employee's exclusive remedy. Because false imprisonment could not be said to be a normal part of the employer-employee relationship, and was criminal conduct, it constituted an exception to the exclusivity rule. The employee had pleaded sufficient facts to prevent pretrial dismissal of the lawsuit. *Fermino v. Fedco, Inc.*, 30 Cal.Rptr.2d 18, 872 P.2d 559 (Cal.1994).

A financial services company in Florida purchased a car buyer's automobile financing contract from an auto dealer in violation of its own retail buying procedures. The car buyer's credit application and his contract indicated that the chances were very low that he would make all the payments under the contract. A year later he returned the car because he could no longer afford it. The company then sold the vehicle and applied the net proceeds to his debt. It sent him two deficiency notices and he contacted the company supposedly to discuss making payments. Instead, he went on a rampage, opening fire on the company's customers and employees. After killing nine people and wounding four others, he killed himself. The company secured workers' compensation coverage for its employees who had been killed. Their personal representatives then filed suit against the branch manager and the company in a Florida trial court, alleging that the defendants knowingly and intentionally directed the employees to work in a credit/lending office when they knew with substantial certainty that the employees were subject to open attacks by armed felons. The branch manager and the company moved for summary judgment on the ground that they were immune from suit, but the trial court denied their motion.

On appeal to the District Court of Appeal, First District, the branch manager and the company asserted that an employer which properly secures workers' compensation coverage for its employees is immune from suit so long as the employer has not engaged in an intentional act designed to result in injury or death or conduct which is substantially certain to result in injury or death to an employee. The court of appeal agreed. It noted that the standard for overcoming immunity required more than a strong probability of injury; it required virtual certainty. Here, even though the car buyer had a criminal history as well as a history of violence and bad credit, it could not be said that harm to the employees was a substantial certainty. Accordingly, the branch manager and the company were entitled to workers' compensation immunity. The trial court's holding was reversed. *General Motors Acceptance Corp. v. David*, 632 So.2d 123 (Fla.App.1st Dist.1994).

A resident of the District of Columbia was hired there by a company, but also worked for the company in the state of Virginia. He sustained a back injury while working in Virginia, and received benefits under Virginia's workers' compensation law. Subsequently, he received a supplemental award under the District of Columbia's workers' compensation law. His employer and its carrier challenged this second award because Virginia law excluded any other recovery "at common law or otherwise." Thus, the District of Columbia should have given the first award "full faith and credit." An administrative order upholding the second award was reversed by the U.S. Court of Appeals, and the case came before the U.S. Supreme Court.

The Court held that the U.S. Constitution's Full Faith and Credit Clause did not preclude successive workers' compensation awards where the second state would have had the power to apply its workers' compensation law in the first place. Here, since the employee could have sought a compensation award from the District of Columbia in the first place, the employer and its insurer would have had to measure their liability exposure by the more generous workers' compensation scheme anyway. Accordingly, Virginia's interest was not enough to prevent the District of Columbia from making the supplemental award. The Court reversed and remanded the case. *Thomas v. Washington Gas Light Co.,* 448 U.S. 261, 100 S.Ct. 2647, 65 L.Ed.2d 757 (1980).

After a South Dakota laundry worker was severely burned when hot water in one of the washers backsplashed, he received workers' compensation benefits. He then sued the company, asserting that he could avoid the exclusivity provisions of South Dakota's workers' compensation law because he had been intentionally injured. The U.S. Court of Appeals, Eighth Circuit, noted that the fact that the company knew that the washers had backsplashed hot water on workers in the past and that the company had failed to take any corrective measures did not indicate that the company intended to burn the worker. Although it may have been foreseeable to a reasonable person that the washers could backsplash and burn someone, it was not *substantially certain* that the washers would backsplash hot water. Accordingly, workers' compensation was the exclusive remedy. *Kuhnert v. John Morrell & Co. Meat Packing, Inc.*, 5 F.3d 303 (8th Cir.1993).

A supervisor at a Florida convenience store was murdered during a robbery. Her personal representative filed a lawsuit seeking damages for gross negligence against certain officers and directors of the corporation that owned the convenience store. A state trial judge dismissed the complaint with prejudice, finding that workers' compensation provided the exclusive remedy to the employee's estate. On appeal, the District Court of Appeal, Second District, examined a 1988 amendment to the Workers' Compensation Law which raised the degree of negligence necessary to maintain a civil tort action against policymaking employees from gross negligence to culpable negligence. The court found that culpable negligence was criminal negligence equivalent to an intentional act and that the amendment abolished all civil causes of action in negligence against managerial/policymaking-type employees without providing a reasonable alternative. The court held the amendment to be unconstitutional.

The issue then came before the Supreme Court of Florida which quashed the appellate court's decision and ordered that the trial court's dismissal of the lawsuit be affirmed. The supreme court noted that culpable negligence was still a form of negligence and was actionable as a civil action under the workers' compensation law regardless of whether criminal charges were filed against a co-employee. Since the amendment at issue merely raised the degree of negligence required to sue a policymaking co-employee, the court found that the amendment did not abolish employees' constitutional rights of access to the courts. Further, even if the amendment did abolish the right of access, the court determined that the workers' compensation law provided a reasonable alternative to a lawsuit. The employee's estate was limited to recovery under workers' compensation. *Eller v. Shova*, 630 So.2d 537 (Fla.1993).

An Illinois man worked as a coal miner for approximately 45 years. When he was 61 years old he filed for black lung benefits with the U.S. Department of Labor. A claim for black lung benefits requires a miner to establish total disability caused at least in part by pneumoconiosis that arose out of employment in a coal mine. The record consisted of a single x-ray and the testimony of three different doctors who came to two different conclusions. However, the administrative law judge concluded that true doubt existed as to whether the x-ray was positive for pneumoconiosis. Believing that the true doubt rule required him to resolve the evidentiary doubt in the claimant's favor, the ALJ found that the claimant had established the presence of pneumoconiosis. The company appealed to the U.S. Court of Appeals, Seventh Circuit. The company asserted that the true doubt rule was at odds with the Administrative Procedure Act (APA) because the rule allowed the ALJ to award black lung benefits to a claimant who has not proven his right to them by a preponderance of the evidence. The true doubt rule states that in the absence of definitive medical conclusions, there is a clear need to resolve doubts in favor of the disabled miner or his survivors. Noting that the U.S. Supreme Court has upheld the true doubt rule, the court of appeals stated that the rule was appropriately applied in this case. The Department of Labor's decision to award benefits was upheld. *Freeman United Coal Mining Company v. Office of Workers' Compensation Program,* 988 F.2d 706 (7th Cir.1993).

A South Carolina life insurance sales representative sued her former employer and her immediate supervisor, claiming that she had been subjected to a pattern of verbal, physical and emotional harassment and abuse by her supervisor while performing her duties. A South Carolina circuit court dismissed the case, stating that the employee's exclusive remedy was workers' compensation. The employee appealed to the Court of Appeals of South Carolina. The court of appeals noted that injury resulting from an assault and battery by a co-employee or manager fits in the definition of a compensable injury under the act. In addition, the co-employee could not be sued because he was performing work incident to the employer's business.

The employee appealed to the Supreme Court of South Carolina. The supreme court affirmed the appellate court's decision that the employee's claims were precluded by the exclusive remedy provision of the workers' compensation act. However, the court reversed the opinion to the extent that it held that the manager could not be held individually liable for an intentional tort he might have committed while acting within the scope of his employment. The court held that a co-employee who negligently injures another while in the scope of his employment is immune under the act and cannot be held personally liable. However, it found that it is against public policy to extend this immunity to a co-employee who commits an intentional tortious act upon another employee. The court stated that the workers' compensation act could not be used as a shield for a co-employee's intentionally injurious conduct. *Dickert v. Metropolitan Life Ins. Co.,* 428 S.E.2d 700 (S.C.1993).

A Texas man was hired by an employment agency, and then sent to work for another company. The employment agency paid his wages and provided workers' compensation insurance for the employee. The company providing work for the employee was named as an alternate employer in the policy. After a work shift, the employee was told to wash his work clothes in a vat of acetone. He did so. The next morning, while he was attempting to wash the acetone out of the work clothes, the acetone fumes ignited and the employee was seriously burned. He sued the employment agency and the company for negligence. Both defendants asserted that workers' compensation was his only remedy, and the trial court agreed. The employee appealed to the Court of Appeals of Texas.

On appeal, the court noted that the employment agency was a "subscriber" under Texas workers' compensation law (the party who hires and pays the employee). However, the company (the party with the right to control) was not a "subscriber." Further, the employee's claim was only barred as against subscribers. Therefore, the claim against the employment agency was barred, but the suit against the company could proceed. Even though the company was named as an alternate employer in the policy, this did not satisfy its obligations under workers' compensation law. *Zavala-Nava v. A.C. Employment, Inc.*, 820 S.W.2d 14 (Tex.App.1991).

A patient representative, employed by a hospital, was robbed, raped and beaten while walking to her car at approximately 2:30 a.m. The hospital had instructed her, prior to the incident, not to request a security guard to accompany her to her car. The employee sued the hospital, contending that it was negligent in failing to provide adequate security. The hospital asserted that the employee's action was barred by the exclusive remedy provisions of the Georgia Workers' Compensation Act. The trial court granted summary judgment to the hospital, and the employer appealed to the Court of Appeals of Georgia. On appeal, the court noted that the exclusive remedy provisions applied to injuries "arising out of and in the course of employment." Here, the injury was causally connected to conditions of employment because the employee was forced to walk alone to her car during early morning hours, thus increasing the risk of attack and subjecting her to a danger which was peculiar to her employment. Accordingly, workers' compensation coverage was the sole remedy available to the employee for her injuries. The court affirmed the grant of summary judgment to the hospital. *Maxwell v. Hospital Authority*, 413 S.E.2d 205 (Ga.App.1991).

A Michigan man fell to his death after being directed to work while standing on an unguarded catwalk. The employer had been told that the catwalk posed a high risk of injury. An action was brought to determine the scope of the intentional tort exception to the exclusive remedy provision of the Workers' Disability Compensation Act. A Michigan trial court found in favor of the employer. Appeal was taken to the Court of Appeals of Michigan. The court noted that the intentional tort exception was not triggered simply because the employer had actual knowledge that an injury was likely to occur. Only where the employer had knowledge that an injury was certain to occur (and did nothing to prevent the injury) would the exception apply. Because such was not the case here, the appellate court upheld the decision of the trial court and ruled that the allegations failed to establish an intentional tort. They did not establish that the employer had actual knowledge that an injury was certain to incur and that it wilfully disregarded that knowledge. *Oaks v. Twin City Foods, Inc.*, 497 N.W.2d 196 (Mich.App.1992).

A South Carolina woman was employed by a sports company as an exercise instructor. She apparently told her employer that she had developed a bladder illness which required surgery. When she told her employer that her physician had advised against exercise and recommended surgery, he apparently told her that she would have to continue performing group exercises for the next three weeks or she would be fired. The exercises caused her to lose control of her bladder, and she brought suit against her employer for intentional infliction of emotional distress. Her employer moved for summary judgment on the grounds that her claim was governed exclusively by workers' compensation laws. The trial court denied the motion, and the employer appealed to the Supreme Court of South Carolina. The supreme court noted that, to fall within the scope of workers' compensation, an injury must be an accident and arise out of and in the course of employment. In this case, the employee alleged that her employer had acted intentionally. Thus, the injury was not the result of an accident, and did not become compensable under workers' compensation. The court allowed the lawsuit to proceed. However, it cautioned that recovery could not be had under both common law and workers' compensation. Because the employee could continue her suit against the employer, she was barred from any further workers' compensation claims for her injury. *McSwain v. Shei*, 402 S.E.2d 890 (S.C.1991).

A Louisiana lab assistant worked for a laboratory which ran tests for a hospital. She administered a skin test to a hospital patient, using a syringe. The syringe was covered with a plastic cap. After administering the test, the lab assistant attempted to recap the needle, but the needle punctured the cap and went into her thumb. The patient was suffering from AIDS and hepatitis. The lab assistant filed a tort action against the hospital in a Louisiana trial court. The trial court determined that the lab assistant was an employee and granted summary judgment in favor of the hospital holding that workers' compensation was her only remedy. The lab assistant appealed to the Court of Appeal of Louisiana.

The lab assistant contended that an employment relationship did not exist. The hospital contended that the lab assistant was acting as an employee while performing the test and her only remedy was workers' compensation. Louisiana workers' compensation law states that when an employer "contracts to execute any work, which is part of his trade, business or occupation, the employer is liable under the workers' compensation statute just as if the contractor were a direct employee." Thus, the employer would be immune from tort liability. To determine if the contract work was part of the employer's trade, business or occupation, the court had to determine: 1) if the work was routine; 2) whether the employer was capable of performing the work; and 3) what the practice was in the industry. The hospital was an acute care hospital and provided laboratory services. The skin test was a routine diagnostic test. Further, laboratory services are routine, customary and a necessary part of the day-to-day operations of any hospital. Accordingly, the court concluded that the lab assistant's work was part of the hospital's trade, business or occupation and it upheld the grant of summary judgment to the hospital, finding that it was immune from tort liability. *Frith v. Motorist Ins. Co.*, 613 So.2d 249 (La.App.1992).

An employee of a metal company was injured while operating a press brake in the course and scope of his employment. He brought a civil action against his employer, alleging that the employer had caused his injury by its knowing removal of (or knowing failure to install) a point of operation guard on the press brake. He asserted that this was a violation of California Labor Code § 4558 which provided him with an exception to the exclusivity principle of workers' compensation law. The employee sought both compensatory and punitive damages. The employer sought to dismiss the employee's claim, but the trial court denied its motion. The employer appealed to the California Court of Appeal, Second District. The appellate court noted that the burden of proof in such a case is greater than it would be for a mere negligence action. The employee must establish that the employer knowingly failed to install or knowingly removed the protective guard. Further, the employee must show that the employer specifically authorized the removal "under conditions known by the employer to create a probability of serious injury or death." Although this higher burden was more difficult to meet, the employee had alleged facts sufficient to bring him within the requirements of § 4558. The court thus allowed the suit against the employer to continue. *Award Metals, Inc. v. Superior Court*, 279 Cal.Rptr. 459 (Cal.App.2d Dist.1991).

A woman in the first trimester of her pregnancy was employed at a restaurant in Illinois. While a computer system was being installed, the restaurant's ventilation and exhaust system failed, and the woman was exposed to carbon monoxide and other fumes for a three-day period. Subsequently, the woman gave birth to a child with severe and disabling birth defects. The child through his mother brought a lawsuit in federal court against the restaurant, alleging that his injuries had been caused by his mother's exposure to carbon monoxide due to the restaurant's negligence. The restaurant moved for summary judgment, asserting that the child's claim was barred by the Illinois Workers' Compensation Act.

The district court noted that the exclusive remedy doctrine of the act provided that lawsuits could not be maintained against employers for injuries or death sustained by employees while engaged in their duties as employees. The sole remedy was under the workers' compensation act. However, in this case, the child was bringing a claim based on his own injuries which occurred while he was still *in utero*. Since Illinois allowed a child to bring a cause of action against a party for prenatal injuries suffered by the child, the court determined that the child could maintain a cause of action against the restaurant for the fetal injuries he incurred. Further, the court determined that its ruling would not lead to discriminatory policies against women in the workplace because of the protections of Title VII and the Pregnancy Discrimination Act. The court thus denied the restaurant's motion for summary judgment and allowed the case to proceed to trial. *Thompson v. Pizza Hut of America, Inc.*, 767 F.Supp. 916 (N.D.Ill.1991).

A Louisiana employee worked as an order filler for a fast food restaurant drive-through. Her supervisor hit her after she admitted to improperly filling an order. The employee had trouble sleeping that night and visited a family practitioner where she received a prescription for her nerves. No marks were evident on the employee nor did she make any complaints of pain, only references that she was nervous and upset. Eventually, she was diagnosed as suffering from post-traumatic stress syndrome. The employee sought both workers' compensation benefits and damages in tort. The district court granted both claims in favor of the employee. The employer appealed.

On appeal, the Court of Appeal of Louisiana affirmed the lower court's decision allowing her to recover under workers' compensation and tort. The court stated, "the penalty for injuries by intentional acts is that the employee can recover both damages in tort and workers' compensation benefits." The employer then appealed to the Supreme Court of Louisiana.

In modifying the lower court's decision the court analyzed the law to determine if the woman could recover in tort law in addition to workers' compensation. The Workers' Compensation Act is a compromise where the employer surrenders immunity for cases where it is without fault, and the employee surrenders his or her right to full damages and instead receives compensation measured as a percentage of wages. However, the exclusivity of workers' compensation was not applicable to intentional acts. The court determined that the intent of the legislature was not to make workers' compensation the exclusive remedy for intentional acts but rather to punish employers for such acts. Thus, the employee could recover tort damages as well as workers' compensation benefits. However, the employee could not be compensated doubly for the same elements. Thus, the court affirmed the lower courts' decision but offset the tort damages against the workers' compensation benefits. *Gagnard v. Baldridge*, 612 So.2d 732 (La.1993).

A Georgia employee suffered burns and other injuries while he was attempting to repair a flange valve on a steam line. He made a claim for and was awarded workers' compensation benefits for his medical expenses and lost wages according to Georgia law. Subsequently, he brought suit against his employer seeking additional compensatory and punitive damages for his injuries. The employer moved to dismiss the complaint, contending that the Georgia Workers' Compensation Act provided the employee with the sole remedy for his injuries. The trial court granted the employer's motion, and the employee appealed to the Court of Appeals of Georgia.

On appeal, the employee asserted that the employer had breached its contractual duty to provide a safe work environment for its employees as set forth in the collective bargaining agreement between the employer and the employee's union. He asserted that the collective bargaining agreement was governed by federal law, and that the exclusive remedy provisions of the workers' compensation act were preempted by federal labor law. The court of appeals, however, noted that Georgia statutory and common law required an employer to furnish a reasonably safe place to work and to exercise ordinary care and diligence to keep it safe. Since this was the same duty owed by virtue of the collective bargaining agreement, the employer's duty to its employees was not expanded. Therefore, the employee could not use federal law to skirt the requirements of the workers' compensation act. The court affirmed the decision of the trial court and held that federal law did not preempt the exclusive remedy provisions. *Dugger v. Miller Brewing Co.*, 406 S.E.2d 484 (Ga.App.1991).

A woman was employed by a large New York bank. The bank ran a store which contained a pharmacy for its employees one level below the lobby of its building. The employee had a prescription filled at the pharmacy and claimed that her ingestion of the prescription caused her serious injuries. She brought suit against the bank and the employee who filled the prescription, alleging negligence and breach of the warranties of merchantability and fitness for a particular use. The bank made a motion for summary judgment, asserting the exclusive remedy defense of workers' compensation. The woman made a cross-motion against the bank. The Civil Court of the City of New York held that the bank could not assert the exclusive remedy of workers' compensation for the woman's injuries. The pharmacy was not open only to employees, but to all the building's tenants and contractors working in the building. An estimated 2500 nonemployees were permitted to use the pharmacy. The court stated that allowing such a large number of nonemployees to utilize the pharmacy denied the bank the right to assert its exclusive remedy defense. Therefore, it granted the motion to strike the affirmative defense of workers' compensation and denied the bank's motion for summary judgment. *Ruiz v. Chase Manhattan Bank,* 588 N.Y.S.2d 251 (N.Y.City Civ.Ct.1992).

II.   CONNECTION WITH EMPLOYMENT

Compensation will not be paid merely because an injured person happens to be employed. The injury must be connected with the employment for benefits to become payable. Either the injury must arise out of and in the course of the employment or it must be an occupational disease. In addition, the existence of a preexisting condition may affect the eligibility of a claim.

A.   Arising from Employment and/or Occupational Diseases

A Nevada employee on temporary assignment at a New Mexico laboratory suffered a fractured wrist when she fell off a bicycle provided by the laboratory for its employees. The laboratory was located in a remote area and the employer anticipated that employees would use the bicycle during breaks to get exercise. The Supreme Court of Nevada reversed a district court order barring an award of benefits and reinstated an administrative decision awarding benefits. The employee was properly deemed in the course and scope of her employment when she was injured, considering the remote locale, the employer's ownership of the bicycle and the employer's expectation of employee use. The injury was not of the type contemplated by the legislature in amending the compensation act to preclude the award of workers' compensation benefits to employees injured in athletic or social events sponsored by employers. *Dixon v. State Ind. Ins. System,* 899 P.2d 571 (Nev.1995).

A Nebraska company held a company picnic at which attendance was not mandatory and an employee was severely injured while participating in a football game. The state workers' compensation court determined that the injured employee was not entitled to receive workers' compensation benefits because the company had not received any substantial direct tangible benefit from holding the event. This result was affirmed by a three-judge workers' compensation review panel and the Nebraska Court of Appeals. The employee appealed to the Supreme Court of Nebraska. The supreme court found that application of the six-part test employed by the court of appeals in its decision was unnecessary. Instead, it employed the three-part test used previously by the state supreme court. The three factors for determining whether a recreational or social activity could be considered within the course of employment included consideration of whether the accident occurred on the employer's premises as a regular incident of employment, whether the employer expressly or impliedly required employee participation, and whether the employer derived substantial direct benefit from the activity, irrespective of employee morale. Employing these factors, the court affirmed the result of the compensation review panel and affirmed the court of appeals' decision as modified. *Shade v. Ayars & Ayars, Inc.*, 247 Neb. 94, 525 N.W.2d 32 (1994).

A Missouri company held a picnic that was advertised by posters and payroll notices. An employee who volunteered to help set up the picnic was assigned to supervise delivery of the ice and had a company check to pay for it. She came to the picnic early, and after the ice was delivered (but before the scheduled picnic) she was injured when she fell from some stilts. She suffered a broken ankle and underwent three surgeries requiring hospitalization. The state commission of labor and industrial relations reversed the determination of an administrative law judge that the employee was not acting within the scope of her employment when she was injured. It awarded her over $26,000 in disability and medical expenses, and the employer appealed to the Missouri Court of Appeals, Eastern District, Division Three.

The court of appeals determined that there was no clear test for determining whether employees were in the course of employment when injured at company picnics. However, some of the factors to resolve this question included whether the picnic was sufficiently related to their employment, whether the employer derived some benefit from sponsorship, whether employees were required to attend, the extent of employer sponsorship, control and participation, and whether the employer benefited by holding the event. In this case, the employee was present at the site before the event began in order to pay for and supervise the ice delivery. Because she was fulfilling a concurrent purpose, she was appropriately considered to have been injured while in the course of employment. Because the business and personal purposes were combined at the employer's request and convenience, the commission had properly awarded workers' compensation benefits. *Ludwinski v. National Courier*, 873 S.W.2d 890 (Mo.App.E.D.1994).

A recently hired Louisiana gas station employee sought employment during the day shift and permission to carry a gun at work because of continuing harassment by her estranged husband. The employer refused these requests and the husband subsequently wounded the employee with three rifle shots while she was working at the station. An administrative hearing officer rejected the employee's claims for workers' compensation benefits, finding that the injuries arose out of a domestic dispute that was totally unrelated to employment. The Louisiana Court of Appeal, Third Circuit, reversed the administrative decision, ruling that the question of work-relatedness was a fact issue that made summary judgment inappropriate. The employer appealed to the Supreme Court of Louisiana, which analyzed the applicable section of the workers' compensation statute. Workers' compensation benefits were intended to compensate employees for personal injuries arising out of and in the course of employment. Liability was precluded where an employer demonstrated that an accident arose out of a dispute with another person or employee over matters unrelated to the injured employee's employment. Although the employee in this case had been injured in the course of her employment, her injuries did not arise out of her employment because of the strictly personal nature of the dispute. Discussions with her employer about the problems created by the relationship did not convert the matter to an employment-related dispute, and the court reversed the decision of the court of appeal. *Guillory v. Interstate Gas Station*, 653 So.2d 1152 (La.1995).

A longtime employee of a Pennsylvania corporation underwent severe stress when the company merged with another corporation and her job duties were substantially increased. She alleged that the increased workload and her many new duties caused her chest pains, severe gastrointestinal problems, headaches and other physical symptoms. She stopped working and filed a claim for workers' compensation benefits, claiming that the physical symptoms she experienced resulted from stress. A workers' compensation referee determined that she was entitled to benefits, but this decision was reversed by the state compensation appeal board. The employee appealed to the Commonwealth Court of Pennsylvania. On appeal, the employer argued that the employee's symptoms were mental injuries and that she had failed to show evidence of an abnormal working condition, because many other employees had also been required to increase their performance. The employee argued that she had suffered physical injuries that did not require the proof of abnormal working conditions. The court agreed with the employee, ruling that her work stress resulted in distinct and identifiable physical injuries, not in a merely disabling mental injury. Accordingly, the employee had established a causal connection between her work conditions and her physical injuries, requiring reversal of the board's order. *Whiteside v. WCAB*, 650 A.2d 1202 (Pa.Cmwlth.1994).

A Maryland computer operator claimed that some of his coworkers harassed him to the point that he became restless and sleepless, had headaches and developed post-traumatic stress syndrome. He claimed that the harassment prevented him from working and submitted a claim for workers' compensation benefits on the basis of an occupational disease. The state workers' compensation commission denied the claim, ruling that the operator did not sustain a mental disorder arising out of and in the course of employment within the meaning of the state workers' compensation act. The operator appealed to a Maryland circuit court, which granted a motion for summary judgment by the employer and its insurer. The Maryland Court of Appeals granted the operator's petition for review. The court disagreed with the employer's argument that purely mental diseases could never be compensable as occupational diseases. However, it agreed with the employer that a claimant must demonstrate a relationship between a particular disease and employment. The court found no inherent relationship between the job duties of a computer operator and the alleged harassment by coworkers. It was insufficient to show that a mental injury was related to general conditions on the job. Because the alleged injury was not compensable under the state workers' compensation act, the court affirmed summary judgment for the employer and its insurer. *Davis v. Dyncorp*, 336 Md. 226, 647 A.2d 446 (1994).

A North Carolina bulldozer operator returned to work at a Florida jobsite with a coworker after spending several days in North Carolina. On the return trip, the workers drank beer. They went directly to the jobsite to check on some water pumps. No other persons were present at the jobsite and they stayed there drinking beer for an hour. As they left the jobsite in a truck, the workers were involved in a serious traffic accident in which the coworker was driving. The employer paid the bulldozer operator for three hours of work on the day of the accident and filed a claim for medical benefits on his behalf with the company's workers' compensation carrier. The operator received over $43,000 in wage loss benefits before retaining an attorney who advised him not to accept any further benefits and to file a personal injury suit against the employer, coworker and other parties. A Florida trial court granted summary judgment to the employer, determining that the coworker was immune from any personal injury lawsuit because the injury was in the course and scope of employment and further claims were barred by the state workers' compensation act.

The Florida District Court of Appeal, First District, observed that the bulldozer operator had never filed a workers' compensation claim, although he had received benefits that had been paid to him voluntarily. Because he had not made a formal claim for compensation and had only passively accepted benefits, it had been inappropriate for the trial court to grant summary judgment against him. Disputed fact issues existed concerning whether the injury occurred during the course and scope of employment, and the operator should not be legally precluded from seeking a personal injury recovery. The compensation carrier would be entitled to a setoff of any recovery he might receive. *Holder v. Waldrop*, 654 So.2d 1059 (Fla.App.1st Dist.1995).

An Ohio employee of a company was a member of a union. A strike occurred and the union directed the employee to walk on the picket line at certain times. While on picket duty, the employee was hit and injured by a company vehicle. He filed a claim for workers' compensation benefits which was denied. He then appealed to the common pleas court, which held that his injury was not received in the course of his employment. He further appealed to the Court of Appeals of Ohio. Under Ohio workers' compensation law, an employee's injury is compensable only if it was "received in the course of, and arising out of, the injured employee's employment." Here, the court noted that the employee was at the time of his injury subsisting on strike benefits paid by his union, from which his union dues were deducted. Although he retained his status as a company employee during the strike, his presence on the picket line at the expense and direction of his union had to be viewed as personal activity and not as activity incidental to his employment duties. Even though the accident took place on or near company premises, and even though the employer had control over the scene of the accident, the employer did not receive any benefit from the injured employee's presence on the picket line. Accordingly, the court affirmed the lower court's ruling in favor of the company. *Koger v. Greyhound Lines, Inc.*, 629 N.E.2d 492 (Ohio App.1st Dist.1993).

A Connecticut salesman who maintained an office in his basement was expected to visit his account holders regularly. He did not observe strict hours and used his own car daily. He suffered a cardiac arrest while shoveling snow in his driveway before going to call on customers. The salesman, who had a history of high blood pressure, died later that day. His widow filed an application for workers' compensation benefits. The state compensation commissioner determined that the salesman suffered the cardiac arrest because of snow shoveling and that the only reason he had been shoveling snow was to call on customers. Therefore, he had suffered a compensable injury under the workers' compensation statute and the widow was entitled to benefits. The Appellate Court of Connecticut affirmed, and the salesman's employer appealed to the Supreme Court of Connecticut.

On appeal, the employer claimed that the salesman was performing a domestic preparatory activity that was not within the scope of his employment. It argued that the court should deny benefits. The court determined that there was no convenient legal distinction to apply in cases of salespersons based in home offices to help distinguish between mere preparatory work and activities that were in the course of employment. Because workers' compensation law was uniquely statutory, the court stated that the legislature would have to propose appropriate guidelines to create any finer distinction than that existing under judicial law. The court dismissed the employer's appeal. *Tovish v. Gerber Electronics*, 229 Conn. 587, 642 A.2d 721 (Conn.1994).

A Connecticut woman worked for a dentist as a dental hygienist for six years. Due to their increased awareness of infection from communicable diseases, both the woman and the dentist received precautionary vaccinations against hepatitis. During this time, the woman's husband was diagnosed as being a carrier of hepatitis type B virus (HBV). As a result of this diagnosis, the woman was tested and also diagnosed as being a carrier of HBV. She stopped working as a dental hygienist when she and the dentist agreed that her condition posed a threat to patients. The woman was awarded workers' compensation benefits and her employer appealed to the Supreme Court of Connecticut.

On appeal, the employer first claimed that the woman had failed to satisfy her burden of proving that HBV falls within the definition of an occupational disease. The court noted that the statutory language required the disease to be "peculiar to the occupation in which the employee was engaged and due to causes in excess of the ordinary hazards of employment as such." Although HBV is contagious, and can be transmitted through means outside the workplace, for dental hygienists it is a disease so distinctly associated with their profession that the necessary causal connection was present. Secondly, the dentist claimed that the woman was not entitled to compensation because she did not have a "partial incapacity." The court noted, however, that the disease itself was an impairment in capacity because it disabled the woman from employment as a dental hygienist and therefore caused her to lose earnings. Thus, the court affirmed the lower court's award of compensation benefits. *Hansen v. Gordon*, 602 A.2d 560 (Conn.1992).

A California worker installed, inspected, maintained and repaired flow regulators used in a waste water treatment plant. His job responsibilities required him to reach his hands into raw sewage to remove equipment for repair. Although he wore gloves, sometimes the equipment would cut his gloves, exposing his hands to raw sewage. At times, his hand would be nicked and he would bleed. In 1987, the worker received treatment at an emergency room which showed he had contracted hepatitis B. He then developed chronic hepatitis B and polyarthritisnedosa with significant neurological deficits involving the use of his hands and legs. The workers' compensation board denied benefits and the worker appealed to the Court of Appeal of California.

Several doctors testified that although there were no studies indicating that hepatitis B could be contracted through raw sewage, several factors pointed to that mode of transmission: 1) the sewage worker was not in a risk group such as intravenous drug use, homosexuality, foreign travel or hepatitis in family or friends, 2) hepatitis B can be spread through blood, punctured skin, or close personal contact, and 3) hepatitis B has been reported in feces and urine. Presumably then, a break in the mucosa of a sewage worker could be implicated in the development of the disease. Accordingly, the appellate court determined that the medical evidence was sufficient to support a finding that the worker developed hepatitis B as a result of his occupational exposure to the sewage and it reversed the decision of the board. *Rosas v. Workers' Compensation Appeals Board*, 20 Cal.Rptr.2d 778 (Cal.App.1993).

An Ohio man worked as a quality assurance inspector. He worked a mandatory minimum schedule of 66 hours per week. He received a physical from his personal physician who advised him not to work more than 40 hours per week, and he was given a note to that effect. The employee next saw the company doctor and presented him with the note from his personal physician. The two doctors spoke with one another on the phone, after which the employee went to the hospital and was placed on medical leave. While in the hospital, the employee was diagnosed with atrial fibrillation, an irregular heart beat. He contended that this was a result of stressful working conditions. He filed a workers' compensation claim which was subsequently denied. That decision was affirmed on appeal to the regional board of review. The state industrial commission refused to hear a further appeal by the employee. He then filed suit in a trial court, which granted summary judgment in favor of the employer. The employee appealed.

The Court of Appeals of Ohio noted that a physical injury caused solely by mental or emotional stress received in the course of, and arising out of, the injured employee's employment was compensable. However, atrial fibrillation could not be compensable within the workers' compensation law without a showing that it caused a physical injury, or, under unique circumstances, that it was a physical injury. Here, there was no evidence of physical injury caused by or resulting from atrial fibrillation. The court determined that atrial fibrillation was a noncompensable injury and affirmed the judgment of the trial court. *Beard v. Mayfield,* 596 N.E.2d 1056 (Ohio App.10th Dist.1991).

While working for a nursery, a Pennsylvania man sustained a spinal cord injury when he fell from a tree while performing his job. He received workers' compensation benefits until he was able to return to work. His employer remained responsible for those necessary and reasonable medical expenses which were causally related to the work injury. Subsequently, the employee and his wife decided that they wanted to have a baby, but due to the employee's injury they could only conceive by means of artificial insemination. The employee sought to be reimbursed for the medical and transportation expenses incurred by him and his wife in their attempt at conception. The workers' compensation referee dismissed the employee's claim because his partial dysfunction did not impair his ability to work. The referee further held that the expenses were neither reasonable nor necessary in that the insemination procedure was not causally related to his work injury. After the appeal board upheld the referee's decision the employee appealed to the Commonwealth Court of Pennsylvania.

On appeal, the court noted that the findings below were in error. First, the employee had established by medical testimony that his dysfunction was connected with his spinal cord injury. Second, the employer had never presented evidence that the procedure was neither reasonable nor necessary. In order for the employee to carry out his inherent right to attempt to have children, artificial insemination was necessary. Further, the procedure could not be carried out without the employee's wife as a participant. Accordingly, the court held that artificial insemination was a compensable medical expense. *Tobias v. WCAB (Nature's Way Nursery, Inc.),* 595 A.2d 781 (Pa.Cmwlth.1991).

A Wyoming mud-logger worked as a unit manager at a secluded oil well drilling site. After a 12-hour workshift, the employee drove from the site to a town about 40 miles away. On his return to the site, the employee was killed in a one-vehicle accident a mile from the well site. His widow sought workers' compensation death benefits. The hearing officer awarded benefits, but the district court reversed the award. The widow appealed. On appeal to the Supreme Court of Wyoming, the court reversed the lower court's decision and awarded benefits. The court held that the unexplained-death rule governed. Specifically, the unexplained-death rule allows a "presumption or inference that the death arose out of the employment" when circumstances indicate the employee was "within the time and space limits of the employment." The presumption supplies the employment connection, unless there is contrary evidence presented. Absent contradictory evidence, therefore, the court granted the widow compensation. *Richard v. State of Wyoming,* 831 P.2d 244 (Wyo.1992).

An Illinois man was a salaried employee of a corporation. His employer circulated a memorandum querying whether he wished to participate in a round-robin tennis tournament. He chose to participate. No wages or salary were deducted from his paycheck and his travel expenses and accommodations were paid for by the corporation. During the tournament, he suffered a fatal heart attack. His widow filed a claim for workers' compensation, and the industrial commission denied benefits. The widow appealed to the Appellate Court of Illinois.

On appeal, she asserted that even though her husband's conduct in participating had been voluntary, the tennis tournament itself was not a recreational activity. She asserted that it was a promotional activity which benefited the corporation. The appellate court stated that the tennis tournament was a voluntary recreational activity regardless of the purpose of the activity. Even if the heart attack could be said to have arisen out of and in the course of the man's employment, the Worker's Compensation Act disallowed compensation for recreational events. The court affirmed the denial of benefits. *Kozak v. Industrial Commission*, 579 N.E.2d 921 (Ill.App.1st Dist.1991).

A New York man was injured while participating in a basketball game during a picnic. The picnic had been organized by a coffee club made up of his coworkers. He filed a claim for workers' compensation benefits, and the state Workers' Compensation Board ruled that he had sustained a compensable injury under the workers' compensation law. The New York Supreme Court, Appellate Division, reversed the decision of the board. It held that the evidence was insufficient to establish employer sponsorship of the activity so as to render the employer liable to the man for the injuries sustained at the picnic. There was no overt encouragement of participation in the picnic by the employer. The court found that the use of employer stationery and telephone lines to organize the picnic was insufficient to establish employer sponsorship under the workers' compensation law. Notwithstanding that the employer assented to the existence of the coffee club on the business premises and derived a general benefit from the picnic in the form of increased morale and efficiency, the court found that the evidence did not provide a basis for a finding of compensability. Therefore, it dismissed the claim for workers' compensation benefits. *Farnan v. NYS Dept. of Social Services,* 589 N.Y.S.2d 713 (A.D.3d Dept.1992).

A Louisiana man worked for two different companies in a two year period as an x-ray technician, inspecting pipe welds and various equipment. He was exposed to gamma radiation at this time. He then contracted testicular cancer which metastasized to his lungs. He brought a petition for workers' compensation benefits, alleging that his exposure to the radiation caused his cancer. He subsequently died, and his mother continued the petition. A trial was held on the evidence, two expert witnesses testified, and the court determined that the cancer did not arise from the decedent's exposure to radiation. His mother appealed to the Court of Appeal of Louisiana. On appeal, the court noted that the more respected expert witness had testified that she was uncertain whether the decedent's exposure to radiation had caused the cancer in question. Her testimony did not establish a "reasonable possibility of causal connection." Accordingly, it was not error for the trial court to credit her testimony over that of the less qualified expert, and to find that no compensation was due. The trial court's decision was affirmed. *McKay v. Assured Inspection Mgt., Inc.*, 588 So.2d 729 (La.App.1991).

A Tennessee man worked as an outside television technician for a large company. In the course of his employment he was furnished a uniform and a service van to make service calls to customers. Company policy provided for a "drop system" where each evening a route person would deliver the next day's assignments to the technician's home by placing a "route sheet" into a bucket in the back of the service van. The route person would collect the money envelope containing the day's cash and checks received from the customers, as well as any parts needed to be repaired at the shop. While attempting to retrieve the route sheet from the service van parked in his driveway, the employee was attacked and pistol-whipped by an unknown assailant. He suffered severe head injuries. A trial court dismissed his suit for workers' compensation benefits, finding that his injuries did not arise out of his employment. The employee appealed.

The Supreme Court of Tennessee reversed the decision of the trial court. It noted that for an injury to be compensable under the workers' compensation law, it must be "by accident arising out of and in the course of employment." The court applied the "street risk doctrine," finding that the employment exposed the employee to the hazards of the street and that a causal connection existed between the injury and his employment. It noted that money and valuables were removed nightly from the service van, making it reasonable to conclude that the employee would be a target for attack. It found that since the company policy mandated that technicians organize their next day's routes at home prior to embarking on the day's first service call, the employee was acting in the course of his employment when the attack occurred. The court thus held the employee eligible for workers' compensation benefits. *Braden v. Sears, Roebuck and Co.*, 833 S.W.2d 496 (Tenn.1992).

A New Jersey couple hired a registered nurse to care for the wife at their home. While at the patient's home, the nurse went down to the garage to throw away a used catheter and, at the patient's request, to place a basket on a shelf. She slipped and fell on an oil spill. The nurse's medical insurance covered her medical expenses but she did not receive any workers' compensation benefits for her period of incapacitation. She filed a personal injury suit against the couple in a New Jersey trial court. The trial court granted summary judgment to the couple and the nurse appealed to the Superior Court of New Jersey, Appellate Division.

The court stated that although the nurse performed nonmedical services to make the wife comfortable, the couple had no control over her actions. It also noted that in previous cases involving home nursing care, the courts ruled that nurses were independent contractors. Thus, the court found that the nurse was an independent contractor and she could sue the couple for her personal injuries. The appellate court reversed the lower court's decision and remanded the case to the trial court to determine liability. *Swillings v. Mahendroo*, 620 A.2d 452 (N.J.Super.1993).

A miner filed a claim for benefits under the Black Lung Benefits Act. At the time of filing he had been totally disabled by pneumoconiosis (black lung disease), and he died while his claim was pending. His widow subsequently filed for survivor's benefits under the same act. After both claims were denied, she requested a hearing before an administrative law judge (ALJ). The ALJ awarded benefits on the miner's claim, but not on the survivor's claim. The widow appealed to the Benefits Review Board (BRB), which affirmed the ALJ. Thereafter, she appealed to the federal court of appeals.

The U.S. Court of Appeals, Fourth Circuit, found that the medical evidence clearly showed that the miner died of pancreatic cancer which had spread to his other internal organs. The immediate cause of death, however, was pneumonia. The statute at issue provided survivor's benefits where the miner's death was due to pneumoconiosis, or where pneumoconiosis was a substantially contributing cause or factor leading to the miner's death. The ALJ had determined that the miner's cancer made him more susceptible to pneumonia, and that pneumoconiosis was not a substantially contributing cause of death. The court, however, adopted the interpretation of the Director of the Office of Workers' Compensation Programs that "pneumoconiosis substantially contributes to death if it serves to hasten death in any way." Because the evidence was unclear whether the pneumoconiosis did hasten the miner's death, which would entitle the widow to survivor's benefits, the court vacated and remanded the BRB's order for a determination of the issue. *Shuff v. Cedar Coal Co.,* 967 F.2d 977 (4th Cir.1992).

A man worked as a maintenance mechanic for an elevator company. He died while on the job site, and his body was found lying face down several feet from an uncovered electrical control panel. The panel was on and the electrical current was "arcing" between two panel contacts. A screwdriver, a tool pouch, and a folded towel that was presumed to be a kneeling pad were found nearby. His widow filed for workers' compensation benefits, and an arbitrator awarded her benefits. On appeal, the Industrial Commission affirmed the arbitrator's decision, and a circuit court affirmed the commission's decision. The employer appealed, claiming that there was no direct or circumstantial evidence to show that the man was electrocuted during the course of his employment.

The First District Appellate Court of Illinois held that the manifest weight of the evidence supported the finding that the man's death arose out of and in the course of his employment. Although there was no direct evidence of electrocution, the circumstantial evidence presented was more than sufficient to support a logical and reasonable inference of a causal connection between the man's employment and his resulting death. The deputy medical examiner affirmed that the man died as a result of low voltage electrocution, notwithstanding evidence of heart disease. The evidence established that maintenance mechanics were sometimes required to place their hands where there was an electrical current, and that electrical shocks were considered a hazard of the trade. Based on the foregoing, the court affirmed the decision of the circuit court in favor of the widow. *Reliance Elevator Co. v. Industrial Com'n,* 600 N.E.2d 4 (Ill.App.1st Dist.1992).

B. Preexisting Conditions

Although an injury may occur on the job or appear to be work-related, it may be the result of a preexisting condition or an aggravation of a preexisting condition. However, such a determination does not necessarily bar a claim for benefits.

A painter was seriously injured after falling 30 feet when a support rope snapped. He filed a claim for workers' compensation benefits against his employer and its insurer. An administrative law judge (ALJ) determined that the employee was permanently, totally disabled and entitled to full benefits. The employer argued that § 8(f) of the Longshore and Harbor Workers' Compensation Act (33 U.S.C. § 908(f)) limited the claim to 104 weeks because the employee had a pre-existing permanent partial disability (alcoholism), known to the employer, without which the employee would not be totally disabled. The employer argued that the employee's alcoholism robbed him of his motivation to rehabilitate himself. The District of Columbia Benefits Review Board vacated the ALJ's decision, finding that despite being rendered a paraplegic who was incontinent, the injury was not severe enough to make full-time employment impossible. The Office of Workers' Compensation Programs of the U.S. Department of Labor appealed on behalf of the employee to the U.S. Court of Appeals, District of Columbia Circuit.

The court of appeals stated that the only question to be resolved was whether the employee's alcoholism was a direct contributing factor to his total disability. In order to do this, the employer would have to show that a subsequent injury alone would not have caused total permanent disability. The employer could not satisfy this standard. There was evidence in the record that work-related injuries caused total disability and that the employee's physical limitations would prevent all but the most ambitious and motivated individual from becoming reemployed. The court vacated the board's decision and reinstated the ALJ's order. *Director, Office of Workers' Compensation Programs v. Jaffe New York Decorating,* 25 F.3d 1080 (D.C.Cir.1994).

An Arkansas employee suffered a work-related injury which resulted in some degree of permanent physical impairment but did not result in any reduction in his wage earning capacity. Eight years later, the worker suffered another compensable injury. The impairment which resulted from this injury was allegedly greater than that which would have occurred but for the worker's previous compensable injury. The Workers' Compensation Commission determined that the Second Injury Fund was not liable because the employee's previous injury was work-related and did not result in a loss of earning capacity. The employer and its workers' compensation carrier appealed to the Court of Appeals of Arkansas.

The employer and the carrier contended that the Second Injury Fund was liable for a portion of the compensation benefits due the worker. The court of appeals utilized a three-part test to determine whether the fund was liable. First, the court agreed with the commission that the employee's earlier injury was a compensable injury. Second, the injury resulted in a permanent impairment. The court determined that the prior impairment need not result in a loss of earning capacity and may be caused by either a work-related or a nonwork-related injury. A contrary holding would impermissibly distinguish between types of handicapped persons. The court did not address the third part of the test which required that the compensable injury combine with the recent injury to produce the current disability status. The court of appeals affirmed the finding that the employee was permanently and totally disabled, reversed the finding as to the liability of the Second Injury Fund and remanded the case for further consideration of the three-part test. *White Consolidated v. Rooney*, 866 S.W.2d 838 (Ark.App.1993).

A New Hampshire employee with a history of back problems allegedly injured his back while shoveling gravel for his employer. The employee filed a claim for a permanent partial disability award with the department of labor. The hearing officer deemed medical evidence insufficient to support a finding that the injury was a result of the shoveling at work. However, the employee appealed, claiming that the hearing officer failed to apply the amended statute allowing permanent partial disability awards for spinal column or spinal cord injuries. Furthermore, the employee claimed the hearing officer erred in determining that any permanent impairment that existed, existed before the alleged injury. On appeal, the Supreme Court of New Hampshire affirmed the hearing officer's finding and dismissed the employee's claims. The court agreed that benefits should not be awarded because the employee did not prove his condition arose from his employment. Moreover, the medical evidence presented showed no evidence of a definite new injury. *Petition of Hyde,* 605 A.2d 228 (N.H.1992).

An Illinois man worked for a company as a truck driver for 17 years. He was involved in a car accident, injuring his neck and back, and was off work for 18 months. Shortly after he returned to work, he injured his back, neck and legs while moving some 50-gallon barrels in the course of his employment. He became depressed, short-tempered and bitter following this accident and was unable to return to work. At a hearing before an arbitrator, he was awarded workers' compensation benefits for permanent and total disability. That decision was affirmed by an Illinois trial court, and his employer appealed to the Appellate Court of Illinois. On appeal, the court noted that a disability caused by a neurosis would be compensable if it resulted from an accidental injury. Here, although evidence had been presented that the employee's psychological condition was preexisting, the work-related accident had aggravated his condition. The accident did not have to be the sole factor contributing to the employee's neurosis. Since the evidence sufficiently showed that the employee was unemployable, and could not be rehabilitated, the appellate court affirmed the trial court's decision granting benefits. *Amoco Oil Co. v. Industrial Commission*, 578 N.E.2d 1043 (Ill.App.1st Dist.1991).

A Nebraska nursing attendant suffered a back injury as a result of transferring a patient from a wheelchair to a bed. The injury occurred from the added weight of the patient she had to support. The employer gave her some time off and workers' compensation benefits for temporary disability. After returning to work, she allegedly began complaining of back pains. She eventually consulted a physician who prescribed some unsuccessful treatment. The physician examined the employee, and concluded that she suffered from a naturally progressing back problem that could have been a congenital condition. The employee and employer presented conflicting evidence regarding whether the initial back injury exacerbated her naturally progressing condition. The Nebraska Workers' Compensation Court denied her claim for benefits. On appeal, the Supreme Court of Nebraska affirmed the compensation court's decision. The supreme court recognized the compensation court's authority to weigh the conflicting evidence and testimony. Additionally, the expert testimony supported the finding that the employee's condition resulted from the natural progression of her back condition. *Liberty v. Colonial Acres Nursing Home,* 481 N.W.2d 189 (Neb.1992).

A Nebraska woman worked as a seamstress for a sewing company for over 30 years. For the last five years of her employment, her duties included attaching collars, cuffs, pockets, and zippers to denim jackets and jeans. Near the end of her employment, her fingers began to tingle, hurt, and get numb. A physician ultimately diagnosed her ailment as bilateral carpel tunnel syndrome. Subsequently, surgery was performed on each of the employee's wrists. The employee filed a petition with the workers' compensation court alleging that she had sustained carpel tunnel syndrome while engaging in constant, repetitive use of her hands. She further alleged that this rendered her permanently and totally disabled. The court awarded benefits to the employee, finding that her condition had indeed left her permanently and totally disabled. The employer appealed to the Supreme Court of Nebraska.

On appeal, the court found that the employee satisfied the necessary criteria for compensation. Normally, there was no indication that the employee's condition was either expected or foreseeable; the injury could be traced to a particular job or activity of the employee and the symptoms could manifest themselves according to the natural course of her work without any independent intervening cause. For these reasons the court found that the workers' compensation court did not err in finding that the employee was totally and permanently disabled. *Schlup v. Auburn Needleworks, Inc.*, 479 N.W.2d 440 (Neb.1992).

A woman worked for a company which manufactured brass items. Her job duties included cleaning and polishing the items, and lifting and carrying heavy trays of small parts which she had to clean. Her previous employment history was irregular. After four months on the job, she notified her supervisor that her wrist was sore. One month later, a doctor diagnosed her as having carpal tunnel syndrome in her right arm, and later, surgery was performed on her right wrist. She subsequently had surgery on her left wrist as well. After filing a workers' compensation claim and asserting that her carpal tunnel syndrome was an occupational disease, an administrative law judge (ALJ) denied her benefits. The employee appealed.

The Court of Appeal of Louisiana held that the employee failed to establish by an overwhelming preponderance of the evidence that her carpal tunnel syndrome was job-related, as required under the statute for the receipt of benefits. Her term of employment with the company lasted only nine months, and her doctor testified that her condition must have been present for quite some time due to the thickening of the affected nerve. He testified that there was really no way to know the cause of the disease. Furthermore, the woman never informed anyone at the company that her problems were job-related. The court affirmed the judgment of the ALJ in denying her benefits. *Ford v. Hart Associates,* 605 So.2d 713 (La.App.2d Cir.1992).

A Louisiana truck driver's normal job was driving a ten-wheeler over medium distances on decent roads. One day, he received instructions to haul auger coal over rough roads on the edge of a mountain. He suffered a heart attack that day and underwent an angioplasty. He did not return to work. The truck driver filed a claim with the Workers' Compensation Board and the matter was decided by an administrative law judge (ALJ). The ALJ determined that the heart attack was not work related. After the Court of Appeals of Kentucky affirmed, the truck driver appealed to the Supreme Court of Kentucky. The truck driver claimed that the stress and strain imposed as a result of a different hauling job greatly contributed to his heart attack. The employer argued that the truck driver was not engaged in substantial arduous labor. He was merely required to shift gears, steer the truck, and avoid holes in the road. The truck driver argued that there was no evidence on the record indicating that the heart attack was caused by any other factor. However, the court noted that the treating physician testified that there was a possibility of a preexisting blocked artery. The appellate court noted that it could only overrule an ALJ's decision for an abuse of discretion. Since the ALJ considered all of the evidence presented and came to a logical conclusion, the court upheld the ALJ's decision and denied workers' compensation benefits. *Roberts v. Estep,* 845 S.W.2d 544 (Ky.1993).

The widow of a man who committed suicide at work applied for workers' compensation death benefits. The decedent employee worked for NBC for several years in a managerial capacity. In 1978, however, the replacement of top-level management brought about major changes for the decedent. He was forced to wear a beeper, received frequent telephone calls at home from the president of NBC, and began working many nights and weekends. Furthermore, in April 1980, he was given the additional responsibility of operating NBC's videotape library, a problem area for the company for decades. As documented in suicide notes, these changes, particularly the operation of the tape library, drove the decedent to take his life in May 1980. The Workers' Compensation Board concluded that the decedent's death was causally related to his employment and awarded benefits to his widow. NBC appealed to the New York Supreme Court, Appellate Division.

The appellate court noted that the record provided substantial evidence for the board's conclusion that the decedent's suicide was the result of a depressive condition which was causally related to stress in his employment. Even though the decedent suffered from an undiagnosed and untreated depression for 20 years, and the job stress merely added to a preexisting mental condition, that did not prevent a finding of causation. It is enough that the work stress be a "contributing cause" of the psychic injury. For these reasons the appellate court affirmed the benefits conferred by the Workers' Compensation Board. *Friedman v. NBC, Inc.*, 577 N.Y.S.2d 517 (A.D.3d Dept.1991).

A 31-year-old Oregon man, who worked for a paper company, was required to bend, twist, and jump down from a waist high table to a cement floor up to 60 times per shift. He began to have pain in his lower back and consulted with a chiropractor more than 50 times during the next four years. After consulting with a neurosurgeon, it was determined that he had a congenital back problem as well as a herniated disk. Subsequently, the employer denied the compensability of his back problems and refused to pay for the surgery. The man sought review of those denials and the referee upheld the denials, concluding that the congenital problem was unrelated to the work activities. The Workers' Compensation Board agreed. The man then appealed to the Court of Appeals of Oregon. The issue was whether the man's work activity was the major contributing cause of any of his lower back problems. The board had relied primarily on the opinions of the man's two doctors. It stated that the doctors agreed that the lower back problems were not caused in major part by his work activities, but by his congenital problems (which were unrelated to his work activities). However, the court disagreed and stated that the board had misinterpreted the doctors' opinions. The doctors stated that they could not determine to a reasonable degree of medical certainty that the work activities were the major contributing cause of his condition. They did not say that the work activities were not the major cause. Therefore, the court reversed the decision of the board and remanded the case for further consideration by the board. *Skochenko v. Weyerhaeuser Company*, 846 P.2d 1212 (Or.App.1993).

C.   The Coming and Going Rule

A Kansas construction worker was employed at a jobsite some distance from his home. His employer provided him with transportation in a company vehicle driven by his supervisor. The worker and supervisor went to a striptease bar after work one evening. After four hours of drinking, the two left with high blood alcohol levels. The worker was killed in a traffic accident and his survivors filed a workers' compensation claim. The employer stated that the employee and supervisor had violated the company vehicle use policy and that the worker's blood alcohol level of .26 precluded recovery. An administrative law judge determined that the death resulted substantially from the worker's intoxication, but an appeals board reversed. The Kansas Supreme Court transferred the employer's appeal from the state court of appeals. It observed that the state workers' compensation act created a no-fault system under which the claimant's behavior is irrelevant to the issue of compensation. The act codified the going and coming rule and contained an exception that allows recovery when travel is a necessary part of employment. Because the worker was expected to live out of town during the work week, and transportation was provided in a company vehicle driven by a supervisor, his claim came within the exception to the going and coming rule. The worker's intoxication was not a violation of law and did not contribute to his death. Because he was killed in an accident arising out of and in the course of employment, the board's decision allowing benefits was affirmed. *Kindel v. Ferco Rental, Inc.*, 899 P.2d 1058 (Kan.1995).

The Supreme Court of Wyoming denied benefits to a claimant injured in a traffic accident while returning to Wyoming from a Colorado worksite. The claimant was a passenger in a vehicle owned by a coworker's wife in which several employees car-pooled from their temporary residence at a motel to the worksite. The court held that the accident had not occurred in the course and scope of the worker's employment under the coming and going rule. The court found that the traffic accident had occurred in a typical Wyoming/Colorado commuting situation involving no special risk and it affirmed the denial of benefits. *Chapman v. Meyers*, 899 P.2d 48 (Wyo.1995).

An Idaho construction worker accepted employment with a construction company at a project in Washington that was 300 miles from his home. The contractor paid the worker $30 per day for "subsistence" without designating any portion as a transportation reimbursement. After completing work on the project, the worker was severely injured in a traffic accident as he returned to Idaho. He submitted a workers' compensation claim that was denied by the state Industrial Commission, which determined that the accident did not arise out of and in the course of employment for the contractor. The worker appealed to the Supreme Court of Idaho, which considered the coming-and-going doctrine. That doctrine states that an employee is ordinarily not in the course of employment while going to or returning from work. The court noted that a number of legal authorities and most states hold that when an employee travels away from an employer's premises, the employee is within the course and scope of employment continuously throughout the trip, except when making a distinct departure for personal business. In this case, the Washington worksite was considered the normal place of work. Because the employee's work did not require him to travel away from the Washington worksite, he was not a traveling employee and was not entitled to workers' compensation benefits. *Andrews v. Les Bois Masonry, Inc.*, 896 P.2d 973 (Idaho 1995).

A New York security guard was required to wear a uniform provided by his employer, and was subject to discipline if he failed to keep it clean. Although he could choose various means to clean it, he used a drycleaning establishment at which the employer maintained an account for the purpose of encouraging guards to have their uniforms drycleaned. The security guard, after dropping off some uniforms on his way home from work, was involved in an automobile accident and sustained serious injuries. The state's Workers' Compensation Board ruled that the guard sustained an accidental injury arising out of and in the course of his employment. The employer appealed to the New York Supreme Court, Appellate Division, which reversed the board's ruling. The court determined that the guard was not on a special errand for the employer because he was not required to have his uniform drycleaned. The security guard further appealed.

The New York Court of Appeals stated that an employee who engages in a work-related errand while traveling between work and home, and is injured during that trip, sustains injuries that arise out of and in the course of employment if the employer both encouraged the errand and obtained a benefit from the performance of the errand. Here, the facts supported the conclusion that the guard was engaged in a special errand at the time of his injury. The employer encouraged its employees to have their uniforms drycleaned by paying for those services, and received a benefit in the form of its employees' appearance being neat and clean. It also received a benefit by virtue of the consolidated accounting; it did not have to reimburse the guard for cleaning services he might have obtained elsewhere. The court reversed the appellate division's holding and reinstated the holding of the Workers' Compensation Board. *Neacosia v. New York Power Authority*, 649 N.E.2d 1188 (N.Y.1995).

A Maryland insurance company executive traveled approximately 20 percent of his time on the job. His employer reimbursed him for travel expenses and mileage during trips, but not for mileage between his home and office. He was injured in a one-car accident while driving from an airport to his home following a business trip. Because a blood test indicated a high level of alcohol, his employer contested the claim he submitted for workers' compensation. The insurer further argued that the employee did not suffer an accidental injury arising out of and in the course of employment. The state workers' compensation commission denied the employee's claim and he appealed to a Maryland county court. The court reversed the commission's decision, granting the employee summary judgment on the issues of whether the accident arose during the course of employment and whether intoxication was the sole cause of injury. The employer and its insurer appealed to the Court of Special Appeals of Maryland.

The court of special appeals determined that the accident had occurred during circumstances constituting an exception to the general rule that employees are not entitled to workers' compensation benefits when coming to or going from work. Because the company had obligated itself to provide for the employee's transportation during business trips and had always reimbursed him for his expenses, the "free transportation exception" to the coming and going rule applied. The court affirmed the trial court's decision on that issue, but found a genuine issue of fact concerning the issue of the employee's intoxication. It vacated the trial court order and remanded the case. *Maryland Cas. Co. v. Lorkovic*, 100 Md.App. 333, 641 A.2d 924 (1994).

A Rhode Island employment agency transported workers to various job sites in its area with vans it owned, operated and maintained. The service was optional and employees paid a small user fee. Employees punched their time cards at work sites rather than at the agency. A machine operator employed by the agency was injured in a traffic accident while riding in an agency van that was returning to the agency from a job site. The state workers' compensation court, after a pretrial conference, awarded benefits to the employee, but the workers' compensation court reversed this decision after a trial. An appellate level workers' compensation court affirmed the trial court decision and the employee appealed to the Supreme Court of Rhode Island. The supreme court noted that a Rhode Island statute excluded the award of benefits to employees who were injured in commuter accidents while being transported to work in voluntary car pools and mass transportation facilities. Such individuals could not be deemed to have been injured in an incident arising out of and in the course of employment. Because the employee in this case had been injured while commuting in a voluntary, employer-supplied program, the trial court had properly found that she was not entitled to workers' compensation benefits. Accordingly, the court affirmed the lower court decisions for the employment agency. *Claros v. Highland Employment Agency*, 643 A.2d 212 (R.I.1994).

An Oregon woman worked for a company as a fabricator. After her shift ended, while she was getting into her car (parked in the employee parking lot) her knee twisted, made a popping noise and she experienced immediate pain. Thereafter, she underwent surgery. She filed a workers' compensation claim for permanent impairment after her knee surgery. The board denied her benefits, and the woman appealed. The Court of Appeals of Oregon held that the knee injury suffered while the woman was getting into her car was compensable under the parking lot exception to the "going and coming rule." This exception applies when the injury occurs on the employer's premises, including an employee parking lot. Since the injury occurred on employer-controlled premises while the woman was traveling from work, it made the incident work-connected. The court reversed the board's decision and held that the woman's injury was within the course of her employment. *Boyd v. SAIF Corp.*, 837 P.2d 556 (Or.App.1992).

III. MODIFICATION AND TERMINATION OF BENEFITS

Benefits can be increased where the injured employee's situation worsens, and they can be decreased where the employee's situation improves. They can be terminated completely if the employee recovers or is able to return to work. They can also be terminated or offset for other reasons.

A housekeeper employed by the Catholic Archdiocese of Seattle complained of sexual harassment by her supervisor. She later injured her hand at work, and required a three-month medical leave. She applied for and received workers' compensation benefits. Her supervisor repeated the harassment when she returned to work. When her hand required further surgery, the housekeeper was absent from work for eight months under assurances that her position would be kept open. However, the archdiocese failed to preserve the job and refused to hire the housekeeper for other vacancies. The former housekeeper filed a lawsuit against the archdiocese for handicap, age and sex discrimination and for retaliatory discharge. She also alleged intentional infliction of emotional distress, negligent supervision, invasion of privacy, outrage and failure to provide a safe workplace. A Washington trial court awarded $150,000 in general damages plus $47,000 in attorney's fees. The Washington Court of Appeals held that the trial court had erroneously refused to offset the damage award in the amount of lost wages under the workers' compensation system. The parties appealed to the Supreme Court of Washington.

The supreme court disagreed with the archdiocese and held that the employee was not required to mitigate her damages under the collateral source rule. The compensation had been made for two different injuries: discrimination and the hand injury. The trial court had not committed error by refusing to set off the general damage award by the employee's workers' compensation benefits. This was because the general damage award did not properly segregate damages to allow determination of the portion representing lost wages. The court reversed and remanded the case. *Wheeler v. Catholic Archdiocese of Seattle*, 880 P.2d 29 (Wash.1994).

A clerk for a California supermarket slipped and fell on a wet floor, sustaining injuries which required medical treatment and vocational rehabilitation. She was paid temporary disability indemnity benefits and received a permanent disability indemnity of 61 percent. She sought a 50 percent increase in her award under § 4553 of the California Labor Code, alleging serious and wilful misconduct by the employer. At an administrative hearing, it was determined that there were no safety mats on the floor, and that employees were advised to walk carefully because safety mats would be a nuisance. The workers' compensation judge found that the employee's injury occurred as a result of serious and wilful misconduct, and ordered a 50 percent increase in her total compensation benefits, including all nonindemnity payments. The employer petitioned for reconsideration and the state Workers' Compensation Appeals Board affirmed the finding that the employee's injury occurred as a result of the employer's serious and wilful misconduct. However, it held that the 50 percent increase in compensation applied only to compensation indemnity and not to nonindemnity benefits. The employee appealed to the California Court of Appeal, First District.

The court held that the 50 percent increase recoverable under § 4553 should include nonindemnity benefits such as medical treatment payments, medical legal fees, and vocational rehabilitation costs. It noted that the state labor code defined compensation to include every benefit or payment conferred upon an injured employee, including vocational rehabilitation. The 50 percent increase did not constitute punitive damages and was not constitutionally excessive so long as the total benefits payable were not more than was necessary to fully compensate the clerk for her damages. The court annulled the board's decision and remanded the case for further proceedings. *Ferguson v. WCAB,* 39 Cal.Rptr.2d 806 (Cal.App.1st Dist.1995).

An Iowa employee's arm was amputated after she caught her hand in a meat grinder. She received partial disability benefits for the impairment to her right arm (a scheduled injury). However, the industrial commissioner denied her benefits for an alleged injury to her central nervous system. Specifically, her doctor testified that pain at the "limb's former situs" caused permanent impairment to her body as a whole (an unscheduled injury). The employee challenged the denial of benefits in a U.S. district court alleging that Iowa statute § 8534(u) entitled her to further compensation for the phantom limb pain. The district court held that, pursuant to paragraph (m), the employee was entitled only to compensation for scheduled injuries. The employee appealed to the Iowa Court of Appeals.

The court of appeals determined that Iowa statute § 8534(2)(a)-(t) provides compensation for scheduled injuries (i.e. the loss of an arm). Paragraph (u) provides compensation for unscheduled injuries (i.e., injury to the body as a whole). Psychological conditions resulting from work-related physical trauma are compensable as unscheduled injuries. Although no Iowa decision addressed compensation for phantom limb pain, New Mexico and Pennsylvania have held phantom limb pain to be a disabling impairment under state workers' compensation law. Here, the court of appeals determined that the phantom pain experienced by the employee at the limb's former situs was analogous to a psychological condition. Consequently, it was a compensable unscheduled injury under paragraph (u). The holding of the district court was reversed and the case was remanded for a determination of the functional loss to the employee's body pursuant to paragraph (u). *Dowell v. Wagler,* 509 N.W.2d 134 (Iowa App.1993).

A Rhode Island painter sustained severe injuries to his right leg when he fell between a roof and scaffolding. He filed a petition for compensation benefits with the Workers' Compensation Commission. The commission awarded him 125 weeks of disfigurement compensation. However, due to complications, the employee's right lower leg was amputated. He then filed a petition with the Workers' Compensation Court seeking additional disfigurement compensation. The trial judge ordered the employer to pay 15 weeks of additional disfigurement compensation. The employee filed an appeal with the Workers' Compensation Court, Appellate Division, which affirmed. The painter then appealed to the Supreme Court of Rhode Island. The employee contended that the disfigurement award of 140 total weeks of compensation was highly inadequate. The court noted that the original disfigurement was 125 weeks for what the physician termed as a crushed leg. However, the assessed compensation for the disfigurement caused by the amputation was for 15 weeks (approximately eight times less than the value of the initial award). Accordingly, the court determined that the award was inadequate and remanded the case to the appellate division for further proceedings to determine the proper assessment based on a comparison of the appearance of the employee's right leg as it existed before and after the amputation. *Johnson v. State,* 634 A.2d 863 (R.I.1993).

A Pennsylvania employee suffered a compression fracture of the spine while in the course of employment and was granted disability benefits. He later returned to light duty work for his employer and benefits were suspended. However, six months after his return, he was laid off because he lacked seniority status in his new department. He then filed a petition for reinstatement of compensation. Following a hearing, the referee concluded that the employer failed to sustain its burden of establishing that work was available to the claimant within his physical, vocational and mental capacities. Therefore, the referee granted his reinstatement petition. In addition, the referee concluded that the employer's contest of benefits was unreasonable and awarded attorney's fees. After the workers' compensation board affirmed, the employer appealed to the Commonwealth Court of Pennsylvania. The employer asserted that the light duty job remained available to the employee within the meaning of the workers' compensation act. Essentially, the employer argued that because the position was available to employees with a higher seniority level, the position was available to the employee. The court disagreed and stated that the position could not be considered open to an employee when that employee was not eligible for the position as a result of his seniority level. Accordingly, the court affirmed the order of the board granting the employee's petition for reinstatement of benefits. The court further awarded the employee attorney's fees. *General Dynamics Land Systems Inc. v. WCAB*, 631 A.2d 728 (Pa.Cmwlth.1993).

A Pennsylvania welder became disabled as a result of exposure to zinc fumes. He received workers' compensation benefits based upon an average weekly wage that included a prorated $2,750 annual bonus. One year later, the welder filed a petition to review the compensation award, claiming that the entire bonus should be included in the quarter in which it was actually paid and that the same quarter should be used in calculating his average weekly wage. He based this argument on a state law governing wage determinations for compensation purposes. The law stated in part that "the average weekly wage shall be the wage most favorable to the employee...." The referee granted the welder's petition and the state Workmen's Compensation Appeal Board affirmed. The board's decision was affirmed by the Pennsylvania Commonwealth Court and the employer and its insurer appealed to the Supreme Court of Pennsylvania. The supreme court determined that the commonwealth court had employed the "most favorable" language of the statute out of context. The statute required selecting the highest average weekly wage from the four 13-week periods in the preceding year in certain cases. However, where the employee was paid a wage that was determined annually, the average weekly wage was to be calculated by dividing the annual wage by 52. Because the bonus had been paid as an annual performance bonus, the welder's wage was an annual wage that required prorating the bonus over 52 weeks. The court reversed and remanded the commonwealth court's decision. *Lane Enterprises, Inc. v. WCAB*, 644 A.2d 726 (Pa.1994).

A Pennsylvania woman died in the course of her employment with a coal mining company. Subsequently, the decedent's widower received compensation benefits in accordance with the Pennsylvania Workmen's Compensation Act. After a period of eight years, the employer filed a petition for termination of benefits, and asserted that the claimant had violated the Act by engaging in a meretricious relationship. At a hearing, the claimant admitted to living with a woman and having sexual relations with her for three and one-half years. As a result of this testimony, the employer's termination petition was granted, and the Workmen's Compensation Appeal Board affirmed. The claimant appealed to the Commonwealth Court of Pennsylvania.

On appeal, the court upheld the termination of benefits. The claimant contended, among other things, that certain provisions of the Act violated his constitutional rights to privacy, due process, and equal protection. The court noted, however, that when the Pennsylvania legislature promulgated the Act, it was properly concerned with fostering good morals and encouraging legally recognized and responsible family relationships while discouraging the formation of illicit relationships. For this reason, among others, the court affirmed the decision of the appeal board for the termination of benefits. On further appeal to the Supreme Court of Pennsylvania, it was determined that the provision of the workers' compensation statute that terminated benefits for engaging in a meretricious relationship was constitutional. *McCusker v. WCAB*, 639 A.2d 776 (Pa.1994).

A Georgia woman worked at a convenience market. She sustained a compensable injury and was paid temporary total disability benefits for almost two years. Those payments stopped, and partial disability payments started, because it was discovered that she had returned to full-time employment. Soon thereafter, however, the woman's new employer fired her because it learned that she was working for it full-time while at the same time receiving temporary disability payments. She then sought total disability payments, and an administrative law judge ordered those payments resumed even though the termination of her most recent employment was the result of her own misconduct. The market appealed this decision to both the State Board of Compensation and the Superior Court, but was unsuccessful. Subsequently, it appealed to the Georgia Court of Appeals.

On appeal, the court noted that in appeals of this nature, employees are entitled to resumption of benefits, even if terminated from subsequent employment because of their own misconduct, if their disabilities prevent them from finding further employment. The burden was on the employee, however, to prove that her inability to find full-time employment was proximately caused by her disabilities. The court found that the woman had not met this burden. There was no evidence to show that the woman could not find other employment because of her disability. The case was reversed and remanded for a determination of the appropriate award of partial disability benefits. *Aden's Minit Market v. Landon*, 413 S.E.2d 738 (Ga.App.1991).

An Ohio woman worked for a steel corporation as a "hot bed person," changing the stops on troughs that hold cut steel stock. In the course of her employment, she fell through an opening in the floor of the machine where she worked. She sought and obtained workers' compensation benefits, then filed an application for an additional award based on an alleged violation of a specific safety requirement (to put a safety cover over or install a railing around the hole). The Industrial Commission of Ohio granted her an additional award because of the safety violation, and the corporation appealed to a trial court, and then to the Court of Appeals of Ohio. On appeal, the corporation argued that the opening into which the employee fell was not a "floor opening" within the meaning of the regulation. The court agreed with the corporation. Here, the opening was not in an area used as a walkway or as a usual route of movement for employees who worked in the general area. Since the opening was not one which needed to be guarded under the regulation, the corporation did not violate a specific safety requirement, and the employee was not entitled to the additional award. The court reversed the award. *State ex rel. LTV Steel Corp. v. Industrial Commission of Ohio,* 590 N.E.2d 9 (Ohio App.1990).

A Pennsylvania woman who suffered an injury during the course of her employment and received workers' compensation benefits rejected the employer's offer to work a replacement job because she was unable to comply with the hours offered. The Commonwealth Court of Pennsylvania held that where the work hours are unrelated to the physical condition of the claimant, the work is not unsuitable just because the work hours are different. Here, the position offered was within the employee's physical capabilities and there was no medical reason for a flexible hourly schedule. Accordingly, the court denied the employee benefits. *Swope v. WCAB,* 600 A.2d 670 (Pa.Cmwlth.1991).

A New Jersey employee sustained work-related injuries and was awarded workers' compensation benefits to last for nine years. The employer miscalculated the amount of weekly payments causing the total amount due to be paid in seven and a half years. The employer, therefore, stopped payment once the total award was made. The employee moved to require the employer to continue the weekly payments until the nine years had expired. The Division of Workers' Compensation ordered the employer to continue the payments. The judge of compensation determined that the employer should pay too much rather than the less acceptable option of the employee not receiving funds. On appeal, the Superior Court of New Jersey, Appellate Division, held that the enforcement of the payment schedule would be contrary to principles of equity. In order to prevent the duplicity of payment for the same disability, the employee was not entitled to continued workers' compensation pay for the remaining year and a half. Additionally, the court directed that upon a finding of overpayment constituting unjustly enriching the employee, the employer could attempt to recover the overpaid amount. *Montgomery v. Abex Corp, Division of Signal Stat,* 602 A.2d 290 (N.J.Super A.D.1992).

A Louisiana man was injured in an accident while unloading trucks for his employer. He was awarded workers' compensation benefits and underwent surgery. The surgery was partially successful, but he was unable to return to work. The employer's agent discontinued benefits due to the doctor's statement that the man wished to return to school and due to the fact that he did not return to the doctor's office for four and a half months. The man sought to have his benefits reinstated but the agent failed to tell him why he had discontinued the benefits. Finally, the man filed suit with the Workers' Compensation Administration. The administration assessed penalties and attorney's fees against the employer and it appealed to the Court of Appeal of Louisiana. The court noted that a Louisiana statute authorized attorney's fee awards and a twelve percent penalty where employers failed to pay compensation within the statutory time period. The employer claimed that it had no knowledge of the claimant's ongoing injury and thus it was entitled to withhold compensation payments. However, the court noted that the claimant was never given a doctor's release. Further, the employer never informed the claimant that his benefits were being discontinued. Accordingly, the court determined the employer's discontinuance to be arbitrary and capricious and upheld the award of attorney's fees and penalties. *Chexnayder v. Schwegmann Giant Supermarket, Inc.,* 620 So.2d 392 (La.App.1993).

A North Dakota man worked as a ranch foreman. While managing the ranch, he was thrown from his horse, and injured his left hip and pelvis. He did not fully recover, and was prevented from performing any physical labor (which precluded his return to ranch manager). He received workers' compensation benefits, including medical, disability, and partial permanent impairment for his injury. The workers' compensation bureau indicated that the man was not employable without retraining, but that he possessed strong academic and mental abilities. A vocational rehabilitation plan was recommended for education that would enable him to return to employment. He resisted retraining and demanded a lump sum equal to the present value of all future disability payments on the grounds that he was totally and permanently disabled. The bureau offered him a lump sum equal to the cost of retraining. The district court found that the employee failed to provide any evidence that a lump sum payment was in his best interest in any way other than economically, and denied his request for payment. He appealed to the Supreme Court of North Dakota.

On appeal, the employee relied on medical testimony which indicated that he was permanently disabled and the pain of his physical limitations was all that he could handle. The court, however, saw no medical opinion in the record that said the employee's physical condition and chronic pain precluded his education and retraining. The employee tested very high cognitively, but was simply unwilling to consider a retraining program. Therefore, the court found that since the employee was a candidate for rehabilitation, the workers' compensation bureau did not abuse its discretion in denying a lump sum payment. *Schiff v. N.D. Workers Comp. Bureau,* 480 N.W.2d 732 (N.D.1992).

A Minnesota man died in the course of his employment with an electric company. His surviving spouse was 24 years old at the time of his death. Her marriage and the birth of two children resulted in the end of her employment outside of the home. However, she was able to complete her studies at a state university and was awarded a bachelor of arts degree. After the death of her husband, the woman and her two children received dependency benefits based on the decedent's weekly wage. In addition, the woman sought approval for a training plan for employment which would require her to earn a master's degree in a field unrelated to her undergraduate degree. The workers' compensation judge ordered the decedent's employer to provide for the retraining, and the workers' compensation court of appeals affirmed. The employer appealed to the Minnesota Supreme Court.

On appeal, the court found that the woman's disinterest in working in the occupation for which she was trained did not justify imposing on her deceased husband's employer the obligation to finance her master's degree. The court stated that the spouse could expect to receive workers' compensation benefits for more than 25 years. Forcing the employer to pay for her education in an unrelated field represented a departure from the aims and purposes of the workers' compensation act. The supreme court reversed and found for the employer. *Wirtjes v. Interstate Power Co.*, 479 N.W.2d 713 (Minn.1992).

Michigan workers' compensation law has been subject to continuing debate and study for almost two decades. In 1981, a statute which allowed "benefit coordination" was enacted, allowing employers to decrease benefits to those disabled employees who were eligible to receive wage-loss compensation from other employer-funded sources. Certain employers then attempted to apply the law to employees injured prior to 1982. The legislature subsequently enacted a law disapproving this practice. The employers sought judicial relief (because the new statute required them to reimburse disabled employees nearly $25 million). The controversy eventually reached the U.S. Supreme Court.

The employers argued that the reimbursement provision violated the Contract Clause and the Due Process Clause of the U.S. Constitution. The Court disagreed. With respect to the Contract Clause, there was no contractual relationship here which had been impaired by the new statute. Although employment contracts existed prior to the new law's enactment, they did not address the specific workers' compensation terms at issue. Further, there was no due process violation because the reimbursement provision was a rational means of meeting a legitimate objective — preserving injured workers' rights to their full benefits. The Court thus held that the Michigan statute did not violate the Constitution. *General Motors Corp. v. Romein*, 503 U.S. 181, 112 S.Ct. 1105, 117 L.Ed.2d 328 (1992).

A 55-year-old Arkansas man worked as a banquet manager for a hotel. He sustained a compensable injury when a stack of eight-foot banquet tables collapsed on his leg. He underwent two complex surgeries and was eventually released for sedentary employment with various restrictions. The employer refused to rehire the banquet manager without a 100% release for all work. He then filed a claim for permanent total disability benefits pursuant to the odd-lot doctrine. The doctrine refers to employees who are able to work only a small amount. Even if they can work a little, they can be considered totally disabled if their overall job prospects are negligible. The workers' compensation commission rejected the employee's claim, concluding that his inability to find a job was not due to his disability, but was attributable to the unavailability of employment. The employee appealed to the Court of Appeals of Arkansas.

On appeal, the court noted that the commission had placed undue emphasis on the employee's eagerness to return to work. The banquet manager's willingness to work did not translate into opportunity. Due to a combination of his advancing age, his level of education, his limited job experience and his disability, suitable work was simply not available. The court thus reversed the commission's decision and granted benefits to the employee. *Lewis v. Camelot Hotel & Royal Ins. Co.*, 816 S.W.2d 632 (Ark.App.1991).

A New Mexico woman was attacked and severely injured at a Santa Fe private school while performing her duties as a security guard. She worked for a security company which had been hired by the school. Her employer's workers' compensation carrier began paying her temporary total disability benefits. She then sued the school to recover damages for her injuries, and settled the action for $7,500. The carrier stopped paying her benefits, and in the lawsuit which followed, summary judgment was granted to the employer and its carrier. That decision was affirmed by the court of appeals. The employee appealed to the Supreme Court of New Mexico.

On appeal, the court rejected an earlier rule which provided that satisfaction of a claim against a third party tortfeasor extinguished a worker's right to compensation arising from the same circumstances. The rule was meant to prevent double recovery by employees with respect to certain injuries. Here, the recovery by the employee ($7,000) was less than she would have been entitled to under the workers' compensation act. Thus, the amount she had received would be credited against what the employer owed her for her injuries, but she would not be denied workers' compensation because of her settlement recovery. The court therefore reversed the appellate court's decision and held in favor of the employee. *Montoya v. Akal Security, Inc.*, 838 P.2d 971 (N.M.1992).

In 1989, a Nebraska maintenance employee was injured in an accident in the course of his employment. He filed a petition in the state workers' compensation court alleging that he was entitled to compensation from his employer and its compensation carrier for his injuries. While this action was pending, the employer commenced a declaratory judgment action in the district court to determine whether an insurance policy provided coverage at the time of the accident. The compensation court awarded a judgment to the employee for disability and medical expenses. The insurance company then requested a rehearing. Following the rehearing, the compensation court dismissed the worker's petition without prejudice on the ground that it lacked jurisdiction to make a final judgment because of the declaratory judgment action pending between the employer and its insurance carrier. The worker then appealed to the Supreme Court of Nebraska. Nebraska statutes provide that compensation courts may order one or more defendants to contribute to the payments when the worker's right to compensation is not at issue, but the issue of liability is raised between an employer and an insurance carrier. In this case, there was no dispute as to the right of the worker to recover compensation. Therefore, the compensation court should have held one or both of the defendants liable for the award. The supreme court awarded compensation to the worker against the employer. *Tyler v. Struve Enterprises, Inc.*, 500 N.W.2d 837 (Neb.1993).

A Tennessee employee was injured in the course of her employment, resulting in a loss of range of motion and the amputation of an index finger. She received temporary total disability benefits until she attained maximum recovery at which point she stopped receiving temporary benefits. Subsequently, the employee died in an automobile accident unrelated to her employment before she could file a claim for further benefits. The employee's estate filed for the recovery of unpaid disability benefits. The trial court found that the employee had been paid all temporary benefits due and held that the estate could not recover any disability benefits. The court dismissed the suit. The estate appealed to the Supreme Court of Tennessee. The estate contended that it was entitled to recover workers' compensation benefits due from the date of injury until the employee's death from a nonwork-related cause, even though the claim had not been adjudicated at the time of death. However, the supreme court disagreed. The unadjudicated claim for permanent disability benefits did not survive the nonwork-related death of the employee. *Estate of Thompson v. WCI Components*, 845 S.W.2d 214 (Tenn.1992).

IV. EMPLOYEE MISCONDUCT

Where an employee commits misconduct in the workplace by, for example, violating known safety rules, the employer can raise this as a defense in an action for benefits. Further, disregard of a doctor's advice may be enough to allow for the cessation of benefits.

While operating a bulldozer, an employee scraped the dirt away from a nest of yellowjackets and received multiple stings. He had a severe reaction and was taken to a clinic by a coworker. After receiving a shot, the employee was told by the doctor not to operate machinery or drive for the remainder of the day. The employee was also given written instructions to that effect. After being returned to work, the employee was offered a ride home by a coworker, but he rejected the offer. The employee became unconscious behind the wheel of his car and had an accident from which he received injuries to his head, neck and back. An administrative law judge (ALJ) denied the employee's request for workers' compensation benefits, stating that the employee's disabilities flowed naturally from his failure to follow reasonable medical advice. The Workers' Compensation Board upheld this decision. The employee appealed to the court of appeals which affirmed the board's decision, and the employee appealed to the Supreme Court of Kentucky.

On appeal, the employee argued that his actions of driving himself home were not unreasonable and that the advice given to him by the doctor was not "medical advice." The supreme court disagreed, noting that the reaction the employee had to the stings, the medication he was given at the clinic, the specific medical instructions he received and the offer of a ride home by a coworker were sufficient to uphold the determination that the employee acted unreasonably. The supreme court also held that the doctor's advice was "medical advice." Medical advice was defined as advice concerning the treatment of the injury which was the immediate cause of the disability. The employee's disability would not have occurred if he would have followed the specific advice of the doctor. It was the employee's responsibility to prevent further injury or disability to himself. The court affirmed the denial of workers' compensation benefits. *Allen v. Glenn Baker Trucking, Inc.*, 875 S.W.2d 92 (Ky.1994).

A Virginia man worked in maintenance at a golf course. He was injured when a foreign object flew into his eye while he was operating a weed eater. At that time, he was wearing his sunglasses, not the safety glasses that were issued to him. The employee acknowledged that the employer had safety rules requiring all employees to use the safety equipment provided. The employee sought workers' compensation benefits which were denied. The workers' compensation commission stated that the employee was guilty of wilful misconduct in violating a safety rule designed for his protection, and that his eye injury occurred as a result. The employee appealed to the Virginia Court of Appeals. On appeal, the court noted that if a safety rule is reasonable and known to the employee, and if he intentionally violates the rule, he is guilty of wilful misconduct. In addition, the question of whether an employee is guilty of wilful misconduct is a question that can properly be resolved by the workers' compensation commission. The court thus affirmed the judgment of the state compensation commission and denied benefits to the employee. *Watford v. Colonial Williamsburg Foundation*, 413 S.E.2d 69 (Va.App.1992).

An Alaska employee worked as a sheet metal worker until he was struck by falling ductwork which injured his back. Several doctors determined that he had a herniated disk and chronic alcoholism as well as other medical problems. The employee required back operations including a disc excision and fusion. His employer paid compensation, medical benefits and vocational rehabilitation expenses. Upon being arrested for public intoxication, the employee resisted arrest and fought with the officer. A struggle resulted in the employee being forced to the ground. The employee's doctor notified the employer that the bone surgery had been displaced and required removal to be re-fused. The employer refused to pay, claiming the employee's conduct was an intervening cause. The Alaska Workers' Compensation Board required the employer to pay for the expenses. The Superior Court affirmed the board's conclusion.

On appeal, the Alaska Supreme Court affirmed the superior court decision. The court determined that the Alaska statute presumed an employee's conduct was not intentional or wilful. Mere recklessness does not give rise to the level of wilful misconduct. Consequently, the employee's conduct did not constitute an intervening cause negating recovery under workers' compensation. In essence, the employer remained liable for the employee's back condition as long as the work-related injury was a substantial factor contributing to the later injury. *Walt's Sheetmetal v. Debler*, 826 P.2d 333 (Alaska 1992).

V. LONGSHORE AND HARBOR WORKERS' COMPENSATION ACT (LHWCA)

The LHWCA was enacted to provide compensation for the death or disability of persons engaged in "maritime employment." It works to supplement state workers' compensation laws rather than replacing them with an exclusive federal remedy.

The Jones Act provides a negligence cause of action for any seaman injured in the course of employment. The act does not define the term "seaman." A supervising engineer employed by a cruise ship company was based in a Miami office but his duties included supervising ship engineering departments at sea. While at sea, a ship's doctor diagnosed the engineer with a detached retina, but postponed treatment for two days. As a result the engineer lost 75 percent of his vision in one eye. After returning to work, the engineer sailed to Germany for six months to work on the ship in drydock. The following year the engineer's employment was terminated and he filed a lawsuit against the company in the U.S. District Court for the Southern District of New York for compensatory damages under the Jones Act. The court instructed the jury that the engineer could be deemed a seaman within the meaning of the act if it determined that he was either permanently assigned to the ship or performed a substantial part of his work on board. It also instructed the jury not to consider the time during which the ship was in drydock. Following a verdict in favor of the shipping company, the engineer appealed to the U.S. Court of Appeals, Second Circuit, which vacated the district court judgment and remanded the case for a new trial. The U.S. Supreme Court granted further review.

The Court observed that the Jones Act and the Longshore and Harbor Workers' Compensation Act (LHWCA) established mutually exclusive compensation systems for seamen and land-based maritime workers, respectively. In order to cope with the lack of a statutory definition for the term "seaman," the Court stated that a status-based standard must be utilized by courts to inquire into the employee's connection to a vessel in navigation. The test had two components, under which the employee's duties must contribute to and have a connection to a vessel in navigation that is substantial in both duration and nature. In this case, the district court had improperly instructed the jury to disregard the time the ship had spent in drydock and directed the district court to reevaluate the case consistently with its new test. *Chandris, Inc. v. Latsis*, 115 S.Ct. 2172, 132 L.Ed.2d 314 (1995).

The LHWCA allows the modification of awards on the grounds of a change in conditions or a mistake in a determination of fact. An injured longshore worker suffered a permanent partial disability of over 20 percent and received a permanent partial disability award under the LHWCA. He returned to work at a reduced wage, but began attending trade school for training as a crane operator. He was then reemployed at an average weekly wage that was three times greater than his preinjury pay rate. His physical condition remained unchanged. His former employer sought to modify the disability award in view of his increased wage-earning capacity, asserting that there had been a change in conditions under the LHWCA. An administrative law judge determined that the modification should take place due to his increased wage-earning capacity despite the absence of a change in physical condition. The employee appealed the termination of his disability payments to the U.S. Court of Appeals, Ninth Circuit, which reversed the decision, ruling that the LHWCA authorizes the modification of awards only on the basis of a change in the claimant's physical condition.

The U.S. Supreme Court agreed to hear the employer's appeal. It found no statutory language that limited the modification of an award to cases in which there was a change in physical condition. The applicable conditions could include increased wage-earning capacity because the LHWCA defined disability as an economic and not a medical concept. A disability award under the LHWCA could be modified whenever there was a change in the employee's wage-earning capacity, despite the lack of change in physical condition. The court reversed and remanded the court of appeals' decision. *Metropolitan Stevedore Co. v. Rambo*, 115 S.Ct. 2144, 132 L.Ed.2d 226 (1995).

A shipbuilding and drydock worker was injured in an on-the-job accident and sought benefits under the LHWCA. He was fired because of medical restrictions that made him unable to perform his former job duties. An administrative law judge determined that the worker was partially disabled and therefore entitled to only partial disability benefits during his period of unemployment. The federal Benefits Review Board affirmed the judgment and held that the company was entitled to discontinue making disability payments after 104 weeks, when the LHWCA special fund would become liable for further payments. The worker did not seek further review, but the director of the Office of Workers' Compensation Programs appealed the findings of partial disability and special fund liability. The U.S. Court of Appeals, Fourth Circuit, held that the director had no legal standing to appeal the board's order, and the director appealed further to the U.S. Supreme Court. The Court found no support for the director's argument that she had standing as "a person adversely affected or aggrieved" under the LHWCA. The director was unable to demonstrate how an erroneous board ruling would interfere with the performance of her assigned duties. The Court affirmed the judgment of the court of appeals. *Director, Office of Workers' Compensation Programs, Dept. of Labor v. Newport News Shipbuilding and Dry Dock Co.*, 115 S.Ct. 1278, 131 L.Ed.2d 160 (1995).

Five employees of a shipbuilding and repair company were injured while involved in shipbuilding or ship repair activities. Although the LHWCA applied to the injuries sustained, they applied for benefits under Pennsylvania's workers' compensation law. The employer asserted that the LHWCA was the exclusive remedy, but the state administrative agency ruled that the LHWCA did not preempt state workers' compensation laws. After this decision was affirmed in the state courts, the U.S. Supreme Court granted review.

The Court noted that the 1972 amendments to the LHWCA, which extended federal jurisdiction landward beyond the shoreline of the navigable waters of the United States, supplemented, rather than supplanted, state workers' compensation law. The idea was to provide complete coverage to maritime laborers so that they wouldn't have to guess which jurisdiction they were supposed to be in before filing a claim. Here, by filing under state law, the workers may have gotten better benefits than under an exclusively federal system, but the LHWCA was enacted to raise awards to a federal minimum because state compensation laws were generally less generous. Thus, the workers were entitled to state benefits. The Court affirmed the state court decisions. *Sun Ship, Inc. v. Pennsylvania,* 447 U.S. 715, 100 S.Ct. 2432, 65 L.Ed.2d 458 (1980).

The U.S. Supreme Court held that a maritime worker in California whose occupation was one of those enumerated in the LHWCA could still be a seaman within the meaning of the Jones Act pending final agency determinations that the injured employee was a crew member. Further, the fact that the employee had received benefits under the LHWCA did not mean that he was barred from litigating his employer's liability under the Jones Act. Since issues of fact existed regarding the employee's seaman status, the case had to be remanded for trial. *Southwest Marine Inc. v. Gizoni,* 502 U.S. 81, 112 S.Ct. 486, 116 L.Ed.2d 405 (1991).

The U.S. Supreme Court held that an employee who worked as a welder on a fixed platform oil rig located in Louisiana territorial waters was not entitled to LHWCA benefits because his employment was not "maritime." Not everyone involved in every task that is part and parcel of offshore drilling can be considered a maritime employee. Congress' purpose under the LHWCA was to cover those workers on a covered situs who are involved in the essential elements of the loading, unloading or construction of vessels. The welding work involved here was far from the traditional work covered by the LHWCA. Further, even though the employee would have been eligible for LHWCA benefits if he had been injured on the continental shelf, such was not the case here. Accordingly, the employee was only entitled to recover state workers' compensation benefits. *Herb's Welding, Inc. v. Gray,* 470 U.S. 414, 105 S.Ct. 1421, 84 L.Ed.2d 406 (1985).

A man worked for an iron works corporation for many years. After he retired, he learned that he suffered from a work-related hearing loss. Upon filing a claim for disability benefits under the LHWCA, an administrative law judge awarded benefits under a combination of compensation systems set forth under pertinent provisions of the LHWCA. The decision was affirmed by the Benefits Review Board. Upon appeal by the corporation, the U.S. Court of Appeals reversed the decisions of the lower tribunals, finding that the worker should have been compensated under the LHWCA's scheduled injury plan. Further appeal was taken to the U.S. Supreme Court.

The U.S. Supreme Court held that claims for hearing loss filed by either current workers or retirees were claims for scheduled injuries which had to be compensated under the system of scheduled injury compensation, rather than under the system providing compensation for retirees who suffered from occupational diseases that did not become disabling until after retirement. As a scheduled injury type of loss, the worker is presumptively disabled simultaneously with the injury. It did not matter that the worker did not notice the hearing loss until after he retired. The Court affirmed the decision of the court of appeals in holding that disability benefits be awarded under the statutorily scheduled injury plan. *Bath Iron Works v. Director OWCP*, 113 S.Ct. 692, 121 L.Ed.2d 619 (1993).

The U.S. Department of Labor applied the "true doubt" rule to resolve claims under the Black Lung Benefits Act and the LHWCA. The rule shifted the burden of persuasion to a party opposing a claim for benefits so that in cases in which the evidence was evenly balanced, the claimant prevailed. In two separate cases arising under these federal acts, administrative law judges awarded benefits to the claimants. However, in the case involving benefits under the Black Lung Act, the U.S. Court of Appeals, Third Circuit, vacated a benefit review board's decision, finding the true doubt rule inconsistent with department of labor regulations. In the LHWCA case, the Third Circuit court reversed the award, ruling that the true doubt rule violated § 7(c) of the Administrative Procedure Act (APA). The U.S. Supreme Court agreed to hear the cases and consolidated them on appeal.

The Department of Labor argued that "burden of proof" applied only to the burden of going forward with evidence (in other words, the burden of production). The employers argued that "burden of proof" included the ultimate burden of persuasion. The Court determined that at the time of the passage of the APA, the term "burden of proof" meant "burden of persuasion." Under the department of labor's true doubt rule, where evidence was evenly balanced, the claimant always won. However, because the APA required that a claimant must lose in the case of evenly balanced evidence, the true doubt rule violated the APA. The department of labor's analysis was incorrect and the employers prevailed. *Director, Office of Workers' Comp. Programs v. Greenwich Collieries*, 114 S.Ct. 2251, 129 L.Ed.2d 221 (1994).

Two maritime employees, who had preexisting injuries, suffered subsequent work-related injuries. Both employees were deemed to have total permanent disabilities preventing them from returning to work. The employees, therefore, were eligible for compensation under the LHWCA. After a hearing, the employees' injuries were deemed the result of a combination of the preexisting and subsequent injuries. Thus, the administrative law judges (ALJs) held that their employer was eligible for relief under § 8(f) which limits an employer's compensation liability to a specific time period. A special fund pays the remaining compensation. The Benefits Review Board of the U.S. Department of Labor upheld the ALJs' findings. The Director of the Office of Workers' Compensation

Programs petitioned for review arguing that the wrong standard was applied in determining the employer's eligibility for relief.

On appeal, the U.S. Court of Appeals, Second Circuit, reversed the board's decisions and returned the cases to have the proper standard applied. The court held that employer liability for relief requires an employer to "show, by medical or other evidence, that a claimant's subsequent injury *alone* would not have caused the claimant's total permanent disability." *Director, Office of Workers' Compensation Programs, United States Dept. of Labor v. Luccitelli,* 964 F.2d 1303 (2d Cir.1992).

A paint foreman was inspecting a pipe on an oil drilling platform when a bolt, serving as a plug in the pipe, blew out under pressure and injured him. He sued his employer under the Jones Act, seeking to recover for its negligence. In a Louisiana federal district court, the jury entered an award for the foreman, finding that he was a "seaman" under the Jones Act. The U.S. Court of Appeals affirmed, holding that the employee did not have to aid in the navigation of a vessel to be considered a seaman. The U.S. Supreme Court granted certiorari.

The Court noted that when the Jones Act was passed in 1920, general maritime law required only that a seaman be employed on board a vessel in furtherance of its purpose to be classed as a "seaman." Although some courts had required that a seaman aid in navigation to be able to bring a suit under the Jones Act, the Court rejected this approach. Further, under the Longshore and Harbor Workers' Compensation Act (which is mutually exclusive of the Jones Act), no coverage is provided for "a master or member of a crew of any vessel." This term was the equivalent of a "seaman." Accordingly, the foreman was not precluded from seaman status even though he did not perform transportation-related functions on board the vessel. The Court affirmed the court of appeals' decision, allowing the foreman to recover for his injuries. *McDermott International, Inc. v. Wilander,* 498 U.S. 337, 111 S.Ct. 807, 112 L.Ed.2d 866 (1991).

Three railroad employees were injured while working at their employers' Virginia terminals, where coal was being loaded from railway cars to ships. Two of the employees were injured while they were cleaning spilled coal from loading equipment to prevent the machinery from fouling. The other employee was injured while repairing a mechanical device necessary for the loading of ships. All three employees brought suit in state court under the FELA (which provides a negligence cause of action for railroad employees), but the trial courts dismissed on the grounds that the Longshore and Harbor Workers' Compensation Act (LHWCA) provided the exclusive remedy. The Supreme Court of Virginia reversed, and the U.S. Supreme Court granted review.

The Supreme Court reversed the lower court's decision, holding that the LHWCA provided the exclusive remedy here. Maritime employment includes not only those who physically handle cargo, but also land-based activity which is an integral or essential part of loading or unloading a vessel. In this case, the employees were maintaining or repairing equipment which was essential to the loading process. Even though the work being performed might be considered traditional railroad work which could be done wherever railroad cars are unloaded, it was being done at a relevant situs and it involved integral elements of the loading process. Thus, the LHWCA applied, and the employees could not bring suit under the FELA. *Chesapeake and Ohio Railway Co. v. Schwalb,* 493 U.S. 40, 110 S.Ct. 381, 107 L.Ed.2d 278 (1989).

VI. OTHER WORKERS' COMPENSATION CASES

A great variety of issues can arise in workers' compensation litigation. This section contains cases that vary in content and do not fit easily into the above sections.

The wife of a Missouri man died in a work-related accident in the parking lot of her employer. Her husband filed a claim for death benefits under Missouri's workers' compensation law. However, the law provided that a widower could not receive death benefits unless he was either mentally or physically incapacitated from wage earning, or unless he could show actual dependency on his wife's earnings. His claim was denied because he did not fit into the statutory parameters, but a state trial court reversed on equal protection grounds. After the Missouri Supreme Court reversed, finding that "the substantive difference in the economic standing of working men and women justifie[d] the advantage that [the law gave] to a widow," the U.S. Supreme Court granted certiorari.

The Supreme Court held that the Missouri law indisputably mandated gender-based discrimination. Further, the discriminatory means employed were not substantially related to the achievement of the important governmental objective of providing for needy spouses. Either all widows and widowers could be paid or only dependent surviving spouses could be paid. The discriminatory law, then, simply did not stand up under the intermediate level of scrutiny applied by the Court in gender discrimination cases. The claim that it was administratively more convenient to have the law structured in this way was not sufficient to justify the different treatment for men. The Court reversed the lower court's decision and remanded the case. *Wengler v. Druggist Mutual Ins. Co.,* 446 U.S. 142, 100 S.Ct. 1540, 64 L.Ed.2d 107 (1980).

A Nebraska taxi company entered into lease agreements with its drivers, which recited that the company rented cabs to drivers and that a lessor-lessee relationship existed between the parties. The lease agreement also contained terms that limited driver control, including limitations on work hours, contribution to a company self-insurance fund and cab calling procedures. Cab drivers were prohibited from subleasing vehicles and were not permitted to use phones or beepers in vehicles. They kept their fares and the company did not withhold taxes. A driver was injured and submitted a claim for workers' compensation. The state workers' compensation court held that he was an independent contractor, not an employee, and was not entitled to workers' compensation benefits. A review panel affirmed the denial of benefits, as did the Nebraska Court of Appeals. The driver appealed to the Supreme Court of Nebraska.

The supreme court stated that the primary method of distinguishing an independent contractor from an employee was the employer's exercise of control over the person doing the work. The equipment lease agreement vested the right of control of the cab and driver in the company in several significant respects. Although control was only one of several factors in determining employee or independent contractor status, it was the most important. Other factors such as the skill required, the type of occupation, supplying of tools, length of time employed, and method of payment also indicated that the driver was an employee. The court reversed and remanded the case. *Hemmerling v. Happy Cab Co.*, 247 Neb. 919, 530 N.W.2d 916 (1995).

Amendments to the Kansas Workers' Compensation Act in 1993 established a board with jurisdiction over workers' compensation appeals. Board members were selected by a representative of the state Chamber of Commerce and Industry and a representative of the Kansas AFL-CIO, both of which are private organizations. Under the amended statute, the compensation appeal board's decisions were subject to review by the Kansas Court of Appeals on questions of law only. Workers who had pending cases before the compensation appeals board filed a lawsuit seeking a declaration that the selection of board members by private entities violated the Kansas Constitution by usurping the power of the executive branch and delegating it to private interest groups. The court petitioned directly to the Supreme Court of Kansas, arguing that because of the great importance of the question, the court should exercise original jurisdiction.

After accepting jurisdiction over the case, the supreme court determined that the comprehensive amendments did not usurp executive powers under the state constitution. The state constitution, unlike the U.S. Constitution, did not restrain the legislature from appointing public officers. However, the court agreed with the workers that the statutory scheme effectively delegated governmental power to private organizations. Because the chamber of commerce and state AFL-CIO chapter had absolute control over the selection of board members, the legislation represented an unconstitutional abdication of legislative authority. The court therefore granted the workers an order dissolving the workers' compensation board, declaring the positions of board members vacant and divesting the board of its power and authority. Claims pending before the board were transferred to the appropriate district court for resolution. *Sedlak v. Dick*, 887 P.2d 1119 (Kan.1995).

A Colorado man worked for a ski resort as a part-time ski instructor in exchange for a ski pass which allowed him to ski free at any time at the resort. Subsequently, the resort notified its ski instructors that it needed persons with CPR qualifications and first aid training to work on ski patrol. The instructor was qualified for this position and, because he already had a free pass, he negotiated an agreement with the ski patrol director to receive daily ski passes for his girlfriend in exchange for his work. He then fell while on ski patrol duty and injured his knees. His workers' compensation claim was contested by the resort and its insurer on the ground that he was a volunteer and not entitled to benefits.

An administrative law judge determined that he was an employee, the court of appeals affirmed, and the Supreme Court of Colorado granted review.

The court found that the instructor was an employee of the resort under the basic definition of that term. Here, the instructor negotiated with his employer and agreed to work only in exchange for the benefit of daily passes for his girlfriend. The court rejected the resort's argument that the instructor was expressly excluded from the definition of employee by an amendment to the workers' compensation act which stated that a "person who volunteers his time or services as a ski patrol person ... for a passenger tramway operator ..." is not an employee. It did not matter that the instructor was not paid wages by the resort. Because he specifically bargained for daily passes for his girlfriend, he was not a volunteer, even if he would have been a volunteer had he only received ski passes for himself. The instructor was entitled to benefits. *Aspen Highlands Skiing Corp. v. Apostolou*, 866 P.2d 1384 (Colo.1994).

The owner of a Missouri automobile repair shop contracted with a bricklayer to construct a concrete block addition to the repair shop, which was to be used as a carwash. The bricklayer supplied his own tools for the job, but the owner provided the materials as the bricklayer requested. Although the owner was present at the job site nearly every day, he never gave instructions to the bricklayer. While working on the carwash, the bricklayer fell and broke his ankle and wrist. The bricklayer claimed he was a statutory employee and thereby entitled to workers' compensation benefits. The Industrial Relations Commission agreed with the bricklayer and awarded him medical and disability benefits. The owner appealed to the Missouri Court of Appeals.

On appeal, the owner asserted that the commission erred in finding he was the bricklayer's statutory employer, because the construction of buildings was not within his usual course of business. The court of appeals cited the three requirements used to determine if the owner was a statutory employer: 1) the bricklayer performed the work under the contract; 2) the bricklayer's injury occurred on premises under the owner's exclusive control; and 3) the bricklayer's injury occurred while performing work within the owner's usual course of business. The owner argued that the bricklayer failed to meet the third requirement because his injury did not occur while repairing an automobile, the owner's usual course of business. The court of appeals agreed, stating that the construction of the addition was not a regular part of the owner's business. The owner was not acting as a general contractor in the construction project as the commission had found. Rather, he was merely the owner of an automobile repair business and should not be classified as a statutory employer. The award of workers' compensation was reversed. *Thomas v. Halbert*, 875 S.W.2d 243 (Mo.App.E.D.1994).

A worker in a stone container plant fell 60 feet to his death when a metal walkway on which he was working collapsed. He had two sons from a previous marriage. His former wife sought to recover death benefits on behalf of his two sons. The Court of Appeal of Louisiana noted that the decedent's sons were neither living with him, nor was the decedent providing child support payments at the time of his death. The intent of the statute was to compensate only those persons entirely dependent upon the deceased worker. Those persons only partially dependent upon the worker could not be compensated under the statute. *Hackney v. G.T. Contractor*, 602 So.2d 268 (La.App.2d Cir.1992).

A New Jersey man was shot and killed while on the job by the mentally disabled boyfriend of a co-employee. The decedent cohabitated with a woman for twelve years. They also maintained a joint bank and utility account and purchased a home as joint tenants. The woman filed for workers' compensation dependency benefits. The judge of compensation denied the petitioner's claim because she was not the decedent's wife within the meaning of the statutes. She then appealed to the Superior Court of New Jersey, Appellate Division. The woman contended that she was entitled to benefits as the "de facto" wife of the decedent. Courts have recognized a de facto marital relationship in certain cases. However, such claims have only been sustained when "the surviving petitioner had entered into a ceremonial marriage unaware of any marital impediment on the part of the decedent employee." The parties in this case did not enter into a ceremonial marriage and the woman was well aware of her single status. Therefore, the court affirmed the decision of the workers' compensation judge denying dependency benefits. *Toms v. Dee Rose Furniture*, 621 A.2d 91 (N.J.Super.A.D.1993).

A part-time newspaper carrier was employed by a New Jersey newspaper. She also held another job on a full-time basis. While delivering newspapers, a truck collided with her car. She suffered severe injuries and suffered a 55 percent permanent partial disability. She applied for workers' compensation benefits. She had worked 17 and a half hours each week for the newspaper and had been paid at the hourly rate of $8.73. The workers' compensation court calculated recovery on a reconstructed 40-hour work week. The employer appealed to the Superior Court, Appellate Division. The appellate court reversed the decision and calculated benefits on an actual work week based on part-time hours. The employee then appealed to the Supreme Court of New Jersey.

The appellate court reversed the decision of the workers' compensation court because of the 1979 Workers' Compensation Act Amendments. Under the amendments, the definition of part-time employment was changed and the appellate court read the language to provide that compensation for part-time employees would consist simply of their hourly rate of pay multiplied by the number of hours in their regular work week. However, the supreme court noted that in concluding that the regular hours of a part-time employee constituted the outer limits of a compensation award, the appellate court had perceived no distinction between part-time employees who suffered temporary disabilities and those who suffered permanent disabilities. The legislative history accompanying the amendments did not refer to several important decisions that used the reconstructed work week. Since the legislature was fully aware of the decisions, it did not intend to alter the practice with respect to calculation of compensation benefits for part-time, permanently injured employees. Therefore, the court reversed the decision of the appellate court and upheld the workers' compensation award. *Katsoris v. South Jersey Publishing Company,* 622 A.2d 219 (N.J.1993).

A man worked as a journeyman electrician for an electric power company. While stringing a new aluminum electrical line to a water well system, his right hand made contact with a 7,200 volt energized conductor. An electrical charge entered the top of his hand and exited at his right hip. His upper torso, comprising 28% of his body, was burned. He sought workers' compensation benefits for the total loss of his right hand and leg, and a jury awarded him lifetime benefits. The employer appealed, arguing that the injury to his right leg did not correspond to any of the injuries listed in the statute that are compensated by lifetime benefits.

The Court of Appeals of Texas affirmed the judgment of the trial court. It held that even though the man's injury (which resulted in total and permanent loss of the right leg at or above the ankle) was not listed in the applicable statute, it necessarily resulted in the loss of the attached foot. The loss of the whole leg was an injury listed within the statute. A medical expert testified that the man was more susceptible to injuries in the future and should not be in situations where he could injure his hand or foot. The court found that the man could not satisfactorily perform the usual tasks of a workman because of the loss of use of his right leg. There was also continuing need for treatment to his thigh and leg. The evidence showed that the man suffered total incapacity and total loss of his right leg at or above the ankle. The court held that he was eligible for lifetime benefits. *Texas General Indemnity Co. v. Martin,* 836 S.W.2d 636 (Tenn.App.1992).

A reforestation company, headquartered in Oregon, but providing work in both Oregon and Washington, hired a temporary employee to do some seasonal work. The employee worked in Washington for two months and then was transferred to an Oregon site where he was injured. The company's Washington coverage for workers' compensation provided the employee with benefits. The employee filed for benefits in Oregon which the company denied. The company argued that the employee was not a subject worker and the company was not a subject employer under the Oregon Workers' Compensation Law. After a hearing, the referee found that the employee was entitled to benefits and the Workers' Compensation Board (board) affirmed. The company sought review of the decision.

On appeal, the Court of Appeals of Oregon affirmed the board's decision. The court held that the permanent employment relation test was the appropriate standard to determine if Oregon's law applied. Specifically, the court highlighted several factors to be considered in assessing "the extent to which the claimant's work outside the state is temporary." Among the factors, the court found that the employee and employer would be subject to Oregon law based on the location of the company headquarters, place of the employee's hiring, variety of locations he could work and the return to Oregon for work assignments. The employee was entitled to benefits. *Northwest Greentree Inc. v. Cervantes-Ochoa and SAIF Corp.,* 830 P.2d 627 (Or.App.1992).

A South Carolina carpenter was hired by a subcontractor to work on a residential site. On his first day of work, he fell from a two story high scaffold and was severely injured. He sought workers' compensation benefits from the contractor. The Workers' Compensation Commission awarded benefits and the contractor appealed to the Supreme Court of South Carolina. The contractor contended that it was not the carpenter's statutory employer. However, the court noted that the contractor sent a letter to its insurer admitting the contractor-subcontractor relationship. Next, the contractor argued that the employee was required to establish that his immediate employer was financially irresponsible before bringing a claim against his statutory employer. However, the court noted that section 42-1-410 does not expressly require proof of the immediate employer's inability to pay. Rather, the contractor was entitled to indemnity from the immediate employer and could either bring a separate action against him for indemnification or join him as a defendant in the action brought by the injured employee. Thus, the court upheld the decision of the Workers' Compensation Commission awarding benefits to the injured employee. *Long v. Atlantic Homes*, 428 S.E.2d 711 (S.C.1993).

An Oregon woman worked as a welder for a shipyard from 1942 to 1945. She was exposed to asbestos during this time. Her work ended with the war, in 1945, after which she did not work or seek work, preferring to stay home and raise her children. She later developed laryngeal cancer, which was determined to be compensable. Her physical condition deteriorated so that, from 1962 on, she was unable to reenter the work force. She applied for permanent total disability (PTD) benefits with the Oregon Workers' Compensation Board, but her application was denied. She appealed to the Court of Appeals of Oregon.

On appeal, she asserted that because her compensable condition rendered her unable to seek gainful employment, she did not need to show that she had "made reasonable efforts" to obtain employment. The court, while agreeing with this argument, stated that an applicant still had to prove that, but for the compensable condition, she would be willing to seek regular gainful employment. Here, the applicant had not shown that she would be willing to work if she did not suffer from laryngeal cancer. Accordingly, the board's refusal to award PTD benefits was affirmed. *Stephen v. Oregon Shipyards,* 838 P.2d 1109 (Or.App.1992).

While working as a journeyman painter for a painting company, a Colorado man sustained an industrial injury to his knee. Because of physical restrictions imposed on him by his doctor, he was unable to return to his painting job. He was placed in a vocational rehabilitation program for 26 months, during which time he was identified as being capable of working as a bookkeeper or a shipping clerk. However, each of these occupations had a pay scale less than 50% of what he had made at the time of his injury. In the hearing to determine whether the painter was permanently and totally disabled, the administrative law judge (ALJ) found that the bookkeeper and shipping clerk positions did not amount to "gainful employ-ment" because their hourly rate of pay was so low compared to what the painter had previously earned.

After the ALJ found the painter to be permanently and totally disabled, a review panel affirmed. On appeal to the Colorado Court of Appeals, that decision was reversed. The court noted that if a claimant could "regain efficiency in some substantial degree in the field of general employment," a finding of permanent total   disability would be precluded. However, in this case, the finding of permanent total disability had been wrongfully premised solely on whether the employment available to the painter was "gainful." There should have been more than a comparison of salary ranges in the determination of whether the employment was gainful. Accordingly, the court set aside the review panel's order and remanded the case for further proceedings. *Prestige Painting v. Mitchusson,* 825 P.2d 1049 (Colo.App.1991).

A woman worked for a company and suffered a compensable lower back injury. She was treated by several physicians, and she and the company ultimately agreed upon an authorized treating physician. The employee later requested the company to authorize treatment by another physician, and the company refused. Subsequently, surgery was performed on the employee by the unauthorized physician. The woman filed for workers' compensation, and the commission directed the company to pay for the surgery. The company appealed, arguing that it did not approve of the surgery and that the physician was not the authorized treating physician. The Court of Appeals of Virginia affirmed the decision of the commission. It held that although the physician who performed the surgery was not the authorized physician, the company was required to pay for the surgery because the employee benefited appreciably from it, and the evidence showed that the extent of her injury was actually greater than that determined by her authorized treating physician. The court found that the woman had acted in good faith by trying to seek the approval of her treating physician and the company before the surgery, and that the surgery was both medically reasonable and necessary. The court held that the evidence was sufficent to support the award of medical expenses to the unauthorized treating physician. *Shenandoah Products, Inc. v. Whitlock,* 421 S.E.2d 483 (Va.App.1992).

A Louisiana man was hurt on the job when he attempted to recoil a hose which flipped up, striking him in the groin. Subsequently, the employee's testicles atrophied and induced sterility. The workers' compensation hearing officer awarded him benefits for 100 weeks pursuant to Louisiana Statutes Annotated § 23:1221(4)(p). The administrative officer reasoned that the loss of function in the testes was a physical impairment which permitted an award of benefits without a commensurate finding of continued disability as generally required by the act. The employer then appealed to the Court of Appeal of Louisiana. The appellate court reasoned that the testes performed a physical function which was prematurely interrupted by the work injury. However, the Louisiana legislature amended § 23:1221(4)(p) to state that the employee must prove that the injured organ was contained within the thoracic or abdominal cavities. The employer argued that the testes were not within the thoracic or abdominal cavities. However, testimony indicated that although the scrotum was not contained fully in the abdominal cavity it could be considered an extension of this section. Further, the court looked to the legislative history of the statute and determined that the legislature did not intend to exclude the male reproductive organs from coverage under the act. Accordingly, the court upheld the decision of the trial court and awarded benefits. *Lindon v. Terminex Services, Inc.,* 617 So.2d 1251 (La.App.1993).

While employed as a carpenter, a Minnesota man injured his back in 1986. As a result, he sustained a nine percent permanent partial disability. After several years, he applied for a carpentry position with a construction company. The preemployment health questionnaire asked specific questions concerning whether he had a previous back injury or had received workers' compensation benefits. He answered no to all the questions. He was subsequently injured and 35% of the injury was attributed to the construction company while 65% went to the previous condition. The workers' compensation judge denied benefits to the worker because of false statements on the health questionnaire. The Workers' Compensation Court of Appeals (WCCA) affirmed the decision, and the claimant appealed to the Minnesota Supreme Court.

The supreme court noted that in 1989, it had ruled that the false representation as to physical condition made by an employee precludes the awarding of workers' compensation benefits. However, the supreme court also noted that only questions that were valid under the Minnesota Human Rights Act would preclude the awarding of benefits. Under that act, only those medical questions that were related to essential job-related abilities were valid. The court examined the health questionnaire and determined that the questions were not designed to elicit responses regarding those disabilities which would prevent the applicant from doing the essential job functions of a carpenter. For instance, one inquiry was whether the applicant had ever injured his back. Having a functioning back was necessary to perform the work of a carpenter; however, having a back that has never been injured was not. Further, the court noted that the construction company asked whether the applicant had ever made any workers' compensation claims. The court determined that this was too broad and not tailored to the needs of the job in question. Therefore, the questions were in violation of the Minnesota Human Rights Act and could not be used to deny workers' compensation benefits. The supreme court reversed the decision of the WCCA and ordered judgment for the worker. *Huisenga v. Opus Corp.,* 494 N.W.2d 469 (Minn.1992).

I. VOLUNTARY SEPARATION

State unemployment compensation systems are designed to provide temporary wage replacement for workers who become involuntarily unemployed through no fault of their own. Major issues in this area include whether the worker is an employee or an independent contractor and whether the employment termination was voluntary or involuntary.

A. Unemployment Caused by Labor Stoppages

A Michigan statute made employees ineligible for unemployment compensation benefits if they provided "financing," by means other than the payment of regular union dues, for a strike that caused their unemployment. Employees of General Motors were required by their union to pay "emergency dues" to augment the union's strike insurance fund. Several local unions went on strike, curtailing operations at other plants. Strike fund benefits were paid to all the workers who were idle. They then sought unemployment compensation benefits, but were denied such benefits by the Michigan Supreme Court. They appealed to the U.S. Supreme Court. The Court agreed with the lower court that the employees' payment of emergency dues amounted to "financing" of the strikes which caused the unemployment. Even though federal labor law protects employee rights to authorize a strike, it does not prohibit a state from deciding to disallow unemployment benefits to employees who cause their own unemployment. The decision to participate in the strike caused the unemployment in this case, making it voluntary rather than involuntary. The Court affirmed the Michigan Supreme Court's decision denying benefits. *Baker v. General Motors Corp.*, 478 U.S. 621, 106 S.Ct. 3129, 92 L.Ed.2d 504 (1986).

Unionized employees of a Pennsylvania hospital notified the hospital that a one-day work stoppage would occur when their collective bargaining agreement expired. They also scheduled a one-day stoppage two weeks later. The hospital decided not to admit new patients and to transfer existing patients elsewhere to avoid endangering them. Union employees reported for work the following day but were told that work was not available because of the threat of the second work stoppage. The employer notified the union that its strike threat had created an unsafe condition for patient admissions. The employees filed claims for unemployment compensation. Benefits were denied for the first week of the stoppage, but granted for the following week. The Pennsylvania Commonwealth Court determined that where unemployment is due to a work stoppage, eligibility for unemployment compensation depends on whether the stoppage is a strike or a lock-out. The party changing the status quo is responsible for the work stoppage. In this case, the union's threat to impose one-day work stoppages two weeks apart did not constitute an offer to continue working for a reasonable time period and made hospital operations impossible. Accordingly, the union had changed the status quo and benefits were denied for the entire period. *Miners Hosp. of Northern Cambria v. Unemployment Comp. Bd. of Review*, 658 A.2d 495 (Pa.Cmwlth.1995).

Employees of a unionized Pennsylvania plant submitted unemployment compensation claims for days they did not work when they claimed that they could not safely cross a picket line established at their plant by a union representing another bargaining unit. Despite evidence of threats and actual damage to an employee's automobile, a hearing referee determined that the workers had participated in the labor dispute and were ineligible for benefits. The state unemployment compensation board of review reversed the referee's decision, and the Commonwealth Court of Pennsylvania affirmed the award of benefits. The claimants were not required to show that actual violence had occurred in order to prove that their refusal to cross the picket line was involuntary. Force or threats that created a fear of violence were sufficient to prove that failure to cross the line had been involuntary. *Stone Container Corp. v. Unemployment Comp. Bd. of Review*, 657 A.2d 1333 (Pa.Cmwlth.1995).

The District Court of Appeal of Florida, First District, agreed with a state unemployment appeals commission ruling that striking workers who had received strike benefits from their union were to be considered employees of the union at the time of their strike. The workers had been required by their union to participate at picket sites for at least four hours per week during the strike, and their $100 weekly strike benefits were considered wages for the purpose of the state unemployment compensation law. *International Assn. of Machinists v. Tucker*, 652 So.2d 842 (Fla.App.1st Dist.1995).

Employees represented by the United Auto Workers Union called a strike after the union was unable to negotiate a new contract for Alabama aircraft product workers. Several weeks after calling the strike, the employer hired permanent replacement employees to replace the strikers. The union workers then filed claims for unemployment compensation that were denied on the basis of an Alabama statute that disqualified claims for unemployment benefits when the unemployment was directly caused by a labor dispute. After the state unemployment compensation division denied the claims, that decision was affirmed by an Alabama trial court and the state Court of Civil Appeals. The employees appealed to the Supreme Court of Alabama.

The supreme court observed that unemployment compensation labor dispute disqualification statutes could be typed into two categories. The first, described as the "stoppage of work" statutes included Michigan, Indiana, Ohio, Colorado, and California. In these states, the mere hiring of permanent replacement workers lifted the statutory labor dispute disqualification. The second type of statute was described as "labor dispute in active progress" statutes, which were used in Wisconsin, Minnesota, Tennessee, Oregon and Arizona. In those states, replaced striking employees were required to show abandonment of the strike and an unconditional offer to return to work before the labor dispute disqualification could be lifted. Although many statutes of the first type had substantially identical language to statutes of the second type, Alabama had patterned its statute after Wisconsin's, which was the first such unemployment compensation statute in the nation. It also contained language that a labor dispute could exist regardless of whether the disputants had an employer and employee relationship. It was consistent with the intent of the legislature to prevent a labor dispute from being financed through unemployment compensation benefits. Because the use of replacement workers was not an event that ended the statutory disqualification for unemployment benefits, the supreme court affirmed the lower court decisions. *Ex parte Williams,* 646 So.2d 22 (Ala.1994).

An Ohio nursing home's employees declared an economic strike. Prior to the strike, members of the union received a memorandum from the home informing them that the home intended to permanently replace any employee who participated in the strike. The home began hiring permanent replacements on the first day of the strike. The hiring of replacements was an ongoing process. During the strike, eleven members of the union crossed the picket line and returned to work. Two months after the strike began, the settlement agreement was signed and the strike ended. The 111 striking members of the union filed claims for unemployment compensation for the weeks of the strike. The administrator of the Ohio Bureau of Employment Services granted these claims. The Unemployment Compensation Board of Review reversed the decision of the administrator and the employees appealed to a state court which reversed the board's decision, finding it unlawful, unreasonable and against the manifest weight of the evidence. The home then appealed to the Court of Appeals of Ohio.

The home contended that the claimants' unemployment was due to a labor dispute other than a lockout and therefore they were disqualified from receiving unemployment benefits. The court noted that if the home had discharged the employees, the resulting unemployment would be the act of the employer. The employer's action and not the labor dispute would be the cause of unemployment. Thus, the court had to determine whether the home's action caused the termination of the claimants' status as employees. In this case, prior to the strike, the home informed the striking employees that it intended to permanently replace striking participants immediately. The home began hiring permanent replacements when the employees went out on strike. Employees were never informed that they had been replaced. Instead, employees were informed that they could work during the strike and eleven employees who had crossed the picket line were returned to work. Accordingly, the evidence indicated that the claimants were not terminated from their jobs by the home and the judgment in their favor was reversed. *Moriarity v. Elyria United Methodist Home*, 621 N.E.2d 576 (Ohio App.1993).

After a Pennsylvania plastics company changed hands, the new owner offered employment to all company employees and extended recognition to their union. However, before hiring the employees, the new employer advised each applicant that although it would continue the same wages, benefits, and other economic conditions, certain employment policies would be different. The new employer and union began negotiations; however, little progress was made. The employees became discontented with the lack of progress and walked out without authorization by the union or notice to the new employer. Two weeks later, the union indicated that the employees would return to work under four conditions. The new employer refused the offer and also advised the union that it had hired permanent replacement employees. Finally, three months later the parties entered into a written agreement providing for the return to work of the striking employees. During this time, some of the striking employees had filed for unemployment compensation benefits which were denied. However, the state Unemployment Compensation Board of Review granted the benefits and the new employer appealed to the Commonwealth Court of Pennsylvania.

On appeal, the new employer argued that the board erred because the striking employees' offer to return to work was conditional. In a previous case, *Acme Corrugated Box Company v. Unemployment Compensation Board of Review,* 570 A.2d 100 (1990), the court held that striking employees who were permanently replaced during a strike were ineligible for unemployment compensation benefits until they made an unconditional offer to return to work. The union contended that it was not bound by the *Acme* decision because the striking employees' jobs had been severed by the new employer by the hiring of replacement employees. However, the court noted that there was no evidence that the new employer would keep the replacement employees if an unconditional offer was made. Therefore, the requirement of an unconditional offer as described in *Acme* was not met. The court reversed the board's decision. *Bruce Plastics v. Unemployment Compensation Board,* 621 A.2d 1130 (Pa.Cmwlth.1993).

B. Resignation

A nursing director at a Wyoming healthcare center was criticized by her immediate supervisor and given specific corrective actions for her to take immediately. The supervisor also stated that he would review the director's performance on a weekly basis and took away some of her duties. The director submitted her resignation the following day and filed a claim for unemployment insurance benefits. The state unemployment insurance commission allowed the claim, but subsequent appeals resulted in the finding that the director quit her job voluntarily without good cause directly attributable to employment. A Wyoming trial court upheld the administrative decisions, and the director appealed to the Supreme Court of Wyoming. The court restated its previous holdings that mere dissatisfaction with working conditions does not constitute good cause for resignation. Where an employer introduces procedures for evaluating job performance, the employee must make a good faith effort to use the procedures, not simply submit a resignation. The court found the administrative decision for the employer consistent with the evidence, and noted that courts in New York, Pennsylvania and Oregon had affirmed agency decisions disallowing unemployment compensation claims for employees who voluntarily left their jobs without good cause following criticism of their job performance by the employer. The court affirmed the decision to disallow the claim. *Weidner v. Life Care Centers of America*, 893 P.2d 706 (Wyo.1995).

After an Ohio man was separated from his printing company, he was awarded unemployment benefits for a year. Four months later he worked at a California printing company on a temporary one-week basis. At the end of one week and as agreed, he left his employment and returned to Ohio. He then filed an application to reopen his existing claim. The unemployment compensation board of review denied benefits and the employee appealed to the Court of Common Pleas of Ohio.

The issue for the court to consider was whether the employee was properly terminated from the unemployment benefits he had been receiving in the state of Ohio when he traveled to California and agreed to take a one-week temporary job there. The board maintained that the employee quit his job in California without just cause. The board's position was that he should have continued to work in California. The appellate court disagreed. The court determined that the only testimony offered was that the employee went to California with a round-trip ticket to visit his adult children living there. While in California, he took a temporary one-week job with another printing company. Both parties were in agreement that this would be temporary employment only. There was no evidence contrary to this conclusion anywhere in the record. Accordingly, the court reversed and determined that the decision of the board of review was against all of the evidence. *Prentice v. Albert and Bassett*, 623 N.E.2d 744 (Ohio Comm.1993).

A Nebraska clerical worker submitted a two-week notice to her employer of her intention to resign. After giving her notice, the employee was told to leave immediately, but she was never told that she had been fired. When she reported for work after the weekend, she was told by her employer to instruct another employee on what needed to be done and then leave without completing the two-week period. She was not paid for the last day she reported to work, and she received no severance pay. After she filed for unemployment insurance benefits, the department of labor determined that she was discharged in the employer's best interests and that she was not dismissed for work-related misconduct. Full benefits were allowed. The employer appealed unsuccessfully to the appeal tribunal and a trial court affirmed the tribunal's decision. The employer further appealed to the Court of Appeals of Nebraska, which affirmed the award of benefits. The court stated that if the employee had been allowed to remain employed during the two-week notice period, the burden would have been upon her to show that she voluntarily left her employment with good cause. However, because the discharge had been for and at the convenience of the employer, the employee was entitled to unemployment compensation benefits without disqualification. *Speedway Motors, Inc. v. Commissioner of Labor*, 510 N.W.2d 341 (Neb.App.1993).

Two Idaho men applied for unemployment compensation benefits after each had voluntarily quit his previous employment to accept offers of new employment. In both cases, the new job offers fell through. Although both claimants were initially determined to be eligible for unemployment compensation benefits, the appeals examiner determined that each claimant had not satisfied the requirements of Idaho Code §§ 09.30.483 and 09.30.484. Both men appealed to the state unemployment commission. The commission upheld the decision, stating that "an employee's decision to quit his or her job in order to take a better job is subjective, personal, and unique to the employee and is not connected to the employee's prior employment." The men appealed to the Supreme Court of Idaho. The court noted that the primary objective in the unemployment compensation act is to prevent involuntary unemployment, not to encourage the voluntary upgrading of employment. In this respect, § 09.30.483 requires the claimant to prove that the leaving of his employment arose from working conditions, job tasks or an employment agreement. Since there was no finding below as to whether the claimants complied with § 09.30.483, the case was remanded to the commission for the necessary findings of fact. *Garner v. Horkley Oil*, 853 P.2d 576 (Idaho 1993).

An Indiana man worked in a floor maintenance position for a discount store. He was offered another floor maintenance position with another store at a better wage. He accepted the position but was discharged approximately one month later over a disputed incident at the store. He thereafter filed for unemployment benefits, and an administrative law judge ruled that he was not entitled to benefits because he voluntarily left his employment with his first employer without good cause in connection with his work and had failed to work for his second employer for the minimum ten-week period required by state law. On appeal, the decision was affirmed by the state review board. The claimant appealed.

The Court of Appeals of Indiana affirmed the decision of the review board. It stated that the claimant's leaving his employment with his first employer to accept a better paying job did not constitute "good cause in connection with work" because it was done to improve his financial condition. His reasons for quitting his job were not objectively related to his previous work conditions. The court held that the ten-week requirement that applies to an unemployment claimant who leaves employment to accept a better paying job and then is fired by a second employer within ten weeks does not violate the Equal Protection Clauses of the United States and Indiana Constitutions because its purpose is to stabilize employment and protect the first employer's interest. This legitimate state interest in supporting the ten-week rule applies to employees who are discharged, with or without just cause, by the second employer. Thus, the man was denied unemployment compensation. *Lafferty v. Review Bd.,* 600 N.E.2d 1378 (Ind.App.2d Dist.1992).

A computer analyst, employed by a wholesale company in Pennsylvania, was asked to alter a computer program, apparently so that the company would be able to avoid reporting all of its cash transactions. When he questioned the owner about the practice and determined that it was illegal, he quit. He then sought unemployment compensation benefits which were awarded to him. The company appealed to the Commonwealth Court of Pennsylvania. On appeal, the company asserted that the analyst had voluntarily terminated his employment and had failed to establish a cause of a necessitous and compelling nature that would make him eligible for compensation under Pennsylvania law. The court, however, noted that even though the company could not have required the analyst to perform an illegal act (because the program was not operational at the time of his separation from the company), this was not a prerequisite to the receipt of unemployment compensation benefits. Here, the analyst believed he would be performing an illegal act and that it would negatively affect his personal and professional integrity. Further, he informed the company's owner of his belief. Thus, he was entitled to receive benefits and the award was affirmed. *Tom Tobin Wholesale v. Unemployment Comp. Bd. of Review,* 600 A.2d 680 (Pa.Cmwlth.1991).

A woman was employed by the American Institute of Architects in Washington D.C. as an executive vice president. Her employment agreement provided for a three-year term of office, and stated that she would not be discharged without substantial and serious cause. Approximately seven months into her term, after an executive committee meeting, five committee members met with the vice president. They asked her for her resignation, and provided her with a draft letter of resignation for her to sign. She was upset by the members' proposal, and went into another room. One of the committee members followed her into the room, and allegedly told her to sign the letter right then because she couldn't win if she decided to fight the proposal. She agreed to sign the resignation letter. Subsequently, she attempted to withdraw her resignation on the grounds that it had been obtained under duress and coercion. Her employer maintained that she had resigned. She then filed a claim for unemployment compensation, but was ruled ineligible for benefits because her resignation had been voluntary. An administrative review resulted in a reversal based on the decision that the employee's resignation was involuntary. The employer appealed to the District of Columbia Court of Appeals.

On appeal, the court noted that an employee's departure from employment is presumed to be involuntary. Thus, the employer had to show that the employee had left voluntarily. In this case, the employee seemed to have been given the alternative of quitting or staying with the company and being miserable, with an implied threat of being fired sometime in the future. Accordingly, the administrative reviewer had come to a justifiable conclusion that the employee's resignation was involuntary. Because the resignation had been held involuntary, the resignation was deemed compensable as a matter of law. The court affirmed the award of benefits to the employee. *Washington Chapter of American Institute of Architects v. DOES*, 594 A.2d 83 (D.C.App.1991).

A Pennsylvania woman worked for a medical center for over three years, holding numerous positions during that time. She initially worked full-time as a medical transcriptionist, and then as a secretary in the marketing department. After she filed charges of sexual harassment against a supervisor, the company moved her to a secretarial position in another department. She thereafter requested and was granted a reduction in her work hours. Unhappy with her position, the employee asked and was assigned to work part-time at home as a medical transcriptionist. During this time the company offered her several full-time positions, but the employee refused, stating that they were not comparable to the position she had left. She began working part-time for a second company while remaining in her position with the medical center. When she was laid off from her second job several months later, she applied for and was granted unemployment benefits. However, the charges were applied against the medical center because she had not worked the statutory number of weeks to be awarded benefits from the second company. In an effort to avoid unemployment charges, the medical center offered her another full-time position, but again the employee refused. A referee then denied her claim for benefits. The employee appealed, and the Board of Review reversed.

Thereafter, the company appealed to the Commonwealth Court of Pennsylvania. That court stated that the company had done everything in its power to accommodate the employee. It stated that since the employee voluntarily quit her full-time position to assume a part-time position and subsequently refused several full-time offers of employment, she was not eligible for unemployment benefits. The court stated that to award her benefits would allow the employee to reap the benefits of a change in her employment position which she initiated and voluntarily accepted. This would circumvent the purpose of the law, which the court noted is to prevent hardships. Thus, the court reversed the decision of the board. *Hamot v. Unemp. Comp. Bd. of Review*, 613 A.2d 116 (Pa.Cmwlth.1992).

C. Personal and Health-Related Emergencies

A Missouri woman worked for a company for about three years, then requested a leave of absence due to pregnancy. The company granted her a "leave without guarantee of reinstatement" which meant that she would only be rehired if a position was available when she was ready to return to work. When she later notified the company of her willingness to return to work, no positions were available. She then filed a claim for unemployment compensation benefits which was denied. A state trial court held that the Missouri statute—which disqualifies a claimant who has left work voluntarily without good cause attributable to the work or the employer—was inconsistent with the Federal Unemployment Tax Act (FUTA). The state court of appeals affirmed, but the Missouri Supreme Court reversed. Further appeal was taken to the U.S. Supreme Court.

The Court held that the Missouri statute was consistent with FUTA. Congress only intended to prohibit states from singling out pregnancy for unfavorable treatment when it decreed that no state could deny any compensation "solely on the basis of pregnancy or termination of pregnancy." Here, the Missouri statute was neutral toward pregnancy. Since the employee had left work for a reason which had no causal connection to either her work or her employer, she was not entitled to unemployment compensation benefits. She had not been denied benefits "solely" because of her pregnancy. The Court affirmed the state supreme court's decision against the employee. *Wimberly v. Labor and Industrial Relations Comm'n,* 479 U.S. 511, 107 S.Ct. 821, 93 L.Ed.2d 909 (1987).

A Florida woman who worked full-time learned that her son had contracted chicken pox. The doctor instructed her to keep the boy out of school. She notified her employer of the situation and promised to return to work as soon as alternative day care arrangements could be made. When a week had passed, her employer called her and notified her that she needn't bother reporting for work if she didn't make it in the next day. She couldn't find a sitter, and failed to report as ordered. When she did return the following day, she was discharged. She sought unemployment benefits. The Unemployment Appeals Commission held that she was disqualified from receiving benefits. She appealed to the District Court of Appeal of Florida. The appellate court found that the employee had not voluntarily abandoned her employment by failing to return to work on the prescribed date. She had acted reasonably by delaying her return until a sitter could be found for her son. Accordingly, she was entitled to receive unemployment benefits. The court reversed the commission's decision. *Dean v. Florida Unemployment Appeals Commission,* 598 So.2d 100 (Fla.App.2d Dist.1992).

A Kansas man took a job in Missouri as the director of maintenance for a trucking company. He moved his family to Missouri with him, but his wife and daughter had serious problems adjusting to life there. His daughter began to get failing grades in school. After returning from work one night, his wife told him that she had rented a truck and that she wanted him to take her back to Kansas. He came to the belief that the only way to "salvage his marriage" was to quit his job and move back to Kansas. He lined up a job there, and told his employer he was quitting. His employer talked him into staying until a replacement could be found. In the meantime, the job he had lined up was lost due to the wait. He then filed for unemployment compensation benefits in Kansas. An administrative board granted him benefits, and a Kansas trial court affirmed that decision.

On appeal to the Court of Appeals of Kansas, the court noted that if the employee had voluntarily terminated his employment due to a personal emergency (and after making reasonable efforts to preserve the work) it would be contrary to good conscience to disallow benefits. Here, the resignation had been determined to be the result of a personal emergency, rather than just a move for personal reasons. Since the evidence supported that finding, the court upheld the award of benefits, abiding by the Kansas statute which allowed for such an award if the personal emergency was sufficiently compelling. *Churchill Truck Lines v. Dept. of Human Resources, Employment Security Bd. of Review,* 837 P.2d 1322 (Kan.App.1992).

An Iowa woman worked as a meat cutter in a turkey processing plant. In a regular medical checkup, she was diagnosed as jaundiced. Later, this turned out to be viral hepatitis. Her doctor told her not to work with food because of the risk of transmission of the virus. As a result, she left her job, then applied for unemployment compensation benefits. Initially, she was granted benefits, but her employer appealed administratively. After a contested hearing, the administrative law judge denied her benefits because her illness was not attributable to her employment, nor was it contributed to by her employer. This decision was affirmed by an Iowa trial court, and the claimant appealed to the Supreme Court of Iowa. On appeal, the supreme court noted that if the employment termination could be deemed involuntary, then the claimant might be entitled to benefits. Here, even though the employee had left voluntarily, she could not do the work required of her because to do so might have imperiled her employer's operations. Accordingly, for purposes of unemployment compensation, the claimant would be deemed to have left her job involuntarily. The supreme court reversed the lower court's decision and granted benefits to the claimant. *Sharp v. Employment Appeal Board,* 479 N.W.2d 280 (Iowa 1991).

II.   CONSTITUTIONALLY PROTECTED SEPARATION

The U.S. Supreme Court has recognized the right of employees to receive unemployment compensation benefits where continued employment interferes with a sincerely held religious belief of the employee. Denial of benefits in these cases has been held to violate the Free Exercise Clause of the First Amendment to the U.S. Constitution.

An Illinois man was offered a temporary retail position by a placement agency. He refused the position because the job would have required him to work on Sunday, a day he considered to be "the Lord's day." He then applied for unemployment compensation benefits, claiming that there was good cause for his refusal to work on Sunday. The Illinois Department of Economic Security denied his application, and a board of review upheld that decision. It found that the applicant's refusal to work was based solely on an entirely personal belief which was not a tenet or dogma of a church, sect or denomination. The Illinois courts also upheld the denial of benefits, and appeal was taken to the U.S. Supreme Court.

The applicant charged that the denial of benefits violated his free exercise of religion, as guaranteed by the First Amendment of the U.S. Constitution. The Court agreed. So long as the applicant had a sincere belief which required him to refrain from the work offered, it did not matter that the belief was not in response to the commands of a particular religious organization. Further, the state had not shown any justification for burdening the applicant's beliefs by denying unemployment benefits. The granting of benefits was not likely to cause a mass movement away from Sunday employment by others. The Court reversed the lower courts and granted benefits to the applicant. *Frazee v. Illinois Dept. of Economic Security,* 489 U.S. 829, 109 S.Ct. 1514, 103 L.Ed.2d 914 (1989).

A Florida jeweler hired a woman to work at a retail jewelry store. Subsequently, the woman became baptized in the Seventh-Day Adventist Church. She informed her supervisor that she could no longer work from sundown on Friday to sundown on Saturday, due to her religious beliefs. After initially accommodating her, the jeweler discharged her. When she filed for unemployment compensation benefits, the jeweler contested payment, asserting that "misconduct" connected with her work was the reason for the discharge. Benefits were denied. Following the Florida District Court of Appeal's affirmance of no benefits, the applicant appealed to the U.S. Supreme Court.

The Supreme Court held that the denial of benefits violated the Free Exercise Clause of the First Amendment. Under a strict scrutiny analysis, the rejection of benefits failed. First, even though Florida law only disqualified applicants for a limited time, rather than making them completely ineligible, the denial could not be justified. Second, it did not matter that the employer did not change the conditions of employment so as to conflict with the employee's religious beliefs, or that the employee converted to the religion during the course of the employment. Benefits had to be paid. Finally, the Court noted that paying benefits here would not be a fostering of religion in violation of the Establishment Clause. *Hobbie v. Unemployment Appeals Comm'n of Florida,* 480 U.S. 136, 107 S.Ct. 1046, 94 L.Ed.2d 190 (1987).

An employee of a foundry and machinery company worked in the roll foundry, fabricating sheet steel for a variety of industrial uses. When the roll foundry closed, the company transferred the employee to a department that fabricated turrets for military tanks. The employee, a Jehovah's Witness, believed that working on weapons would violate the principles of his religion. Because there were no "nonweapons" jobs in the company and because the company refused to lay him off, he quit. He then applied for unemployment compensation, which was denied. The Indiana Court of Appeals awarded benefits, but the state supreme court reversed. Further appeal was taken to the U.S. Supreme Court.

The Supreme Court held that the denial of benefits violated the applicant's First Amendment right to the free exercise of his religion. It did not matter that another Jehovah's Witness was willing to work on tank turrets. The religious belief in question need not be shared by all the members of a religious sect. Here, the important thing to consider was that the employee had quit for religious reasons. The Court stated that a person may not be compelled to choose between the exercise of a First Amendment right and participation in an otherwise available public program. It thus reversed the lower court and granted benefits to the applicant. *Thomas v. Review Bd. of Indiana Employment Security Div.,* 450 U.S. 707, 101 S.Ct. 1425, 67 L.Ed.2d 624 (1981).

An employee was discharged by her South Carolina employer because she refused to work on Saturday. She was a Seventh-Day Adventist. When she was unable to find other employment because of her religious refusal to work on Saturdays, she filed a claim for unemployment compensation benefits. The South Carolina Employment Security Commission denied her benefits because she failed, "without good cause," to accept suitable work which had been offered. The denial of benefits was affirmed by a trial court and the Supreme Court of South Carolina, and the case came before the U.S. Supreme Court. The Court held that the denial of benefits imposed a burden on the claimant's free exercise of religion in violation of the First Amendment. Here, the claimant was being forced to choose between following her religion (and thus forfeiting benefits) and abandoning the precepts of her religion to accept work. The Court reversed the state supreme court's decision and remanded the case, holding that the claimant was entitled to be paid unemployment compensation benefits. *Sherbert v. Verner,* 374 U.S. 398, 83 S.Ct. 1790, 10 L.Ed.2d 965 (1963).

A drug rehabilitation organization fired two employees because they ingested peyote, a hallucinogenic drug, for sacramental purposes at a Native American church ceremony. When the two men applied for unemployment compensation benefits, their applications were denied on the ground that they had committed work-related misconduct. The Oregon Court of Appeals reversed that determination, finding that the denial of benefits violated the Free Exercise Clause of the First Amendment. The state supreme court affirmed, and the case reached the U.S. Supreme Court which held that a remand was required to determine whether religious use of peyote was legal in Oregon. *Employment Division, Dept. of Human Resources v. Smith,* 485 U.S. 660, 108 S.Ct. 1444, 99 L.Ed.2d 753 (1988).

On remand, the Oregon Supreme Court held that the applicants' religious use of peyote was against the law in Oregon because no exception was made for sacramental use of the drug. However, the court then decided that the prohibition against use of the drug was invalid under the Free Exercise Clause. Thus, the state could not deny unemployment benefits to the applicants. The case again came before the U.S. Supreme Court. The Supreme Court stated that Oregon could prohibit sacramental peyote use without violating the Free Exercise Clause and, accordingly, could deny unemployment benefits to persons discharged for such use. Here, a law of general applicability, which was religiously neutral, prohibited the possession of controlled substances (including peyote) without making exceptions for religious use. This was permissible. It only incidentally affected religion. The Court reversed the state supreme court's decision, and held that unemployment benefits could be denied. *Employment Division, Dept. of Human Resources v. Smith,* 494 U.S. 872, 110 S.Ct. 1595, 108 L.Ed.2d 876 (1990).

Congress enacted the Religious Freedom Restoration Act of 1993 to create a statutory prohibition against governmental action which substantially burdens the exercise of religion, even if the burden results from a rule of general applicability, unless the government can show that the action is the least restrictive means of furthering a compelling governmental interest.

III. MISCONDUCT

Employee misconduct is often a valid reason for denying benefits upon termination. Even if it is not a full bar to unemployment compensation, it may reduce the amount of benefits payable by, for example, denying eligibility for a certain number of weeks.

A Nebraska employer adopted an antidrug policy calling for a drug-free workplace and requiring its employees to submit urine samples for drug testing. One employee tested positive for marijuana use and was fired. He applied to the state department of labor for unemployment insurance benefits. The claim was allowed when the department determined that the employer did not fire the employee for misconduct in connection with work. A state appeal board reversed the department's decision, but the state labor commissioner obtained reversal in a Nebraska trial court. The employer appealed to the Supreme Court of Nebraska.

The court observed that some states have held that a positive drug test without proof of impaired work performance does not result in disqualification from unemployment benefits. These states include Oregon, Arizona, Washington and Virginia. Another group of states has held that a positive test result indicates evidence of controlled substance use at work and may provide the basis for an intentional violation of drug-free work policies. These states include Oklahoma, Arkansas, Nevada, Louisiana and Illinois. Under the Nebraska unemployment statute, misconduct was behavior that constituted wanton and wilful disregard of the employer's interest, a deliberate rules violation, disregard of standards of behavior set by the employer, or negligent disregard for the employer's interests. The supreme court determined that there need not be a showing of work-related misconduct to disqualify an unemployment compensation claimant. A worker who knowingly violated a work rule was guilty of wanton or wilful disregard of the employer's interests, deliberate violation of rules and disregard of employer standards. The court reversed the district court decision. *Dolan v. Svitak,* 247 Neb. 410, 527 N.W.2d 621 (1995).

The Idaho Supreme Court affirmed a ruling by the state Industrial Commission awarding unemployment compensation benefits to a skate shop cashier and manager who had been fired for making negative comments, creating scheduling problems and bringing her children to work. Evidence produced at administrative hearings failed to identify any specific misconduct by the employee. Although the employer claimed that she was inflexible about scheduling, there was no evidence that she had ever failed or refused to work. Negative statements attributed to the employee had been based on hearsay and none had been documented. There was sufficient evidence that the employee had brought her children to the workplace in order to participate in figure skating programs and that this did not interfere with her own employment. Accordingly, the employee was entitled to receive unemployment benefits. *Wulff v. Sun Valley Co.*, 896 P.2d 979 (Idaho 1995).

A customer service representative at a Delaware bank made a sexually explicit proposition to another representative. The remark was overheard by another employee who monitored telephone calls for quality control purposes. The bank fired the representative for violation of its written sexual harassment policy, which had been published and distributed to all employees. The representative filed a claim for unemployment compensation benefits which resulted in a determination that he had been dismissed for just cause. His administrative appeals were unsuccessful and he appealed to the Delaware Superior Court. The court ruled that an employee's sexually explicit proposition to a coworker constituted misconduct that justified the denial of unemployment benefits. It observed that a New York appellate division court had found similar conduct sufficient to justify the denial of a compensation claim even in the absence of a written sexual harassment policy. *Tuttle v. Mellon Bank of Delaware*, 659 A.2d 786 (Del.Super.1995).

A locomotive engineer employed by the Alaska Railroad Corporation (ARRC) submitted three specimens for random urinalysis over a period of several hours. Only one specimen was adequate for urinalysis, and this sample tested positive. ARRC fired the engineer, and he applied for unemployment benefits. The state commissioner of labor determined that the employee had been terminated for misconduct and was therefore disqualified from receiving unemployment compensation benefits. An Alaska trial court affirmed the commissioner's decision and the engineer appealed to the Supreme Court of Alaska. The engineer argued that he had been coerced into waiving his rights of nondisclosure to the state employment security division and that there was insufficient evidence of unlawful marijuana usage. The supreme court disagreed with the engineer's arguments. Evidence indicated that he had knowingly withdrawn his objection to the release of confidential medical information in the administrative proceeding because of the threat of denial of benefits. Although the engineer was unrepresented by counsel at that time, there was no evidence of coercion in the waiver of his confidentiality rights. The court was also not convinced by the engineer's argument that the third specimen he had produced was a false positive caused by medicine or second-hand smoke. A doctor testifying for the railroad had introduced contrary testimony that passive inhalation of marijuana smoke could not produce the level of drugs found in the engineer's specimen. The supreme court affirmed the trial court's decision. *Risch v. State of Alaska*, 879 P.2d 358 (Alaska 1994).

A Texas truck driver injured his elbow on the job. He was diagnosed with tendonitis but eventually returned to work. However, the pain returned and he made a workers' compensation claim. After a period of treatment, a doctor advised the employee to return to full duty and stated that if he could not perform his job he should change his occupation. Shortly after returning to work, the employee reinjured his elbow and missed more work. When he next reported for work, he was assigned duties that required truck unloading. The driver stated that he would need help because of his elbow and offered to do clerical work instead. The supervisor fired the driver, who then sought unemployment benefits from the state employment commission. The commission determined that the employee had refused to perform assigned work and was therefore disqualified from receiving unemployment benefits. It observed that the driver had failed to present verifiable medical evidence that he was unable to perform his job duties. This constituted "misconduct" under the state unemployment benefits act. A Texas trial court vacated the commission's judgment and the commission appealed to the Court of Appeals of Texas, Houston. The court of appeals held that the driver was not guilty of misconduct according to the statutory definition, which included action or inaction, neglect that jeopardizes life or property, intentional wrongdoing or malfeasance, violation of law or violation of a policy or rule adopted by the employer. Evidence indicated that the driver had performed his work commendably and he did not violate any employer policy by asking for help. The trial court had properly set aside the commission's decision. *Texas Employment Comm. v. Morgan*, 877 S.W.2d 11 (Tex.App.—Houston 1994).

A California man was employed as a housekeeper for a company which maintained living quarters for oil drill workers on offshore drilling platforms. The company's drug-free policy subjected employees to random drug testing by the company, the owner of the platform, and the U.S. Coast Guard. After the housekeeper returned from shore leave, he refused to take a drug test and was discharged. He applied for unemployment compensation benefits which were denied. His union then sued the unemployment insurance board in a state trial court. When the court ruled in the board's favor, the union appealed to the California Court of Appeal, Second District. The issue before the court was whether the worker had been discharged for misconduct connected with his work so as to make him ineligible for unemployment compensation benefits. The court held that the refusal to submit to the drug test was misconduct. Here, the housekeeper worked in a hazardous work environment. The employer had a strong safety interest and the drug screening requirement was reasonable. Even though the housekeeper's job might not be considered "safety sensitive" in another location, the hazardous environment in which he worked made it so in this case. Further, his privacy expectations were minimal since he knew when he took the job that he could be tested at any time. His refusal to take the test was sufficient to deny him unemployment benefits. *AFL-CIO v. Calif. Unemployment Ins. Appeals Bd.*, 28 Cal.Rptr.2d 210 (Cal.App.2d Dist.1994).

A South Dakota truck driver was convicted of driving while under the influence of alcohol. As a result, his driver's license was suspended for one year. He was granted a work permit; however, federal regulations require commercial truck drivers to possess a commercial driver's license (CDL). Because the employee could not obtain a CDL, the company could not allow him to continue working as a truck driver. He was offered alternative continued employment operating a grinder, but experienced difficulties with the machine and was discharged. His claim for unemployment insurance benefits was denied, and a state circuit court upheld that denial. The claimant appealed to the Supreme Court of South Dakota. The supreme court held that if the employee had been discharged for his off-duty traffic violation and consequent inability to obtain a CDL, the discharge would have been for work-connected misconduct that would disqualify him from receiving unemployment insurance benefits. The employee's voluntary conduct in driving drunk was a knowing and substantial disregard of an obligation he owed his employer. However, he had been discharged because of his inability to operate a grinder. South Dakota law states that the failure to perform as the result of inability or incapacity is not misconduct. Accordingly, the employee's discharge was not for work-connected misconduct and he was entitled to receive unemployment compensation benefits. *Rasmussen v. South Dakota Dept. of Labor*, 510 N.W.2d 655 (S.D.1993).

A Florida security guard worked on a rotating schedule including both day and night shifts. His duties included monitoring closed circuit surveillance of the activities in the plant while sitting in a five- by seven-foot, windowless room. He was required to remain in this room for his entire shift, including meals, leaving only briefly to go to the restroom. In 1992, he nodded off for a few minutes and was discovered by his supervisor. As a result of the single incident, he was fired. The policy handbook for employees provided that sleeping on the job was a serious offense. After the unemployment commission denied his claim for benefits, the security guard appealed to the District Court of Appeal of Florida. The court noted that an isolated act of negligence is rarely of such a degree as "to manifest the culpability, wrongful intent, or evil design" sufficient to prove misconduct. Accordingly, the employer would have to prove that the security guard intentionally took a nap on this one occasion or that he repeatedly fell asleep on the job. Otherwise, the claimant would be entitled to benefits. Since the employer had failed to meet this burden, the commission's decision was reversed with directions to award unemployment compensation to the security guard. *Paul v. Jabil Circuit Co.*, 627 So.2d 545 (Fla.App.1993).

During the course of a conversation between a white employee and two coworkers who were African-American, the white employee made the following remark in describing her heavy workload: "Please excuse me, but they're working me like a nigger." The next day both the coworkers filed incident reports with the employer. The employer suspended the employee pending further investigation into the incident and subsequently discharged her for inappropriate behavior regarding the racial slur. The employee applied for unemployment benefits which were denied. She then appealed to the Commonwealth Court of Pennsylvania. She argued that the unemployment compensation board erred as a matter of law in determining that her conduct constituted wilful misconduct. The court noted that the employee's statement was so offensive that it should have been obvious to the employee that its use was inimical to the employer's interest, and in complete disregard of the standards of behavior which the employer had a right to expect from its employees. Accordingly, the court affirmed the denial of benefits. *Witkowski v. Unemployment Compensation Board of Review*, 633 A.2d 1259 (Pa.Cmwlth.1993).

A Pennsylvania truck driver was involved in three traffic accidents. The accidents resulted in damages in excess of $14,000 to his employer. The employer then fired the driver. After discharge, the driver applied for unemployment compensation benefits. The Pennsylvania Department of Labor and Industry Office of Employment Security determined that he was ineligible for benefits due to his wilful misconduct. The driver then appealed to a Pennsylvania trial court, arguing that he did not commit wilful misconduct and that the referee had based her decision on objectionable, hearsay evidence. The trial court determined that, while the police reports were hearsay, they were supported by testimony. The driver appealed to the Supreme Court of Pennsylvania. The driver argued that the employer's testimony was hearsay and did not support the police reports. The supreme court agreed and determined that the employer's testimony regarding the accidents was itself hearsay evidence. The employer was not at the scene of any of the accidents and his testimony regarding them was based on what others had told him. Therefore, the employer had failed to present any competent evidence indicating the driver's intentional disregard of the employer's interest. Accordingly, the court reversed the decision of the trial court and determined that the three traffic accidents did not constitute wilful misconduct sufficient to justify the denial of unemployment benefits. *Myers v. Commonwealth of Pennsylvania Unemployment Compensation Board of Review*, 625 A.2d 622 (Pa.1993).

A Utah man was fired for damaging his employer's forklift. A maintenance worker claimed that the employee had intentionally damaged the forklift by beating on it, resulting in damage to the battery cover. The employee applied for unemployment compensation after his discharge. The Utah Department of Employment Security denied his claim for benefits. The employee appealed the ruling and a hearing was held before an ALJ, who reversed the department's decision. He determined that the employee's testimony was more credible than that of his coworker. The Board of Review adopted the ALJ's findings, and the employer appealed to the Court of Appeals of Utah.

On appeal, the court had to decide whether the board had correctly concluded that the employee was not discharged for just cause and thus entitled to unemployment benefits. The employer bears the burden of proving just cause for the termination. To establish just cause, the employer must show that the employee's conduct involved three factors: culpability, knowledge and control. If the conduct is an isolated incident of poor judgment and there is no expectation that the conduct will be continued or repeated, potential harm may not be shown and therefore it is not necessary to discharge the employee. The employer challenged the board's finding that the employee did not intentionally damage the forklift. The evidence came down to conflicting testimony between two employees. The ALJ had found the discharged employee's testimony to be more credible. There was substantial evidence to support a finding that the employee did not wilfully destroy the employer's property. The court found that the employee's conduct did not rise to the level of culpability required to deny unemployment benefits and upheld the decision of the board. *Albertsons, Inc. v. Dept. of Employment Security*, 854 P.2d 570 (Utah App.1993).

A Wyoming man worked intermittently for a company during a two-year period. The company instituted a drug and alcohol testing policy between the time the man left his job and the time when he was rehired. As a condition for his reemployment, he was tested, and the test results were negative in all respects. Several weeks after he was rehired, the employee was told to go to a medical center to be tested under the testing policy or be fired. The employee refused to take the test, and was fired. He applied for and was granted unemployment benefits. The employer appealed, and an appeals examiner determined that the employee was not eligible for benefits because his refusal to take the test constituted misconduct. Upon review by the commission, it determined that he had not committed misconduct and benefits were reinstated. On appeal by the employer, a state district court found that the employee had committed misconduct and reversed the commission's decision. The employee appealed.

The Supreme Court of Wyoming noted that a Wyoming statute disqualified workers from receiving unemployment compensation benefits and required the forfeiture of accrued benefits if the discharge was for misconduct connected with work. The company had a policy which provided for testing upon "reasonable cause." The burden was on the company to prove misconduct. Because the company did not follow its own established policy, the employee's refusal to take the drug-alcohol test was not misconduct which would disqualify him from receiving unemployment compensation benefits. The court stated that unemployment compensation statutes are to be liberally construed in favor of claimants. Because the company's evidence was disputed and uncertain, unemployment compensation benefits were granted to the employee. The court thus reversed the decision of the district court. *Wyoming Dept. of Emp. v. Rissler & McMurry*, 837 P.2d 686 (Wyo.1992).

A North Dakota woman worked as a clerk in the medical records department of a hospital. The hospital had a policy that allowed employees or their relatives to have their medical records locked in the medical supervisor's desk so that other employees would not have access to them. The clerk, who was in the process of obtaining a divorce, discovered part of her husband's medical report which had been previously misfiled. She put the report in her lunch sack in the bottom drawer of her desk, where it was discovered by a coworker, who gave it to the records supervisor. Consequently, the clerk was fired for breach of confidentiality. A state unemployment compensation hearings referee determined that she was not entitled to benefits because she was discharged for misconduct. This decision was affirmed by another administrative agency and a state district court. The Supreme Court of North Dakota noted that the clerk had been discharged for unauthorized access to medical records, which violated the hospital's policy of confidentiality. The clerk did not have permission to have access to her husband's records. The court found that the clerk had committed misconduct by violating the unwritten policy against removal and retention of medical records, and that this instance of misconduct was sufficient to disqualify her from unemployment compensation benefits. Even though she neither disclosed the records to anyone else nor understood the specifics of what was in her husband's records, the court reasoned that the breach was severe enough to deny benefits. The hospital had an important interest in maintaining the confidentiality of disclosure of medical information contained in hospital records. Accordingly, the court affirmed the decision of the district court. *Tehven v. Job Service North Dakota,* 488 N.W.2d 48 (N.D.1992).

An Alaska man worked for a retail store as a cashier. At one point, he accepted a credit card charge from a customer which was over the floor limit of $50 without obtaining management authorization. He also accepted a check made out to a different store. Management then gave him a performance evaluation report, reprimanding him for his actions. He was notified that any further insubordination or noncooperation would result in his discharge. A month later, he accepted a credit card transaction for more than $50 without management authorization because no one responded to his public address call for assistance. The store fired him. He unsuccessfully sought unemployment benefits from a state agency, and his case eventually reached the Alaska Supreme Court. The supreme court noted that there was evidence in the record to support the department of labor's determination that the employee had been discharged for misconduct, and that he was ineligible for unemployment compensation. Despite the employee's contention that he faced circumstances beyond his control, he knew or should have known of the importance of the policy to the store. Because he had been warned a month previously about the policy, his actions constituted misconduct and he was not entitled to unemployment compensation benefits. The trial court's decision was affirmed. *Smith v. Sampson,* 816 P.2d 902 (Alaska 1991).

A Virginia man worked as a stockman for a grocery store. He suffered a disabling back injury and also depression which kept him off work for several months. During a meeting with company officials to determine whether he was capable of returning to work, the employee was fired by the chief executive officer for using vulgar language toward him. The employee then applied for unemployment benefits, which were denied by the commission because of "misconduct connected with his work." He appealed to a trial court, which reversed the commission's denial of benefits. The company appealed.

The Court of Appeals of Virginia noted that employees who are discharged for "misconduct connected with their work" are disqualified from receiving unemployment benefits. The misconduct must be a violation of a company rule and be of such a nature or recurrence as to manifest a wilful disregard of the employer's interests and the duties and obligations the employee owes the employer. The court found that the company had no rule prohibiting the use of vulgar language in the workplace, and that the employee's behavior was not recurrent. Further, the employee's remarks were not overheard by other store employees or customers and they did not disrupt or interfere with store business. Additionally, the employee had no record of misconduct in over 20 years with the company. Therefore, the court affirmed the decision of the trial court. *Kennedy's Piggly Wiggly v. Cooper,* 419 S.E.2d 278 (Va.App.1992).

An Oklahoma man worked for a drilling company which instituted a drug testing policy that provided for random testing. All the company's employees were given a letter to sign which indicated that they were aware of the program and that refusal to submit to the test would result in termination. One month later, the employee refused to take a drug test upon the company's request. He was fired. He then sought unemployment benefits. The Oklahoma Employment Security Commission denied benefits on the grounds that the employee's refusal to take the test amounted to misconduct. After several unsuccessful appeals by the employee, the case reached the Oklahoma Court of Appeals. The employee argued on appeal that a private sector employee's refusal to take a drug test is not misconduct if the employer does not have reasonable suspicion that the employee is impaired. The court disagreed. An employee's refusal to follow the employer's reasonable work rules and policies constitutes a "deliberate violation or disregard of standards of behavior" that the employer may reasonably expect from its employees, and this is sufficient misconduct to allow for the denial of unemployment benefits. *Doby v. Oklahoma Employment Security Commission,* 823 P.2d 390 (Okl.App.1991).

A Pennsylvania part-time secretary was asked to perform extra duties as a result of financially-based staff reductions. One duty required picking up the mail daily. The secretary was concerned about the "wear and tear" on her car; consequently, the company provided three alternatives: use of a company van, a company sedan, or reimbursement for use of her own car. The employee rejected these alternatives. The company discharged her. The employee then applied for unemployment compensation benefits. The Office of Employment Security (OES) denied her benefits because her discharge was the result of her wilful misconduct. At a hearing, the referee reversed the OES decision. The company appealed to the Unemployment Compensation Board of Review (UCBR) which reversed the referee and reinstated the denial of benefits. The employee appealed. On appeal, the Commonwealth Court of Pennsylvania affirmed the UCBR ruling. The court found that the request to perform extra duties was reasonable because of the reduction in personnel as a result of financial concerns. While the employee's refusal to drive the van was justified, the court found that her refusal to use her own car and be reimbursed was not justified based on the employment circumstances. Therefore, the court held that her refusal constituted wilful misconduct making her ineligible for benefits. *Hershey v. UCBR,* 605 A.2d 447 (Pa.Cmwlth.1992).

A Minnesota man worked for a corporation as a punch press operator on the third shift. The corporation transferred him and other third shift employees to the first shift. He wanted to remain on the third shift because of his child care situation, so he discussed the situation with a union representative. He left work in an angry mood one day, squealing his tires by flooring the accelerator of his pickup truck. He then had to slam on his brakes to avoid hitting a car, missing it by inches. An investigation by the company revealed that several employees were walking in the parking lot at the time of this incident; as a result, the company decided to fire the employee for seriously endangering the health and safety of his fellow employees. His claim for unemployment compensation benefits was turned down on the grounds of misconduct. He appealed to the Minnesota Court of Appeals, asserting that his behavior had been an isolated hotheaded incident which did not interfere with his employer's business. Thus, he should not be disqualified from receiving benefits. The court, however, found that the employee's actions could have resulted in serious physical injury. An employer had the right to expect its employees not to engage in conduct which seriously endangers people's safety. The court affirmed the denial of benefits to the claimant. *Hayes v. Wrico Stamping Griffiths Corp.,* 490 N.W.2d 672 (Minn.App.1992).

A North Carolina woman worked for a company for approximately three years. She was then discharged because she did not comply with the company's no-fault attendance policy. She then filed a claim for unemployment compensation benefits. The North Carolina Employment Security Commission denied her claim. On appeal, a referee determined that she was disqualified from receiving nine weeks of benefits because she was substantially at fault in her job separation. The commission affirmed this decision, and the ex-employee unsuccessfully appealed to a state trial court. She appealed again to the Court of Appeals of North Carolina. The court noted that state law allowed the denial of benefits for a period of four to 13 weeks if the individual's discharge was due to "substantial fault on her part connected with her work not rising to the level of misconduct." Substantial fault included reasonable control by an employee over acts or omissions which violated reasonable job requirements. Here, the ex-employee had been tardy numerous times and had several excused absences. She had reasonable control over her ability to comply with these job requirements. Further, the requirements themselves were reasonable. The court thus concluded that the ex-employee had been discharged for substantial fault connected with her employment, and it affirmed the trial court's decision denying benefits for nine weeks. *Lindsey v. Qualex, Inc.*, 406 S.E.2d 609 (N.C.App.1991).

A man worked as a body shop painter in an Ohio automobile shop. He had a third grade level of education and was functionally illiterate. As the state of technology for automobile paints advanced, his job required an ability to read in order to correctly blend and match the colors. On several occasions the employee mixed the wrong colors together, which resulted in costly corrections by the employer. The employer offered on numerous occasions to send the employee to school to learn to read, but the employee ignored the offers. Thereafter, the employee was issued repeated warnings of poor work performance, followed by a suspension and discharge. The employee filed a claim for unemployment compensation which was subsequently denied. A board of review affirmed the denial. A trial court reaffirmed the board's decision. The employee appealed.

The Court of Appeals of Ohio stated that the issue was whether the employer had just cause to terminate the employee, thus precluding unemployment compensation. It noted that discharge for just cause required a finding that the employee was at fault in some way. The employee argued that the technological advances were beyond his control, and that he was, therefore, not at fault and should not be deprived of benefits. However, the court found that while inability to perform may not be just cause for discharge, a lack of effort or willingness to perform is just cause for denial of benefits. Here, the employee refused the help and assistance of his employer and coworkers. He did not demonstrate a good faith effort to improve his performance. The court affirmed the decision of the trial court. *Lee v. Nick Mayer Lincoln,* 598 N.E.2d 1238 (Ohio App.8th Dist.1991).

An employee of a bank, who worked as a teller, pled guilty to a misdemeanor charge of theft of property. The theft took place at a department store while the teller was off duty from her employment at the bank. The bank subsequently discharged her because the Federal Deposit Act prohibited the bank from allowing "any person convicted of a criminal offense involving dishonesty to participate in the conduct of affairs of the bank in any manner without prior written consent" from the FDIC. The teller filed a claim for unemployment compensation, but her claim was rejected. A trial court granted summary judgment against the teller, and she appealed to the Court of Civil Appeals of Alabama.

On appeal, the court affirmed the denial of benefits. There was no genuine issue as to any material fact, and the evidence showed that the employee had been discharged for misconduct. Even though the theft took place outside of the teller's employment and away from the bank's premises, it was connected with her employment by virtue of the Federal Deposit Act. The teller had been properly denied benefits. *White v. Allen,* 594 So.2d 129 (Ala.Civ.App.1991).

In her application for employment as a secretary with a company, an Iowa woman stated that she could type 35 words per minute, and also represented that she had computer experience. The company hired her for the job. She had in fact attended only one day of computer class training, and took over 20 minutes to type a 40-word invoice. The company then terminated her employment, and she applied for unemployment compensation benefits. In resisting her application for benefits, the company cited unsatisfactory work as the only ground for termination. The hearing officer found that the employee had not been dismissed for misconduct, and that she was thus entitled to unemployment benefits. The company appealed to an ALJ who reversed the hearing officer's decision. A trial court upheld the ALJ's decision, and the employee appealed to the Supreme Court of Iowa. On appeal, the court noted that although the woman could have been fired for her misconduct in connection with the work application, she was not fired for that reason. The department of employment services had adopted a definition of misconduct which stated that "mere inefficiency, unsatisfactory conduct, failure in good performance as the result of inability or incapacity ... is not to be deemed as misconduct." Since she had only been fired for her incompetence, she was entitled to unemployment benefits. The supreme court reversed the trial court's decision and directed that the woman be awarded benefits. *Larson v. Employment Appeal Board*, 474 N.W.2d 570 (Iowa 1991).

A Louisiana man was employed as a pipeline worker by a corporation involved in transporting volatile materials. He was discharged for misconduct resulting from his arrest and conviction for distribution of marijuana. The district manager held several discussions with the employee requesting him to keep the corporation informed of the criminal proceeding. The employee failed to do so. As a result, he was terminated for violating the corporation's drug policy, failing to apprise the corporation of the criminal proceeding, and failing to tell the truth. He filed for unemployment benefits. On the application for benefits, the employee did not mention the felony and consequently became eligible for unemployment benefits. The corporation appealed. An ALJ found that the employee was discharged for misconduct connected with his employment creating a basis for denial of the unemployment benefits. The Board of Review adopted the ALJ's findings. On appeal, a district court reversed that decision and awarded benefits. The district court deemed the evidence insufficient to show a violation of the corporation's drug policy. The corporation appealed the decision.

On appeal, the Court of Appeal of Louisiana reversed the district court's decision. The appellate court upheld the ALJ's finding that the corporation had an unwritten drug policy in place before the employee's violation. Further, the employee stated that he was aware of the company's rules. He had also pled guilty to the criminal charge. The fact that the corporation implemented the drug policy in writing after the violation was irrelevant. The court also found that the nature of the corporation's business, the transportation of volatile materials, allowed the corporation to require its employees to be drug free. *Landry v. Shell Oil Co.,* 597 So.2d 521 (La.App.1st Cir.1992).

An Iowa woman worked for an insurance brokerage firm for 17 years. She was a vice president and head of a department that administered group insurance trusts. Several problems occurred involving incorrect bank statements, employee turnover, and a malfunctioning computer system. An audit of the department showed errors totaling $136,000 in the trust accounts. Subsequently, the woman was discharged. A job service representative approved the woman's application for unemployment benefits, and found that her former employer had not established that she was discharged due to misconduct on the job. Her employer appealed, and the administrative law judge found that the woman was discharged for negligence or irresponsibility in the management of her department and an attempt to mislead the employer by disguising that negligence. The administrative law judge found that the employee was guilty of "misconduct" and thus was not entitled to unemployment benefits. The woman appealed to the Supreme Court of Iowa. The court found that there was no question raised as to the woman's abilities. When no issue was raised as to her capabilities, this factor had no bearing on whether she was guilty of misconduct, nor was it evidence of misconduct. Otherwise, the court noted, every capable employee who failed to perform to the employer's satisfaction would be guilty of misconduct. Because inability or incapacity to perform well is not intentional, it cannot be deemed misconduct. The court reversed and remanded the case for computation and payment of unemployment benefits. *Richers v. Iowa Dept. of Job Service*, 479 N.W.2d 308 (Iowa 1991).

IV. INDEPENDENT CONTRACTORS

In order to be eligible for unemployment compensation benefits, the separated worker must have been employed on terms that meet statutory definitions of "employee." If the worker is held to be an independent contractor, there is no entitlement to unemployment compensation upon separation, and there can be no employer liability for state unemployment compensation taxes.

The South Carolina Employment Security Commission investigated the employment status of persons performing work for a telephone sales business. The investigation was brought to determine whether the company should be liable for unemployment taxes on two classes of workers, telephone solicitors and delivery drivers. Solicitors were required to make phone calls from the office during office hours. The company designated break periods and set maximum work hours for phone solicitors, and provided them with potential customer lists, required them to fill out sales reports, and guaranteed a specific minimum wage drawn against their commissions. Solicitors were then paid the higher of the guaranteed minimum wage or their commission. Drivers were required to report to the office to pick up daily delivery routes and products. They were paid a commission only for completed deliveries, and wore company name badges and shirts. The drivers provided their own vehicles, gas, and insurance and determined their own routes. They were responsible for any product loss or damage, but were not responsible for bad checks. The employment commission determined that the telephone solicitors and delivery drivers were employees and that the company was therefore liable for unemployment taxes. The company appealed to the Court of Appeals of South Carolina.

The court held that substantial evidence supported the finding that telephone solicitors were employees of the company. The company had the authority to control and direct the work of solicitors, including the placing of restraints on their schedules, and the imposition of maximum hours and mandatory breaks. Also significant was the guaranteed minimum wage and the use of company phones, customer lists and scripts. Conversely, there was no substantial evidence supporting the finding that drivers were employees, because the company did not have the right to control their work performance. The lack of supervision over drivers during deliveries, lack of an hourly wage, and use of personal vehicles, gas and insurance indicated that they were independent contractors. The court reversed that part of the commission's decision concerning the status of the drivers and affirmed the part concerning the solicitors. *Smoky Mountain Secrets, Inc. v. South Carolina Employment Security Comm.*, 439 S.E.2d 288 (S.C.App.1993).

Two Illinois men worked as chauffeurs for a limousine service. When their employment at the service ended, both filed for benefits under the state unemployment insurance act. They were granted benefits, and the limousine service appealed. The decision was affirmed by a state board of review. The limousine service appealed to a state trial court, which affirmed the decision of the board of review. The limousine service again appealed.

The Appellate Court of Illinois found that the chauffeurs were employees rather than independent contractors and were covered under the unemployment insurance act for purposes of unemployment compensation. It found that the limousine service exerted general control over the chauffeurs. The limousine service mandated that the chauffeurs wear a dark business suit and tie which was essentially a uniform requirement. The commission that the drivers received was set by the limousine service and was not negotiable. The service retained the right to stop leasing its limousines, even though the drivers could set their own hours and decline customers. The court found that the drivers were not engaged in an independent business because their allegedly independent business was under the complete control of the limousine service. The drivers had no assets, as the limousine service provided both the cars and the customers to the drivers. Accordingly, the court found that the chauffeurs were employees and entitled to unemployment compensation benefits. It affirmed the judgment of the trial court. *O'Hare-Midway Limousine Service v. Baker,* 596 N.E.2d 795 (Ill.App.1st Dist.1992).

A publishing company employed sales representatives to travel throughout the northwestern United States and Canada to solicit the purchase of advertisements to appear in its magazines. These sales people operated under an independent contractor agreement and received a set commission for all advertisements sold. The company provided lodging, sales forms, reporting forms, a company telephone credit card number, and company gas credit cards. In 1990, the unemployment insurance division of the Montana Department of Labor and Industry determined that the commissioned sales representatives working for the publishing company were employees of the company for purposes of unemployment insurance taxation. The Department of Labor and Industry affirmed the decision and the publishing company appealed to a Montana trial court. After the trial court affirmed the decision, the publishing company appealed to the Supreme Court of Montana.

The publishing company argued that the sales persons were independent contractors. Montana statutes define independent contractors as individuals who provide their services in the course of an occupation and who are engaged in an independently established trade, occupation, profession, or business. The court noted that the record was devoid of evidence in support of the publisher's position that its sales people were engaged in an independently established business. When the persons' relationship with the publishing company terminated, their business terminated as well. The court concluded that the sales people were employees, not independent contractors. The supreme court affirmed the decision of the lower court and determined that the publishing company owed unemployment insurance taxes. *Northwest Publishing v. Montana Dept. of Labor and Industry,* 846 P.2d 1030 (Mont.1993).

V.   OTHER UNEMPLOYMENT BENEFITS ISSUES

An Arizona subcontractor installed cabinets for a general contractor at a California worksite. The subcontractor became unable to complete the project and folded its operations, terminating all of its employees. The general contractor hired four subcontractor employees who had been employed at the worksite to complete the cabinet project. Two months later, when the work was finished, the general contractor terminated their employment. The former employees applied for unemployment compensation with the state Department of Economic Security, which determined that the general contractor was liable for unemployment insurance benefits because it had "acquired and continued" the business of the subcontractor. An appeals board affirmed the administrative decision and the general contractor appealed to the Arizona Court of Appeals, Division One. The court of appeals held that there had been no continuity of management or ownership between the general contractor and subcontractor and that the only relationship between them was the retention of the employees to finish the project. There was no sale or transfer of assets and the general contractor's motivation for hiring the employees was simply to complete the project. Retention of the employees was not an acquisition under Arizona law that would create liability for the purposes of unemployment insurance, and the administrative decisions were reversed and remanded. *Empire West Companies, Inc. v. Arizona Dept. of Economic Security,* 893 P.2d 746 (Ariz.App.Div.1 1995).

An unemployment insurance benefits claimant was qualified to receive benefits. She was overpaid more than $2,000 but the overpayment was not due to a wilful misrepresentation. Three years later, the claimant became unemployed again and received benefits. The New York State Department of Labor set off 50 percent of her benefits to recover the prior overpayment. It rejected the claimant's offer to repay the prior overpayment in smaller installments. The claimant filed a complaint in a New York trial court, seeking a declaration that the department's recovery methods violated state law and that the department had failed to comply with the rulemaking requirements of the state administrative procedure act. The trial court dismissed the complaint and a state appellate division court affirmed its decision. The claimant appealed to the Court of Appeals of New York.

The court of appeals observed that the state legislature had repealed a prohibition on recovery of overpaid benefits in cases not involving fraud. The labor commissioner's right to recover improperly paid benefits extended not only to civil suits, but to setoff. However, the department's inflexible policy of recovering 50 percent of current benefits was applied without regard to individual circumstances. Accordingly, it was a rule within the meaning of the state administrative procedure act. This required the department to comply with the act's rulemaking procedures. Because the commissioner had not complied with this requirement, the claimant was entitled to a determination of the benefits that would not have been set off had her individual circumstances been considered. The court reversed the appellate division court's decision. *Schwartfigure v. Hartnett*, 83 N.Y.2d 296, 632 N.E.2d 434 (1994).

A Pennsylvania man petitioned the Commonwealth Court of Pennsylvania for review of the Unemployment Compensation Board of Review's decision to deny him benefits under § 404(d) of the Unemployment Compensation Law. The board had concluded that his pension benefits were deductible from his weekly unemployment compensation benefit rate and he was ineligible for unemployment compensation because 100 percent of his prorated pension of $304 exceeded the weekly unemployment benefits of $291. In addition, the board concluded that he was involuntarily separated from his employment after his retirement date.

Section 404(d) provides that pension benefits shall be deducted from any unemployment compensation benefits. The claimant argued that the board erred in deducting his pension benefits from any unemployment compensation benefits otherwise owed to him because he was involuntarily terminated prior to his retirement date. However, the court noted that Section C states that "the phrase prior to retirement date shall mean prior to the claimant's attainment of the age specified in the retirement plan or program at which the employee may be retired with full or reduced pension rights." The board determined that the employee was eligible to retire with full benefits after having achieved 30 years of service. Additionally, the court noted that the legislative intent in enacting the amendment offsetting unemployment compensation benefits otherwise due against any pension benefits received was to preserve the funds for those who truly needed them. Thus, even though he apparently had no plans to retire officially and voluntarily at the time of the plant closing, the court concluded that the fact that he was admittedly eligible to retire after achieving 30 years service was determinative. For the above reasons, the court affirmed the decision of the board to deny unemployment benefits. *Grace v. Unemployment Compensation Board of Review*, 631 A.2d 748 (Pa.Cmwlth.1993).

In 1978, Congress enacted the Airline Deregulation Act (ADA), effectively terminating a longstanding system of economic regulation of air carriers and introducing a system in which market forces would play a dominant role in determining rates and market entry in the commercial airline industry. Section 43 of the ADA established an employee protection program (EPP) designed to insure that "the public benefits flowing from deregulation would not be paid for by airline employees who had relied on the heavily regulated nature of the industry in deciding to accept and retain their positions."

After an airline suffered major losses and ceased operations in 1982, a group of employees sought to obtain unemployment compensation benefits under the EPP of the ADA. After benefits were denied, the Airline Pilots Association and the National Brotherhood of Teamsters challenged the conclusion of the Department of Transportation (DOT) that certain airline work force reductions were not qualifying dislocations making the former employees eligible for the special unemployment benefits of the ADA.

The unions argued that the DOT's determination that the deregulation was not the major cause of the employees' dislocation was inconsistent with other DOT decisions. The court agreed and noted that the DOT had come to a different conclusion in a similar fact situation with a different airline. Accordingly, the court held that the department's determination that deregulation was not the major cause of the employee dislocation at the airline, so as to entitle the former employees to receive unemployment compensation, was unreasonable. *Air Line Pilots Assn. v. Federal Aviation Admin.*, 3 F.3d 449 (D.C.Cir.1993).

APPENDIX A

UNITED STATES CONSTITUTION

Relevant Provisions with respect to Employment Law

ARTICLE I

Section 1. All legislative Powers herein granted shall be vested in a Congress of the United States, which shall consist of a Senate and House of Representatives.

* * *

Section 8. The Congress shall have Power To lay and collect Taxes, Duties, Imposts and Excises, to pay the Debts and provide for the common Defence and general Welfare of the United States; but all Duties, Imposts and Excises shall be uniform throughout the Unites States;

To borrow money on the credit of the United States;

To regulate Commerce with foreign Nations, and among the several States, and with the Indian Tribes;

To establish an uniform Rule of Naturalization, and uniform Laws on the subject of Bankruptcies throughout the United States;

* * *

To promote the Progress of Science and useful Arts, by securing for limited Times to Authors and Inventors the exclusive Right to their respective Writings and Discoveries;

* * *

To make all Laws which shall be necessary and proper for carrying into Execution for the foregoing Powers, and all other Powers vested by this Constitution in the Government of the United States, or in any Department or Officer thereof.

* * *

Section 9. * * * No Bill of Attainder or ex post facto Law shall be passed.
* * *

Section 10. No State shall * * * pass any Bill of Attainder, ex post facto Law, or Law impairing the Obligation of Contracts, or grant any Title of Nobility.

417

ARTICLE II

Section 1. The executive Power shall be vested in a President of the United States of America. * * *

ARTICLE III

Section 1. The judicial Power of the United States, shall be vested in one supreme Court, and in such inferior Courts as the Congress may from time to time ordain and establish. The Judges, both of the supreme and inferior courts, shall hold their Offices during good Behaviour, and shall, at stated Times, receive for their Services a Compensation, which shall not be diminished during their Continuance in Office.

Section 2. The judicial Power shall extend to all Cases, in Law and Equity, arising under this Constitution, the Laws of the United States, and Treaties made, or which shall be made, under their Authority; - to all Cases affecting Ambassadors, other public Ministers and Consuls; - to all Cases of admiralty and maritime Jurisdiction, - to Controversies to which the United States shall be a party; - to Controversies between two or more States; - between a State and Citizens of another State; - between Citizens of different States; - between Citizens of the same State claiming Lands under the Grants of different States, and between a State, or the Citizens thereof, and foreign States, Citizens or Subjects.

* * *

ARTICLE IV

Section 1. Full Faith and Credit shall be given in each State to the public Acts, Records and judicial Proceedings of every other State. * * *

Section 2. The Citizens of each State shall be entitled to all Privileges and Immunities of Citizens in the several States.

* * *

Section 4. The United States shall guarantee to every State in this Union a Republican Form of Government, and shall protect each of them against Invasion; and on Application of the Legislature, or of the Executive (when the Legislature cannot be convened) against domestic Violence.

ARTICLE V

The Congress, whenever two thirds of both Houses shall deem it necessary, shall propose Amendments to this Constitution, or, on the Application of the Legislatures of two thirds of the several States, shall call a Convention for proposing Amendments, which, in either Case, shall be valid to all Intents and Purposes, as part of this Constitution, when ratified by the Legislatures of three fourths of the several States, or by Conventions in three fourths thereof, as the one or the other Mode of Ratification may be proposed by the Congress; Provided that no Amendment which may be made prior to the Year One thousand eight hundred and eight shall in any Manner affect the first and fourth Clauses in the Ninth Section of the first Article; and that no State, without its Consent, shall be deprived of its equal Suffrage in the Senate.

ARTICLE VI

* * *

This Constitution, and the Laws of the United States which shall be made in Pursuance thereof; and all Treaties made, or which shall be made, under the Authority of the United States, shall be the supreme Law of the Land; and the Judges in every State shall be bound thereby, any Thing in the Constitution or Laws of any State to the Contrary notwithstanding.

The Senators and Representatives before mentioned, and the Members of the several State Legislatures, and all executive and judicial Officers, both of the United States and of the several States, shall be bound by Oath or Affirmation, to support this Constitution; but no religious Test shall ever be required as a Qualification to any Office or public Trust under the United States.

* * *

AMENDMENT I

Congress shall make no law respecting an establishment of religion, or prohibiting the free exercise thereof; or abridging the freedom of speech, or of the press; or the right of the people peaceably to assemble, and to petition the Government for a redress of grievances.

* * *

AMENDMENT IV

The right of the people to be secure in their persons, houses, papers, and effects, against unreasonable searches and seizures, shall not be violated, and no Warrants shall issue, but upon probable cause, supported by Oath or affirmation, and particularly describing the place to be searched, and the persons or things to be seized.

AMENDMENT V

No person shall be held to answer for a capital, or otherwise infamous crime, unless on a presentment or indictment of a Grand Jury, except in cases arising in the land or naval forces, or in the Militia, when in actual service in time of War or public danger; nor shall any person be subject for the same offence to be twice put in jeopardy of life or limb; nor shall be compelled in any criminal case to be a witness against himself, nor be deprived of life, liberty, or property, without due process of law; nor shall private property be taken for public use, without just compensation.

AMENDMENT VI

In all criminal prosecutions, the accused shall enjoy the right to a speedy and public trial, by an impartial jury of the State and district wherein the crime shall have been committed, which district shall have been previously ascertained by law, and to be informed of the nature and cause of the accusation; to be confronted with the witnesses against him; to have compulsory process for obtaining witnesses in his favor, and to have the Assistance of Counsel for his defense.

AMENDMENT VII

In Suits at common law, where the value in controversy shall exceed twenty dollars, the right of trial by jury shall be preserved, and no fact tried by jury, shall be otherwise re-examined in any Court of the United States, than according to the rules of the common law.

AMENDMENT VIII

Excessive bail shall not be required, nor excessive fines imposed , nor cruel and unusual punishments inflicted.

AMENDMENT IX

The enumeration in the Constitution, of certain rights, shall not be construed to deny or disparage others retained by the people.

AMENDMENT X

The powers not delegated to the United States by the Constitution, nor prohibited by it to the States, are reserved to the States respectively, or to the people.

AMENDMENT XI

The Judicial power of the United States shall not be construed to extend to any suit in law or equity, commenced or prosecuted against one of the United States by Citizens of another State, or by Citizens or Subjects of any Foreign State.

* * *

AMENDMENT XIII

Section 1. Neither slavery nor involuntary servitude, except as a punishment for crime whereof the party shall have been duly convicted, shall exist within the United States, or any place subject to their jurisdiction.

Section 2. Congress shall have power to enforce this article by appropriate legislation.

AMENDMENT XIV

Section 1. All persons born or naturalized in the United States, and subject to the jurisdiction thereof, are citizens of the United States and of the State wherein they reside. No State shall make or enforce any law which shall abridge the privileges or immunities of citizens of the United States; nor shall any State deprive any person of life, liberty, or property, without due process of law; nor deny to any person within its jurisdiction the equal protection of the laws.

* * *

Section 5. The Congress shall have power to enforce, by appropriate legislation, the provisions of this article.

APPENDIX B

SUBJECT MATTER TABLE
OF RECENT LAW REVIEW
ARTICLES

Arbitration

Adler, Sara. *Arbitration and the Americans with Disabilities Act.* 37 St.Louis U.L.J. 1005 (1993).

Atkinson, Carolyn. Note. *A change in policy*: Litton *and the Court's disfavoring of arbitrability of post-expiration grievances.* 22 Cap.U.L.Rev. 207 (1993).

Bales, R. *A new direction for American labor law: individual autonomy and the compulsory arbitration of individual employment rights.* 30 Hous.L.Rev. 1863 (1994).

Berger, Mark. *Can employment law arbitration work?* 61 UMKC L.Rev. 693 (1993).

Bricker, Timothy R. Note. *A labor arbitrator's ability to modify a termination order based on employer violations of the grievance procedure.* 9 Ohio St.J.on Disp.Resol. 373 (1994).

Buse, Michele M. Comment. *Contracting employment disputes out of the jury system: an analysis of the implementation of binding arbitration in the non-union workplace and proposals to reduce the harsh effects of a non-appealable award.* 22 Pepperdine L.Rev. 1485 (1995).

Fox, Diane. Note. *Evolution of the post-expiration duty to arbitrate grievances.* [Litton v. NLRB, 111 S.Ct. 2215 (1991)]. 9 Ohio St.J.on Disp.Resol. 161 (1993).

Hayford, Stephen L. and Anthony V. Sinicropi. *The labor contract and external law: revisiting the arbitrator's scope of authority.* 1993 J.Dispute Resol. 249.

Hayford, Stephen L. and Michael J. Evers. *The interaction between the employment-at-will doctrine and employer-employee agreements to arbitrate statutory fair employment practices claims: difficult choices for at-will employers.* 73 N.C.L.Rev. 443 (1995).

Irvine, Mori. *Mediation: is it appropriate for sexual harassment grievances?* 9 Ohio St.J.on Disp.Resol. 27 (1993).

Mayes, Gregory T. Recent decision. *Labor law — the Third Circuit defines the public policy exception to labor arbitration awards.* [*Exxon Shipping Co. v. Exxon Seamen's Union,* 993 F.2d 357 (3d Cir.1993)]. 67 Temp.L.Rev. 493 (1994).

Silberman, R. Gaull, Susan E. Murphy and Susan P. Adams. *Alternative dispute resolution of employment discrimination claims.* 54 La.L.Rev. 1533 (1994).

Tien, Wendy S. Note. *Compulsory arbitration of ADA claims: disabling the disabled.* 77 Minn.L.Rev. 1443 (1993).

At-will employment and wrongful discharge

Brown, Gian. Note. *Employee misconduct and the affirmative defense of "after-acquired evidence."* 62 Fordham L.Rev. 381 (1993).

Dietrich, Sharon. *Crossroads: wrongful discharge in Pennsylvania.* 1 Hybrid: J.L.& Soc.Change 39 (1993).

Dominquez, David. *Lost cause protection: will the demise of employment at will breathe new life into collective job security?* 28 Idaho L.Rev. 283 (1991-1992).

Duffy, Dennis P. *Intentional infliction of emotional distress and employment at will: the case against "tortification" of labor and employment law.* 74 B.U.L.Rev. 387 (1994).

Erdman, Laurie A. Casenote. *When can an employee be discharged? Ask the Legislature.* [Gantt v. Sentry Insurance, 1 Cal.4th 1083, 824 P.2d 680, 4 Cal.Rptr.2d 874, (1992)]. 25 Pac.L.J. 107 (1993).

Fabiano, Michael D. Note. *The meaning of just cause for termination when an employer alleges misconduct and the employee denies it.* 44 Hastings L.J. 399 (1993).

Fahleson, Mark A. *The public policy exception to employment at will — when should courts defer to the legislature?* 72 Neb.L.Rev. 956 (1993).

Ferguson, John W., Jr. Note. *Texas Supreme Court refuses to recognize a "whistleblower" exception to the at-will employment rule for private employment.* [Winters v. Houston Chronicle Publishing Co., 795 S.W.2d 723 (Tex.1990)]. 22 Tex.Tech L.Rev. 1215 (1991).

Franczak, Michael S. Note. *The Model Employment Termination Act (META): does it violate the right to trial by jury?* 10 Ohio St.J. on Disp.Resol. 441 (1995).

Greenlee, Steven G. Casenote. *Contract law — employee handbooks: at-will or not at-will? A question of form over substance.* [McDonald v. Mobil Coal Producing, Inc., 820 P.2d 986 (Wyo.1991)]. 28 Land & Water L.Rev. 289 (1993).

Ho, Debbie. Recent decision. *Employment law — exceptions to the at-will doctrine — the adoption of the public policy exception in two specific situations could signal the adoption of additional exceptions to the doctrine.* 64 Miss.L.J. 257 (1994).

Kane, Michael. Comment. *Whistleblowers: are they protected?* 20 Ohio N.U.L.Rev. 1007 (1994).

Kirk, Valerie P. and Ann Clarke Snell. *The Texas Whistleblower Act: time for a change.* 26 Tex.Tech L.Rev. 75 (1995).

Lund, Matthew J. Casenote. *Employment contracts — oral contracts for employment — oral assurances may not necessarily create employment contracts terminable only for just cause.* [Rowe v. Montgomery Ward & Co., 473 N.W.2d 268 (Mich.1991)]. 69 U.Det.Mercy L.Rev. 427 (1992).

Malin, Martin H. *The distributive and corrective justice concerns in the debate over employment at-will: some preliminary thoughts.* 68 Chi.-Kent L.Rev. 117 (1992).

Marks, Keith S. Note. *RICO law — wrongful discharge and RICO conspiracy standing: the* Holmes v. Securities Investor Protection Corp. *direct-injury test resolves the standing issue.* [Holmes v. Securities Investor Protection Corp., 112 S.Ct. 1311 (1992)]. 16 W.New Eng.L.Rev. 365 (1994).

McCormick, Kathleen T. *Wrongful discharge of private employees in Texas: status quo or statute?* 19 T.Marshall L.Rev. 45 (1993).

McLane, William P. Legislative survey. S*triking down the Workplace Fairness Act: the death of an employee's right to return to the job.* 19 Seton Hall Legis.J. 375 (1994).

Muhic, Peter A. Recent decision. *Labor law—drug testing and the employment at-will doctrine: Third Circuit defines new cause of action for wrongful discharge.* [Borse v. Piece Goods Shop, Inc., 963 F.2d 611 (3d Cir.1992)]. 66 Temp.L.Rev. 327 (1993).

Mullings, Sandra J. Wieder v. Skala*: a chink in the armor of the at-will doctrine or a lance for law firm associates?* 45 Syracuse L.Rev. 963 (1995).

Muoio, Reid Anthony. *An independent auditor's suit for wrongful discharge.* 58 Alb.L.Rev. 413 (1994).

Pennington, Christopher L. Comment. *The public policy exception to the employment-at-will doctrine: its inconsistencies in application.* 68 Tul.L.Rev. 1583 (1994).

Przbylo, Gregory A. Casenote. *Call off the funeral:* Toussaint v. Blue Cross & Blue Shield of Michigan *is alive under ...* [Rood v. General Dynamics Corp., 507 N.W.2d 591 (Mich.1993)]. 11 T.M.Cooley L.Rev. 947 (1994).

Roberts, Bonita K. *The more things change, the more they stay the same: the employment-at-will doctrine in Texas.* 25 St.Mary's L.J. 435 (1993).

Schmedemann, Deobrah A. and Judi McLean Parks. *Contract formation and employee handbooks: legal, psychological, and empirical analysis.* 29 Wake Forest L.Rev. 647 (1994).

Schwab, Stewart J. *Life-cycle justice: accommodating just cause and employment at will.* 92 Mich.L.Rev. 8 (1993).

Tepker, Harry F., Jr. *Oklahoma's evolving employment law: clarifying the at-will rule.* 45 Okla.L.Rev. 629 (1992).

Terminating at-will employment contracts in Utah subsequent to [Berube v. Fashion Centre, 771 P.2d 1033 (Utah 1989)]. 1990 B.Y.U.L.Rev. 987.

The status of the employment-at-will doctrine in Ohio: Ohio incorporates a public policy exception. 52 Ohio St.L.J. 315 (1991).

Wynkoop, Steven M. and Elizabeth Scott Moise. *Employee handbooks in South Carolina: the employers' dilemma.* 42 S.C.L.Rev. 323 (1991).

Discrimination

Age

Barklow, Beatrice Kathleen. Comment. *Rethinking the age sixty mandatory retirement rule: a look at the newest movement.* 60 J.Air L.& Com. 329

Beall, Jim. Note. *The charge-filing requirement of the Age Discrimination in Employment Act: accrual and equitable modification.* 91 Mich.L.Rev. 798 (1993).

Bodensteiner, Jill R. Note. *Post-OWBPA developments in the law regarding waivers to ADEA claims.* 46 Wash.U.J.Urb.& Contemp.L. 225 (1994).

Finkelstein, Michael O. and Bruce Levin. *Proportional hazard models for age discrimination cases.* 34 Jurimetrics J. 153 (1994).

Frier, Daniel B. Comment. *Age discrimination and the ADA: how the ADA may be used to arm older Americans against age discrimination by employers who would otherwise escape liability under the ADEA.* 66 Temp.L.Rev. 173 (1993).

Harper, Michael C. *Age-based exit incentives, coercion, and the prospective waiver of ADEA rights: the failure of the Older Workers Benefit Protection Act.* 79 Va.L.Rev. 1271 (1993).

Lyons, Edward C. Student case comment. *Collective bargaining agreements and Age Discrimination in Employment Act claims: what counts as retaliation under ADEA section 4(d)?* [EEOC v. Board of Governors of State Colleges and Universities, 957 F.2d 424, 7th Cir.1992, cert. denied, 113 S.Ct. 299 (1992)]. 20 J.C.& U.L. 241 (1993).

Marinelli, Arthur J. *Age discrimination and reductions in force.* 20 Ohio N.U.L.Rev. 277 (1993).

Mitchell, Patricia A. Note. *Extending the disparate impact doctrine to ADEA claims.* [Hazen Paper Co. v. Biggins, 113 S.Ct. 1701 (1993), *vacating* 953 F.2d 1405 (1st Cir.1992)]. 29 Gonz.L.Rev. 675 (1993/94).

Moberly, Michael D. *Reconsidering the discriminatory motive requirement in ADEA disparate treatment cases.* 24 N.M.L.Rev. 89 (1994).

Reardon, Gavin J. Recent development. *The Age Discrimination in Employment Act preempts the National Labor Relations Act.* [Britt v. Grocers Supply Co., 978 F.2d 1441 5th Cir.1992, cert. denied, 113 S.Ct. 2929 (1993)]. 68 Tul.L.Rev. 241 (1993).

Sloan, Michael C. Comment. *Disparative impact in the Age Discrimination in Employment Act: will the Supreme Court permit it?* 1995 Wis.L.Rev. 507.

Stith, Rebecca S. and William A. Kohlburn. *Early retirement incentive plans after the passage of the Older Workers Benefit Protection Act.* 11 St.Louis U.Pub.L.Rev. 263 (1992).

Sweeney, Michael T. Note. *Employment arbitration — Age Discrimination in Employment — arbitrability of claims under Age Discrimination in Employment Act upheld pursuant to arbitration agreement.* [Gilmer v. Interstate/Johnson Lane Corp., 111 S.Ct. 1647 (1991)]. 22 Seton Hall L.Rev. 540 (1992).

Disability

Conway, John A. Comment. *The Americans with Disabilities Act: new challenges in airline hiring practices.* 59 J.Air L.& Com. 945 (1994).

Daley-Rooney, Rose. Note. *Reconciling conflicts between the Americans with Disabilities Act and the National Labor Relations Act to accommodate people with disabilities.* 6 DePaul Bus.L.J. 387 (1994).

Dryovage, Mary. *Compliance and litigation resources for implementing the Americans with Disabilities Act of 1990.* (Reviewing Gary Phelan and Janet B. Arterton, *Disability Discrimination in the Workplace*; and Mark Daniels, *Employment Law Guide to the Americans with Disabilities Act.*) 14 Berkeley J.Emp.& Lab.L. 318 (1993).

Dubault, Robert A. Note. *The ADA and the NLRA: balancing individual and collective rights.* 70 Ind.L.J. 1271 (1995).

Dunworth, Kimberly B. Note. *Drawing the line at obesity?* [Cassita v. Community Foods, Inc., 856 P.2d 1143 (Cal.1993)]. 24 Golden Gate U.L.Rev. 523 (1994).

Flynn, John L. Note. *Mixed-motive causation under the ADA: linked statutes, fuzzy thinking, and clear statements.* 83 Geo.L.J. 2009 (1995).

Frier, Daniel B. Comment. *Age discrimination and the ADA: how the ADA may be used to arm older Americans against age discrimination by employers who would otherwise escape liability under the ADEA.* 66 Temp.L.Rev. 173 (1993).

Harger, David. Comment. *Drawing the line between reasonable accommodation and undue hardship under the Americans with Disabilities Act: reducing the effects of ambiguity on small businesses.* 41 U.Kan.L.Rev. 783 (1993).

Hartnett, Patricia. Note. *Nature or nurture, lifestyle or fate: employment discrimination against obese workers.* 24 Rutgers L.J. 807 (1993).

Holtzman, Gerald T., Kyle L. Jennings, and David J. Schenck. *Reasonable accommodation of the disabled worker — a job for the man or a man for the job?* 44 Baylor L.Rev. 279 (1992).

Johnson, Kathryn A. Comment. *Constructive discharge and "reasonable accommodation" under the Americans with Disabilities Act.* 65 U.Colo.L.Rev. 175 (1993).

Knych, Lianna C. Note. *Assessing the application of* McDonnell Douglas *to employment discrimination claims brought under the Americans with Disabilities Act.* 79 Minn.L.Rev. 1515 (1995).

Lee, Barbara A. *Reasonable accommodation under the Americans with Disabilities Act: the limitations of Rehabilitation Act precedent.* 14 Berkeley J.Emp.& Lab.L. 201 (1993).

Mastrangelo, Rebecca. Comment. *Does the Americans with Disabilities Act of 1990 impose an undue burden on employers?* 32 Duq.L.Rev. 269 (1994).

McAtee, Richard S. Comment. *The Americans with Disabilities Act and the National Labor Relations Act: a unionized employer's road map to reasonable accommodations.* 33 Duq.L.Rev. 105 (1994).

Miller, Frances H. and Philip A. Huvos. *Genetic blueprints, employer cost-cutting and The Americans with Disabilities Act.* 46 Admin.L.Rev. 369 (1994).

Oliver, Ranko Shiraki. *The impact of Title I of the Americans with Disabilities Act of 1990 on workers' compensation law.* 16 U.Ark.Little Rock L.J. 327 (1994).

Petersen, Scott. Comment. *Discrimination against overweight people: can society still get away with it?* 30 Gonz.L.Rev. 105 (1994/95).

Postol, Lawrence and David Kadue. *An employer's guide to the Americans with Disabilities Act: from job qualifications to reasonable accommodations.* 24 J. Marshall L.Rev. 693 (1991).

Prewitt, R. Bradley. Comment. *The "direct threat" approach to the HIV-positive health care employee under the ADA.* 62 Miss.L.J. 719 (1993).

Pugsley, Mark W. Note. *Nonsmoking hiring policies: examining the status of smokers under Title I of the Americans with Disabilities Act of 1990.* 43 Duke L.J. 1089 (1994).

Ravitch, Frank S. *Beyond reasonable accommodation: the availability and structure of a cause of action for workplace harassment under the Americans with Disabilities Act.* 15 Cardozo L.Rev. 1475 (1994).

Robinson, David A. *Discovery of the plaintiff's mental health history in an employment discrimination case.* 16 W.New Eng.L.Rev. 55 (1994).

Singleton, Denise C. Comment. *Nonconsensual HIV testing in the health care setting: the case for extending the occupational protection of California Proposition 96 to health care workers.* 26 Loy.L.A.L.Rev. 1251 (1993).

Tucker, Bonnie P., et al. *Discrimination on the basis of disability: the need for a Third Wave Movement.* 3 Cornell J.L.& Pub.Pol'y 253 (1994).

Willis, Christopher J. Comment. *Title I of the Americans with Disabilities Act: disabling the disabled.* 25 Cumb.L.Rev. 715 (1994-1995).

Wolverton, Kathy Ann. Comment. *Protecting alcoholics under the Americans with Disabilities Act and New York law: a statutory tug of war.* 57 Alb.L.Rev. 527 (1993).

Zablocki, Michael, Luellen G. Lucid and James Reilly. *Americans with Disabilities Act update.* 15 Whittier L.Rev. 177 (1994).

Zeldin, Jessica. Note. *Disabling employers: problems with the ADA's confidentiality requirement in unionized workplaces.* 73 Wash.U.L.Q. 737 (1995).

Generally

Crocenzi, Michael. Comment. *IRCA-related discrimination: is it time to repeal the employer sanctions?* 96 Dick.L.Rev. 673 (1992).

Cunniff, Thomas A. Note. *The price of equal opportunity: the efficiency of Title VII after ...* [St. Mary's Honor Center v. Hicks, 113 S.Ct. 2742 (1993)]. 45 Case W.Res.L.Rev. 507 (1995).

Edwards, Patrick M. Casenote. *Civil rights — Title VII employment discrimination.* [St. Mary's Honor Center v. Hicks, 113 S.Ct. 2742 (1993)]. 71 U.Det.Mercy L.Rev. 693 (1994).

Essary, Melissa A. *The dismantling of* McDonnell Douglas v. Green: *the High Court muddies the evidentiary waters in circumstantial discrimination cases.* 21 Pepperdine L.Rev. 385 (1994).

Foster, Sheila. *Difference and equality: a critical assessment of the concept of "diversity."* 1993 Wis.L.Rev. 105.

Goldian, Donna G. Note. *New reason to lie: the end of proving discriminatory intent by proving pretext only after ...* [St. Mary's Honor Center v. Hicks, 113 S.Ct. 2742 (1993)]. 30 Willamette L.Rev. 699 (1994).

Goldstein, Richard. *The comparison of models in discrimination cases.* 34 Jurimetrics J. 215 (1994).

Greer, Cristopher. Note. *"Who, me?": A supervisor's individual liability for discrimination in the workplace.* 62 Fordham L.Rev. 1835 (1994).

Humphress, Stephen B. Note. *State protection against marital status discrimination by employers.* 31 U.Louisville J.Fam.L. 919 (1992-93).

Kaufman, Eileen. *Employment discrimination: recent developments in the Supreme Court.* 11 Touro L.Rev. 465 (1995).

Lamberson, Phillip. Comment. *Personal liability for violations of Title VII: thirty years of indecision.* 46 Baylor L.Rev. 419 (1994).

McGinley, Ann C. *Reinventing reality: the impermissible intrusion of after-acquired evidence in Title VII litigation.* 26 Conn.L.Rev. 145 (1993).

Muth, William M., Jr. Note. T*he after-acquired evidence doctrine in Title VII cases and the challenge presented ...* [Wallace v. Dunn Construction, 968 F.2d 1174 (11th Cir.1992)]. 72 Neb.L.Rev. 330 (1993).

Patterson, Michael F. Note. *English-only rules in the workplace.* [Garcia v. Spun Steak Co., 998 F.2d 1480, Cert. denied, 114 S.Ct. 2726 (1994)]. 27 Ariz.St.L.J. 277 (1995).

Peluso, Marie Elena. Note. *Tempering Title VII's straight arrow approach: recognizing and protecting gay victims of employment discrimination.* 46 Vand.L.Rev. 1533 (1993).

Ratz, James P. Note. *Requiring discriminatory intent and relevant statistical evidence in Title VII cases.* [Equal Employment Opportunity Commission v. Chicago Miniature Lamp Works, 947 F.2d 292 (7th Cir.1991)]. 16 Hamline L.Rev. 1003 (1993).

Rutherglen, George. *Discrimination and its discontents.* 81 Va.L.Rev. 117 (1995).

Rutherglen, George. *From race to age: the expanding scope of employment discrimination law.* 24 J.Legal Stud. 491 (1995).

The Civil Rights Act of 1991: A Symposium. Articles by Roger Clegg, Glen D. Nager, Julia M. Broas, C. Boyden Gray, John O. McGinnis, R. Gaull Silberman, Susan E. Murphy, Susan P. Adams and Nelson Lund. 54 La.L.Rev. 1459 (1994).

Tighe, J. Hagood. Note. *The refined pretext-plus analysis: employees' and employers' respective burdens after ...* [St. Mary's Honor Center v. Hicks, 113 S.Ct. 2742 (1993)]. 46 S.C.L.Rev. 333 (1995).

Verkerke, J. Hoult. *Notice liability in employment discrimination law.* 81 Va.L.Rev. 273 (1995).

Weinstein, Jason M. Note. *No harm, no foul?: The use of after-acquired evidence in Title VII employment discrimination cases.* 62 Geo.Wash.L.Rev. 280 (1994).

White, Rebecca Hanner and Robert D. Brussack. *The proper role of after-acquired evidence in employment discrimination litigation.* 35

B.C.L.Rev. 49 (1993).

Whitis, Norma G. Note. *The Title VII shifting burden stays put.* [St. Mary's Honor Center v. Hicks, 113 S.Ct. 2742 (1993)]. 25 Loy.U.Chi.L.J. 269 (1994).

Wiley, David T. Note. *Whose proof?: Deference to EEOC guidelines on disparate impact discrimination analysis of "English-only" rules.* 29 Ga.L.Rev. 539 (1995).

Race

Braswell, Michael K., Gary A. Moore and Stephen L. Poe. *Affirmative action: an assessment of its continuing role in employment discrimination policy.* 57 Alb.L.Rev. 365 (1993).

Burstein, Paul and Mark Evan Edwards. *The impact of employment discrimination litigation on racial disparity in earnings: evidence and unresolved issues.* 28 Law & Soc'y Rev. 79 (1994).

Crespi, Gregory S. *Market magic: can the invisible hand strangle bigotry?* [*Reviewing Richard A. Epstien,* Forbidden Grounds: The Case against Employment Discrimination Laws]. 72 B.U.L.Rev. 991 (1992).

Flagg, Barbara J. *Fashioning a Title VII remedy for transparently white subjective decisionmaking.* 104 Yale L.J. 2009 (1995).

Haney, Craig and Aida Hurtado. *The jurisprudence of race and meritocracy: standarized testing and "race-neutral" racism in the workplace.* 18 Law & Hum.Behavior 223 (1994).

Larson, David A. *Title VII compensation issues affecting bilingual Hispanic employees.* 23 Ariz.St.L.J. 821 (1991).

McAlister, James L. Comment. *A pigment of the imagination: looking at affirmative action through Justice Scalia's color-blind rule.* 77 Marq.L.Rev. 327 (1994).

Perea, Juan F. *Ethnicity and prejudice: reevaluating "national origin" discrimination under Title VII.* 35 Wm.& Mary L.Rev. 805 (1994).

Selmi, Michael. *Testing for equality: merit, efficiency, and the affirmative action debate.* 42 UCLA L.Rev. 1251 (1995).

True, Gary E. Note. *A dilution of the right of nonminorities to equal protection under the Fifth Amendment or a temporary aberration in affirmative action jurisprudence?* [Metro Broadcasting, Inc. v. FCC, 110 S.Ct. 2997 (1990)]. 35 St.Louis U.L.J. 710 (1991).

Sex

Bowden, Ellen M. Student article. *Closing the pay gap: redefining the Equal Pay Act's fourth affirmative defense.* 27 Colum.J.L.& Soc.Probs. 225 (1994).

Brown, Thomas D. Recent development. *When counseling is not enough: the Ninth Circuit requires employers to discipline sexual harassers.* [Intelkofer v. Turnage, 973 F.2d 733 (9th Cir.1992)]. 71 Wash.U.L.Q. 901 (1993).

Buff, Dawn M. Note. *Beyond the Court's standard response: creating an effective test for determining hostile work environment harassment under Title VII.* [Harris v. Forklift Systems, Inc., 114 S.Ct. 367 (1993)]. 24 Stetson L.Rev. 719 (1995).

Burns, Sarah E. *Evidence of sexually hostile workplace: what is it and how should it be assessed after* Harris v. Forklift Systems, Inc.*?* 21 N.Y.U.Rev.L.& Soc.Change 357 (1994-1995).

Cigoy, Penny L. Comment. *Harmless amusement or sexual harassment?: The reasonableness of the reasonable woman standard.* 20 Pepp.L.Rev. 1071 (1993).

Claps, Thomas E. Note. *Employment law — sexual harassment.* [Lehmann v. Toys "R" Us, Inc., 132 N.J. 587, 626 A.2d 445 (1993)]. 24 Seton Hall L.Rev. 2915 (1994).

Cooper, Stacy J. Student article. *Sexual harassment and the Swedish Bikini Team: a reevaluation of the "hostile environment" doctrine.* 26 Colum.J.L.& Soc.Probs. 387 (1993).

Dolkart, Jane L. *Hostile environment harassment: equality, objectivity, and the shaping of legal standards.* 43 Emory L.J. 151 (1994).

Dowd, Nancy E. *Liberty vs. equality: in defense of privileged white males.* [*Reviewing Richard A. Epstein,* Forbidden Grounds: The Case Against Employment Discrimination Laws]. 34 Wm.& Mary L.Rev. 429 (1993).

Fishman, Leta L. Note. *Preemption revisited: Title VII and state tort liability after ...* [International Union v. Johnson Controls, 111 S.Ct. 1196 (1991)]. 66 St.John's L.Rev. 1047 (1993).

Flynt, Bobbie Loper. Note. *Sex discrimination: psychological injury from hostile work environment sexual harassment.* [Harris v. Forklift Systems, Inc., 114 S.Ct. 367, interim ed. (1993)]. 20 U.Dayton L.Rev. 1049 (1995).

Gomez, Mary C. Comment. *Sexual harassment after* Harris v. Forklift Systems, Inc. *— is it really easier to prove?* [Harris v. Forklift Systems, Inc., 114 S.Ct. 367 (1993)]. 18 Nova L.Rev. 1889 (1994).

Hebert, L. Camille. *Sexual harassment is gender harassment.* 42 U.Kan.L.Rev. 565 (1995).

Hyche, J. Tod. Student comment. *The reasonable woman standard in sexual harassment cases: is it reasonable?* 24 Cumb.L.Rev. 559 (1993-1994).

Johnson, Paul B. *The reasonable woman in sexual harassment law: progress or illusion?* 28 Wake Forest L.Rev. 619 (1993).

Kennedy, Ruth A. Comment. *Insulating sexual harassment grievance procedures from the chilling effect of defamation litigation.* 69 Wash.L.Rev. 235 (1994).

Keyes, Stephen. Note. *Affirmative action for working mothers: does* Guerra's *preferential treatment rationale extend to childrearing leave benefits?* [California Federal Savings and Loan Association v. Guerra, 479 U.S. 272 (1987)]. 60 Fordham L.Rev. 309 (1991).

Konopka, Patricia A. Comment. *Combating sexual harassment in the workplace without risking a wrongful discharge lawsuit: an employer's dilemma?* 42 U.Kan.L.Rev. 437 (1994).

Kruse, Katherine. Comment. *The inequality approach and the BFOQ: use of feminist theory to reinterpret the Title VII BFOQ exception.* 1993 Wis.L.Rev. 261.

Levy, Michael J. Note. *Sex, promotions, and Title VII: why sexual favoritism is not sexual discrimination.* 45 Hastings L.J. 667 (1994).

Lewis, Frederick J. and Thomas L. Henderson. *Employer liability for "hostile work environment" sexual harassment created by supervisors: the search for an appropriate standard.* 25 U.Mem.L.Rev. 667 (1995).

McGaw, Wayne T. *Investigating sexual harassment: a practical primer for the corporate lawyer.* 40 Loy.L.Rev. 97 (1994).

Michelsen, Jan. Note. *A class act: forces of increased awareness, expanded remedies, and procedural strategy converge to combat hostile workplace environments.* 27 Ind.L.Rev. 607 (1994).

Miller, Shawn O. *Sexual harassment and the Illinois Business Corporation Act.* 19 S.Ill.U.L.J. 459 (1995).

Oshige, Miranda. Note. *What's sex got to do with it?* 47 Stan.L.Rev. 565 (1995).

Perry, Sarah H. Comment. *Enough is enough: per se constructive discharge for victims of sexually hostile work environments under Title VII.* 70 Wash.L.Rev. 541 (1995).

Pfenninger, Lisa. Comment. *Sexual harassment in the legal profession: workplace education and reform, civil remedies, and professional discipline.* 22 Fla.St.U.L.Rev. 171 (1994).

Phillips, Michael J. *The dubious Title VII cause of action for sexual favoritism.* 51 Wash.& Lee L.Rev. 547 (1994).

Radford, Mary F. *By invitation only: the proof of welcomeness in sexual harassment cases.* 72 N.C.L.Rev. 499 (1994).

Sneirson, Amy M. Case comment. *One of these things is not like the other: providing liability under the Equal Pay Act and Title VII.* [Tidwell v. Fort Howard Corp., 989 F.2d 406 (10th Cir.1993)]. 72 Wash.U.L.Q. 783 (1994).

Symposium: The Gender Gap in Compensation. Articles by Warren F. Schwartz, Jane Friesen, James Albrecht, Susan Vroman, Richard A. Epstein, Gillian K. Hadfield, Sharon M. Oster, Jennifer Roback, George Rutherglen and Rosemary Hunter. 82 Geo.L.J. 27 (1993).

Weddle, Justin S. Note. *Title VII sexual harassment: recognizing an employer's non-delegable duty to prevent a hostile workplace.* 95 Colum.L.Rev. 724 (1995).

Wiener, Richard L. *et al. Social analytic investigation of hostile work environments: a test of the reasonable woman standard.* 19 Law & Hum.Behavior 263 (1995).

Werner, Rhonda. Student article. *Exposing employers in the hostile work environment: appearance standards that lead to sexual harassment.* 15 Hamline J.Pub.L.& Pol'y 145 (1994).

Drug Testing and Privacy Issues

Blackburn, John D., Elliot L. Klayman and Richard O. Nathan. *Invasion of privacy: refocusing the tort in private sector employment.* 6 DePaul Bus.L.J. 41 (1993).

Brightman, Richard J. Note. *Employment law——employment-at-will—— an employer may randomly drug test an at-will employee in a safety-sensitive positive position without violating public policy which protects the employee's privacy interest.* [Hennessey v. Coastal Eagle Point Oil Company, 129 N.J. 81, 609 A.2d 11 (1992)]. 24 Seton Hall L.Rev. 483 (1993).

Cavico, Frank J. *Invasion of privacy in the private employment sector: tortious and ethical aspects.* 30 Hous.L.Rev. 1263 (1993).

Flanagan, Julie A. Note. *Restricting electronic monitoring in the private workplace.* 43 Duke L.J. 1256 (1994).

King, David Neil. Note. *Privacy issues in the private-sector workplace: protection from electronic surveillance and the merging "privacy gap."* 67 S.Cal.L.Rev. 441 (1994).

Marculewicz, Stefan Jan. *Some tough questions for challenges to preemployment drug testing.* 10 J. Contemp.Health L.& Pol'y 243 (1994).

Muhic, Peter A. Recent decision. *Labor law—drug testing and the employment at-will doctrine: Third Circuit defines new cause of action for wrongful discharge.* [Borse v. Piece Goods Shop, Inc., 963 F.2d 611 (3d Cir.1992)] 66 Temp.L.Rev. 327 (1993).

Witt, Lois R. Comment. *Terminally nosy: are employers free to access our electronic mail?* 96 Dick.L.Rev. 545 (1992).

Employee Benefits

ABA. Section of Business Law. *Subcommittee on Employee Benefits and Executive Compensation of the Committee on Federal Regulation of Securities. International employee stock plans and the federal securities laws.* 49 Bus.Law. 797 (1994).

Bartrum, Thomas E. Note. *Fear, discrimination and dying in the workplace: AIDS and the capping of employees' health insurance benefits.* 82 Ky.L.J. 249 (1993-94).

Bryan, J. Keith. Comment. *Expiration of retiree benefit plans during reorganization: a bitter pill for employees.* 9 Bankr.Dev.J. 539 (1993).

McKee, Christopher J. Note. *Integrating benefits and the older worker.* 1993 Colum.Bus.L.Rev. 365.

Preston, Patrick Joseph. Note. *The retention of severance benefits during challenges of waivers under the Age Discrimination in Employment Act.* 27 Ind.L.Rev. 157 (1993).

Simon, William H. *The prospects of pension fund socialism.* 14 Berkeley J.Emp.& Lab.L. 251 (1993).

Zanglein, Jayne E. *Employee benefits law.* 25 Tex.Tech L.Rev. 645 (1994).

Employer Liability

Acoff, Valerie L. Student note. *References available upon request ... Not! — employers are being sued for providing employee job references.* 17 Am.J.Trial Advoc. 755 (1994).

Church, Janice M. *Tort immunity revisited: what is the present test for statutory employer?* 54 La.L.Rev. 587 (1994).

Franklin, Rhett B. *Comment. Pouring new wine into an old bottle: a recommendation for determining liability of an employer under respondeat superior.* 39 S.D.L.Rev. 570 (1994).

Gallagher, Sean W. Note. *The public policy exclusion and insurance for intentional employment discrimination.* 92 Mich.L.Rev. 1256 (1994).

Hallinan, Kathleen M. Student article. *Invasion of privacy or protection against sexual harassment: co-employee dating and employer liability.* 26 Colum.J.L.& Soc.Probs. 435 (1993).

Horkan, Edward R. Note. *Contracting around the law of defamation and employment references.* 79 Va.L.Rev. 517 (1993).

Kelly, George. Note. *An employer's right to health protection or a woman's right to equal employment? A critical look at fetal protection policies.* 26 New Eng.L.Rev. 1101 (1992).

Kionka, Edward J. *Recent developments in the law of joint and several liability and the impact of plaintiff's employer's fault.* 54 La.L.Rev. 1619 (1994).

Machson, Robert A. and Joseph P. Monteleone. *Insurance coverage for wrongful employment practices claims under various liability policies.* 49 Bus.Law. 689 (1994).

Mark, Valarie. *The flip side of fetal protection policies: compensating children injured through parental exposure to reproductive hazards in the workplace.* 22 Golden Gate U.L.Rev. 673 (1992).

Matheny, Kenneth. *Achieving safer workplaces by expanding employers' tort liability under workers' compensation laws.* 19 N.Ky.L.Rev. 457 (1992).

Platt, Bruce D. Comment. *Negligent retention and hiring in Florida: safety of customers versus security of employers.* 20 Fla.St.U.L.Rev. 697 (1993).

Ravitch, Frank S. *Hostile work environment and the objective reasonableness conundrum: deriving a workable framework from tort law for addressing knowing harassment of hypersensitive employees.* 36 B.C.L.Rev. 257 (1995).

Segal, Scott S., Jeffrey V. Mehalic and Mark R. Staun. *Workplace injury litigation.* 95 W.Va.L.Rev. 995 (1993).

Siegel, Howard J. *Self-publication: defamation within the employment context.* 26 St.Mary's L.J. 1 (1994).

Weber, Rochelle Rubin. *"Scope of employment" redefined: holding employers vicariously liable for sexual assaults committed by their employees.* 76 Minn.L.Rev. 1513 (1992).

Employment generally

Baker, Tim A. *Survey of recent labor and employment law developments for Seventh Circuit practitioners.* 27 Ind.L.Rev. 1205 (1994).

Clore, Lawrence H. and David M. Thomas. *Labor law and employment law.* 24 Tex.Tech L.Rev. 705 (1993).

Clore, Lawrence H. and Robin W. Coopwood. *Labor and employment law.* 26 Tex.Tech L.Rev. 717 (1995).

Cooperider, Dan, and Stephan Wiss. *Student survey. Employment law.* 25 Golden Gate U.L.Rev. 119 (1995).

Dau-Schmidt, Kenneth G. *Meeting the demands of workers into the twenty-first century: the future of labor and employment law.* 68 Ind.L.J. 685-703 (1993).

Fast, Scott L. Comment. *Breach of employee confidentiality: moving toward a common-law tort remedy.* 142 U.Pa.L.Rev. 431 (1993).

Gallagher, Michael J. Note. *Statutory rights and predispute agreements to arbitrate in contracts of employment.* 66 St.John's L.Rev. 1067 (1993).

Hall, W. Wendell. *Employment and labor law.* 47 SMU L.Rev. 1055 (1994).

Holloway, Ian. *The constitutionalization of employment rights: a comparative view.* 14 Berkeley J.Emp.& Lab.L. 113 (1993).

Hulen, Myron et al. *Independent contractors: compliance and classification issues.* 11 Am.J.Tax Pol'y 13 (1994).

Hyde, Alan, Frank Sheed and Mary Deery Uva. *After* Smyrna: *rights and powers of unions that represent less than a majority.* 45 Rutgers L.Rev. 637 (1993).

Hylton, Keith N. *Efficiency and labor law.* 87 Nw.U.L.Rev. 471 (1993).

Kraamwinkel, Margriet. *Women's work and law: new perspectives on the labor market strategy.* 26 New Eng.L.Rev. 823 (1992).

LaBerge, Robert A., Thomas G. Eron and John G. McDonald. *Employment law.* 44 Syracuse L.Rev. 243 (1993).

1993-1994 Annual Survey of Labor and Employment Law. 36 B.C.L.Rev. 305 (1995).

Note. *Labor-management cooperation after* Electromation: *implications for workplace diversity.* 107 Harv.L.Rev. 678 (1994).

O'Neill, Terry A. *Employees' duty of loyalty and the corporate constituency debate.* 25 Conn.L.Rev. 681 (1993).

Smith, Rebecca R. Comment. *Workplace smoking in New Jersey: time for a change.* 24 Seton Hall L.Rev. 958 (1993).

Stadler, James R. and Mary C. Bonnema. *Employment and labor law.* 40 Wayne L.Rev. 675 (1994).

Strader, Kent D. Comment. *Counterclaims against whistleblowers: should counterclaims against* qui tam *plaintiffs be allowed in False Claims Act cases?* 62 U.Cin.L.Rev. 713 (1993).

Student survey. *Employment-related crimes.* 32 Am.Crim.L.Rev. 213 (1995).

Wallace, Roger W. and Max Scoular. *The North American Free Trade Agreement and United States employment.* 24 St.Mary's L.J. 945 (1993).

Whitley, Ann B. Note. *Collective institutional guilt: the emergence of international unions' RICO liability for local union crimes.* 21 Am.J.Crim.L. 291 (1994).

Wonnell, Christopher T. *The contractual disempowerment of employees.* 46 Stan.L.Rev. 87 (1993).

Employment practices

Bryan, J. Keith. Comment. *Expiration of retiree benefit plans during reorganization: a bitter pill for employees.* 9 Bankr.Dev.J. 539 (1993).

Dolatly, George C. Student article. *The future of the reasonable accommodation duty in employment practices.* 26 Colum.J.L.& Soc.Probs. 523 (1993).

Ezra, David B. *"Get off your butts": the employer's right to regulate employee smoking.* 60 Tenn.L.Rev. 905 (1993).

Greenberg, Thomas R. Comment. *E-Mail and voice mail: employee privacy and the Federal Wiretap Statute.* 44 Am.U.L.Rev. 219 (1994).

Hines, Carol M. Comment. *"A modest proposal" for defining "gross misconduct" for COBRA coverage disqualifications.* 42 DePaul L.Rev. 463 (1993).

Kraus, Anthony W. *Absolute protection for intracorporate personnel communications under defamation law: a philosophical reappraisal of the nonpublication doctrine.* 25 U.Memphis L.Rev. 155 (1994).

Lapham, John S. Note. *Enhancing employee productivity after* Electromation *and* Du Pont. 45 Wash.U.J.Urb.& Contemp.L. 255 (1994).

Malin, Martin H. *Fathers and parental leave.* 72 Tex.L.Rev. 1047 (1994).

McCartney, Donald R. Comment. *Electronic surveillance and the resulting loss of privacy in the workplace.* 62 UMKC L.Rev. 859 (1994).

McGraw, Edward J. Note. *Compliance costs of the Americans with Disabilities Act.* 18 Del.J.Corp.L. 521 (1993).

Pace, Kimberly A. *What does it mean to be a salaried employee? The future of pay-docking.* 21 J.Legis. 49 (1995).

Saxton, Bradley. *Flaws in the laws governing employment references: problems of "overdeterrence" and a proposal for reform.* 13 Yale L.& Pol'y Rev. 45 (1995).

Schuchmann, Mona L. Note. *The Family and Medical Leave Act of 1993: a comparative analysis with Germany.* 20 J.Corp.L. 331 (1995).

Stickler, K. Bruce and Patricia L. Mehler. *Employee participation programs after* Electromation: *they're worth the risk!* 2 Annals Health L. 55 (1993).

Suve, Heather A. Note. *State-legislated family leave: the FMLA's panacea or ERISA's scourge?* 73 Wash.U.L.Q. 665 (1995).

Yamada, David C. *The regulation of pre-employment honesty testing: striking a temporary(?) balance between self-regulation and prohibition.* 39 Wayne L.Rev. 1549 (1993).

ERISA

Darroch, Elaine McClatchey. *Twelfth Annual National Labor Law Writing Competition. The Supreme Court's dismantling of civil enforcement under ERISA.* [Mertens v. Hewitt Associates, 113 S.Ct. 2063 (1993)]. 1994 Det.C.L.Rev. 1089.

Flint, George Lee, Jr. *ERISA: anti-alienation superiority in bankruptcy.* 94 W.Va.L.Rev. 411 (1991-92).

Flint, George Lee, Jr. *ERISA: jury trial mandated for benefit claims actions.* 25 Loy.L.A.L.Rev. 361 (1992).

Goldstein, Jared A. Note. *Employment discrimination claims under ERISA section 510: should courts require exhaustion of arbitral and plan remedies?* 93 Mich.L.Rev. 193 (1994).

Kelly, Michael W. Note. *Multiemployer pension plan withdrawal liability: limitations without limits.* 42 Case W.Res.L.Rev. 255 (1992).

Maslow, Louis, II. Comment. *Dual liability: the growing overlap of the Age Discrimination in Employment Act and section 510 of the Employee Retirement Income Security Act.* 58 Alb.L.Rev. 509 (1994).

Morris, Jack E. Comment. *Small employers and group health insurance: should ERISA apply?* 52 La.L.Rev. 971 (1992).

Muir, Dana M. *Plant closing and ERISA's noninterference provision.* 36 B.C.L.Rev. 201 (1995).

Rappaport, Anna M. *Policy environment for health benefits: implications for employer plans.* 43 DePaul L.Rev. 1107 (1994).

Schacht, Laura J. Note. *The Health Care Crisis: improving access for employees covered by self-insured health plans under ERISA and the Americans with Disabilities Act.* 45 Wash.U.J.Urb.& Contemp.L. 303 (1994).

Schmall, Lorraine. *Toward full participation and protection of the worker with illness: the failure of federal health law under* McGann v. H & H Music Co. 29 Wake Forest L.Rev. 781 (1994).

Statutory claims under ERISA: is arbitration the appropriate forum? [Southside Internists Group PC Money Purchase Pension Plan v. Janus Capital Corp., 741 F.Supp. 1536 (N.D.Ala.1990)]. 1991 J.Dispute Resolution 171.

Freedom of Speech and Religion

Berman, Geoffrey D. Note. *A New Deal for free speech: free speech and the Labor Movement in the 1930's.* 80 Va.L.Rev. 291 (1994).

Bingham, Lisa B. *Employee free speech in the workplace: using the First Amendment as public policy for wrongful discharge actions.* 55 Ohio St.L.J. 341 (1994).

Brant, Joanne C. *"Our shield belongs to the Lord:" religious employers and a constitutional right to discriminate.* 21 Hastings Const.L.Q. 275 (1994).

Collins, Michael E. Student comment. *Pin-ups in the workplace — balancing Title VII mandates with the right of free speech.* 23 Cumb.L.Rev. 629 (1992-1993).

Harper, Mike. Note. Connick v. Myers *and the First Amendment rights of public employees.* [Connick v. Myers, 461 U.S. 138 (1983)]. 16 Hastings COMM/ENT L.J. 525 (1994).

Ides, Allan. *The text of the Free Exercise Clause as a measure of* Employment Division v. Smith *and the Religious Freedom Restoration Act.* 51 Wash.& Lee L.Rev. 135 (1994).

Volokh, Eugene. Comment. *Freedom of speech and workplace harassment.* 39 UCLA L.Rev. 1791 (1992).

Labor relations

Becker, Craig. *Democracy in the workplace: union representation elections and federal labor laws.* 77 Minn.L.Rev. 495 (1993).

Becker, Craig. *"Better than a strike": protecting new forms of collective work stoppages under the National Labor Relations Act.* 61 U.Chi.L.Rev. 351 (1994).

Bierman, Leonard and Rafael Gely. *Striker replacements: a law, economics, and negotiations approach.* 68 S.Cal.L.Rev. 363 (1995).

DeChiara, Peter D. *The right to know: an argument for informing employees of their rights under the National Labor Relations Act.* 32 Harv.J.on Legis. 431 (1995).

Dubault, Robert A. Note. *The ADA and the NLRA: balancing individual and collective rights.* 70 Ind.L.J. 1271 (1995).

Epstein, R. Tali. Comment. *Should the Fair Labor Standards Act enjoy extraterritorial application?: A look at the unique case of flags of convenience.* 13 U.Pa.J.Int'l Bus.L. 653 (1993).

Estlund, Cynthia L. *Economic rationality and union avoidance: misunderstanding the National Labor Relations Act.* 71 Tex.L.Rev. 921 (1993).

Estes, R. Wayne and Adam M. Porter. Babcock/Lechmere *revisited: derivative nature of union organizers' right of access to employers' property should impact judicial evaluation of alternatives.* 48 SMU L.Rev. 349 (1995).

Estreicher, Samuel. *Employee involvement and the "company union" prohibition: the case for partial repeal of section 8(a)(2) of the NLRA.* 69 N.Y.U.L.Rev. 125 (1994).

Feldman, George. *Workplace power and collective activity: the supervisory and managerial exclusions in labor law.* 37 Ariz.L.Rev. 525 (1995).

Flynn, Joan. *The costs and benefits of "hiding the ball": NLRB policymaking and the failure of judicial review.* 75 B.U.L.Rev. 387 (1995).

Goldin, Jonathan B. Comment. *Labor-management cooperation:* Bath Iron Work's *bold new approach.* 47 Maine L.Rev. 415 (1995).

Gonick, Peter B. Note. *Shoring up employer bargaining power by sandbagging nonunion workers.* [Bravo v. Dolsen Cos., 71 Wash.App. 769, 862 P.2d 623 (1993), review granted, 124 Wash.2d 1001 (1994)]. 70 Wash.L.Rev. 203 (1995).

Hacker, Jonathan D. Note. *Are trojan horse union organizers "employees"?: A new look at deference to the NLRB's interpretation of NLRA section 2(3).* 93 Mich.L.Rev. 772 (1995).

Hall, W. Wendell and Renee A. Forinash. *Employment and labor law.* 48 SMU L.Rev. 1135 (1995).

Holdsclaw, Susan Lillian. Note. *A call for putting standards back into the Fair Labor Standards Act.* [Wilson v. City of Charlotte, 964 F.2d 1391 (4th Cir.1992), rev'g 702 F.Supp. 1232 (W.D.N.C. 1988)]. 71 N.C.L.Rev. 1996 (1993).

Kannar, George. *Making the Teamsters safe for democracy.* 102 Yale L.J. 1645 (1993).

Kullman, William F. *Recent decision. Labor relations—right of privacy: whether the public interest in collective bargaining outweighs federal employees' privacy interests in their homes and occupations.* [Federal Labor Relations Authority v. United States Department of the Navy, 966 F.2d 747 (3d Cir.1992, en banc.)]. 66 Temp.L.Rev. 343 (1993).

LeRoy, Michael H. *Employer treatment of permanently replaced strikers, 1935-1991: public policy implications.* 13 Yale L.& Pol'y Rev. 1 (1995).

McHugh, Richard W. *Fair warning or foul? An analysis of the Worker Adjustment and Retraining Notification (WARN) Act in practice.* 14 Berkeley J.Emp.& Lab.L. 1 (1993).

Moore, Maureen F. *Hit and run strikes — protected activity or suicidal actions under the Railway Labor Act?* 59 J.Air L.& Com. 867 (1994).

Morris, Charles J. *A blueprint for reform of the National Labor Relations Act.* 8 Admin.L.J.Am.U. 517 (1994).

Pfander, James E. *Federal jurisdiction over union constitutions after Woddell.* 37 Vill.L.Rev. 443 (1992).

Post, Frederick R. *Do compelling economic considerations actually exist under the National Labor Relations Act.* 25 Conn.L.Rev. 321 (1993).

Rangarajan, Banumathi. *Labor law.* 1994 Det.C.L.Rev. 829.

Rolling, E. Jane. Comment. *Around the world on eight dollars a day: the binding effect of maintenance rate provisions in collective bargaining agreements.* 18 Tul.Mar.L.J. 317 (1994).

Schor, Juliet B. The Piper Lecture. *Worktime in contemporary context: amending the Fair Labor Standards Act.* 70 Chi.—Kent L.Rev. 157 (1994).

Teeter, John W., Jr. *Between the buttons: employer distribution of antiunion insignia.* 24 N.M.L.Rev. 69 (1994).

Westbrook, James E. *A comparison of the interpretation of statutes and collective bargaining agreements: grasping the pivot of Tao.* 60 Mo.L.Rev. 283 (1995).

Woodson, Frederick J. Note. *Signaling the need for revision of the NLRA.* [NLRB v. Health Care & Retirement Corp. of Am., 114 S.Ct. 1778 (1994)]. 14 J.L.& Com. 301 (1995).

Woolf, David J. Student article. *The legality of employee participation in unionized firms: the Saturn experience and beyond.* 27 Colum.J.L.& Soc.Probs. 557 (1994).

Trade Secrets and Noncompete Agreements

Cundiff, Victoria A. *Maximum security: how to prevent departing employees from putting your trade secrets to work for your competitors.* 8 Santa Clara Computer & High Tech.L.J. 301 (1992).

Curley, Gregory M. Casenote. *The use of noncompetition agreements to protect proprietary information.* [Baxter International, Inc. v. Morris, 976 F.2d 1189 (8th Cir.1992)]. 27 Creighton L.Rev. 915 (1994).

Feldman, Miles J. Comment. *Toward a clearer standard of protectable information: trade secrets and the employment relationship.* 9 High Tech.L.J. 151 (1994).

Pynnonen, Brett D. Comment. *Ohio and Michigan law on postemployment covenants not to compete.* 55 Ohio St.L.J. 215 (1994).

Schulman, Edward M. *Economic analysis of employee noncompetition agreements.* 69 Denv.U.L.Rev. 97 (1992).

Unemployment Compensation

Casebeer, Kenneth M. *Unemployment insurance: American social wage, labor organization and legal ideology.* 35 B.C.L.Rev. 259 (1994).

Frey, Kirsten Hagedorn. Comment. *Employment law — the erosion of the voluntary quit disqualification from unemployment compensation benefits.* [Reep v. Commissioner of the Dept. of Employment & Training, 593 N.E.2d 1297 (Mass.1992)]. 19 J.Corp.L. 183 (1993).

Johns, Daniel V. Note. *Risk of exposure to toxic hazards in the workplace and the unemployment compensation system: proposing a rebuttable presumption of good cause.* 13 Va.Envtl.L.J. 683 (1994).

Lee, Thomas W. Comment. *Deducting unemployment compensation and ending employment discrimination: continuing conflict.* 43 Emory L.J. 325 (1994).

Matheny, Ken. *Labor dispute disqualification for unemployment compensation benefits.* 95 W.Va.L.Rev. 791 (1993).

Worker safety

Collyer, Rosemary M. and J. Michael Klise. *Rights of mine access for miners' representatives: has a walk around the mine become a run around the law?* 95 W.Va.L.Rev. 617 (1993).

Kopin, Jonathan A. Note. *Occupational exposure to asbestos: OSHA's major changes affecting construction, shipyard and general industries.* 1 Envtl.Law 625 (1995).

Mattingly, William S. and Martin E. Hall. *Federal black lung update: the standard of disability causation for federal black lung benefits.* 94 W.Va.L.Rev. 787 (1992).

Quigley, Thomas E. *Employee involvement in the OSHA settlement process.* 1990 Det.C.L.Rev. 579.

Rhinehart, Lynn K. Note. *Would workers be better protected if they were declared an endangered species? A comparison of criminal enforcement under the federal workplace safety and environmental protection laws.* 31 Am.Crim.L.Rev. 351 (1994).

Squire, Madelyn C. *Arbitration of health and safety issues in the workplace: employees who refuse work assignments because of fear of AIDS contagion.* 44 Maine L.Rev. 315 (1992).

Weil, Matthew F. *Protecting employees' fetuses from workplace hazards: Johnson Controls narrows the options.* 14 Berkeley J.Emp.& Lab.L. 142 (1993).

Workers' compensation (see also — Employer liability)

Brenneman, Deborah S. Case note. *Sexual harassment claims and Ohio's workers' compensation statute.* [Kerans v. Porter Paint Co., 575 N.E.2d 428 (Ohio 1991)]. 61 U.Cin.L.Rev. 1515 (1993).

Carlson, Scott A. Comment. *The ADA and the Illinois Workers' Compensation Act: can two "rights" make a "wrong"?* 19 S.Ill.U.L.J. 567 (1995).

Caruso, Gabrielle Lee and Michael R. Alberty. *Workers' disability compensation.* 38 Wayne L.Rev. 1273 (1992).

Cole, Jeffrey. Comment. *Causation in workers' compensation heart attack cases: an argument for a new standard.* 37 S.D.L.Rev. 549 (1992).

Collins, Debbie. Note. *A new exception to the exclusivity provision of the North Carolina Workers' Compensation Act.* [Woodson v. Rowland, 407 S.E.2d 224 (1991)]. 14 Campbell L.Rev. 261 (1992).

Copeland, John D. *The new Arkansas Workers' Compensation Act: did the pendulum swing too far?* 47 Ark.L.Rev. 1 (1994).

Elward, Brad A. *Survey of Illinois Law: workers' compensation.* 17 S.Ill.U.L.J. 985 (1993).

Girdwood, Derek R. Comment. *Can I collect workers' compensation benefits if my job drives me crazy?* 1992 Det.C.L.Rev. 591.

Hynes, Dennis. *Chaos and the law of borrowed servant: an argument for consistency.* 14 J.L.& Com. 1 (1994).

Johnson, H. Alston. *Workers' compensation.* 54 La.L.Rev. 817 (1994).

Kaiser, Amanda C. Case Comment. *Workers' compensation: Tennessee Supreme Court specifies elements required to establish a cause of action for retaliatory discharge in workers' compensation cases.* [Anderson v. Standard Register Co., 857 S.W.2d 555 (Tenn.1993)]. 24 Mem.St.U.L.Rev. 835 (1994).

Murphy, James P. *Proving a defense of fraudulent employment application in workers' compensation accident claims.* 13 Bridgeport L.Rev. 857 (1993).

Quinones, Carlos M. Note. *Workers' compensation law — the sexual harassment claim quandary: workers' compensation as an inadequate and unavailable remedy.* [Cox v. Chino Mines/Phelps Dodge, 115 N.M. 335, 850 P.2d 1038 (Ct.App.1993)]. 24 N.M.L.Rev. 565 (1994).

Rabaut, Louis C. *Worker's disability compensation.* 39 Wayne L.Rev. 1035 (1993).

Spieler, Emily A. *Injured workers, workers' compensation, and work: new perspective on the workers' compensation debate in West Virginia.* 95 W.Va.L.Rev. 333 (1992-93).

Sullivan, J. Thomas. *The Arkansas remedy for employer retaliation against workers' compensation claimants.* 16 U.Ark.Little Rock L.J. 373 (1994).

Symposium on Workers' Compensation. Articles by Mark C. de St. Aubin, John R. Bradley, James E. Higginbotham, II, Alison Steiner and R. Pepper Crutcher, Jr. 62 Miss.L.J. 511 (1993).

Twing, Shawn D. Case note. *Retaliatory discharge in Arkansas workers' compensation cases.* [Wal-Mart Stores, Inc. v. Baysinger, 306 Ark. 239, 812 S.W.2d 463 (1991)]. 45 Ark.L.Rev. 939 (1993).

APPENDIX C

TABLE OF RECENT AND IMPORTANT
UNITED STATES SUPREME COURT EMPLOYMENT CASES

Affirmative Action

Adarand Constructors, Inc. v. Pena, 115 S.Ct. 2097, 132 L.Ed.2d 158 (1995).

Martin v. Wilks, 490 U.S. 755, 109 S.Ct. 2180, 104 L.Ed.2d 835 (1989).

City of Richmond v. J.A. Croson Co., 488 U.S. 469, 109 S.Ct. 706, 102 L.Ed.2d 854 (1989).

Johnson v. Transportation Agency, Santa Clara County, 480 U.S. 616, 107 S.Ct. 1442, 94 L.Ed.2d 615 (1987).

U.S. v. Paradise, 480 U.S. 149, 107 S.Ct. 1053, 94 L.Ed.2d 203 (1987).

Wygant v. Jackson Bd. of Education, 476 U.S. 267, 106 S.Ct. 1842, 90 L.Ed.2d 260 (1986).

Firefighters Local Union No. 1784 v. Stotts, 467 U.S. 561, 104 S.Ct. 2576, 81 L.Ed.2d 483 (1984).

County of Los Angeles v. Davis, 440 U.S. 625, 99 S.Ct. 1379, 59 L.Ed.2d 642 (1979).

Discrimination

Commissioner of Internal Revenue v. Schleier, 115 S.Ct. 2159, 132 L.Ed.2d 294 (1995).

McKennon v. Nashville Banner Pub. Co., 115 S.Ct. 879, 130 L.Ed.2d 852 (1995).

Landgraf v. U.S.I. Film Products, 114 S.Ct. 1483, 128 L.Ed.2d 229 (1994)

Rivers v. Roadway Express, Inc., 114 S.Ct. 1510, 128 L.Ed.2d 274 (1994)

Harris v. Forklift Systems, Inc., 114 S.Ct. 367, 126 L.Ed.2d 295 (1993).

Hazen Paper Company v. Biggins, 113 S.Ct. 1701, 123 L.Ed.2d 338 (1993).

St. Mary's Honor Center v. Hicks, 113 S.Ct. 2742, 125 L.Ed.2d 407 (1993).

Astoria Federal Saving and Loan Ass'n v. Solimino, 501 U.S. 104, 111 S.Ct. 2166, 115 L.Ed.2d 96 (1991).

Gilmer v. Interstate/Johnson Lane Corp.,   500 U.S. 20, 111 S.Ct. 1647, 114 L.Ed.2d 26 (1991).

Stevens v. Dept. of the Treasury, 500 U.S. 1, 111 S.Ct. 1562, 114 L.Ed.2d 1 (1991).

EEOC v. Arabian American Oil Co., 499 U.S. 244, 111 S.Ct. 1227, 113 L.Ed.2d 274 (1991).

International Union, UAW v. Johnson Controls, 499 U.S. 187, 111 S.Ct. 1196, 113 L.Ed.2d 158 (1991).

Public Employees Retirement System of Ohio v. Betts, 492 U.S. 158, 109 S.Ct. 2854, 106 L.Ed.2d 134 (1989).

Jett v. Dallas Independent School District, 491 U.S. 701, 109 S.Ct. 2702, 105 L.Ed.2d 598 (1989).

Patterson v. McClean Credit Union, 491 U.S. 164, 109 S.Ct. 2363, 105 L.Ed.2d 132 (1989).

Will v. Michigan Dept. of State Police, 491 U.S. 58, 109 S.Ct.2304, 105 L.Ed.2d 45 (1989).

Lorance v. AT&T Technologies, Inc., 490 U.S. 900, 109 S.Ct. 2261, 104 L.Ed.2d 961 (1989).

Wards Cove Packing Co., Inc. v. Atonio, 490 U.S. 642, 109 S.Ct. 2115, 104 L.Ed.2d 733 (1989).

Price Waterhouse v. Hopkins, 490 U.S. 228, 109 S.Ct.1775, 104 L.Ed.2d 268 (1989).

Watson v. Fort Worth Bank and Trust, 487 U.S. 977, 108 S.Ct. 2777, 101 L.Ed.2d 827 (1988).

Goodman v. Lukens Steel Co., 482 U.S. 656, 107 S.Ct. 2617, 96 L.Ed.2d 572 (1987).

School Bd. of Nassau County, Fla. v. Arline, 480 U.S. 273, 107 S.Ct.1123, 94 L.Ed.2d 307 (1987).

Ansonia Bd. of Education v. Philbrook, 479 U.S. 60, 107 S.Ct. 367, 93 L.Ed.2d 305 (1986).

Local No. 93, International Ass'n of Firefighters v. City of Cleveland, 478 U.S. 501, 106 S.Ct. 3063, 92 L.Ed.2d 405 (1986).

Local 28 of Sheet Metal Workers v. EEOC, 478 U.S. 421, 106 S.Ct. 3019, 92 L.Ed.2d 344 (1986).

Bazemore v. Friday, 478 U.S. 385, 106 S.Ct. 3000, 92 L.Ed.2d 315 (1986).

Meritor Savings Bank, FSB v. Vinson, 477 U.S. 57, 106 S.Ct. 2399, 91 L.Ed.2d 49 (1986).

Western Air Lines, Inc. v. Criswell, 472 U.S. 400, 105 S.Ct. 2743, 86 L.Ed.2d 321 (1985).

Andersen v. Bessemer City, 470 U.S. 564, 105 S.Ct. 1504, 84 L.Ed.2d 518 (1985).

Alexander v. Choate, 469 U.S. 287, 105 S.Ct. 712, 83 L.Ed.2d 661 (1985).

U.S. Postal Service Bd. of Governors v. Aikens, 460 U.S. 711, 103 S.Ct. 1478, 75 L.Ed.2d 403 (1983).

Connecticut v. Teal, 457 U.S. 440, 102 S.Ct. 2525, 73 L.Ed.2d 130 (1982).

County of Washington v. Gunther, 452 U.S. 161, 101 S.Ct. 2242, 68 L.Ed.2d 751 (1981).

Texas Dept. of Community Affairs v. Burdine, 450 U.S. 248, 101 S.Ct. 1089, 67 L.Ed.2d 207 (1981).

Vance v. Bradley, 440 U.S. 93, 99 S.Ct. 939, 59 L.Ed.2d 171 (1979).

International Brotherhood of Teamsters v. U.S., 433 U.S. 324, 97 S.Ct. 1843, 52 L.Ed.2d 396 (1977).

Dothard v. Rawlinson, 433 U.S. 321, 97 S.Ct. 2720, 53 L.Ed.2d 786 (1977).

Trans World Airlines, Inc. v. Hardison, 432 U.S. 63, 97 S.Ct. 2264, 53 L.Ed.2d 113 (1977).

Massachusetts Board of Retirement v. Murgia, 427 U.S. 307, 96 S.Ct. 2562, 49 L.Ed.2d 520 (1976).

Albemarle Paper Co. v. Moody, 422 U.S. 405, 95 S.Ct. 2362, 45 L.Ed.2d 280 (1975).

McDonnell Douglas Corp. v. Green, 411 U.S. 792, 93 S.Ct. 1817, 36 L.Ed.2d 668 (1973).

Griggs v. Duke Power Co., 401 U.S. 424, 91 S.Ct. 849, 28 L.Ed.2d 158 (1971).

Phillips v. Martin Marietta Corp., 400 U.S. 542, 91 S.Ct. 496, 27 L.Ed.2d 613 (1971).

Employee Benefits

Milwaukee Brewery Workers' Pension Plan v. Jos. Schlitz Brewing Co., 115 S.Ct. 981, 130 L.Ed.2d 932 (1995).

Curtiss-Wright Corp. v. Schoonejongen, 115 S.Ct. 1223, 131 L.Ed.2d 94 (1995).

John Hancock Mutual Life Ins. Co. v. Harris Trust and Savings Bank, 114 S.Ct. 517, 126 L.Ed.2d 524 (1993).

Mertens v. Hewitt Associates, 113 S.Ct. 2063 (1993).

Commissioner of Internal Revenue v. Keystone Consolidated Industries, Inc., 113 S.Ct. 2006 (1993).

Bath Iron Works v. Director, OWCP, 113 S.Ct. 692 (1993).

District of Columbia v. Greater Washington Bd. of Trade, 113 S.Ct. 580, 121 L.Ed.2d 513 (1992).

Nationwide Mutual Ins. Co. v. Darden, 503 U.S. 318, 112 S.Ct. 1344, 117 L.Ed.2d 581 (1992).

Ingersoll-Rand Co. v. McClendon, 498 U.S. 133, 111 S.Ct. 478, 112 L.Ed.2d 474 (1990).

FMC Corp. v. Holliday, 498 U.S. 52, 111 S.Ct. 403, 112 L.Ed.2d 356 (1990).

Rutan v. Republican Party of Illinois, 497 U.S. 62, 110 S.Ct. 2729, 111 L.Ed.2d 52 (1990).

Mead Corp. v. Tilley, 490 U.S. 714, 109 S.Ct. 2156, 104 L.Ed.2d 796 (1989).

Massachusetts v. Morash, 490 U.S. 107, 109 S.Ct. 1668, 104 L.Ed.2d 98 (1989).

Firestone Tire and Rubber Co. v. Bruch, 489 U.S. 101, 109 S.Ct. 948, 103 L.Ed.2d 80 (1989).

Fort Halifax Packing Co. v. Coyne, 482 U.S. 1, 107 S.Ct. 2211, 96 L.Ed.2d 1 (1987).

Connolly v. Pension Benefit Guaranty Corp., 475 U.S. 211, 106 S.Ct. 1018, 89 L.Ed.2d 166 (1986).

Central States, Southeast and Southwest Areas Pension Fund v. Central Transport, Inc., 472 U.S. 559, 105 S.Ct. 2833, 86 L.Ed.2d 447 (1985).

Metropolitan Life Ins. Co. v. Massachusetts, 471 U.S. 724, 105 S.Ct. 2380, 85 L.Ed.2d 728 (1985).

City of Los Angeles Dept. of Water v. Manhart, 435 U.S. 702, 98 S.Ct. 1370, 55 L.Ed.2d 657 (1978).

Employer Liability

Atchison, Topeka and Santa Fe Ry. Co. v. Buell, 480 U.S. 557, 107 S.Ct. 1410, 94 L.Ed.2d 563 (1987).

Employment Practices

California Federal Savings and Loan Ass'n v. Guerra, 479 U.S. 272, 107 S.Ct. 683, 93 L.Ed.2d 613 (1987).

Attorney General of New York v. Soto-Lopez, 476 U.S. 898, 106 S.Ct. 2317, 90 L.Ed.2d 899 (1986).

Free Speech

Texas v. Johnson, 491 U.S. 397, 109 S.Ct. 2533, 105 L.Ed.2d 342 (1989).

Dun & Bradstreet, Inc. v. Greenmoss Builders, Inc., 472 U.S. 749, 105 S.Ct. 2939, 86 L.Ed.2d 593 (1985).

Brockett v. Spokane Arcades, Inc., 472 U.S. 491, 105 S.Ct. 2794, 86 L.Ed.2d 394 (1985).

Connick v. Myers, 461 U.S. 138, 103 S.Ct. 1684, 75 L.Ed.2d 708 (1983).

Labor Relations

North Star Steel Co. v. Thomas, 115 S.Ct. 1927, 132 L.Ed.2d 27 (1995).

NLRB v. Health Care & Retirement Corp., 114 S.Ct. 1778, 128 L.Ed.2d 586 (1994).

ABF Freight System, Inc. v. NLRB, 114 S.Ct. 835, 127 L.Ed.2d 152 (1994).

Livadas v. Bradshaw, 114 S.Ct. 2068, 129 L.Ed.2d 93 (1994).

Hawaiian Airlines, Inc. v. Norris, 114 S.Ct. 2239, 129 L.Ed.2d 203 (1994).

Thunder Basin Coal Co. v. Reich, 114 S.Ct. 771, 127 L.Ed.2d 29 (1994).

Lechmere, Inc. v. NLRB, 502 U.S. 527, 112 S.Ct. 841, 117 L.Ed.2d 79 (1992).

Litton Financial Printing v. NLRB, 501 U.S. 190, 111 S.Ct. 2215, 115 L.Ed.2d 177 (1991).

Air Line Pilots Ass'n International v. O'Neill, 499 U.S. 65, 111 S.Ct. 1127, 113 L.Ed.2d 51 (1991).

Martin v. OSHRC, 499 U.S. 144, 111 S.Ct. 1171, 113 L.Ed.2d 117 (1991).

Groves v. Ring Screw Works, 498 U.S. 168, 111 S.Ct. 498, 112 L.Ed.2d 508 (1990).

English v. General Electric Co., 496 U.S. 72, 110 S.Ct. 2270, 110 L.Ed.2d 65 (1990).

NLRB v. Curtin Matheson Scientific, Inc., 494 U.S. 775, 110 S.Ct. 1542, 108 L.Ed.2d 801 (1990).

Trans World Airlines v. Independent Fed'n of Flight Attendants, 489 U.S. 426, 109 S.Ct. 1225, 103 L.Ed.2d 456 (1989).

Communications Workers of America v. Beck, 487 U.S. 735, 108 S.Ct. 2641, 101 L.Ed.2d 634 (1988).

McLaughlin v. Richland Shoe Co., 486 U.S. 128, 108 S.Ct. 1677, 100 L.Ed.2d 115 (1988).

Landers v. National Railroad Passengers Corp., 485 U.S. 652, 108 S.Ct. 1440, 99 L.Ed.2d 745 (1988).

Citicorp Industrial Credit, Inc. v. Brock, 483 U.S. 27, 107 S.Ct. 2694, 97 L.Ed.2d 23 (1987).

Fall River Dyeing & Finishing Corp. v. NLRB, 482 U.S. 27, 107 S.Ct. 2225, 96 L.Ed.2d 22 (1987).

Icicle Seafoods, Inc. v. Worthington, 475 U.S. 709, 106 S.Ct. 1527, 89 L.Ed.2d 739 (1986).

Cuyahoga Valley Railway Co. v. United Transportation Union, 474 U.S. 3, 106 S.Ct. 286, 88 L.Ed.2d 2 (1985).

NLRB v. International Longshoremen's Ass'n, AFL-CIO, 473 U.S. 61, 105 S.Ct. 3045, 87 L.Ed.2d 47 (1985).

Cornelius v. Nutt, 472 U.S. 648, 105 S.Ct. 2882, 86 L.Ed.2d 515 (1985).

NLRB v. Action Automotive, Inc., 471 U.S. 1049, 105 S.Ct. 984, 83 L.Ed.2d 986 (1985).

Tony and Susan Alamo Foundation v. Secretary of Labor, 471 U.S. 290, 105 S.Ct. 1953, 85 L.Ed.2d 278 (1985).

Allis-Chalmers Corp. v. Lueck, 471 U.S. 202, 105 S.Ct. 1904, 85 L.Ed.2d 206 (1985).

Barrentine v. Arkansas-Best Freight System, 450 U.S. 728, 101 S.Ct. 1437, 67 L.Ed.2d 641 (1981).

Termination

Lingle v. Norge Division of Magic Chef, Inc., 486 U.S. 399, 108 S.Ct. 1877, 100 L.Ed.2d 410 (1988).

United Paperworkers International Union v. Misco, Inc., 484 U.S. 29, 108 S.Ct. 364, 98 L.Ed.2d 286 (1987).

Caterpillar Inc. v. Williams, 482 U.S. 386, 107 S.Ct. 2425, 96 L.Ed.2d 318 (1987).

Unemployment Compensation

Frazee v. Illinois Dept. of Employment Sec., 489 U.S. 829, 109 S.Ct. 1514, 103 L.Ed.2d 914 (1989).

Hobbie v. Unemployment Appeals Comm'n of Florida, 480 U.S. 136, 107 S.Ct. 1046, 94 L.Ed.2d 190 (1987).

Baker v. General Motors Corp., 478 U.S. 621, 106 S.Ct. 3129, 92 L.Ed.2d 504 (1986).

Thomas v. Review Board of Indiana Employment Security Div., 450 U.S. 707, 101 S.Ct. 1425, 67 L.Ed.2d 624 (1981).

Workers' Compensation

Director, Office of Workers' Compensation Programs, Dept. of Labor v. Newport News Shipbuilding and Dry Dock Co., 115 S.Ct. 1278, 131 L.Ed.2d 160 (1995).

Chandris, Inc. v. Latsis, 115 S.Ct. 2172, 132 L.Ed.2d 314 (1995).

Metropolitan Stevedore Co. v. Rambo, 115 S.Ct. 2144, 132 L.Ed.2d 226 (1995).

Director, Office of Workers' Comp. Programs v. Greenwich Collieries, 114 S.Ct. 2251, 129 L.Ed.2d 221 (1994).

Thomas v. Washington Gas Light Co., 448 U.S. 261, 100 S.Ct. 2647, 65 L.Ed.2d 757 (1980).

Wengler v. Druggist Mutual Ins. Co., 446 U.S. 142, 100 S.Ct. 1540, 64 L.Ed.2d 107 (1980).

APPENDIX D

GLOSSARY

Administrative Law Judge - (ALJ) an officer who presides at administrative hearings. ALJs are empowered by employment and agency statutes to serve as initial fact finders in many employment cases including workers' compensation and unemployment benefits claims and many labor disputes. Although courts must give ALJ findings of fact considerable weight, they are not bound by an ALJ's conclusions of law.

Age Discrimination in Employment Act (ADEA) - The ADEA, 29 U.S.C. § 621 *et seq.*, is part of the Fair Labor Standards Act. It prohibits discrimination against persons who are at least forty years old, and applies to employers which have twenty or more employees and which affect interstate commerce.

Americans With Disabilities Act (ADA) - The ADA, 42 U.S.C. § 12101 *et seq.*, went into effect on July 26, 1992. Among other things, it prohibits discrimination against a qualified individual with a disability because of that person's disability with respect to job application procedures, the hiring, advancement or discharge of employees, employee compensation, job training, and other terms, conditions and privileges of employment.

Bona fide - Latin term meaning "good faith." Generally used to note a party's lack of bad intent or fraudulent purpose.

CBA - Collective bargaining agreement.

Class Action Suit - Federal Rule of Civil Procedure 23 allows members of a class to sue as representatives on behalf of the whole class provided that the class is so large that joinder of all parties is impractical, there are questions of law or fact common to the class, the claims or defenses of the representatives are typical of the claims or defenses of the class, and the representative parties will adequately protect the interests of the class. In addition, there must be some danger of inconsistent verdicts or adjudications if the class action were prosecuted as separate actions. Most states also allow class actions under the same or similar circumstances.

Collateral Estoppel - Also known as issue preclusion. The idea that once an issue has been litigated, it may not be re-tried. Similar to the doctrine of *Res Judicata* (see below).

Due Process Clause - The clauses of the Fifth and Fourteenth Amendments to the Constitution which guarantee the citizens of the United States "due process of law" (see below). The Fifth Amendment's Due Process Clause applies to the federal government, and the Fourteenth Amendment's Due Process Clause applies to the states.

Due Process of Law - The idea of "fair play" in the government's application of law to its citizens, guaranteed by the Fifth and Fourteenth Amendments. Substantive due process is just plain *fairness*, and procedural due process is accorded when the government utilizes adequate procedural safeguards for the protection of an individual's liberty or property interests.

Employee Retirement Income Security Act (ERISA) - Federal legislation which sets uniform standards for employee pension benefit plans and employee welfare benefit plans. It is codified at 29 U.S.C. § 1001 *et seq.*

Enjoin - (see Injunction).

Equal Pay Act - Federal legislation which is part of the Fair Labor Standards Act. It applies to discrimination in wages which is based on gender. For race discrimination, employees paid unequally must utilize Title VII or 42 U.S.C. § 1981. Unlike many labor statutes, there is no minimum number of employees necessary to invoke the act's protection.

Equal Protection Clause - The clause of the Fourteenth Amendment which prohibits a state from denying any person within its jurisdiction equal protection of its laws. Also, the Due Process Clause of the Fifth Amendment which pertains to the federal government. This has been interpreted by the Supreme Court to grant equal protection even though there is no explicit grant in the Constitution.

Establishment Clause - The clause of the First Amendment which prohibits Congress from making "any law respecting an establishment of religion." This clause has been interpreted as creating a "wall of separation" between church and state. The test now used to determine whether government action violates the Establishment Clause, referred to as the *Lemon* test, from *Lemon v. Kurtzman,* 403 U.S. 602, 91 S.Ct. 2105, 29 L.Ed.2d 745 (1971), which asks whether the action has a secular purpose, whether its primary effect promotes or inhibits religion, and whether it requires excessive entanglement between church and state.

Ex Post Facto Law - A law which punishes as criminal any action which was not a crime at the time it was performed. Prohibited by Article I, Section 9, of the Constitution.

Exclusionary Rule - Constitutional limitation on the introduction of evidence which states that evidence derived from a constitutional violation must be excluded from trial.

Fair Labor Standards Act (FLSA) - Federal legislation which mandates the payment of minimum wages and overtime compensation to covered employees. The overtime provisions require employers to pay at least time-and-one-half to employees who work more than 40 hours per week.

Federal Employers' Liability Act (FELA) - Legislation enacted to provide a federal remedy for railroad workers who are injured as a result of employer or co-employee negligence. It expressly prohibits covered carriers from adopting any regulation, or entering into any contract, which limits their FELA liability.

Federal Tort Claims Act - Federal legislation which determines the circum-stances under which the United States waives its sovereign immunity (see below) and agrees to be sued in court for money damages. The government retains its immunity in cases of intentional torts committed by its employees or agents, and where the tort is the result of a "discretionary function" of a federal employee or agency. Many states have similar acts.

42 U.S.C. §§ 1981, 1983 - Section 1983 of the federal Civil Rights Act prohibits any person acting under color of state law from depriving any other person of rights protected by the Constitution or by federal laws. A vast majority of lawsuits claiming constitutional violations are brought under § 1983. Section 1981 pro-vides that all persons enjoy the same right to make and enforce contracts as "white citizens." Section 1981 applies to employment contracts. Further, unlike § 1983, § 1981 applies even to private actors. It is not limited to those acting under color of state law. These sections do not apply to the federal government, though the government may be sued directly under the Constitution for any violations.

Free Exercise Clause - The clause of the First Amendment which prohibits Congress from interfering with citizens' rights to the free exercise of their religion. Through the Fourteenth Amendment, it has also been made applicable to the states and their sub-entities. The Supreme Court has held that laws of general applicabil-ity which have an incidental effect on persons' free exercise rights are not viola-tive of the Free Exercise Clause.

Incorporation Doctrine - By its own terms, the Bill of Rights applies only to the federal government. The Incorporation Doctrine states that the Fourteenth Amendment makes the Bill of Rights applicable to the states.

Injunction - An equitable remedy (see Remedies) wherein a court orders a party to do or refrain from doing some particular action.

Issue Preclusion - (see Res Judicata).

Jurisdiction - The power of a court to determine cases and controversies. The Supreme Court's jurisdiction extends to cases arising under the Constitution and under federal law. Federal courts have the power to hear cases where there is diversity of citizenship or where a federal question is involved.

Labor Management Relations Act (LMRA) - Federal labor law which preempts state law with respect to controversies involving collective bargaining agreements. The most important provision of the LMRA is § 301, which is codified at 29 U.S.C. § 185.

National Labor Relations Act (NLRA) - Federal legislation which guarantees to employees the right to form and participate in labor organizations. It prohibits employers from interfering with employees in the exercise of their rights under the NLRA.

Negligence per se - Negligence on its face. Usually, the violation of an ordinance or statute will be treated as negligence per se because no careful person would have been guilty of it.

Occupational Safety and Health Act (OSHA) - Federal legislation which requires employers to provide a safe workplace. Employers have both general and specific duties under OSHA. The general duty is to provide a workplace which is free from recognized hazards that are likely to result in serious physical harm. The specific duty is to conform to the health and safety standards promulgated by the Secretary of Labor.

Overbroad - A government action is overbroad if, in an attempt to alleviate a specific evil, it impermissibly prohibits or chills a protected action. For example, attempting to deal with street litter by prohibiting the distribution of leaflets or handbills.

Preemption Doctrine - Doctrine which states that when federal and state law attempt to regulate the same subject matter, federal law prevents the state law from operating. Based on the Supremacy Clause of Article VI, Clause 2, of the Constitution.

Prior Restraint - Restraining a publication before it is distributed. In general, constitutional law doctrine prohibits government from exercising prior restraint.

Pro Se - A party appearing in court, without the benefit of an attorney, is said to be appearing pro se.

Remand - The act of an appellate court in returning a case to the court from which it came for further action.

Remedies - There are two general categories of remedies, or relief: legal remedies, which consist of money damages, and equitable remedies, which consist of a court mandate that a specific action be prohibited or required. For example, a claim for compensatory and punitive damages seeks a legal remedy; a claim for an injunction seeks an equitable remedy. Equitable remedies are generally unavailable unless legal remedies are inadequate to address the harm.

Res Judicata - The judicial notion that a claim or action may not be tried twice or re-litigated, or that all causes of action arising out of the same set of operative facts should be tried at one time. Also known as claim preclusion.

Section 504 of the Rehabilitation Act of 1973 - Section 504 applies to public or private institutions receiving federal financial assistance. It requires that, in the employment context, an otherwise qualified individual cannot be denied employment based on his or her handicap. An otherwise qualified individual is one who can perform the "essential functions" of the job with "reasonable accomodation."

Section 1981 & Section 1983 - (see 42 U.S.C. §§ 1981, 1983).

Sovereign Immunity - The idea that the government cannot be sued without its consent. It stems from the English notion that the "King could do no wrong." This immunity from suit has been abrogated in most states and by the federal government through legislative acts known as "tort claims acts."

Standing - The judicial doctrine which states that in order to maintain a lawsuit a party must have some real interest at stake in the outcome of the trial.

Statute of Limitations - A statute of limitation provides the time period in which a specific cause of action may be brought.

Summary Judgment - Federal Rule of Civil Procedure 56 provides for the summary adjudication of a case if either party can show that there is no genuine issue as to any material fact and that, given the facts agreed upon, the party is entitled to judgment as a matter of law. In general, summary judgment is used to dispose of claims which do not support a legally recognized claim.

Supremacy Clause - Clause in Article VI of the Constitution which states that federal legislation is the supreme law of the land. This clause is used to support the Preemption Doctrine (see above).

Title VII, Civil Rights Act of 1964 (Title VII) - Title VII prohibits discrimination in employment based upon race, color, sex, national origin, or religion. It applies to any employer having fifteen or more employees. Under Title VII, where an employer intentionally discriminates, employees may obtain money damages unless the claim is for race discrimination. For those claims, monetary relief is available under 42 U.S.C. § 1981.

U.S. Equal Employment Opportunity Commission (EEOC) - The EEOC is the government entity which is empowered to enforce Title VII (see above) through investigation and/or lawsuits. Private individuals alleging discrimination must pursue administrative remedies within the EEOC before they are allowed to file suit under Title VII.

Vacate - The act of annulling the judgment of a court either by an appellate court or by the court itself. The Supreme Court will generally vacate a lower court's judgment without deciding the case itself, and remand the case to the lower court for further consideration in light of some recent controlling decision.

Void-for-Vagueness Doctrine - A judicial doctrine based on the Fourteenth Amendment's Due Process Clause. In order for a law which regulates speech, or any criminal statute, to pass muster under the doctrine, the law must make clear what actions are prohibited or made criminal. Under the principles of the Due Process Clause, people of average intelligence should not have to guess at the meaning of a law.

Writ of Certiorari - The device used by the Supreme Court to transfer cases from the appellate court's docket to its own. Since the Supreme Court's appellate jurisdiction is largely discretionary, it need only issue such a writ when it desires to rule in the case.